Robert never fails to cut through the fog of theories, presenting wisdom and guidance in all matters P3M, and all based on knowledge and experience gained the hard way, out there doing the job! He is the author of the most readable and digestible books on these subjects.

Jayne Redfern, Associate Professor, University of Warwick, UK

Robert Buttrick is the most inspirational project manager that I have ever worked with. His decades of experience shine through in the simple, clear and practical language of his books.

Marion Thomas, Extraordinary Project Management, UK

Selecting the method or approach to apply to your project is rarely as simple as selecting on or off on a switch. More often, a rheostat is needed to dial in the appropriate mix needed to realize the benefits for your business. Robert's work provides the practitioner with the broad understanding of today's globally recognized standards, methods, and approaches needed to dial up success.

Charles J. Lesko, Jr. Ph.D., Professor, East Carolina University, USA

I know no one with Robert's encyclopaedic knowledge and experience of project and programme management. This fantastic book is an invaluable companion for anyone working with projects and programmes.

Phillip Stanton, Partner at Firewood Ltd and PRINCE2 author, UK

Robert Buttrick's book, *The Programme and Portfolio Workout* is an excellent guide and reference for those engaged in managing projects, programmes, and portfolios. Robert's insights into this critical topic come from his long history of working in this field and his extended support of developing standards on the management of projects, programmes, and portfolios. This is a must-read for those engaged in this field.

Dave Violette, MPM, PMP retired, Former Program Manager for Supplier Automation, Duke Energy Corporation, USA

With this new distinctive intelligent product, *The Programme and Portfolio Workout*, Robert brilliantly provides the two subjects to complement *The Project Workout*. Together, these books form a complete operational picture for every professional involved in project management.

Babissakana, PMP, PMO-CP, President of the Pan-African Project Management Conference, Nigeria Former Chair of Technical Development Group (TDG) of ISO/TC 258 Project, Programme and Portfolio Management

A must-read book to provide business and programme managers, who pursue the success of their organization, with practical 'workouts' that seek to ensure that everyone in their organization works towards the same strategic goals. A perfect companion for Robert's very successful book, *The Project Workout*.

Juan Verástegui M, CESEL Ingenieros -Management System and Project Control Manager, Perú

Robert and I worked together on a series of transformation initiatives for a portfolio of major programmes across BT Global Services which resulted in the accreditation of these programmes at CMMI Capability Level 3 - the first achieved within BT. In this book Robert shares with you the lessons he learned on this and other transformation journeys.

Stephen Woods, Founder, PMO ELITE Network, UK

I have greatly benefitted from Robert's work. He is a leader in the world of project and programme management and a real authority on creating and running project-based frameworks for managing change. I welcome the publication of *The Programme and Portfolio Workout* to sit alongside the companion volume, *The Project Workout*, to build on the range of practical advice and techniques available to ensure your organization succeeds.

David Byrne, Knowledge Management Consultant and Artist (Ad Hoc Art) Ex- Senior Business Support Manager BT, UK

Robert is a thought leader in the true sense when it comes to project, programme and portfolio management. His experience, knowledge and ability of creating best practices, while also being pedagogical, makes his writings, lectures and discussions easy to digest and apply.

Klas Skogmar, Management Consultant within PPP - Sweden

If you truly understand your topic you can explain it in terms that anyone can understand. *The Project Workout* has demonstrated Robert's deep knowledge and ability to put 'projects' in terms that will support any practitioner, no matter what your experience level. *The Programme and Portfolio Workout* is a fabulous extension on the foundations laid by *The Project Workout* and a truly invaluable resource for all practitioners.

Jo-Anne Harrison, Chair, Standards Australia Mirror Committee – Project, Programme and Portfolio Management

The Programme and Portfolio Workout

Implementing change is needed in every business. But how do you get started and ensure you actually realize the benefits you need? How do you direct and manage the tens, hundreds, or even thousands, of projects and the other pieces of work your business is undertaking? How do you make sure everyone is working towards the same goals? Building on five previous editions of *The Project Workout*, this book focusses on programme and portfolio management. It is a valuable companion for every business executive and programme manager as well as a comprehensive resource for students of business, portfolio and programme management.

The Programme and Portfolio Workout provides practical advice and techniques to direct and manage your business in a structured, yet agile, way. Aimed at both business and programme managers, it takes you through different approaches to portfolio, programme and project management and shows you how they can work together. The practical approach is enhanced throughout with a series of 'Workouts': exercises, techniques and checklists to help you put the book's advice into practice. The Workouts are supported by an on-line resource of tools.

This expanded edition contains a wealth of new material on the governance and management of portfolio and programmes, including how to work with standards and methods, such as GovS 002, ISO 21504, BS6079 and MSP. The companion to this book, *The Project Workout*, deals with directing and managing individual projects. It uses the same concepts and approaches so that you know, when directing your portfolio or programme, that your project sponsors and managers are taking the same approach. Together, these books give you what you need to ensure your organization succeeds.

Robert Buttrick has an impressive track record of introducing and practising programme and portfolio management in major organizations. He is a contributor to management methods, best practice, government and international standards. He is a consultant and Visiting Teaching Fellow at the University of Warwick.

The Programme and Portfolio Workout

Directing Business-Led Programmes and Portfolios

Robert Buttrick

LONDON AND NEW YORK

First published 2020
by Routledge
2 Park Square, Milton Park, Abingdon, Oxon OX14 4RN

and by Routledge
52 Vanderbilt Avenue, New York, NY 10017

Routledge is an imprint of the Taylor & Francis Group, an informa business

British Library Cataloguing-in-Publication Data
A catalogue record for this book is available from the British Library

Library of Congress Cataloging-in-Publication Data
Names: Buttrick, Robert, author.
Title: The programme and portfolio workout : directing business-led programmes and portfolios / Robert Buttrick.
Description: Abingdon, Oxon ; New York, NY : Routledge, 2020. | Includes index.
Identifiers: LCCN 2020004511 (print) | LCCN 2020004512 (ebook) | ISBN 9781138721210 (paperback) | ISBN 9780367502508 (hardback) | ISBN 9781315194608 (ebook)
Subjects: LCSH: Project management.
Classification: LCC HD69.P75 B8848 2020 (print) | LCC HD69.P75 (ebook) | DDC 658.4/04—dc23
LC record available at https://lccn.loc.gov/2020004511
LC ebook record available at https://lccn.loc.gov/2020004512

ISBN: 978-0-367-50250-8 (hbk)
ISBN: 978-1-138-72121-0 (pbk)
ISBN: 978-1-315-19460-8 (ebk)

Typeset in Myriad Pro
by Apex CoVantage, LLC

Contents

Workouts

Foreword

The forward progress of organizations has always depended heavily on the management of projects. New plants, new products, new organizations, new methods, new ventures – all required dedicated teams working to strict timetables and separate budgets. But today there's a vital difference. The project management mode has broadened and evolved to the point where managers may spend as much time in interdisciplinary, cross-functional, interdepartmental project teams as they do in their normal posts.

Many factors have contributed to this unstoppable development – among them the increased complexity of all businesses, the closer inter-relationships within organizations and with customers and suppliers outside and the mounting pressure for speed. The latter demands synchronous working. Organizations can no longer afford to play pass-the-parcel, with each department or function waiting for the others to finish. There simply isn't enough time to waste.

That pressure demands not only speed but effective delivery, on time, on specification, and on budget. That will not happen by accident – and Robert Buttrick's book, based on his extensive corporate experience, is an invaluable, lucid and practical guide to a crucial area of management which has been crying out for the treatment it receives in these pages. Unlike management in general, project management is self-contained and dedicated to clearly defined ends. The organizations and the managers who best master the methods and maxims in this book will not only achieve their specific objectives, but they will also win the whole game.

Robert Heller

Acknowledgements

This book is built on the experience and knowledge of many people I have worked with over the years in corporate life, as a consultant and on the BSI and ISO working groups. If I named them all the list would be as long as the credits at the end of an epic film . . . and we all walk out of the cinema before they've finished rolling, don't we?

Unlike many books, this one was written by one of the 'infantry': I am not an academic. I would like to thank Alan Fowler, of Isochron, for his stunning insights into benefits management; to the one and only Dr Eddie Obeng, for introducing me to his frameworks and concepts relating to project types; to Oded Cohen of the Goldratt Institute, who opened my eyes to the Theory of Constraints; to Chris Worseley at CITI, for his work on project manager profiling; and to John Anderson, for his insights into portfolio management. Many thanks to those I worked with in the UK's Cabinet Office when developing their project delivery standard; the projects they deal with are among the largest and most complex in the world.

I'd also like to thank those business leaders who, frankly, never 'got it' and just love their corporate silos and hierarchies; without them, there would be no competitive advantage for those who do 'get it'!

Most important of all, I would like to thank my wife, for hours of sense-checking and proofreading, and the solid support she has given me to ensure this venture succeeds.

Robert Buttrick, 2020, projectworkout.com

About the author

Robert Buttrick is an international authority on business-led strategic programme and project management. He has a successful track record for introducing strategic portfolio management to a wide variety of blue-chip companies as well as in government.

Robert is currently an independent consultant and Visiting Teaching Fellow at the University of Warwick. He is an author of the 2017 edition of PRINCE2® and lead author for the UK government's project delivery standard. He is an active contributor to programme and project management practice, writing articles and presenting at conferences. He received a Distinguished Service Certificate from BSI for services to national and international project management standards. He is a Member of the Chartered Institute of Marketing, a Chartered Engineer and an Honorary Fellow of the Association for Project Management.

His most recent corporate role was as BT's PPM Method Director. Prior to that, he was accountable for creating and running a portfolio-based framework for managing change within Cable and Wireless, enabling the planning and development of new systems, products, services and capabilities to meet ever growing customer needs.

Before taking up a corporate career in 1993, Robert worked for PA Consulting, where he specialized in business-led project management. Clients included Lloyds TSB Bank, National Rivers Authority, Property Services Agency, Avon Industrial Polymers, NatWest Bank and RHM.

Robert's early career was as a civil engineer. After graduating from the University of Liverpool with a first-class honours degree, he joined Gibb Ltd, providing consulting and design services for infrastructure projects worldwide. He has lived in countries as diverse as Kenya, Mauritius, Yemen, Senegal and Sudan, working on the evaluation, design and supervision of marine and water resource projects. He also worked at the World Bank in Washington, D.C. on investment appraisals.

Robert can be contacted via his website, projectworkout.com.

Introduction

This book is about driving change in your organization by ensuring everything you do, whether business-as-usual, projects or programmes, is targeted at achieving your business objectives. The approach is to keep to some basic principles supported by only a few rules, giving the executive or director the freedom to direct their business, and the managers the freedom to manage their work to suit the circumstances and their own style.

In the mid-1990s, Sir Ian Gibson, then President – Nissan Europe, said:

> *"As organizations we must become increasingly able to change quickly and easily. This means building on and around people's abilities rather than limiting them for the convenience of recognizable roles."*

He recognized the need for a new way of managing change within our organizations; one that is flexible and not tied to specific departments and job titles, where people can be used to the best effect and where what they do (their role) counts more than the department or function they come from (their job). In such organizations, reporting structures are flat, job titles are secondary and most personnel moves are sideways. This applies from top to bottom and no one should ever say, "I won't do that, it's not my job!" Change is built into the way they work.

Today, the term 'corporate agility' is often used, not least by McKinsey and Company. In this context, McKinsey argues that being 'agile' is all about 'adhocracy' rather than 'bureaucracy'. In an adhocracy, action and decisions are focussed on business objectives and purpose across functional boundaries; some organizations have attained this vision, but many have not. Since it was first published in 1997, *The Project Workout* (which is the precursor to this book) has been using this 'new way' of looking at businesses, drawing on the core principles of project management. Project management has been with us for a long time, usually buried deeply within our IT, technical and engineering departments. It is now, however, increasingly being recognized by business and governments alike as a valuable discipline in any management context where change is needed.

Since the first edition of *The Project Workout* was published in 1997, there is evidence of many more organizations taking deliberate steps to use project management-based methods. Yet, in some organizations, the support and training given to those sponsoring or managing programmes and projects is pitifully small; all too often projects are targeted at delivering 'things' in separate departments rather than ensuring the achievement of specific business objectives for the organization as a whole. Managers are often given a project to sponsor or manage because it is 'good for their development'. True, but not if they have to invent how to 'do it' for themselves with no grounding whatsoever or if the organization sets them up to fail by fostering an environment which is hostile to cross-functional working. I have never heard of an accountant who was expected to do his job 'from first principles'. Newcomers to project management are often termed 'accidental' project sponsors or managers. Billions of pounds, euros and dollars rest on their shoulders, yet many major organizations do not provide the corporate environment, training, methods or tool kit to support them in undertaking their roles. As we will learn in Part I of this book, the wrong corporate culture undermines project success no matter how good the project team is at their jobs.

Management is man-made; it is not an inherent physical construct, which means there are many 'right' ways of achieving the same aims. When someone talks about 'project management' or 'programme management', they might have a very different mental picture than you. This book uses the concepts I have found to work in practice and is consistent with those from publicly available standards and methods, many of which I have been instrumental in writing.

The core discipline of project management is often made to look too bureaucratic and complicated, frequently misunderstood and poorly practised. Consequently, some managers seek to avoid it, as their real-life experience has shown that it does not deliver the promised rewards. They haven't grasped that unsupported, uninformed and unskilled people, working in an organization which has no project-based management structures, cannot perform well. Whether you are a senior executive, manager, sponsor, project manager or 'one of the infantry', I aim to:

- explain the challenges faced by many companies;
- outline lessons and advice from leading companies;
- propose a framework for directing and managing organizations from a business-led perspective;
- explain the key roles;
- provide best practice techniques for managing portfolios, programmes and projects.

Reading this book will benefit you as:

- the 'mystique' of portfolio and programme management is exposed, making it simple to understand and accessible to finance, sales, marketing, customer services, administrators, engineers, scientists and technologists alike;
- the content is not tied to any formally published 'methods' but is positioned as 'common sense', which overrides them all.

The book is divided into six parts:

- Part I covers the challenges and lessons.
- Part II looks at the essence of project management.
- Part III looks at how to organize your business into portfolios to focus on your strategic needs.
- Part IV deals with programme management.
- Part V provides a range of techniques you'll need to become familiar with, whether working at portfolio, programme or project level.
- Part VI contains some thoughts on making sure all this works for you in your organization.

Many of the key points are restated in different sections throughout the book. This is intentional, both as reinforcement and to enable you to dip into separate chapters without the need to follow up multiple cross-references. This cross-connectivity emphasizes how the 'real world' is not divided into a series of discrete, neatly labelled topics but comprises an ever-changing mix of topics, each affecting the other. Successful programme and portfolio management is a complete system, and to describe elements of it in isolation would be deficient.

Management is an 'art'. To be effective, it requires both structured management skills (hard skills) and powerful interpersonal skills (soft skills). I have concentrated on the former as this is where the myths cluster. I do, however, refer throughout to the essential soft skills you need for success.

When the first edition of this book was published in 1997, the term 'project' was not always understood in the same way as it is now. A project was regarded as a delivery vehicle for technical, IT or engineering outputs. Few saw it as a means to achieve business outcomes. I was one of a few advocates of business-led project management. The practice of project management has moved on to incorporate the 'business-led' project, perhaps not as fast as I would have liked, but many methods and standards now recognize this more powerful use of the discipline.

Back in 1997, there was no consensus on the meaning of the words 'programme' and 'portfolio'. Often the words 'project' and 'programme' were interchangeable and for some people, they still are. Whilst many still argue this point, the various standards bodies (including ISO and BSI), professional bodies (such as APM, IPMA and PMI) and method providers (like AXELOS for PRINCE2®, MSP®, MoP®) are beginning to use a common language. There are, however, still 'ragged edges' across these organizations' publications and even within them!

In the first four editions of *The Project Workout*, I covered running one project at a time and running many projects at once in a single volume. Now, however, I have made *The Project Workout* into two separate books, as it was getting rather fat:

- *The Programme and Portfolio Workout* (this book) looks at how to deal with many projects at once, together with all the other work done in an organization in order be successful. It includes what much of the project management literature now refers to as 'programmes', 'portfolios' and 'organizational project management'.

- *The Project Workout* is about directing and managing a single project, covering the essential techniques and winning behaviours.

To make each book self-sufficient, there is deliberately some overlap and reinforcement of key principles and content. I have included cross references between the books to point to more detailed content which builds to create a whole approach. Whilst a great programme manager or business manager needn't be a great project manager, they do need to understand the principles to be effective in their roles. Similarly, a great project sponsor or project manager should understand the needs of programme or business portfolio managers and why they are essential to overall success.

The workouts

The book contains a number of exercises, problem posers and techniques to help put the 'book work' into practice. They are intended to be both a stimulant and a practical help.

Case studies

The case studies are derived from real-life incidents, but some have been simplified to make them more concise in conveying the particular message being illustrated.

"Change the name and it's about you, that story."

HORACE 65–8bc

Points of interest

I have included a number of points of interest relating to the core theme of each chapter. They provide you with a greater understanding of the subject but may be glossed over on first reading so you can concentrate on the main message. If this book were a presentation, these would be the questions which interrupt the presenter or the anecdotes the presenter uses to help bring the story to life.

Definitions of all those important words

In the field of project management, there is a converging consensus on what words mean, but there are still instances where opinions differ; my work on international standards hit this problem time and again. Someone else's definition of a word or phrase is not necessarily wrong but might simply be 'differently right'. What is important is any terminology you adopt must be used consistently or confusion will reign. In this book, you will find a number of words which might be new to you or old words which have been used in a new way. I have therefore included a jargon-busting glossary in Appendix A. I also include commonly used alternatives.

"How often misused words generate misleading thoughts."

HUBERT SPENCER

Principles

Principles are the basic values or practices you need to apply if you are to succeed. You should ensure that any 'rules' or procedures you develop and use within your organization are compatible.

Key points

Key points are short checklists to keep you on the right track.

Cartoons

In many of the chapters I have used cartoons to emphasize a point. The cartoons are all set 2,000 years ago in the Roman Empire and show how, if the Romans had run their affairs as many modern organizations do, they would have failed miserably. The cartoons illustrate how project management is essentially applying common sense that has been with us for a very long time.

The question 'why' is very powerful

The website and tools

The website – projectworkout.com

Much of the practical content of this book is ready for you to print out and use from the accompanying website. I have also included a number of the templates, including the Health Check, MS Project views and control logs.

At my own website, **projectworkout.com**, you can find:

- my blog, containing informal articles and 'thought pieces';
- frequently asked questions;
- articles;
- an outline of the services I provide, including consulting support and seminars;
- a contact form.

BusinessOptix evaluation system

Throughout this book, I have made use of flow charts to demonstrate the sequence of activities you need to undertake some aspects of portfolio, programme and project management. Nowadays, processes and methods are becoming a way of life in many organizations, particularly those moving up the maturity levels and adopting models such as SEI's CMMI for Development. Unfortunately, there are few 'easy to use' business modelling tools on the market but one I use very effectively in my day-to-day corporate life is BusinessOptix. You can see some examples on my website.

Every owner of *The Programme and Portfolio Workout* can obtain an evaluation licence of BusinessOptix. For more details, see **process.projectworkout.com**.

PART I

CHALLENGES TO BE FACED

"Minds are like parachutes; they only work when open."

LORD DEWAR, 1864–1930

In this part of the book I set out the challenges many organizations face in driving through the changes necessary to achieve their strategic objectives. This is followed by a review of good practice used by some of the world's leading companies.

How to use Part I

Part I is for you to read and learn from. Put aside your own situation and the problems in your organization. Open your mind to what others are saying and doing. If you find yourself thinking "but we don't do it like that, we are different!" pull yourself back – you are different. So is everyone else. BUT other people's experience, even from dissimilar industries or sectors, may give you a clue to dealing with the issues confronting you.

The workouts in Part I are designed to help you think about your organization and your programmes and projects; they should prompt you to think about, discuss and take action on the aspects you feel will benefit you most. You won't be able to address everything at once; there will be too much, bearing in mind you also have a business to run! Part VI of this book will, however, give you some ideas on how to decide your priorities.

You can share your own experience with the author on projectworkout.com.

1

Challenges we need to face

Problems, more problems

Initiatives fail, are cancelled, or never get started – why?

In our new world of the twenty-first century no organization is immune from 'shut down' if it fails to perform.

"Facts do not cease to exist because they are ignored."

ALDOUS HUXLEY, 1894–1963

Problems, more problems

All organizations have problems with the way they undertake their work and tackle change. Problems might be related to any aspect of the business, technology, people, processes, systems or structure. There is always something somewhere that needs to be created, dropped or improved. A plethora of techniques are available to business leaders to enable them to improve their organizations, most with three- or four-letter acronyms to add to their mystique; some even gain cult status. These include, but are by no means limited to:

- Business agility;
- Management by Objectives (MBO);
- Total Quality Management (TQM);
- Quality Function Deployment (QFD);
- Design for Manufacture and Assembly (DFMA);
- Business Process Reengineering (BPR);
- LEAN Six Sigma;
- Value Management and Engineering.

All these approaches, and many more, have contributed to the performance of a significant number of organizations, but it is a sad fact that many organizations have failed to secure the enduring benefits initially promised. What has gone wrong? Maybe we are not all as good as we should be at managing and controlling change and achieving sustained benefits from such initiatives.

'Grand' initiatives of the kind just mentioned are not the only ones that can fail. Organizations must continually strive to solve problems or achieve specific objectives. For example:

- new products and services need to be developed and old ones are updated or withdrawn;
- supply chains need rationalizing;
- manufacturing processes are altered to take account of new methods and technologies;
- sales channels are developed;
- new plant and offices are opened and old ones are closed;
- key business functions are outsourced; some are brought back in-house;
- businesses are disposed of; others are acquired and integrated into the mainstream business;
- information systems are built to give greater efficiency and add to the overall effectiveness of the operation.

Again, many of these initiatives fail. Either they:

- didn't fit the organization's strategy;
- cost too much;
- take too long;
- are inadequately scoped and specified;
- don't work as expected, having undesired side effects;
- or simply don't realize the expected benefits.

This amounts to failure on a scale which costs billions every year and can result in the demise of an organization.

This amounts to failure on a scale which costs billions every year and can result in the demise of an organization. It happens in the private, public and charitable sectors, small undertakings and major multinational enterprises. In the twenty-first century, no organization is immune from 'shut down' if it fails to perform.

Initiatives fail, are cancelled or never get started – why?

A review of a representative cross-section of large companies reveals a common pattern of cause and effect with two fundamental causes:

- Organizations don't know HOW to control change. There is no 'organization-wide' way of undertaking business change initiatives and management. Consequently, team members follow different or even conflicting approaches and have different norms of behaviour.
- Organizations don't know WHAT they should be doing or WHY. There is no clear strategy driving requirements or decision making. Consequently, an organization can waste money on the wrong projects or activities.

This book concentrates on solving the first of these root causes (how), but because success also relies heavily on the latter (strategy) being in place, you will see frequent references to business strategy throughout the book.

What can go wrong, other than the sponsor or manager of the initiative just doing a bad job? Without a clear strategy, you cannot hope to ensure your initiatives are aligned. As a result, decisions might be contradictory, and people will tend to focus on short-term needs because that is all they can be certain about. In some cases, the wrong projects are started, and the right ones never see the light of day. If it is left to each departmental head to decide how their people work, cross functional working will be problematic, with each team using different approaches, terminology and concepts which are likely to be incompatible. There might not be a consistent list of current initiatives as each department might use different names or not even have a list at all. Too many projects might be started, resources might get overloaded and then each departmental head might reallocate those

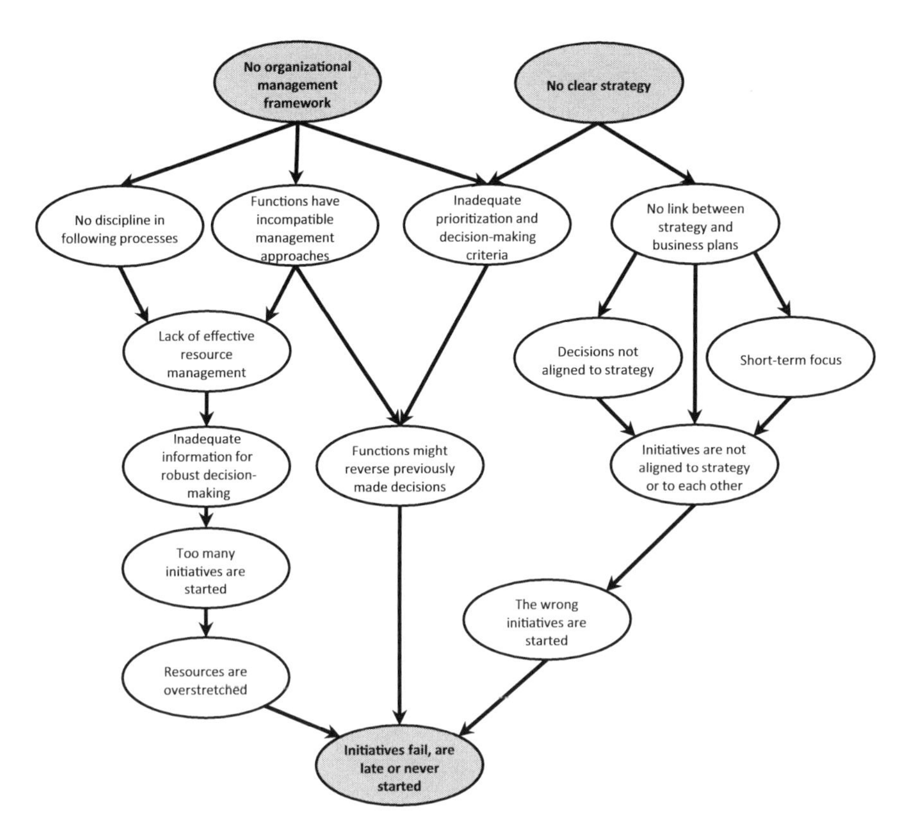

Figure 1.1 Problem analysis

A cause and effect analysis of the reasons for the failure of business initiatives shows two fundamental reasons: (a) a lack of clear strategy and (b) a lack of a rational way of managing the required changes. If your initiatives fail, then ultimately so will your business. Note how many of the problems can't be solved at a project or initiative level but require a shift in how the organization, as a whole, is directed and managed.

resources based on their own priorities, rather than what is best for the organization as a whole.

It all sounds like a bit of a disaster, but even in such chaos, departmental managers can often meet their annual cost centre targets, giving the false impression of everything being under control. As we will see in this book, nothing could be further from the truth.

Figure 1.1 shows many of the issues facing organizations. Notice how most issues included in the figure can only be solved by changing the way the organization, as a whole, is directed and managed. An individual programme sponsor, project manager or functional manager is powerless to make a difference. Some organizations are so poor at providing the right enterprise wide environment and support that they are condemning their project teams to inevitable failure, and only the rare 'heroic' sponsor or manager will succeed, and then, despite the organization, not because of it.

If any of the problems identified in this chapter or drawn out from Figure 1.1 are familiar to you and recognizable in your organization, you will need to solve a number of issues:

- the solution to issues relating to the undertaking of a large number of programmes and projects, together with 'business-as-usual', is known as **business portfolio management**;
- the solution to issues relating to groups of closely connected projects and other related work, is known as **programme management**;
- the solution to issues relating to single initiatives in isolation, is known as **project management**.

Organizations must be competent at all three of these management approaches. Further, those management approaches must be implemented in a mutually consistent way if the organization to work both effectively and efficiently.

Workout 1.1 – Self-diagnosis

This workout is best done by a group of executives or business leaders from across the organization. Remember, business initiatives cross functional and departmental boundaries, so doing this within a single department will not help you. The term 'initiative' is used here to represent a project or a programme.

1. Use the following questions as prompts to establish the areas of competence you might need to address.
    - Have you a list of all the initiatives being undertaken in your organization?
    - Can you establish a clear link between your organization's business strategy and each of your initiatives?
    - Is it clear why you are undertaking each initiative?
    - Do you find upper and middle management communicate and pass on instructions accurately?
    - Do you find it easy to get decisions made?
    - Does your organization have any documented criteria against which decisions on whether or not to undertake initiatives are tested? If so, are they actually used in practice?
    - Is there a disciplined method or way of managing initiatives across your organization?
    - Is there always enough time to do those things which must be done?
    - Do your managers and employees commit themselves to and meet the targets set for them?
    - Do you have the resources to complete what you have already started?
2. Do you really KNOW, and can you DEMONSTRATE:
    - Who benefits from each initiative?
    - Who is the sponsor and who is the manager for each initiative?
    - Who makes the decisions on each initiative?
    - Who will be adversely impacted by your project?
    - The cost and benefits of your initiative, both to date and projected?
    - What activities your resources are committed to and what, if any, free time they have?
3. Build a cause and effect diagram similar to Figure 1.1 for your organization. By creating this yourself, you will identify the pain points which are most pertinent to your organization.
    - Start with 'Initiatives fail, are terminated, late, or never started' written on a Post-it® Note at the bottom of a flip chart.

- Ask yourself why this happens. Write each possible reason on a Post-It® Note and place these on the flip chart.

4. For each new Post-It® Note, ask the reason why, writing these on more Post-It® Notes. Eventually, if you are honest, you will discover a core reason(s), picking up many symptoms on the way.

2

Advice the best organizations give us

The organizations chosen for the study had clearly demonstrated success in their own fields and markets. Despite the diverse industries, there was a marked similarity in approach taken.

"Example moves the world more than doctrine."

HENRY MILLER 1891–1980

The study

The problems outlined in the previous chapter are significant and far reaching. This chapter looks at practical solutions to these problems. The advice is based on research undertaken by the author, verified through experience of working within major organizations, across a number of industries. The research questions were not explicitly related to project management, thereby avoiding preconceptions on the part of those involved on what a 'project' is. Rather, the questions related to 'product development' as the development and launching of products or services touches almost every part of every organization, whether public or private. Product development is an excellent business area for learning about complex, cross-functional projects and how organizations address them. If an organization cannot develop products and services efficiently, it is probable that it cannot tackle any other form of cross-functional work effectively either. In a business context, a project is a project, regardless of whether it is technology based, for cultural change, complex change or whatever else.

The study had the following characteristics:

- The research was undertaken through face-to-face interviews, thereby ensuring both the questions and answers were properly understood. Each interview lasted about three hours and was conducted by two researchers.
- The study was predominantly qualitative with only a few quantitative questions added to obtain the 'hard data' available. It was considered more important to find out how people worked rather than collect statistics which, in all likelihood, would not be comparable. Obtaining statistics which are truly comparable across different organizations and sectors is difficult.

The objective was to 'learn from the best', hence the inclusion of a number of industries, in both growing and mature markets:

- aerospace; complex, customized manufacturing;
- computer hardware;
- telecommunications;
- manufacturing;
- management consulting;
- systems integrators;
- software development;
- corporate financial services and retail banking;
- architecture and engineering and construction.

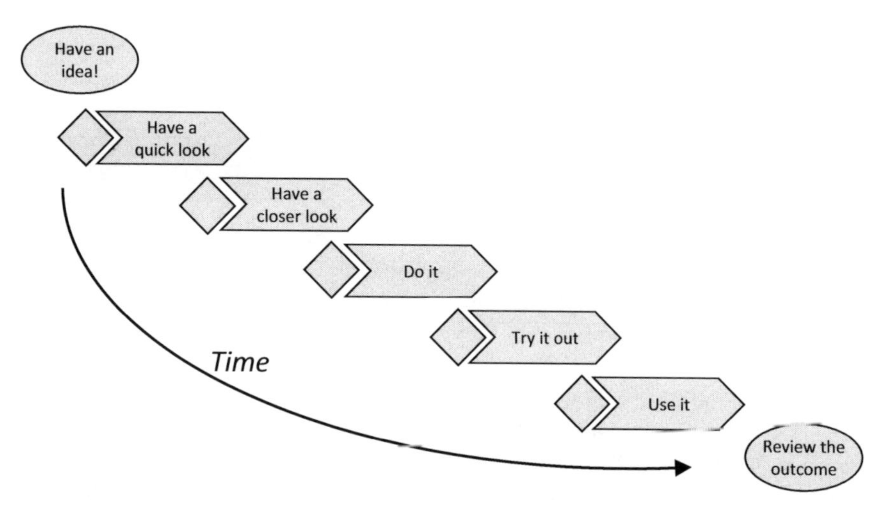

Figure 2.1 A typical staged project framework

A staged approach to projects starts with a preliminary look at the objectives and possible solutions and results, via more detailed investigation, development and trial stages, in the release of the outputs into the operational environment. You should not start any stage without meeting the prescribed criteria at the preceding gate. This includes checks on strategic fit and 'do ability' as well as financial considerations.

The organizations chosen for the study had clearly demonstrated success in their own fields and markets. Although diverse, there was a clear similarity in the approach taken. They all used or were implementing a 'staged', 'cross-functional' framework within which to manage their product development projects (Figure 2.1). The number of stages differed from organization to organization, but all have the characteristic of incrementally investing a certain amount of the organization's resources to obtain more information across the full range of activities which impact a project and its outcome, namely:

- market;
- operational;
- technical;
- commercial and financial.

An additional finding was that some organizations did not limit their approach to product development but also applied it more generally to business change projects, i.e., to everything they did which created change in the organization. In other words, they had a common business-led management framework.

There, however, the similarities between organizations end and the individual cultures and the nature of the different industries takes over. Figure 2.2 illustrates how any process or method (including those for portfolio, programme and project management) sits within a context of culture, systems and organization structure; alter

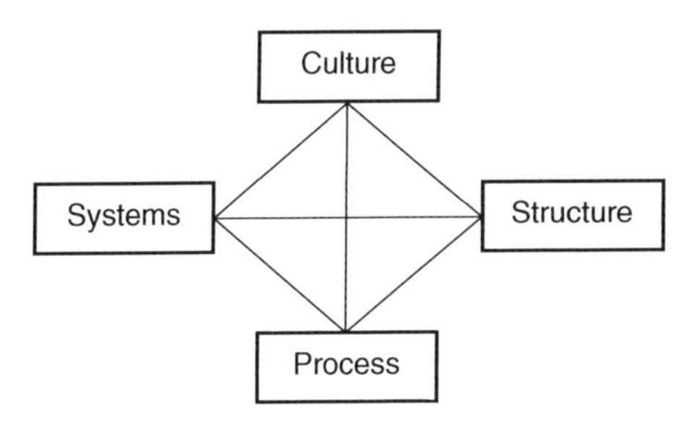

Figure 2.2 The organizational context for programme and portfolio management and other processes

No process or method sits in isolation. How you are organized, the systems and tools you use to support the process and the prevailing culture of the organization all affect how well any process works.

any one and it will affect the others. This is an important diagram, and one we will return to throughout the book.

This single observation means that although a process might be similar in principle in many organizations, the culture and behaviours making it work are different. Logically, if a proven process appears to break down, the fault might lie outside the process itself, in different aspects of the organization. This observation means that a process which works well in one organization will not necessarily work in every organization. One CEO told me, "We know our process is logical and has worked well in the past; if it stops working, we look first at the behaviours of the people trying to make it work rather than at the process itself." This company had a well-established enterprise-wide project management approach, in which it had a high degree of confidence. It still, however, maintained the good practice of continually improving its approach by promoting feedback and having quarterly performance reviews. Another organization had a very effective project gating process (see lesson 2), which totally failed after a new management team took over the company.

It was notable that certain industries were excellent in particular aspects of managing projects because of the nature of their business.

It was notable that certain industries were excellent in particular aspects of managing projects because of the nature of their business. Often, they took this for granted; to use a learning and development maxim, they were 'unconsciously competent' at such activities. For example: *"Concentrate on the early stages"* was a message which came across loud and clear, but it was the organizations that relied on bids or tenders for their business which really put the effort in up front as the effect of failure was obvious: they lost the bid or won unprofitable work.

"Manage risks" was another message. The only organization to tell me, unprompted, that it was excellent in risk management was an avionics business. Interestingly, the company did not claim to use very sophisticated risk-management techniques but rather designed its whole approach with a risk-management bias. It cited

its staged process as a key part of this: you will hear a lot about staged approaches as you work through this book.

"Measure everything you do" was also a common message. Organizations which needed to keep a track of man hours to bill their customers (e.g., consultants, system development houses) also have the most comprehensive cost and resource planning and monitoring systems. These provide a view of each individual piece of work plus a collation and summary of the current status for all their work, giving them a quantum leap in management information most other organizations lack.

The lessons and their implications

The lessons learned from the research are summarized below and described more fully on the following pages. The quotations preceding each lesson are taken from the study notes.

The first seven lessons apply at all times. They indicate what is required for each item of work and the characteristics the organization needs to have to create an environment which promotes rather than hinders success:

1. Make sure your work is driven by benefits which support your strategy.
2. Use a simple and well-defined framework.
3. Address and revalidate the marketing, commercial, operational and technical viability of the work throughout its life.
4. Involve selected users and customers in the work to understand their current and future needs.
5. Build excellence in project management techniques and controls across the organization.
6. Break down functional boundaries by using cross-functional teams.
7. Use dedicated resources for each category of development and prioritize within each category.

   The next three lessons apply to particular stages in a project:
8. THE START

   Place high emphasis on the early stages of the project.
9. THE MIDDLE

   Build the business case into the company's forward plan as soon as the project has been formally approved.
10. THE END

    Close the project formally to build a bridge to the future, learn any lessons and ensure a clean handover.

1. Make sure your projects are driven by benefits which support your strategy

"If you don't know why you want to do a project, don't do it!"

All the organizations were able to demonstrate explicitly how each project undertaken fitted their business strategy. The screening out of unwanted initiatives and projects as soon as possible was key. At the start of any project, there is usually insufficient information to decide economic or financial viability, but strategic fit should be assessable from the beginning. Not surprisingly, organizations with clear strategies were able to screen more effectively than those without. Strategic fit was often assessed by using simple questions, derived from the strategy, such as:

- Will this product ensure we maintain our leadership position?
- Will the results promote a long-term relationship with our customers?

The less clear the strategy, the more likely projects are to pass the initial screening. This results in more projects competing for scarce resources with the company losing focus and jeopardizing its overall performance.

The less clear the strategy, the more likely projects are to pass the initial screening.

2. Use a simple and well-defined framework, with a staged approach

"Our usual process is our fast-track process."

The use of a staged project framework (life cycle) was found to be well established in most of the study participants' organizations. It is rarely possible to plan a project in its entirety from start to finish; there are simply too many unknowns. By using a number of defined project stages, it is possible to plan the next stage in detail, with the remaining stages planned in summary. As you progress through the project, from stage to stage, the endpoint should become clearer and your confidence in delivery should increase. It was apparent that organizations were striving to make their project frameworks as simple as possible, minimizing the number of stages and cutting down the weight of supporting documentation.

Further, the same generic stages were often used for all types of project (e.g., for a new plastic bottle, or a new manufacturing line; for a project costing £1,000 to one of £10m) so that senior management is able to cross compare the status of each project. This makes the use and understanding of the framework easier and avoids the need to learn different frameworks and processes for different types of project. This is particularly important for those sponsoring projects or who are infrequently involved in projects. By having one basic framework they are able to understand their role within it and do not have to learn a new language and approach for each situation.

What differs is the work content of each project, level of activity, nature of the activity, degree of risk, resources and expertise required and the stakeholders and decision makers needed.

A common criticism of a staged approach is that it slows projects down. This was explored in the research and found not to be the case. In contrast, a staged approach was believed to speed up desirable projects. Of particular relevance is the nature of the decision to start a new stage of a project, often called gates. Some organizations used them as 'entry' points to the next project stage rather than the more traditionally accepted 'exit' point from a previous stage. This simple principle has the effect of allowing a stage to start before the previous stage has been completed. In this way, stages can overlap without increasing the risk to the business, provided the gate criteria are met.

In all cases, the organizations said that their 'usual process' was the fast track.

The existence of so-called 'fast-track' processes to speed up projects was also considered. In all cases, the organizations said that their 'usual process' was the fast track. Doing anything else, such as skipping stages or going ahead without fully preparing for each stage, increases the risk of the project failing. The message from the more experienced organizations was 'going fast' by missing essential work actually slowed them down; the amount of rework required was generally greater than the effort saved. When people talk of fast tracking, they usually mean raising the priority of a project so it is not slowed down by a lack of resources.

Isn't this just old-fashioned 'waterfall'? No!

Don't make the common mistake of confusing a project framework or life cycle as discussed here with IT waterfall delivery, which is just one very particular form of development life cycle. In a generic project life cycle, the stages can be defined however you want them to be defined and incorporate any development or delivery method. The problem is that so many IT people grew up on waterfall software development that they assume all project management is 'waterfall'. Changing this mind-set can be difficult!

3. Address and revalidate the marketing, commercial, operational and technical viability of the project throughout its life

"We are very good at slamming on the brakes if we see we cannot achieve our goals."

All the organizations addressed all aspects throughout the life cycle of a project. No single facet is allowed to proceed at a greater pace than the others as, for example, there is little point in:

No single facet is allowed to proceed at a greater pace than the others

- having an excellent technological product which has no adequate market rationale and cannot be economically produced;
- developing a new service with no delivery or billing capability;
- creating a superb new staff appraisal system if there are no administrative processes to make it work in practice.

As the project moves forward through its life cycle, the level of knowledge should increase and hence the level of risk should decrease (lesson 2). The only exception is where there is a particularly large area of risk and work can be brought forward to understand the problems and manage the consequences as part of a planned risk-management strategy.

Coupled with this, the ability of organizations to stop (terminate) projects was seen to be important. Some expressed themselves to be experts at this. A problem in any one aspect of the project (e.g., market, operations, technology and finance) can lead to termination. For example, one company, with a product leadership strategy, killed a new product just prior to launch as a competitor had just released a superior product. It was better to abort the launch and work on the next generation product than proceed with releasing a new product which could be seen, by the market, as inferior. If the company had gone ahead, its strategy of product leadership and premium pricing would have been compromised, with the technical press rubbing their hands with glee!

Naturally, the gates prior to each stage are the key decision points for revalidating a project. The best organizations also monitor the validity of the project between gates and are prepared to stop if their business objectives are unlikely to be met. At all times, the project timescale, cost, scope and benefits need to be kept in balance (Figure 2.3).

4. Involve stakeholders in the work to understand their current and future needs

"The front line customer interface has been and is our primary focus."

The involvement of stakeholders, such as users, customers and those impacted by the project, is seen as essential in all stages of a project to validate the requirements and proposed solution. Usually, the earlier the involvement, the better the result.

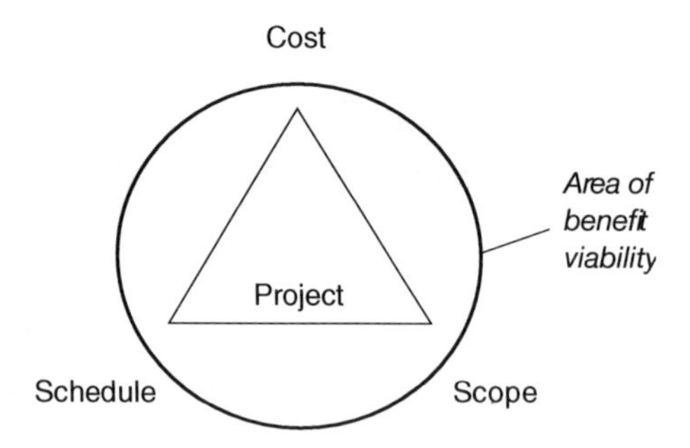

Figure 2.3 The project balance

A project comprises a defined scope, to be delivered in an agreed timescale at an agreed cost. These must be combined in such a way to ensure that the project is always viable and will realize the expected benefits. If any one of these falls outside the area of benefit viability, the others should be changed to bring the project back on target. If this cannot be done, the project should be terminated.

The more 'consultancy-oriented' organizations must, by the nature of their business, talk to customers to ascertain their needs. Yet, even these organizations said they often misinterpreted the real needs of the customer, despite great efforts to avoid this. Where project teams are more removed from their users or customers, there is even greater scope for error.

Many innovative ways have been used to obtain this involvement, including:

- focus groups;
- facilitated workshops;
- early prototyping;
- simulations.

Involving the stakeholders is a powerful mover for change, whilst ignoring them can lead to failure.

Involving the stakeholders is a powerful mover for change, whilst ignoring them can lead to failure. When viewed from a stakeholder's perspective, your project may be just one more that the stakeholder has to cope with as well as fulfilling their usual duties; it might even appear irrelevant or regressive. If the stakeholders' knowledge is needed to understand the requirements and their consent required to make things happen, ignore them at your peril! People who are familiar with agile software development methods (like scrum) will recognize this as an active and engaged 'customer' is a vital role.

5. Build excellence in project management techniques and controls across the organization

"Never see project management as an overhead."

All the organizations I interviewed saw good project management techniques and controls as prerequisites to effecting change. Project management skills are most conspicuous in the engineering-based organizations, particularly those with a project/line matrix management structure. However, other organizations had taken, or were taking, active steps to improve this discipline across all parts of the business.

There should be project management guidance, training and support for all staff connected with projects. This should include senior managers who sponsor projects and programmes or make project-related decisions, and departmental managers who provide resources. Core control techniques identified in the organizations included planning, reporting and managing risk, issues, changes and assurance.

Planning as a discipline was seen as essential.

Planning as a discipline was seen as essential. If you have no definition of the project and no plan, you are unlikely to be successful. Without a plan, it is virtually impossible to communicate your intentions to a team and stakeholders. Further, if there is no plan, phrases such as 'early', 'late' and 'within budget' have no meaning. Planning should be holistic, encompassing schedule, resources cost, scope and benefits refined in light of resource constraints and business risk (Figure 2.4).

Risk was frequently mentioned: using a staged approach (as described in lesson 2) is itself a risk management technique with the gates acting as formal review points where risk is put in the context of the business benefits and cost of delivery. Projects are risky and it is essential to analyze the project and its intended outcomes, determine which are the inherently risky parts and take action to reduce, avoid or, in some cases, insure against those risks.

Despite good planning things do not always go smoothly. Unforeseen issues do arise which, if not resolved, threaten the success of the project. Monitoring and forecasting against the agreed plan is a discipline which ensures events do not take those involved in the project by surprise. This is illustrated by the 'control cycle' in Figure 2.5. The appropriate frequency for the cycle depends on the nature of the work, its stage of development and inherent risk. Monthly is considered the most appropriate by many of the organizations, although in certain circumstances this is increased to weekly. For agile software delivery it is daily!

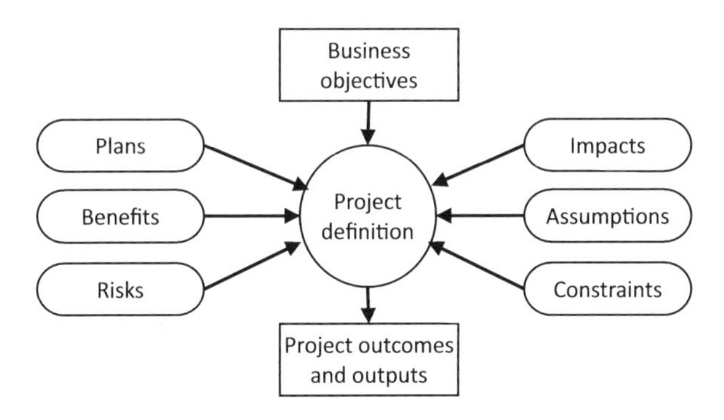

Figure 2.4 Planning

Planning should be holistic, encompassing . . .

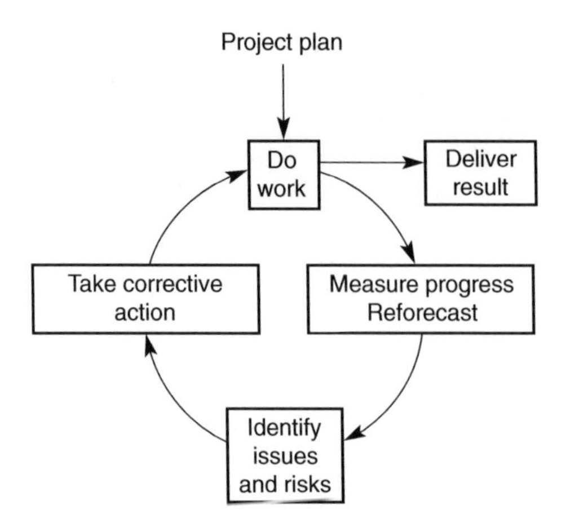

Figure 2.5 Control cycle

The control cycle comprises doing the work as set out in your plan, measuring progress against that plan, identifying any risks, opportunities or issues and taking corrective action to keep the project on track. From time to time, results, in the form of deliverables, are generated. (Copyright © PA Consulting Group, London)

Such monitoring should focus more on future benefits and performance than on what has been completed. Completion of activities is evidence of progress but not sufficient to predict milestones will continue to be met. Managers should check continually to ensure the plan is still fit for its purpose and likely to realize the business benefits on time. Here, the future is more important than the past.

It is a sad fact that many programmes and projects are late, or never reach completion. One of the reasons for this is 'scope creep'. More and more ideas are incorporated into the programme or project resulting in higher costs and later delivery. Controlling change is critical to ensuring the benefits are achieved and the work is not derailed by 'good ideas' or 'good intentions'. Changes are a fact of life and cannot be avoided. Good planning and a staged approach reduce the potential for major change but cannot prevent it. Changes, even beneficial ones, should be controlled to ensure that only those enabling the benefits to be realized are accepted. Contractors are particularly good at controlling change, as their income is directly derived from projects undertaken for customers – doing 'that bit more' without checking its impact on their contractual obligations is not good business. Why should it be any less so when dealing with internal projects?

The full project environment

Lesson 5 says use 'good project management tools and techniques', BUT it is only one of ten findings which provide the full environment for projects to work. Is this why some organizations say, "We do project management, but it doesn't work for us."

6. Break down functional boundaries by using cross-functional teams

"No one in this company can consider themselves outside the scope and influence of projects."

The need for many programmes and projects to draw on people from a range of functions, perhaps even from different organizations, makes a cross-functional team approach essential. Running 'projects' in functional parts with coordination between them always slows down progress, produces less satisfactory results and increases the likelihood of errors. All the organizations in the study recognized this and had working practices which encouraged lateral cooperation and communication (Figure 2.6). In some cases, this went as far as removing staff from their own departmental locations to group them in team work spaces. In others, departments which frequently worked together were located as close as practical in the company's premises. Generally, the closer people work, the better they perform. Although not always possible, closeness can be compensated for by frequent meetings and good communication.

Cross-functional team working, however, is not the only facet. It was also seen that setting direction and decision making also have to be on a cross-functional basis. Decision making and the associated processes was an area where some of the organizations were less than satisfied with their current performance. Either decision makers took too narrow a view or insufficient information was available.

Setting direction and decision making also have to be on a cross-functional basis.

Another requirement of cross-functional working is to ensure both corporate and individual objectives do not conflict. For example, one company found that team members on the same project received different levels of bonuses merely because they belonged to different departments.

The more functionally structured a company is, the more difficult it is to implement effective cross-company working, as is needed in effective portfolio, programme and project management. This is because these, by their nature, cross functional boundaries. For success, the balance of power usually needs to be tipped away from line management (vertical) towards the horizontal portfolio, programme and project structures. For a 'traditional', functionally led company, this is often a sacrifice its leaders refuse to make . . . at the expense of overall business performance.

7. Use dedicated resources for each category of development and prioritize within each category

"We thought long and hard about ring fencing (dedicating) resources and decided, for us, it was the best way to minimise internal conflict."

The management and allocation of resources was acknowledged by many organizations to be their most intransigent problem. There is continual competition for scarce

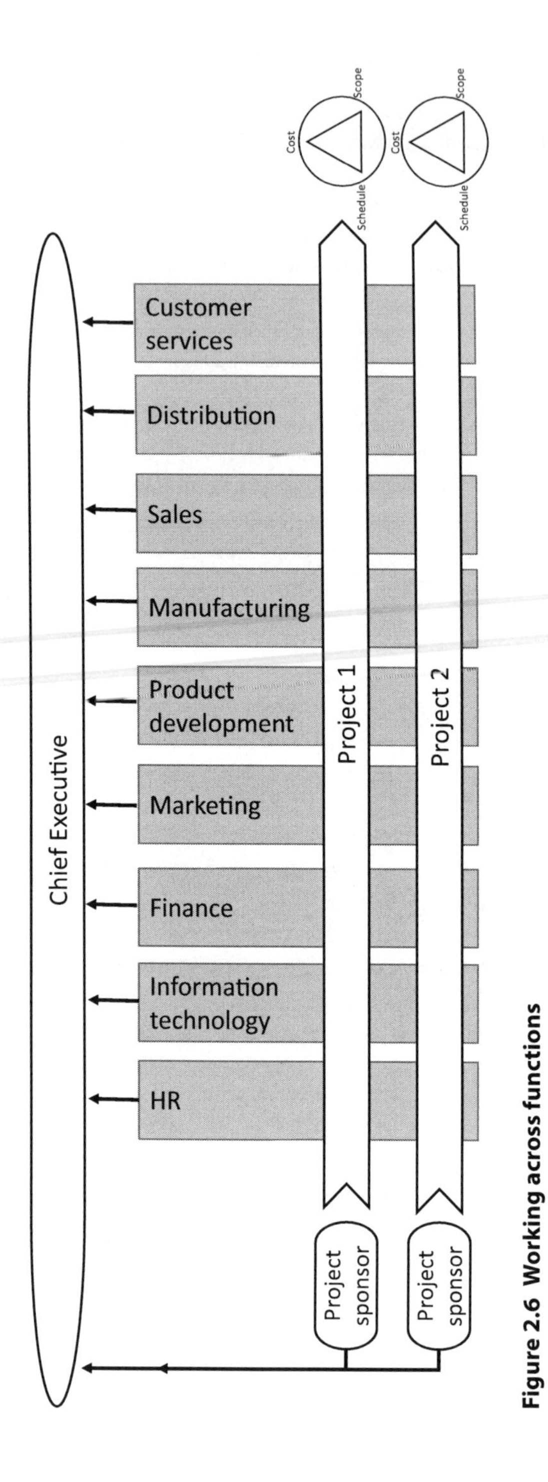

Figure 2.6 Working across functions

A project is a set of activities aligned to achieve a defined result. It draws in people from across the organization who provide their particular expertise and knowledge.

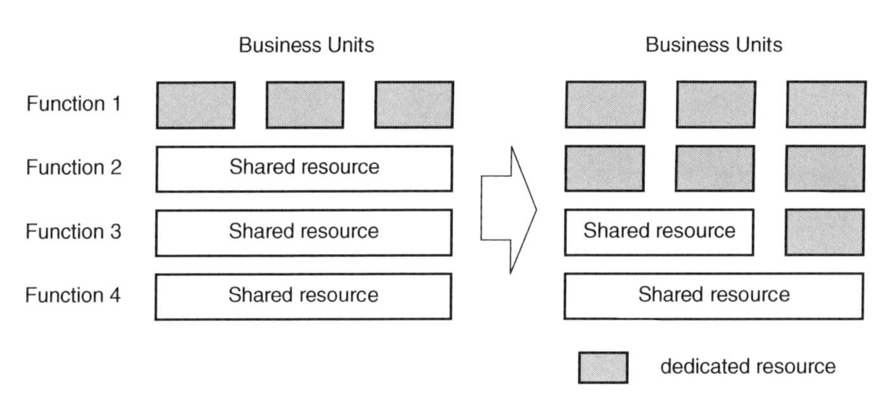

Figure 2.7 Apply dedicated resource to each category of projects (e.g., by strategic business unit, market sector) as deeply as possible

Some organizations, as a result of their organizational structure, share most of their resources across a number of categories. This allows them to deploy the most appropriate people to any project regardless of where they are in the organization. It also minimizes duplication of functions within the organization. Other organizations separate their resource to a greater extent and confine it to working on a single business unit's projects. This allows quicker and more localized resource management but can lead to duplication of functional capabilities.

resources between managers, whether for projects or 'business-as-usual'. In one company, this had reached such a level that it was proving destructive, with very few projects actually being completed, as too many projects were started and few were finished as resources were moved around to deal with the latest crisis.

I discovered that resourcing could be approached in two ways, both of which have their merits.

The first (Figure 2.7) is to apply dedicated (separate) resources for each category of project (say, aligned around a business unit, portfolio or programme) and take this principle as deep as possible into the company. In this way, potential conflicts are limited whilst decisions and choices are more localized. In fact, the more separate and dedicated your resources, the more local your decision making can be, providing you only need to draw resources from that single pool. By 'pool,' I don't mean a single department. A pool can be any number of departments. For example, a global company could have one pool for each of its regions, with the regional lead structuring the organization as they see fit. The downside of such an approach is that you will have to reorganize and resize your resource pools continually to meet demand. In a fast-moving industry, this can mean you might have the right number of people, but they might be deployed in the wrong places; it can be very inefficient. Most traditional, functionally organized companies follow this approach, with each department manager deciding on the number of people they need to undertake the anticipated volume of work for the next financial year.

The second extreme is to have all staff in a single, shared resource pool and use effective matrix management support tools for resource allocation and forecasting (Figure 2.8). This method was adopted, to a greater or lesser extent, by the consulting

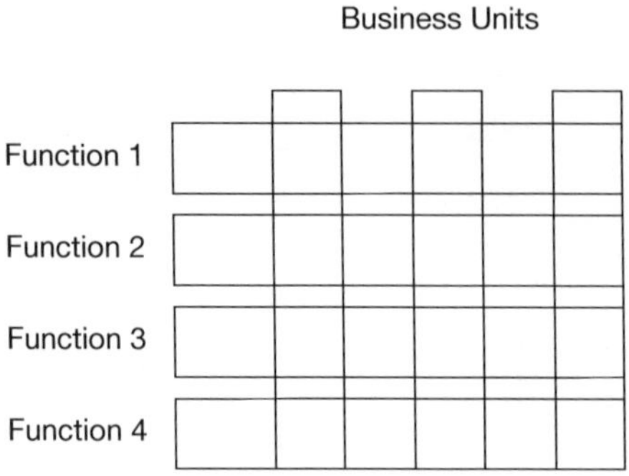

Business Units

Function 1

Function 2

Function 3

Function 4

Figure 2.8 Resources from all functions are applied anywhere, to best effect

In this model, anyone from any function can work on any project. It is the most flexible way of organizing but, without good control systems, is the most complex.

and engineering organizations. A person might work on up to ten projects in a week, and there may be 300 projects in progress at any one time. It is very effective, conceptually simple and totally flexible. Major reorganizations are less frequent but it is also the most difficult to implement in a company with a strong functional management bias, as it means line managers having to defer to 'others' for decisions, something they resist on the basis of their mistaken belief that unless they own the resources and have ultimate decision-making authority, they can't be held accountable.

In practice, a hybrid between the two extremes provides the simplicity of purely functionally based organizations with the flexibility of full matrix-managed organizations. The implication is, however, that:

- roles and accountabilities need to be rigorously defined in both dimensions of the matrix, with no overlaps or gaps;
- the resource management and accounting systems must be able to view the company in a consistent way from both perspectives.

8. Place high emphasis on the early stages of the project

"Skipping the first stage is a driver for failure."

All organizations see the early stages of a project as fundamental to success. Some could not stress this enough. High emphasis for some meant that between 30 to 50% of the project life is spent on the investigative stages before any final output is physically built. One company, from the USA, had research data explicitly demonstrating how this emphasis significantly decreased time to completion. Good investigative work means clearer objectives and plans; work spent on this is rarely wasted. Decisions taken

Decisions taken at the early stages of a project have a far-reaching effect and set the tone for the remainder of the project.

at the early stages of a project have a far-reaching effect and set the direction for the remainder of the project. In the early stages, creative solutions can slash delivery times in half and cut costs dramatically. Once development is under way, however, it is rarely possible to effect savings of anything but a few percent. Good upfront work also reduces the likelihood of change later, as most changes to projects are actually reactive to misunderstandings over scope and approach rather than proactive decisions to change the project for the better. The further you are into the project, the more costly change becomes.

Despite this, there is often pressure, for what appear to be all the right commercial reasons, to skip the investigative stages and 'get on with the real work' as soon as possible (so-called fast tracking, see lesson 2). Two organizations interviewed had found through bitter experience that you cannot go any faster by missing out essential work. One told me, "Skipping the investigative stages led to failure"; the other, "Whenever we've tried to leave a bit out for the sake of speed, we've always failed and had to do more extensive rework later which cost us far in excess of anything we might have saved."

But isn't this lesson flying in the face of agile delivery?

Agile delivery is well established as a great way to determine what your real requirements are. Good agile delivery requires discipline and a rational approach, with each sprint and release building on preceding work. Defining what should be worked on from the backlog and in which sprint is crucial, and it should be risk based. By doing this well, the real requirements and a working solution will emerge sooner; the early sprints are the upfront work. Also, couple this lesson with lesson 2, and you can see that the project stages can be seen as the equivalent to agile releases; the concepts are very similar. You can even look at the classic project life cycle as being 'macro-agile'.

9. Build the business case into the organization's forward plan as soon as the project has been formally approved

"Once it is authorized, pin it down!"

Projects are the vehicles for implementing future strategic change. The most mature organizations are always sure the projects they undertake will produce what they need and fit the company's wider objectives (see lesson 1). Organizations usually have far more proposals for projects than they can handle. In order to choose which to undertake, it is essential to know what future resources (cash, manpower, etc.) have already been committed and what benefits (revenues, cost savings, etc.) are expected. Unless this is done, the 'gap' between where the company is now and where it wants to be is unknown, making the choice of projects to fill the gap more difficult (Figure 2.9).

Organizations handle this by having set points in the project life cycle (see lesson 2) at which resource commitment, cost and benefit streams are built into the business plan. This is usually when a full business case is approved, which is the point at which 'what you want to do' becomes 'what you are going to do'.

Projects do not recognize fiscal quarters

Clearly, financial planning and resource systems must be able to be updated at any time as projects do not recognize fiscal quarters as relevant to start or finish dates. Also, any such information systems must be a part of the business and not an 'add-on' outside the usual pattern of planning, forecasting and accounting. Information systems are looked at in more detail in Part VI of this book.

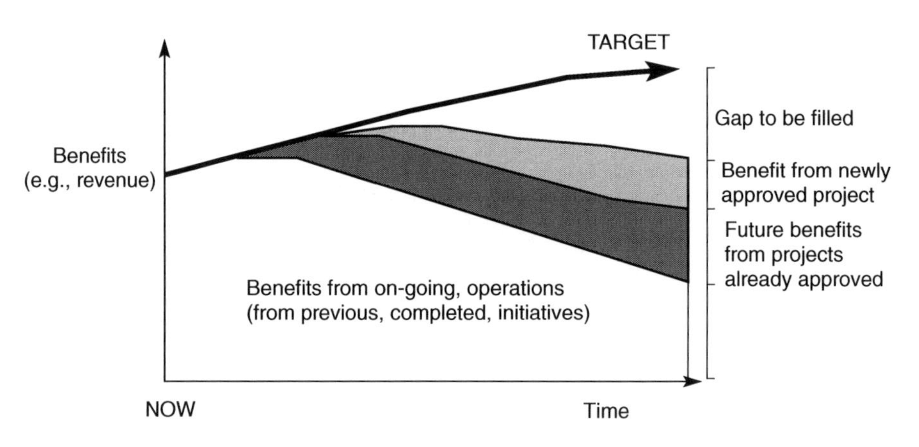

Figure 2.9 Build the project into your business plan as soon as it is authorized

The figure shows the revenue generated by the organization if no new projects are started. It then shows the revenue which will be generated by projects which are currently in progress. The gap between the sum of these and the target revenue needs to be filled. This can be by starting off new projects which will cause this to be generated or/and by starting initiatives in the line which will deliver the extra revenue to fill the gap.

10. Close the project formally to build a bridge to the future, to learn any lessons and to ensure a clean handover

"We close projects quickly to prevent any left-over budget from being wasted."

Closing projects formally is essential for some organizations. For example, low margin organizations must close the project accounts down to ensure no more time is spent working on completed projects, no matter how interesting! Their tight profit margins simply won't allow this luxury. From another angle, component products in an aircraft can be in service long after the project team has dispersed or even well after some team members have retired. Not to have full records (resurrection documents) on these critical components at times of need, such as an air accident, is unthinkable.

All organizations interviewed either had a formal closure procedure or were actively implementing one. This usually takes the form of a closure report, which highlights any outstanding issues, ensures explicit handover of accountabilities and makes it clear to those who need to know that the project is finished.

Another key reason given for formal closure was the provision of an opportunity to learn lessons and improve the workings of the organization. One company left 'closure' out of its process in the original design but soon realized it was vital and added it in. It simply found that if it did not close projects the list of projects it was doing was just growing by the day and funds were leaking at an unacceptable rate.

Workout 2.1 – Review of the ten lessons

1. As a management team, review the ten lessons given in this chapter and ask yourself how well you apply them in your organization at present. Agree a mark out of 10 and mark the relevant column, from Table 2.1, with an 'X'.
   10 = we currently apply this lesson fully across our organization and can demonstrate this with ease.
   0 = this is not applied at all.
2. Ask the sponsors of a number of your programmes or projects (say, at least five) to answer the same question, mark their responses with an 'S'.
3. Ask the managers of a number of your programmes or projects (say, at least five) to answer the same question, mark their responses with a 'P'.
4. Ask your line managers (say, at least five) to answer the same question, mark their responses with a 'L'.
5. Discuss, as a management team, your responses and those of the other groups. Did you all agree or were there differences of opinion? If so, why do you think this is? Which lessons are not being applied? Why not?
6. What do you propose to do about any large variations?

Table 2.1 The ten lessons based on the research findings

	Poor										*Excellent*
Lesson	*0*	*1*	*2*	*3*	*4*	*5*	*6*	*7*	*8*	*9*	*10*
1 My project is driven by benefits which support the organization's business strategy.											
2 We use a defined project framework (life cycle), with a staged approach.											
3 We address and revalidate the marketing, commercial, operational and technical viability of the project throughout its life.											
4 We engage stakeholders to understand their current and future needs.											
5 We promote excellence in project management techniques and controls across the project.											
6 We use a cross-functional team.											
7 We always have the resources we need, when we need them.											
8 We place(d) high emphasis on the early stages of the project.											
9 We built (or will build) the business case into the organization's forward plan as soon as the project was formally approved.											
10 At project closure we will learn any lessons and ensure a clean handover with an explicit project "end" point.											

Organization context: we're all different!

Organizations can only succeed if their processes (or methods) for undertaking work (such as in portfolios, programmes and projects) are supported by compatible accountabilities, culture and systems (as shown previously in Figure 2.2). The lessons in this chapter describe how organizations use or are moving towards a staged approach, even though the environments in which they operate are very different. So, when you hear the plaintive cry of, "This won't work here, we're different!" you can confidently answer, "Yes, we are different but we can make it work if we really want to."

The following sections describe some of the wide range of approaches taken by different organizations.

Structure and accountabilities

Organization structures vary from pure project to pure functional; this impacts the ease of cross-functional working and hence the effectiveness of project management. Figure 2.10 shows the range of organization shapes and the effect they tend to have on cross functional management, especially programme and portfolio management. In heavily functionally driven organizations, programme and project manager are generally very weak, disempowered and at the mercy of the functional

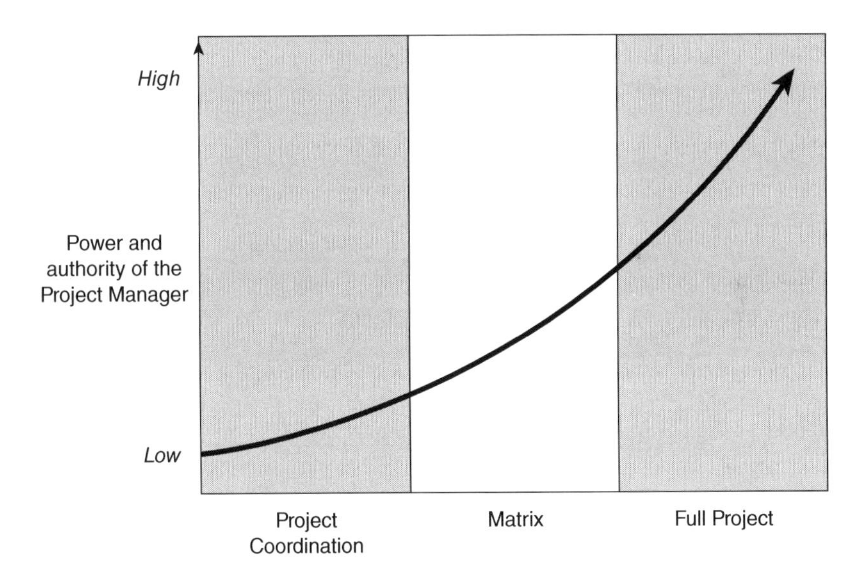

Figure 2.10 Project organizations

Organizations can be structured with differing emphasis on line and project management authority. When the most power is invested in line management, project managers are reduced to a 'coordination' role. In full project structures, the project manager has greater power than the line manager. The line manager is there to satisfy the resourcing needs of the projects and business as usual processes only. The mid-point between these extremes is the 'matrix', where there is a balance of power which is derived from the role someone takes as well as their position in the line.

heads of department. They are often called "project coordinators" which is very apt. In full project organizations, the project managers have greater power and influence over and above heads of department. In the middle is matrix management. This is a much-maligned structure but one which can be very effective in organizations which require a relatively stable functional structure but still need to have the efficiency advantages of a cross-functional approach. People often say "Matrix organizations don't work, they just confuse people." Yes, that can be true if they are implemented in an environment with no suitable controls and incompatible line and project roles, accountabilities and processes. Generally, those organizations which have moved the balance of power away from the line (vertical) and towards the horizontal structures such as projects, have found cross-functional working more effective and reap greater rewards. Another reason why matrix organizations fail is because they have been set up on a false premise. Sometimes a matrix is described as a structure where power and authority is 'shared' between the line manager and project manager; if that's what people are working to, no wonder matrices don't work. The role of a line manager and that of a project manager are different. Two people cannot be accountable for the same work or decision – 'sharing' is not relevant; clarity of role is.

Generally, in a matrix:

- **Line managers** are accountable for deploying the right people on projects; the methods and processes used for the specialist work undertaken by their people, including quality assurance and control; ensuring their people are trained and skilled as needed; day-to-day human resource tasks (such as career planning, training, absence monitoring, adherence to organization-wide policies and procedures);
- **Portfolio, programme and project managers** are accountable to the respective sponsor for delivering a successful programme or project; fostering a team approach, ensuring the work undertaken will deliver the required outcomes and realize the benefits in time, to proven quality and within the cost constraints; ensuring the team members understand their role and what others need from them for the programme or project to succeed.

The acceptance of clear definitions of roles, accountabilities and relationships for the key players are most apparent in those organizations which are comfortable with their processes. Further, the separation of 'role' from job title is seen as crucial to maintaining simplicity as, in cross-functional, programme and project environments, the role a person takes (e.g., as a portfolio sponsor, programme manager, project manager or team manager) is more important than their job title or position in the functional hierarchy.

Some organizations set up cross-functional groups to undertake particular tasks on an on-going basis. The most obvious are those groups which undertake the screening of proposals prior to entry to the project process. In this way, the structures created match the process (rather than leading or following the process). This must also apply to any review or decision-making bodies which are created. The one most commonly found to be adrift is that relating to financial authorizations. Many organizations have parallel financial processes shadowing their project processes, demanding similar but different justifications and supporting material. This is usually found where finance functions have disproportionate power and act as controllers rather than in an assurance or business partner mode. The more mature organizations ensured that there was little divergence between decisions required for finance and those relating to strategy. They make certain that financial expertise is built into the plan in the same way as any other discipline, with finance people being included on the programme or project team.

Programmes and projects are 'temporary' and cease to exist once completed. Clear accountability for on-going management of the outputs in the line ensures that the right people are involved, and the handover is clean and explicit. Career progression and continuity of employment for people involved in programmes and projects is an important consideration. Programmes and projects are about change and the future of your organization. Good organizations ensure the people who create these changes are retained, and projects are seen as stepping stones to career progression and not as career limiting or the fast track to redundancy. You need your best people to create your future organization, so make sure you keep them.

You need your best people to create your future organization, so make sure you keep them.

Don't use structure to solve a cultural problem

A large, global company was having difficulty ensuring its people worked cooperatively across department and functional boundaries (typical silo behaviour). This had been raised on a number of occasions at senior team level. One day, the chief executive officer told me he had fixed the problem. "How?" I asked. "I've put all problem functions under Andy," he replied. "How does an extra management tier and the creation of an even bigger silo solve the problem?" I asked. There was silence lasting for a full minute. "Well, that's what I've done," he eventually said.

Clearly, this chief executive officer had not fully understood the problem and was merely offloading it onto someone else. Further, he was using a structural solution in an attempt to solve a cultural problem. (You will recall Figure 2.2.)

Culture

Culture is probably the least reproducible facet of an organization and the most intangible. It has a very significant impact on how people behave and how programmes and projects are directed and managed. Unfortunately, many cultural factors are outside a managers' ability to influence and need to be addressed at programme, portfolio or corporate level.

For example, the corporate attitude to risk and the way an organization's people behave if high-risk projects have to be stopped will have far reaching effects on the quality of the outputs produced. In avionics, the 'least risk' approach is generally preferred to the 'least cost', despite being within an industry in which accepting the lowest tender is a primary driver.

One company interviewed, explicitly strives to make its own products obsolete as it clearly sees itself as a product leader. It is forever initiating new projects to build better products, quicker and more frequently than the competition. This same company focusses its rewards on teams, not individuals, and takes great care to ensure its performance measurement systems avoid internal conflict. Another company admitted that its bonus schemes were all based on functional performance and not team performance despite 60% of the staff working cross-functionally. An example was given of a staff member who received no bonus for his year's work whilst all his colleagues on the same project (in a different department!) had large bonuses. This was not seen as 'fair' and was the result of basing bonuses on something that could be counted easily rather than on something that actually counted!

Following Dr W. Edwards Deming's belief that individual performance schemes are counterproductive, another company had no annual bonus scheme below senior management level but provided immediate 'Well Done' awards for individuals they consider merit them. These are given almost immediately after the event which prompted the award and are well appreciated. This same company was 100% employee owned and had a sales force who did not receive sales commissions.

Most of the organizations interviewed encouraged direct access to decision makers as it improved the quality of decisions. Roles, rather than 'job descriptions', promote this. Functional hierarchies tend to have a greater 'power distance' and decision makers become remote from the effects of their actions or the issues involved. You'll also find departmental managers massaging the reports provided by their staff in order to show their department in a more favourable light, rather than telling the truth

As a paradox, those organizations which have the most comprehensive control systems (project accounting, resource management, time sheeting, etc.) are able to delegate decision making lower in the organization and hence empower their people. Through the use of such systems, senior management does not lose sight of what is happening and always knows who is accountable and, hence, who to contact if they need to.

Practise what you preach?

A major producer of project scheduling software confided in me that when it came to managing its own internal business projects, all the good practice and advice the company advocated as essential to its customers was ignored. The culture of the company's management simply does not fit the product it sells. Organizations can be very successful without any rational approach to business projects but are unlikely to remain successful for long.

Workout 2.2 – What happens to project managers in your organization when the project is finished?

(a) They are kept on the payroll and assigned to a manager for "pay and rations" until a new project or suitable alternative work is found.
(b) They are put on a redeployment list and then made redundant if no suitable opening is found for them within x months.
(c) They leave the organization straightaway if no suitable opening is found for them.
(d) They leave the organization.
(e) I don't have this problem as they are all contracted in when needed.

If you answered (b) to (d) you are probably very functionally driven, and projects tend to be difficult to undertake and those working on them have little stake in completing them. If you answered (e) you may be in a very fortunate position to be able to source such key people OR you are in the same situation as (b) to (d).

If you answered (a) you are probably in a good position to reap the rewards of project working or are already doing so!

Debate with your colleagues: what motivates your staff to work on projects?

If you answered (b) to (d), do you really expect to have your best people volunteering to work on your projects? Why would they do this?

Systems and tools

A number of those interviewed stated that the accounting systems must integrate process, project and line management. Programmes and projects must not be seen as an 'add-on'.

Resource management and allocation was found to be a problem for many organizations. Those which had the least difficulty centrally managed their entire resource across all their departments, and the departments and the projects used the same core system; only the reporting emphasis was different.

Other organizations had developed systems to cope with what they saw as their particular needs; for example, risk management or action tracking.

The USA-based organizations had acquired the practice of constantly validating their processes and systems through benchmarking.

Conclusion

The study confirmed that:

- The staged framework is widely used for business change projects and is delivering better value than more traditional functionally based project processes.
- A holistic, enterprise-wide cross-functional management-approach, such as portfolio and programme management, is essential for success.

What is apparent, however, is that the infrastructure varies considerably across the organization which took part in the study – in particular, the quality and immediacy of information decision makers have to support them. For example, it is usually relatively easy to decide if a project in isolation is viable or not, but if you need to decide which of a number of projects should go ahead it becomes more difficult. You'll have to assess the relative merits of each project, and to do this, you need answers to the following questions:

- what overall business objectives is each project driving towards?
- on what other projects does each project depend?
- what other projects depend on this project?
- when will we have the capacity to undertake each project (in terms of people and other resources)?
- can the business, suppliers and customers accept this change together with all the other changes being imposed? If so, when?
- do we have enough cash to carry out all the projects?
- after what length of time will each project cease to be viable?
- how big is the overall risk to the organization with and without this project?

The challenge lies in having processes, systems, accountabilities and a culture which address these questions, both at a working level and at the decision-making level. If this is not dealt with, the result will be:

- the wrong projects being undertaken;
- late delivery;
- failure to realize the expected benefits.

When your boss reports to you!

In one company, it was not unusual to find directors reporting to graduates on projects. The directors are on the project teams to add their particular knowledge and skills and not to lead the project. This company saw nothing strange about this arrangement. The most appropriate people were being used in the most appropriate way.

Reorganizing isn't always the solution!

*Quotation from Gaius Petronius Arbiter, AD66

Enemies Within

Running a project is difficult enough, but we often make it more arduous than need be by creating problems for ourselves. Here are a few examples:

Reorganizing – either the company or a part of it. Tinkering with your structure is usually NOT the solution to your problems; it just confuses people. The Romans realized this 2,000 years ago (see the cartoon). If, however, you are a senior executive, this is a great way to hide non-delivery!

Functional thinking – not taking the helicopter, the organization-wide view. This often happens when executives' or individuals' bonuses are based on targets which are at odds with the organization's needs, e.g., sales bonus rewarded on revenue, regardless of profit or contribution.

Having too many rules – the more rules you have, the more sinners you create and the less happy your people become. Have you ever met a happy bureaucrat?

Disappearing and changing sponsors – without a sponsor there should be no project. Continual changing of the 'driver' will cause you to lose focus and forget WHY you are undertaking the project. Consider terminating such a project to see who really wants it!

Ignoring the risks – risks don't go away, so acknowledge them and manage them. If I said that a certain airplane is likely to crash, would you fly on it? And yet, every day executives approve projects when a simple risk analysis shows they are highly likely to fail.

Dash in and get on with it! – if a project is that important, you haven't the time NOT to plan your way ahead. High activity levels do not necessarily mean action or progress.

Analysis paralysis – you need to investigate, but only enough to gain the confidence to move on. Analysis paralysis is the opposite to dash in and ignore the risks. It is also a ploy used to delay projects: "I haven't quite enough information to make a decision, just do some more study work."

Untested assumptions – all assumptions are risks; treat them as such.

Forgetting what the project is for – if this happens terminate the project. If it is that useful, someone will scream and remember why it is being done.

Executive's 'pet projects' – have no exceptions. If an executive's idea is really so good, it should stand up to the scrutiny that all the others go through. He or she may have a helicopter view, but he might also have his head in the clouds.

3

Portfolios, programmes and projects

We need to take a value and benefit-based approach, directing and managing our work across the departments (horizontal management), where the work is aimed at achieving specific business objectives.

> *"We cannot solve our problems with the same thinking we used when we created them."*
>
> ALBERT EINSTEIN, 1879–1955

- **Be value or benefit focussed, not just budget constrained.**
- **Some people need to work on both existing operations and creating new capabilities.**
- **Portfolios are governed through a business plan.**
- **Programmes and projects are governed through business cases.**
- **Think about how best to manage something, not what it is you are managing.**

Managing horizontally

Chapter 1 looked at the problems faced by many organizations through not being able to achieve all they want though the lack of funds and resources, whilst wasting those same resources and funds because of their inability to co-ordinate their current work. At the same time, demands for new work continue to arrive, adding to the pressure on scarce resources and finance. Chapter 2 took examples from real life organizations which can help solve this management problem. The solution depends on adopting a different management perspective; rather than trying to manage the organization through its traditional departmental structure and control work through cost centres (vertical management), we need to take a value or benefit based perspective, directing and managing our work across the departments (horizontal management), where the work is aimed at achieving specific business objectives. This should support the organization's strategy by harnessing the true power of matrix management, applying it in a common sense and practical way.

All but the very simplest of organizations operate in two main areas:

- **managing the day-to-day operations**, providing the products or services that are the basis of whatever the organizations offers;
- **changing** (and hopefully improving!) the current way 'business as usual' works, such as creating and delivering new and better products and services and implementing more efficient and effective ways of doing business.

Projects are increasingly being used to manage 'change' activities, but business is rarely so simple that a single project can achieve all that is needed to direct and manage all the necessary changes. This requires a number of projects, each aimed at delivering a required outcome to realize the benefits the organization needs. The most important questions in respect are:

- Why are you doing this project?
- What business objective and outcomes are you hoping to achieve?
- What benefits do you hope to realize?

Don't jump to solutions!

None of the three questions posed earlier concerns the solution. Unless you understand your overall business objectives and aims, you cannot define a suitable solution. Too often, people 'jump to solutions' rather than take the time to understand the business issue or opportunity. Having understood your objective, look at different ways this could be addressed, finally choosing the solution to meet the need.

Usually a number of initiatives are necessary to achieve an organization's aims.

Usually a number of initiatives are necessary to achieve an organization's aims. For large organizations, this can mean hundreds, or even thousands, of projects and other types of work) being undertaken in a year, together with solving a myriad of business as usual and operational problems. If that organization also uses projects to deliver its day-to-day operations (such as for an engineering contractor or software development house), the number of projects increases further.

Lesson 4 in Chapter 2 emphasizes the need to involve stakeholders. If, for example, you are developing a new service management approach, it is a good idea to include the service managers in the design, testing and validating of a solution. Success relies on them using the new system and they probably know more about service management in their business than the people creating the new tools. In most cases, therefore, certain people and resources need to be shared between the change activities and business as usual activities; you cannot totally separate them.

If a business or organization is to be successful, the managers need to understand:

- how bundles (or portfolios) of projects are used together with other business activities to further their aims and;
- how resources and funds need to be allocated as a result.

If managers don't grasp this, they will continue to be dogged by the problems highlighted in Chapter 1 and be overtaken by competitors who do 'get it'. This chapter covers the management structures you need to use to reap the rewards of being a value focussed business or organization (see Figure 3.1). These management structures include:

- **business portfolios** – everything you are doing;
- **programmes** – bundles of projects and other work, aimed at a common objective;
- **projects** – initiatives aimed at filling a specific business need;
- **other work** – initiatives which are either not run as projects or comprises any other type work required to support the business;
- **work packages** – where the 'real work' happens.

The formal definitions of these words are given later in this chapter and covered in greater detail in Parts III to V of this book.

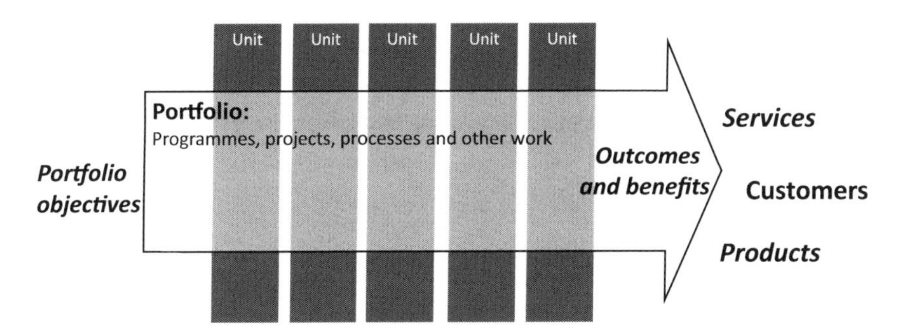

Figure 3.1 Taking a 'horizontal', value-based perspective

The solution to many management problems depends on us having a different management perspective; rather than trying to manage the organization through its traditional departmental (unit) structure and control work through cost centres (vertical management), we need to take a 'value-based' approach, directing and managing our work across the departments (horizontal management), where the work is aimed at achieving specific business objectives, which in turn should support the organization's strategy.

An example of a simple business portfolio

A business portfolio is best explained by using a simplified example.

Building a better and growing business

Assume you are the CEO of a small manufacturing business in a specialist product market. Your board has challenged you to increase revenue from £10m to £15m in two years, whilst increasing profitability.

After six months, you report back to board telling them you've chosen to meet the objective by increasing your share of an under-exploited segment of your target market. Your alternative would have been to withdraw from that market and save the associated costs (always consider alternatives, including 'do nothing'!) and then look for new markets; this is considered too risky.

In order to achieve the required increase in revenue, you have decided to run five projects (see Figure 3.2) with the aim of:

- enhancing your current product to include some new features and thereby stay ahead of the competition. (Project 1 – enhance old product.);
- developing a new product to exploit an unfulfilled need identified in the market. To do this quickly, you had decided to launch a basic version of the new product, as soon as practical, to start engaging the market, using existing manufacturing capability. (Project 2 – the basic new product.) The launch is being followed up four months later with an enhanced product which meets the full needs. (Project 2A – the enhanced new product.);
- decreasing delivery time to protect revenues; speed of delivery is a buying factor for your target market, and you consider your current delivery channels are too

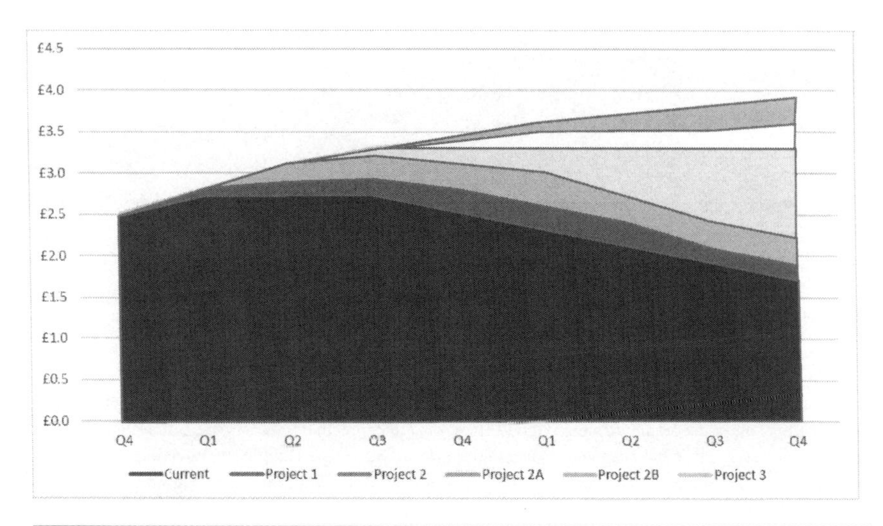

Schedule	Q4	Q1	Q2	Q3	Q4	Q1	Q2	Q3	Q4
Initial quest									
Project 1									
Project 2									
Project 2A									
Project 2B									
Project 3									

Revenue £m	Q4	Q1	Q2	Q3	Q4	Q1	Q2	Q3	Q4
Current	£2.5	£2.7	£2.7	£2.7	£2.5	£2.3	£2.1	£1.9	£1.7
Project 1		£0.1	£0.2	£0.2	£0.3	£0.3	£0.3	£0.2	£0.2
Project 2			£0.2	£0.3	£0.3	£0.4	£0.3	£0.3	£0.3
Project 2A				£0.1	£0.2	£0.3	£0.6	£0.9	£1.1
Project 2B					£0.1	£0.2	£0.2	£0.2	£0.3
Project 3						£0.1	£0.2	£0.3	£0.3
Total	**£2.5**	**£2.8**	**£3.1**	**£3.3**	**£3.4**	**£3.6**	**£3.7**	**£3.8**	**£3.9**

Figure 3.2 Example business portfolio

The schedule for the projects within the business portfolio is shown in the middle; each bar represents a project, with its start and end point. The top part of the figure shows the revenue expected as a result of each project coming to fruition, layered on the revenues you expect from the current product. The revenue is shown numerically at the bottom of the figure.

slow. If the speed of delivery can be increased, it will enhance revenues by enabling you to win business from competitors. (Project 2B – decrease delivery time.);

- aiming to protect your reputation and hence, revenue by addressing a quality problem in manufacturing the current product. Whilst the levels of faults have been acceptable to the target market in the past, this is not expected to be the case in the future; customers have higher expectations. If faults stay at present levels, customers will choose competitors' products. (Project 3 – reduce manufacturing faults.).

You point out to the board that the five projects are aligned to your overall strategy and each provides a discrete business benefit. Most are independent, with the exception of Project 2A, which depends on Project 2, as you cannot enhance a product until you know what that product is. You have decided to split the new product development into two phases (Projects 2 and 2A) in order to gain an early foothold in the market and earn revenue earlier than would otherwise be the case. Often, organizations make their projects too big or lengthy but you know that if you can deliver the required outcomes in smaller 'chunks of change' and start to realize benefits sooner, you are more likely to be successful in gaining market share and implementation will be easier. Having four independent streams means that delays in one will not threaten the success of the others; you have spread the risk.

Finally, you emphasize to the board the need to ensure the benefits from the existing product are in fact realized by ensuring 'business as usual' is not disrupted. Your aim is to obtain a total of £15m revenue. The benefits from your current product and future projects and initiatives need to be sufficiently high to meet that target.

As a business manager, you are not particularly concerned with the individual performance of each project and product, but in the total benefit. You know that everything is unlikely go as planned, some projects will do well, others not so well. Thus, if the current products start to sell better than expected, a delay in one of the new projects might not be too significant. A drop in benefits from the current product set might lead to cash flow difficulties, meaning the five projects might not all be affordable; trade-offs and choices might need to be made.

How did the projects come about?

How did the CEO and leadership team derive their approach and end up with the five projects described earlier? The starting point was a problem for the directors of the organization: the board required higher profits. The directors therefore needed to look at their current mix of products and markets and decide the most likely areas for gaining the additional, profitable revenue, as well as considering possible new products and markets. Project 0 was therefore initiated to analyze the situation and recommend possible solutions. One option identified by the analysis was either to take a minimum prescribed market share of a particular segment or withdraw from it completely. It was considered untenable to keep the status quo. This would lead to a decline in revenue to about $7m per year. This conversation is firmly within the domain of business strategy and planning, and what is needed now is to act on this. The review might have recommended three independent projects:

- enhance the existing product (Project 1);
- develop a new product (Project 2);
- reduce faults (Project 3).

Each project fulfils the definition of a business project by realizing discrete benefits as defined in its business case. Each project will further the aims of the organization to attain more revenue. By being independent of each other, the risks are spread as delays in one are not likely to affect the other projects.

The team working on Project 2, however, found a time constraint on manufacturing the new product. It was not possible to complete this project in the time required and hence a decision was made to create the new product in two phases (i.e., two projects). We now have four projects:

- enhance the existing product (Project 1);
- develop a new product (Project 2);
- enhance the new product (Project 2A);
- reduce faults (Project 3).

Once Project 2 was under way, the team discovered, as part of their market research, that delivery time was a far more important buying factor than realized. If amendments to Project 2 were made to incorporate this, it would have slipped, and the revenue targets missed. Consequently, a separate project was initiated to take this aspect into account (Project 2B, decrease delivery time).

The five projects reported on by the CEO to the board could not have come about directly as the result of the strategic review. The organization simply would not have known enough at that time to reach that conclusion. Only three projects were envisioned as a result of the review; the other two came about as a result of what was discovered whilst undertaking those projects. This highlights an important feature of business portfolios; they are not predetermined but emerge as a result of what is happening inside the organization and in its wider business context. People have to manage business portfolios against an ever-moving backdrop and flow of new information; nothing is fixed and wholly predictable and the constituent parts of a portfolio are likely to change. Portfolios are continuous and, unlike programmes, projects and work packages, are not time-bound, although they do include time constrained targets.

Note that each project in the example business portfolio is defined such that it delivers a slice of benefit, either independently or, as in the case of Projects 2 and 3, in series. Also notice how the business solution has been broken into discrete pieces. This has the effect of making them easier to implement, enabling benefits to be realized earlier than if the full scope was undertaken in a single project. You can proceed with some projects as soon as you're ready, as they are relatively straight-forward, whilst for other projects you might still be looking for a solution. Some projects are riskier than others, and you can deal with this by taking each project forward a stage at a time (see lesson 2, from Chapter 2), making decisions on what to do next as more reliable information becomes available. None of the decisions noted here can be taken by the project sponsor or manager of the individual projects but require the high-level perspective that business portfolio management provides.

Definitions for business portfolios, programmes and projects

The example, earlier, is far simpler than the situations you are likely to find in practice. Most business portfolios comprise many more initiatives (often thousands for large organizations). Nevertheless, the example demonstrates some key aspects of business portfolios:

- business portfolios are continuous. The overall portfolio should last as long as the organization it represents;
- the scope of a business portfolio changes; it can comprise a large number of initiatives, each proceeding to different timescales;
- new information (problems and opportunities) emerge from the work being undertaken within the portfolio;
- the business context surrounding the portfolio is continuously changing;
- the viability of the portfolio (as a whole) is more important than that of any component part;
- the portfolio should be constructed to reflect the risks you are willing to take.

A **business portfolio** comprises current benefit generating business activities, together with a loosely coupled but tightly aligned portfolio of programmes, projects and other work, aimed at realizing the benefits of part of a business plan or strategy. A business portfolio comprises all or part of an organization's investment required to achieve its objectives. For large or diverse organizations, a business portfolio can include other portfolios in order to ensure the span of control is manageable and to allow a degree of independence between business portfolios and hence more local decision making. Good scoping of portfolios minimizes interdependencies. A business portfolio is governed through its business plan. Business plans tend to be drawn up to reflect the organization's fiscal year and might cover a period of time of a number of years, with regular review points. I expect most of us have been involved in quarterly performance reviews (QPRs) for our parts of the businesses we work for or who work for us!

A **programme** is a tightly coupled and tightly aligned grouping of projects and other work managed as a temporary, flexible organization created to coordinate, direct, oversee and deliver outputs, outcomes and benefits related to a set of strategic objectives. Programmes can be undertaken in one or more phases, each of which is structured around distinct step changes in capability and benefit realization and is itself managed as a programme. Programmes are governed through a business case. A programme's business case covers the period from the start of the programme until it is closed but should reflect in any financial or economic analysis the resultant cash flows following the closure of the programme (if any).

A **project**, in a business environment, is a piece of work with a beginning and end, undertaken in stages, within defined cost and time constraints, directed at achieving stated business outcomes and benefits. A project can be standalone within a business portfolio or part of a programme. If a project is standalone, it should be governed through its business case; if it is part of a programme it should be governed by the programme's business case, although it might also have its own business case within the constraints of the programme's business case. A project's business case covers the period from the start of the project until it is closed but will reflect in any financial or economic analysis the resultant cash flows following the closure of the project.

Different definitions are used by different people

The use of the terms 'project', 'programme' and 'portfolio' varies from organization to organization and even within organizations. Colloquially, the words 'programme' and 'project' are often used interchangeably and might not have any foundation in any published standard or methodology. The terms used in this book might not match the definitions you have in your head or which have been prescribed in your organization. To be clear, I have used the term 'business portfolio' rather than simply 'portfolio' as the term 'portfolio' on its own, is widely used (and useful!) in many other contexts. Often, in general conversation, these differences in terminology don't matter as the context of the conversation usually makes the meaning clear. When you are explaining how they fit together in a process or methodology, the distinctions, however, becomes important. The terms used in this book are consistent with those that you'll find in the ISO standards, professional bodies of knowledge and published methodologies, such as those by AXELOS. I have, however, made the definitions in this book more flexible by drawing on what I consider are the best features of the published definitions and which match the messages and techniques within this book and in the its companion, *The Project Workout*. I have no doubt that definitions will continue to evolve and arguments continue to rage, but that's life. It is however, up to you to choose what the terminology for your organization is and use it consistently. I have advice on that in Part VI of this book.

Projects and programmes are not the only management structures required to run a business in the form of a business portfolio. For example, 'business as usual' does not fit into those definitions as it is a continuous stream of work. In addition, 'projects' are not the only vehicles for managing change; we have an ever-growing range of management methods which can be used independently of a project. For example, if I want to improve performance on the production lines in my factory, I might apply LEAN/Six sigma methods to the current manufacturing process, ensuring a continuous stream of incremental improvements are implemented as the work proceeds. I might also use agile software development to continually upgrade the features on a service platform. We therefore need another management structure to represent the 'non-project' work; I have simply called this 'other work'.

Other work is work within a business portfolio or programme which is not managed as a project. Examples include:

- business as usual operations;
- service delivery;
- support services such as finance and HR;
- on-going improvement initiatives not run as projects, but using a defined approach, such as agile delivered platform-based upgrades and LEAN six sigma.

The introduction of 'other work' as a management structure is vital for the effective implementation of business portfolio and programme management, as it gives you the freedom to use whatever management method is appropriate in your organization;

this makes the business portfolio management approach future-proof in the event of new management techniques being invented. After all, 'project management' is not the answer to everything!

Business portfolios, programmes and projects are merely management constructs. They only create outputs which are useful for management (such as plans and business cases); they don't actually create any outputs useful to end users or customers. They are simply a way of shaping the management of your organization and, as such, a vital aspect of governance (governance is addressed in detail in Chapter 4). You will, however, hear people in a project context talk about the 'real work', which is the actual coding of software, pouring concrete, laying track, fitting out an office, serving a customer, making a sale or whatever relates to the business objective you are aiming to satisfy. The management structure used for 'real work' is called a work package.

Business portfolios, programmes and projects are merely management constructs.

A **work package** is a set of information relevant to the creation of one or more deliverables or outputs. It comprises a description of the outputs required and details of any constraints; it is managed through its work plan. As it is simply a 'chunk of work', it can be part of a project or 'other work'.

For completeness, we'll define **business portfolio, programme and project management** as an integrated way of meeting an organization's ambitions, driving better decisions and increasing the likelihood of successful outcomes.

Be outcome focussed, not just fixated on outputs

You might be thinking: "But I was told that projects create outputs and programmes deliver outcomes and realize benefits; are you now telling me projects can also deliver outcomes and realize benefits?"

Yes, I am. A lot of people see the key difference between a programme and a project is that projects only deliver outputs. You can have projects which just deliver outputs, and that is often how contractors see the world. If you want to simplify your management structures, however, you should not limit yourself to this viewpoint. The UK government certainly takes the view that projects can (and should) be used to deliver outcomes and realize benefits. Their thinking (and mine!) is that it is outcomes that make the difference, whether for business or social change. As a result, a project should not be considered completed until you have achieved an outcome; that is to say, enough change has happened and enough benefits have started to flow to know you will meet your business objectives. We have all heard of IT systems that are developed, made live and then not used because the so called 'business project' wasn't done properly. If we all thought first in terms of outcomes and benefits, and then work out what has to happen in order to achieve these, we would end up with fewer 'white elephant' outputs, adding no value whatsoever. The main tenet of this book and its companion, *The Project Workout*, is to be business and benefit driven. Outputs are necessary, have to be defined and delivered but they don't, on their own, add value. We'll return to this theme throughout the book and provide techniques to do this.

Figure 3.3 shows the hierarchical relationship between the organization, portfolios, programmes, projects, other work and work packages. Each higher-level component comprises the sum of all connected lower level components.

Figure 3.4 shows the relationship between the activities (and therefore methods or processes) for managing business portfolios, programmes, projects and other work.

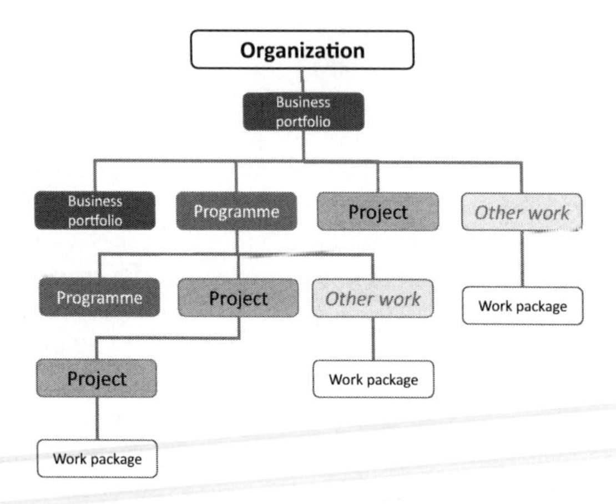

Figure 3.3 Relationship between portfolios, programmes, projects, other work and work packages

This figure shows the hierarchical relationship between work components, with each higher-level component comprising the sum of all connected lower level components. A business portfolio comprises a loosely coupled but tightly aligned portfolio of programmes, projects and other work. For large or diverse organizations, a portfolio can include other portfolios in order to ensure the span of control is manageable. A Programme might include 'sub-programmes', projects and other work. Work packages are defined pieces of work within a project or 'other work' component.

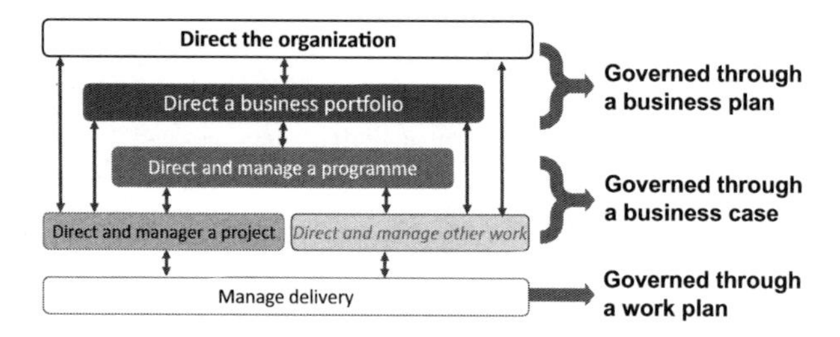

Figure 3.4 Organization, portfolio, programme, project management and delivery activities

The activities, and therefore methods or processes, for managing business portfolios, programmes, projects and other work, define the flow of information and should reflect the hierarchy of the elements. For example, a project might be directed from the host organization, or from a business portfolio, within the host organization or from a programme, which is itself part of a business portfolio. Downward arrows denote providing direction and advice and information on the higher-level context and risk; upward arrows show denote reporting, escalation and requests for advice or direction.

Whose programme or project is it?

Internal and customer programmes and projects

Go to any organization and you'll find there are 'programmes and projects', but what one person calls a 'project' might differ from your own perception. Sometimes the words 'programme' and 'project' are used interchangeably. Whilst you might not be able to control how the words are used throughout your organization, if you are managing a portfolio or programme, you need to ensure your team has a common understanding.

Typically, an organization uses programme or project management to change its own operations, such as developing a new product or service, improving its manufacturing or operational systems, launching a market initiative, taking over another company or building its infrastructure. Organizations undertake programmes and projects to further their business objectives and realize certain benefits. Let's call this an internal programme or project, as it is done internally, within the organization. An **internal programme or project** is one which an organization is undertaking directly for its own benefit.

Additionally, many organizations use programme and project management to control work they are doing for their customers. The primary benefit gained is revenue as payment for the services provided. For example, a building contractor would undertake the construction of an office block as a project but have no interest in the office once it is handed over to the customer and paid for. Let's call this a **customer programme or project** because it is done for a client.

Promoting and contracting organizations

Initiating an internal programme or project is a company's own decision.

Initiating an internal programme or project is a company's own decision. Even if the project is intended to implement a new legal or regulatory requirement, the organization has a choice. If they want to stay in that business, they must comply . . . but no one is compelling them to stay in that business. A bid is an internal project, as it is the company itself which decides whether to bid for the work; there is no compulsion. Once, however, a bid has been won and a contract signed, a 'customer project' is created and the organization has an obligation to undertake the work, within the terms of a legal agreement or contract.

From the previous information, it follows there are primarily two reasons for undertaking a programme or project:

1 to develop the capabilities of own organization: **promoting**;
2 to provide services to another organization: **contracting**.

Promoting organizations identify a business, strategic or political need, translate this into a set of objectives and, using a programme or project as the vehicle of change, create the outputs and business changes needed to ensure those objectives are met. A promoting organization might undertake all the work themselves or sublet part to a contracting organization or supplier.

Contracting organizations identify an opportunity through market analysis, or an invitation to tender, prepare a response and then, if successful, undertake the work as a programme or project. The relationship between the contractor and customer is defined by a formal contract. In most cases, the contractor's work forms only part of the work needed by their customer (a promoter) to gain the full benefits they need. Note, sublet work within a promoting organization's internal programme or project would be a contracting organization's 'customer programme or project'. Yes, you can get lost very quickly.

Figure 3.5 illustrates this. In the top diagram, Company X is the promoting organization and has an internal project, comprising four work packages, WP1 to WP4. Company X is doing all the work internally. The middle diagram illustrates the same situation, with Company X promoting an internal project, but work package WP4 is contracted to Company Y to fulfil. Company Y would see work package WP4 as a customer project undertaken for Company X. The relationship between Company X and Company Y would be determined by a contract. In the lower diagram, Company Y has sublet part of their contracted work, work package WP4.2, to Company Z. Company Z would then see work package WP4.2 as a customer project. The relationship between Company Y and Company Z is determined by the sub-contract, which may itself be determined by the terms of the contract between Company X and Company Y.

A person in Company X would say the project is 'their project' and the project sponsor is accountable for the whole of it, looking after Company X's business interests. A person in company Y would say that WP4 is 'their project' and the person accountable in that company would look after the business interests of Company Y within the constraints of the contract they have signed. Similarly, a person in Company Z would say that WP 4.2 is 'their project' and would look after the business interests of Company Z within the constraints of their sub-contract. Without an understanding of the breakdown of the work, even a simple situation in Figure 3.5 could become confused and have serious consequences on governance.

All work done by the promotor

Project

WP 1

WP 2

WP 3

WP 4

Company X

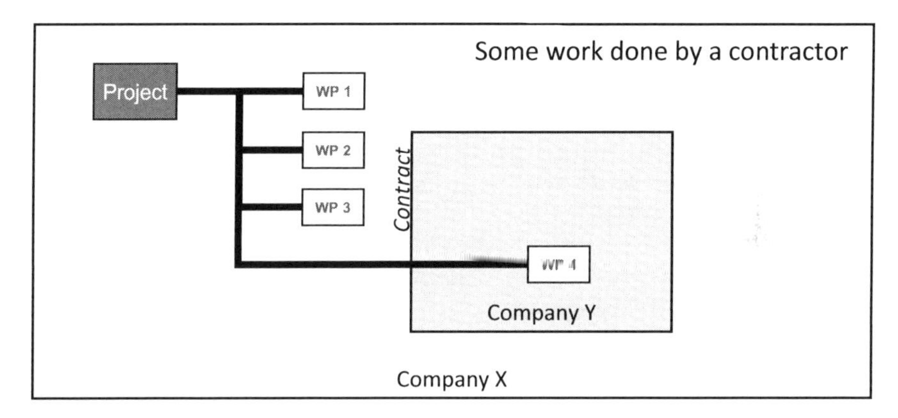

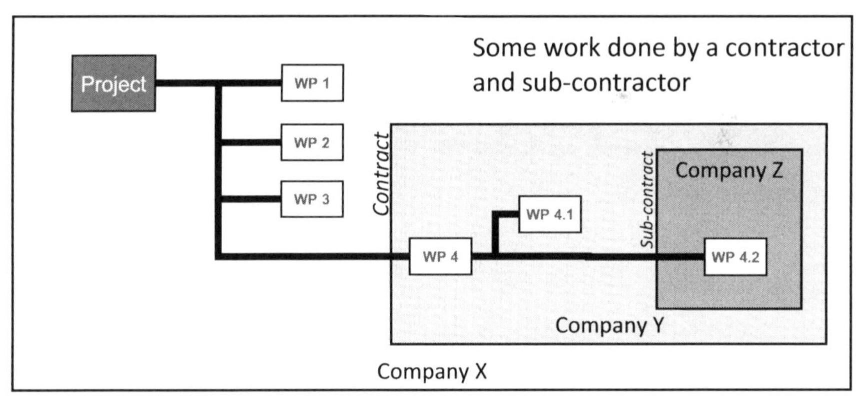

Figure 3.5 Promoting and contracting organizations

Top diagram: Company X owns the project and is doing all the work themselves. Company A is the promoting organization., Middle diagram: Company X has contracted part of the work (Work Package 4) to Company Y, who sees this as 'their project' and manages it as such. Company Y is a contracting organization. Bottom diagram: Similarly, Company Y sublets part of their work (Work Package 4.2) to Company Z, who in turn, sees this as 'their project'. To understand whose project is whose, you need to understand both the scope and the commercial context.

And it can get even more confusing!

The definitions in this chapter and used throughout this book simply describe the characteristics of each management structure (business portfolio, programme, etc.). These definitions are not rules telling you what management approach to use in each circumstance. In other words, you cannot start with those definitions and say, unequivocally, what management approach you should be using. Rather, you need to look at the work needed and decide which of the management approaches is the most appropriate in your circumstances; context is very important. Don't think in terms of whether something *is* a portfolio, programme or a project; think in terms of whether it is best *managed* as a portfolio or programme or *managed* as a project.

The boundaries between each structure overlap (see figure 3.6). A chunk of work might equally be managed as a:

- portfolio or a programme;
- programme or a project;
- project or a work package.

By calling something a 'programme', you have chosen to manage it as a programme and all that entails.

This does not mean that a business portfolio and a programme, or a project and a programme are the same. By calling something a 'programme', you have chosen to *manage* it as a programme and all that entails. In most cases, it is obvious which is the most appropriate management approach. In some cases, however, you have a choice, and your decision will depend on the context of your work within your organization, as well as the nature of the work itself. The following case studies should give you an idea of these choices.

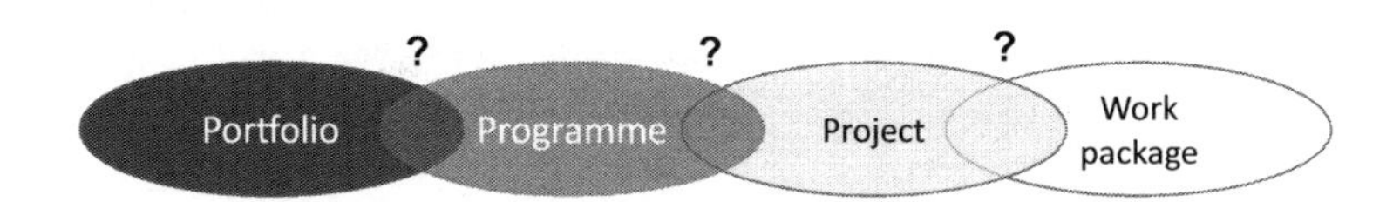

Figure 3.6 It is not always obvious which management structure to use

The boundaries between each structure overlap. The work might be managed as a portfolio or a programme; programme or a project; or project or a work package. The choice is yours and very much depends on the context.

Business portfolio or programme?

A major communications supplier won a £1bn contract lasting ten years for the provision of health care information systems. The contract included the development of about 40 applications, deploying these in over 200 locations and managing the on-going use of the service, including platform upgrades to reflect volume of usage and new technologies. They chose to run this as a single programme, with four sub-programmes, three of which were directed at the three delivery sectors (primary care, secondary care and GPs/local clinics) and the fourth at business improvement. The programme had a single overarching business case and each sub-programme had its own business case with tolerances set to keep them within the overall case.

Bearing in mind the scale and length of the contract (dwarfing most people's entire business!), it could have been run as a portfolio (controlled through a business plan), with three programmes covering the three sectors and a fourth business improvement programme. Each programme would be controlled through its business case, which would be aligned to the overall business plan.

Programme or project?

The requirement was to provide project managers with improved financial information, to provide more immediate visibility of costs and enhance forecasting. The new information systems were to be delivered and rolled out in three phases, the first containing the minimum required capability and the subsequent two adding more features and reporting options. It was decided to run this as a project, with a single business case, as there would be a single manager in overall charge, supported by the specialist software, hardware and change management teams.

It could have been run as a programme, with one project for the design and build of the base capability and then two projects for the subsequent capability drops. This approach was not chosen as it added a spurious extra tier of management which added no value.

Project or work package?

The deployment of a new service management capability required the implementation of new software, deployment of devices and infrastructure, configuration and testing, data migration, user validation and the development and roll-out of end user of administration training. The technical aspects could have been managed as a project, with the training aspect dealt with in a separate project. It was, however, decided that as all the work was aimed at a single outcome and 'go live' date, the technical elements would be managed as work packages within a single deployment project, not a separate 'IT project'. The work relating to training very much depended on deliverables from the IT stream and if treated separately, the number of interdependencies between the projects effectively meant that they needed to be under the same management and within the same project life cycle. If two projects have a large number of interdependencies, they are usually better managed as a single project. Managing the IT work as work packages within a single project was simpler.

Note, that if the IT aspect had been managed as a separate project, the whole deployment initiative would be managed as a programme, adding an extra tier of management, with little or no added value.

So why, if it is better to treat some work as a work package rather than as a project (or as a project rather than a programme), do so many organizations manage their work in a way that adds more management tiers and overheads? The reasons are either that they take a dated and dogmatic view of the project management or, possibly, their financial systems drive them in this direction. For example, if an organization controls its costs based on annually budgeted cost centres, each department has already been allocated funds for the work they are forecast to do during the year. Each departmental head therefore controls their department's spend and work agenda to make sure they stay within their budget, often setting up new cost centres for work they call a 'project' and which might even be labelled a 'project' in the finance systems. If three separate departments need to be involved, each will have their own budget and cost centre and see the work as 'their project'.

Workout 3.1 – Starting to build your business portfolio

1 List the primary business objectives of your organization on Post-It® Notes.
2 Brainstorm all the initiatives and activities you are currently doing in your organization. Think in terms of the programmes, projects and other work as defined in this chapter. Write each on a Post-It® Note. (Don't worry about work packages as they are far too detailed.) Use yellow for projects, blue for programmes and green for other work.
3 Start placing them on a wall or large white board in approximate chronological order.
4 Group together, in bands across the board, those which you believe are targeted at fulfilling the primary business objective, selected from your list from step 1.
5 Identify any interdependencies (for example, where one project relies on the deliverable(s) from another in order to meet its objective). Draw an arrow from the Post-IT® creating the deliverable to the one requiring the deliverable.
6 You might have a very complicated picture by now, and this should make you think how your people can navigate it, doing the right thing when required. Further, with all those interdependencies, how does anyone actually get anything completed?! We will pick up on this later in Workout 11.3.

Keep your structures simple

4

Governance

The governance of portfolios, programmes and projects should be an integrated part of overall organizational (or corporate) governance and not an added extra.

"Truly good governance has to be lived."

DAME SUZI LEATHER, b1956–

- **Governance is about being good, not just looking good.**
- **Governance is not a structure, nor a process – think in terms of a framework.**
- **Use matrix management to make your business agile.**
- **Understand what influences and constrains governance in your organization.**
- **Build time and money for governance into your plans.**
- **Know who guards your guards.**
- **Keep an eye on the risks and act accordingly if they start to rise.**

What is governance?

The Oxford Dictionary's definition of governance is simply:

1 conduct the policy, actions and affairs (of a state, organization or people) with authority;
2 control, influence or regulate (a person, action or course of events).

The OECD defines corporate governance in its *Principles of Corporate Governance* (2015), as:

> *Corporate governance involves a set of relationships between a company's management, its board, its shareholders and other stakeholders. Corporate governance also provides the structure through which the objectives of the company are set, and the means of attaining those objectives and monitoring performance are determined.*

The OECD, with the G20, sets out in this document what it believes are the essential features of corporate governance a state should promote to build an environment of trust, transparency and accountability necessary for fostering long-term investment, financial stability and business integrity, thereby supporting stronger growth and more inclusive societies. The objective is that countries should enshrine the principles in their own legislative and regulatory frameworks, to improve business practices and hence, performance.

The public sector shares many of the same challenges as the private sector and so adopts many of the same principles of corporate governance. For example, in the UK public sector, governance is covered in *Managing Public Money* (2015) and in *Corporate governance in central government departments: code of good practice* (2017). These concentrate mostly on roles and accountabilities but also cover risk management. The code of practice states:

> *Corporate governance is the way in which organisations are directed, controlled and led. It defines relationships and the distribution of rights and responsibilities among those who work with and in the organisation, determines the rules and*

procedures through which the organisation's objectives are set, and provides the means of attaining those objectives and monitoring performance. Importantly, it defines where accountability lies throughout the organisation.

Clearly, 'governance' is a hot topic. All private and public sector organizations run programmes and projects, and these should always be undertaken within the context of a higher-level organization and its governance. In fact, the governance of portfolios, programmes and projects should be an integrated part of overall organizational (or corporate) governance and not an added extra. There needs to be consistency and compatibility between the governance of parts of an organization's activities and governance of the whole organization.

How can governance be applied in practice in the context of portfolio, programme and project management? The characteristics for effective governance are a mix of:

- **purpose**: to set the vision, values and objectives which are compelling and achievable and take a long-term view to achieving the organization's objectives;
- **systems**: an understanding of the organisation and political, economic, social and technological context it operates within;
- **culture**: in terms of behaviour, ethics, reputation, integrity;
- **process**: to enable the right level of control, delegation, operational efficiency and effectiveness;
- **structure**: having the right tiers of accountability.

These characteristics, shown in Figure 4.1, are wide-ranging and can help you challenge some misconceptions about governance:

- governance is NOT a structure, although structure is a vital element;
- governance is NOT a process, although processes are a vital element;

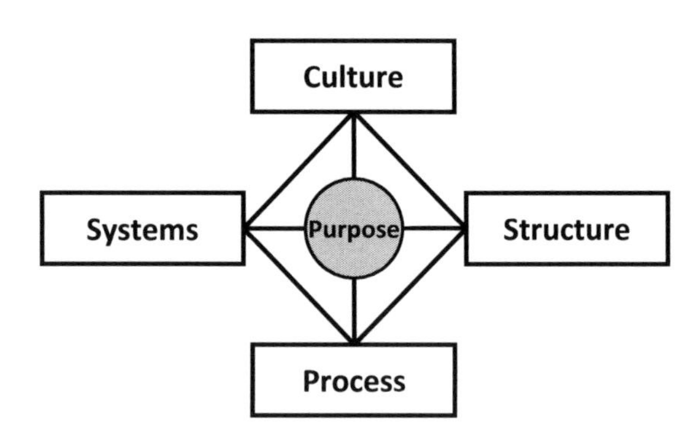

Figure 4.1 The characteristics for an effective governance framework

In Chapter 2, Figure 2.2, which showed us that process or method, systems and tools, structure and accountability and culture and behaviours do not sit in isolation but each affect the other. Good governance relies on using each of these four levers appropriately and proportionately in order to achieve the organization's purpose.

- governance is NOT just about decision making, although decision making is a vital activity within governance.

If you restrict your perception of 'governance', you limit how you apply governance and how other people perceive governance, and as a result, ignore people's behaviours and attitudes. As previously shown in Figure 2.2 and emphasized in Figure 4.1, process or method, systems and tools, structure and accountability and culture and behaviours do not sit in isolation, for each affect the other; good governance relies on using each of these four levers together, appropriately and proportionately.

If you restrict your perception of 'governance', you limit how you apply governance

The term 'structure' in OECD's definition of corporate governance can be interpreted as 'organization' or 'arrangement', and I believe that is what the OECD meant. Unfortunately, the word 'structure' is so often interlinked with 'organization structure' in the business world, it can be misinterpreted. Often 'governance structure' is used simply as the reporting line of senior management boards within the company; this does need to be defined, but it is not enough for good governance.

Similarly, the term 'process' can simply mean 'activities', but in a management context it frequently refers to the formal management of activities where an input is converted to an output, using resources. Governance is not just about blindly following a process, although following defined processes is often an essential part of governance.

Decisions are a vital aspect of governance, but if governance is concerned solely with decision making, that could lead to the right decisions being implemented in an illegal or unethical way. For effective governance, the leadership team needs to ensure their organization has proper policies, processes and systems in place but must also promote the right attitudes and have structure in terms of accountability. To achieve this, the leadership team needs to:

1. work effectively, both as individuals and a team;
2. understand its role;
3. ensure delivery of organizational purpose;
4. exercise effective control;
5. visibly behave with integrity;
6. be accountable.

Sometimes, you will see a requirement to be 'open'. In some organizations and in some situations, openness can be difficult or even contravene statutory or legal requirements. For example:

- there are restrictions relating to publicly quoted companies on what the directors may say at particular times in the year (so called closed periods);
- certain work is classified under secrecy legislation (such as the *Official Secrets Act* in the UK);
- information might be restricted for commercial reasons.

Rather than 'open', I would say that leaders need to visibly display the types of behaviour they wish to promote – leading by example.

I will lie to you, only if I have to

The new Chief Executive of a publicly quoted company held a drinks reception for staff in the head office to introduce himself and his way of working. In his talk, he promised never to lie to them . . . but added the rider, "Except when the rules of the City determine that I must. Funny world, isn't it?"

Leadership team?

At an internal project management conference, the Chief Executive of a major international airline told us about his early days in the company. Soon after being appointed, he asked his leadership team members to walk through the atrium and the open areas of offices, rather than take the express lifts from the car park to the executive floors each morning. He wanted them to be visible, 'feel the mood' in the building and talk to people. One morning, he was walking through the atrium when a person came up to him saying, "You are our new CEO, aren't you?"

"Yes, I am," replied the CEO, "and you are?"

"Don't worry about that. Tell me, as CEO you are head of the leadership team; correct?"

"Yes, that's right."

"Did you know, 'leadership team' is an oxymoron here; they do not lead and neither are they a team?"

The CEO told us he was stunned for a few seconds until he realized this person was absolutely right and had reminded him of his highest priority as a leader (and that 'walking about' is really worthwhile).

Governance in context

Governance is nearly always associated with two other words: 'risk' and 'accountability'.

'Governance' is an important word and one which can make our business and public sector leaders prick up their ears. Governance is nearly always associated with two other words: 'risk' and 'accountability'. Twenty years ago, governance was rarely talked about but now it is enshrined in law, regulations and codes of conduct. What happened? In the private sector, there were a number of well publicized cases of financial irregularities, such as Enron in the USA and Tesco in the UK. These events severely and immediately impacted their respective share prices and, more importantly, knocked people's confidence in business generally. The Enron scandal happened in 2001, but despite the publicity and increasing regulation, organizations continued to go wrong, led from the top, as evidenced by Tesco's profit scandal in 2014 and a rash of news reports in 2018 around financial irregularities in major charities.

Governance, however, is not just about avoiding scandal. Good governance promotes good performance, whether in the public, private or charitable sectors. In the opening pages of *Good Governance, A Code for the Voluntary and Community Sector* (2001), Dame Suzi Leather, Chair of the UK's Charity Commission, said:

> *"The central importance of good governance to all sectors of the economy is now clearer than ever. The crisis which beset our financial system has highlighted how dangerous a tick-box approach can be. Truly good governance has to be lived. Each and every trustee and board member needs to embrace its values, and apply them to the particular needs and circumstances of their organisation."*

This code was updated in 2017, and at the top of the list of changes were:

- a new section on the importance of effective leadership;
- recognition that culture and behaviours are as important as structures and processes.

In other words, it's about *being* good not just *looking* good, starting at the top of an organization.

Tesco – UK – 2014

In September 2014, Tesco, the UK's largest grocery retailer, suspended four senior executives and called in investigators following the discovery that its profits had been artificially inflated by £250m. More than £2bn was wiped off the company's value when it became clear that payments from suppliers were being incorrectly allocated and profits inflated. Analysts believed that Tesco was focussing on making money from supplier contracts rather than customers' shopping trips, leading to a £6.3bn loss in 2015. At the time of writing, the full damage and implications of the scandal are still unknown: three executives faced prosecution but were cleared of wrongdoing in a ruling that raises serious questions about why the company agreed a £129m plea bargain with the Serious Fraud Office since no one has been convicted. There was also £100m civil law suit brought by over 125 investors and potentially two US class actions claiming up to $150m.

Enron – USA – 2001

The Enron scandal led to the bankruptcy of the Enron Corporation, an American energy company, and to the closure of Arthur Andersen, then one of the five largest audit and accountancy partnerships in the world. Enron's Chief Financial Officer, Andrew Fastow, and other executives were able to hide billions of dollars in debt from failed deals and projects. This was achieved by using accounting loopholes and poor financial reporting. They misled Enron's board of directors and audit committee on high-risk accounting practices and pressured their auditor, Arthur Andersen, to ignore the issues.

Many executives at Enron were prosecuted for a variety of charges; some went to prison. Enron's auditor, Arthur Andersen, was found guilty of illegally destroying relevant documents, which voided its license to audit public companies and effectively closed the business. Enron lost the majority of its customers and ceased operating; employees and shareholders received limited returns in lawsuits, despite losing billions in pensions and stock prices.

As a consequence of the scandal, new regulations and legislation were enacted to in the USA to improve the accuracy of financial reporting for public companies. The Sarbanes-Oxley Act was introduced, which increased penalties for destroying, altering or fabricating records in federal investigations or for attempting to defraud shareholders; it also increased the accountability of auditing firms to act independently of their clients.

Is Sarbanes-Oxley really a deterrent?

Sarbanes-Oxley is implemented in many organizations as a process, relying on the right controls being in place and the right signatures being collected to confirm that business leaders are taking their accountabilities seriously. Unfortunately, the fact that such a process is in place might not, on its own, stop bad behaviours. If someone is intent on fraud, is a signature likely to actually stop them? For example, shares in BT plunged 21% in January 2017, cutting its stock market value by £8bn in one day, after the company revealed that it expected the cost of the accounting fraud inside its Italian unit to reach £530m.

Constraints on governance

You do not have total freedom to apply governance

Now you understand what governance is, you should also realize that you do not have total freedom to apply governance to your particular business portfolio, programme or project. Constraints are imposed by external factors, as well as the organization itself. Organizational constraints should not be regarded as 'bad'. The more consistent an organization is in its approach to directing and managing its work, the less time is wasted in deciding 'who is accountable' when decisions are needed. This especially applies to an organization's most senior people: they simply haven't the time and energy to find out all the different nuances of naming and lines of authority on every programme or project they are the sponsor for or stakeholders in. Consistent governance leads to good practice. A business portfolio, programme or a project is simply a set of activities within a larger organization and the leaders of that organization have an obligation to apply effective governance to everything the organization does. As such, business portfolio, programme or project governance is a part of their corporate governance; you should be able to trace different aspects of governance from the top to the bottom of the organization.

Constraints on governance come from a number of sources such as:

- legal, regulatory and codes of practice;
- corporate polices;
- technical conformance;
- processes and methods to be used;
- contracts with suppliers;
- contracts with clients and customers.

Legal and regulatory

In any country, the legal and regulatory frameworks are paramount. All business activities must comply with both civil and criminal law. In many cases, there are also regulators and voluntary codes of practice which prescribe certain behaviours, processes and practices. Some industries, like pharmaceuticals, telecommunications, finance, utilities, railways and aviation, are more highly regulated than others.

Management policies

To protect its reputation and operate within the law and other binding agreements, organizations have policies dictating the boundaries of governance for particular topics, such as diversity, safety, environment and sustainability, as well as the more routine human resource and technical topics. Policies determine the way processes are designed and which practices are used; they set the overall vision for each topic.

Technical conformance

With the rise of platform-based product, service and management systems, many organizations seek to promote operational efficiencies by ensuring the maximum reuse of standard solution components. This might be a financial or ERP platform, like SAP or Oracle, or an automotive chassis which serves a number of car models. It could be that only certain components or 'parts' are selected from specific preferred suppliers or from the organization's internally certified catalogue of products or components.

Processes and methods

Using consistent processes and methods creates the opportunity for people to work together more efficiently.

Standard processes and methods dictate or advise how to undertake certain activities. Some (processes) are very rigid, others (methods) are looser, leaving a lot of discretion in their application. Using consistent processes and methods creates the opportunity to share experience and for people to work together more efficiently.

Contracts

Contracts with the suppliers limit your degrees of freedom and may impose, on both parties, particular governance requirements, say for meetings, procedures and payment triggers. The contract with a customer might also limit management's degrees of freedom and impose, on both parties, particular requirements influencing how governance is applied. For example, the roles of any joint boards and the contractual basis on which they take their authority – it might dictate that a supplier has to inform a customer as soon as they believe a delay or overspend is likely; it might define how changes to the contract scope are approved and paid for; it will always define how and when payments will be made. See Chapter 26 for more on contracts.

Making governance work in practice

Think in terms of a governance framework

In simple terms, a leadership team sets the long-term vision and protects the reputation and values of its organization. Central to this is a focus on accountability and risk. As 'governance structure' and 'governance process' are inadequate vehicles for defining governance, I refer to 'governance framework', as this is more inclusive and can mean all the aspects shown in Figure 4.1.

A governance framework needs to be established which meets the need of any overriding legal and policy constraints. The framework should include the authority limits, decision-making roles and rules, degree of autonomy, assurance needs, reporting structure, accountabilities and responsibilities, together with the more detailed management frameworks for business portfolio, programme and project management, as well as for any other type of work you might define. Looking at governance in this way means that it encompasses how the entire organization works (or should work) as a whole. In that respect, this entire book is about governance as it deals with how portfolios, programmes and projects relate to each other and how they are directed and managed. To make this easier to grasp, the book is structured into its component topics:

- Part II – project management;
- Part III – portfolio management;
- Part IV – programme management;
- Part V – techniques that can be used for all three.

Harness the matrix

Lesson 6 from Chapter 2, Breakdown functional boundaries by using cross-functional teams, is fundamental to making business portfolio, programme and project governance work. That chapter also discussed the implications of this on structure and accountabilities. By working across departmental or functional boundaries you are operating a matrix. You probably have the accountabilities and targets defined for each function (or department) but, in a matrix you also need to define them for the 'horizontal' dimension, where activity follows the value chain rather than the cost centre budget. In the modern world, I would argue that every organization is operating in a matrix, but many do not recognize this. In a matrix you need to define:

- roles which work across the departments, independent of jobs;
- processes designed and enabled to end working, including whatever activities from whatever departments are needed;
- systems which support the cross-functional processes;
- structures to show tiering, so that there is traceability from organization to work package and vice-versa.

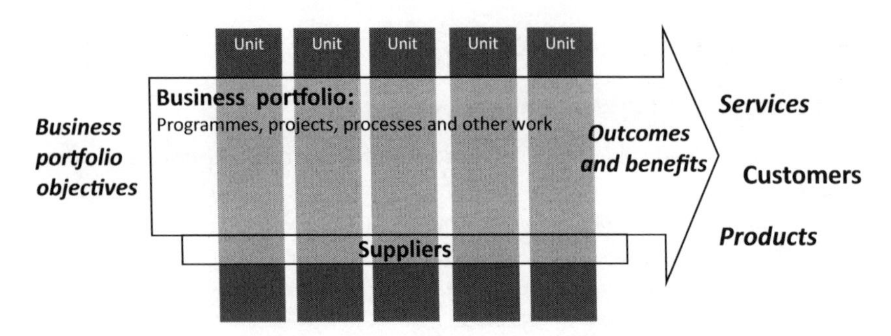

Figure 4.2 Portfolios, programmes and projects are key management structures in a matrix

In a matrix, the driving force follows the value chain, rather than the cost centre budget. This concept is at the heart of what is often termed as 'business agility'.

These horizontal facets are not to be used instead of the traditional vertical structures but in addition to them. The vertical and horizontal roles, processes, structures and systems need to be defined to work together. See Figure 4.2.

The following sections in this chapter will look at three key aspects of governance:

- roles and accountabilities;
- decision making;
- assurance.

Other features of good governance are then discussed.

Implementing a matrix structure

Part of a major organization wanted to implement matrix management, as they frequently shared resources over a number of projects and suffered from all the problems outlined in Chapter 1. They worked out what the respective accountabilities of the vertical and horizontal dimensions were and ensured there were no overlaps or gaps. The processes were revised to support the matrix accountabilities. They checked that the management information systems could provide the information to those who needed it. Whilst they believed they had done everything needed, unfortunately, it didn't work out that way. Some line managers continued to make decisions and redeploy staff as they always had done, with little regard to the new accountabilities. A bad situation became even worse. Where did they go wrong? Making a change to matrix operations involves changing the power dynamics in an organization. If the managers involved do not want it to happen, or do not fully understand the new operating model, they will continue to work as they always have done. The staff will be used to the line managers making decisions and are unlikely to challenge them, after all, they've been doing it for years. Some managers will, however, start working to the new rules and might come into conflict with those working to the old rules. Instead of running an operation with a weak matrix, as before, the situation degrades into chaos as not only do different verticals come into conflict but also the verticals and the horizontals. This failure wasn't because 'matrices don't work' but rather because the cultural and behavioural dimension (shown earlier in Figure 4.1) was not adequately addressed. If the people involved in the change do not subscribe to the change, it simply won't happen.

Take account of complexity

The greater the complexity, the greater the risk of not delivering the intended outcomes and outputs and hence realizing the benefits.

Complexity is an indicator of how difficult it is to undertake a programme or project. The greater the complexity, the greater the risk of not delivering the intended outcomes and outputs and hence realizing the benefits.

Complexity can be measured in relative terms or absolute terms. **Absolute complexity** relates to how inherently difficult the work is to undertake, regardless of the organization undertaking it. It is therefore useful for benchmarking across organizations. **Relative complexity** deals with how difficult an individual organization would find undertaking the work. It is useful for identifying aspects of the programme or project that contribute to risk and might therefore need special governance arrangements or the support of specialist suppliers. This would especially relate to:

- the organization's prior experience and track record of similar work;
- what makes the work new or innovative;
- whether the organization has the skills, knowledge and tools needed to undertake the work are available to the organization;

In most cases, the application of relative complexity is more useful for portfolio and programme managers. For this reason, tools have been developed to support this, of which Workout 4.3 is an example. This example uses a range of topics to illustrate different dimensions to complexity, including:

- Business criticality: how important the work is to the organization;
- Reputation exposure: the damage that could be done, if it goes wrong;
- Financial exposure: the amount you stand to lose;
- Interdependencies: how complicated the schedule network is;
- Legal, regulatory constraints: the level of externally binding constraints;
- Business transformation: how much you need to change the organization;
- Schedule flexibility: how rigid your target dates are;
- Requirements and scope: the extent to which you know what you want;
- Output innovation: whether you have done this before;
- Delivery processes: whether you already have processes to undertake the work;
- Team dynamics and size: how well-established or dispersed the team is;
- Supplier involvement: the extent you need to rely on suppliers.

These might not be the most significant factors for your organization but should give you an idea of the types of topics you could consider in your own model. If you do not want each factor to carry equal weight, you can apply weightings.

Complexity should be assessed regularly as it can change through the life of a programme or project. On long standing programmes, the necessary tools and processes might be developed, the team could become well-established, requirements better

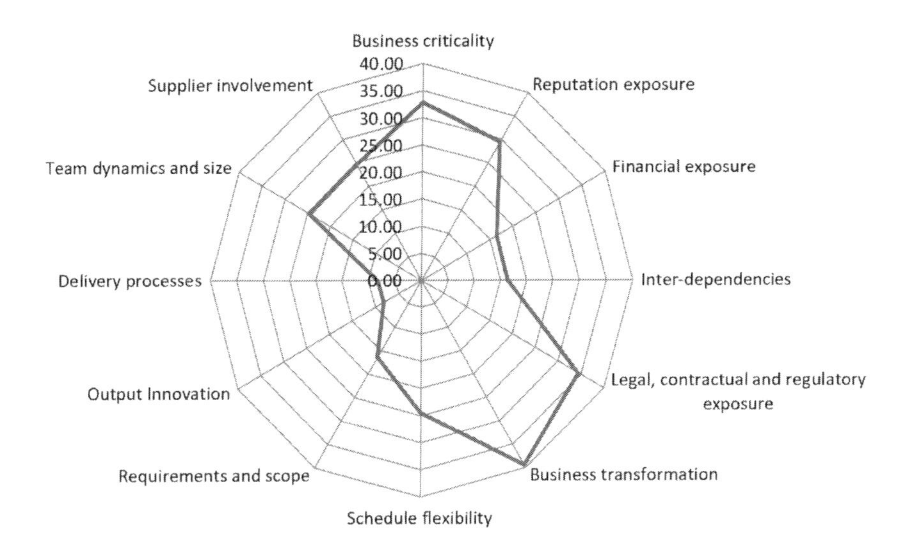

Figure 4.3 Typical complexity assessment

A radar diagram is a good way to represent the different dimensions of complexity. In this example, whilst the core of the work seems straightforward and affordable, the programme is being undertaken in a highly regulated environment, involves major transformational change, is critical to the business and, if it goes wrong, could severely damage the reputation of the organization. This is not a programme to undertake lightly.

understood and so complexity (and hence risk) can reduce. Furthermore, by assessing a portfolio in terms of the complexity of its component parts, the business portfolio manager can critically examine each in terms of their risk and enable them to be managed according to the organization's risk appetite, applying available resources and skills in the best way to deliver the most desirable outcomes. It can also be used to make the organization's senior managers aware of the most complex, and therefore risky, work in their portfolio and prompt appropriate assurance and management attention to be applied. If applied consistently within an organization, a complexity assessment might also form part of the review prior to a 'go', 'no go' or deferral gate decision. Figure 4.3 shows a typical output from an assessment tool; see Workout 4.3 as an example.

Complexity assessments can be extended to support other decisions, such as recommending the grade of programme or project manager required for a particular piece of work. This can be very useful, especially when convincing a human resources department of the reasons you need, what might seem to them, an expensive programme manager.

For customer programmes or projects (see Chapter 3), you can use the tool to assess the work you are bidding for from the customer's viewpoint. In which case you would also complete the assessment as if you were the customer. This can throw up some startling results, the most striking being that what might seem to you a trivial piece of work could, for the customer, be a 'make or break' point for their entire organization. If the work failed, you could shrug it off, but the customer might go into liquidation. This is often the case when procurement chooses so called 'safe' suppliers, on account of their scale and market power; perhaps, not always so safe!

The vast scope of complexity theory

Complexity theory is an expanding area of study and has been applied in a wide range of circumstances including linguistics, where people have measured how inherently complex a language is (absolute complexity) as opposed to the effort a person needs to put in to learn that language (relative complexity). Complexity is also used in system engineering and applied to the complexity of a product, solution or output; we will look at this in Chapter 24 and its effect on quality.

Roles and accountabilities

Tiered and traceable roles

If you are not accountable to anyone, you can't be held to account

The roles and accountabilities of those working within a business portfolio, programme or project need to be defined as a whole. This includes, but is not limited to, who each role holder is accountable to and what activities, outputs or outcomes they are accountable for. If you are not accountable to anyone, you can't be held to account; neither is anyone counting on you, so your efforts might be futile.

In Chapter 3 we defined the relationship between an organization and the related business portfolio, programme and project management activities. Figures 3.3 defined the structure and Figure 3.4 the processes. Figure 4.4 uses these figures as the basis for defining the roles, ensuring they are consistent with both structure and process. The people at each level in the hierarchy are accountable to those at the next higher level in the hierarchy. At each level, there are two primary roles: one senior role, which has overall accountability for setting direction, and a lower level role, which has day-to-day management accountability. For example, a project manager is accountable to a project sponsor for the day-to-day management of the project; a team manager is accountable to the project manager for the delivery of a work package. The roles associated with 'other work' are dependent on what that other work is and should follow the same two-level pattern.

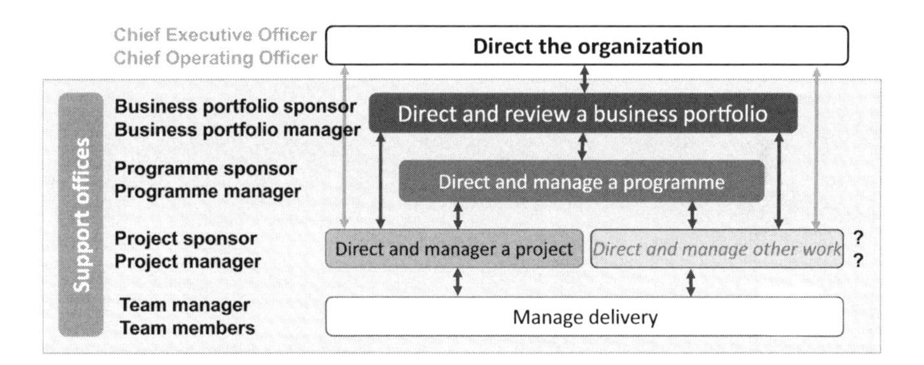

Figure 4.4 The primary portfolio, programme and project management roles

The people at each level in the hierarchy are accountable to those at the next higher level in the hierarchy. At each level, there are two primary roles: one senior role, which has overall accountability, and a lower level role, which has day-to-day management accountability. The roles associated with 'other work' will be dependent on what that other work is and should follow the same two-level pattern.

The 'top' level

The top level is not strictly part of business portfolio, programme or project management, but if it is not defined, the business portfolio management team would not be clear on their reporting lines. In a private sector organization, the primary roles at this level are usually the chief executive officer (CEO) and the chief operating officer (COO); the former is usually accountable to the company board for the overall performance and direction of the company. The chief operating officer is usually accountable to the CEO for the effective and efficient operation of the company (both present and future). As business portfolio management and all it entails doesn't happen by accident and is a deliberate way to direct and manage an organization, two specific roles are needed:

- **business portfolio management director**, accountable to CEO, deputy CEO or COO for the adoption and direction across the whole organization;
- **business portfolio design authority**, accountable to the business portfolio management for the operational architecture (accountabilities, process, systems and culture).

See Chapter 27 for more on these.

Business portfolio sponsor

The business portfolio sponsor is accountable to the chief executive officer (or equivalent) for the direction and governance of the business portfolio, ensuring it realizes the required benefits at an acceptable level of risk. The business portfolio sponsor provides leadership and direction and owns the portfolio strategy and plan.

See Chapter 5 for more on sponsorship and Chapter 11 for more on business portfolio management roles.

Business portfolio manager

The business portfolio manager is accountable to the business portfolio sponsor for managing a business portfolio as a whole and ensuring its work components are sufficient to meet the objectives, including monitoring spend against budget and benefits realization. The business portfolio manager coordinates the effective and efficient operation of business portfolio management and ensures the flow of information to decision makers.

See Chapter 11 for more detail on business portfolio management roles.

Programme or project sponsor

The programme/project sponsor is accountable to the business portfolio sponsor for ensuring a programme or project meets its objectives, delivers the required outcomes and realizes the required benefits. The programme/project sponsor owns the business case and is accountable for all aspects of programme or project governance.

See Chapter 5 for more on sponsorship and Chapters 18 and 7 for more on programme and project management roles respectively.

Programme or project manager

The programme/project manager is accountable to the sponsor for establishing the governance framework and for the day-to-day management of a programme/ project, to deliver the desired outcomes and products and realize the required benefits.

See Chapter 18 for more detail on programme management roles and Chapter 7 on project management roles.

Coach or facilitator

The coach or facilitator is accountable for supporting the project manager, project sponsor and project board. This may be by pure coaching or giving advice, facilitation and guidance on project management. Both approaches will help project teams, experienced and inexperienced, to perform beyond their own expectations. This role which is seldom included but can prove extremely effective.

Support (such as programme management office)

Support provides expertise, specialist advice and guidance on aspects of portfolio, programme and project management. They are often given names such as project office, project management office or project support office. They support the programme or project manager to establish the most appropriate governance strategy and implement planning and control mechanisms, methods, processes and tools. They also undertake many of the routine administrative functions.

See Chapter 27 for more detail on support roles.

Team manager

A team manager is accountable to either to a project manager or manager of 'other related work' for supervising the individual members of the team to deliver the assigned work package. See Chapter 7 for more detail.

Other roles

Other roles should be defined to suit the needs of the work required, for example those managing the development of specialist outputs. This includes roles relating to service and operations management, business change, communications and various engineering disciplines.

Multiple layer models

For simplicity, Figure 4.2 only shows a single level for each of business portfolio, programme, project and work package. In practice we know there could be multiple levels such as a portfolio having sub-portfolios and a programme having sub-programmes (see Figure 3.3). This affects the lines of accountability. For example, a manager of a sub-programme would be accountable to the programme manager rather than to the programme sponsor directly. A team manager for a low-level work package might be accountable to the manager of the next highest-level work package and not to the project manager. It might seem obvious, but this does need spelling out to ensure those involved are absolutely clear.

Job titles and 'different' role titles

You need to distinguish between the roles described here and a person's given job title; people who have grown up in functional hierarchies often find this a difficult concept to grasp. A job title might bear no relation to the role they are playing, say, as a project manager. Thus, the chief executive might have such a personal interest in a particular project that he takes on the project sponsor role. Very simple and obvious. The problem comes when job titles and the roles use the same words or appear related. In many organizations the HR department decides on a person's job title because it is associated with a particular salary and benefits package. In such approaches it is often assumed that a programme manager is 'superior' to a project manager and should attract a commensurately higher benefits package. Further, people are often assigned a 'director' title as opposed to 'manager' to describe a job with higher responsibility. Hence, job titles such as Project Director as opposed to Project Manager. It is not unusual for a person to have a job title of Programme Manager and have nothing to do with programmes, as defined in this book; it is simply that the benefits package is the right one. By separating 'job' from 'role', a Programme Director (job title) can undertake a project manager role or a Project Director could be the head of a project support office. The roles simply set out the accountabilities; there is no implication of the complexity, worth or importance of a work package, project or programme. A work package might require a far greater level of skill and experience to manage than a simple programme. The important point is to ensure that work is assigned to people with the right skills and experience to manage it, regardless of their job title. Being role based simplifies processes and methods considerably. With less than a dozen primary roles, you can define a business portfolio, programme or project management process or method, regardless of the number of related job titles. If you have ever tried writing and maintaining a process based on job titles, you'll know how difficult and convoluted they become as those job titles and their holders shift and change.

Dealing with egos

So, how do you treat a person, with a Project Director job title managing a particularly difficult work package but refuses to be called a 'team manager' as they perceive that devalues them? First, let them keep their job title and use it in their email signatures and business cards. It is, after all, who they are. As far as the project goes, however, the management plan should make it clear they are accountable to a project manager for a particular work package, using the 'manage delivery' process, shown in Figure 4.4. For organizations familiar with matrix management, this situation is not unusual; it's an everyday fact of matrix life where what you do, and your authority is based on the role you are undertaking. People in organizations which are still primarily run as siloes will find this situation difficult to reconcile. Remind yourself of lesson 6 in Chapter 2.

But where are the boards?

Many projects have a project board to ensure direction and decisions are in the best interest of the organization. In some cases, a board supports the project sponsor role, whilst in others, it is a higher-level entity to which the project sponsor is accountable.

In all cases, a board's purpose and the limits of its authority (including decision making) should be clear. For programmes and projects, I generally start with the view that the sponsor has the primary, single point accountability, and the board supports them in that role (PRINCE2® also takes that stance); the sponsor would be the chair of the board. The board's terms of reference define what decisions a sponsor can take independently and what might require board voting. If a project is part of a programme, the overall programme board might take the place of multiple project boards. There is no point in having a board if it doesn't add any value.

The membership and operating rules for a board should be defined in terms of reference, which should include:

- purpose of the board; why does it exist?
- specific responsibilities of the board;
- membership and roles;
- what authority the board has; rules for voting (if needed); authority of board members and chair;
- quorum required if the authorities are to be exercised; this might be in terms of numbers or a requirement that certain members should be present;
- working method or protocol: meeting frequency; meeting format (timing, location, face to face, telephone, video-conference, etc.);
- record keeping: style of minutes and location where agenda, briefing notes and minutes are stored.

Unless the role of the board is defined, you cannot decide its membership or way of working.

Choosing the board members is a prime consideration, as the mix of personalities and skills determines its effectiveness. Unless the role of the board is defined, you cannot decide its membership or way of working. If the board is there to support a sponsor, you need to decide if it is purely advisory and can be overruled by the sponsor or if some decisions require a consensus or even a vote. The 'rules' for a board affect the behaviours of its members. Board members solely representing the interests of their own departments or divisions and rarely make a good contribution, as they will invariably place the needs of their own departments over the needs of the wider organization. Beware of having boards with too large a membership; a board is not a stakeholder engagement device, and treating it in this way leads to a lessening of its authority, or it risks becoming a mere 'talking shop'.

Boards relating to business portfolio management are discussed in Part III; boards relating to projects and programmes are dealt with in Parts II and IV, respectively.

Rearranging the deck chairs

Naming roles and bodies can be very difficult. Each needs to be as self-explanatory as possible so that people can intuitively understand what each role is for. This can be doubly difficult in a project environment where the words 'project' and 'programme' can take on so many different meanings. I have chosen a set of role names which are consistently applied throughout the book and draw on associated terminology. I tend to use 'sponsor' where the role is 'directing' and 'manager' where the role is 'managing'. Practical considerations are:

- make sure role names are distinct;
- don't choose names which will date;
- keep the roles separate from job titles;
- if referring to boards, keep the roles separate from the board titles;
- having chosen your role names, don't keep changing them.

Keeping roles and job titles separate enables a number of roles to be undertaken by a single person or body, thereby saving you from having to rewrite all your processes simply because of a minor change in personnel. For example, the CEO's Leadership Team might take on the role of the business strategy and planning board and the portfolio review group. Changing role names is a common ploy by new directors to show they 'have arrived', but all it usually does is create confusion. A colleague of mine once referred to this as 'rearranging the deck chairs on the Titanic'.

Decision making

An organization's performance is really no more and no less than the sum of the decisions it makes

An organization's performance is really no more and no less than the sum of the decisions it makes and implements. A new organization chart or new process can't make much difference unless it somehow leads to better, faster decisions and implementation. In the context of portfolios, programmes and projects, decisions might relate to:

- approving a strategy;
- initiating a programme, project or other work;
- starting a new project stage (e.g., decision point/gate) or a new programme tranche;
- suspending or terminating work;
- selecting suppliers;
- deciding options for further study;
- selecting the solution;
- approving plans and baselines.

Decisions should be holistic, taking account of what else is happening within the organization, of the external context and the whole life of outputs (such as in life service and disposal). Decisions should be made in light of any known, negative impacts and may be:

- phased to take into account risk;
- conditional, with responsibility for fulfilling such conditions defined.

Always distinguish between a decision and a review

People can often be confused about decisions and reviews, so when depicting them diagrammatically, make sure they are denoted with different icons. Figure 4.5 shows a project life cycle with the decision point prior to starting each project stage clearly marked (often called 'gates') and the reviews, which happen prior to them. Decisions can often be taken in a few minutes provided the right information is at hand, whilst reviews can take hours or even days, requiring the right expert reviewers to be available. The conclusions from a review should be part of the information required in later decisions.

Decisions should be made in a timely manner by evaluating alternative choices against agreed criteria. Stakeholders and subject matter experts should be consulted and informed of the outcome.

The setting of decision rights for a modern, matrix organization can be difficult and controversial. For a bureaucratic hierarchy, it is simple: whoever 'owns' that part of the business makes the decisions. Today's integrated organizations are more

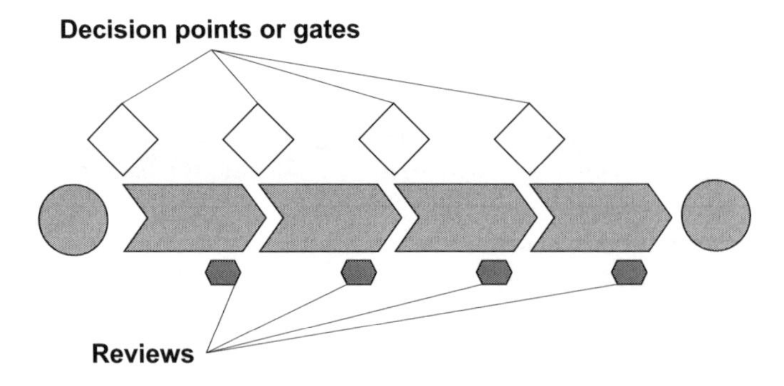

Figure 4.5 Decisions and assurance reviews

People often confuse about decisions and reviews, so when depicting them diagrammatically, make sure they are denoted with different icons. This example shows a project life cycle with the decision point prior to starting each project stage clearly marked (often called 'gates') and the reviews, which happen prior to them.

complicated, with many decisions impacting many parts of the business. Badly constructed decision rights (or schemes of delegation) can lead to an inefficient, sluggish and moribund organization. To optimize decision making, decisions need to be made as close as possible to where the work is done. Nick Pudar, Director of planning and strategic initiatives at General Motors, said, "If I know someone in the organization's lower levels can make a tough call *that won't affect other parts of the company*, then it's their call." I have italicized what I believe are the most crucial words. Delegation is a good thing, but the prime risk associated with placing decisions making at lower levels is that the lower level manager's motivations and aims might not align with those of the organization's leaders. The way you allocate decisions, therefore, must take this into account, particularly in the way the hierarchy and flow of decisions are designed.

Effective decision making relies having enough information at the right time.

Effective decision making relies having enough information at the right time. To achieve this, processes and support systems need to be designed to enable the flow of information to the decision maker, with the right stakeholders being involved. I would argue that you cannot design a 'decision-making process', but you can ensure processes support the decision maker. The costs of this, however, have to be commensurate with of value of the information gained. Any gaps in knowledge require assumptions, which represent a risk. General wisdom in corporate governance is that single point accountability for each decision is essential.

In this context, portfolio, programme and project management practices promote good decision making, through the web of roles, work breakdown structure, processes and individual practices. The crucial part is ensuring decision making at one level (say, project level) dovetails into decision making at the next higher level, such as programme, business portfolio or sponsoring organization. Decisions should be traceable. The failure to ensure decisions fit into the governance of the wider organization is fundamental to why even well-run projects fail. Hence, in the quest to ensure every project succeeds, more and more attention is directed at high-level management techniques such as programme and portfolio management.

Assurance

Imagine you are a business leader of a large organization or sponsor of a complex programme, where it is impossible for to oversee everything that is going on or be involved in every decision; how do you know that the work is progressing well and risks are being contained? You can't be everywhere at once. This problem is what assurance seeks to address.

Assurance is the systematic set of actions necessary to provide confidence to senior leaders and stakeholders that work is controlled, on track to deliver and aligned with strategy.

If you have good governance, you should be confident that:

- the people managing and undertaking the work are competent and experienced;
- they are following well managed processes and using defined methods;
- behaviours are conducive to good working relationships;
- plans are rigorous and viable;
- reports are complete and reliable;
- risks and issues will be escalated to you, when necessary.

By having good governance, you actually have assurance that you are highly likely to meet your objectives. You will know that if things start to go wrong, you will hear about it in time to take preventative or corrective action.

Imagine if the programme you are sponsoring, with over 600 people involved, plus a number of suppliers and contractors, was being managed in an ad-hoc way, with each project manager and team manager deciding how they organize their decisions, plans, progress monitoring, metrics, reports, communications and interfaces. How would you know the status of the programme as a whole? How would the team know when to escalate issues to you? In what form would all this information he held and where? Even if each project manager was separately following a best practice standard, such as BS6079, it would be virtually impossible to manage the programme as a whole. It might sound progressive to allow each team to decide its own approach but that won't necessarily mean the project or the programme will be successful. Having common working methods and processes are vital for simplifying management and communication. This is why so many organizations choose to build enterprise-wide portfolio, programme and project management methods and encourage or expect their people to use them. That doesn't mean teams can't be self-organizing; in fact, they should have the freedom to apply the methods to suit the particular context and circumstances of their work. This is called tailoring.

Tailoring alters or adapts methods or processes for use in a particular situation. At organizational level, a single method will not suit every situation and will need to be adapted to suit. Similarly, for most organizations, one enterprise-wide method or process is not appropriate for every type of work in every circumstance. Some adaptation is normally needed if the work is to be run both effectively and efficiently, to suit both the type of work and the people involved. Tailoring guidelines describe what can and cannot be modified in a process or method.

As part of good governance, organizations should have a defined and consistent approach to assurance.

As part of good governance, organizations should have a defined and consistent approach to assurance. Assurance should be undertaken on at least three levels:

- **1st line:** carried out by, or on behalf of, the operational management that own and manage risk to ensure appropriate standards, processes or methods are being used;
- **2nd line:** undertaken by, or on behalf of, those who have no first line responsibilities, to ensure first line of defence is properly designed, in place and operating as intended;
- **3rd line:** carried out independently, by internal audit, to provide senior management with an objective opinion on the effectiveness of governance, risk management and internal controls, including the effectiveness of the first and second lines of defence.

Organizations interpret these lines of defence in different ways and might even have more levels, with each higher level overseeing the lower levels. In effect this is a formal way of answering the question, "Who guards the guards?"

In a programme or project context the second line of defence is concerned with:

- ensuring the methods and processes are used effectively, through observation and analysis of metrics;
- undertaking reviews prior to significant decisions or when a significant issue has arisen; the initiator is usually the programme and project sponsor, as that role is accountable for assurance.

Assurance reviews should be scheduled prior to significant decisions (such as gates) to provide decision makers with an assessment of the status and outlook for the work. Such reviews should be planned to minimize the impact on the programme and project teams and workload of the reviewers. This can be done, for example, by combining project and programme reviews or combining a number of project reviews.

The third line of defence is usually concerned with audits; these might be externally driven, say through ISO 9000 quality audits or by the organization's senior management and undertaken by an internal audit group. Audits are normally defined and planned well in advance as part of an annual audit plan which addresses where the organization sees the risks.

Project governance or governance of project management?

Don't confuse project or programme governance with the governance of project or programme *management*. Project and programme governance are concerned with how a project or programme is actually directed and managed. The governance of programme or project management is concerned with the methods and processes for directing and managing programmes and projects: how they are created and approved, how they are updated and how you ensure they are being used.

Parts III and V deal with project and programme governance respectively. Part VI includes Chapter 27 which describes the governance of programme and project management.

The many aspects of governance

The preceding sections in this chapter covered those aspects of governance which are of primary concern to senior management. However, governance is more far reaching. Fundamentally, an organization undertakes its activities to realize benefits. To achieve this, its people need to be effective at both managing and doing the specialist work at the core of the business. There is little point in being in the automotive industry if you haven't the capability to design, manufacture and distribute cars, no matter how good your project managers are. Nor is it beneficial to be able to create a superb product if you cannot get it to your customers. Table 4.1 lists some other aspects governance which need to be covered.

Table 4.1 Different aspects of governance

Roles	Ensuring people, from top to bottom know what they are accountable for and who they are accountable to. Key in this is the 'sponsor' role, who is accountable for ensuring the organization's business interest are maintained.
Decisions	Knowing who will take each decision, the criteria for the decision and who will support them.
Assurance	Helping the sponsor exercise their business leadership role.
Specialist assurance	Ensuring specialist areas of work are undertaken effectively and efficiently, such as: • technical assurance – checking the solution is the right one and will work; • user assurance – checking users get what they need; • service assurance – ensuring customers are served appropriately.
Customer contract	Ensuring we know and meet our obligations and that our customer does the same.
Supplier contract	Ensuring suppliers know and meet their obligations and that we do the same. Ensure we know explicitly who is accountable for each contractual obligation.
Meetings	Who meets whom, when and why?
Prioritisation	Determining who can make decisions when there is a conflict of priority. In business-led projects, the choice should relate to maximizing benefit to the organization, bearing in mind the associated risks.
Escalations	Ensuring accountabilities can be met, even when things fail.
Reporting	Ensuring the right people have the right information in order to undertake their accountabilities.
Controls	Monitoring progress to be reassured everything is on track and to prompt action when things start going wrong. Key in this is the creation of a plan (baselined), the management of risks and issues and the introduction of changes to the plan in a controlled way, keeping focussed on the required benefits. A key pillar of control is the work break down structure.
Processes and procedures	Defining how a work is set up, managed and controlled.
Project gating	Ensuring only those projects which should be started are started and only those which should continue, do continue.
Quality	Ensuring we achieve the quality of outputs that we need and that the specified quality really does meet the stakeholders' needs.

Most of the aspects in Table 4.1 are covered in this book. I would, however, like to emphasize the breadth and interaction between them by looking at:

- harnessing the work breakdown structure to make simplify governance;
- developing plans which allow for governance;
- using baselines effectively.

Don't be solely driven by bookkeeping

Harness the work breakdown structure

A well thought through work breakdown structure is the basis of good multi-level governance. It ensures every activity in the plan is directly traceable, through the various levels of accountability from the team member undertaking the work, via the project manager to the project sponsor and up to the business portfolio sponsor. Conversely, a poorly thought through work breakdown structure is a recipe for confusion, duplication and omission. A good work breakdown structure provides:

A well thought through work breakdown structure is the basis of good multi-level governance.

- clear accountability, at every level in the hierarchy for scope, time, cost and schedule;
- obvious point of accountability when a 'level manager' goes missing (the higher-level manager is accountable for filling the gap);
- clear escalation path, without the need to negotiate the corporate structure;
- clear lines for reporting and escalation;
- clear view of who has the decision rights over whom and for what.

Don't confuse a work breakdown structure with an organization structure. On the face of it, they might look similar, with team member reporting to team manager reporting to project manager. A single individual could, however, work on a number of separate work packages, reporting to a different team manger on each and even be acting as a team manager on others; see Figure 4.6.

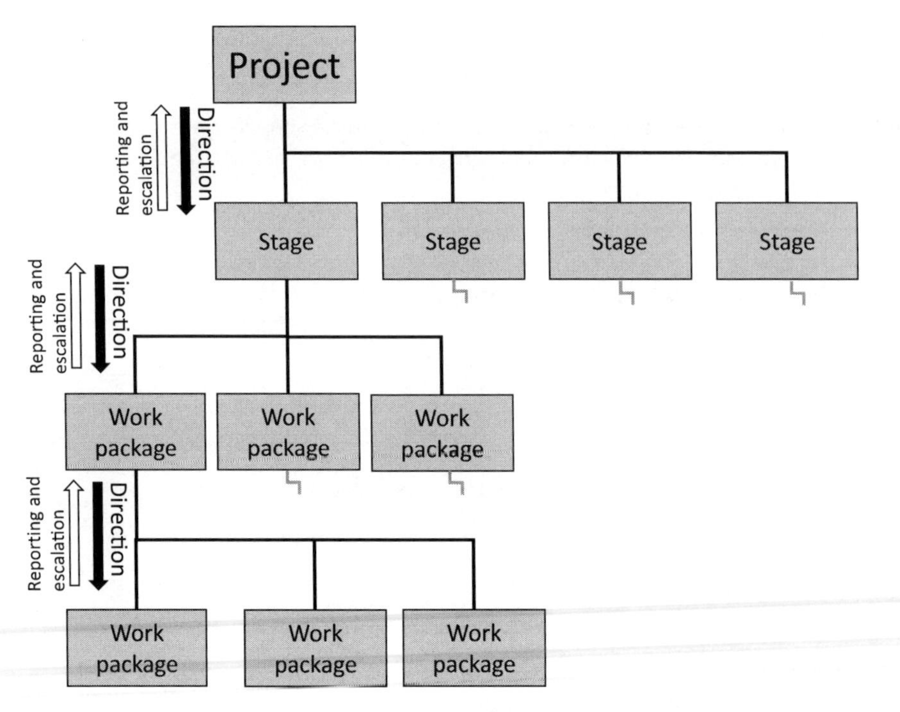

Figure 4.6 The work breakdown structure as an essential element of governance

A properly constructed work breakdown structure provides clear accountability at every level in the project, for planning, delegation, escalation, reporting and decision rights. This example shows the tiers of accountability within a project. By combining this with Figure 3.3, you can ensure traceability of all decision and direction from the top of the organization to the lowest levels, where the 'real work' is done.

Build time for governance into your plans

Governance is not 'free'. It takes effort, time and money. For this reason, when developing plans, take account of the time governance can take. In particular, look at decision making. Certain deliverables might require extensive peer review before they can be approved. In system engineering, it is not unusual to have preliminary and critical design reviews, each lasting a week, when the subject matter experts look into every aspect of the design before making any recommendations. Project gate decisions usually require senior level approval and in many organizations, this will be at a board which might only meet monthly. Look at all the reviews, approvals and decisions required in your plan and check whether.

- any individuals are overloaded, having too many decisions to make;
- you allowed enough time for reviews to take place;
- decisions are linked into regular (heartbeat) boards or will you sometimes need extraordinary meetings to maintain momentum.

Figure 4.7 shows a real-life example of the number of the number of decisions required each month on a transformation programme comprising nine projects. It peaks at about 54 decisions a month, when the various project teams are completing their investigative stages; that is 54 decisions on top of the decisions the directors have to make as a part of the day-to-day running of the business.

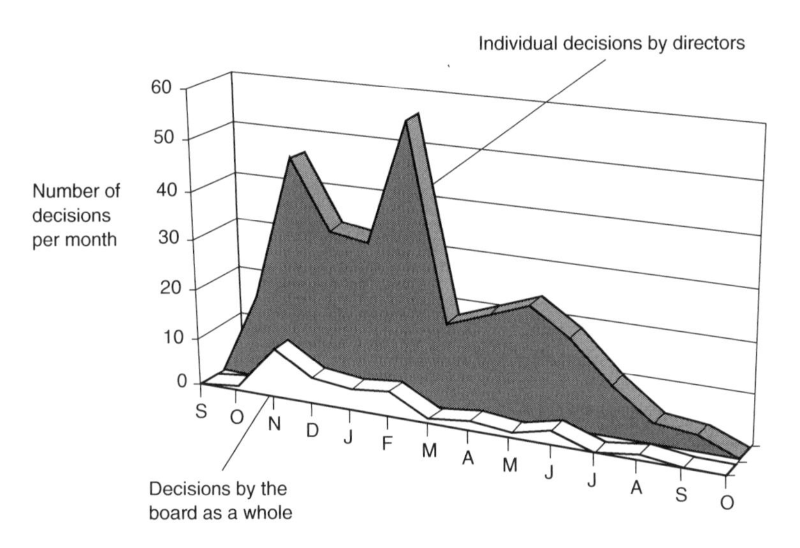

Figure 4.7 Decisions

In the planning stages of a complex change programme, the project managers identified each point which required either a board decision or the decision of one of the directors. In all, over 200 decisions were identified, spanning nine strategic change projects.

You need to consider whether the decision makers actually have the time to devote to the decisions required of them. The programme in this example relates to the re-engineering of a manufacturing company which was rationalizing its product offerings and channels to market, upgrading production lines and consolidating all its operations on a new single site. It was clear that the decision makers themselves might become the bottleneck and actually impede progress. Possible responses to this are to:

- combine closely related decisions;
- pre-book weekly programme board meetings for the duration of the programme (previously the board members only met monthly at their regular senior team meeting);
- delegate as many decisions as possible whilst at the same time, through the use of good processes, ensuing top-down visibility;
- increase the contingency in the schedule in case a decision maker is not available and to allow for slippage on critical path activities.

Use baselines effectively

The management of baselines is an essential part of governance. At any point in time you need to know three aspects:

- the plan baseline: in terms of schedule, costs, scope and benefits (see Chapter 22);
- the solution baseline: comprising requirements, design and product (see Chapter 24);
- contract baseline: relating to a customer (if any) and suppliers (see Chapter 26).

These three baselines are not independent. It is vital that every requirement and solution component can be traced to the planned work being undertaken in relation to it. In addition, requirements should be traceable to any contract clauses (both up to the customer and down to a supplier – allocated requirements) to which they relate. Without this level of control, changes, an inevitable fact of life, cannot be adequately assessed and, if implemented, the effects cannot be adequately communicated to those who need to know. We will look at change control in Chapter 23.

Plan baseline

The plan baseline covers what the approved plan is, in terms of benefits, schedule, costs, resources and scope, against which progress will be measured.

Solution baseline

The solution baseline explains everything about the output the project is going to create. This is made up of three parts. The requirements baseline is the definitive set of requirements driving the project. The design baseline provides the configuration of the various components of the solution and the detail for each part of the solution. The product baseline is the solution 'as built' and handed over for steady state operation. You might not be familiar with this terminology, which is derived from system engineering, but you are sure to have definitions or descriptions of your outputs in text or diagram form, electronically or in documents which are used in a similar way.

Contract baseline

The contract baseline is the contract, as signed, together with any agreed variations (changes). This can apply to a customer or to suppliers.

Workout 4.1 – The governance of your projects

Consider each project you are either sponsoring or is within a portfolio or programme you are managing or directing.

1. Use Table 4.1 as the basis to create your own table for defining what influences the governance of each of your projects; discard any aspects which don't apply and add any special ones you believe are missing.
2. State whether you have already covered this aspect (Yes/No).
3. Finally, use the last column to say how each aspect is, or should be, dealt with in your organization.

Roles	Ensuring people, from top to bottom know what they are accountable for and who they are accountable to. Key in this is the 'sponsor' role, who is accountable for ensuring the organization's business interests are maintained.	Yes
Decisions	Knowing who will take each decision, the criteria for the decision and who will support them.	Yes
Assurance	Helping the sponsor exercise their business leadership role	Yes
Specialist assurance	Ensuring specialist areas of work are undertaken effectively and efficiently, such as: • technical assurance – checking the solution is the right one and will work; • user assurance – checking users get what they need; service assurance – ensuring customers are served appropriately	Yes
Customer contract	Ensuring we know and meet our obligations and that our customer does the same	N/A
Supplier contract	Ensuring suppliers know and meet their obligations and that we do the same. Ensure we know explicitly who is accountable for each contractual obligation.	Yes
Meetings	Who meets whom, when and why?	

Workout 4.2 – Chains of accountability

Pick up your results from Workout 3.1. If you haven't completed it, finish it now!

1 Based on what you now know about the importance of roles and breakdown structures, verify:
   a Who, by name and role, is accountable to whom, within the portfolio and each of its constituent components (programmes, projects and other work). Cover the portfolio director, portfolio manager, programme sponsor, programme manager, project sponsor and project manager roles together with any other roles associate with 'other work'.
   b The governance of each portfolio component dovetails with higher-level components with no gaps or overlaps in accountability.
2 Who is accountable for the following:
   a Decisions on starting new programmes and projects and any phases and stages within them.
   b Decisions on whether work should be terminated.
   c Decisions on which work takes priority over another?
   d Decision on whether the quality of deliverables is adequate?
3 Does each individual, named on your structure, understand their accountabilities?
   a Do they know who they take direction from and report to?
   b Do they know who is expecting direction from them?
   c Do they understand what particular aspects of governance they are accountable for exercising?
   d Do they know what decisions they are entitled to take and which they are entitled to be consulted on?
4 If there are any answers to questions 2 and 3 such as 'unknown' or 'not sure', or if you find two or more people seem to be accountable for the same decision or activity, you need to clarify those accountabilities.

Note, in poorly defined matrix organizations, and ones run primarily on departmental hierarchy, this will not be a simple exercise and you might not give you the clarification you need. If this is the case, you'll need to ensure the risks associated with this situation are at least recognized and then work towards creating an environment where the accountabilities are clear. The workouts in the remainder of this book will help you.

Workout 4.3 – Programme or project complexity

Use the table below to determine what factors you need to pay special attention to when designing your governance framework. You can present the results as a figure like Figure 4.3.

FACTOR		*DESCRIPTION*		
Business criticality	0 = This work is not at all critical to the organization	3 = A division of the organization will suffer if this work is not completed	5 = The organization will suffer significantly or even fail, if this work is not done	
Reputation exposure	0 = This work has no impact on reputation	3 = Organization reputation will suffer, perhaps with minor impact on share prices and/or customer perception	5 = The organization reputation will suffer significantly (share impacting) if this work fails	
Financial exposure	0 = No financial exposure	3 = Financial exposure would impact an operating division such that Vice President level escalation would be needed	5 = Significant (share impacting) financial exposure, which could damage the organization	
Inter-dependencies	0 = the work is totally self-contained. No inter-dependencies.	3 = The work has numerous, identified dependencies	5 = The work has multiple dependencies outside the management control of the manager	
Legal and regulatory exposure	0 = There is no discernible legal, contractual or regulatory exposure from the work	3 = There are legal, contractual or regulatory constraints which need some management	5 = significant regulatory and/or legal, contractual issues involved – high level of risk if not carefully governed	
Business transformation	0 = the work includes very little organization transformation aspects	3 = The work includes changes to processes, tools and culture and the operating vision is clear	5 = The work involves significant changes to process, tools and culture and the operating vision is unclear	

FACTOR		*DESCRIPTION*		
Schedule flexibility	0 = there is total flexibility on when the work can be finished (self-imposed constraint)	3 = Intermediate and end dates for the work are fixed through legal, regulatory or contractual mechanisms but can be moved by negotiation	5 = Intermediate and end dates for the work are fixed due to an unmovable end date, such as an event	
Requirements and scope	0 = Requirements and scope are absolutely clear	3 = Requirements and scope are defined in outline with some acceptance criteria known	5 = the requirements and scope are not defined and need to be determined as part of the work	
Output Innovation	0 – the output from the work is standard	3 = some aspects of the solution rely on new technologies or capabilities (new to the organization, but not new to the world)	5 = The output requires the development of completely new capabilities and technologies	
Delivery processes	0 = The work is so trivial that no standard processes are required	3 = How the work is undertaken is partially defined and the organization has good experience of this type of work	5 = There are no defined processes and methods for how much of the work should be undertaken	
Team dynamics and size	0 = very small (say, 2–5), co-located core team, used to working with each other	3 = The core team is moderate in size (say, 5–15) and from a number of business areas; most have not worked together before	5 = Large, multi-disciplinary core team (say, 20) dispersed across the world	
Supplier involvement	0 = no suppliers involved in the work, 1= 1 or 2 suppliers, which the organization is used to working with.	3 = a number of suppliers are used, some of which the organization has experience of working with	5 = multiple key suppliers are required for significant aspects of the work, which the organization has no experience of working with	
			TOTAL	

5

Sponsorship

The sponsor

Who will you need to work with?

Your leadership style

Some tough choices

As a sponsor, where do I fit?

Business portfolio, programme and project sponsorship are all concerned with business leadership, outcomes, benefits and risk.

"Do I dare disturb the universe?"

T. S. ELIOT, 1888–1965

- **Sponsorship involves being a business leader, decision maker and change agent.**
- **The sponsor is the primary risk-taker.**
- **Ensure work is at all times viable, if not, terminate it!**
- **Be forward looking; focus on the business objectives, outcomes and benefits.**
- **The way a sponsor is perceived, as a leader has a significant impact.**

The sponsor

An underlying principle of business portfolio, programme and project management is 'single point accountability'. This is meant to stop things 'falling down the cracks' and applies not only to individual pieces of work but also to the direction of a business portfolio, programme or project; there should be only one sponsor per portfolio, programme or project. In this respect, the term 'sponsorship' should not be used in the same sense as 'sponsoring Tom to run a marathon', where the objective is to have as many sponsors as possible.

Most people associate the term 'sponsor' with directing a project, but the term can also be applied to programmes and business portfolios. I have used it in this book as there is more in common between what a business portfolio sponsor, programme sponsor and project sponsor does than there are differences. They are all concerned with business leadership, outcomes, benefits and risk. Chapter 3, however, demonstrated how programmes and projects are governed through their business cases whilst business portfolios are governed through a business plan; Chapter 4 showed that they are all part of governance but fit in different places within governance, depending on the context. Because of the similarities, I have drawn together, in this chapter, some aspects of sponsorship which apply throughout. The specific parts of this book on projects (Part II), business portfolios (Part III) and programmes (Part IV) will highlight what is different in each.

They are all concerned with business leadership, outcomes, benefits and risk.

As an executive, you are a leader within your organization. For some of you, still ascending the corporate ladder, sponsorship might be a new experience. You will be in the position of advocating a new order, acting in the interest of the wider needs of the company rather than those of the department or line director you serve. For the first time, you might be operating outside your own departmental or functional structure. You might have to work with people you don't have direct authority over, and this will require all your influencing and leadership skills to achieve your aims.

As a sponsor, you are the business advocate accountable for ensuring business objectives are met and benefits realized.

As a sponsor, you are the business advocate accountable for ensuring business objectives are met and benefits realized. If a sponsor is to be effective, rather than just someone who gives out money, you will need to be:

- a business leader;
- a change agent;
- a decision maker.

This applies regardless of whether you are sponsoring a business portfolio, a programme or a project. What changes with each of these roles is your position in the hierarchy of accountabilities and hence, what you are accountable for and who you are accountable to. As always, it is the context which matters.

The sponsor as a business leader

As a sponsor, you are accountable for the outcomes and realization of the benefits. You are therefore also accountable for any shortfalls, making you the primary risk taker. It is *your* portfolio, programme or project and all risks are *your* risks. Sponsorship is an active role and includes ensuring every piece of work undertaken always makes sound business sense, involving all benefiting units, setting direction, approving key deliverables and making decisions or recommendations at critical points.

Sponsorship is not merely a 'figurehead' role.

Sponsorship is not merely a 'figurehead' role. A sponsor is fundamentally accountable for ensuring 'why' the organization is spending time and resources on particular piece of work. You must ensure the vision and associated business objectives are articulated and communicated clearly and whatever is being created is needed and fulfilled in a viable way. You need to keep your head up, making sure the need remains relevant and the capabilities produced continue to meet that need. The importance of sponsorship roles cannot be over-emphasized; current research indicates that a prime cause of project failure is lack of effective sponsorship and stakeholder engagement (stakeholders are dealt with in Chapter 25).

The sponsor as a change agent

You might see a change agent and leader as synonymous. If so, that is good. For others, I have separated these out so it can be related to what many consultants and academics often refer to as 'the management of change'. Every business portfolio, programme and project will create some change in the organization, otherwise there is no point in undertaking it! Some changes are less problematic to implement than others as they align with the status quo and do not cross any politically sensitive boundaries. In essence, most people carry on as they always have done. Other changes, however, are fundamental and result in shifts in power bases internally to the organization or even affect external agencies, such as with unions, suppliers or customers.

All organizations are 'political' to some extent and the greater the change to the status quo, the more those involved need to be aware of the opinions and interests of others. The change created by a programme or project might not necessarily be beneficial to everyone it touches and might trigger a political dimension to the sponsor's role. Suffice to say, you need to acknowledge any political aspects, understand the sources and motivations of the key players and then develop an appropriate approach. Naturally, if your work is concerned with public and social change, the political dimension might go far beyond organizational politics.

You can find more on the management of change in Chapter 25.

You must be able to communicate your vision and stay engaged

The sponsor as a decision maker

The decisions a sponsor needs to make fall into three broad types:

- setting direction or objectives, in which you set the course for future work without defining exactly how this should be achieved;
- go/no go decisions at the start of each piece of work and subsequent phases, decisions regarding how to react to issues and possible changes and decisions on whether to terminate work;
- approval of certain deliverables relating to particular outputs or outcomes.

If you are not comfortable with making choices and decisions and, especially, being held to account for those decisions, the sponsor is not likely to be a role you will be comfortable with. Many of the decisions you make will be predictable (in terms of timing, if not outcome!) and backed up by evidence provided by the programme or project manager. The standard management documentation, such as business plan, business case, feasibility report and closure report, is designed to provide the information you need. Ensuring your team supports you by providing options, risks and 'pros and cons' relating to each decision is part of your 'assurance' role. It is better to be surrounded by positive challengers who provide the advice you need rather than being told only what you want to hear.

The programme or project sponsor's champion

Often a programme or project requires high level sponsorship from either a vice president or even the company CEO or president. Unfortunately, senior ranks do not always have the time to carry out all the duties of a sponsor. Here, it is best if the role is delegated. Half-hearted sponsorship can be demotivating for the team and might even lead to the failure. Alternatively, aspects the role can be delegated to a 'champion' who is as committed to the benefits as the sponsor. In all practical terms, the champion acts on a day-to-day basis as the sponsor, only referring decisions upwards as required.

Attribute of a sponsor

If being a leader, change agent and decision maker are required of a sponsor, what sort of personal attributes does a good sponsor need to have? There is nothing magic in the answer; as sponsorship is essentially a business role, then the attributes are what you would expect for any good business executive. The exception is that, in a portfolio, programme or project managed context, business leadership crosses departmental boundaries (See Chapter 2, lesson 6) and might not be able to rely solely on 'position power' get his or her way.

Performance in a role can be looked at as a combination of four factors: knowledge, experience, skill and behaviours as shown in Table 5.1. At such a leadership

Table 5.1 Attributes of a sponsor

Knowledge	*Skills*
Strategic perspective	Ability to inspire and motivate
Market and customer	Communication
Supplier and supply chain	Relationship building
Professional and technical	Analysis and problem solving
Business law	Creativity and innovation
Financial	Learning
Behaviours	*Experience factors*
Honesty	Evidence of business change leadership
Ability to delegate	Evidence of endurance and perseverance
Confidence	Evidence of adaptability
Commitment	Evidence of intuition
Positive attitude	

level, however, the behavioural attributes should be paramount. Gaps in knowledge and skills can be compensated for by building a team to ensure completeness, or by appointing board members for their particular skills.

Who will you need to work with?

In some organizations the sponsor roles are well defined and established. You will find your accountabilities, and everyone else's, detailed in process documentation or methods. In other organizations, nothing will exist, and you will have to create the role and accountabilities for yourself. You will need to work harder to influence those around you to undertake complementary roles, such as programme and project managers or board members. There is little point in being the perfect sponsor when those you are relying on do not understand your role and the demands you are placing on them. Similarly, you have to set the expectations of your peers and the executive team to whom you either report or rely on for resources and expertise. You have to agree with them the degrees of freedom you have and the formal authority they have vested in you.

The more mature an organization is in working across the organization in programmes and projects, the easier it will be to exercise your role as a sponsor. Conversely, the less mature organization, the more difficult you will find that role ... but as a leader, you will relish that challenge!

Who you interact with depends on the context of your role. Look back at Chapter 3, which shows the relationships between business portfolios, programmes, projects and other work; the sponsor role needs to follow the same relationship. Table 5.2 outlines the key interactions, covering who you are accountable to and your direct reports.

There is, therefore, a tiering of sponsorship roles. This is necessary, as one person cannot have the energy and time to undertake all the sponsorship roles themselves.

Table 5.2 Context for the sponsor roles

	Business portfolio sponsor	*Programme sponsor*	*Project sponsor*
Accountable to:	Chief executive or higher-level portfolio sponsor	Business portfolio sponsor	Business portfolio sponsor (for a standalone project) or programme sponsor (if part of a programme)
Direct reports:	Business portfolio manager	Sponsor for subsidiary business portfolios (if any) Programme manager	Project manager
Who else might take on the role?	The chief executive	The business portfolio sponsor	If part of a programme, the programme manager can be assigned the project sponsor role.
Board		Executive programme board	Project board

Each sponsor is effectively taking a chunk of the higher-level sponsor's objectives and working on their behalf. In some cases, it is possible and acceptable for a sponsor to act at more than one level, say as the business portfolio sponsor and the sponsor for a particularly important programme within that portfolio. They might even work as a project sponsor on a project in someone else's business portfolio.

Any interactions you have as a sponsor, whether formal, informal, written or verbal should take into account who you are interacting with and what their accountabilities are relative to your own. If you are personally confused as to who is accountable for what and to whom, that uncertainty will ripple through the team and stakeholders, resulting in conflicts. Time spent establishing the roles is well spent and will lead to less potential for disagreements later. If you are leading at a business portfolio or programme level, you have to be confident that the sponsor and manager of each of the projects under your remit are working together effectively. Any failure by them is your failure.

Time spent establishing the roles is well spent and will lead to less potential for disagreements later.

Rank and organization hierarchy

Rank and organization hierarchy are secondary to placing the right people in the role, no matter what level. People who are driven by traditional status and organizational hierarchy might find this difficult to accept. An organization which includes too many people with this viewpoint will not be able to reap the full benefits of business portfolio management and is likely to remain as a traditionally structured organization, driven through annual cost centre and capital budgeting.

Your leadership style

There are probably more books and seminars on effective leadership styles than any other management topic and yet, time and time again, things go wrong for very human reasons. During the 1990s, it was estimated that ten academic papers a day were published on the subject and nowadays, virtually every organization includes leadership as a topic within their management or executive development programmes, Few actually address cross-functional sponsor roles, such are those covered in this chapter. The UK government is a notable exception and has a specific educational programme, the Major Projects Leadership Academy, for their programme and project sponsors (they call this role 'Senior Responsible Owner').

As a sponsor:

- you might be leading across an organization, impacting people and capabilities outside your traditional line management remit;
- traditional hierarchy and ranks might be side stepped, with apparently senior line managers accountable to managers perceived to be more junior;
- you might have no direct authority over the programme and project managers and teams as seen from a line management perspective. The normal disciplinary sanctions for non-performance of individuals might not exist.

In such situations, certain aspects of 'pushy' or 'blue' styles, such as assertion and persuasion, can be ineffective. Persuasion is useful if the issue is open to rational debate and you are perceived as being competent in the topic under discussion. It is notoriously poor in a highly charged emotional environment. Assertiveness can be powerful if your needs are legitimate and you stand to lose if those needs are not met. The accountabilities associated with your role give you legitimacy but do check what incentives or sanctions you can use to gain agreement or compliance with your wishes. If you can provide neither, assertion can be fruitless.

'Pull' or 'green' styles such as bridging and attraction might be more effective. Bridging involves gaining others' commitment and is most valuable if you are seen to be open to influence and value their opinions. Look at your stakeholders and you will probably find this form of influence will be appropriate for many situations involving them. Attraction or envisioning is all about generating enthusiasm and excitement, taking people beyond the everyday to new possibilities. It is often seen as totally irrational but is no less effective for that. If shared values and trust are needed to achieve your aims, this is a good influencing style.

The 'best style' is to use depends on the situation you are in and who you are trying to influence. In western cultures, open, even-handed styles which foster a common sense of purpose and trust usually win in the long run over leadership based on bullying and fear.

Try to be aware of how you come across; you might not see yourself as others see you. If you find yourself saying the following, think again:

- "Don't come to me with problems, come with solutions."
- "I only accept 'can do' as an option."
- "Don't come moaning to me; just do it."
- "I want action NOW!"

All these expressions might lead to over optimistic reports of progress, the truth being hidden and blaming others for failure to deliver.

Finally, remember success is concerned with meeting business objectives. An enabling part of that is producing deliverables on time, to quality and to budget. Against this background, a programme or project team can perform as expected or can fail. For example, if the project is well planned, the team should not be expected to produce a higher quality, quicker and cheaper solution than the one defined. If the expectations are higher, the project should be planned to meet those higher aspirations. If carried out properly, the investigative stages of the project will assure the most appropriate solution is chosen and defined; this is when the big gains are made or lost, not during the later development and build stages of the project. A project which completes on time and to budget is not necessarily an easy project, it could be a very difficult project which has been managed well by the project manager. You should give credit where credit is due.

If the expectations are higher, the project should be planned to meet those higher aspirations.

Some tough choices

People within organizations seldom act as you expect them to. Agreed roles and accountabilities can help prevent misunderstandings but will not guarantee it. Often, senior managers will do what they want to do, regardless of any agreements, 'rules' or best practice. The more immature an organization and/or the more political the senior tiers, the more likely you are to come across potentially dysfunctional behaviour. Four potentially difficult situations are described later. These are all described in the context of a project sponsor, but the underlying messages apply to programmes and business portfolios.

Being given a project which does not fit the strategy

If you are asked to sponsor a programme or a project for which you are either unable to see a link to strategy, or which you believe is counter to the stated strategy, what should you do? Should you:

1. decline to sponsor it?
2. sponsor it regardless?

Both actions are potentially career limiting. On the former, you might be perceived as an ineffective or timid manager. On the latter, you will be tying your reputation to something you do not believe in and for which you may ultimately be held to account.

If you can engage the executive who requested you to be the sponsor of the programme or project and discuss the potential problem that is well and good. If your organization already has business portfolio management defined and established, you'll be able to determine the legitimacy of the request. If not, you'll have to work that out for yourself. First, you need to understand why the senior executive wants the project undertaken and where they perceive the strategic fit lies. You also need to understand the power base which enabled them to give you the instruction in the first place; Workout 5.1 can help with that.

If engagement is difficult, you should harness the principles of business-led project management and stakeholder engagement to build a coalition or case for (or against) the project by taking a staged approach (see Chapter 8). During the investigative stages, poll the thoughts of other impacted parties to determine whether it is you who is out of line or your senior executive. Based on such information, decide whether, in the context of the whole business, this project is something which really matters. If not, keeping a low profile and undertaking it might be an option, although a potential waste of money and time. If it does matter, ensure you keep your senior executive engaged:

- ask her to address a meeting of key stakeholders to explain the imperatives behind the project; make sure the questions you need answering are asked by the participants;
- ask her to chair the project board to hear on-going questions and queries as they arise. This will ensure direct involvement in key decisions, especially at major decision points, such a project gates;
- refer crucial decisions to her and ensure she makes them – give your own views and recommendations;
- ensure she personally underwrites all crucial communications to make it clear to everyone where the drive for the project is coming from.

By ensuring the senior executive's involvement, you increase the chances of:

- correcting any misperceptions you might have;
- protecting yourself by making the executive visibly own her own decisions
- exposing the executive to counter arguments and hence opening the opportunity for a reversal of the decision, without losing face. ("The detailed investigation resulting from the project has uncovered some important new facts and has led me to review this project. As a result, I have decided to terminate it.")

Terminating a project which is no longer viable

Throughout this book, you will see many references to the advice that if a project ceases to be viable, it should be terminated.

Termination can be difficult to make happen in practice.

This is very obvious, but termination can be difficult to make happen in practice. Some projects simply refuse to die! As the sponsor, you are in a prime position to determine whether termination is required. You are, after all, accountable for the outcomes and realization of the benefits and if they are unlikely to flow, you will fail to meet your objectives. Do not expect the project manager to recommend termination. Unless the deliverables are proving impossible to deliver, the project manager and team are likely to want to carry on regardless. Expecting them to terminate their source of employment is like expecting turkeys to vote for Christmas. The following actions should lead you to a correct decision:

- Have whatever event prompted you to consider termination placed in the issues log (see Chapter 23). Use workshop techniques to define the source problem, look for possible solutions (including termination) and gain consensus from the key stakeholders.
- If termination is the recommended option, treat this as a formal 'change' to the project. Undertake an impact assessment on what effect termination will have on other projects, operations and the ability of the organization to meet the objectives in the business portfolio plan.
- If termination is the preferred action, do it without delay, in an orderly and controlled way.

Remember, it is not usually sufficient for you alone to know termination is the right course of action. Many people at a senior or influential level might be personally associated with the project and regard termination as 'losing face' or failure. Some would rather see the project continue than face reality. You need to bring the stakeholders with you and make the decision 'safe' by phrasing it in as positive way as possible; after all, think of the money and reputation you have saved by stopping something which would either deliver nothing or worse, reflect badly on the organization.

We can't afford to terminate that project. Really? Why?

It was quite clear that the project ought to be stopped. The proposed solution was never going to meet the needs and continuing would just throw good money after bad. Termination was the right option. Unfortunately, the finance team disagreed, saying, "We can't afford the write-off we if terminate it, so you'll just have to sort it out and start delivering." Unfortunately, this scenario is not uncommon and generally relates to the organization's financial treatments. Accounts are meant to be prudent with sales and assets not being recognized until they are certain to materialize. If you can't 'afford the write-off', it probably means that the work to date has been over-valued and risks have either not been recognized by the project team or not been taken into account in the financial statements by the finance managers. This situation can be indicative of a company under stress to perform beyond its capabilities with 'making the numbers up' replacing 'making the numbers'. It could be fraud.

On being given a strategic project

It might sound like a career-enhancing dream to be asked to sponsor a 'strategic' programme or project and be at the leading edge of the company. However, treat such opportunities with caution. 'Strategic' projects usually happen at the top of the business cycle, often associated with a new executive appointment and sometimes relate to the latest management fad. In good times, the threshold for spending large sums of money on such projects is very low. When the downturn comes, organizations usually focus on cash and efficiency, neither of which many strategic projects can deliver in the short term.

Real strategic projects are concerned with ensuring the longer-term sustainability of the organization. If you have been given a strategic project, make sure you can demonstrate true strategic linkage and that the project is likely to be a sound investment. If you cannot demonstrate this, chunk the project into smaller packages of deliverables to keep interest from stakeholders, demonstrate progress through successive wins and maintain momentum.

Real strategic projects are concerned with ensuring the longer-term sustainability of the organization.

As a sponsor, where do I fit?

In many organizations, how the management of programmes and projects across departments can be opaque. In addition, there might not be anything covering business portfolio management. If this is your situation, you will need to do some detective work to determine who you are accountable to with respect to the project and it might not necessarily be your line director or the CEO. Ask yourself:

- who asked me to undertake the role?
- what authority do they have to ask me to do this?
- what resources do they have to contribute?
- what level of interest or supervision will they exert?
- where does this project sit relative to others?
- who else may think they can legitimately direct me on this role?
- who has the authority to terminate the project?

If the Chief Executive has asked you to undertake the role, your accountability line is clear. However, make sure you have interpreted what you perceive you heard correctly. Corporations are full of 'the CEO said' projects, which the CEO had no intention of initiating or of taking a personal interest in. Often, they are merely 'flying a kite'. Also, check what level of authority you have if there are no company guidelines to define them. Again, many CEOs' intentions to investigate a problem are incorrectly interpreted as 'spend a fortune to do xyz'. In other words, if you hear the words 'approval' or 'authority', don't jump to the conclusion you have carte-blanche to do whatever you want. It does no harm to confirm your understanding in writing.

If the direction is not from the Chief Executive, it might still be valid, but check with the relevant person that your understanding and theirs match. Remember 'your project' may be just one of a number and might not be the highest priority. A short, open conversation, supported by a 'Proposal' document (see Chapter 8), should help to clarify minds and significantly reduce the likelihood of misunderstandings.

Look for who else might believe they have a legitimate right to direct you. Find out why this should be the case. Perhaps they are a more appropriate reporting line but a word of warning, the less mature your organization is in project management, the more likely it is to have the senior reporting line, in project terms, completely wrong. A common example is where it is believed an IT Director or CTO, should have ultimate accountability for any projects containing significant IT deliverables (an 'IT Project'). However, at the senior end, projects should be directed on the basis of the desired outcomes and the benefits they realize rather than the deliverables they produce. For example, a customer service director would be more appropriate as a sponsor for a new customer relationship management system than the IT Director. The IT Director should have accountability for the architectures and quality of the IT deliverables and as such, will be a key to delivery and a candidate for membership of the programme or project board, but that is quite different from being the programme or project sponsor.

Projects should be directed on the basis of the desired outcomes and the benefits they realize rather than the deliverables they produce.

Workout 5.1 – Picking up a programme or project in mid-flight

Some organizations undergo an almost continuous stream of reorganization which can lead to a sponsor leaving the company or being deployed elsewhere. Even in stable organizations, people often move on. It is therefore possible you will be asked to take on the sponsorship of a programme or a project which is already under way. What should you do? Just as when you take over another company, you need to apply 'due diligence' and undertake a formal review of the project to understand what you are taking accountability for. The following actions should help you gain an understanding of the project.

1. Interview the project manager. You need to build a relationship, so start as soon as you can. Ask for:
   a. their perception of the business objectives and likelihood of meeting them;
   b. a list of stakeholders who have been or need to be engaged;
   c. a copy of the most recent formal documentation (Proposal, Project Definition, etc.);
   d. a progress update covering performance against cost and schedule; the key risks and issues are and what the outlook is for the remainder of the project.
2. Interview (if still available) the outgoing sponsor:
   a. determine if their departure is related to the project;
   b. ask for a two-minute summary: what outcomes a project will deliver, why it is needed, the benefits which will be realized and the scope;
   c. find out the stakeholders who have been or need to be engaged;
   d. ask where the key risks lie and what the key issues are currently being faced;
   e. ask for copies of recent assurance and audit reports, if any.
3. Interview some key stakeholders to determine their views on the project, its strategic fit, desirability and current health.
4. Use the gate checklists in Chapter 8 on project frameworks, to determine whether the work is proceeding on a sound footing.
5. Compare the views you have gathered from discussions and formal documentation and note any significant mismatches.
6. Meet with the executive who appointed you and gain their perspective; cross check any discrepancies with them and agree any actions that need to be taken as a result.

Such a review will meet two objectives:

- you will meet most of the key players, demonstrate your willingness to listen and make the hand-over of the sponsorship role to you explicit. No one should be in any doubt that the role holder has changed;
- you will gather facts and rumours upon which you can make a value judgement on the overall health of the project and what needs to be addressed as a priority.

PART II
THE ESSENCE OF PROJECT MANAGEMENT

"Take calculated risks. That is quite different from being rash."

GENERAL GEORGE S. PATTON, 1885–1945

To be successful at managing programmes and portfolios, you need to have a thorough understanding of project management. That doesn't mean you have to be a great project manager, but without understanding how project management works, you are unlikely to have a successful programme and that might be very costly. Projects often fail due to poor direction from those leading programmes or portfolios, not because the project sponsor or project manager was inadequate. By providing the right 'top-cover' you can give your people the freedom to manage. This doesn't mean that you can be totally hands-off; if you create a vacuum at the top, your projects are almost guaranteed to fail.

- **Make sure your projects are driven by benefits supporting your strategy.**
- **Understand the context for each project.**
- **Ensure roles are defined, assigned and understood.**
- **Contain risk by taking a staged approach to managing the project.**
- **Ensure project governance is appropriate and proportionate.**

How to use Part II

In this part of the book, I set out the key features of projects and how they are directed and managed, highlighting those aspects you, as a programme or business portfolio sponsor or manager, need to pay particular attention to. The workouts in Part II are designed to help you challenge your project sponsors and managers in a positive way, helping you ask the right questions to take things forward, not to make the team feel inadequate. Remember, a failed project is not just the team's failure, it is *your* failure.

If you want to know about project management in greater detail, read *The Project Workout*. This is the companion volume to this book and goes into far more detail about how an individual project should be run.

6

Project management in context

Projects as vehicles of change

Positioning the project

Business-led and enabling projects

Making sure your scope meets the business need

Context matters; business portfolio and programme leaders must understand the bigger picture within which each project sits.

"Life is really simple, but we insist on making it complicated."

CONFUCIUS, 551 – 479 BC

- **Business-led projects are about making change happen.**
- **Understand the context for the project.**
- **A business-led project includes all the work necessary to achieve the outcomes.**
- **Enabling projects create outputs and should be part of a programme.**
- **The justification for doing a project and for choosing a solution is different.**
- **Don't make your management over-complicated.**

Projects as vehicles of change

Projects are rapidly becoming the way organizations manage change; projects apply not only to work such as large construction or IT initiatives but also to any change initiative aimed at putting a part of a business strategy (or for the public sector, policy) in place. Projects, in the modern sense, are vehicles for implementing strategy and project management is now a core competence which many organizations require their leaders and managers to have.

Most organizations are never short of ideas for improvement. Ideas can come from anywhere within the organization, or even outside, from competitors, customers or suppliers. Deciding which of ideas business leaders should actually spend time and money on is not easy. This decision is one that those involved with business portfolio management are responsible for; they must take care in selecting projects, as:

- there is probably not enough money, manpower or management energy to pursue all of the ideas;
- undertaking projects which cannot be reconciled with the organization's strategy will, almost certainly, create internal conflicts between senior managers, confuse the direction of the business and ultimately, reduce the return on the company's investment.

Business portfolio managers should consider for selection only those projects which:

- have a firm root in the organization's strategy;
- meet the business portfolio's needs;
- will realize real benefits;
- are derived from gaps identified in business portfolio plans;
- and are achievable.

Programme managers will have similar choices to make, except programmes generally have more constrained objectives than portfolios, giving fewer options.

This is the challenge for business portfolio and programme managers. Projects therefore need to be directed and managed in such a way as to ensure the right information flows to those managers at the right time.

Positioning the project

Part I of this book describes what business portfolios, programmes and projects are, and how they relate to each other. To be successful as a leader in business portfolio or programme management, you need to ensure you understand Chapters 1 to 5. Refer back to them, as necessary because they form the foundations of everything else in this book.

Some business portfolio or programme managers might have been project managers at some time in their career and have a good understanding of what is entailed and what can go wrong. Many portfolio and programme managers, however, will not have any significant project management experience but they still need to understand how project management works in practice, if they are to be successful.

Many project sponsors and project managers complain of working in a vacuum and therefore have little understanding of, the pressures and issues the organization is facing that might impact their projects. Consequently, in the absence of this understanding, inappropriate decisions might be made. The challenge for any portfolio or programme manager is to ensure the project sponsors and managers within their remit have a sufficient understanding of how a project fits into the wider aims of the programme or business portfolio. Too often, senior managers assume their direct reports have the same information as themselves. Put yourself into the shoes of your project sponsors and managers and ask, in their position, what would you need to know to direct and manage this project? Conversely, drowning them in information can be as bad because they would need to analyze it for themselves and might come to different conclusions.

Context matters because portfolio and programme leaders need to understand the bigger picture surrounding each project.

Context matters because portfolio and programme leaders need to understand the bigger picture surrounding each project. If the organization is a jigsaw, how does each project fit with everything else? Portfolio and programme leaders should always understand why they are undertaking a project. Each project should be worthwhile, delivering desired outcomes for stakeholders and realizing the required benefits as part of a whole.

Let's remind ourselves of the lessons in Chapter 2 and see how these relate to projects.

- **Lesson 1**: Make sure your work is driven by benefits which support your strategy. In other words, understand why you should do this project. Approaches to this are covered in Part III of this book, which looks at how to select projects.
- **Lesson 2**: projects should be undertaken in stages (a project life cycle), proceeding incrementally and, if no longer viable, should be terminated. We'll look at this in more detail in Chapter 8.

- **Lesson 3**: Address and revalidate the marketing, commercial, operational and technical viability of the work throughout its life. To be a truly business-led project, everything that enables the outcomes and benefits you need has to be considered.
- **Lesson 4**: Involve selected users and customers into the work to understand their current and future needs. If you don't understand the users, customers or those impacted by the project and its results, you won't recognize what the right solution is. We'll look at this in Chapter 24.
- **Lesson 5**: Build excellence in project management techniques and controls. A project must be 'governed'; there needs to be a management framework, with roles, methods and processes to define how the project is directed and managed. This is covered in Chapters 7 to 10.
- **Lesson 6**: breakdown functional barriers by using cross-functional teams. Good solutions require input from many different specialties working together effectively. All those aspects which are implied in lesson 3 need to have people involved in the project, working together, to 'make it happen' in a matrix.

Business-led and enabling projects

Business portfolio and programme context

As this book is about portfolio and programme management, we will make the assumption that a project is either standalone within a portfolio or that it is part of a programme; see Figure 6.1. I have used the definitions of business portfolio and programme given in Chapter 3.

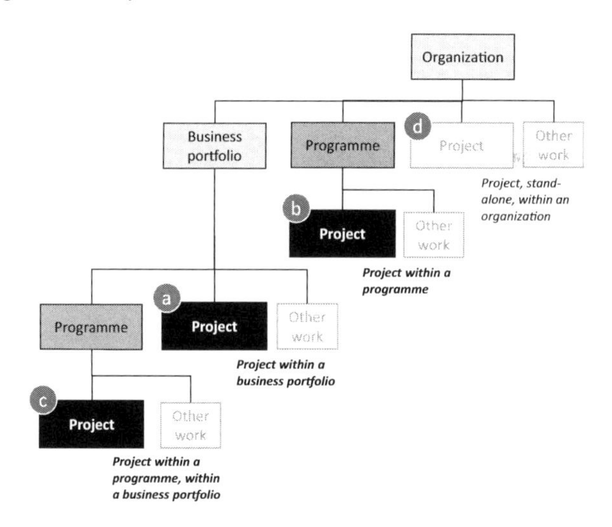

Figure 6.1 Projects in context

A project might be (a) standalone within a business portfolio; (b) part of a programme, which is standalone within the organization; (c) part of a programme which is itself part of a portfolio; (c); and (d) standalone within the organization. Unless you understand where your project sits, you will not know who has overall accountability.

Figures 6.2 and 6.3 show this relationship in a different way,

Figure 6.2 shows a standalone project, within a portfolio. It would be self-contained and have its own business case.

Figure 6.3 shows a project within a programme, within a business portfolio. Such a project would come under the remit of the programme's business case.

By understanding where your project sits, you will know who the project sponsor is accountable to. Otherwise, a fundamental aspect of governance, namely traceability of accountability, will be missing and it won't be clear who needs progress reports, who acts on such reports, who issues should be escalated and who can take which decisions.

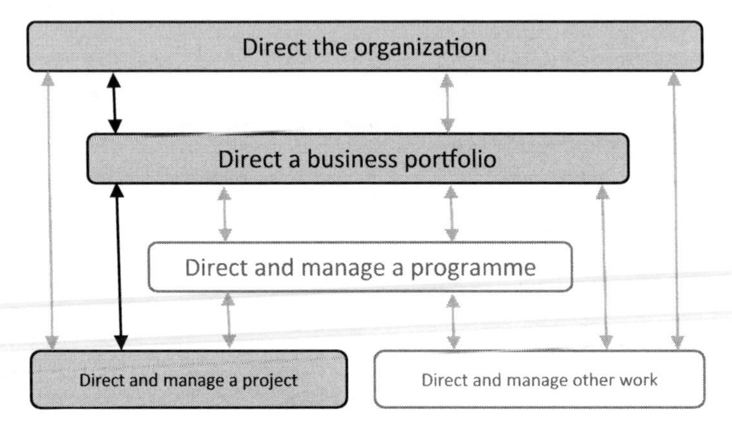

Figure 6.2 Projects within a business portfolio

When a project is part of a business portfolio, its direction comes from that portfolio and its objectives should contribute to the overall objectives for the portfolio. The direction for the portfolio comes from organizational level.

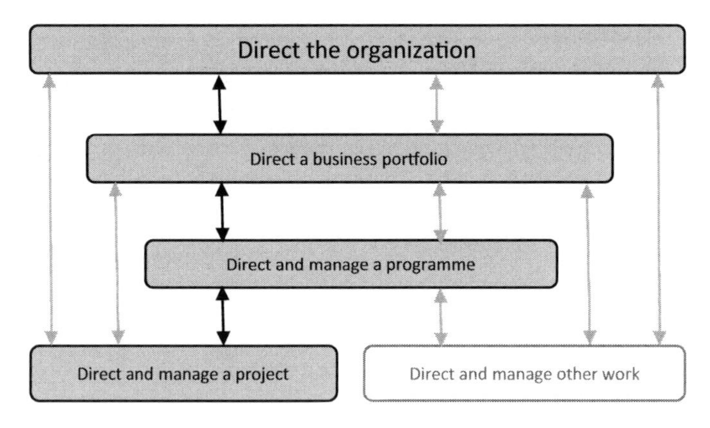

Figure 6.3 Projects within a programme

When a project is part of a programme, its direction comes from that programme and its objectives should contribute to the overall objectives for the programme. The programme would come under the direction of the business portfolio to which it belongs.

Business-led projects

All projects should be driven by a business need and result in benefits for the sponsoring organization. Chapter 3 showed how the organization might be a promoter or a contractor. For a promoter, the benefits can be wide-ranging but primarily concern one or more of the following:

All projects should be driven by a business need and result in benefits

- increasing the company's revenues through the development and provision of its products and services;
- reducing costs though more efficient working, innovation and choice of working platforms;
- reducing the need for working capital.

Benefits are considered in detail in Chapter 21.

Contractors also need to deal with these issues but realize benefits primarily in the form of payments received for the services provided to other organizations, such as building bridges or developing bespoke software. A promoter undertakes projects for themselves, whilst a contractor does them for someone else.

The test of any business-led project, regardless of whether it is for a promoter or a contractor, is that of financial or economic viability: will the benefits outweigh the costs over a defined time period? This is justified in a **business case**, which demonstrates the viability and the associated risks. In short, business projects have business cases and are relatively self-contained as their scope covers all the work necessary to drive the business changes (outcomes) needed to realize the benefits.

Enabling projects

There are situations, however, when an individual project might not need its own business case or be viable on its own. Such projects should be part of a programme and enable something else to happen, which would lead to outcomes and benefits being realized. For this reason, such projects are often called **enabling projects**. An enabling project has no direct benefit for the project sponsor as is seen in what are often termed 'IT projects'. For example, a project creates new software for an application which is then picked up within another project to be deployed and implemented. Benefits will start to flow only after the system is in use. But you might say, surely every project should be justified, otherwise there will be anarchy? You are right. Even though an enabling project can't have its own business case, it should be incorporated within the scope of a higher level business case (a programme business case), which includes the other projects and work required to deliver the outcomes and realize the benefits. Writing a business case for an enabling project on a marginal basis would serve no purpose.

Even though an enabling project does not need a business case, your choice of solution still needs to be justified. Not only should the solution meet the requirements, but it should do so effectively and efficiently; 'value for money' is a term

Don't confuse the justification for undertaking a project with the justification for the choice of solution

you'll often hear. This usually requires analyzing the options to select the most appropriate solution. Don't confuse the justification for undertaking a project with the justification for the choice of solution; in some organizations, they call both aspects 'business case'!

But my organization doesn't have any business portfolios?

You might think that your organization hasn't any business portfolios. What you should really be thinking is that your organization hasn't any *formal* portfolios. Regardless of whether you recognize it or not, your organization is your business portfolio. You still need to select what projects to do, check performance, assign resources and stop unviable work. Otherwise, you might simply be abdicating the leadership of the organization to the various heads of department, hoping they work together, each within their own targets and constraints, to come up with the right directives for the organization as a whole. That is hardly likely to happen. If this is your situation, start to look at the organization as being the business portfolio and then work to improve how this runs as a whole. This is covered in more detail in Part III of this book.

Making sure your scope meets the business need

A business-led approach

If your project is to realize the benefits you need, everything necessary to enable those benefits has to be in place; something has to change. In order for things to change, you need to create outputs which enable that change (or outcome) to happen. The linkage between outputs, outcomes and benefits is often known as benefit mapping. This is covered in more detail in Chapter 21.

For now, let's look at a simple example. You need to reduce the costs of service management in your organization by increasing efficiency and reliability. Your customer base is now so large that your customer service assistants can no longer find the relevant records when a customer calls in. You have decided to install a proprietary customer management platform to access all records from a customer's name or address. Installing that platform is not enough to get any benefits as you will also need to migrate records from existing systems, redesign the organization for the new way of working and train and support your employees in its use (customer service assistants and IT operations staff). You might also have to install computers for staff to use, wide and local area networks and power supplies for the new kit, screens, ergonomic furniture and a data management process to comply with prevailing law. There might also be on-going support contracts. Figure 6.4 illustrates this. A business-led project would include all the work necessary to achieve the outcomes in its scope. The

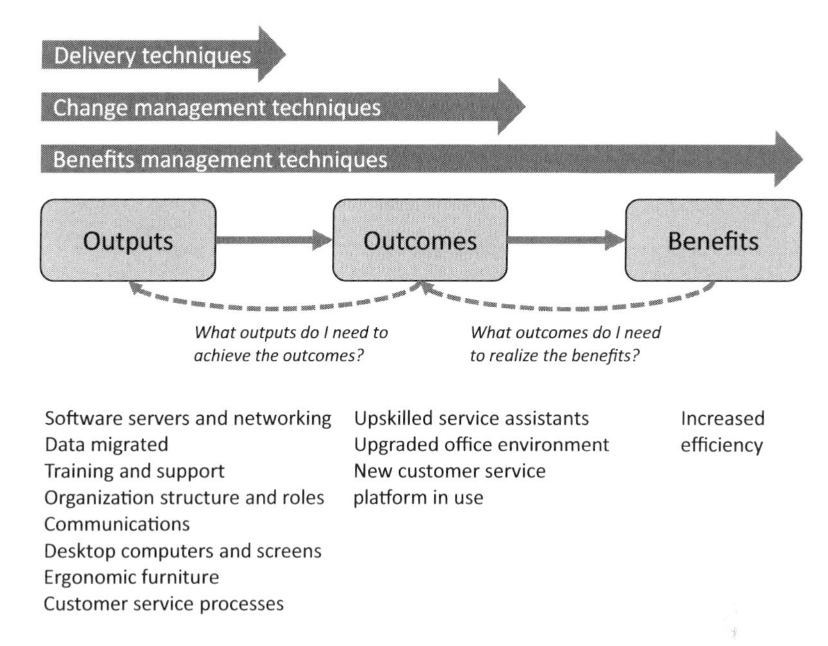

Figure 6.4 Scoping a business-led project

The scope of a business-led project should include all the work necessary to achieve the outcomes in its scope, so that the benefits can be realized. Delivery techniques are used to create outputs, business change techniques to ensure outcome materialize and benefits management techniques are used to ensure it is financially viable.

project team would comprise people from a range of functions, like software, hardware, networking, training, business change management and workplace design. To do this a range of management techniques would be used:

- **delivery techniques** used by the project teams to develop their specialist outputs;
- **change management techniques** to ensure the outcomes needed actually materialize;
- **benefits management techniques** to determine whether the resultant benefits are likely to justify the costs of the outputs and business change.

By building your project's scope in this way and directing and managing it as a single project, you are more likely to achieve your objectives. The team, as a whole, would be focussed on the outcomes rather than just delivering their bit. When things go wrong, solutions to issues in one function can often be solved by changes in another function. Figure 6.5 shows that effective project management takes away the uncertainty by providing direction, discipline and drive towards a business outcome.

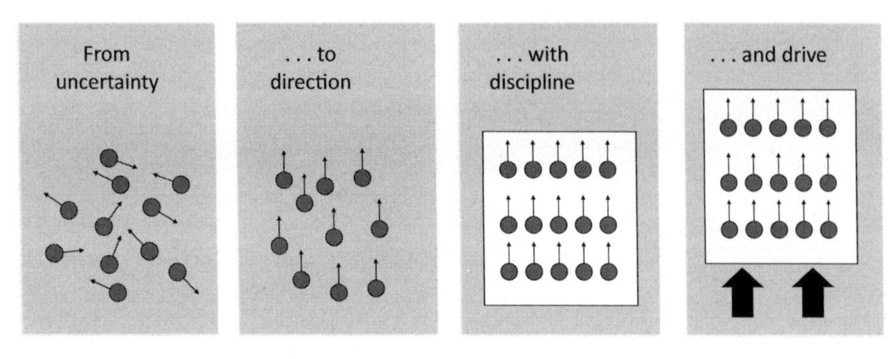

Figure 6.5 Business-led project management

Business-led project management takes you from uncertainty, applying direction, discipline and drive to 'make it happen'.

An alternative approach

Often organizations tackle a 'project' like that described earlier as a series of separate projects, focussing on each output. This is particularly the case in siloed organizations, where each department draws on their own annual budget to fund the work. So, the software development department would have a project to customize and install the software, the infrastructure department a project for the hardware and networking, L&D a training project and facilities, an office upgrade project. Each would run 'their project' in whatever way they saw fit and hope it joins up to 'go-live' on a particular date. Some might not manage their work as a project at all. Sometimes the term 'workstream' is used to undertake each function's work, although there is very little consensus on what a 'workstream' is and certainly no methods or approaches published for how to manage them. The necessary coordination, focus and drive that true project management provides would be missing as lessons 3 and 6, in particular would be ignored. My advice is avoid any management approach that uses 'workstream' unless you understand what the term means, how it is managed and its relationship to a project and a programme.

You could manage such an initiative as a programme, comprising a number of coordinated projects. Most of the projects would be 'enabling projects' scoped by outputs rather than outcomes, perhaps with a business-led project drawing it together. In many cases, however, this would complicate the governance and management far beyond what is necessary, and business is complicated enough without adding unnecessary management overhead. Part IV of this book examines programme management.

The cost of getting the scope wrong

The technology development team in a major organization created a stunning service platform, years ahead of the competition. By bolting a super-fast computer onto a standard telecommunications switch they were able to make what became known as the 'intelligent network' a reality. By calling a single number, from anywhere in the country, your call could be directed to the local branch of, say a shop or other business. Unfortunately, that was all that was developed. The missing element was how to provide such services to their customers and how to bill the customers. That took another three years to work out, by which time the rest of the industry had caught up. If the development of the 'intelligent switch' had been seen as just one part of a service development project, with service management and billing as part of the scope, these enabling systems would have been ready years earlier rather than considered as an after-thought.

Uncertainty, direction, discipline and drive

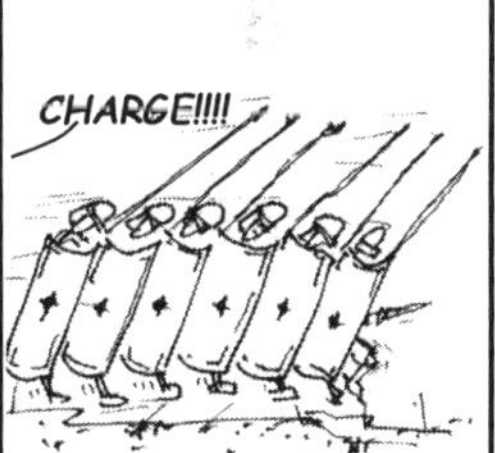

Workout 6.1 – Do your projects actually drive benefits?

Take the output from Workout 3.1, which should be a list of programmes, projects and other initiatives you are doing as a list and as a dependency map.

Make up a table listing them as follows:

Reference	*Name*	*Programme? Project? Other work?*	*Direct or enabling*	*Business case?*	*Sponsor*	*Comment*
Z001		Programme	Direct	Yes	Jan White	Possibly some work missing?
Z002		Project	Enabling	Z001	Viv Waters	
Z003		Other work	Enabling	Z001	Alex Saunders	
F005		Project	Direct	No	?	Sponsor not known
H008		Project	Enabling	?	Cley Aspen	Business case not identified

1. Look at each item in turn and decide it is being managed as a programme, project or other type of work.
2. Decide which of these directly lead to benefits and which are 'enabling'.
3. Those which directly lead to benefits should have a business case (or equivalent' justifying why they are being done.
4. The enabling ones should be covered under a business case somewhere else. Can you identify which one? If so, insert a cross reference to the programme or project whose business case covers the work.
5. Do you know who is sponsoring the work?
6. Add any comments or queries you believe are relevant.
7. Unless you are already very competent at portfolio management, you will find a number of gaps or 'unknowns'. The challenge is to complete these. Look for:

   - work for which you cannot identify the management approach being taken;
   - work you are undertaking with no justification;
   - mutually dependent projects with no overall programme management.

When undertaking this type of analysis, you might find the boundary you have chosen is inappropriate. For example, if the boundary only covers part of the organization, you could find that projects essential for a programme are missing. This is a sure indication that you need to look more closely at how you define your portfolios. There is more on this in Part II.

7

Who does what in a project

Roles

Who are the key people in project management?

Project sponsor

Project board

Project manager

Project team managers and team members

Assurance, support and coaching

High performing teams don't happen by accident.

In the long run, teams with a clear purpose and good working relationships drive better business results.

"Even emperors can't do it all by themselves."

BERTOLT BRECHT, 1898–1956

- **A project sponsor directs the project.**
- **A project manager manages the project.**
- **Team managers manage delivery.**
- **Separate assurance from project support.**
- **Use coaching to help your people excel.**

Who are the key people in project management?

People are at the heart of projects; without them, nothing happens

People are at the heart of projects; without them, nothing happens. It is people who communicate a vision, set targets, plan work, do work, use the outputs and, too often, change their minds. For that reason, how we direct and manage a project needs roles and working practices to reflect this.

This is a good point in the book to remind yourself of the roles and accountabilities for business portfolios, programmes, projects and work packages described in Chapter 4. Having understood the context, we can now look in more detail at the roles which are specific to managing a project. The important roles are shown in Figure 7.1 and drawn from those already outlined in Chapter 4:

- **The project sponsor** has an opportunity to exploit or a problem to solve and could be supported by a **project board**.
- **The project manager** reports to the project sponsor and is accountable for the day-to-day running of the project.
- **Team managers**, accountable for particular work, report to the project manager. Each team manager has a team of people, **team members**, who actually do the work.
- **Project support** might provide advice or management services to the project manager and team.
- **Project assurance** aids the sponsor in ensuring the project achieves its objectives.
- **A project coach** can be used to support all or any of these roles.

As a business portfolio or programme director or manager, you will deal either with the project sponsor or the project manager (depending on the context) but it is essential to understand the other roles for you to create the right environment for your projects to succeed. As shown in Part I, many projects fail despite having good sponsors, managers and teams, simply because the portfolio or programme manager stacked the odds against success, either in terms of personal behaviours, working environment or the resources and systems provided.

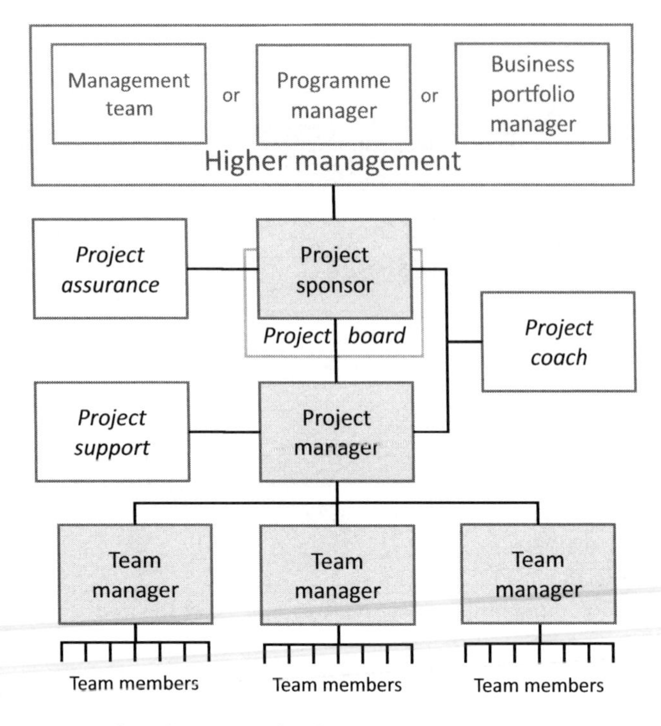

Figure 7.1 A typical project organization structure

The project sponsor who requires the benefits is accountable to, depending on the context, either a management team, programme manager or sponsor or to a business portfolio sponsor. The project manager reports to the project sponsor and is accountable for the day-to-day running of the project. Team managers, accountable for particular work report to the project manager. Each team manager may have a team of people, team members, who actually undertake the specialist work. A project coach supports these key roles. The project sponsor may be supported by a project board. Project assurance aids the sponsor in making sure the project will achieve its objectives. The project manager may be supported by project support.

Their failure is your failure

If you are leading at a business portfolio or programme level, you have to be confident that the sponsor and manager of each of the programmes and projects under your remit are working together effectively. Any failure by them would become your failure.

Project sponsor

Chapter 5 covers the sponsor role in detail. As a reminder, the project sponsor is primarily outcome and benefits focussed, directing the project to make sure their required outcomes are achieved and benefits realized. Such benefits might continue to accrue long after the project is over.

The project sponsor is an essential role on a project and is accountable to higher level management for the overall success of the project. Depending on the context, this might be to a programme sponsor (if the project is part of a programme) or to the business portfolio manager. The project sponsor is the primary risk taker and should champion the project's business objectives, engage senior stakeholders, make key decisions, intervene in high priority issues, approve key deliverables and make decisions or recommendations at critical points in the project's life. The project sponsor is usually a director, executive, or senior manager and should:

- ensure a real business need is being addressed by the project;
- approve the business case;
- define and communicate the business objectives in a concise and unambiguous way;
- ensure the project remains a viable business proposition;
- initiate project reviews;
- ensure the delivered solution matches the needs of the business;
- represent the business in key project decisions;
- sign off key project deliverables and project closure;
- resolve project issues that are outside the control of the project manager;
- chair the project board (if one is required);
- appoint the project manager and facilitate the appointment of team members;
- engage and manage key stakeholders.

Project board

A project board is usually required for projects spanning a number of processes or functional boundaries and/or where the benefits are directed to more than one market segment or function. In the example organization structure in Figure 7.1, the project board is there to support the project sponsor role and chaired by the project sponsor. In other cases:

- the project board might be at a higher level to which a project sponsor is accountable;
- the role can be undertaken by a board at programme or portfolio level;
- a project board might not even be necessary.

Whilst I prefer a project board to support the sponsor, as it emphasises the principle of single point accountability, there is no right or wrong approach. In all cases, however, it must be clear what the board's purpose is, the line of accountability and the limits of authority (including decision making), especially in relation to the accountability and authority of the project sponsor. For example, in PRINCE2®, a project board, is required to cover the interests of:

- the business, to ensure the project remains viable;
- those supplying the project resource (supplier) without which, progress cannot be made;

- those who will be impacted by the outcomes (users), who, if ignored, might mean the required business changes do not materialize.

Such accountabilities and authorities should be defined in terms of reference. A project board is often called a steering committee, steering group or steering board.

A project board, which supports the project sponsor, should:

- advise on direction, review progress, manage key issues and risks (as escalated) and agree any actions which are necessary to keep the project on track;
- monitor the project's progress, to ensure the interests of the organization are best served and the project's outcomes are achievable;
- provide a forum for taking strategic, cross-functional decisions, removing obstacles and resolving issues.

Project manager

The project manager is primarily 'action focussed' towards the achievement of the defined objectives. Managing the project's activities, they ensure the delivery of the outputs and outcomes required by the project sponsor. The project manager is accountable to the project sponsor for managing the project on a day-to-day basis and should:

- mobilize the project team, with the agreement of appropriate line managers;
- prepare the business case, project definition and detailed plans;
- define the processes and procedures to be used on the project;
- define the accountabilities, work scope and targets for each team member;
- monitor and manage the project's progress;
- monitor and manage risk and opportunities;
- manage the resolution of the project's issues;
- manage the scope of the project and control changes;
- forecast likely business benefits;
- deliver the project's deliverables on time, to budget, at agreed quality;
- monitor and manage suppliers' performance;
- communicate with stakeholders;
- manage the closure of the project.

This list applies, no matter how simple or complex the project. When selecting the right person for the job, consider complexity and ensure the individual you select has the right level of experience. The bodies of knowledge of various associations seek to define the attributes or competencies of project managers for a range of project types and many organizations build this into their capability and salary band frameworks. This is not always easy to apply in practice, so, to put them in context, consider three levels of project manager competence:

- **Intuitive** project managers are capable of managing a small or simple project effectively with a small team. They rely on their own acquired common sense, much of which is inherent good practice in project management. Intuitively, they engage stakeholders, seek solutions, plan ahead, allocate work and check progress. Many 'accidental' project managers fall into this category.

- **Methodical** project managers are capable of managing larger, more complex projects where it is not possible to keep the whole venture on track using simple tools and memory. Formal methods, procedures and practices are put in place to ensure the project is managed effectively.
- **Judgmental** project managers can cope with highly complex and often difficult projects. They can apply methods creatively to build a project approach and plan which is both flexible and effective, whilst keeping true to all the principles of good project management.

Performance in a role can be looked at as a combination of four factors: knowledge, experience, skill and behaviours, as summarized in Table 7.1:

- **Knowledge** comprises learning a set of tools and techniques necessary for effective project management.
- **Skills** are the application of tools and techniques.
- **Behaviours** represent the attitude and style used by the project manager towards team members, sponsor, board and stakeholders.
- **Experience** measures the depth to which any knowledge, skills or behaviours have been applied.

Table 7.1 Attributes of a project manager

Knowledge	**Skills**
Project definition	Team building
Project planning	Facilitation and coaching
Benefits management	Conflict resolution
Schedule management	Analytical thinking and problem solving
Financial management	Organization
Risk and opportunity management	Administration
Issues management	Technical expertise
Change control	Communication (verbal; written and active listening)
Behaviours	**Experience factors**
Integrity	Evidence of delivery
Self-motivated – proactive	Evidence of problem solving
Comfortable with ambiguity	Size and complexity of teams managed
Open	Number of projects managed
Even-handed	Complexity of projects managed
Approachable	Evidence of effective leadership

The preceding paragraphs give the criteria to look for when selecting a project manager and are sufficient to discuss a brief with other managers or your Human Resources department. When it comes down to it, however, you'll need to consider how you distinguish between people with similar skill sets and what you should look for or avoid.

Good reasons for selecting a particular project manager include the following:

- **Inherent enthusiasm**. They need to understand the role and what it entails, or be willing to learn, and have the aptitude to cope. Look for the spark that tells you they really want this to succeed.
- **High tolerance of uncertainty**. They need to be able to work effectively across the organization, without formal line authority or rank authority. They need to be able, especially in the investigative stages, to deal with the many potentially conflicting needs and signals as the project hunts its way towards a solution.
- **Team-building**. People are at the heart of projects, both as team members and stakeholders. If the project manager doesn't have the necessary 'people' skills, the project is unlikely to be a success.
- **Client orientation**. This means they need to understand the expectations and differing success criteria of the various stakeholders, especially the project sponsor.

Poor reasons for selecting a project manager, if taken in isolation, include the following:

- **Availability**. The worst reason to appoint a person is simply because they are available. Why are they available? What aptitude do they have? This tends to happen in organizations with a low level of maturity in project management, as 'project staff' are often not seen as part of the normal work of the organization and having them 'do something' rather than 'nothing' is seen as more important.
- **Technical skill**. This can be useful on a project but not essential. The project manager can draw on technical experts as part of the core team. If the project manager is also the technical expert, there is a danger of them concentrating on the technical area of interest to the exclusion of everything else. For example, a good systems programmer may ignore the roll out, training and usability of a new system, as they are more interested in the technical architectures and features.
- **Toughness**. The 'macho' project manager who closely supervises every aspect of the project, placing demand upon demand upon the team (or else!), is guaranteed to demoralize a team. Add to this, the likelihood of many of the team working part time, it may be a fast way of losing the very people who are vital to a successful outcome. Yes, a project manager needs to be emotionally tough and resilient, but this should not translate into being a bully.
- **Age**. Grey hairs do not necessarily indicate a more experienced project manager. Maturity in project management comes from exposure to a wide range of different situations and projects, not just length of service. Managing a single project over five years is quite different to managing five projects each of 12-month duration. Length of time alone is not an indicator of experience.

Project team managers and team members

Project team managers and team members are the people who do the 'real' work. Everyone else is simply 'management', whose job is to make sure the right project is being done and make the doing of that project as stress free as possible and focussed on its objectives. Just as a project manager has to understand what the sponsor's needs are, so the team managers need to understand the project manager's needs. A team manager who is kept in the dark over the context of their work and the potential risks is unlikely to respond in an appropriate way if problems arise. Nor are they likely to spot opportunities for improving the performance of the project as a whole or the desired outcomes.

Team managers are the 'doers' who report to the project manager and are accountable for prescribed work packages and deliverables. This might range from a complete subproject to a single deliverable. It is essential to bring the full experience of the team to any problems or solutions from the start. Project teams often comprise two parts:

- **The core team** – those members working full time on the project and reporting directly to the project manager. A core team size of six to ten people is about right.
- **The extended team** – those members who report to the core team (team managers) and who may be part or full time.

It is essential that each person working on a project has a clearly defined:

- role and reporting line to the project manager;
- scope of work and list of deliverables (both final and intermediate deliverables);
- level of authority (i.e., directions on what decisions he/she can and cannot take on behalf of his/her line function).

All groups or individuals associated with the project and making up the team should be identified and listed with their role, scope and accountabilities.

The team managers are accountable to the project manager and should:

- be accountable for such deliverables as are delegated to them by the project manager, ensuring they are planned and completed on time and to budget;
- liaise and work with other team managers and members in the carrying out of their work;
- contribute to and review key project documentation;
- monitor and manage progress on their delegated work scope;
- manage the resolution of issues, escalating any they cannot deal with to the project manager;
- monitor changes to their work scope, informing the project manager of any requiring approval;
- monitor risk associated with their work scope;
- be responsible for advising the appropriate team managers and/or project manager of potential issues, risks, or opportunities they have noticed;
- manage the individual members of the team.

Team managers form the bedrock of a successful project. Not only do they have to be competent in the specialist work relating to their assigned deliverables but also need to be competent in a range of project management techniques. From the accountabilities listed earlier, you will notice that many aspects including planning, reporting, risk and issues management, change control and stakeholder management are the same as those required by a project manager. It is not unusual to find that work scopes for some team managers' work packages dwarf other project manager's projects in terms of team size and spend. For this reason, many organizations include project management techniques as a core part of every manager's training and development. If team managers are not competent at the management aspect of their role, as part of a project team, it is the project manager's accountability to brief them on what is needed and, if necessary, tailor the techniques to suit the competence levels of those using them and provide support where needed.

Assurance, support and coaching

If you have a project sponsor, project manager, team managers and team members, you have the right roles to undertake a project; for a simple project, nothing more is necessary. Most projects, however, are not simple and a number of additional roles might be needed.

Project assurance

The project sponsor is accountable for project assurance. The sponsor owns the business case and is the primary risk taker, and so assurance is inherent in the role. Specific responsibilities include assuring:

- fit with the overall business strategy;
- the project remains needed and viable;
- focus on the business need is maintained;
- risks are controlled;
- users' needs and expectations are met or managed;
- constant reassessment of the value-for-money solution;
- the right people are involved;
- an acceptable solution is being developed;
- the scope of the project is not 'creeping upwards' unnoticed;
- internal and external communications are working;
- applicable standards are being used;
- legislative, regulatory or contractual constraints are being observed.

Everything undertaken by project assurance is the accountability of the project sponsor. Thus, in the absence of project assurance, the sponsor is accountable for the activities. The most common reason for creating a project assurance function is simply because a sponsor hasn't the time or competence to undertake this role effectively.

By having a project assurance function, the time pressure can be relieved and more experienced people used when needed.

Those undertaking assurance roles need to take an independent view

Those undertaking assurance roles need to take an independent view to enable them to challenge and confront any troublesome issues. Often the major issues are well known within a project team, but political or other constraints can prevent those involved from speaking up about the 'elephant in the room', which everyone can see but no one acknowledges; or to point out the facts behind the 'emperor's new clothes' where some aspect of the project is exposed, whilst all those involved pretend it is well covered. Those undertaking assurance must have the gravitas and management style to be trusted by the project team and stakeholders and need to provide constructive and practical views based on insight and experience. Assurance undertaken on the basis of scoring points off the project team or doggedly sticking to checklists will not be beneficial to anyone. Finally, don't confuse 'project assurance' with 'quality assurance'; the former is about ensuring every aspect of the project is run to ensure the business objectives will be met, whilst the latter is focussed on the processes, procedures and practices which ensure quality is built into the deliverables.

Providing assurance services on a project by project basis can be very expensive and for this reason, assurance is sometimes provided from a central group at programme or portfolio level. As a business portfolio or programme manager you can provide assurance assistance for all the projects within your remit. By doing this, you can ensure consistency in approach and rapid feedback of common issues.

Project support

The project manager is accountable for managing the project and all that entails, including planning, reporting, managing risks and issues, controlling change, engaging stakeholders and managing communications. For a small project, this can be done by one person; the project manager. When a project is large, however, the project manager might simply run out of hours in the day and need others to help. If a project is part of a programme or business portfolio, support services can be provided more consistently and efficiently through a central service, with, perhaps some activities provided locally. Chapter 27 looks at support services in detail, but for now, as a business portfolio or programme manager, you need to understand that project support is one part of the 'right environment' you need to provide for your teams to succeed.

Specific responsibilities may include the following:

- define and establish project governance arrangements;
- set up and maintain project files;
- establish document control procedures;
- compile, copy and distribute all project management deliverables;
- collect actuals data and forecasts;
- update project plans;

- assist with the compilation of reports;
- administer the document review and approval process;
- administer meetings;
- monitor and administer risks, issues, changes and defects;
- provide specialist knowledge (for example, governance, processes, estimating, risk management);
- provide specialist tool expertise (for example, planning and control tools, risk analysis)

Notice project support ranges from high value-added to simple administrative functions.

Notice project support ranges from high value-added to simple administrative functions. Project support is by no means a low-level role. Take care, however, to make sure those undertaking a support role do not also play a part in project assurance. Assurance has to be independent, if it is to be credible.

Central services

Remember that efficiency should not be the only driver for centralizing project support services. Central services are rarely effective if they are remote from the people they are supporting, and hence good working relationships cannot be formed.

Always prioritize having an effective team over an efficient one. Project management makes up 5 to 10% of a project's cost and far less in terms of benefits. Providing inadequate project management could lead to errors and inefficiencies in the 'real work', dwarfing any savings in support costs.

The place to look for efficiencies is in the provision of management information systems, which need to serve every component of a programme or portfolio.

Coaching

Rarely is a single project able to afford coaching services but coaching can be powerful, making the ordinary person or team become extraordinary. It is highly unlikely for everyone on a project team to be fully competent and experienced to undertake their role. If there are gaps in capability and experience of the team, you as leader, should ensure the gap is filled. Melding a group of individuals into a team goes a long way to doing this; the more experienced individuals should help the others as, if you have set the right parameters, it is the team as a whole which succeeds or fails; if the team fails, every individual has failed, including you. Coaching can also be seen as a management style, where a manager challenges and develops their staff to develop their skills and achieve the best results, as self-sufficiently as possible. In other words, if you manage as a coach, your staff members learn and grow through working. Because of the power of coaching, either peer to peer or manager to sub-ordinate, many organizations include coaching techniques as a part of their general management development programmes. If many members of a team are from different organizations, a programme manager might have to provide such techniques training as part of induction or on-going training and development. In some cases, however, the needed experience isn't contained within the team and external coaches might be needed. This might be external to the project, say for a programme or portfolio team, or it could be external to the organization, from consultant coaches.

Coaching can take many forms but has one characteristic; a coach should not shoulder the accountabilities of the person they are coaching. At its simplest, coaching can be as informal as when you bounce ideas off a friend. In other cases, it can be formal, timetabled and directed at a particular issue. Sometimes coaching is helping people to use the standard processes, methods and tools effectively or facilitating workshops (team coaching).

Except on very large projects, providing coaching on a project by project basis is not cost effective, whereas, providing it for a complete programme or business portfolio can be worthwhile.

High performing teams don't happen by accident

High performing teams need firm and constructive leadership and a belief in certain principles. For example, the Agile Alliance's agile manifesto, rooted in software development, is supported by 12 principles, four of which relate directly to team performance. These principles are so important that many people say you cannot *do* agile but can only *be* agile, as it is inherent in how you behave. The relevant Agile principles are:

- business people and developers must work together daily throughout the project (Agile Principle 4);
- build projects around motivated individuals. Give them the environment and support they need, and trust them to get the job done (Agile Principle 5);
- the most efficient and effective method of conveying information to and within a development team is face-to-face conversation (Agile Principle 6);
- the best architectures, requirements and designs emerge from self-organizing teams (Agile Principle 11)

Notice this requires trust on two dimensions:

- trust between team members (horizontal);
- trust between levels of management (vertical).

I am not advocating using agile delivery on everything, only where it is appropriate. What I am pointing out is that the 'agile' behaviours cited earlier, which are seen as 'new' by some people, are valid in any team and have been recommended as a part of good project management for a long time.

Research by Carl Wiese and Ron Ricci at Cisco cites ten characteristics of high performing teams:

1. people have solid and deep trust in each other and in the team's purpose – they feel free to express feelings and ideas;
2. everybody is working towards the same goals;
3. team members are clear on how to work together and how to accomplish tasks;
4. everyone understands both team and individual performance goals and knows what is expected;
5. team members actively diffuse tension and friction in a relaxed and informal atmosphere;
6. the team engages in extensive discussion, and everyone gets a chance to contribute – even the introverts;
7. disagreement is viewed as a good thing and conflicts are managed. Criticism is constructive and is oriented towards problem solving and removing obstacles;
8. the team makes decisions when there is natural agreement – in the cases where agreement is elusive, a decision is made by the team lead or sponsor, after which little second-guessing occurs;
9. each team member carries his or her own weight and respects the team processes and other members;
10. the leadership of the team shifts from time to time, as appropriate, to drive results. No individual members are more important than the team.

Notice the emphasis on 'team', not individual and on being tough on problems, not on people. The way a team works together needs to be agreed and goes beyond the role descriptions and processes in this book. Workout 7.1 paves the way for collaborative success by providing clarity to build trust between team members. With this in place, you'll be able to unlock the potential value of your people by empowering them to contribute. In the long run, teams with a clear purpose and good working relationships drive business results. Job satisfaction goes up, people stay engaged with their work and everybody wins. Most members of high-performing teams say that it's fun and satisfying to work on collaborative teams because they are asked to contribute at their highest potential and learn a lot along the way.

In terms of project management, team managers have to be familiar with both the specialist (or technical) aspects of their assigned work and project management techniques. A team manager's work package might dwarf a project manager's project. Sometimes very good specialists have poor project management skills and, further, some simply aren't interested! Sherlock Holmes would not be a good project manager. This can lead to significant challenges for a project manager, such as:

- a refusal to plan or predict completion dates or costs;
- reluctance to attend project team meetings;
- over optimism in delivering a solution (i.e., ignoring risks);
- not providing any progress updates or providing the sporadically and late.

In other words, the project team is not a team at all. Good team set up (as in Work-out 7.1) with supportive coaching can be used to lead such individuals to fulfil all aspects of their role.

Adopt an open, even handed style to encourage communication

If team managers misbehave, it might be you who is at fault!

A number of specialist team managers refused to predict the cost or delivery date for their work packages because they were hunting their way towards a solution. They also knew, from hard experience, that whatever costs or date they provided, they would be held to and it could impact their annual bonus or performance appraisal. They learned that it was better to say nothing and deliver whenever it was ready. This approach made the management of the project impossible. The project manager had no reliable project plan and little understanding of the risks. A number of discussions and workshops were held to try to resolve this issue. The outcome was that a team manager was allowed to predict a range of possible costs or dates or put a confidence indicator against their prediction (high confidence, medium confidence, low confidence). This simple change to reporting changed the behaviours, as every person reading or using the reports was aware how hard or soft the forecasts were. This also opened up discussions on what the risks were and what could be done to alleviate them

Workout 7.1 – Getting a team started on the right track

This is best done in a relaxed atmosphere without any tables acting as barriers between people. The 'board room' arrangement is not recommended. Team meetings are best in rooms with space to move around and wall room for flip charts. Confined and cramped rooms confine and cramp thinking. This workout can be applied at any level in the portfolio to work package hierarchy.

The first time a team gathers is very important and can set the tone for the rest of the project. Some individuals might know each other (and you) well. Others might know no one. Some might have worked together before. Even if some have not met before, they might have preconceived ideas of others on the team based on gossip and rumour from other colleagues, which may or may not be accurate. It is you, as a leader, who must bond this disparate group into a committed team. One way of doing this is to encourage the group members to respect each other and to create a set of team rules which are seen, by all, as fair!

Respect each other

1. Ask all present to introduce themselves and say a little about their interests outside work. Ask them to tell the others something about themselves none of the others knows.
2. Ask each person to say what his/her commitments are to the project, why he/she would like to see it succeed and what that person will do to help success become a reality.
3. When the individual has finished, each of the other team members should build on what that individual has said about him/herself by saying what skills and competencies they know or feel the person has which they respect. Keep to positive and strong points only.
4. On receiving this acknowledgment, the individual should not be embarrassed. 'Thank you' is all he or she needs to say.
5. Steps 1 to 3 should be gone through for every person in the group. This may sound contrived, but it does work if treated seriously. It can remove or dispel rumour. It brings people onto a personal footing.

Team values

Creating a set of 'rules' that the team accept as fair and which each of them agrees to live by and uphold, is also a powerful way of bonding:

1. Brainstorm a set of values or rules for the team to live by. Put these on a flip chart.
2. The team should then select those which it wants to live by.
3. Display the values prominently in the team's workroom and at every team meeting.

During the brainstorm, individuals will often shout out things that annoy them. For example, if someone really gets heated if meetings start late, he may want the rule/value

'All meetings start on time'. The brainstorm list, therefore, becomes a set of potential 'hot buttons' which can turn each person from a likeable, rational soul into an angry unreasonable one. It's good to know what these are at the start! Some of the most powerful values can also appear very shallow. One senior team had 'chocolate' as a value. At every meeting someone was accountable for bringing one or two chocolate treats, often from a country they recently visited on business. It became a symbol of 'looking after each other' and something to joke about to lighten the tension when business issues were weighing heavily, and the team could not agree a way forward. If one member became over excited, another would simply offer him or her a chocolate as a reminder that the team had the same objectives and all its members are on the same side.

8

The project framework

Managing your risks a step at a time

Project life cycle, gates and stages

An example project life cycle

Proposal – before the project starts

Initial investigation stage

Detailed investigation stage

Develop and test stage

Trial stage

Release stage

Post implementation review – after the project is completed

When used well, a good project life cycle simplifies not only the management of individual projects but also the oversight of the many projects you have to keep track of.

"The middle of everything looks like a mistake; the middle of every successful project looks like a disaster."

ROSABETH MOSS CANTOR, b1943

- **Projects tend to be riskier than day-to-day operations.**
- **A staged approach is essential to good governance.**
- **Drive risk down as you progress through the life cycle.**
- **Gates are decision points at the start of each stage.**
- **Stages are periods of time when work is undertaken.**

Managing your risks a step at a time

Understanding the project life cycle is one of the most important concepts in this book. A good project life cycle simplifies not only the management of individual projects but also the oversight of the many projects you have to deal with as a business portfolio or programme manager.

The difference between working on a project, rather than on day-to-day operational work, is that projects often break new ground. Sometimes the solution to a problem or opportunity is not known; perhaps the problem is not fully understood. As projects tend to be riskier than day-to day operations, how we manage a project needs to take account uncertainty. As a project proceeds, the amount of money invested increases. This investment should be aimed at reducing the risks associated with the project. Your objective is to ensure such risks are driven down as the project moves up from idea to reality, as shown in Figure 8.1. By the time you start spending a lot of money, enough work should have been done to demonstrate

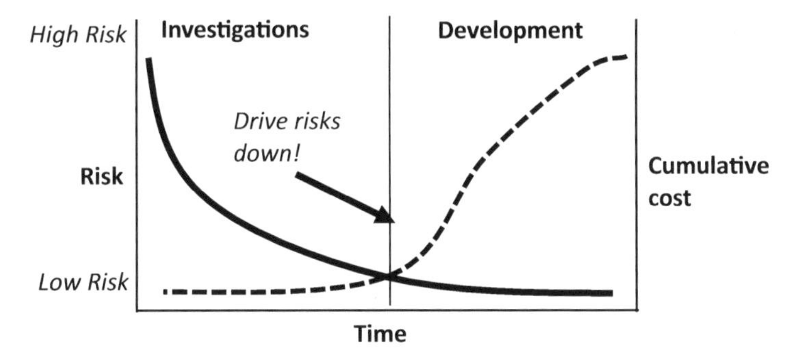

Figure 8.1 Using the project life cycle to manage risk

The investigative stages are crucial and you should hold back significant development work until your investigations show you know what you are doing and have proved to yourself that the risks (solid line) are acceptable before you start spending big money (dashed line).

that the risks are acceptable. The investigative stages are therefore crucial, and you should hold back development work until your investigations show you know what you are doing and how you are going to do it. This is achieved by taking a staged approach, where you authorize the start of each stage only if you are confident that moving forward is likely to be more beneficial than stopping the project. You therefore release the funds a stage at a time, only when you are satisfied that the project is viable and you have an agreed (and detailed) plan for the next stage with an outline plan for the rest of the project. In this way, each stage serves as a launch pad for the subsequent stage.

Project life cycle, gates and stages

The project life cycle

A **project life cycle** is a phased approach for the governance of a project and underpins the project plan, from start to finish. It comprises a number of stages, each of which is preceded by a decision point, known as gate, at which authorization for the next stage is given . . . if the project is still justified.

Stages

Stages are specific time periods during which work on the project takes place: information is collected, outputs created and outcomes recognized. For each stage of the project, you should carry out the full range of work covering the entire scope of functional inputs required (Figure 8.2). As we learned in Chapter 2, lesson 6, those working on the project should work as a cross-functional team, in a continuous dialogue with each other to develop the best overall solution. In this way, knowledge develops and increases on all fronts at a similar pace. Solutions are designed, built and tested in an integrated way and no one area of work should advance ahead of any other. Consequently, you should be able to create a pragmatic solution which is best for your organization as a whole not one function alone. This has the benefits of shortcutting the functional hierarchies, creating a flat, lean structure as it forces people with different perspectives to work together rather than apart. Further, you should limit the work undertaken in any stage to that needed at the next gate: there is little point in spending effort and money until needed.

During each stage of the project, it is essential for the project manager to forecast and reforecast the benefits likely to be gained and the time, resources and costs needed to complete the project. The relevant function managers should be kept informed of progress and the on-going viability of the project confirmed; there is little point in continuing a project which is no longer justifiable. This continuous cycle of doing and checking is illustrated by the 'project control cycle' in Figure 8.3 and is the heartbeat of every project stage.

Stage or phase?

In this book and its companion, *The Project Workout*, I have used the term 'stage' as the primary parts of a project. The term 'phase' is also used. Some people can become very heated over whether 'stage' or 'phase' is right. Relax, they are just 'differently right' words for the same concept. Whichever you choose to use, use it consistently.

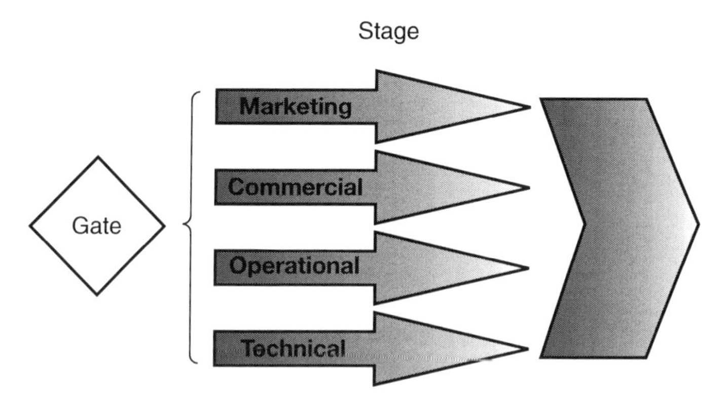

Figure 8.2 Address all aspects of the project in parallel

For each stage in the project, you should carry out the full range of work covering the entire scope of functional inputs required. In this way your knowledge develops and increases on all fronts at a similar pace and solutions are designed, built and tested in an integrated way.

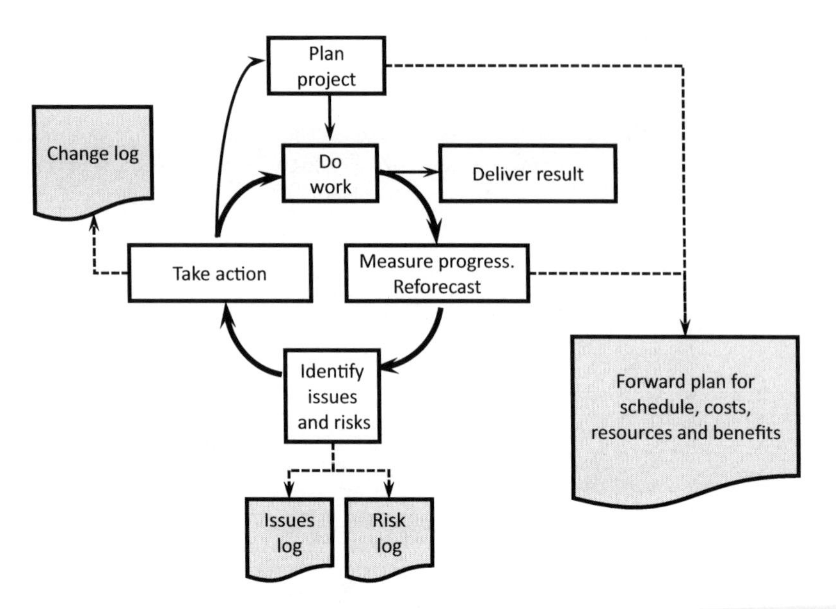

Figure 8.3 The project control cycle

A stage can be represented by the project control cycle together with the plan and key control tools you need to manage it (these are described in Part 5).

Gates

Gates are the decision points preceding every stage. Unless specific criteria have been met, as evidenced by certain approved deliverables or verifiable outcomes, the subsequent stage should not be started. Being a decision 'point', a gate is a special milestone on the project. Gates serve as points to:

- check the project is still required, viable and the risks are acceptable;
- confirm its priority relative to other projects;
- agree the plans for the remainder of the project;
- make a go/no go decision regarding continuing the project.

You should not regard gates as 'end of term exams' but rather the culmination of a period of continual assessment, with the gates acting as formal review and decision points.

Gate criteria are often reinforced at consecutive gates to ensure the same strands of the project are followed through as the project progresses. The further into the project you move, the more confidence you should have when responding to the criteria.

At each gate, three distinct questions need to be answered:

- is there a real need for this project and is it viable in its own right?
- what is its priority relative to other projects?
- do you have the funding to continue the project?

The first question concerns the need for and viability of the project. Does it fit your strategy? Does it make business sense? Are the risks acceptable? Have you the resources to undertake the work and operate its outputs?

The second question (priority) concerns the context of the project. It might be a worthy project but how does it measure against all the other projects and work you want to do or are currently undertaking? Are there more worthwhile things to spend time and money on? Is it 'a risk too far', bearing in mind what you are already committed to? This question is dealt with in Part III on business portfolio management where I will show you a method of managing such decisions.

The third question involves funding. Traditionally, organizations have discrete and formal rules concerning the allocation of funds, generally managed by a finance function. The project might be viable and the most beneficial of those proposed BUT have you the cash-flow to finance it?

Gates – an end or a beginning?

Gates have traditionally been looked at as endpoints to the preceding stage. The logic is that the work in the stage culminates in a review (viz. end of stage assessment) where a check is done to ensure everything is complete before starting the next stage. This misconception has come about as people often confuse system or software development processes with project life cycles. For example, a software development process concentrates on quality and hence the need for completeness before moving on to the next step in the process. Project management, however, is not a process and is aimed at managing business risk. Due to time pressures, it is often necessary to start the next stage before everything in the previous stage has been finalized. For example, the typical project framework (shown later in Figure 8.4) shows it can make sense to undertake the trial of a new output before all the processes, training and communication elements of the final product are completed. What is essential is to cover sufficient work to start the trial stage with confidence. If you treat a gate as the end of a stage, this could extend the timescale for the project and could give rise to the difficulty of having a traditional 'rule' that common sense encourages us to break.

The solution to this dilemma is to treat gates as entry points to the next stage. In this way, the next stage can begin as soon as you are ready, regardless of whether or not the full work scope of the previous stage has been completed. You do, however, need to define your entry criteria (what really must be completed), ensure the risks are acceptable and that the resources and time to complete the unfinished work are built into your plan. In this way, stages can overlap, reducing timescales but without increasing the risk associated with the project. This can be on a planned basis or in reaction to prevailing circumstances

This also opens another powerful characteristic of this approach. Gates are compulsory; stages are not. In other words, provided the work needed to meet the criteria to pass into the next stage is done, how you arrived there is not so important. This allows you to follow the strict principles of the staged framework, even if a stage is omitted, thereby enabling you to tailor the life cycle for 'simple' projects.

If you still aren't convinced, think of this from a senior executive's point of view. How many executives do you know who like to make decisions on what has already happened? Senior executives make decisions about what they are going to do next; this fits in with the 'entry gate' approach perfectly. They like to announce they are investing untold millions over the next six months into the next stage of the company's development. Personally, I have never met an executive who led by looking backwards.

Packaging your deliverables helps avoid chaos

An example project life cycle

In this book and its companion, *The Project Workout*, I use a five-stage project life cycle. This is shown in Figure 8.4 as a bar chart and in Figure 8.5 as a diagrammatic overview. I have found this five-stage model fits most circumstances but other models, with different stages are equally acceptable if they suit the need, environment and culture of your organization. I will cover adapting the five-stage model for your particular circumstances in Chapter 9.

The steps in a five-stage project life cycle are:

- proposal – the activities needed prior to the project starting;
- initial investigations stage;
- detailed investigation stage;
- develop and test stage;
- trial stage;
- release stage;
- post implementation review, after the project is completed.

Notice the pre- and post-project activities; these provide the link to the project's context, such as whether it is part of a programme or business portfolio.

Each stage is described in the following sections, together with workouts you can use at the associated gates. In many cases you'll be relying on the project sponsor to provide the answers to many of the questions.

- **The staged project framework enables you to direct projects which are benefit driven, user focussed, take risk into account, allow parallel working, build in quality and draw on resources from across the organization.**
- **Stages are periods of time during which the work happens. Stage names vary from company to company and method to method, but all involve investigative stages and build/development stages.**
- **Gates are milestones, used as check points to verify the project is still required, its priority relative to other projects, the plans for the remainder of the project and whether a decision to continue is in the best interests of the company. Gates are entry points to stages.**
- **Each gate has defined criteria which must be met before the next stage is task. The project sponsor is the key decision maker at the gates.**
- **Your focus and attention will change as the project moves through its life cycle.**

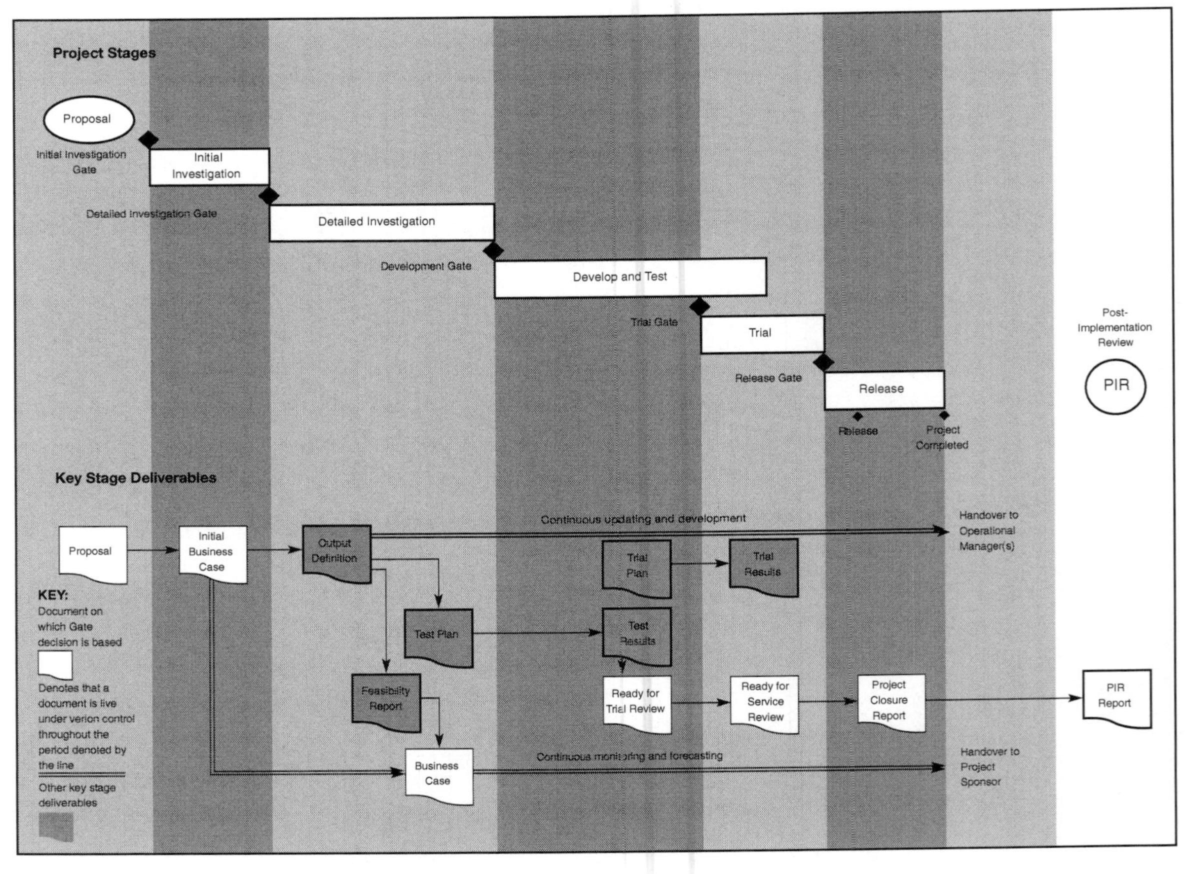

Figure 8.4 The project life cycle as a bar chart

The project life cycle is shown here in 'bar chart format' at the top, with the document deliverables for each stage shown at bottom.

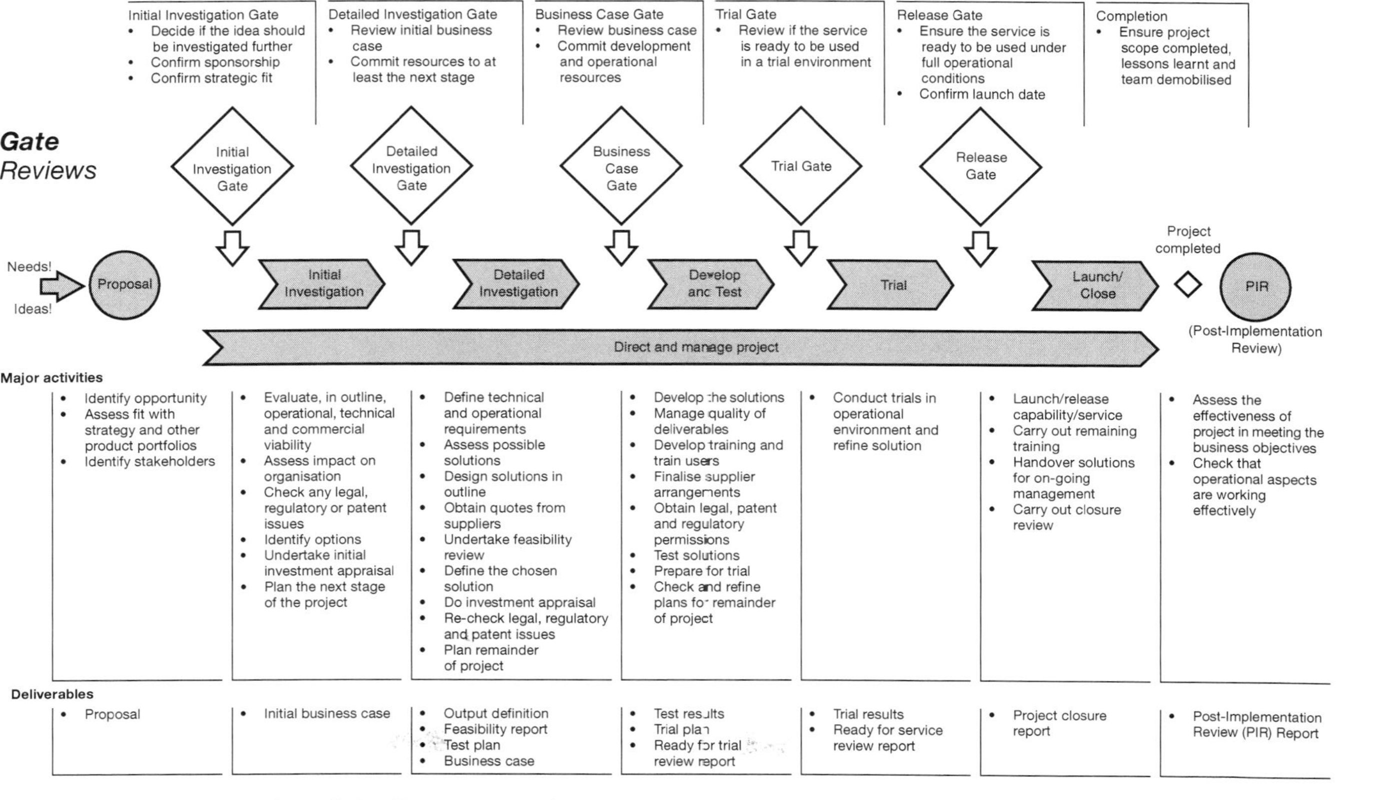

Figure 8.5 The project life cycle in diagrammatic form

The project life cycle is shown here in a format which clearly distinguishes between the gates and the stages. It also shows the activities and deliverables relating to each stage and the main questions to ask at each gate.

Proposal – before the project starts

Overview

This is when a need or opportunity is first formally recognized by describing why you want to initiate a project. This should be described in terms of business outcomes you need or want to achieve. The proposal should be discussed with potential stakeholders. This work culminates in the initial investigation gate, which is the first decision point when resources are committed to the project and it is formally recognized as a project.

Key deliverable

The proposal outlines the business need the project will meet, the desired outcomes what it is intended to produce (if known), its benefits and how it fits with current strategy. If apparent, the likely impact on the organization (market, technology and operational), broad expectations of benefits and cost, and time required to completion can also be included. The proposal does not need to contain any detail other than the business need; anything else is a bonus. If time is spent fleshing out the proposal, it is in effect jumping ahead and starting the investigative work. A proposal can ask far more questions than it answers.

Focus on

This is the start point and only one thing should be certain: the project is aligned to strategy and meets a recognized need or opportunity. If you do not identify the business need adequately, it is highly likely the project team will not be able to meet that need. Also check that there are no other projects already under way addressing the same need.

What can go wrong?

- Without a defined proposal, no one can have a clear idea of what has to be achieved, whilst pretending they do! Ensure work in the initial investigation stage concentrates on clarifying any aspects of the proposal which are unclear.
- Money and resource are wasted on ill-conceived objectives.
- The business objectives of the project do not match the needs of the business or align to strategy.
- The proposal states what the solution should be, which is only possible on the simplest of projects or when the projects is part of a programme.
- A proposal can be sparse or detailed but whatever it contains must already be known. If you insist on putting too much detail in a proposal, you will in effect be starting the initial investigation stage prior to the project being authorized and hence force the creation of an 'invisible project' which no one can sign up to.

Workout 8.1 – Check list for starting the initial investigation stage

Before approving the start of the initial investigation stage, you should ensure your proposal reflects the business need and is in line with the organization's strategic direction and priorities.

Business need and strategic fit

- Does the Proposal fit the organization's strategy?
- Is the opportunity attractive (size, share, cost saving, contribution, etc.) relative to alternative proposals?
- Is the Proposal likely to be acceptable to customers, users and other stakeholder groups?
- Do any competitors have capabilities similar to this and. if so, will the result of this Proposal provide any competitive advantage?
- Have you provided detailed terms of reference for the initial investigation stage to ensure the project manager focusses on the key issues as you see them?

Accountabilities

- Is your project sponsor clear to whom they are accountable for this project? Has this been agreed?
- Has a project manager been identified for the initial investigation stage?

Resources

- Can resources be committed to the initial investigation?
- Does the organization have or is it able to develop or acquire the required capabilities to support the Proposal?
- Is the Proposal technically feasible with current technology?
- Has or can the organization acquire operational capability to support the outcome?

Initial investigation stage

Overview

The goal of the initial investigation stage is for the project manager and team to examine the proposal as quickly as possible, identifying possible solutions and approaches. They need to determine if the intended project is likely to be viable in financial, operational, technical and customer terms.

As the investigative stages of the project are the most influential, a programme manager or business portfolio manager is likely to be involved in many of the decisions and discussions which will steer the project sponsor and team in a preferred direction. Expect to be asked your opinion on ranges of options and possibilities; whilst you may leave the project manager and team to derive and investigate these, you need to be making those decisions which you have not delegated to the project sponsor.

Key deliverables

The initial business case contains the business rationale for the project. It outlines WHY you need the project, WHAT options you intend to investigate, HOW it will be done and WHO is needed to make it happen. It also answers, in outline, the question HOW MUCH? The Initial Business Case does not comprise a full analysis but is only sufficient to enable you to decide if it is worthwhile continuing the project.

Focus on

You need to ensure that the project sponsor and manager have engaged the right team and understand the business need and any constraints to creating a solution. Be prepared to allow modifications to the statement of the business need if this adds greater clarity and understanding or keeps the project viable. Focus on the constructive testing of assumptions and trawling for a wide range of solutions. Investigate those potential solutions which are likely to meet the needs soonest with maximum benefits and at an acceptable level of risk.

What can go wrong?

- The project team don't understand the business context and takes too narrow a view on the scope of the project.
- Insufficient creative thinking is applied to the possible solutions. Consider them all, no matter how 'off the wall', then choose the best three for detailed investigation in the next stage.
- Spurious accuracy is placed on time and cost estimates. At this point it is better to think in ranges and not absolutes. Absolute values are erroneous and might only pander to senior management insecurity.

Workout 8.2 – Check list for starting the detailed investigation stage

At this gate you should check the project against the organization's business plans and reconfirm its strategic fit, priority and whether it is likely to be viable in commercial, technical and operational terms. If you can tick-off all these, you can approve the start of the detailed investigation stage.

Business need and strategic fit

- Is it clear which business unit(s) or function(s) plan the project supports?
- Does the project fit the strategy?
- Is there a real business need and is the opportunity attractive compared to others which may consume the same resources?
- Are the risks acceptable and is a management plan in place to deal with any high risks?
- Is the initial business case and investment appraisal acceptable?

Deliverables

- Is there an outline schedule, resource and cost plan for the full project which takes into account the known risks and constraints?
- Is there a detailed schedule, resource, and cost plan for the detailed investigation stage?
- Have all the relevant teams been involved in creating and reviewing the deliverables?
- Are the proposed solution options likely to represent value for money?

Accountabilities and resources

- Have you identified a project sponsor? Have you met to agree the approach to be taken, stakeholders to be engaged and how key risks should be managed?
- Does the sponsor have the 'right team' identified to undertake the detailed investigation stage?

Operational and technical

- Is the project technically feasible with current technology, or is there a possible technical development path to provide the capability or service?
- Does the organization currently have the operational capability to support it? If not, is it likely this can be put in place when needed?

Detailed investigation stage

Overview

During the detailed investigation stage, the project manager and team should identify and recommend the optimum solution and financial proposition. The next gate (the development gate), for which this stage is preparation, is critical as it is the last point at which you can stop the project before substantial financial commitments are made. At the end of this stage, you should have confidence in all aspects of the project; this is when, 'What you want to do' becomes 'What you are going to do!'

Key deliverables

The blueprint describes the outcome and output of the project in terms of operating model, process, organization, systems, technology and culture. It integrates the individual systems, people, process and platform requirements and specifies how they work together. The blueprint should continue to develop as the project proceeds and will be handed over to the appropriate operational manager(s) before project completion.

The feasibility report builds on the initial business case. It includes the recommendation for which option should be adopted as the solution, comparing it against rejected solutions in financial and non-financial terms.

The business case contains the business rationale. It is derived from the initial business case and feasibility report. It is the document on which the decision is made to authorize funding for the remainder of the project and the building in of costs and benefits to the business plan.

The project plan includes the detailed, viable, schedule, resource and cost plans for the develop and test stage, with the remaining stages in summary.

The test plan defines the tests required to verify performance of any outputs from the project, both in isolation and working as a complete system.

Focus on

The focus here is on deciding the solution, checking it meets the organization's needs and ensuring key stakeholders are engaged and supportive (or, at least, not hostile). During this stage you will decide the approach to be taken which will set the direction for the remainder of the project and be reflected in a viable plan which takes account of known risks. Once this is decided, the scope for improving the performance of the project is very small. You will need to ensure:

- the concept is researched with the target users and/or customers;
- possible options are evaluated to identify your preferred solution;
- the preferred solution will meet the defined needs;

- process, technical and operational requirements are defined, where appropriate;
- any legal or regulatory issues have been checked;
- possible suppliers and partners have been evaluated.

What can go wrong?

- The proposed change, whilst technically and operationally feasible, is not viable in the prevailing economic, social or political environment. It might be the right solution at the wrong time.
- The feasibility work is either omitted or rushed with only one solution really being taken seriously in the often lame hope that the project will be quicker. Creative solutions, however, often take less time. In some cases, creative might mean phasing the delivery rather than meeting all the needs in one hit.
- The necessary stakeholders are ignored, forgotten or simply missed. If you need a person or group to achieve the outcomes you want, you must have engaged them by the end of this stage – but the earlier the better.
- The project plan is just a vague idea of what might possibly happen, containing little in the way of activities, deliverables or resource requirements. Without a decent plan, how can anyone have any confidence in what will happen?
- The plan ignores the risks. All risks should be mitigated in one way or another, with no high risks remaining. Sensitivity and scenario analyses are good tools for assessing the possible outcomes – use them! Look at simulation approaches, like Monte Carlo analysis.
- Insufficient time is built into the plan for decision making or reviews. Done properly, such activities add value.
- Contingency for known risks is 'removed' from the plan to make it look more attractive or to give the illusion of 'keeping tight control'. Risk is risk and pretending it isn't there is naïve. Finance managers, beware!
- The trial stage is left out of the plan to decrease time to market/release. All this usually does is deliver a potentially inadequate solution quicker. Always assume you need a trial and then (if you can) prove you do not.
- Note, of all the 'things that can go wrong', this stage has the most as it is the stage when you decide what you are going to do. Everything which follows is reliant on the decisions and choices made here.

Workout 8.3 – Check list for starting the develop and test stage

At this gate, you should evaluate the project approach recommended by the project sponsor, the proposed functionality and features of the solution, including business processes, systems and organization/roles.

Business need and strategic fit

- Is it still clear which business unit(s) or function(s) strategy and plan the project supports; does it still fit the strategy?
- Is the business case ready to be built into the overall business plan?
- Have the key sensitivities and scenarios for the recommended option been checked and are they acceptable?

Project plan

- Is there an outline schedule, resource, and cost plan for the full project?
- Is there a detailed schedule, resource and cost plan for the develop and test stage?
- Are there sufficient assurance reviews in the plan to maintain confidence that the project will not deviate off course?
- Is it clear when major contractual commitments are to be made? Is there a review point planned prior to these?
- Has the project plan been designed to eliminate known high risks? Is a trial stage required to mitigate risk?

Resources

- Are there resources to undertake the develop and test stage?
- Have formal resource commitments been made by the relevant resource owners?
- Have suppliers been identified and short-listed?

Operational and technical

- Is it technically feasible with current technology?
- Does the organization have the operational capability to support it?

Solution

- Have the development concepts (e.g., marketing) been researched and tested on target segments and the need reaffirmed?
- Is the blueprint complete?
- Is it clear how the output will be tested and, if needed, trialled?

Develop and test stage

Overview

The develop and test stage is when the bulk of the costs relating to the project are spent. It comprises the completing the outstanding detailed design, development, creation and build of the chosen solution and its supporting applications, manuals, business processes and training. It concludes with a full test in a controlled environment.

During this stage, you will need to make the decision to start the trial stage. This decision can be taken prior to completion of the full work scope for this stage, as only activities required for the trial need be completed.

Key deliverables

The test results verify that any testing has been completed in accordance with the test plan and acceptance criteria, prior to preparing for the trial review.

The trial plan documents the way in which the output will be piloted to validate the expected outcomes will be realized. It includes the criteria for determining whether the trial is successful.

The ready for trial review report confirms all deliverables, resources and prerequisites across all functions required for starting the trial are in place.

The business case should be updated to demonstrate the project is still needed and viable.

The project plan: the schedule, resource and cost plan should be viable.

Focus on

You've already set the direction by approving the start of this stage, and it is now up to the project manager to deliver the solution you agreed on. Focus here is on ensuring the outcomes you need are still attainable. You need to confirm the original business need is still valid, especially when matters arise which result in a change to the project. In such cases, focus only on those aspects which will either increase benefit realization or bring it forward. Look for evidence of progress, don't always take everyone at their word; get out of your office and look for yourself and challenge people. 'Show me' and 'Demonstrate that' should be what you are asking.

What can go wrong?

- There can be a post-authorization lull when the project has key staff changes, and a new team might emerge which is not fully briefed or aligned. They need to be focussed, energized and bonded as well as introduced to the project; many of them will not have been present in the often-heated discussions which defined the solution. Unless they understand the solution fully, there is a danger they will want to start to redesign it as they go along.

- In the dash for delivery, the overall business objective is forgotten, and the need vanishes or changes without anyone noticing.
- The plan is abandoned and the project lurches forward on a day by day basis. Coupled with this, the risks, identified in the investigative stages, are overlooked and forgotten. Look for yellowing and out of date project plans and progress reports pinned to walls as evidence of this.
- Deliverables start arriving late and contingency time is squeezed. Eventually slippage is inevitable but is not reported as there is blind hope it will all come right in the end. It seldom does.
- Progress reports continue to say everything is going well. Don't believe it; look for yourself and for evidence.
- Time spent on testing is reduced as pressure comes on delivery, almost regardless of quality.
- Stakeholders are ignored or forgotten
- Scope starts to creep. New features keep being added for what might on their own be good ideas, but not at the cost of delivering nothing. Perfection is the enemy of the good!

Berlin's new airport

Delays on many high profile national projects pale into insignificance against the trials and tribulations of Berlin's new Brandenburg airport. After almost 15 years of planning, construction began in 2006. Originally planned to open in October 2011, the airport has encountered a series of delays and cost overruns due to poor construction planning, execution, management, as well as corruption. The opening date is still unclear; at the time of writing it was promised for October 2020.

Crossrail – Elizabeth Line

The Elizabeth line, as it will be known once services begin, will link Reading and Heathrow airport, west of London, with Shenfield in Essex and Abbey Wood in southeast London. As late as July 2018, the management team was reporting that the line would open on time in October 2018. A Public Accounts Committee report was scathing about the management of the project, saying over-optimism was prevalent throughout and has proved hugely damaging to the programme.

> *"Given the amount of work still to be done, it is clear that Crossrail Ltd did not have a full appreciation of the scale and complexity of the outstanding work until recently, particularly the work to bring together all the infrastructure and systems required for the railway to begin operations."*

Anyone simply walking past the construction sites in the summer of 2018 could see how far work had progressed with their own eyes even if the integration effort was invisible (see Chapter 24). The work is not likely to be fully complete until 2021.

Workout 8.4 – Check list for starting the trial stage

This gate comprises the decision point prior to undertaking any trials with 'real' users or even customers. You should be confident the trial has been planned fully and addresses those aspects which are the source of the major risks.

Business need and strategic fit

- Is the project still a good business proposition?
- Is the project still correctly reflected in the overall business plan?
- Have all high risks been eliminated?

Project Plan

- Is the project plan up to date, full and complete?
- Is there an outline plan for the remainder of the project?
- Is there a detailed schedule, resource and cost plan for the trial stage?
- Do we have sufficient resources to undertake the trial?

For the trial

- Have the tests been finished and the results accepted?
- Has the trial plan been prepared and approved?
- Have the trial acceptance criteria been agreed?
- Have checklists been prepared for the customers and users?
- Have customers/users been identified and trial agreements drafted?
- Have the business processes been finalized?
- Are all relevant functions and units ready for the trial?
- Is the communications material ready?
- Are trial results monitoring systems in place?
- Is there time and resource allowed in the plan to undertake modifications to any deliverables, should they be needed?

Trial stage

Overview

During the trial stage, the partially proven solution is checked in the operational environment with live users and/or customers. The purpose of this stage is to validate that the solution is acceptable to users and customers, works in a 'real world' context and is likely to result in the achievement of your business objectives. It is better that something goes wrong during a limited trial than after full scale implementation.

Key deliverables

The trial results confirm the trials have been completed in accordance with the trial plan's acceptance criteria. If validated, the developed solution is now ready to move to the release stage. Any outstanding risks and issues should be noted.

The ready for service (RFS) review report is a short report confirming all deliverables and prerequisite activities required before starting the release stage have been completed.

The business case should be updated to demonstrate the project is still needed and viable.

The project plan: a viable and detailed schedule, resource and cost plan for the release stage.

Focus on

You need to ensure the solution is likely to meet the need in customer and operational terms. Focus on the reactions of those engaged in the trials, ensuring critical feedback is acted on. Critical feedback is that which if not acted on, will threaten the success of the project. You should aim to reduce or neutralize outstanding risks and issues. Your most important decision comes at the end this stage: should the solution be put into full-scale use? Focus here is on the state of readiness of the organization and how it will receive the solution. A poor decision at this point threatens the entire investment and your reputation.

What can go wrong?

- The trial starts prematurely 'to maintain the dates' and the media notices the problems which ensue, damaging your organization's reputation.
- The scale of the trial was totally underestimated. By now it's a bit late but it's better to recognize this that try to hide it. Look at the two case studies under the 'develop and test stage' earlier.
- Insufficient notice is given to those involved in the trial and they are not available when needed or are inadequately briefed.
- No time is provided in the plan to correct any errors discovered.
- The trial is curtailed as it started late, and the team is still under pressure to deliver on time. Look at the risks this will raise!

Workout 8.5 – Check list for starting the release stage

This gate represents one of your biggest decisions. Until now the project has been internal or at least contained (such as the trial). If terminated now, the costs will have been for nothing . . . but that is not what counts. What matters is you deciding whether it is still in the best interests of the company to release the new order and start reaping the rewards the project was set up for in the first place. Moving ahead when the circumstances are not right, or the work is incomplete, might severely damage the organization and its standing with customers, employees and shareholders. It could also be career limiting for you!

Business need and strategic fit

- Is the project still a good business proposition?
- Have all high and medium risks been eliminated from the project?

Ready for service (RFS)

- Have the right stakeholders been engaged and consulted concerning the RFS decision?
- Are you absolutely sure, beyond reasonable doubt, it will work? (Your reputation and that of your organization is at stake!)
- Have process designs across the organization (and to third parties if needed) been accepted and is all training completed?
- Have the operational parts of the business and any suppliers confirmed they are ready to start using and maintaining the new capabilities? Are contracts ready to be placed?
- Are benefits/results/operational monitoring processes and systems in place?
- Have the costs and benefits been reforecast against the business plan?

Project plan

- Is the project plan updated, full and complete?
- Is there a detailed schedule, resource and cost plan for the release stage?
- Is the launch/release date(s) defined?
- Do you have the resources to undertake the release stage?

Release stage

Overview

This is the stage when 'the rubber hits the road'. You unleash your 'new order' on the world and start to realize the benefits your project was set up to create. In addition, work is carried out post release to ensure the environments left by the project are 'clean', e.g., old data removed from computer applications. This stage ends with a project closure review when the project is formally closed. This stage is not necessarily short in duration as it includes a period of initial operational running, which is essential to tune the solution in its early phases of operation.

Key deliverable

Project closure report contains the notes of solution hand over and project closure, including 'lessons learned' from the project in terms of how the processes, organization, systems and team worked (i.e., the efficiency of the project). Terms of reference for the Post-Implementation Review is also included.

Focus on

The bulk of the project's deliverables should now be completed, but that does not mean they are being put to beneficial use. During this stage, ensure the handover of the solutions and capabilities to the operational managers and those with on-going accountabilities are smooth and complete. Do not expect perfection, but do ensure there are management actions in place to deal with any problems. After everything is handed over, the buck stops with you, as the project team will have been disbanded.

What can go wrong?

- Look for signs of corners being cut, deliverables left incomplete, processes not working adequately, accountabilities being confused.
- Users reject the solution (it's a bit late for this to be found out now and a damning indictment on the effectiveness of the stakeholder engagement so far)
- The project closure is not done, and remaining funds are diverted to 'pet initiatives' or propping up other overspending projects.
- The lessons aren't learned, and the same mistakes are made again and again on future projects.
- No one thanks and rewards the project sponsor, manager and team for a job well done.

Workout 8.6 – Check list at project completion

The solution is now in operation, and it is time to close the project formally. You must be satisfied everything planned was done. Don't let anyone off the hook until the work is completed. All too often this part of the project is rushed as attention has moved on to new things but losing focus at this point in time could adversely impact benefits realization.

Business need and strategic fit

- Has the business forecast been updated to take into account the benefits arising from your project?
- Have you decided who will monitor the benefits and how?
- Have review points and metrics for measuring the benefits been defined?
- Have all suppliers been paid?
- Has the project account been closed so that no more costs can be incurred?

Post implementation review (PIR)

- Have you agreed the need for, timing and terms of reference for the PIR?
- Have the terms of reference, management and timing for the post implementation review been defined?

Risks and Issues

- Have all issues been resolved or handed over to a named person in the operational environment or another project?
- Has ownership of each outstanding risk been accepted by a named person in the line or in another project?

Team/stakeholders

- Have all who need to know about the closure of the project been identified?
- Have team appraisals relating to the project been completed?
- Have you acknowledged those who deserve special thanks and recognition?

Lessons learned

- Have lessons learned been recorded and communicated to the relevant process and documentation owners?

Post implementation review – after the project is completed

Overview

You should carry out a post implementation review when sufficient time has elapsed for the benefits of the project and the operation of the outputs to be assessable. The review cannot cover every aspect, but it should establish whether:

- the predicted benefits were realized or are on track to be realized;
- the desired outcomes are a reality;
- the most effective operational systems, processes and structures were designed;
- the solution really met the business needs, both for users and customers.

As you are the one who wanted the benefits and for whom the project was undertaken, it is in your interest to initiate the review. This review should result in plans for improvement where necessary and hence help in the achievement of the benefits. It will also inform any necessary changes to the programme or business portfolio the project was part of. For major projects this review might be carried out by an audit function, but in all cases, it is better (although not essential) if it is conducted by someone independent from the project team. To be effective, the review must not be used as a 'witch hunt'. If you use it in this way, you'll never have the truth presented to you again!

Key deliverable

The post implementation review report assesses the success of the project against predefined conditions of satisfaction given in the business. It assesses how effective the project was in meeting its business objectives, how well the outputs are operating in practice and includes recommendations for improvements.

Focus on

Your focus here is on confirming the solutions operating to expectations and the benefits are being realized. Look for any deviations and ensure corrective action is put in place. Confirm the original business need has in fact been fulfilled or that the changes are embedded sufficiently to be sustainable.

What can go wrong?

- This review is often not done either because interest has waned and the world has moved on, or because it is felt the outcome of the review will be embarrassing. If we are not 'big enough' to learn from mistakes, we are probably not fit to lead major change.
- The wrong people are engaged in the review, and it concentrates on 'how the project went' rather than if the solution worked effectively and if the benefits were realized.
- The identified shortfalls are not noted and hence not built into the future work schedule for the programme or business portfolio.

Workout 8.7 – Post implementation review

The outputs from the project have been in use for some time and you should be seeing evidence of benefits being realized.

Business need

- Are the benefits being realized as expected?
- Are there any unexpected costs or dis-benefits?

Operational aspects

- Are all aspects of the solution working as envisaged?
- Are there any unexpected side-effects or issues?
- Are changes being sustained?

Action

- Has a corrective action plan been put in place to address any shortfall in expected benefits?
- Has a corrective action plan been put in place to address any shortfall in operational aspects?
- Have lessons learned been recorded and communicated to the relevant stakeholders?

9

Applying the project framework

Using the project framework in practice

Building your own standard project life cycle

The project framework can be used for any type of project, for any purpose. It is not concerned with the technicalities of how specialist deliverables are created.

"Take calculated risks.
That is quite different from being rash."

GENERAL GEORGE PATTON, 1885–1945

- **Create a standardized project life cycle for your organization.**
- **Make your standardized project life cycle business-led.**
- **Tailor the standardized life cycle to suit each project type.**
- **Tailor again to suit the circumstances of each project.**
- **Ensure the reduction of risk is central to your project life cycle.**

Using the project framework in practice

In the previous chapter, I took you through a five-stage project life cycle which can be used for all your projects. This life cycle can be used:

- in a modified form to meet the needs of different projects;
- as a basis to create your own standardized project life cycle.

The advantages of a standardized project life cycle are not always understood by individual project sponsors or managers but for portfolio and programme managers it is vital. If all the projects in your portfolio or programme follow (or can at least be aligned to) the same life cycle, you are able to compare where each is by tracking the last gate approval. This enables you to have the management information you need for managing the whole portfolio of projects but which would not be available if every project followed a different life cycle. This is described in detail on Part V of this book.

Using a standard project life cycle, however, does not mean that every project has go through all five stages. Simpler projects generally require fewer stages than more complicated ones. This chapter explains how to tailor the five-stage project life cycle to meet the needs of your projects and your programme or business portfolio.

Obeng's four types of project

In *All Change, the Project Leader's Secret Handbook*, Eddie Obeng describes four types of projects, each dealing with a different kind of change. These are shown these in Figure 9.1.

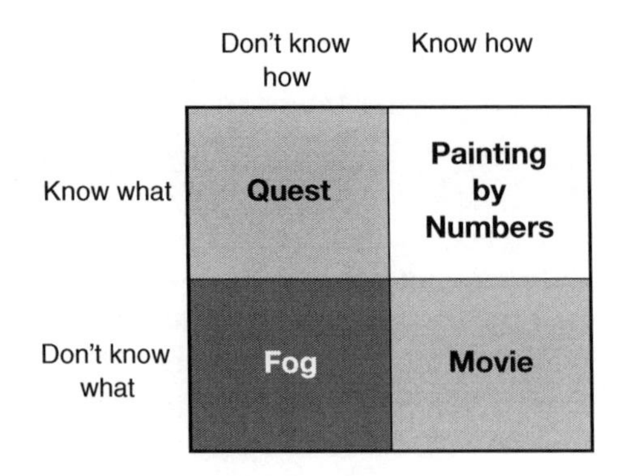

Figure 9.1 Different types of change project

If you know what you are doing and how you are going to do it, you have a 'painting by numbers' project. If you know how but not what, you have a 'movie'. A 'quest' is when you know what you want, but not how you will achieve it. Finally, a 'fog' is when you don't know what you want, nor how to achieve it.

Painting by numbers

Painting by numbers projects have clear outputs and a well-defined set of activities to be carried out. You know what you want to achieve and how to achieve it.

Going on a quest

This is named after the quest for the Holy Grail. You are clear on what is to be done but not the means (how) to achieve it. The secret of this type of project is get your 'knights' fired up to look for solutions in different places at the same time and ensure that they all return to report their findings on a fixed date. In other words, you might have a number of investigative stages before you settle on a solution. Quests give 'permission' for your people to explore 'out of the box' possibilities. If you don't keep strict control over costs and timescales they are, however, notorious for overspending, being very late, or simply delivering nothing.

Making movies

In this type of project, you are certain of how you will do something but have no idea what to do. Typically, your organization has built up significant expertise and capability and you are looking for ways to apply it. There must be several people committed to the methods you will use.

Walking in the fog

This type of project is one where you have no idea what to do nor how to do it. It is often prompted as a reaction to a change in circumstances (e.g., political, competitive, social), although it can be set off pro-actively. This project needs to be managed like a quest. You need to have tight control over costs and timescale and investigate as

Table 9.1 Obeng's project types [on one page – do not split]

Project type	*Type of change it helps create or man*	*Application*
Painting by numbers	Evolutionary	Improving your continuing business operations
Going on a quest	Revolutionary	Proactively exploring outside current operations and ways of working
Making a movie	Evolutionary	Leveraging existing capabilities
Lost in a fog	Revolutionary	Solving a problem or exploring areas outside your current operations and ways of working

Adapted from Eddie Obeng *Putting Strategy to Work* (London: Pitman Publishing, 1996)

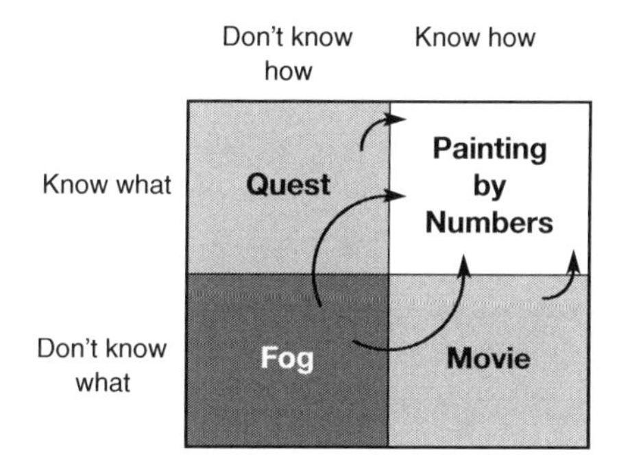

Figure 9.2 Creating a project you can implement

By the time you reach the development gate, that you should know what you are going to do and how. That is to say, at the development gate, you will have a painting by numbers project. You may, however, start off as any of the project types – the investigative stages are the means by which you arrive at your solution.

many options as possible in parallel. Like a quest, these projects can end up in delivering nothing unless firmly controlled.

Each of these project types has different characteristics, requiring different leadership styles. They are also suited for different purposes, as shown in Table 9.1.

The staged framework requires that, by the time you reach the development gate, you know, with a reasonable level of confidence, what you are going to do and how to do it (see Figure 9.2). The investigative stages are there to discover an appropriate solution to your problem and finalize your plan. The proposal should state why you need the project, but your level of background knowledge will differ for each proposal you want to address. This will have a considerable impact on the way you undertake the investigative stages and the level of risk associated with the project at the start. Painting by numbers projects tend to be less risky than the other types, but not always. The clarity of your scope, timescale, costs and benefits will improve as you gain more knowledge. In addition, as we learned earlier, the level of risk should decrease as you progress through the project.

Just to make your day, there are circumstances when you should allow a project to continue past the development gate as a fog, movie or quest. For example, when the risks of not proceeding outweigh the risks of proceeding. The level of risk would be higher than under normal circumstances but that is your choice. As a business portfolio or programme manager, your objective is to ensure the risks in your portfolio or programme are acceptable as a whole.

How do I deal with a simple project?

You might know a great deal about a simple project before you even start. By the time you finish the initial investigation stage, you might have fully defined the project outputs and your plan. Your confidence level will be as high as for a more complicated project at the development gate, so undertaking the detailed investigation stage is either trivial or unnecessary. Full authorization to complete the project can therefore be given at the detailed investigation gate (see Figure 9.3). You must, however, meet the full criteria of the development gate before you start the develop and test stage. In this way, you have used the principles of the framework, checking at every gate but avoided doing any unnecessary work.

How do I deal with a complicated or complex project?

A complicated project is like a quest or fog project. You might not want to risk authorizing an expensive and time-consuming investigative stage in which you have little confidence in the outcome, but you still want to see what the possibilities are. You can therefore add additional investigative stages and limit your exposure, as shown in Figure 9.4.

A different five stage project life cycle

The UK government has a five-stage project life cycle in its project delivery standard. It includes three investigative stages, in contrast to the two proposed in this book. This is because experience has shown that the size and complexity of government projects is such that two investigative stages is usually insufficient for managing the risks.

What about agile?

Agile can be problematic because there are many different interpretations of what 'agile' is. In relation to iterative development methods (like Scrum), I find it simpler not to think in terms of 'agile project management' but rather 'agile delivery' and consider 'agile methods' as applying to work packages, not whole projects. Do not try to map agile steps into specific project life cycle stages. Instead, put your agile managed work packages in whatever life cycle stage makes sense, bearing in mind risk and dependencies on other work. Some people refer to this as a 'hybrid' approach.

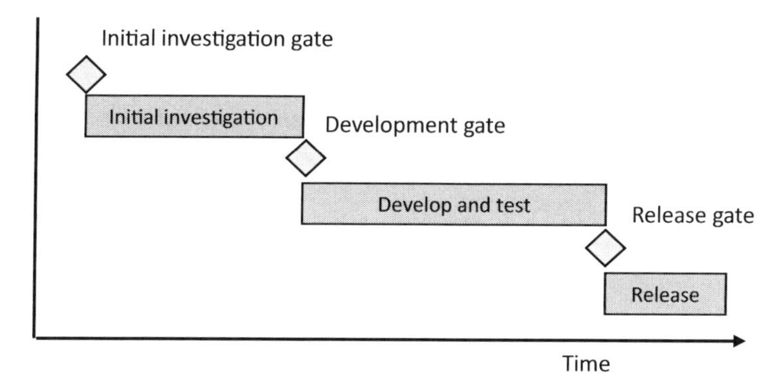

Figure 9.3 The stages for a simple project

The diagram represents a case where no further investigative work needs to be done after the initial investigation. The project is checked against the criteria for the development gate and, if acceptable, moves straight into the develop and test stage. In this case, a trial stage is not considered necessary.

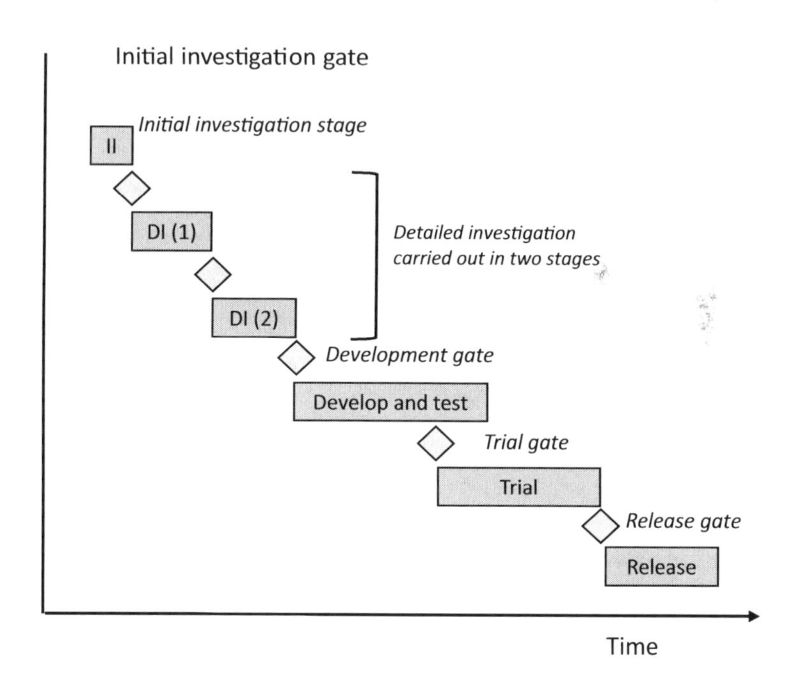

Figure 9.4 The stages for a riskier project

The diagram represents a case where the risks of authorizing a single detailed investigation stage are too high, and so an additional investigative stage is added.

Agile and the staged approach to projects

Look back at Obeng's project types at the start of this chapter, especially at 'going on a quest' and 'walking in a fog'. These sound very similar to agile scrum, don't they? Do a bit in a time box. Review; do the next bit. Agile advocates often criticize a staged project life cycle as being 'non-agile', but actually you can consider it as 'macro-agile' if you can leave your prejudices behind.

Is a trial stage really needed?

"I have already tested this rigorously. Surely, I don't really need to trial it as well? Won't this just delay the benefits?" Whilst this is a valid question, the answer, as always, is "It depends." The choice of 'to trial or not to trial' comes down to risk. What is the likely impact on your business if this goes wrong? How confident are you that it won't go wrong? With this in mind, you might choose to subject certain aspects to a trial more rigorously than others – balancing the speed to benefits realization with the risks.

It is prudent to assume you always need a trial and omit it only if you have proved to yourself and your stakeholders that it will not add any value to your project. Never skip the trial because you are in a hurry! If in doubt, try it out. In some cases, two trial stages might be needed, one to check functionality and the other scalability.

If in doubt, try it out!

Using the project framework on different types of project

The project framework can be used for any type of project, for any purpose. As it is not concerned with the technicalities creating specialist deliverables, it is flexible and provides project managers with the opportunity for tailoring to suit the requirements of individual projects. This ensures an optimum path through the generic project framework rather than one tied by bureaucracy. Particular types of project require their own methods and steps but provided you know how they match the overall high level framework, they can be used with confidence in an environment where you, as a business portfolio or programme manager, know what is happening. A common project framework in an organization will ensure alignment between different parts of the organization with clearer communication and understanding. Table 9.2 shows how a range of different projects and their key activities can fit into the framework.

Table 9.2 Mapping different project types into the project framework

	Initial investigation stage	*Detailed investigation stage*	*Develop and test stage*	*Trial stage*	*Release stage*
Product development	Concept	Alternatives and feasibility	Develop and test	Market validation	Market launch
Product withdrawal	Initial investigation	Detailed investigation	Develop and test	Pilot withdrawal	Close operations
Information systems	Analysis	Logical and outline physical design	Detailed design, build and test	Pilot	Cutover
Bid or tender	Receive request and evaluate	Prepare detailed tender	Develop, build, internal test	Commissioning trials	Handover
Construction	Inception study	Feasibility study, tender design	Detailed design and construction	Commissioning trials	Handover
Publishing	Proposal	Prepare manuscript	Edit, typeset	Final proof	Launch
IT waterfall	Requirements review	Analysis and design	Build	Beta test	Cutover
DSDM/agile	Feasibility	Foundation	Evolutionary development	Deployment	Deployment

Workout 9.1 – Tailor your own five stage project framework

Consider the list of different types of project in Table 9.2. Do you recognize any from your own organization? Can you add to the list? If so, ask those who are familiar with those project types to reproduce Figure 4.7 with modified activities, deliverables and gate review criteria. There is a blank template for this on the website for you to use. At the end of this workout, you will have a set of project frameworks, summarizing each project type.

Building your own standard project life cycle

How many gates and stages should I have?

First, as a gate is the decision point for starting a stage, you should always have the same number of gates as stages, plus a 'project completion' gate at the end. To decide the right number of stages, consider the types of project undertaken in your organization. Do they fit the generic stages described earlier? Are there some modifications you would like to make? Some organizations have only four stages, others six or more. Generally, the fewer the better, but they must reflect the risks and fit the majority of projects you are likely to do. My experience is that three is too few and five fits most purposes, so if in doubt try five. Of the five stages used in this book, the trial stage is often either left out or merged in with the develop and test stage. I prefer to have the trial as a distinct stage to differentiate it from testing. Testing is very much an internal, 'private' activity. A trial, on the other hand, is often 'public', involving real users and customers. You are therefore open to poor media comment or hostile reactions from employees and suppliers. Making the trial a distinct stage forces people to focus on whether they really are ready for it.

You might find instances of organizations with anything up to a dozen stages. This usually happens because the industry and project type requires a more granular approach. In regulated industries, like aerospace, the gating often reflects mandatory regulatory approvals. In the UK rail industry, Network Rail has a project life cycle called GRIP (Guide to Rail Investment Process) which has eight stages; like aerospace, the rail industry is regulated as safety is paramount. The UK government's standard life cycle has five stages, three of which are investigative, following the Treasury's desire to limit expenditure until the solution is clear.

What should I call the stages and gates?

The stage and gate names I have used throughout this book and in *The Project Workout* have evolved over a number of years and are based on my experience of working in several organizations on many different business projects. What you choose to call the stages in your project life cycle is up to you, but that decision is not trivial. Words are emotive and can be either powerful movers or inhibitors of change. In all organizations there are words which mean:

Words are emotive and can be either powerful movers or inhibitors of change.

- something particular to everyone;
- different things to different people.

You can build on the former by exploiting them in your project framework, provided the meaning is compatible with what you wish to achieve.

You should avoid the ambiguity of the latter and choose different words, even making up new words if the dictionary cannot help you. For example, working in one company I found the word 'concept' problematic. 'Concept', to some people, was a high level statement of an idea (the meaning I wanted to convey), but to others it meant a detailed assessment of what has been decided should be done (this was not what I wanted). Rather than try to re-educate people in their everyday language, I used a different word (proposal) which had no strong linkages to current use of language. There were similar problems with the word 'implement': it has so many preconceived meanings, it is better not to use it at all! Implement can mean launch the plan and get on with the meaty part of the project, whilst to others it is put whatever you created into beneficial use. 'Execute' is another interesting word but to some people it is more associated with capital punishment than undertaking projects! For this reason, the International Standards Organisation's committee on project management avoids the use of the word and its derivatives, despite its liberal use by 'hard-nosed' businesspeople as a verbal marker to show how effective they are. Table 9.3 includes some of the alternatives I have seen.

Table 9.3 Alternative names for project stages

Names used in this book	*Possible alternatives*	
Proposal "Identify the need."	Concept Start up Initiation	Idea generation Identification Ideation
Initial Investigation "Have a quick look."	Pre-feasibility Initial assessment Initial planning Preliminary investigation	Evaluation/Evaluate Research Justification/Justify Incubation
Detailed Investigation "Have a closer look."	Feasibility Appraisal/Appraise Definition/Define Planning/Plan Scope	Specification/Specify Design Business case Evaluation/Evaluate Authorization
Develop and Test "Do it."	Implementation/Implement Execution/Execute Realization/Realize Development/Develop	Production Construction/Construct Build Do
Trial "Try it."	Beta test Validation/Validate	Commissioning Pilot
Release "Use it."	Initial operation Finalization/Finalize Launch Completion	Implementation/Implement Handover Acceptance/Accept Closure/closedown/Close
Post-Implementation Review "How did it work out?"	Business review Post-project review	Post project evaluation Post investment review

The same issues apply to the naming of the gates. For these, however, it is better to name each one according to the stage it precedes. This emphasizes the 'gate as an entry point' concept. An alternative approach is to name the gate after the document used as the control on the gate. You will see I have mixed these. Again, this is your choice, but ensure the same terminology is used across the whole organization.

I do, however, strongly advise against referring to the stages and gates by a number or letter. It will cause difficulties later (including significant cost) if you need to revise your framework. You will not believe the number of times a 'Gate 0' or 'Stage 0' has to be added to the front of a framework. Using proper names is simpler, more memorable and will not box you in for the future if you do not get it right at the start or there are real pressures to change.

What is the best way to depict a project framework?

If your project framework is to be understood, you need to communicate it in a consistent and unambiguous way, making sure it is clear that stages and gates serve different purposes. I use circle, arrow and diamond icons:

- a circle depicts activities which happen before a project starts or after it is completed;
- a diamond represents a gate;
- an arrow represents a stage.

This approach is used in Figure 8.5 and has withstood the test of use in many diverse organizations and is now incorporated in the British Standard on project management (BS6079) and the UK government's project delivery standard (GovS 002).

Workout 9.2 – Create your own project framework

This is best done in an informal workshop.

1 Take the set of project frameworks from Workout 9.1. Find out from those who created them what problems they had in producing them.
   a Do the gates reflect all the big 'go/no go' decisions?
   b Could they fit into the five stages or did they need more or less?
   c Are all the essential activities and deliverables covered in the stages?
   d Does the flow lead to risk decreasing through the life cycle?

2 Determine which of the project frameworks represent 'business-led projects' and which represent 'enabling projects'. Separate them into two groups.
3 Using the project framework in Figures 8.4 and 8.5, and your own project frameworks from step 2, create a project framework which reflects the business-led projects in your organization.
   a Start with the big decisions. These reflect 'gates'. Each gate should precede a stage.
   b Check the gates can be mapped to any current project authorization process or finance rules you have.
4 Once you have an outline project framework, start adding the detail, drawing on those you produced in Workout 9.1. The aim is to create a generic life cycle to which they all align.

If you have no business-led projects, it is likely that your projects are scoped based on your departments. You will need to simplify and focus how you run projects in your organization if you are to be successful at programme and portfolio management.

10

Directing and managing a project

Project management and supporting processes

The project management processes

The supporting processes

Project frameworks or life cycles

Implications for a business portfolio or programme manager

The project life cycle is driven by time and the need to reduce risk to an acceptable level. On the other hand, processes are iterative.

"You know my methods. Apply them."

SIR ARTHUR CONAN DOYLE, 1859–1930

- **The project life cycle and a project process are different.**
- **A project life cycle is time dependent.**
- **A process is iterative.**

Project management and supporting processes

Love them or hate them, processes are key to making sure people know what they are meant to do and for ensuring consistency in how activities are undertaken. Processes are essential but care needs to be taken as, on their own, they are not sufficient for good project management. The project management processes are the core of the any rational management method. The processes should include the essential activities to be carried out by the decision makers, project sponsor, project manager and team managers, such as managing risks and issues, planning and reporting. The project management activities draw together all the information and, for this reason, they can be also called 'integrating' processes. You will notice, however, many activities, such as managing risks not only apply to a project but also to each work package. These are therefore, grouped as supporting processes and detailed separately; see 'The supporting processes' mentioned later. The advantage of this approach is that when integrated with enterprise-wide programme and business portfolio methods, the same supporting processes and systems for can be used for the programmes and business portfolios (see Chapters 16 and 20). It would be wasteful and counter-productive for individuals on the same team to adopt different approaches, processes and tools for the same activity.

The project management processes

The project management processes are shown in Figure 10.1 and described in the following sections.

Direct higher level

This process is not part of the project management process but is included as it provides the context for the project. The higher level could be a business portfolio or a programme. Another term used to represent the higher level is 'sponsoring organization'. Its purpose is to make sure that the project continues to be valid; that is to say, aligned to the higher-level objectives and justifiable. This is where any of the project sponsor's queries are answered, escalations dealt with and decisions and direction made. If the higher level is a business portfolio, the business portfolio management processes are used (see Chapter 16). If the higher level is a programme, the programme management processes are used (see Chapter 20).

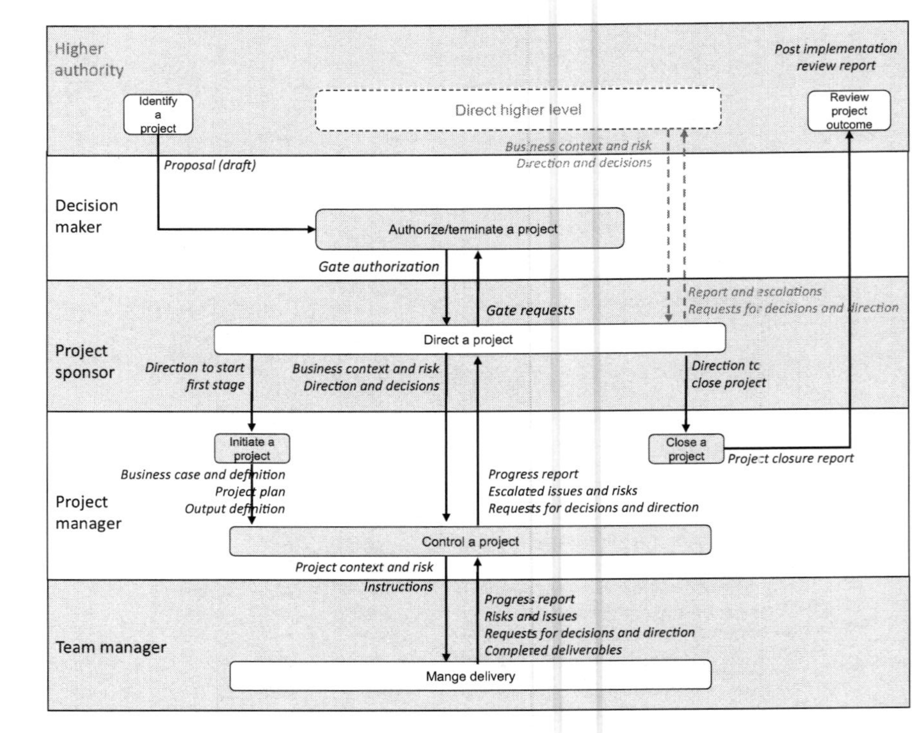

Figure 10.1 Project management processes

The key project management processes and their relationships (inputs and outputs) are shown here, with each activity in a swim lane to show which role is accountable. Notice the 'higher authority' lane. Who undertakes this depends on the context; this could be a programme manager, business portfolio manager or another corporate role. This is the person to whom the project sponsor is accountable.

Authorize/terminate a project

The purpose of this process is to ensure each stage of the project is started in the knowledge that the project is still required, has a viable plan and the risks are acceptable. In addition, the process is used to suspend (place on hold) a project if there are doubts over its viability and, if necessary, terminate it.

I have not presumed who the ultimate decision maker should be, although the person undertaking the project sponsor role should, as a minimum, submit the authorization requests to the decision maker. In some cases, the sponsor can also be the decision maker. In practice, most organizations have a 'scheme of delegation' with a list of criteria, often financially based, stating who has the delegated authority to make a particular decision. This is organizational and context specific.

Direct a project

This process is undertaken by the project sponsor to ensure the business interests of the organization undertaking the project are paramount. You will find more about sponsorship in Chapter 5.

Initiate a project

This process is undertaken by the project manager, supported by the team, to ensure the project is properly set up and planned.

Control a project

This process is undertaken by the project manager, supported by the team, to ensure the project is managed throughout its life. It also includes the activities to prepare for the authorization of each stage.

Close a project

Close a project is undertaken by the project manager, supported by the team, to ensure the project is closed, either because it is complete or because it has been terminated early.

Manage delivery

The purpose of this process is to ensure the deliverables from the project are developed to the right quality, within in the cost and time constraints and that the required outcomes, or business changes, happen. This process is the accountability of a team manager (sometimes called a work package manager or leader), supported by the project team members. Specialist processes would be used for undertaking the work to develop the solution, so don't confuse these with the project management processes (see Chapter 24). Team managers would use the same supporting processes as the project manager for controlling their individual work packages.

The supporting processes

Figure 10.2 shows the most commonly used supporting processes and the relationships between them. If you are to have formal processes, it is important to define the interfaces, otherwise accountabilities become muddled. The supporting processes ensure those techniques which are essential for effective management are used consistently by all role holders at all levels, be it business portfolio, programme, project or work package. This simplifies reporting and communication dramatically. It also enables you to have a more cost-effective tools strategy and provide the same training. Most of the topics essential to project management are described in Part V of this book, but you might wish to add others to reflect the needs of your organization.

Project frameworks or life cycles

In Lesson 2, in Chapter 2 I proposed using a single project framework for every type of project, tailored to reflect different work undertaken. This was looked at in more detail in Chapters 8 and 9. The advantage is that, top-down, all projects look similar to senior, business portfolio and programme management, who will invariably have to sponsor many different types of project. Unfortunately, many people confuse project life cycles with processes, and it is important that you understand the difference. The project life cycle is driven by time and the need to reduce risk to an acceptable level. It shows the typical activities to be undertaken in each stage in order to arrive at a successful conclusion. On the other hand, a process is iterative. A given activity always happens in a process, but each process can be used many times in different stages of the project:

Unfortunately, many people confuse project life cycles with processes

- identify a project – always happens before a project starts;
- initiate a project – always happens at the start of the first stage of the project;
- approve/terminate a project, direct a project, control a project and manage delivery happen throughout the project;
- close a project – always happens at the end of the final stage or a project or at any point when a project is terminated;
- review project outcome – always happens after the end of the project.

Figure 10.3 shows the relationship between the project life cycle and the management and supporting processes.

For more detail on project life cycles refer to Chapters 8 and 9 or for an in-depth view, look at *The Project Workout*.

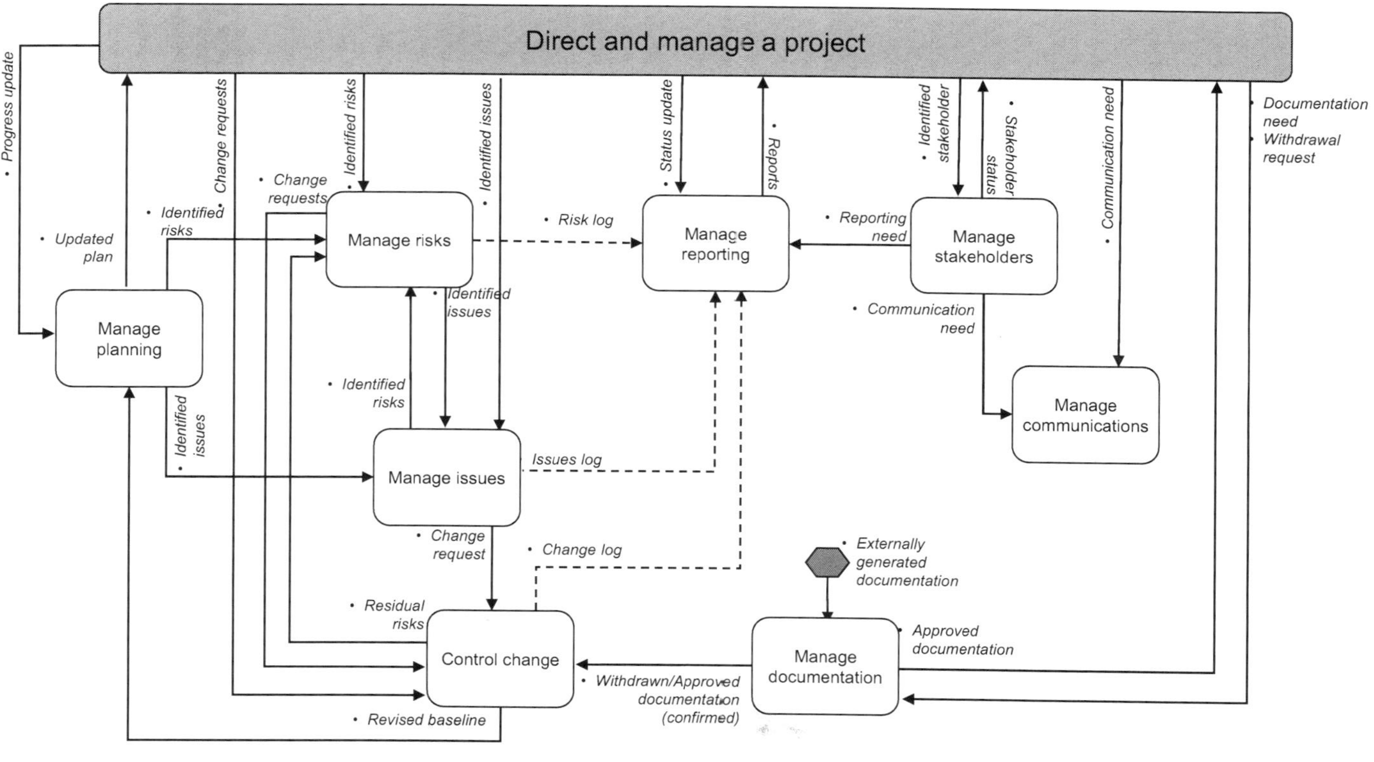

Figure 10.2 The supporting processes

Some of the most commonly used supporting processes and their relationships (inputs and outputs) are shown here. Unless you define an overall architecture, such as this, you will find the interfaces between processes become muddled, which in turn leads to muddled accountabilities.

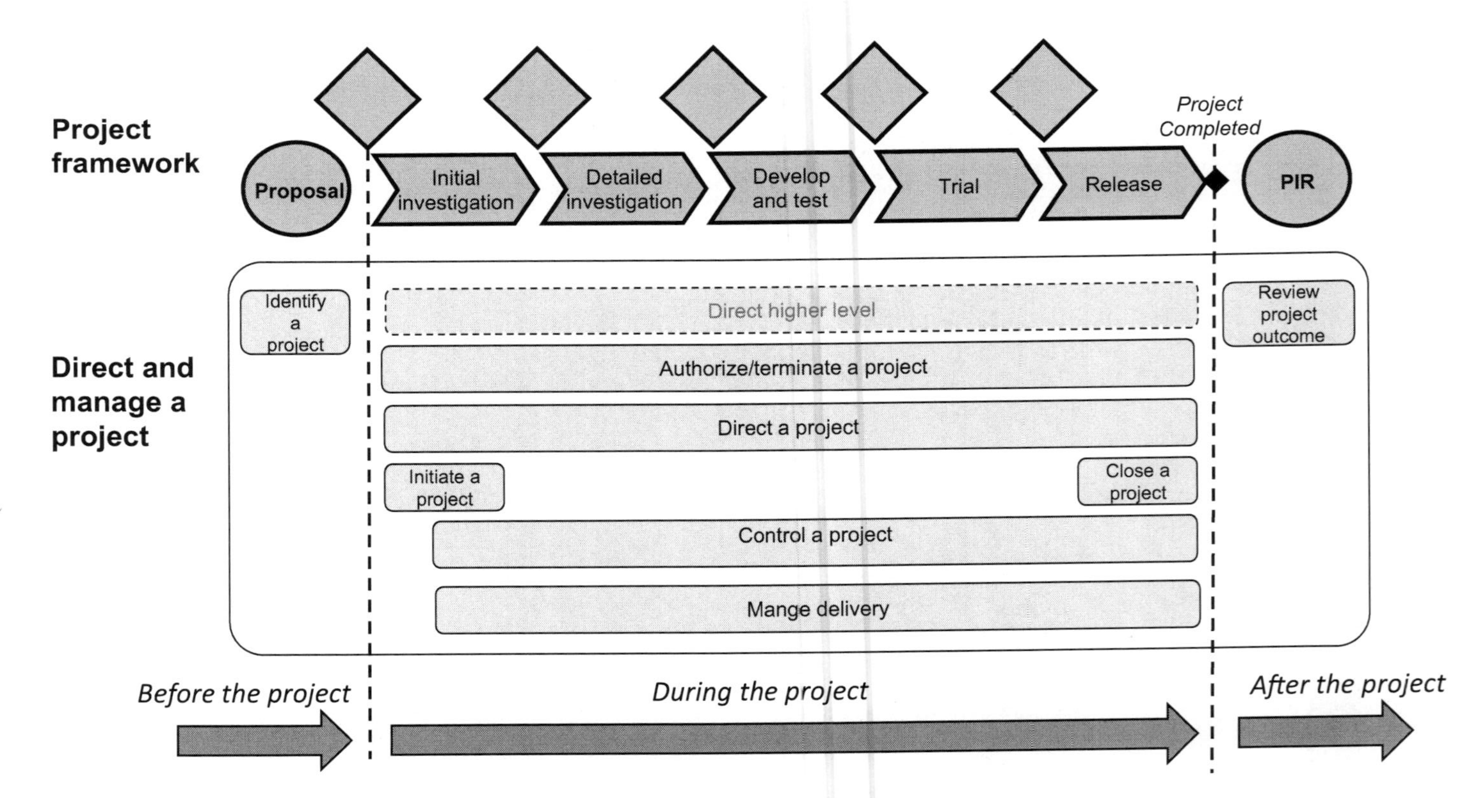

Figure 10.3 The relationship between the project life cycle and the management processes

The management processes and project life cycle should not be confused. This diagram shows the project stages each process is typically used within.

Implications for a business portfolio or programme manager

Think 'top-down'

As a business portfolio or programme manager, you need to concentrate on the activities related to the 'higher authority', 'decision maker' and 'project sponsor' roles (see Figure 10.1). You are the higher authority and, therefore, deciding which project needs to be started, and when, is central to your role. You will also need to make decisions which you have not delegated to others and, in some cases, you might also take on the formal project sponsor role. You'll need to make sure the business environment hasn't changed so much over time as to make the project no longer viable. Finally, you'll want to check that the project achieved, whatever it was you wanted it to achieve.

At business portfolio and programme levels, everything is concerned with governance and management, which means you'll need to:

- decide who takes on which role;
- define the processes you want to be followed.

Assign the roles to the right people

Every project should have a project sponsor who acts as the link between the higher authority and the project manager. If the higher authority is at business portfolio level the sponsor is the person who has the most to lose or gain and should be working in alignment with the business portfolio strategy. If the higher authority is at programme level, the project sponsor might be the same person as the programme sponsor, the programme manager or another person. It all depends on the context, the span of control and how busy key individuals are.

In lesson 1 in Chapter 2 we discussed strategic alignment; in practice this means that the senior people are aligned, as it is only through people that direction and decisions are made. If those undertaking the leadership roles, whether at business portfolio, programme or project level, are not aligned, no amount of project management expertise will compensate for this or correct it. It is true, a skilful project manager might be able to influence the sponsor and higher-level roles, but if they cannot agree among themselves, they should blame no one except themselves for any subsequent failure. Leadership has to be explicit and visible, and there is no place leaders who abdicate their responsibilities.

Put the right processes in place

Having got the right people doing the right roles, you'll need to be satisfied that you have processes in place to support those roles and which make it clear where the boundaries are with respect project management. It is possible to assemble the activities in Figures 10.1 and 10.2 in a number of different ways to emphasize different approaches or reflect an organization's culture. For example, in Figure 10.1, I have shown the gate requests going from 'Direct a project', as I have taken the view that as it is the project sponsor's project, he or she is the person who should make the request. This approach emphasizes the role of the project sponsor as a leader, rather than letting them abdicate the role to the project manager. Alternative approaches might show the gate request going from the project manager, after verifying it with the project sponsor. Neither approach is better than the other; they are 'differently right' and a matter of choice. PRINCE2® combines what I call 'Approve/terminate a project' with 'Direct a project', as it makes the presumption that the project sponsor usually makes gates decisions. In my experience, for large organizations, the project sponsor rarely has such authority and significant gate decisions are made by a higher-level board.

BS6079, PRINCE2® and ISO 21502 are structured in a very similar way to the processes outlined earlier (see Chapter 29). This is because the management processes are role based and therefore show what each role is accountable for and the information flows between the different team members. No project should be undertaken in isolation and therefore the concepts in this chapter are built on in Chapter 16, in relation to business portfolio management and Chapter 20 in relation to programme management so that the processes for business portfolio, programme and project management are mutually consistent.

Workout 10.1 – Building your own project management processes

Use Figure 10.1 as a guide to start building your own project management process. Make sure you include all the important roles. Use the role names you believe fit your organization.

Pay attention to where you place the 'Approve/terminate project' process. For example, it could be as shown in Figure 10.1 or it could be combined with 'Direct a project'. Choose the approach that is either current practice in your organization or the approach you want people to follow in the future. Check your organization's scheme of delegation and make sure this is consistent.

Consider the interface from the project to the 'higher level' carefully. This needs to be tightly defined so that people know the boundaries of their authority, who they are accountable to and the default line of reporting and escalation.

Once you have your own version of Figure 10.1 you can start defining the next level of activities. Draw on the content of *The Project Workout*, PRINCE2® and the British and international standards for the detail and use Part VI of this book to guide you.

PART III

PORTFOLIO MANAGEMENT – DEALING WITH MANY PROJECTS AND BEYOND

"Great things are not done by impulse, but by a series of small things brought together."

GEORGE ELIOT, 1819–1880

We will start at the top. Your organization exists to serve a particular purpose or need. It might be commercial (for profit), it might be social or might be related to government. Everything you do within that organization should support that need. In this respect, business portfolio management represents the management of your organization, but not in the traditional, line hierarchy sense.

- **Balance the risks across your business portfolio.**
- **Build the business cases into your portfolio's business plan as soon as each project has been authorized.**
- **Make informed decisions on which work you allow to continue.**
- **Prioritize benefits, not projects or work.**
- **Ensure that you have the freedom to change by having 'white space'.**
- **Keep a list of all the projects and other work you are undertaking.**

How to use Part III

In this part of the book I start by looking at portfolios of projects, as most people intuitively find it this easy to understand in concept. As you already know from Chapter 3, portfolios are not just about projects; they can comprise any type of work you choose to invent, including 'business-as-usual'. I will then extend the basics of portfolio management to include these other types of work. The workouts in Part III are designed to help you understand what is actually going on inside your organization, how the different activities relate and how you might better organize them.

11

Business portfolios

The advantage of a 'business portfolio approach' is that you can divide an organization's strategy into discrete and achievable pieces to manage the implementation in a coordinated way.

"Luck is what happens when preparation meets opportunity."
SENECA, c. 4 BC – A.D. 65

- **Focus on organizational benefit, not just what is best for a single department.**
- **Portfolio management is integral to running the business, not an added extra.**
- **Consider strategic alignment capability, balance, risk, capability to do what's needed and the capacity to absorb change.**
- **Make sure your governance boards mirror your processes.**

What's different about business portfolio management?

Business portfolios support business plans

Business portfolio management provides a framework and practical tool for managing multiple programmes, projects and other work in pursuit of defined strategic objectives. Business portfolio management complements programme and project management but takes a much broader, enterprise-wide view as it should also include benefits from current operations. Benefits from projects usually start towards the end of a project whilst benefits from business portfolios start to flow as soon as the first project within the business portfolio has been completed and its outputs incorporated into 'business-as-usual' (Figure 11.1). The key focus for business portfolio management is ensuring that current activities, plus the programmes and projects as a whole, provide the overall benefit, regardless of the performance of individual components. Other differences are highlighted in the Table 11.1.

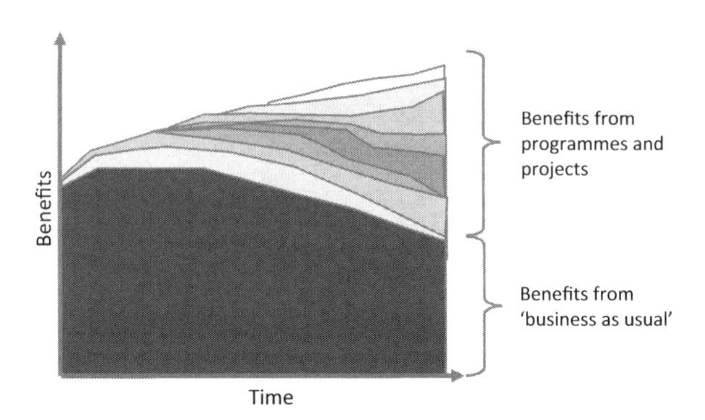

Figure 11.1 Benefits from existing operations and from 'new stuff'

The organization will continue to realize a stream of benefits from its existing 'business as usual' operations; this will probably decline over time. New programmes and projects will create capabilities and outcomes which will add new benefits streams at some point in the future. Together these benefit streams will take you towards your target position.

Table 11.1 Business portfolios compared to programmes and projects

Business portfolio management	*Programme and project management*
Broadly spread activity, concerned with overall strategic objectives as part of a business plan; a continuous activity, with no defined endpoint	Focussed activity aimed at achieving required outcomes and realizing a 'slice' of benefit to the business portfolio as defined in a business case; programmes and projects have a defined start and endpoint
Suitable for managing and balancing a large number of constituent programmes, projects and other types of work, with complex and often changing interdependencies	Best suited to delivering achievable deliverables with a discrete objective
Suitable for managing the impact of and benefits from a number of aligned programmes and projects to ensure a smooth transition from the present to the new order	Suitable for delivering defined benefits and outcomes within a given environment
Includes benefits from current operations and from the outcomes of current and future projects	Includes future benefits of the project or programme itself
Governed and constrained by organization cash flow often seen as an annual budget	Governed and constrained by a discrete programme or project budget defined in a business case.

The advantage of a 'business portfolio approach' is that you can, as we have seen from the simple example in Chapter 3, divide an organization's strategy into discrete and achievable pieces to manage the implementation in a coordinated way. The resultant changes are therefore less likely to appear chaotic to the recipients (be they your own employees, suppliers or customers) and you are likely to see them completed. You are also able to focus on the true business objectives of the portfolio rather than be lost in the minutiae of delivery within each project or component of the portfolio. This enables you to spot gaps in the expected outcomes and benefits (either due to late projects or under-performance in current operations) and take the necessary preventative and corrective action.

You are also able to focus on the true business objectives

Focus on the benefits and outcomes, not the solution

Different meanings of 'portfolio'

I have already mentioned the difficulties certain words can create; 'portfolio' is just such a word. There will always be someone, somewhere who takes a different view on what a 'portfolio' is. I expect there are many readers who will challenge my definition of business portfolio – neither of us is wrong; just 'differently right'. The key point is that, in your organization, *you* should decide what *you* want particular words to mean, then make sure you use the words consistently in all your communications, written and verbal. If you use the language consistently, people will gradually pick it up. In Chapter 3 in this book, I distinguish business portfolio from programme from project, building on the terms I developed when the book was first published in 1997 and taking into account those which have emerged as international standards since. I have adapted already existing meanings to suit what I want to do; you should do the same.

In a small organization, the business portfolio might represent the entire organization, in which case the term 'business portfolio' becomes redundant – the organization *is* the business portfolio; the activity of business portfolio management, however, is still relevant. In larger organizations, the business might need to be divided into a number of subsidiary businesses, each run as a business portfolio, with its own plan.

To test if you are using the term, 'portfolio' in the same way as me, remind yourself of the definition in Chapter 3 and then look at Figure 11.2. Business portfolios are above the 'authorization process'; they are the entities from which programmes and projects are initiated. Business portfolios are governed by business plans, the approval for which usually gives no authority for actual work to take place or money to be spent. Programmes and projects are below the 'authorization process', being governed by business cases, which are the basis for authorizing funding and committing the required resources.

Business portfolios are governed by business plans

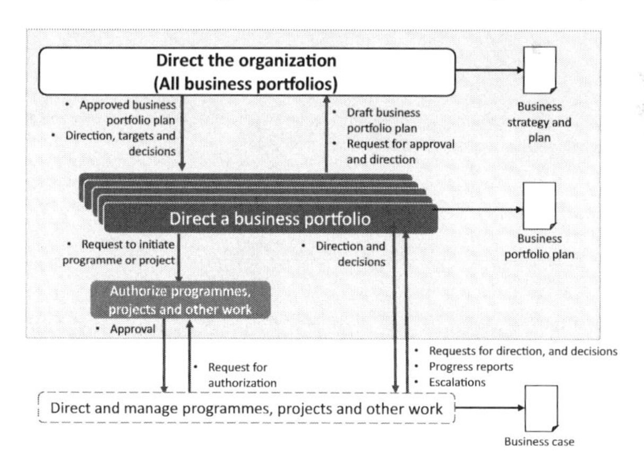

Figure 11.2 Business portfolio management

The organization can comprise any number of business portfolios, each of which is governed by a **business portfolio plan**, the approval for which usually gives no authority for actual work to take place. Programmes and projects are below the 'authorization process', being governed by **business cases**, which are used as the basis for authorizing funding and resources to start work. Each level is accountable to and receives direction from the level above.

Business portfolio management imperatives

Chapter 1 identified a number of commonly found deficiencies in how organizations manage their projects. A key factor in the success of your organization is the speed and effectiveness with which you can stay ahead of, or respond to, changing circumstances. Unless deficiencies in implementing the necessary changes are addressed, you will always lose time and energy in fighting internal conflicts rather than addressing real external opportunities or threats. No organization, however, has just a single project, there are always several running and (as we have seen from the example in Chapter 3) 'projects spawn projects', and there will always be more to come, either as part of a programme or as stand-alone initiatives. Directing this 'portfolio' of projects is a senior management task, as it is this 'bundle' of projects (together with other programmes and work) that will take you from where you are now to your, hopefully, better future. When doing this, you need to keep five imperatives in mind (Figure 11.3):

- strategic alignment;
- strategic balance;
- risk;
- aligned capabilities;
- capacity for change.

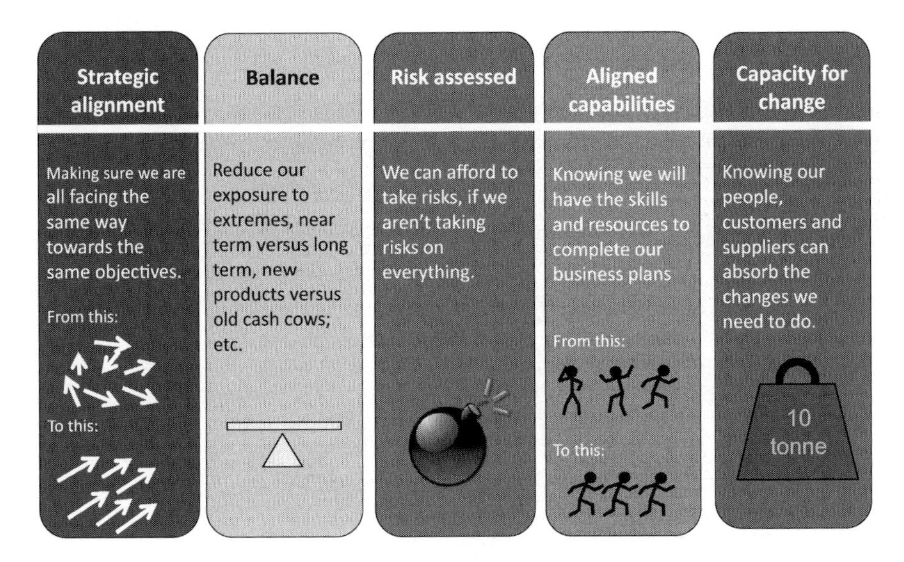

Figure 11.3 Five imperatives of business portfolio management

You need to ensure that your projects (and other work) are aligned to strategy, you have the resources to undertake the work and that those impacted can cope with the resultant changes. Further, you need to be sure everything you are doing does not destabilize the organization's balance nor introduce an unacceptable level of risk.

Strategic alignment

The first imperative is to identify which of the organization's strategic objectives are relevant to the business portfolio and then make sure that each component within the business portfolio is aligned to those objectives. It is the very first lesson from Chapter 2, 'Make sure your projects are driven by benefits which support your strategy'. It is so fundamental that you will come across this again and again as you work through this book.

Balancing the portfolio's aims

Ensure on-going balance across the business portfolio such that the organization does not move, for example, to an extreme market position or sacrifice long-term sustainability to short-term gain. The aims of organizations are varied and so deciding what 'balance' means can only be done with a good understanding of the organization's context and strategic objectives.

Turning down 'good' work in order to preserve the long-term future of the company

A company which worked both in its UK (home) market and overseas found that over 80% of its work came from its overseas market, which, whilst in the short term was profitable, was known to be gradually declining as the local client countries became able to undertake the work themselves. The company took a deliberate step to increase its market share in the UK to be in a good position when the overseas market eventually declined. This move also had the effect of forcing the company into developing higher, value added expertise and services, which could then be exported later.

Balancing the risk

In the context of financial services, a portfolio is a range of investments held by a person or organization. A business portfolio, as described in this book, is a special type of portfolio. Like investments in the stock market, a business portfolio should be balanced with respect to risk. At business portfolio level, the performance of individual projects (or even programmes) becomes less critical. You can accept some being terminated, some being late, some costing too much or simply delivering the wrong thing. What is more critical is that the portfolio, as a whole, performs well enough to move your business forward effectively and efficiently. You should have some (but not too many!) projects which are risky, which should they succeed will create a step change in your organization's capability. Without these, you will be too rooted in today's paradigms and not reaching for new horizons. You should, however, not allow the risk on an individual project or groups of projects to become so high that they threaten the existence of the organization.

Making sure you have the capability to do the work

No matter how well your project aligns with your strategy or how robust your business case, it is worthless unless you can actually complete the project and operate the outputs it creates. This means you need the right capabilities (resources, materials, money and skills) to undertake the work required in the business portfolio. Often, the main constraint in many organizations is the availability of the right people at the right time. Even with the right resources, choosing how to deploy them can be a challenge, as we found out in lesson 7 form Chapter 2, as there is often tension between ensuring the efficient use of resources and being effective in getting the work done. Chapter 14 looks into this challenge in more detail.

From a business portfolio perspective, a lack of capabilities and resources hindering the progress of the organization might be dealt with by triggering a range of initiatives such as recruitment, business transformation, acquisition or continuous improvement projects. One thing is certain, if you carry on authorizing work which cannot be carried out, you'll be wasting money and needlessly stressing the people who are trying to achieve unreachable targets. If there is no way to get the capabilities you need, an alternative approach needs to be taken. New entrants to markets are often far quicker to spot alternative approaches as they do not have the legacy investment and mind-set of more established companies to hold them back. It is impossible for any person working at project level to drive such radical changes and that is why business portfolio management is necessary; looking after such challenges is what the business portfolio team is there for; it is true business leadership.

Ensuring the changes can be absorbed

Even with the 'right' project identified and resources available, you might still not be on to a 'winner'. If the outputs from the project are to make any difference, they need to trigger business changes (outcomes) which would in turn lead to benefits being realized. Inevitably those outcomes will involve people changing the way they work, learning new skills or working to new processes. What if they are already taking on changes from other projects? What if they are also trying to come to terms with changes introduced earlier through recently completed projects? Those people will soon become overloaded or fatigued with change. You might consider that is part of their job and they simply need to face up to it, after all, I am sure we have all been told work-life is about 'change-as-usual' and you'd better get used to it. But what if those people are your suppliers or even your customers? What if those people are your citizens (as in a government project)? Customers and suppliers do not have to work with you and simply might walk away. Citizens could vote you out of office. You often hear people talk about 'being easy to do business with'; if you keep changing how you 'do business', your customers and suppliers might start pushing back, unless it also makes it easier for them. As a business portfolio sponsor or manager, it is your task to make sure that each time you submit or approve a project (or other work) for authorization, those impacted by the subsequent changes are likely to be able to cope with the change on top of everything else they are doing. See Chapter 25 for more on the management of change.

Portfolio of anything you want!

You can use the word 'portfolio' to represent any bundle or grouping of projects or other work you have selected for the convenience of management, reporting or analysis. After all, projects are investments of time and resources made by organizations to achieve benefits. Thus, the full set of projects undertaken within an organization is its 'organizational portfolio'. The set of projects held by a project sponsor is a 'sponsorship portfolio'. The set of projects managed by a person or function is a person's 'management portfolio'. Those undertaken in a particular part of the world are regional portfolios.

Business portfolio roles and accountabilities

If a business portfolio is a chunk of the business plan, who is accountable for it and what are those accountabilities? For small organizations, we have seen that 'business portfolio' might be a redundant term – the organization is the business portfolio. It therefore follows that the role of the CEO or President and their senior executives is relevant. These roles are concerned with the leadership of change, and this requires both sponsorship (benefit/needs) and management (making it happen).

If you have a number of business portfolios in your organization, you will need somebody (an individual or group) accountable for directing them. There is no accepted term for such a body; I will call this the 'business strategy and planning board'. It could be the organization's main management board or an offshoot of it.

You also need roles to direct and manage each business portfolio; I will call these roles 'business portfolio sponsor' and 'business portfolio manager' respectively. You can use whatever role titles you want to fit the culture and language of your organization. Finally, you need a role which authorizes the start of each portfolio's programmes, projects or other work; I'll call this the 'portfolio review group'.

Together, these business portfolio roles (shown in Figure 11.4 aligned to processes and in Figure 11.5 as a structure) form a key part in the governance of the organization. The other aspect of governance is authorization, where 'permission' is required before any work is started or funds spent. I deal with this in Chapter 13.

Business strategy and planning board

The business strategy and planning board is accountable to the chief executive for setting business strategy, directing corporate change and ensuring the business portfolios realize the benefits required. In particular, this board should:

- set the organization's strategic direction, policy and priorities;
- set business outcome and benefits realization objectives and constraints for the organization as a whole and for each business portfolio, to ensure maximum benefits and progress towards the strategic vision;
- allocate funding and resources to each business portfolio, through the approval of the organizations business plan and its subsidiary business portfolio plans;
- monitor and review benefits realization, delivery and costs from all business portfolios, directing corrective action where appropriate.

Portfolio review group

The portfolio review group is accountable to the business strategy and planning board for cross-functional (or cross-process) decisions relating to authorization, prioritization,

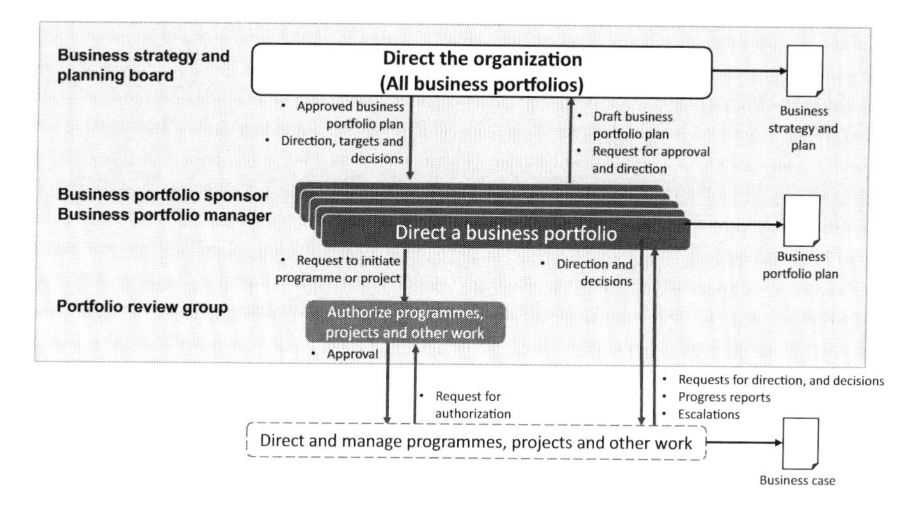

Figure 11.4 Business portfolio management and its associated roles

This figure builds on Figure 11.2. The **business strategy and planning board** sets policy and direction for the whole organization which are set out in the business strategy and plan. They approved the plans for each business portfolio, each of which is directed by a **business portfolio sponsor** and managed by a **business portfolio manager**. Programmes and projects are initiated by the business portfolio manager, through the authorization process, managed by the **portfolio review group**.

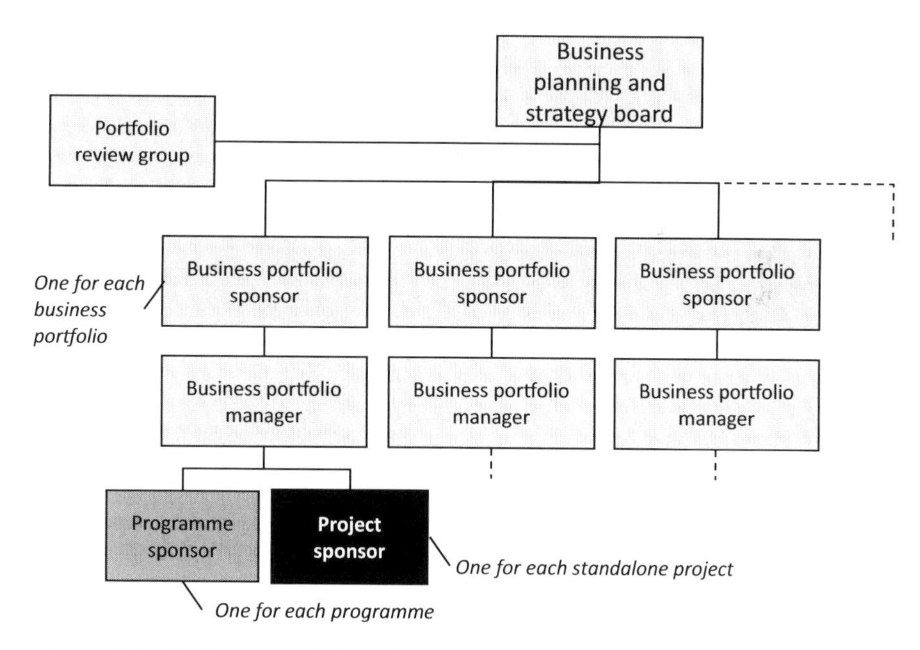

Figure 11.5 Business portfolio roles structure

The business planning board is accountable for setting the strategy and direction for the whole organization and each business portfolio. The sponsor for each business portfolio is accountable to the business strategy and planning board for the assigned portfolio. Each sponsor for each component within the portfolio is accountable to the respective business portfolio sponsor. The portfolio review group is accountable to the business strategy and planning board for the commitment of resources and finances.

issues escalation and resource allocation. Its primary aim is to keep the pipeline of projects and other work flowing. In particular, the portfolio review group should:

- authorize programmes, projects and other work;
- oversee the delegation of authority, where appropriate;
- ensure the business portfolio can be delivered within existing funding allocations and resource constraints;
- ensure the organization's business plan reflects the components of the portfolio (programmes, projects, etc.);
- ensure each project or change is committed to by those required to develop it and operate the outputs post-release;
- identify options for resolution of issues involving resources and escalate for resolution if necessary;
- ensure that departments have planned in 'white space' resources to undertake initial investigations;
- communicate/publish the current status of the organization's business portfolio;
- act as the change control point for the organization's business portfolio;
- be the owner of the authorization process.

We will look more deeply into this important role in Chapters 13 and 14.

Business portfolio sponsor

The business portfolio sponsor is accountable to the business strategy and planning board for directing a business portfolio, ensuring that their assigned portfolio realizes the required benefits. In particular, the business portfolio sponsor should:

- provide business direction to the business portfolio in terms of making decisions, initiating new work, terminating unwanted work and resolving issues;
- approve the business portfolio plan prior to authorization by higher authority;
- ensure the combined benefits for the business portfolio are realized;
- ensure the scope of the business portfolio covers the needs of the business;
- direct priorities between contending work within the business portfolio.

A business portfolio board can be created to support the business portfolio sponsor in carrying out his/her accountabilities, particularly in respect of senior management alignment and engagement.

Business portfolio manager

The business portfolio manager is accountable to the business portfolio sponsor for day-to-day management of the business portfolio, ensuring that the portfolio is planned and managed to ensure maximum focus and speed of benefit realization. In particular, the business portfolio manager should:

- prepare and maintain a plan of scope, timescale, benefits and costs for the business portfolio, including reserve for as yet unidentified work;

- select and manage the projects and other components within the business portfolio to realize the required benefits and to ensure that the contributions of all parts of the organization are taken into account;
- assign the sponsor role for each programme or project and leadership role for other components within the business portfolio;
- approve or authorize projects and other work, as delegated;
- monitor performance against the business portfolio plan, initiating corrective action and ensuring the integrity of the plan (including interdependencies);
- provide regular progress reports to the business portfolio sponsor and senior management;
- ensure use of best practice methods and organizational procedures.

A business portfolio office is likely to be needed to support the business portfolio manager with the necessary administration, expertise, knowledge and resources to ensure the previous accountabilities are undertaken effectively. See Chapter 27 for more on support offices.

Business portfolios and cross-organization leadership

Test the business portfolio roles. Replace the words business portfolio sponsor with CEO and the business with shareholder. Notice the fit? The implication is that the role is truly one of leadership and not one of functional management. Business portfolio sponsors might have some functional accountability, but in the world of business portfolios, they need to take on a cross-organization role, as any single function can achieve very little on its own. (See lesson 6 in Chapter 2) You will see a similar correlation between COO (or deputy CEO) and business portfolio manager.

Defining your own roles

Organizations are very different, and it is not possible to design a 'one size fits all' set of roles and accountabilities. For example, I have separated the portfolio review group role from the strategy and planning board, as the former deals with decisions as part of operations. It is also focussed on the practicalities of implementation and is likely to meet more frequently that the strategy and planning board and have different membership. Notice it doesn't deal with the questions of whether a project *should* even be undertaken, only whether it *can* be undertaken (the business portfolio sponsor is accountable to the strategy and planning board concerning whether it is the right project). In some organizations the portfolio review group and strategy and planning group could be combined, if membership is common and the different focus of the two groups is not lost. Also, you can call these roles whatever you want to fit your organization's pattern and language. What you should do, however, no matter how you design your approach, is make sure the accountabilities listed are taken on by somebody or some group.

Prerequisites for effective business portfolio management

So, what are the prerequisites for managing a business portfolio? Much depends on what scope you decide your business portfolio is to cover. We'll look at this in detail in the next chapter, but for now, let's start on the assumption that the main part of your portfolio is concerned with dealing with a lot of projects and so the central 'plank' to managing your business portfolio is that projects are reliably managed, as these are the vehicles for introducing change. No matter how you scope your portfolio, this aspect will need to be covered. To do this, you need a staged approach to directing your projects to enable key decisions to be made at known points (gates), together with good project management and control techniques. See Part II. To make these work, you must provide an organization-wide (not just departmental!) approach for:

- **maintaining strategic alignment**: ensuring you choose the 'right' projects to turn your strategy into action;
- **decision making**: you must make decisions which are respected, are the right ones and are made in the best interest of your organization;
- **allocating resources**: you must ensure that you have visibility of the availability and consumption of resources you need to undertake your projects and operate the outcomes;
- **business planning, forecasting and reporting**: you should make the management of your portfolio a part of the management of your business – it is not an optional extra. When a project is fully authorized, it should 'lock in' to the business plan;
- **maintaining your project and other work component register**: you need to know what projects and other work you are doing, when, why, who for and who's impacted. You need to know which pieces of work are 'stand-alone' and which are part of a programme;
- **managing finance**: you should ensure funding follows the projects you want to undertake and is not just allocated to the departments who carry out the work to make their own decisions on how to spend it;
- **managing change**: you should have you the skills to know how to assess what stress your people, customers and suppliers are currently experiencing and to manage the transition from the current way of working to what you want to happen;
- **enterprise risk management**: Nothing is certain and whilst each programme or project manager will be looking at the risks to their programme or project, should understand what the overall risk to the organization is and how to keep this within an acceptable level.

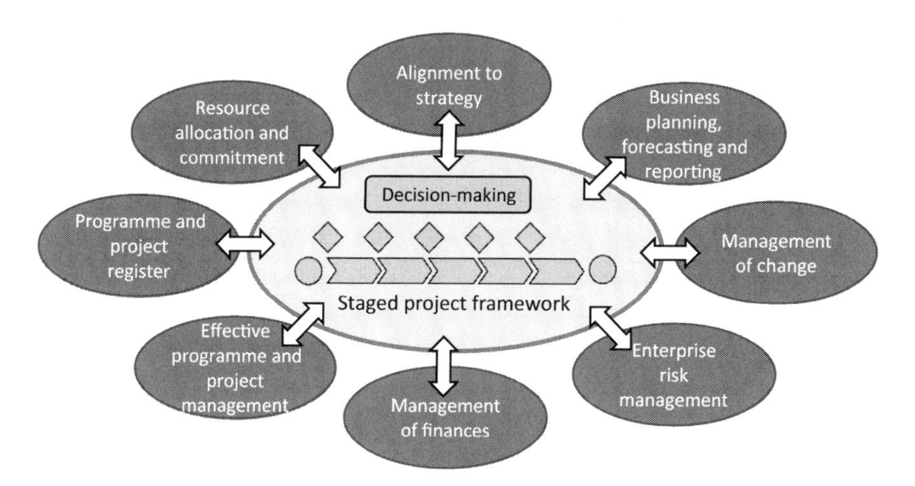

Figure 11.6 The environment for managing your business portfolio

The staged project framework is the central 'plank' around which the key aspects of managing the portfolio revolve. Whilst shown as separate items they in fact have a large degree of interdependence.

I have taken it for granted that you understand the operations of your business or organization! The lack of any of the capabilities described earlier and in Figure 11.6 has implications:

- **poor strategic alignment:** you may end up doing the wrong projects;
- **poor decision making:** decisions made in one part of the organization might be overturned by another part, decisions could take too long or too many projects could be initiated;
- **poor resource management:** you don't know if you have sufficient resources to finish what you've started, let alone start anything new and operate the new processes, systems and capabilities you have introduced;
- **poor business planning, forecasting and reporting:** if you do not integrate the future as created by your projects into your organization's business plan, how will the plan make any sense and how will you know if you have anyone to use the outcomes? If you don't provide the right people with the information needed to undertake their roles, how can you expect them to make the right decisions?

- **poor project register management:** if you have no list of or method for tracking your projects and other work, they won't be visible, and people are unlikely to know what has been authorized and what has not. You will not know which projects are interdependent. You might even have two or more projects trying to solve the same problem;
- **poor fund management:** you won't know if you have the funds to complete the projects you have started or be able to fund new ones. You will spend your money on the wrong things;
- **poor management of change:** despite your project managers delivering what is required of them, you won't realize the benefits as the business changes and outcomes simply do not materialize;
- **poor enterprise risk management:** you have too many high-risk projects which threaten the sustainability of the organization. If, as 'Murphy's Law' predicts, what can go wrong does go wrong, you might be left without a business at all.

Business portfolios are a key tool which enable you to tackle these needs. Business portfolios are chunks of your strategy and your business plan. They are the link between what you do now and what you will do in the future. They therefore also form the most appropriate vehicle for dividing up your organization's spending, with the highest priority business portfolios attracting the greatest investment. Finally, business portfolio management provides the control environment for ensuring you do not overload your organization with too much change. Notice what this implies: business portfolios are an integrated part of the organization and not something separate that is 'done to the business' on top of everything else. As such they should work seamlessly with all your organization's systems and processes, such as:

business portfolios are an integrated part of the organization

- individual and team performance management;
- human resource management;
- financial management;
- procurement;
- communications management.

The wrong people approving procurement

An organization had its projects under control within business portfolios. Projects were funded based on their business cases and run cross-functionally, drawing on resources from wherever needed. Project gating was working well, with very few problems on over-commitment of resources. The senior team was satisfied that their implementation of business portfolio management was starting to reap rewards for the business. Unfortunately, the procurement system was still configured to work on the old 'silo' basis, where the authorizing manager for each procurement was the line manager of the person making the procurement. Further, the larger the procurement cost, the more levels of approval were required, sequentially up the organizational hierarchy. This led to approvals for procurement often being done without the project sponsor or project manager having any involvement (or even knowledge), despite them being accountable for the spending on the project. Until this issue was fixed, the project manager had to put in place a 'prior approval' process to gain visibility of procurement requests before they went into the procurement system, adding a layer of bureaucracy and cost which, if thought about earlier, would not have been necessary.

Workout 11.1 – The business portfolio management environment

The list of factors needed to control a project portfolio is long. In this workout you should assess your current 'health' and use that as a prompt for discussion to help you decide which might need attention in your organization. Take each in turn and with respect to projects and change initiatives in your organization:

1. Assess, without any in-depth analysis, the effectiveness of each competence – 0 = no capability, 5 = excellent in your organization.
2. Discuss the implications on your organization of any lack of competence in each area and note them down. Do not expect to be excellent in every area.
3. If you are basically satisfied with your assessment, consider whether the competencies you have actually work together as whole.

Competence	*Score*	*Implications*
Project life cycle management		
Programme and project management		
Strategic alignment		
Decision making		
Resource management		
Business planning, forecasting and reporting		
Project register		
Finance management		
Management of change		
Enterprise risk management		

If you have work components in addition to programmes and projects, you will need to define how these are directed and managed.

If you have other work components in addition to programmes and project, these would need to be included in the register.

Workout 11.2 – Forecasting cycles

How often do you do your business forecasting? Annually? Quarterly? Monthly? If you do it annually, consider how you can have confidence in the forecasts. Do you really know so much about the future that you can confidently predict your outcomes a year in advance? Is your organization really in such a slow-moving, competitive environment?

Note: forecasting is predicting what your management accounts and information systems will tell you in the future. Setting a target is not forecasting.

Workout 11.3 – Starting to understand your portfolio

Take your output from Workout 3.1, which should be a diagram of the work your organization is doing (programmes, projects and other work). Unless yours is a very simple organization, this picture is likely to be very complicated with a lot of boxes and numerous lines criss-crossing your white board or wall.

1 Try to rationalize the number of items on the board. Projects with arrows going both ways between them are probably the same project even if you've defined them as separate. To test this, ask yourself if either one of the projects on its own produces any benefit to the business. If both projects are needed, they are either the same project or projects within the same programme. Look for clusters of linked projects which have no arrows between them and other clusters. These clusters might be your business portfolios. Look for projects which don't have significant benefits: mark them for possible termination.
2 Look at interdependencies; the more complicated and interwoven, the riskier the portfolio becomes. Think of ways of re-scoping projects to create a set of programmes and projects which are relatively independent (minimum interdependencies) and will realize benefits early. Re-scoping entails moving the accountability for producing a deliverable from one programme or project to another.

12

Defining your business portfolio

Do the right thing?

Strategic and business planning context

Choosing the business portfolio's scope and boundaries

Setting your mission, vision and values

Understanding your current performance and prospects

Recognising your constraints

Describing your business portfolio's objectives

Now, do it all over again!

Strategic alignment, a key tenet of portfolio management, is impossible without a clearly defined and communicated strategy.

"If you always take the short term view, you are always in trouble."

CARL-PETER FORSTER, b1954,

- **An effective organization is more likely to thrive than one which is merely efficient.**
- **Strategy is pointless unless communicated in a way that is understood and actionable.**
- **Effective business portfolio management is value driven for the benefit of the organization as a whole.**
- **The clearer your mission, vision and values, the easier it is to set the business portfolio's objectives.**
- **A business portfolio's objectives need to be described as outcomes, not outputs.**

Do the right thing?

Defining the business portfolio is the first and most critical step in business portfolio management. This is where objectives are set; everything that happens afterwards depends on this being right. You have probably heard about 'doing the right thing' and 'doing it right'. The former is about undertaking activities to further strategic aims and the latter is about doing them in a consistent way. 'Doing the right thing' is related to effectiveness, whilst 'doing it right' is more about efficiency. An effective organization is more likely to survive and thrive than one which is merely efficient. Being effective and efficient provides a sound basis for success as an organization.

This book is about 'doing it right'; it provides the concepts to undertake business portfolio management. It cannot, however, tell you what 'the right thing' is for your organization to do. Setting the strategic direction is a fundamental accountability of the senior leadership team and no book, process, method, consultant or observer can relieve them of that accountability. If you are a senior leader, this book can only prompt you to ask yourself the questions which will provide you with useful answers and encourage you to organize your business to maximize its effectiveness.

Defining a business portfolio depends on having a thorough understanding your organization, its aims and how it works. This is as true of a government department as for a multi-national corporation, private company, partnership, non-government organization (NGO) or charity, regardless of size. If you do not understand the purpose and aims of the organization and how it is currently performing, you cannot hope to be successful. Without a clear strategic direction:

- business plans will not be aligned;
- short-term focus is likely to prevail, to the neglect of the long term;
- projects and other work might conflict;

- priorities might be confused or come into conflict;
- decisions might be contradictory.

Without a 'right way' of working:

- there will be inadequate information for decision makers;
- too many projects might be started;
- resources might become overstretched;
- processes might be incompatible;
- roles and accountabilities might be confused, overlap or be missing.

Any of the mentioned problems could lead to organizational failure.

Strategic and business planning context

Often the development of strategy is treated as external to, and hence an input to, portfolio management. I would argue, however, that the development of strategy and the defining of the business portfolio should be part of the same process. The reasoning for this is if 'definition' is about setting objectives to support strategy, those who set the strategy should also set the objectives. The setting of strategy and objectives is generally done by the senior leadership team.

A strategy is pointless unless communicated in a way that is understood and actionable. Strategic alignment, a key tenet of portfolio management, is impossible without a clearly defined and communicated strategy. The interface between those who develop strategy and those who set portfolio objectives and their respective accountabilities must be clear. If business strategy and objective setting are undertaken in isolation, by separate teams, they are less likely to be aligned, leading to misunderstanding, crossed accountabilities and extra cost.

There are many different views on what a portfolio is. As a business portfolio sponsor or manager, you need to understand where your portfolio sits in an organizational context and what its scope is. Does the portfolio cover the whole or a part of the organization? Is it simply the work undertaken by one function? Does the business portfolio include 'business as usual' as a component, as well as programmes and projects? It is vital to understand the context because the management level above the portfolio should set the objectives (or, as a minimum approve those objectives) and define any constraints. Further, accountabilities should be traceable down and across the whole organization. For example, if the business portfolio:

- covers an entire company, the objectives should be set and approved by the senior management team;
- covers a division or region in a company, the objectives should be set by the 'parent' company;
- is part of a higher-level portfolio, the objectives should be set by the sponsor of that higher portfolio.

Choosing the business portfolio's scope and boundaries

Objectives need to reflect the business portfolio's scope and boundaries; there is little point in giving a portfolio sponsor an objective that he or she has no influence over. If yours is a simple organization, it is likely that you will have just one portfolio, so there is no need to decide what parts of the operation are in which portfolio, as there would only be one. You will, however, still need to select the scope or extent of the activities to be included within the portfolio (and hence managed as a business portfolio). The following sections look at some common permutations together with the pitfalls and advantages of each.

Objectives need to reflect the business portfolio's scope and boundaries

A portfolio of programmes and projects

Figure 12.1 shows an organization with five units (departments or functions, depending on your terminology), where the portfolio (a) includes just the programmes and projects. All of unit V and the rest of the other units' activities (b) are run separately by the respective unit heads on traditional cost centre lines. By managing the programmes and projects as a portfolio, you can make sure they are aligned, determine the scope of each to minimize interdependencies and make effective and efficient use of resources. Such programmes and projects, however, deliver into 'business as usual', the accountability for which is under the separate

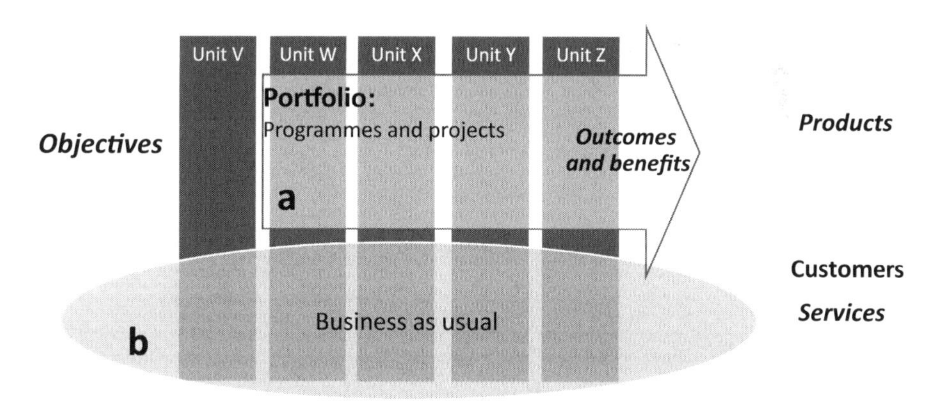

Figure 12.1 A portfolio which covers an organization's programmes and projects only

An organization with five units (departments or functions, depending on your terminology), where the portfolio (a) includes just the programmes and projects. All of unit V and the rest of the other units' activities (b) are run separately by the respective unit heads on traditional cost centre lines.

leadership of each unit head. The portfolio on its own would not, therefore, include everything needed to ensure the organization's strategy is realized. You might also find some resources have to be shared between projects and business as usual; if so, you'll need to decide who sets the priorities and makes decisions when these come into conflict. Many people from a project management background relate to this type of portfolio as it only covers programmes and projects, not other work, such as business as usual.

Programmes, projects and 'other work'

Notice the definition of a business portfolio in Chapter 3 includes 'other work' (such as business-as-usual), implying business as usual should be included within the scope of a business portfolio. By including business-as-usual in the scope of a business portfolio, the portfolio sponsor can manage them together, balancing resources and funding across both elements and reacting to any sudden downturns or changes in the volume of business as usual work. How you breakdown business-as-usual depends on your business model and its associated value chain and business processes. Each business process should be associated with a value chain and treated as a specific category of 'other work'.

Figure 12.2 illustrates a portfolio (a) which includes business as usual (represented in the diagram as processes and other work). The processes would be cross-functional and focussed on customer needs; they would be 'joined up' and represent the flow of work, across the units, needed to operate the business. This approach is

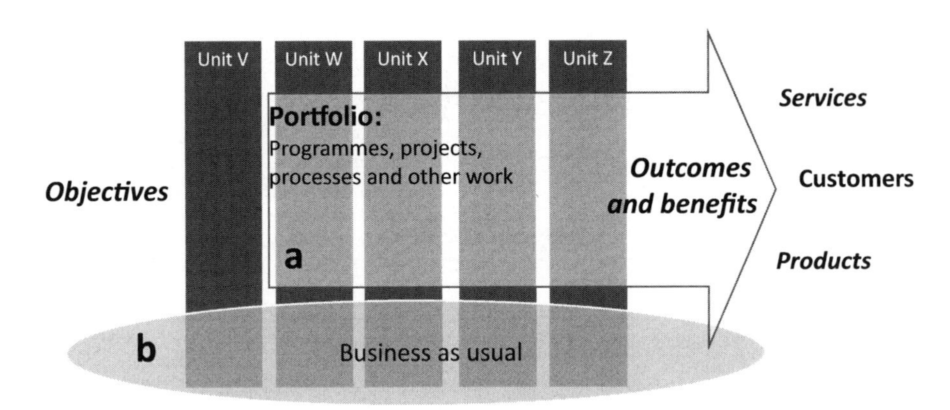

Figure 12.2 A portfolio which covers programmes and projects and part of an organization's business as usual operations

A portfolio (a) which includes business as usual (called in the diagram, processes and other work). The rest of the organization's work (b) is run outside the portfolio.

more responsive than one where each unit has its own targets and processes and 'coordinates' (or not!) across unit boundaries. The business portfolio is run on the horizontal dimension of the organizational matrix, driven by customer need and value. Note that the portfolio still only covers part of the activities for four units; all of unit V and some parts of units W to Z (b) are still outside the scope of the business portfolio; these would be run on traditional cost centre lines. The business portfolio's funds would be allocated on a project by project and process by process (or portfolio component by portfolio component) basis rather than to each unit's cost centre. Direction would be given by a portfolio sponsor and programme/project sponsor (or business lead for other work) rather than divided between each unit manager. This avoids the tendency of unit managers to sub-optimize their part of the operations to meet their budget targets and what they see as their objectives. This approach occurs where central services, such as for HR and finance, are managed as traditional costs centres, or when the business portfolio only covers part of the operations, such as one product or service line.

A complete business portfolio

Figure 12.3 goes one step further and shows an organization where the business portfolio covers the entirety of its operations. Organizations might move to this complete model when they have common ERP and finance platforms, as is increasingly the case in todays connected businesses.

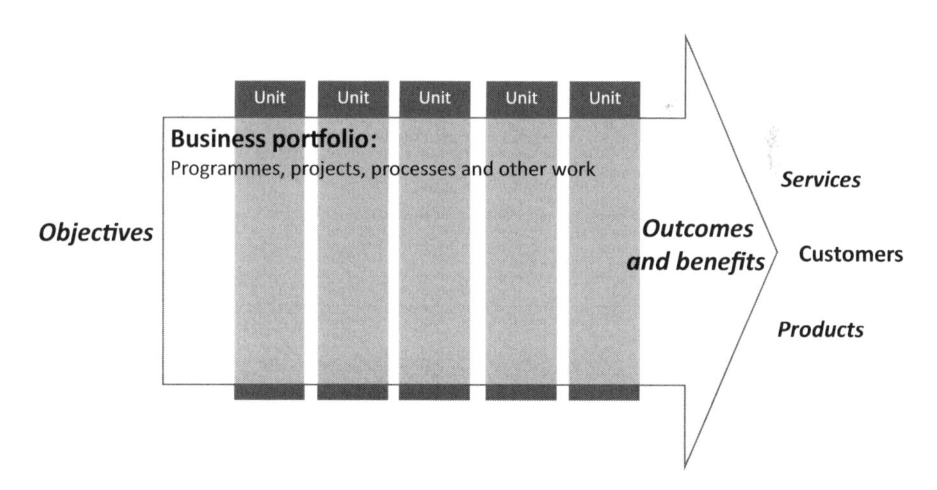

Figure 12.3 A portfolio which covers the entirety of an organization.

A business portfolio which covers the entirety of an organization's operations, including programmes, projects and business as usual.

An organization with a number of business portfolios

An organization always has at least one business portfolio.

An organization always has at least one business portfolio. In a large and diverse organization, it is often necessary to have more than one portfolio (what are effectively sub-portfolios), each of which is directed towards particular objectives. For example, one large multinational company I worked with had five business portfolios. Three portfolios were targeted at different market segments, one at service development as most of the services in the customer segments were built on the same platforms and one for the central services, like finance, facilities and HR. Each of these had sub portfolios, reflecting the objectives (outcomes) they were targeted with. The scope of the business portfolios was such that interdependencies between them were minimized. The service development and central services were separated out as it was not cost effective for each of the three market segments to have its own. Figure 12.4 illustrates an organization with multiple portfolios. Note the portfolio in Figure 12.4, could be treated as a single portfolio with sub-portfolios, as long as the relationships and accountabilities are clear and traceable; labelling the levels is your choice.

There is no set pattern for defining a business portfolio's scope and boundaries; each needs to be designed to suit its circumstances; the permutations are limitless. The aim is to run the organization driven by customer needs and value rather than on a purely cost constrained basis. Each business portfolio or sub-portfolio should be as independent as possible (i.e., with minimum interdependencies), bearing in mind the cost effectiveness of shared services. By taking this approach, direction and decisions should be focussed on value and benefits. This avoids the situation where decisions made by the head of a unit are driven by each unit's manager based on cost centre budgets and annually determined objectives. Such decisions are not necessarily aligned and frequently sub-optimal; objectives can become out of date, especially in fast moving environments.

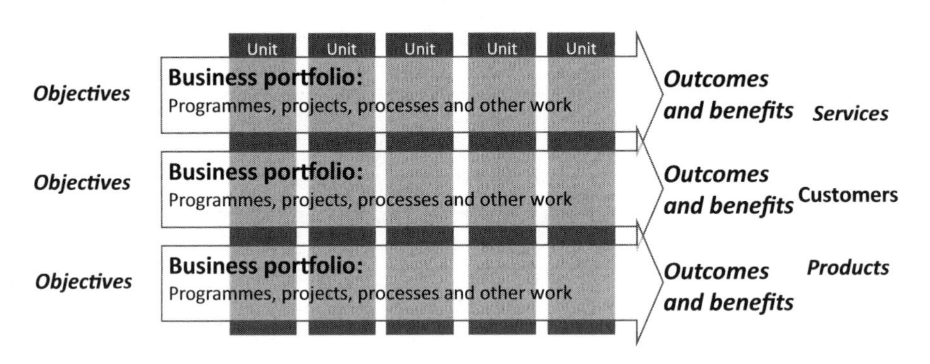

Figure 12.4 An organization with three business portfolios

An organization, which is too large to direct as a single business portfolio, can be managed with multiple portfolios.

When a 'portfolio' is useful but is not a business portfolio at all

If the portfolio is the collection of work undertaken by a particular function, say 'IT projects' undertaken by an internal IT department, the question of who sets objectives can become problematic. Effective business portfolio management as advocated in this book is value driven for the benefit of the organization as a whole. An IT portfolio, as described in Figure 12.5, is simply a collection of tasks undertaken by IT specialists for other parts of the business. IT specialists, however, should not be setting objectives for, say customer services, manufacturing or financial processing but providing capabilities to meet the needs of those groups, each of which should have their own business objectives. The objective of 'portfolio management' in such cases is usually to optimize the use of the IT department's resources and budgets. The danger of treating this type of portfolio as if it is a value based business portfolio, is that it makes it more likely to be driven by departmental costs and efficiency rather than overall business effectiveness, thereby deflecting the direction of the organization away from what really needs to be done. To avoid confusion, it is best to not call such an entity a 'portfolio'; it is simply the work the IT department does. Whilst 'IT' has been used as an example here, the same logic applies to any functional group.

Effective business portfolio management as advocated in this book is value driven for the benefit of the organization as a whole.

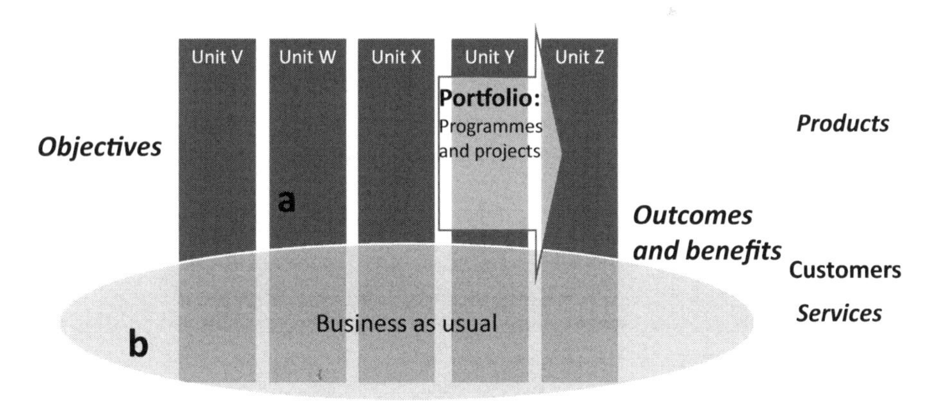

Figure 12.5 Not really a business portfolio at all

This is probably the commonest portfolio of all, contained within a single department. It is a way of ensuring the departments resources are used efficiently.

Setting your mission, vision and values

To set a business portfolio's objectives, the organization's mission, vision and values must be clear:

- **the mission** states the purpose of the organization, why it exists, what it does and who for:
- **the vision** sets out the organization's aspirations for the future;
- **values** influence behaviours and the way the organization achieves the outcomes defined in its vision.

The mission spells out what the organization is all about, the 'strategic intent', centred on the here and now.

The vision is the purpose guiding the whole organization towards a clear outcome and ensures focus for taking your organization forward, whilst staying true to the mission. Everything done within an organization should be aligned with and traceable to its mission and vision.

Values influence and constrain the behaviours of people within the organization to stop the end justifying the means. Simply complying with the law and regulations is often not enough. There are many activities and practices leaders choose not to do, as they consider them unethical, even if legal. Values can hurt; if your values are in the public domain, any infringement, no matter how small, could attract adverse publicity. That's tough but exactly what values are for, so get them right!

The clearer your mission, vision and values, the easier it is to set the business portfolio's objectives.

The clearer your mission, vision and values, the easier it is to set the business portfolio's objectives. As a vision doesn't usually include enough detail to provide explicit direction, it ought to be broken down into a number of 'focus areas' (four to six usually works). These often relate to topics found in the various strategy frameworks, such as the Ansoff matrix, McKinsey's strategic horizons or Treacy and Wierseman's value disciplines. The following are examples, but you can create others more appropriate to your organization.

- **Compliance**: what you need to do simply to stay in business, as driven by relevant legal or regulatory requirements.
- **Market expansion**: taking your products or service to new geographic areas or customer groups.
- **Market balance:** ensuring all your eggs are not in one basket (high risk).
- **Product leadership**: providing new products and services, either through innovation or 'first follower' approaches.
- **Stakeholder engagement**: for example, improving customer satisfaction by engaging your customers, or encouraging preferred suppliers to want to work with you.
- **Customer intimacy:** encouraging customer loyalty and repeat business for the same or new products and services.

- **Operational efficiency:** providing your services or products at a cost to achieve the required margins or stay within a pre-defined cost envelope, thereby keeping prices low.
- **Employee relations**: providing conditions to attract and retain the number and quality of staff you need; this is especially relevant if your business relies on specific skills.

Be aware that even if the mission and vision are stable, focus points might need to change. In other words, you could change how you will achieve the mission.

Choosing a focus point

When Mercury Communications was set up as part of the telecommunications duopoly in the UK to challenge the previously state-owned British Telecom, 'customer intimacy' was selected as a focus. 'Product leadership' was rejected as the services were not innovative nor particularly new. 'Operational efficiency' was rejected as it was recognized the business was not efficient; the view was that competitive pricing was attracting customers and being efficient at a time when margins were still high would not achieve the customer growth needed. 'Customer intimacy', however, was likely to work. At that time, people loved to hate British Telecom (on account of their poor customer service record), and an alternative provider was attractive, even though it wasn't that much better! As a result, a lot was invested on branding and how call centre staff related to customers, defusing complaints and focussing on customer retention. It worked. Of course, as time passed, Mercury had to deal with operational efficiency as BT's prices came down, new market entrants appeared, margins were squeezed and telecom services became more like commodities.

Developing and agreeing mission and vision statements is difficult. I expect many of you have sat through tedious meetings where individual words are argued over until you just want to escape. For that reason, some leaders either don't bother, accept anything or abdicate the responsibility to others, such to a consultant or their strategy department. The danger in this is that the business leaders might not understand the vision and values themselves and even inadvertently start to work against them. By all means, leaders should use specialists and consultants but when the definition work is complete, the words should reflect **the leadership team's** vision and values, both as individuals and as a senior team. People who are actually involved in the 'word-smithing' are more likely to have a deeper understanding of the statements as they have been on a journey, with their colleagues, to understand viewpoints, opinions and the way certain words are interpreted. Only when this level of understanding is reached will they be ready to communicate it more widely within the organization and convey the necessary level of passion. If an organization is serious about business portfolio management, the business portfolio sponsors and managers should be part of the senior team and involved in setting the mission and vision from which their portfolio's business objectives will be derived. If people truly believe the mission and vision, what they say will be seen as authentic and more likely to be taken notice of.

Passion trumps all

Organizations with poorly articulated missions and visions (or none at all!) can succeed. Leaders who exhibit unified purpose and passion instinctively communicate their mission and vision. You often find this in start-ups, where the founder is the owner and has a huge influence. As the organization grows and matures, however, this can get diluted through the layers of management and extended teams, such that a more explicit approach is needed.

There are countless books and papers on setting strategy and objectives as well as numerous supporting tools. All aim to help channel your thinking. Some tools, like Cascade Strategy, draw on a range of different approaches, allowing you to tailor the approach to suit your needs and then track progress. Other tools, such as BusinessOptix, enable you to model your organization and see through the layers of complexity to what really matters by controlling today and navigating tomorrow.

Once you understand the organization's mission and vision, start considering the business portfolio's objectives, each of which should be aligned with and traceable, via a focus point, to the vision, influenced and constrained by the values and be the source for the objectives of the component parts of the portfolio (such as projects). See Figure 12.6.

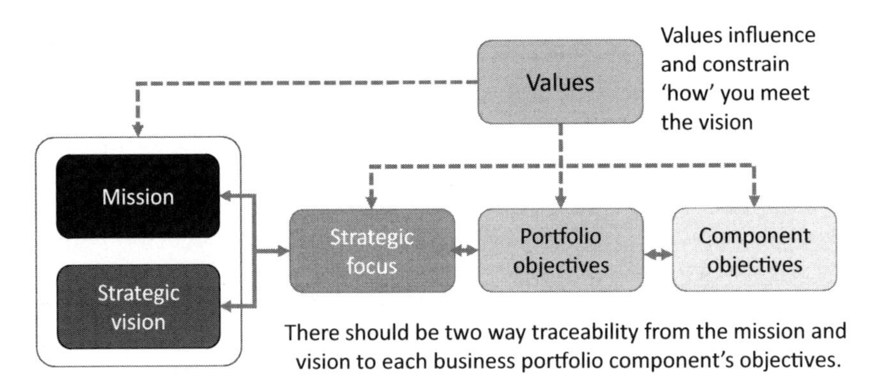

Figure 12.6 Business portfolio vision, values, focus and objectives

Each of the business portfolio's objectives should be aligned with and traceable, via a focus point, to the vision and will be influenced and constrained by the organization's values.

Understanding your current performance and prospects

Very rarely is a business portfolio defined from a totally new venture; there is usually a legacy of operational performance. Poor performance or performance which is below that expected in your sector, is an indication of where action is needed and new or revised objectives setting. Similarly, the possible futures for your organization need to be understood. Will your services or products still be in demand? What are competitors doing? Do entrants to your market have radically different offerings or operating models? Are disruptive technologies emerging or likely to emerge? Are there any social, environmental or legal issues which could impact you?

the possible futures for your organization need to be understood.

Poor performance and a pessimistic forecast for future performance might be an indicator that you should withdraw from a particular activity and concentrate on other priorities to reach your vision. A key problem with any on-going organization is that it just keeps 'doing what it has always done' with little thought to whether this is still relevant. This is sometimes referred to as 'following a recipe'. All too often, each year's budget is simply the previous year's budget plus (or minus) 5%. This is particularly evident in organizations which concentrate on keeping costs down as a priority over other objectives. It is true that everything should be affordable, but affordability relies just as much on the revenue as on costs.

An on-going organization will have a number of programmes, projects or initiatives under way, which are already consuming resources but should move the organization forward on reaching fruition. Again, just because they have been started, it does not mean they have to be (or can be) completed. If an initiative no longer aligns with the strategy, there is no point in carrying on spending with little chance of any return; carrying on might even be detrimental to other products or services. You need to understand how each initiative, project or programme serves the vision and what aspect it focusses on. Organizations seldom fail because one project went awry; business failure comes when the totality of the change doesn't make sense or is unachievable.

Recognizing your constraints

Whilst objectives should not be too constrained, some attention should be paid to business realities. Funds, resources and energy are not unlimited, and a totally unconstrained objective could be ridiculed by those tasked with meeting it; we have all heard stories about strategists having their heads in the clouds. On the other hand, objectives should require people to think and plot a new course if the one they are on will not achieve the aims. Just because something is difficult, it doesn't mean it is unrealistic. Lord Rutherford once said, "We've got no money, so we've got to think."

"We've got no money, so we've got to think."

Those setting objectives need to be cognizant of the:

- availability of funds and resources;
- overall risk across the portfolio and how it relates to the organization's risk appetite;
- organization's capability and capacity to ensure the portfolio can be delivered;
- impact on those affected by the outcomes and whether they can take on the changes.

It is important is to ensure both short- and long-term objectives are covered. Generally, the 'short-term' should feed and fund the 'long-term'. Early benefits are good, but neglecting the long term is usually bad, as emphasized by Carl-Peter Forster, when he was Group CEO at Tata Motors (including that of its British unit, Jaguar Land Rover), "In my opinion, if you always take the short-term view, you are always in trouble."

Some things must be done in the right order

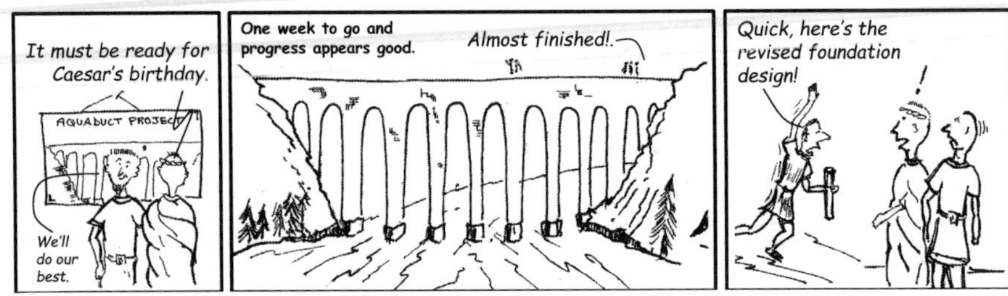

Describing your business portfolio's objectives

Most people are familiar with 'SMART' objectives, which has a few variations, some of which are shown in brackets:

S – specific (significant, stretching)
M – measurable (meaningful, motivational, matter of fact)
A – agreed (attainable, achievable, acceptable, action-oriented)
R – realistic (relevant, reasonable, rewarding, results-oriented)
T – time-bound (timely, tangible, trackable)

'SMART' can be a good basis for writing business portfolio objectives, but be careful not to mix up different interpretations of this commonly used acronym. For example, 'Agreed' simply means what it says: the objective is agreed between the person who is accountable for meeting the objective and the person who sets the objective. This is very different from 'attainable', which is similar to 'realistic', as something which is not attainable can hardly be called realistic! I like 'Matter of fact' as it doesn't force you to use metrics but allows you to verify achievement of outcomes in other ways, such as observation.

In practice, a business portfolio should have two to five objectives. Too few will not give sufficient coverage and too many might risk losing focus and not meeting them all.

Business portfolio objectives need to be described as 'outcomes', not 'outputs'; they should describe a changed state for the organization; something the business will be doing differently in the future. An output is simply a deliverable and is not enough; for example, a business portfolio aimed at providing a seamless customer experience which delivers a customer service platform which is not used has not actually achieved anything. What happens as a result of the platform being used is what matters. And if that platform doesn't work, then another way has to be found to meet that objective.

Do not dwell too deeply on 'measurable', or you might simply do what you can measure rather than what you need to do. If something is hard to measure, think of other means to verify that the change has happened. For instance, some changes can simply be observed a 'matters of fact' without needing measuring at all.

There are always financial constraints and targets, but these should happen as a result of doing the right things. Setting objectives solely in financial terms does not help anyone align to anything, as the numbers could be achieved by any means. Financial targets should be considered more as constraints. Anyone can set a budget of £1m or demand a cost cut of 15%; it takes a true leader to set a vision and determine how that vision can be met in practice.

Now, do it all over again!

Whether you are working in a new organization or one which is already running, defining a business portfolio is difficult, but unless the business portfolio is defined and objectives are set, the organization will lack direction. All organizations are constrained by the practicalities of cash flow and resources and the objectives should reflect this. Consequently, there is likely to be some iteration in defining objectives before they are finalized. Further, as all organizations operate in a real and changing world, the mission, vision, values, focus and objectives will need to be reviewed and possibly changed to reflect this.

Workout 12.1 – What is the scope of your portfolio?

1. Draw a figure like Figures 12.1 to 12.5 to show the extent of your portfolio.
2. Which model does it most closely resemble?
3. Which issues hinder you in directing or managing your portfolio? List them.
4. What changes could be made to make it easier to run your portfolio whilst maximizing value to the organization?

Workout 12.2 – Challenge your existing values statements

1. Look at your organization's values statements (if it has them!) and try to understand what each word and phrase tells you. Is it clear what every part of it means?
2. As a portfolio sponsor or manager, does it provide boundaries or constraints on how you conduct business? Is it ambiguous?
3. Test the statements by verifying each of your major initiatives or activities against them? Do they fit or is there some ambiguity?
4. Test the statement against initiatives you believe are ridiculous to see if they fit.

Workout 12.3 – Discovering your values

This is best done as a group with facilitation.

You already have values, regardless of whether they are written down. People tend to take values for granted; they are the beliefs and principles that serve as a hidden foundation for what you choose to do and how you choose to get things accomplished.

1. As individuals, each person writes what they believe are the organization's values. One value per Post-IT® sticker and as many as people want. Make each statement up to five or six words. Make sure you include a verb as values are about behaviour, so a 'doing word' is vital! Values expressed as a single word, such as 'Open' are likely to be interpreted in different ways.
2. The facilitator should place each on a wall, reading it out and checking that people in the room understand what is meant. As each new Post-IT® is added, the facilitator should cluster those that cover similar topics.
3. The group should then come to a consensus on those to be discarded.
4. The group should then decide which of the remaining clusters should be kept. Try to aim for four to six at the most.
5. Work as a group to rephrase each cluster with a single statement.
6. Come to an agreement on which you believe reflect the organization as it is.
7. Challenge whether the values from step 6 are appropriate for the future. Are they enough? Do they need to change?

Workout 12.4 – Testing your organization's mission and vision

The mission is a statement about the here and now. The vision is a view of the future.

1 Look at your organization's mission and vision statements (if it has them!) and try to understand what each phrase and words tells you. Is it clear what every part of it means? Beware of words like 'world-class', 'global' and 'best-in-class'.
2 Is the vision unique to your organization or could it be applied to any organization?
3 As a portfolio sponsor or manager, does it help you set the direction for your business portfolio? Is it ambiguous?
4 Test the statements by verifying each of your major initiatives or activities against them? Do they fit or is there some ambiguity?
5 Test the statement against initiatives you believe to be ridiculous to see if they fit.

Workout 12.5 – Testing your organization's focus areas

1 Identify your organization's focus areas. These might be difficult to find, but the strategy document should contain something along those lines. Remember, different organizations will use different terminology.
2 If you succeed in all the focus areas, will the vision be achieved? If not, you will need to challenge and revise the focus areas until, as a whole, they cover every part of the vision.
3 Test each of your major initiatives or activities against the focus areas? Do they fit? Are all focus areas covered?

Workout 12.6 – What, no mission, vison or focus?

If your organization has no mission, vision or focus statements, setting objectives for a business portfolio and checking strategic alignment is likely to be difficult, if not impossible. In such cases, you will need to make assumptions to create your own mission, vision and focus points and have those verified when the business portfolio objectives are set and agreed. This approach reduces the likelihood of misunderstandings by being open, at least within the senior team, about your base assumptions. It is better for disagreements to surface early, rather than after significant funds and resources have been committed. When writing the statement, use plain language that is easy to understand, avoids ambiguity and stays true to your values. This is best done as a group with facilitation.

1 Define your mission
    - Brainstorm the following:
        - Make it clear **what** business you are in.
        - Make it clear **why** you are in this business.

   - Describe **how** you conduct your business. This will be related to your values.
- Rephrase this into a memorable statement and ensure it is customer focussed.

2 Define your vision

- Imagine you are five to ten years in the future and brainstorm:
   - What a successful organization is doing; and what it has achieved.
   - What services products is it offering and to whom?
   - How are people using those services? How is it benefiting them?
- Rephrase this into an inspirational statement which will arouse emotion or passion.
   - Make it clear why the organization is different from its competitors.
   - Have a powerful introduction that captures the memory.
   - Make it ambitious but achievable.
   - Describe the outcome in concise language.
   - Write in the future tense.

These are necessarily simple, but this should give you're a start and at least prompt you to ask the right questions; there are whole books and consulting services devoted to this one topic.

Workout 12.7 – Setting business portfolio objectives

1 Look at your current objectives.
Do they describe an outcome?
Are they 'SMART'?
Do they align to the mission, vision and values of the organization?

2 Test the each of your major initiatives or activities against the objectives? Do they fit?

3 If the answer to any of the questions is 'no', decide what corrective action is needed to get a positive answer.

13

There are too many projects to do!

Principles for selecting projects

Project authorization

Far too many projects!

Putting the brakes on

By having a staged approach, you do not need to make all the decisions at the same time. A staged framework enables you to make the necessary choices when you have adequate information to hand, rather than being forced into premature and ill-conceived choices.

"When you choose anything, you reject everything else."

G K CHESTERTON, 1874–1936

- **Do not put a lid on the creation of new ideas for projects.**
- **As soon as you can, make an informed decision on which projects to continue.**
- **Having decided to do a project, do it, but stop if circumstances change.**

Principles for selecting projects

There are always far more ideas to change a business than resources or money can support. To make matters worse, if your strategy is not clearly articulated, people will compound the problem by coming up with even more ideas.

How can you:

- make sure you undertake only those projects you need to?
- limit the number of projects without stifling the good ideas?
- kill off the projects which have no place in your organization?
- ensure that speed through the project life cycle is sustained?

The staged framework within which each project is managed, coupled with effective decision making and business planning, is the key to ensuring you can do all of this. By having a staged approach, you do not need to make all the decisions at the same time. A staged framework enables you to make the necessary choices when you have adequate information to hand rather than being forced into premature and ill-conceived choices. Keeping to three basic principles will help you do this.

1 Do not put a lid on the creation of new ideas for projects.
2 As soon as you can, make an informed decision on which projects to continue.
3 Having decided to do a project, do it, but stop if circumstances change.

This chapter uses the gates and stages of the project framework described in Chapter 8 and repeated in Figure 13.1, but you can adapt it to suit your own life cycle and terminology.

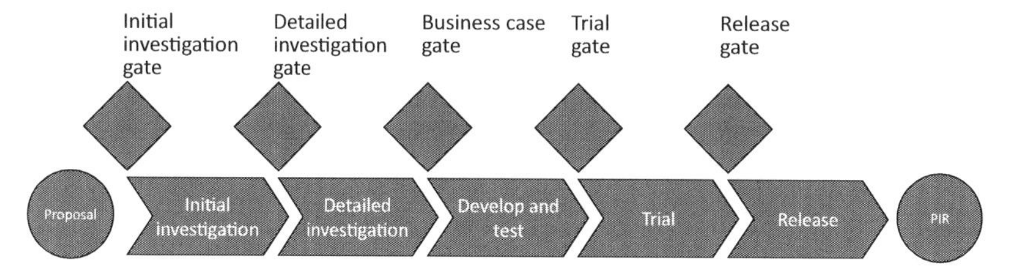

Figure 13.1 The project framework or life cycle used in the chapter

This chapter is based on the project life cycle described in Chapter 8 and illustrated in Figures 8.4 and 8.5.

Do not put a lid on the creation of new ideas for projects

Encourage the creation of as many ideas as possible, letting them originate in any part of the organization and from any source, even suppliers and customers! Stifle creativity and you risk stifling the future growth of your organization. The use of a targeted proposal template should ensure that enough information is collected about an idea (or need) to enable the organization to review and approve or discount it on the grounds of strategic fit. Remember, a project should always have a champion (project sponsor) who needs the benefits it is intended to realize.

The decision to start a project is taken at the initial investigation gate and is only concerned with the first of the three gate questions, "Is there a real need for this project and, in its own right, is it likely to be viable?" Once the authorization is given, the initial investigation stage should start.

A reminder of the key questions

The decision points prior to the start of each stage are called gates and answer three distinct questions:

1 Is there a real need for this project and, in its own right, is it viable?
2 What is its priority relative to other competing projects?
3 Is there funding to undertake the project?

If you are uncertain of your strategy, you are likely to create more proposals than if you really understand the direction the organization is to take. However, if a proposal passes this first gate, you know that at least one person (the project sponsor) believes the proposal does fit the strategy and should, therefore, be evaluated. In this way you will benefit from knowing how your senior managers are converting their understanding of strategy into action. The aim of portfolio management is to make projects visible: the 'outing of projects'. If a manager is undertaking projects his colleagues consider to be outside the needs of the business or of low priority, this will be exposed. Consider also what else such a manager may be doing which may be contrary to the direction of the business but is invisible!

I cannot over-emphasize the impact that a clearly communicated strategy and business plan has on the effectiveness of selecting projects for your business portfolio.

As soon as you can, make an informed decision on which projects to continue

The first gate in the project framework enables you to start investigating the unknowns on the project. You should know why you are undertaking the project but, on some projects, you might not know what your solution is or how you will achieve this. The objective of the project's initial investigation stage is to reduce uncertainty. The output of the initial investigation should provide sufficient knowledge to:

- confirm strategic fit;
- understand possible options and implications;
- know what to do next.

In other words, you will have the information at hand which will enable you to make an informed decision on whether the project should continue rather than one based on your own 'feel' and limited knowledge.

Priority only becomes an issue if you have insufficient resources to do everything you want to do, when you want to do it. If you have only one project to do, its priority is easy to assess. It is PRIORITY ONE. If you have more than one project to review, the question of priority has no significance if you have the resources and funding to do them all when they are required. Priority only becomes an issue if you have insufficient resources to do everything you want to do, when you want to do it.

Priority only becomes an issue if you have insufficient resources to do everything you want to do, when you want to do it.

As relative priority should be assessed on an informed basis, it cannot happen until you reach the detailed investigation gate when the output from the initial investigation stage is available. Once each project sponsor has confirmed that they still need the benefits their projects will realize you will need to concentrate on:

- the 'doability' of the projects;
- their fit within the overall portfolio.

Doability takes for granted a project sponsor's assessment of strategic fit and the soundness of the project on a stand-alone basis. Doability concentrates mainly on whether:

- you have the resources to undertake all the projects;
- you have the funding to undertake all the projects;
- those impacted by the projects' outcomes can cope with the changes required.

The portfolio assessment looks at the balance of risk and opportunity for the proposed projects together with those within the current project portfolio. The aim is to assess whether this mix is moving the organization in the desired direction and risks are contained to an acceptable level.

If you are unable to undertake all the new projects, you will need to make comparisons between the projects and choose which should continue. This implies the need to batch your projects at the detailed investigation gate to make this decision. In practice, you will be deciding which projects should proceed, but it is more powerful, from a decision-making viewpoint, to prioritize the benefits the projects produce rather than the activities the project comprises.

It is more powerful, from a decision-making viewpoint, to prioritize the benefits the projects produce rather than the activities the project comprises.

After all, the benefits are what you need, not the projects. By prioritizing benefits, you will:

- stay focussed on why you are doing the project;
- trap the projects, which have little or no real benefit!

If the prioritization decision coincides with a review and reforecast of your business plan as a whole, you will be able to build whichever projects and benefits you need into the business portfolio plan. This should ensure the totality of future benefits from 'business as usual' and projects adds up to the figures you need (Figure 13.2).

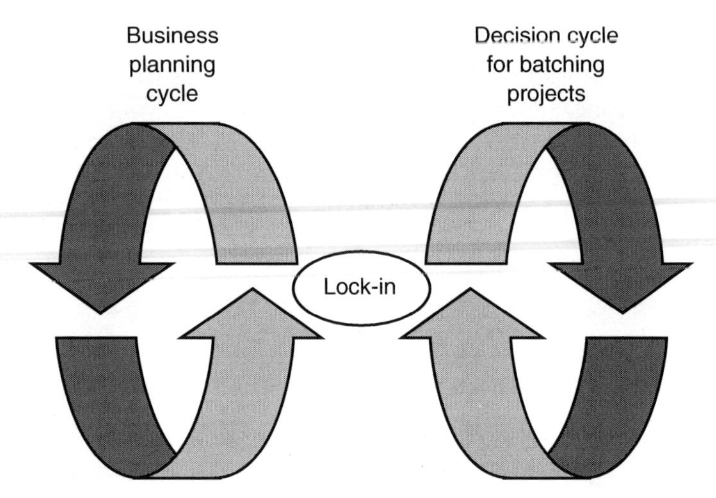

Figure 13.2 Matching the batching time frame to your business planning cycle

If the decision as to which projects should continue coincides with a review and reforecast of your business plan as a whole, you will be able to build whichever projects you need into the plan, whilst ensuring the totality of future benefits from 'business as usual', and projects add up to the figures you need.

Beware of trying to do too much!

Enough information?

Decisions can always be avoided by saying there is not enough information. This is a very effective tactic for blocking anything you do not want. There will never be enough information for decision making. You need to assess what is at stake if your decision is wrong and balance this against what is gained if your decision is right. With a staged approach to projects, coupled with good control techniques, you are be able to 'de-risk' decision making to the extent of answering the question, "Can I continue confidently with the next stage of this project?" You very rarely find you are making life and death choices.

Having decided to do a project, do it – but stop it if circumstances change

Having decided to carry on with a project after the review at the detailed investigation gate, it is useful to presume it will continue. You, therefore, need only assess the relative merits of the new projects you wish to introduce to your business portfolio. This avoids going back over previous decisions and puts an end to the 'stop – go' mentality ineffective authorization processes can cause. It is a strange phenomenon that today's 'good ideas' tend to look more attractive than yesterday's and raise the temptation to ditch yesterday's partially completed projects in favour of new ones. The result is that not a lot is finished!

It is a strange phenomenon that today's 'good ideas' tend to look more attractive than yesterday's

A presumption that on-going projects will continue does not mean a project should never be stopped. For example, imagine there are sufficient resources to do all except one new project and this cannot be done because a key, scarce resource is already occupied on an on-going project. In such circumstances, the presumption is the on-going project continues and the new project is delayed. The new project, however, might have considerably more leverage, resulting in greater benefit, in a shorter time and at less risk than the existing one. Hence, you might take the view that it serves the overall interest of the organization better to terminate the existing project and start the new one. Such decisions should be very rare, otherwise your portfolio will be unstable, running the risk of delivering nothing of value. If this happens a lot, it might be symptomatic of poor business planning and a lack of clearly understood strategy.

Note that if you do this, you will be either suspending or terminating a perfectly good project; it is sacrificed for the greater good of the organization but this is not likely to make the decision makers popular with the sponsor of the affected project. This is, however, a feature of good business portfolio management, and it is through such choices that better decisions can be made. It's a business decision, not personal.

Ability to change – decision making

To what extent does the ability to devolve decision making influence the speed of change? In the planning stages of a complex change programme, the project managers identified each point requiring either a board decision or the decision of one of the directors. In all, about 200 decisions were identified, spanning nine change projects (Figure 13.3). This begs some questions:

- were the board members capable of making that number of decisions in the timescales required, on top of all their 'business as usual' decisions?
- could any of the decisions have been delegated to relieve the senor team of the burden?
- what impact would the decision overload have had on the programme?

Notice the shapes of the two graphs. The board as a group has most of its decisions towards the front. As the projects get under way and alignment achieved, most of the decisions are made by individual directors. The shape of the curve for the directors has both a front-end peak and peaks towards the back. This is because they not only authorize the initial work but also authorize putting into use the outputs from the projects. This does, however, also highlight a common failing of many boards: losing interest after the initial decisions!

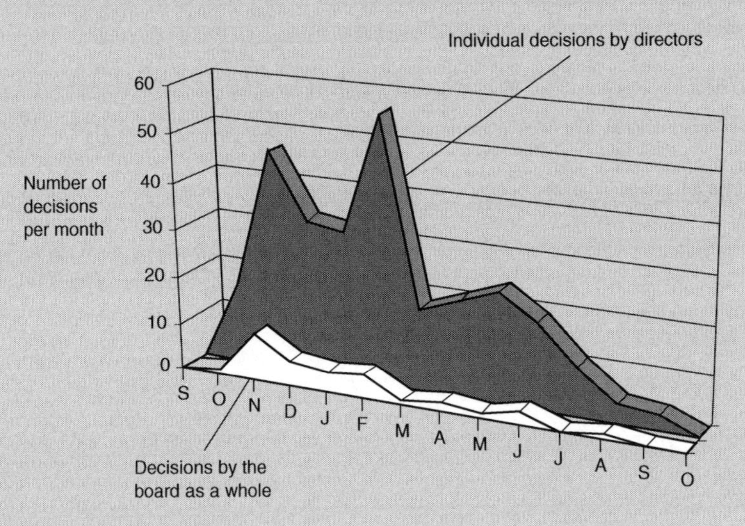

Figure 13.3 Decisions

In the planning stages of a complex change programme, the project managers identified each point which required either a board decision or the decision of one of the directors. In all, about 200 decisions were identified, spanning nine change projects.

Project authorization

Harnessing the project framework

The management of projects within a business portfolio relies on a basic staged project framework being in place, such as in Figure 13.1. To ensure speed through the project stages you should minimize referral to any decision-making bodies outside the project sponsor. Inefficient decision making at gates can double a project's timescale. Nevertheless, there must be sufficient referrals, at appropriate points, to ensure the business portfolio is under control, stable and likely to meet the organization's needs. Referrals from the project organization to the portfolio management organization usually happens at the gates as shown in Figure 13.4. Thus:

- the management of a project is concerned with the work within the stages leading up to a gate decision;
- the management of the portfolio is concerned with ensuring decisions are made at the gates.

Where an issue on a project requires a change, a referral needs to be made from project management to business portfolio management during the course of a stage.

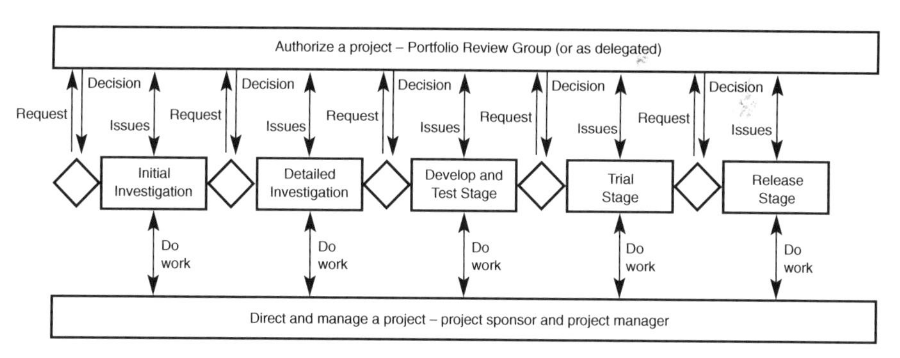

Figure 13.4 Interaction between managing a project and managing the portfolio

Referrals from the project to the 'authorization process' happen primarily at the gates. Where a problem (issue) on a project requires a change, a referral may be made during the course of a stage. In this diagram, the portfolio review group is shown as the authorizing body; for large organizations, there is likely to be some delegation, say to the Business Program Manager.

The choice of who contributes to the decisions is crucial. The decision is the culmination of the three distinct questions we addressed earlier. The roles relating to these are as follows:

- **The project sponsor** answers the gate question 1 – is there a real need for this project and is it viable? The project sponsor is the person who requires the benefits the project will realize and who assesses its fit to strategy.
- **The portfolio review group** answers the gate question 2 – what is the priority? It assesses the 'doability' and integrity of the portfolio as a whole.
- **The investment review group** answers gate question 3 – do we have the funding? It ensures that the financial 'rules' are applied, the project makes sound business sense and funds are available to do it.

I have shown the roles of the investment review group and the portfolio review group separately. In practice it is better, but not essential, if the roles are combined into a single body, such as by putting a finance representative(s) on the portfolio review group. Note how both these role titles are used to illustrate a role required in the governance of projects and make it easier to describe them in this book; what you choose to call them is up to you; there are no commonly accepted terms. Also, you may choose to combine a number of roles in a single body.

Gate decisions

Assuming the project, on its own, makes sound business sense, what else does the portfolio review group need to know about a project or investment before it can commit itself to it?

- What are the project's overall business objectives and do they align with the organization's strategy?
- When will we have the resources to carry out the project (people and facilities)?
- Do we have enough cash to fund the project?
- How big is the overall risk of the portfolio with and without this project?
- Can the organization accept this change on top of everything else we are doing?
- After what time will the project cease to be viable?
- On what projects does this project depend?
- What projects depend on this project?

Let us look at each gate in the project framework from the perspective of a decision maker.

Initial investigation gate

Whilst all gates are held by the portfolio review group, this first one is often delegated to a business portfolio sponsor or manager. Any proposal which they believe is worthy of further study should pass into the initial investigation stage without undue delay, with a defined timescale and budget (Figure 13.5). Some organizations have a special group to review proposals and take decisions on which should proceed, but an effective business planning process should make such a group unnecessary. In most cases, except for extreme reactions to market or business conditions, the business plan should spawn the proposals, hence they will have effectively already been approved, at least in outline.

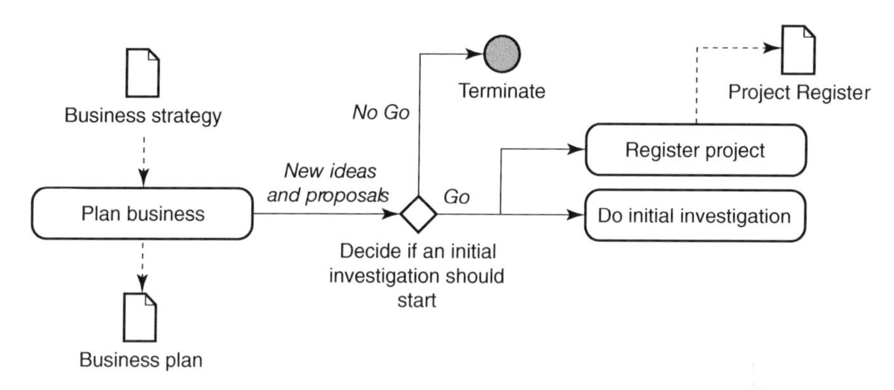

Figure 13.5 Decision process at the initial investigation gate

Any idea that the project sponsor wishes to study further should be investigated without delay.

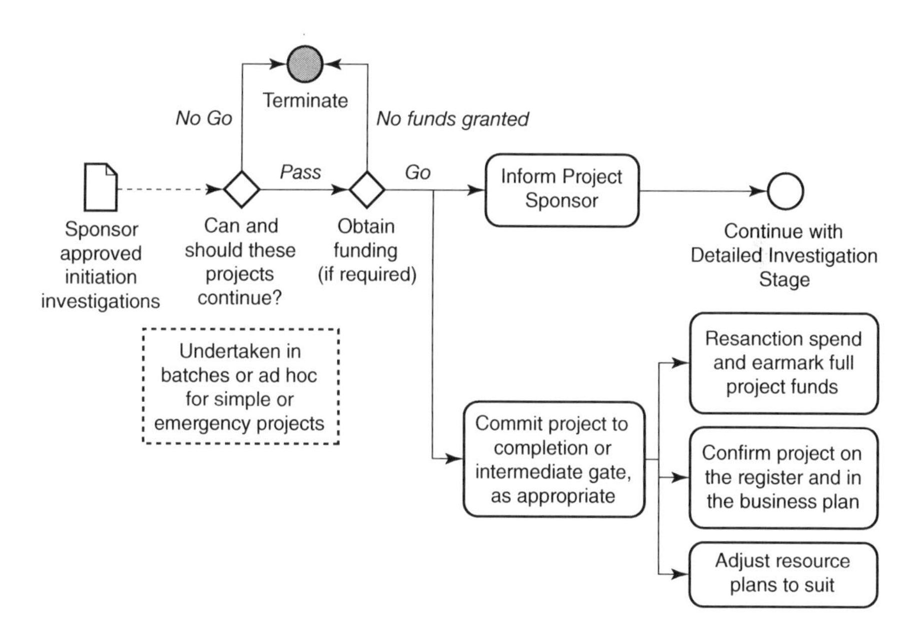

Figure 13.6 Decision process at the detailed investigation gate

Decide which out of a number of projects should proceed to the next gate. This can be done either in batches, to aid comparison, or on a controlled ad-hoc basis.

Detailed investigation gate

Assuming each project has been approved by the project sponsor, the candidate projects are batched, and an informed choice is made as to which should be authorized to proceed into detailed investigation (Figure 13.6). Four basic questions need to be asked by the portfolio review group:

- Is it likely that all these projects can be completed?
- Can the changes be absorbed?
- Is the overall risk acceptable?
- If we include them all, is the portfolio balanced?

If the answer to these questions is 'yes', the full batch of projects proceeds into the detailed investigation stage. If, however, all the projects cannot be done, then those in contention need to be compared and a decision made as to which of them should proceed. Alternatively, the constraint might be identified and, if possible, released (e.g., by rescheduling a project, by sourcing new resources or raising additional finance). The intention should be that any project allowed past the detailed investigation gate is going to move to completion unless it loses its viability or becomes unacceptably risky. For this reason, you can think of this as the NO gate, i.e., where the business says "No, we will not consider that project further." A project in which confidence to complete it is relatively high and committed to completion need not be referred back to the portfolio review group unless it hits an issue requiring a reassessment of the project viability and resourcing which impacts other work.

If the portfolio review group lacks the authority to approve the funding, the investment review group should then decide if funding should be approved to complete either the project or at least the detailed investigation stage.

The capacity of the whole organization is the capacity of the bottleneck

When the portfolio review group assesses whether a project can be done, it must satisfy itself that ALL aspects can be done: operational, technical, marketing, process, etc. If one part is missing, there is little point in doing any of the other work. Your ability to complete projects is, therefore, constrained by the bottlenecks imposed by scarce resources for a particular aspect of work. By undertaking a formal 'doability' check, you can identify any such constraints and assess the cost to the organization of missing or insufficient resource. This cost is the sum of the benefits from the projects you could not do because that resource was not available. This simple concept is the basis for what is called Critical Chain in Eli Goldratt's Theory of Constraints.

Business case gate

At the business case gate, the portfolio review group is concerned only with those projects it could not previously commit to completion. Again, the same questions are asked at the detailed investigation gate. In principle, any project which has reached this gate is one which the business wants to continue. Forward planning should have earmarked the resources required to complete the project. As the presumption is to continue the project unless circumstances dictate otherwise, what is looked for here is confirmation that the project can continue. For this reason, the development gate should be considered as the YES gate. The investment review group provides funding to complete the project if this had not been given earlier. At this point, the project and subsequent operational costs, benefits and resource needs should be locked into the business plan. The process is shown in Figure 13.7.

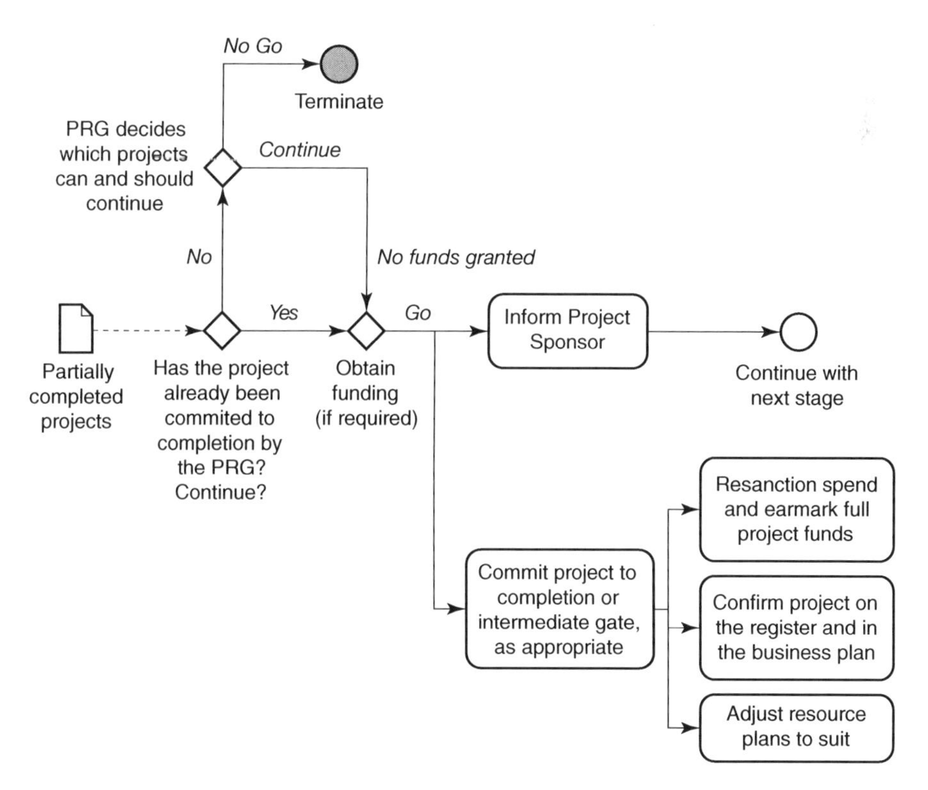

Figure 13.7 Decision process after the detailed investigation gate

If the project has already been committed for completion and is still within the scope, timescale and cost approved at the detailed investigation gate, no referral to the portfolio review group is needed. The project just continues, obtaining extra funding, if not already allocated. For all other projects, the portfolio review group needs to confirm it within the project portfolio.

Trial gate

The project sponsor is often delegated accountability for approving the move into trial. This is usually based on advice given by project assurance or the project manager and team. The project sponsor holds the decision, as it is he/she who requires the benefits. Trials are often the first time a change is presented to the outside world, and it is in the interests of the sponsor to ensure that premature exposure does not compromise downstream benefits. The portfolio review group needs to be consulted only if there are any prioritization issues. In such cases, the same process in Figure 13.7 is followed.

Release gate

Again, this is primarily the project sponsor's decision. As with a trial gate, the sponsor does not want the benefits jeopardized by releasing the project output prematurely. Alternatively, depending on the scale of the change, this decision could be made by a portfolio management board, project board, or even the organization's main board. The portfolio review group only needs to be consulted if there are prioritization or resource issues or if this gate decision has been explicitly retained by them. In such cases, the process in Figure 13.7 is followed.

Summary of decision-making roles at each gate

Table 13.1 summarizes the decisions at the gates and who is involved. A business portfolio board may delegate the decision to a project board or to the project sponsor. Consider this table as a starting point for you to assess the appropriate decision-making bodies and levels in your organization. Remember, as the project definition document contains a list of deliverables and who has approval accountability, you are able to choose the most appropriate people or groups for each project on a case-by-case basis if your usual rules are not appropriate.

Table 13.1 Example decisions for each role

	Initial investigation gate	*Detailed investigation gate*	*Business case gate*	*Trial gate*	*Release gate*
Business portfolio board	Decides if an initial investigation should start	Confirms the project should continue	Confirms the project should continue	Confirms the project should continue	Confirms the output should be released
Portfolio review group	Not usually required	Decides if the detailed investigation should start	Decides if the project should be completed	No referral needed	No referral needed
Investment review group	Not usually required	Provides funding for the detailed investigation	Provides funding to complete the remained the remained of the project	No referral	No referral
Project sponsor	Approves proposal prior to submission	Approves initial business case and plan prior to submission	Approves business case and plan prior to submission	Approves business case and trial report prior to submission	Approves business case and RFS report prior to submission
Document on which gate decision is based	Proposal	Initial business case	Business case	Ready for trial report	Ready for service report
NOTES	*Projects start as soon as practical*	*Projects batched for a comparative decision*	*Stage starts as soon as practical*	*Stage starts as soon as practical*	*Stage starts as soon as practical*

Issues requiring a high-level decision

Not all projects go according to plan. There are instances when changes to an authorized project are desirable. Unless this is managed, scope, timescales and costs will creep, and the project pipeline will become choked. There will be too much work to do and not enough people or cash to do it. Small changes can be dealt with either by the project manager or project sponsor. However, where a proposed change has an impact on other commitments, the impact must be assessed and the approval of the portfolio review group obtained. The process for handling escalated changes is very similar to that for the gate decisions described earlier. It is just that the need for the decision is driven by unexpected events rather than by reaching a predictable milestone (Figure 13.8).

The proposed change is reviewed by the portfolio review group and, if it can be accommodated within the portfolio, approval is given to proceed. Authorization for any extra funding should also be given, if required. In some cases, the portfolio review group may choose to alter the relative priorities of projects if there are resources or funding constraints. See Chapter 23 for a fuller treatment of change control.

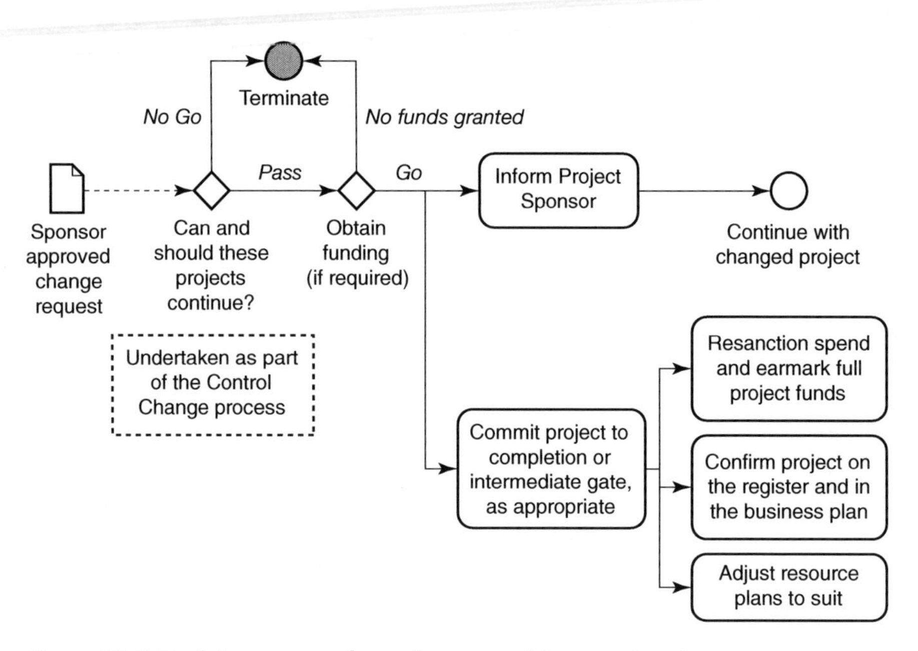

Figure 13.8 Decision process for an issue requiring a major change

The proposed change is reviewed by the portfolio review group and, if it can be accommodated within the portfolio, approval is given to proceed. Authorization for any extra funding should also be given, if required.

Batching projects

Earlier I said that you would need to batch potential projects at the detailed investigation gate to make an informed decision regarding which should continue. If you do not have batching, prioritization can become meaningless. Resources are likely to be allocated to projects on a first come, first served basis rather than on a 'biggest win for the organization' basis. Batching, however, begs two questions:

- how frequently should I do the batching?
- will this slow down the projects by introducing a pause?

As far as frequency is concerned, you need to select a time period which enables a reasonable number of initial business cases to be drawn up and compared with one another whilst not introducing too long a delay:

- annual batching would be too infrequent. The business environment would have changed so much in that time that the exercise would be futile;
- weekly could be too frequent. There would be an insufficient number of projects to allow meaningful decisions to be made;
- between a month and a quarter is probably about right.

Batching does not usually slow projects down in terms of delaying the final delivery date. Unless there is spare resource available to undertake **all** the project immediately, approving them will actually slow everything down. Nevertheless, there might be cases where delaying a project to allow batching to occur might not be in the best business interests of the organization. These cases are for:

- 'simple' projects;
- emergencies;
- exceptions.

Simple projects

Simple projects were discussed in Part II. They are projects where you can see clearly to project completion by the time the initial investigation is completed. They also tend to consume few resources and little money. In such cases, the portfolio review group could allow such a project to proceed into detailed investigation without delay, as the chances of the project compromising future 'better projects' are slim. A project might be thought of as 'simple' by the project manager, but it is the portfolio review group that should decide this. I would also argue that defining, in quantitative terms, what constitutes 'simple' might be a time-consuming and difficult exercise. Further, once you have defined it, you might find that project sponsors and managers massage their initial business cases to fall within the defined threshold to ensure their projects go through without delay. This is not the behaviour you should encourage. It is more pragmatic to phrase the definition of 'simple' in terms of principles and allow the portfolio review group to exercise its own discretion. After all, it should be made up of responsible managers and not merely administrators of predefined 'rules'.

Emergency projects

Emergencies are another exception to batching. I define an emergency as a project which, if delayed, would severely damage the organization. An emergency is not a panic as a result of poor management in a particular part of the organization. Unlike simple projects, emergencies might need to displace resources from on-going projects, thereby causing earlier commitments to be broken. If they are not true emergencies, you will simply be moving the problem from one part of the organization to another. As these projects can have a disruptive effect, the approval for them at the detailed investigation gate should rest with top management (e.g., board), following a detailed impact assessment by the portfolio review group.

Exceptions

Exceptions are any other type of project, other than emergency or simple projects that you wish to continue without going through a batching process. In other words, a pragmatic, but open and deliberate, decision within the principles of business-led portfolio management, which you deem to be in the organization's interest. It is pointless to dream up possible scenarios and rules for these; just deal with them as they arise. By definition, exceptions are 'exceptional', and dealing with exceptions is exactly what senior managers are there for.

Beyond batching by becoming great at portfolio management

The whole reason for batching is for you to decide, from among many contenders, which projects are the 'right' ones to take on.

The whole reason for batching is for you to decide, from among many contenders, which projects are the 'right' ones to take on. By insisting on a named project sponsor, you are obtaining an unequivocal statement that at least one senior manager believes the project is the right project to be doing. By having a portfolio review group, you are making a decision body accountable for ensuring the resource is available and the mix of projects within the business portfolio is right. Poor business portfolio planning makes the jobs of the project sponsor and portfolio review group more difficult. Conversely, good business portfolio planning makes it far easier. Add good information on the current and future commitment of resources and expected benefits and the portfolio review group's task simplifies further. Good business portfolio planning will spawn the right proposals which, in turn, spawn the right projects. This being the case, batching might become less necessary as you become better at portfolio management. If you have a reliable view of what is in the pipeline, ready to arrive at the detailed investigation gate, you will be able to allow more projects to proceed between batches without compromising future projects. Consultants and contractors do this all the time; can they wait and batch up which bids they would like to respond to? No, they have to take a view on their workload, assess the likelihood of success, the availability of resources and the impact on them if they succeed. They then make a choice either to bid or not bid. Remember which organizations were found to have the best resource management systems? See Part I.

Giving up some personal power

Who has the authority to commit resources:

- in a department in your organization?
- in a function within your organization?
- anywhere within your organization?
- in another supplier organization?

Treat the word 'organization' as independent operating division if you are in a global organization. The answers to these questions will probably be, respectively, the head of department, the head of function (often a director or vice president title), the CEO or chief operating officer and someone in that other organization. In other words, the power to apply and commit resources usually lies within the functional or line management hierarchy. If this is the case and organizations need to draw on resources from anywhere to undertake projects, there is only one person (maybe two people) in the organization empowered to do this: the CEO and COO (if you have one). No person, no matter what their title is, has the authority to commit resources which are outside their domains. Unless an organization has structures to make cross-functional commitments, the top people will become overloaded with operational issues. Hence the need for a cross-organization decision-making body, such as a portfolio review group. In effect, the owners of the resources (line and department managers) are giving up part of their power to a cross-functional decision-making body, and it therefore also holds that they should respect the decisions of the group and not unilaterally withdraw resources for their own departmental needs. If the lines of communication work and their representative on the group plays their part, this should pose no problems.

Far too many projects!

So far I have concentrated on decision making on projects where the resources are the limiting factor. This is not always the case. It might be that decision making itself becomes more critical. I have already explained how a portfolio review group can work to ensure that you commit only those projects you have the capacity and capability to implement. There may, however, be too many of these for a single group to deal with and although you might have the capacity to implement them, you might lack the capacity to decide! The first case study in this chapter is an example of this.

In the benchmarking study from Part I, we noted that organizations have some resource which is shared and some which is separate. The former led to greater flexibility, whilst the latter led to easier, more discrete decision making. With separate resources, you can have a dedicated portfolio review group. You will need to rely on business planning to check that the level of resource applied is in line with strategy, as it will not be easy to reallocate these people. Where there is shared resource, you have greater difficulty. How can you divide the portfolio review group into a number of subsidiary parts, capable of handling the volume of projects you have? The options for this include:

- by business area (function);
- by target market plus 'corporate';
- by driver.

If you choose to make decisions based on function, you will fall straight back into the trap of encouraging function-based projects, working in isolation. This is not a rational choice if you want a benefits-driven, cross-functional approach.

You could choose to have the portfolio review groups based on your target markets, bringing the advantage of aligning projects to your customers' needs. Further, if there is little sharing of projects between segments, a logical division would be apparent. You would need to have a 'corporate' level portfolio review group to deal with those projects which did not sit wholly within any particular segment.

Another way is by driver. This has the advantage that you are quite clear as to what the reason is for the project being undertaken. In this approach, you categorize your projects by factors which are directly related to:

- the service or products you offer;
- increasing your capacity to offer more of the same service or product;
- increasing the efficiency of your operations;
- building new overall capability or infrastructures.

Regardless of how you choose to cut up your portfolio review group, you will find:

- decisions from two or more groups will come into conflict at some time. It is vital that you have an escalation route to settle these;

- it will sometimes be difficult to categorize a project. This does not really matter, as all projects should be following the same staged framework, which itself leads to more informed decision making regardless of how you label the project.

Finally, when it comes down to making choices between projects, you will need to ensure the proposed and current projects are aligned and balanced with your corporate strategy. You can encourage this by linking the funding of projects to decision making. Two examples of this conclude the chapter.

Example 1

If portfolio review groups are based on market segments, you could decide, based on your strategy, which is the most critical and which the least important and ration funds accordingly. Thus, if the strategy in segment A is to 'milk cash and withdraw' you would have no funding for new capabilities or operational improvements unless they can also be applied to other segments. You would allocate the major share of the development funds to the most important emerging segment.

Example 2

If portfolio review groups are based on drivers, you decide, from your strategy, what relative importance you need to put to each driver. For example, if you see a need to increase operation efficiency, you would have more funds for the 'efficiency' budget than for the others.

Putting the brakes on

So far, this chapter has dealt with the approach to deciding what to continue; however, business led projects do not always work out as we expect. In some cases, the development of the outputs proves too difficult, lengthy or expensive. In other cases, the opportunity identified has either diminished or disappeared. In both cases, the project might no longer be viable. If following the approach in this book, such circumstances would lead to an issue being raised (see Chapter 23), which would be escalated to the project sponsor or higher for resolution. Remember, it is the project sponsor who is accountable for the business outcome, and therefore it should not be in his or her interest to continue with an unviable project.

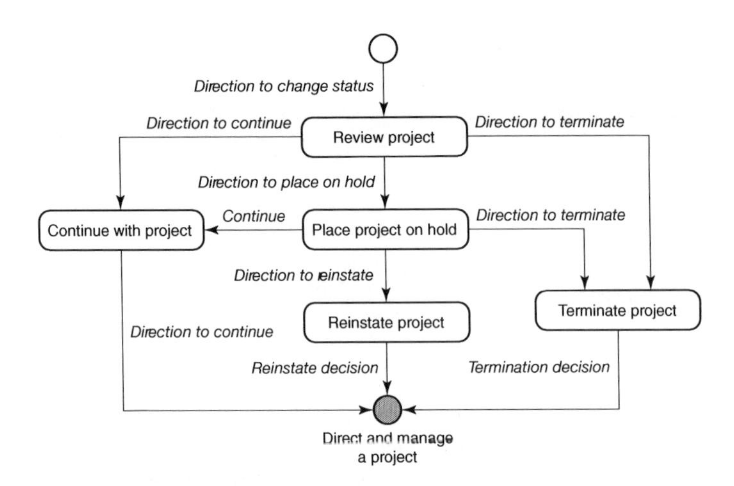

Figure 13.9 Terminating a project

Once the need to terminate a project is recognized, the project should be reviewed to verify this. The review may result in the project continuing, being placed on hold or being terminated. If on hold, the project may later be continued or terminated

The approach to take is shown in Figure 13.9. The first step is to review the project and find out the facts. Exactly what has gone wrong? What possible solution may there be? Workout 23.2 is a good approach for this. Do not make a knee-jerk decision in the absence of the facts and implications. Undertake the review as quickly as possible; there will be an opportunity later for a deeper investigation, if needed. Following the review, you have three possible courses of action:

- **continue** the project: this may be in an altered form, and therefore you may need to apply change control to approve any changes to the business case;
- **terminate** the project if the project is never likely to be viable;
- **place on hold:** the project is suspended, pending further investigations.

Placing a project on hold (suspending it) is a 'halfway house' between continuing and terminating and gives you time to make a considered decision. When a project is on hold, you should not take on any further commitments or start new stages. You should minimize the amount of work undertaken, balancing the need to reduce costs, if it is terminated and maintaining momentum, should it continue. On a practical basis, the 'on hold' status ensures you can retain your core project team and facilities in case you need to restart the project. In addition, there can be instances where health and safety issues require some work to continue, for example, in civil engineering, ensuring tunnels are kept drained. The on hold period is useful if the organization undertaking the project is not able to make a termination decision in isolation but still needs to protect its interests. Thus, a contractor might place a project on hold, pending the client formally terminating it or issuing a change request. Another organization might need to wait for funding decisions from its banks or other fund providers.

Workout 13.1 – Your decision-making bodies

This workout is for you to investigate who contributes to and makes decisions regarding your business projects and when.

1. Identify all the individuals or groups in your organization that contribute to and make decisions regarding your organization's projects. List them on the left of a flip chart or white board.
2. Show what decisions these each make, e.g., I have shown the decision-making bodies proposed in this chapter.
3. Consider and discuss:
   a. Are all three questions represented in your organization?
   b. Are the decision making accountabilities covered?
   c. Has each individual or body the authority to make the decisions?
   d. Is sufficient information available to those involved?
   e. Is question 2 considered 'cross-functionally?' If not, consider what effect this has on projects which require resources from a number of different functions.
4. Finally, decide who is accountable. Remember, accountability cannot be shared.

Individual or group	*Question 1: Soundness of individual project*	*Question 2: Priority versus other projects*	*Question 3: Funding*	*Remit*
Project sponsor				Ensure project is viable
Business portfolio manager	X	X in own portfolio		Ensure portfolio is viable
Portfolio review group		X across the organization		Ensure organization is viable and resources are available
Investment review group			X	Ensure investment criteria are met

14

Do I have the resources?

Obtaining resources and holding on to them can be very problematic, especially in functionally oriented organizations where the balance of power is firmly held by line-management. In these circumstances, resources are often committed to projects on the basis of good intention, rather than good information.

> *"You've got a goal, I've got a goal. Now all we need is a football team."*
>
> GROUCHO MARX, 1890–1977

- **Know how resources are being consumed on a project by project basis.**
- **Understand what resources are available, or soon to be available, within the forecasting horizon of your organization.**
- **Committing resources should be based on clear information, not wishful thinking.**
- **Ensure there is 'White Space' to react to unexpected opportunities or threats.**

Conditions for total resource planning

As long ago as 1993, the University of Southern California analyzed 165 teams in a number of successful organizations to assess the effectiveness of teamwork. Two reasons for teams failing to deliver were found:

- project objectives were unclear;
- the right people were not working on the project at the right time.

In looking for solutions to these two timeless issues, they found that a 'projects approach' gave significant benefits in clarifying objectives. On the question of resources (whether people, material, facilities or equipment), they found that having visibility of available resources and obtaining commitment of the required resources was key. In other words, if you haven't got the right resources you can't expect to complete your project.

Obtaining resources and holding on to them can be problematic, especially in functionally oriented organizations where the balance of power is firmly held by line management. In these circumstances, commitment to projects is often on the basis of good intention, rather than good information. Consequently, resources can be withdrawn, at whim by the owning department manager if he or she believes that his own need is greater than that of the project sponsor. The result is that resource and skill shortages do not become apparent until there is a problem.

Commitment to projects is often on the basis of good intention, rather than good information.

A method of resource allocation and commitment is, therefore, needed and to be effective should meet three conditions:

- **Condition 1**: you have a clear view of how resources are being consumed on every project and other work component in the business portfolio.
- **Condition 2**: you have visibility of the resources available, or soon to be available, within the forecasting horizon of your organization.

- **Condition 3**: commitment of resources should be based on clear information and forms the basis of an 'agreement' between the departments providing the resources and those managers consuming the resource.

Meeting these conditions enables you to anticipate potential resource conflicts before they become a problem and threaten the achievement of your organization's objectives.

Many of the problems faced by organizations in trying to allocate their resources efficiently arise as a result of some misconceptions regarding projects and resources. These misconceptions are:

- people work only on projects and do nothing else;
- resources are allocated to projects;
- project managers can choose whoever they want to work for them.

In practice you find:

- in most organizations, much of the work is not done on projects, but as part of running the business on a day-to-day basis (for example, when I worked on product management, 25%of time was spent on development projects, 15%on general management and administration, 40%on product management and 20%to cover absence for sickness and training).
- work is given to people. Your core employees are there all the time and being paid, regardless of whether they are working or on paid leave. There are some people you can turn on and off like a tap (temporary or agency staff), but I doubt if these are your key people.
- a project (or other) manager states what he needs for the project and the line manager allocates who they believe is the most appropriate (or convenient!) people. The line managers should know their people and their capabilities. They should be competent in the field of work they are accountable for and hence be best placed to decide who will fit a given role.

In the study described in Chapter 2, I found that the organizations best at managing and committing their resources were the consultancies. Their systems and processes were well tuned for this. Tight margins require that they have their staff on fee-paying work for as much of the working year as possible. They also need continually to form and reform teams from across the organization to address assignments. Further, they are never quite sure when a client is going to want their services but when a client does, they need to respond fast. There is, therefore, a conflict between:

- their employees being gainfully engaged on fee paying work, i.e., they need to drive staff utilization up;
- the need to have enough slack in the allocation of resources to enable them to respond to new requests quickly, i.e., don't drive utilization up too high.

Compare this with the need on business projects for an initial investigation of a proposal as soon as possible, whilst trying to carry on all the work which has already been approved – it's very similar. Rather than talk theoretically, I will explain a basic but very effective resource management method from one of these types of organizations.

The organization was an engineering consultancy with about 1,200 employees in numerous design offices and construction sites worldwide. In the past, margins were very high and, as long as staff were working on assignments (projects), good profits were made. Management systems did not need to be sophisticated. The organization had a time-recording capability for all its employees for time to be booked to assignment accounts and charged on to clients. Time for non-assignment work was also captured, either as process activities (marketing, sales, etc.) or as overheads (training, paid leave, sickness), i.e., the organization met **condition 1** for resource management.

When the competitive and economic environment changed, the organization was rapidly drawn into a lower margin industry. It was essential to 'commercialize' the management systems of the organization if the leadership team was to retain control and the organization remain profitable. The first attempt was to collect three sets of data from assignment managers, each required by a different central function:

- the invoicing department wanted a forecast of the invoices which would be sent out to ensure they were staffed up to despatch the invoices quickly (invoice management);
- the financial controller wanted a forecast of when cash was due in so he could manage the working capital required and the payment of suppliers (cash flow management);
- the operations director wanted to know who was allocated to assignments and who was coming free to know what work he could accept (resource management).

Not surprisingly, the assignment managers did not look on these three separate sets of 'new demands' kindly. Nevertheless, they did their best, completing the forms the invoicing department, finance controller an operations director wanted.

When looked at together, however, the three apparently separate sets of information proved very interesting. The forecast of work, in hours, could be multiplied by a factor to give a good approximation of the invoice values. The cash received should be the same as that invoiced (less bad debts). The only difference between the three sets of figures should be timing:

- the time from doing the work to invoicing represents work-in-progress days;
- the time between invoicing and cash received represents debtor days.

Even taking account of the timing difference, the three sets of figures produced by the assignment managers could not be reconciled, meaning the forecast was unreliable and inconsistent.

The solution implemented to deal with this problem was very simple. The same data was requested but collected at the same time on two linked data sheets:

- a manpower sheet;
- a financial sheet.

The manpower sheet: each assignment manager listed the people (by name, or grade/discipline) required on the project. Against each, the number of hours each would book in a given month was forecast. There was a cap on the maximum hours each month to allow for unexpected work and down time. (Look ahead to Figure 14.1 for an example.)

The financial sheet: the hours from the manpower sheet were automatically costed at actual pay-roll rates and entered into a financial sheet as time costs (cost of labour). To this sheet, the assignment manager added the forecast of non-labour costs. The forecast of the value and timing of invoices was added at the top of the sheet, with a line below showing when the cash was expected to be received. In short, this ensured all necessary data were collected at the same time, using the same form. The whole forecast was input to a computer, added and sorted to obtain summary reports and analyses. The result was consistent data giving consistent forecast reports. No matter who needed the information, it was compatible with that used by others for different purposes. It was so good that the marketing department was able to provide a full analysis of the business on a segmented basis every month, both historic and future. Previously, such an analysis used to take up to three months to complete. (Look ahead to Figure 14.2 for an example.)

One of the reports produced from this system was for the heads of department; they each received a listing of all the people within their department, together with the assignments each was committed to and for how many hours each month. The organization, therefore, had visibility of its future resource needs, i.e., the organization met **condition 2**, visibility, for resource management. (Look ahead to Figure 14.3 for an example.)

The first few months of operation were problematic as people adjusted the forecasts to take account of what they had learned, but after a short time it stabilized and became a reliable source of management information. From thereon, whenever the organization had a request for work from a client or was invited to tender for work, it could assess whether it was likely to have the resources available to meet the need and/or design the bid to fit around its known commitments. Also, as the requesting assignment manager completed the resource forecast, this became the agreement between the assignment manager and the supplying department, i.e., they fulfilled **condition 3** for resource management.

The frequency of reforecasting was initially set at quarterly intervals as it was expected that the effort of constructing the forecast would be too onerous on a monthly basis. The assignment managers were, however, given the option to do it monthly. In practice they all chose to do a monthly forecast as it was easier to maintain and amend on this more frequent basis rather than start at a lower level of knowledge on a quarterly basis.

This organization:

- knew what each project and activity in the organization consumed by way of resources (condition 1);
- had clear visibility, at a high level, of its resource availability (condition 2);
- made future commitments based on knowing current commitments and who was available without compromising previously made obligations (condition 3).

In short, this company achieved a level of knowledge about the application of its resources only dreamt of by many organizations. Did this process provide reasonable figures? The financial controller predicted the year-end results, six months in advance, to within an accuracy of 2%, excepting extraordinary accounting items. The company was also able to arrange finance well in advance, based on reliable figures. Whilst individual assignments within the business portfolio exhibited a fair degree of instability in forecasting, the total, for the portfolio as a whole, was very stable.

This example dealt with a consultancy organization where a tight hold on resources is essential. In the manufacturing or service sectors, the management of resources becomes less visible and is often hidden within functional hierarchies. Consider, however, how even these organizations rely on 'knowledge workers' to achieve their aims, even if the bulk of the work is machine based, thus having more in common with consulting organizations than in the past. Certain parts might be exceptionally well managed (such as individual manufacturing units, warehousing, call centres), but these are usually contained within a given function and deal with day-to-day business rather than change. Business projects frequently draw on resources from across an organization, not just from one function. If just one part is unable to deliver its contribution to a project, the entire venture is at risk. Few organizations have, or yet see the need for, the capability to manage their entire employee workforce as a block of resources to be used anywhere, at any time, just as in a consultancy organization. However, as in consultancy organizations, managers should ensure that their people are being applied to productive work rather than merely playing a numbers game with head count and departmental budgets. This just leads to sub-optimization, which might be of no benefit to the organization at all.

Managers should ensure that their people are being applied to productive work rather than merely playing a numbers game with head count and departmental budgets.

Project: YT2Z/Triton 2000
Detailed Investigation Stage

MANPOWER - ROLLING FORECAST (HOURLY)

Period: 4 wks to 28 Sept 2011

Resources	F'cast Month	ACTUAL TO DATE Month	Year	Life	FORECAST Oct	Nov	Dec 2010	Jan 2011	Feb	Mar	Apr	May	J				Q3	Q4	Q5	Q6	Beyond	F'cast Outturn
					134	**134**	**157**	**127**	**134**	**172**	**119**	**119**	**172**	**134**	**127**	**172**	**432**	**425**	**425**	**432**		
Category 1	70	70	280	560	56	70	70	70	84	112	28											1050
Category 2	75	75	300	600	60	75	75	75	90	120	30											1125
Category 3	30	30	120	240	24	30	30	30	36	48	12											450
Category 4	95	95	380	760	76	95	95	95	114	152	38											1425
Mann. J P	130	130	520	1040	104	130	130	130	156	208	52											1950
Fuller, W	100	100	400	800	80	100	100	100	120	160	40											1500
TOTAL HOURS	500	500	2000	4000	400	500	500	500	600	800	200											7500
CUMULATIVE					4400	4900	5400	5900	6500	7300	7500	7500	7500	7500	7500	7500	7500	7500	7500	7500	7500	

This is the guide to the maximum hours per month

Forecast may be by resource category or by individual

This number of hours are forecast by the Project Manager to complete this stage

Figure 14.1 Manpower – rolling forecast by project

This is a typical report on which manpower needs can be forecast. In this case, the figure shows the forecast for the detailed investigation stage of a project. It shows, on the left, the actual hours already booked to the stage and, on the right, the forecast hours and total. The guide for the maximum hcurs is shown below the date line. If this report is costed it provides the data required for the time cost line in the financial forecast (see Figure 14.2).

Project: YT2Z/Triton 2000
Project Sponsor: Kelly, PJ
Project Manager: Jeffries J

PROJECT – ROLLING COST FORECAST

Period: 4 wks to 28 Oct 2011

$ 000s		ACTUAL TO DATE			COST FORECAST																	
	F'cast Month	Month	Year	Life	Oct	Nov	Dec 11	Jan 12	Feb	Mar	Apr	May	Jun	Jul	Aug	Sep	Q3 O-D 12	Q4 J-M 13	Q5 A-J 13	Q6 J-S 13	Beyond	F'cast Outturn
Initial Investigation			53	53																		53
Time costs			50	50																		50
Purchases			3	3																		3
Detailed Investigation	6	7	30	55	6	7	5	5	18	10	4											110
Time costs	5	5	20	40	4	5	5	5	6	8	2											75
Purchases	1	2	10	15	2	2			12	2	2											35
Develop/Test												15	26	33	6	6	13					99
Time costs												5	25	32	5	5	12					84
Purchases												10	1	1	1	1	1					15
Trial																	13	11	2			26
Time costs																	12	10	2			24
Purchases																	1	1				2
Release																			22			22
Time costs																			18			18
Purchases																			4			4
TOTAL COST	6	7	83	108	6	7	5	5	18	10	4	15	26	33	6	6	26	11	24			310
Time cost	5	5	70	90	4	5	5	5	6	8	2	5	25	32	5	5	24	10	20			251
Purchases	1	2	13	18	2	2			12	2	2	10	1	1	1	1	2	1	4			59
CUMULATIVE COST					114	121	126	131	149	159	163	178	204	237	243	249	275	286	310	310	310	

Labour (time) costs are calculated from the 'hours' for ecast

For each stage you can see the labour and non-labour costs

Total cost for the project

Total cost for the project

Figure 14.2 Typical report used for building a financial forecast

This report gives a stage-by-stage summary of the total costs for a project and is ideally suited for building the forecast. For example, the time cost line could be derived from a manpower forecast such as that given in Figure 14.1.

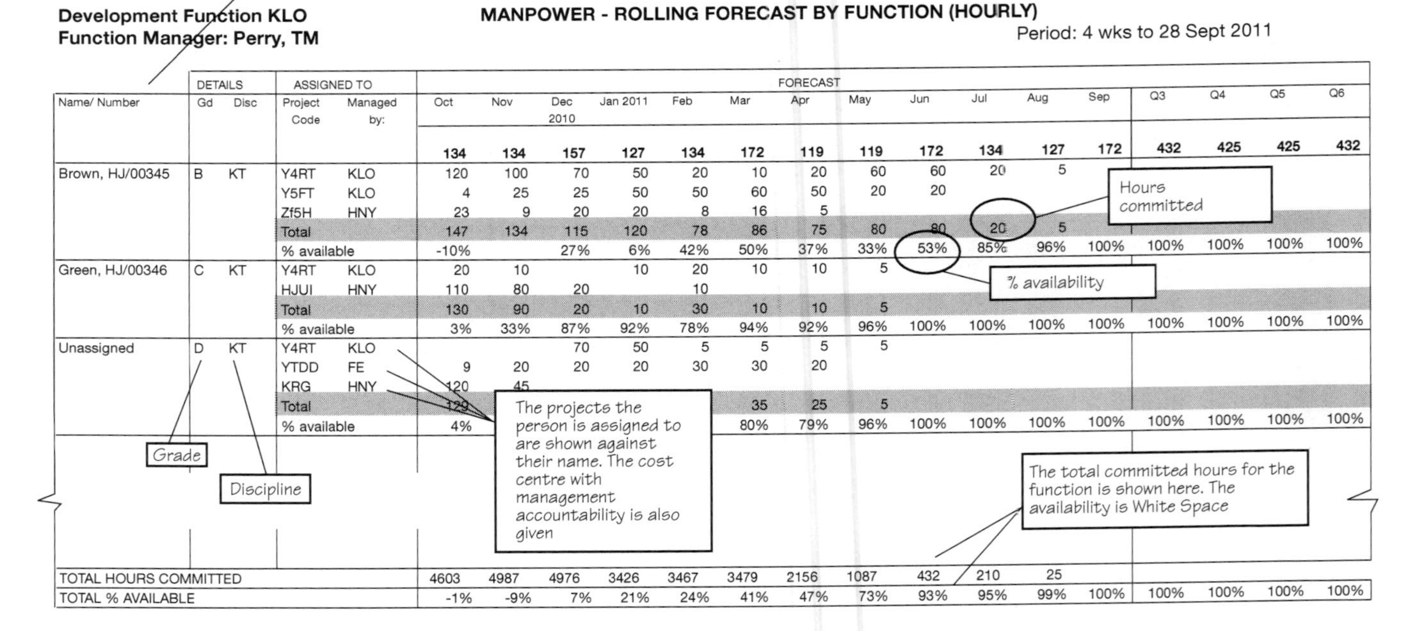

Development Function KLO
Function Manager: Perry, TM

MANPOWER - ROLLING FORECAST BY FUNCTION (HOURLY)
Period: 4 wks to 28 Sept 2011

DETAILS			ASSIGNED TO		FORECAST															
Name/ Number	Gd	Disc	Project Code	Managed by:	Oct	Nov	Dec 2010	Jan 2011	Feb	Mar	Apr	May	Jun	Jul	Aug	Sep	Q3	Q4	Q5	Q6
					134	**134**	**157**	**127**	**134**	**172**	**119**	**119**	**172**	**134**	**127**	**172**	**432**	**425**	**425**	**432**
Brown, HJ/00345	B	KT	Y4RT	KLO	120	100	70	50	20	10	20	60	60	20	5					
			Y5FT	KLO	4	25	25	50	50	60	50	20	20							
			Zf5H	HNY	23	9	20	20	8	16	5									
			Total		147	134	115	120	78	86	75	80	80	20	5					
			% available		-10%		27%	6%	42%	50%	37%	33%	53%	85%	96%	100%	100%	100%	100%	100%
Green, HJ/00346	C	KT	Y4RT	KLO	20	10		10	20	10	10	5								
			HJUI	HNY	110	80	20		10											
			Total		130	90	20	10	30	10	10	5								
			% available		3%	33%	87%	92%	78%	94%	92%	96%	100%	100%	100%	100%	100%	100%	100%	100%
Unassigned	D	KT	Y4RT	KLO			70	50	5	5	5	5								
			YTDD	FE	9	20	20	20	30	30	20									
			KRG	HNY	120	45														
			Total		129					35	25	5								
			% available		4%					80%	79%	96%	100%	100%	100%	100%	100%	100%	100%	100%
TOTAL HOURS COMMITTED					4603	4987	4976	3426	3467	3479	2156	1087	432	210	25					
TOTAL % AVAILABLE					-1%	-9%	7%	21%	24%	41%	47%	73%	93%	95%	99%	100%	100%	100%	100%	100%

Figure 14.3 Manpower – rolling forecast by function

Once all the project manpower forecasts have been collated, they can be sorted to give each line manager a listing of the people in his/her department or function, stating to which projects each are committed.

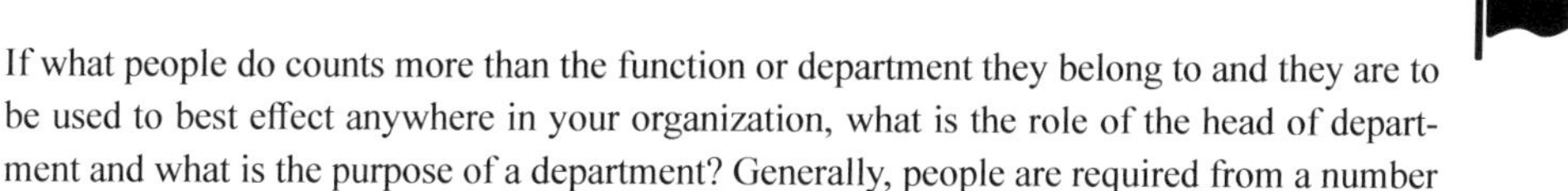

The future of heads of department?

If what people do counts more than the function or department they belong to and they are to be used to best effect anywhere in your organization, what is the role of the head of department and what is the purpose of a department? Generally, people are required from a number of areas contributing to the processes, activities and projects you are undertaking within a business.

In the traditional organization hierarchy, each head of department decides not only the strategic direction of their department but also what each and every one of his/her employees will do and how it will be done. The danger, if departments are too dominant, is that they will drive the business as they see fit from their own perspective. This might not be in line with the direction the organization leadership wants to effect, despite such heads of department appearing to meet their targets. The outcome is that the organization could become out of balance. For example, efficiency is often seen as a good goal, as is responsiveness to customer needs. The latter requires excess capacity to meet customer needs at short notice. If one department is driving 'efficiency' up by reducing capacity whilst another is creating a proposition around responsiveness there is likely to be a mismatch and dissatisfied customers.

A portfolio managed approach aligns the required skills and capabilities around the attainment of a business objective. In the case of a process, the objective is better operations. In the case of a project, the objective is change for the better. Thus, the heads of department are not leaders in driving the business but rather suppliers of people and expertise to projects and processes. The accountability of a head of department is to ensure that the right people are available in the right numbers to service the needs of the business. They will be accountable for pay, employee satisfaction and personal development. Other key roles will become apparent. There will need to be experts at particular disciplines, who will create strategy, develop and maintain business and technical architecture, manage programmes and projects or manage people. This will not be done just in the context of a single department but rather in the context of the complete organization, working wherever needed across departmental boundaries to achieve the business objectives.

This also leads to examining the role of an organization's directors or executives. Many are really 'mega-heads' of department (e.g., marketing director) but with the concept of business portfolios and cross-functional working, such traditional titles become meaningless. The 'top people' should be leaders of the business (all the business). with incentives tied to cross-business achievement, not just on developing suboptimal improvements in their own departments in order to operate within a departmental budget.

White space – the freedom to change

I call the gap between what your resources are committed to and the total resource you have available '**white space**'. White space is the resources that you have not yet committed to a given project or activity. If you fulfil conditions 2 and 3, you will know your white space:

White space = resources available –resources already committed

In the very short term this should be small and grow as you look further into the future.

White space is fundamental to an organization's on-going health. If there is no white space in the short to medium term, you are paralyzed. There will be no one available to change the business to meet new threats or exploit new opportunities unless you withdraw them from previously committed work. White space provides the resources to effect change in the future. "We are in a fast-moving environment" is the common cry nowadays. If this is truly the case, then you need to ensure 'white space' resources are ready to meet the need when it arises. You know the people will be required but you are not yet sure exactly when or what for, but if you have no people to change things, things won't change. White space must cater for four distinct needs:

White space provides the resources to effect change in the future.

- undertaking initial investigations on projects resulting from new proposals. These people must be available at short notice and must be highly knowledgeable if the investigations are to have any value;
- providing the resources to undertake the projects themselves, following approval at the detailed investigation gate;
- providing the ability to run 'business-as-usual', the volume of which might fluctuate;
- being able to respond to risks and issues as they are recognized or arise.

Think about a company putting a bid together – if done by inappropriate people, the bid could be lost or the company might commit itself to a financial disaster. Just because business projects are 'internal', it does not mean you need not apply the same rigor as you would with external matters. Your organization's future is at stake in both cases.

Figure 14.4 represents white space in graph form. The figure could apply to a complete organization, a division, a business portfolio or whatever. Unless you can build this picture, you will be taking risks every time you need to trigger another initiative or respond to a risk or issue.

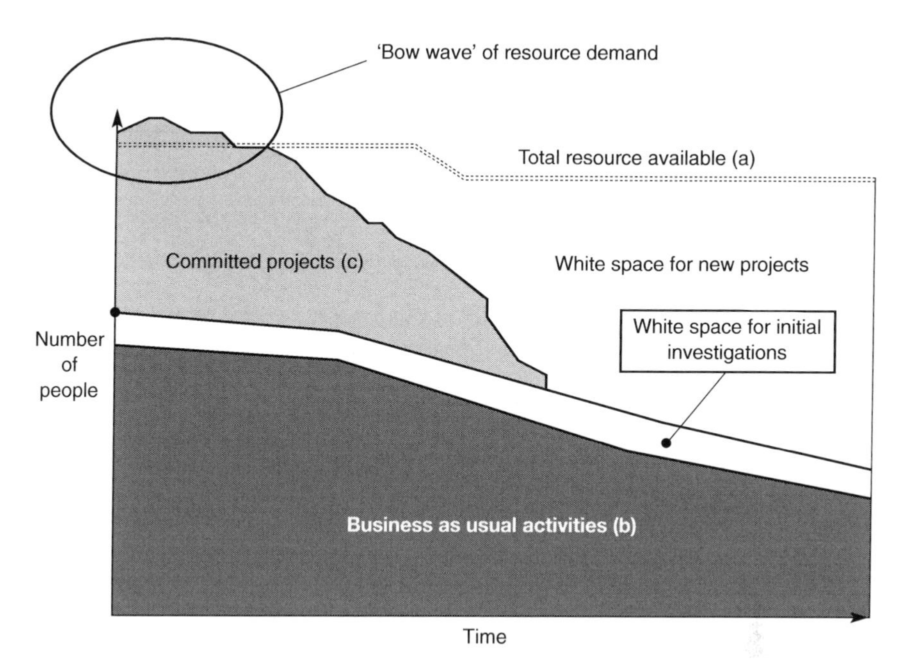

Figure 14.4 White space

White space is the gap between the resources you have (a) and those already committed (b + c). In the very short term this should be small. It will grow as you look further into the future. Notice the short-term bow wave which results from optimistic demands to the immediate needs.

How can I meet the three conditions?

The extent to which you need to employ formal systems to collate the past and future use of your resources depends on your organization. At one extreme, you need time recording to know what people have been working on; at the other you can rely on the line managers filling that gap with their personal knowledge of what their people are doing.

Time recording

Organizations which require time recording for other business critical needs will, like as not, already have it. Few organizations who don't, won't. It is an emotive system to implement as it can look and feel like bureaucracy gone mad. Some people are so against it they will leave an organization rather than fill in a time sheet. It is often bound up in emotive words such as 'trust'. "If you can't trust me to work on the right thing, I don't want to work for you." Few finance or marketing functions are on time recording but it is common in engineering and technical departments.

Some countries even outlaw time-recording! Despite this, time recording can be the key to:

- making a flat structure work;
- enabling people to be accountable for activities and projects ranging far beyond their department's patch;
- enabling job enrichment;
- enabling delegation without losing visibility and control.

If implementing time recording, you need to balance the cost with the information gained. Consider:

- what the reports provided by the system will tell you;
- how current the information is;
- how they are structured;
- who has access.

Consider also, the schedule for implementing a time-recording system. The reason for the system is for the reports it produces; if they don't help to meet your needs, don't do it yet. If the basic understanding and acceptance of their use is not in place, you will have an uphill struggle to make them work. Preferably, wait until those within your organization (project sponsors, project managers, resource managers) have identified the need for such a system themselves.

Finally, remember, if there is not some kind of time recording, you will not know how much your projects are costing. If your projects include a significant 'people' element, that makes management of project costs almost impossible. Consequently, you will rely on line management reports for controlling costs, which in turn keeps the balance of power firmly in the line management camp rather than shifting it towards the project view of life as advised in Chapter 2's, lesson 6. Time recording, if properly implemented with appropriate reporting, will give you an extra degree of freedom to manage your business and make life richer and more varied for your staff as they can change roles, without the risk of leaving their job.

Time recording, if properly implemented with appropriate reporting, will give you an extra degree of freedom to manage your business

Manpower forecasting

Manpower forecasting is a natural follow-on from time recording. It is merely a prediction of how many hours will be booked by each person against a particular activity or project. Forecasts can be created by one of three different roles.

- **Each individual** forecasts his/her own time input based on what he/she has already been briefed on and is committed to doing. Unfortunately, in most cases, individuals will not have sufficient visibility of the work. They will only be able to forecast the work they have been told to do, not what their managers know needs to be done but for which no briefing has, as yet, been given. Forecasts on this basis will be short term and of limited use.

- **The resource manager** forecasts the people required to meet commitments already made. This lets the 'supply' side drive the forecast. The estimates are likely to be good BUT unless well-coordinated with every project manager, the timing might be very wrong. The total of such forecasts might show no deficit of resources, but the departmental resource managers might have made choices impacting project priorities and not rightfully their decisions to make.
- **Each person who requires the resources** (such as a project manager) forecasts the people he/she expects and requires to work on the project, based on the project plan (see Figure 14.2). This lets the demand-side drive the forecast. Estimates will match the plan timescales and should be agreed with the individuals on the project team. The total of these forecasts might show that certain resources are allocated beyond their capacity in which case a business decision is needed to decide on how to deal with the conflicts (see Figure 14.3).

On the whole, the third method (demand driven forecasts made by those requiring the resources) is more likely to serve the needs of the business than the other two. It enables those people who are driving business change to set their demands in accordance with their business objectives. This approach highlights any conflicts or constraints, and enables a business decision to be made, rather than one being made by the limiting or constraining department. Further, it enables the project manager to increase or decrease the demand for resources openly.

In Chapter 13 one of the principles discussed was: "Having decided to do a project, do it; but stop if circumstances change." In other words, the project manager should continue to flex the resource forecast to complete the project, based on current knowledge. If the manpower forecast is costed and tied into financial forecasts, then the project will be reviewed if cost exceeds the sanctioned amount. The business portfolio manager can make an assessment of whether the project should continue. It is their decision, not that of the individual functions supplying the resources.

Over the short term, the demand for resources normally exceeds availability.

Upon adding up the total of resources required, there is usually a 'bow wave' as shown in Figure 14.4. That is, over the short term, the demand for resources normally exceeds availability. Managers are optimistic about the work they believe will be done in the next month, but not enough attention is paid to the reactive work that people have to do in addition to their project duties nor unexpected downtime, such as sickness and special leave. Placing a cap on the maximum hours forecast per person is a simple and effective way of dealing with the 'bow wave'. Assume that a month has four weeks, each of 36 hours, i.e., 144 hours.

It is highly unlikely anyone will actually book 144 hours against a single project or activity on their time sheet. It is even less likely that a large population would all book 144 hours; some would be sick, be assigned to urgent work elsewhere, go on training courses, attend a presentation to a key customer, resign or whatever. This situation can be dealt with by making a simple rule that if a person is full time on an activity, they should forecast only 85% of 144 hours (122 hours). Depressing the maximum forecasting capacity in this way provides contingency (white space) which enables other reactive work to be undertaken or current work to overrun without compromising the plan. In this respect it acts a buffer. Experience with forecasting will lead to calculating the right percentage for your organization.

How detailed does resource forecasting need to be?

High-level forecasting versus detail

The objective of resource management is to give sufficient visibility of the use and availability of resources to enable new projects and activities to be started without compromising the completion of committed work. It follows, then, that the forecast does not need to be fully detailed. All forecasts are, crudely, a range of very good to very poor guesses, the likely deviations in elements comprising the forecast can be significant whilst not affecting the total figure very much.

Forecasts can be on two levels:

- outline – this is equivalent in manufacturing of a master production schedule;
- detailed – this is equivalent in manufacturing to a shop schedule.

The outline or high-level forecast is key in managing business portfolios. The detailed forecast is the accountability of the line and project managers; they decide when the work should be done and by whom. Do not try to combine the two. In the example I used to explain resource management, the organization used the following for its high-level forecasting:

- forecast, by person or skill group/grade in hours;
- per month, for the next 12 months;
- per quarter, for the following year;
- per year, for the next 3 years;
- beyond that as a single figure.

This was in the context that at the start of any financial year, this organization had half of its resources for the year already committed. The reason hours were used was simply because that was the basis on which clients were charged and hence how time sheets were completed and actuals were reported. Forecasting frequency was monthly; weekly forecasts would have given little, if any, extra value. Manpower (or time sheet) frequency and reporting was weekly. Monthly was too infrequent as deviations from plans would not be spotted in time for corrective action to be taken.

In contrast, another organization, at the start of the financial year only had a quarter of its resources for the year already committed and therefore, used to forecast by person only, in days per week. 'Days' were used as the measurement unit as, again, that was how clients were charged and hence how the time-recording system captured and reported the data. The frequency for forecasting was weekly for manpower and monthly for other costs.

Pipeline stability

Sales pipelines are often seen as difficult to estimate, especially in industries where the buying pattern is a few large purchases rather than the mass market consumer pattern. An industrial engineering organization had a pipeline of about 350 prospects, totalling potential revenue of £300m which, after factoring in the probability of the customer wanting to proceed and the probability of the bid being won, totalled £50m. Despite this being made up of inputs from six different people, in six different divisions on three continents, with one-third of the prospects churning every quarter and potential sales and win probabilities changing frequently, this pipeline stayed very consistent in total, displaying only a minimum shift month to month.

Avoiding micro planning – a solution by applying constraints theory

The primary constraint for a project is usually the resource that can be applied. If there are no resources, there is no progress. Micro planning every activity for every person on every one of maybe 50 to 500 projects, is likely to be a fruitless and futile exercise. Reality changes too fast and estimating is not that reliable. So how can we find a way through this to ensure estimates and commitments to undertake the work are realistic and 'good enough'?

Micro planning every activity for every person on every one of maybe 50 to 500 projects, is likely to be a fruitless and futile exercise.

Every system, process, or organization has a constraint which limits how much it can achieve (its throughput). In corporate, multi-project environments, there is usually a single department or work group which is the constraint. In very complex organizations, it can be difficult to identify; however, most people intuitively know where the problems lie. Comments such as, 'Oh, it's those people in IT', or 'we'd better design this so Technology don't need to be involved' are telling. It is sometimes argued that it can be assumed that there is no resource constraint at all; we just spend our time flitting from task to task in a complex round, wasting energy. If we organized better, there would be plenty of resources to do what we really need to do. Others say there are many constraints, not just one, each sheltering behind the other. Whatever your view, be you a purist, saying, "There is only one constraint," or a realist, saying, "It's all a constraint," the problem remains and needs to be addressed.

A solution lies in the practical application of the 'Theory of Constraints'. If it is difficult to find the bottleneck, simply choose a department or unit to be the appointed constraint. Plan the workflow through this single department to achieve maximum throughput. This means ensuring the designated department:

- receives early warning of work;
- receives the work as soon as it is ready (no hand-off delays);

- works only on this (or a defined minimum number) and clear it as soon as possible (that is to say, they avoid bad multi-tasking).

There is also a need to ensure delays on one project (or other work) do not have a knock-on effect on all subsequent projects. This is achieved by ensuring that between each project, the resource has sufficient safety margin built in to absorb unexpected delays. This is called a **capacity buffer**.

By protecting the constraint in this way, the flow of projects in the organization is staggered and it is only necessary to schedule this one resource fully. The constraint becomes, in effect, a drumbeat to which all other departments march. Each work item can be planned independently, but, by tying them to the 'drum', it is possible to stagger them in a rational way. The safety (or buffers) provided around the drum resource also provides safety time for work in other departments. Figure 14.5 illustrates this.

- Planning is used to resolve as many problems as early as possible.
- Monitoring is achieved by managing the buffers.
- There would need to be a strong hold on when projects are released for work; this would be the accountability of the portfolio review group.

If applying this method, individual projects should also be planned in such a way as to increase the reliability of delivery. This is discussed in more detail in *The Project Workout*.

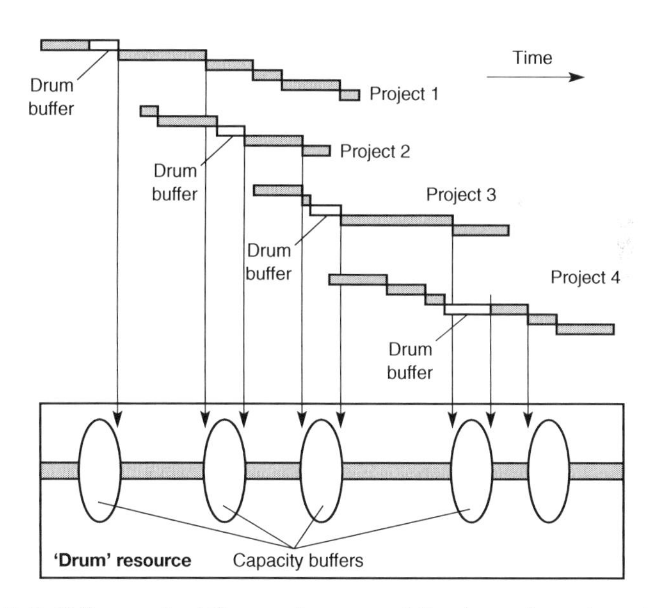

Figure 14.5 Building project timescales around the drum department

The projects are scheduled so that work required in the 'drum' department is done in a logical sequence without bad multi-tasking. A drum buffer in each project protects the resource from delays within each project. A capacity buffer protects the knock-on effects of delays in one project on all downstream projects.

The theory of constraints – dealing with bottlenecks

The theory of constraints (TOC) is a management philosophy, described by Eli Goldratt in his 1984 book, *The Goal*. It aimed at helping organizations continually achieve their goals. Goldratt adapted the concept to project management with his book, *Critical Chain*, published in 1997. Goldratt views any manageable system as being limited in achieving its goals by a very small number of constraints. There is always at least one constraint, and his approach uses a focussing process to identify the constraint and restructure the rest of the organization around it. The theory of constraints adopts the common idiom: 'a chain is no stronger than its weakest link'. This means that processes, organizations, structures and systems are vulnerable because a breakage in the weakest element will adversely affect the outcome.

Who is responsible?

The critical chain solution is not easy to put in place. It requires some fundamental changes in behaviour:

- **senior executives** will have to stagger the release of new projects and new project stages. (Havoc in multi-project environments is often wrought by top managers wanting, "Just one more project . . . NOW!");
- **resource managers** will have to reduce bad multi-tasking habits in their departments (perhaps no more favours!);
- **team managers and members** will have to undertake their work as fast as possible, and deliver their outputs as soon as they can, not just in time for a specified delivery date.

Organizations in cash-rich industries find this difficult because there is little financial imperative to change their behaviours.

Resource management systems

I was speaking at a PMI conference in Sweden and a straw poll of the delegates at a presentation on resource management found:

- all the delegates worked in matrix organizations;
- 30% had a resource management process;
- 20% had tools to support resource management;
- only 2% had been trained on their process and supporting tools.

All of them had big issues with how resource management worked (or more accurately, didn't work) in their organizations. Some ignored the problem as just 'too difficult', whilst others created enormous spreadsheets to try and get a grip on the issue of making sure the organization has the resources to do the work that needs doing. By enormous, I mean at the limit of Microsoft® Office Excel as a tool.

In 2010, Forrester said that there was a significant increase in investment of PPM tools specifically to:

- obtain an accurate view of resource usage;
- manage investment aligned to strategy.

Today, Gartner says the need for resource management is one of the top three reasons companies invest in PPM tools. Not a lot has changed over the years. The vision of many senior managers is to be able to drill down at the touch of a screen to get any information needed at the level they need it . . . but few can do this reliably.

A major pitfall of putting in systems to enable visibility of resources is that they can be too complicated and consume too much inconsequential data. Take the following scenario:

A major pitfall of putting in systems to enable visibility of resources is that they can be too complicated and consume too much inconsequential data.

1. The project schedule and scope drive resource needs.
2. Resources can be assigned in project plans using project-planning software and a profile obtained of who is required and when.
3. This can be downloaded into a central database and analyzed for the organization as a whole.
4. Resource conflicts are spotted by the 'system' which, based on priority rules, automatically levels the conflicting resources by moving lower priority activities back in time.
5. The output from the global resource analysis is fed back to the individual project plans, showing the resultant slippage, which to the owner of the plan can look random.

Software is available to handle all this in an integrated way, so, no doubt there are organizations who manage it this way. However, this level of integration and automation is neither always necessary nor desirable. For example, it would mean that every project team would need someone capable of using the same or closely compatible, planning software and every plan would need to be fully resourced at activity level. On its own, this has dubious value, when all is needed is enough visibility of resources to enable decision making on overall resource availability. Detail is not necessarily needed.

Provided the same high-level work breakdown structures and work components (such as projects) are used as the basis for the forecasts, the resource data can be held in a separate, simpler database. This can be used to analyze and report on those resources where demand looks as if it is likely to exceed capacity – this in turn indicates which projects or other work might come into conflict. The project managers and resource managers of the contentious projects and resources can then discuss and agree how the conflict should be handled. If they cannot agree, the issue should be escalated to the portfolio review group. There is often no need for sophisticated analysis and resource levelling rules; managers can manage it.

In time, with the progress of data handling and artificial intelligence, tools will become available to take the drudgery out of resource management; those organizations who are early adopters will have a competitive advantage. On the other hand, it is possible to simply end up being seduced by technology which is either not yet capable of delivering on the promises made in its sales hype or which enough people in the organization cannot use.

Different types of resources

This chapter has concentrated on the commonest type of resources, people. Within this type, however, the range of different skills and experience is vast. They are not, however, the only types of resources. Resources can be categorized as:

- reusable;
- replenishable;
- exhaustible.

Reusable resources are basically people and equipment. People and equipment can be moved from job to job as and when needed. For example, a test environment for an IT system might be needed for a number of projects, or an excavator could be moved from one construction site to another.

Replenishable resources are those which can be 'topped-up' if they start to run out. The most obvious is fuel. A construction site in a remote location, is likely to have its own fuel depot but the manager will need to ensure it always contains sufficient fuel for work to continue, by planning appropriate deliveries.

Exhaustible resources are those that once they have run out, that is it. Today's global supply chains are such that you can usually obtain what you need from somewhere. The more localized your operations, the more likely you are to come across this constraint.

The methods demonstrated in this chapter deal with reusable resources. Dealing with replenishable resources is more about logistics, and working with exhaustible resources makes risk management essential.

You need ALL your resources to succeed

Workout 14.1 – What's your white space?

This workout is for you to use as a discussion point or to identify the capacity your organization has available to change itself. Assume any projects to change your current way of working need to be managed and staffed from within your current head count. Try to construct a picture, like the one in Figure 12.1. As a start, look 12 months ahead only.

Hints

Break up the problem by function if this helps.

Use the list of projects you derived from Workout 3.1 – number each project.

Try to cluster similar groups of people together and build the picture in the following order;

1. total head count (a);
2. people (either grouped or as individuals) running the current operations (processes) (b);
3. people (either grouped or as individuals) working on projects which are currently in progress (c).

Your percentage of white space is (a – (b + c))/a %;

Consider how fast your business and competitive environment is moving and in this context discuss the following points:

1. Will the amount of white space allow you to develop enough new products and sufficiently improve your operational and management systems and processes to maintain or enhance your position in the market?
2. How far into the future does white space become available? If you had a requirement NOW, how long would you have to wait before you could start working on it without displacing any of your current projects or activities?
3. Is there hidden capacity in your business? How do you know?
4. Do you have any people who can be deployed quickly onto new projects and who probably do not know what they will be doing next week (i.e., resources for initial investigations)?
5. Have you ever started off a set of change projects or initiatives which people say they are keen on but which fail to deliver because insufficient resource is made available for them? If so, what does this tell you?

15

Selecting the right projects

None of the methods is fool proof; you cannot make a process for decision making, you can only make a process for the flow of the information required to support decision makers.

"The cancellation rate of [IT] projects exceeds the default rate of the worst junk bonds – yet bonds have lots of portfolio management applied to them. [IT] investments are huge and risky. It's time we do this."

DOUGLAS HUBBARD

- **Integrate portfolio management with business planning.**
- **Design your selection process and methods carefully.**
- **Use simple tools to start with to promote discussion.**
- **The benefits from good selection will dwarf 'slash and burn' cost cutting approaches.**

Project selection and business planning

Why selection?

Why do so many enterprises:

- waste scarce funds and resources on worthless projects and other work;
- have little understanding of what benefits will accrue from their portfolios;
- struggle interminably with annual budget setting?

Research by the Gensight Group suggested that 35 to 50%of all investment is directed at unsuccessful projects, whilst about 30%of project investment by FTSE 100 organizations actually destroyed shareholder value!

The demand for improved returns from project investment is now pervasive, from public and private sectors alike. Yet most organizations still struggle with deciding what projects (work) to select as well as when to do them. Business portfolio management is a discipline that can increase significantly the value derived from investments. The concepts have been established for over 50 years in the financial investment community and can be applied to deciding which projects to choose to put in a portfolio.

Business portfolio management ensures projects (and other work) are aligned to each other and to the strategy of the organization. As such, portfolio management should be an integral part of business planning. It should enable an organization to select those projects which are likely to create the greatest value, whilst at the same time:

As such, portfolio management should be an integral part of business planning

- ensuring strategic balance;
- handling risk explicitly;
- keeping within resource, funding and risk constraints;
- respecting any dependencies between the selected projects.

In demanding times, this is should be an aim for all enterprises, yet it is rarely applied effectively, despite reliable methods now being available.

Doing it 'the old way'

When creating the next year's business plan and annual budget, most organizations extrapolate from the previous year's expenditure, making adjustments for changed circumstances, with some superficial analysis of priorities. This is usually done within the organization's functional or departmental 'silos'. The aim is generally concerned with keeping within a top-down defined budget, often with capital and operational (revenue) expenditure dealt with in different, unrelated streams. Sometimes, consideration is given to resource constraints and the level of change the organization can cope with. This approach might work, to a limited extent, for steady-state bureaucracies but not for organizations undergoing substantial change. In such cases, the results can be dubious, with little objective attention to:

- the relationship between capital and operational expenditure, which can be unknown or ignored;
- the impact of budget cuts on benefit realization, which is usually not understood;
- priorities, which are often contentious;
- the point at which projects must be rejected, which can be nearly impossible to determine;
- resource constraints and project relationships, which are often seen as too complex.

Scepticism regarding the value of some organization's business planning methods can also apply to outside observers. An analyst at Prudential-Bache said of a FTSE 100 organization in which top-down cuts had been imposed: "Our provisional conclusion is that the current management have finally prescribed strong medicine. It remains to be seen how much life remains in the patient." Not very comforting!

A range of methods you can use

Choosing how to decide between competing projects can cause a great deal of concern. Five methods I have seen used are outlined as follows:

- executive decision;
- economic or financial return;
- scoring;
- visualization;
- optimization.

I would, however, point out that none of the methods is fool proof; a process for decision making cannot be made, only a process for the flow of information required to support decision makers. Ultimately, decisions come down to a choice made by a person or group, not by a process or clever business model. Nevertheless, there are approaches which can help significantly to improve the quality, objectivity and transparency of the decisions.

Executive decision

Just choose, based on the information and opinions to hand. This is a simple and often effective method, especially if you do not have to justify your decisions! Sometimes, decisions are so marginal, it does not matter what you decide, as long as a decision is made!

What colour do you want our cars?

The commercial director of an engineering organization interrupted the chief executive, asking him what colour the new chauffeur cars should be. The chief executive picked up the phone and asked his personal assistant to come in.

"What colour should our new cars be?" he asked.

"Red," the personal assistant replied.

"There, you have your answer."

After the commercial director had left the room, the chief executive commented, "I like easy decisions which I can make quickly – it makes me feel good. But that was ridiculous!"

Four bright red cars were in fact delivered, BUT the organization's brand colours were blue and white! The chief executive was simply making a point, at the cost of his brand uniformity, that all his directors ought to understand the fundamentals of the business and its strategy and not simply live in their own functional siloes, as the commercial director clearly did.

Economic or financial return

Investment appraisal methods based on discounted cash flow are commonly used in many organizations to justify projects. The aim is to either maximize the net present value (NPV) and/or increase the internal rate of return (IRR). In addition, the 'payback period' can also have an influence. For example, some organizations will insist a project returns at least 15%IRR and has a pay-back period of less than two years. The IRR hurdle rate is set to capture projects with returns greater than that required by the market and the payback period is set to control cash flow and ensure the benefits stream is not too distant. Different organizations set different hurdle rates. Those with short product life cycles tend to set short pay-back periods and higher IRR targets.

The aim is to either maximize the net present value (NPV) and/or increase the internal rate of return (IRR).

Making the numbers up?

In one organization I worked with, all the projects coming up for authorization or selection into the business plan had internal rates of return in the hundreds or even thousands. This organization should have been enormously profitable, but, unfortunately, it was not. Despite these 'excellent projects' and more than adequate operational performance, the organization lost money. I found two things were happening:

- the investment appraisals were 'doctored', giving a far better impression than was the case. Optimism was rife, with 'making the numbers up' being the acceptable approach.
- different projects claimed the same chunk of benefit, resulting in benefits being double counted (or sometimes counted up to seven times!).

These symptoms are classic in organizations with poor business planning capabilities and where project selection and portfolio management are divorced from whatever business plan does exist. They are often unduly influenced by the finance function, with project selection and authorization being perceived by the business leaders as 'bureaucracy getting in the way of what we want to do'.

Scoring techniques

Scoring techniques seek to maximize the value of a business portfolio. They build on the discounted cash flow method described earlier, taking into account factors such as net present value, probability of technical success, probability of commercial success, project cost and the on-going operating costs. From these, the expected commercial value can be calculated and the projects ranked according to those with the highest value, enabling the selection of those that can be completed within the limited budget. Table 15.1 is a simple example for nine projects (in reality you could have tens or hundreds of projects). If you had a Year 1 annual constraint of a £20m spend, you would select the five projects with the highest commercial value: C, A, I, D and H. This would use £17.7m of the available budget.

The use of the 'strategic importance factor' demonstrates how to use scoring to favour projects with particular characteristics (in this case, link to strategy). Some organizations use a scoring model to take into account a wide number of factors, each of which can be weighted. It can become very complicated and subjective and for this reason alone some senior managers are sceptical if the answers they want to see are not forthcoming!

A modification would be to determine the ranking by dividing the expected commercial value by the constraining factor. In this way those projects giving the greatest return for whatever your limited resource is can be favoured. Hence this is often referred to as the 'most bangs for the bucks' approach. Once the projects have been ranked, keep selecting projects, in rank order, until the constraining resource is exhausted. In the example in Table 15.2, I have used the development cost as the constraining resource, but you could choose anything, such as a particular skill group.

Table 15.1 Scoring – maximizing economic value

Project	*NPV (£m)*	*Strategic importance (SI)*	*Income PV (£m)*	*Commercial success*	*Technical success*	*Project cost PV (£m)*	*Project cost Yr1*	*Project cost Yr2*	*On-going cost PV*	*ECV (£m)*	*Rank*
A	£5.30	2	£11.5	80%	80%	£2.7	£3.0	£0.0	£3.4	£9.2	2
B	£3.79	1	£9.3	80%	70%	£2.7	£3.0	£0.0	£2.8	£0.5	9
C	£3.92	3	£9.3	70%	75%	£2.6	£2.0	£0.9	£2.8	£9.9	1
D	£9.64	1	£22.9	85%	90%	£6.4	£7.0	£0.0	£6.9	£5.0	4
E	£1.94	2	£13.2	75%	60%	£7.3	£8.0	£0.0	£3.9	£2.2	6
F	£5.28	1	£17.0	80%	85%	£6.6	£7.3	£0.0	£5.1	£0.6	8
G	£5.09	1	£9.7	70%	70%	£1.7	£1.0	£1.0	£2.9	£1.0	7
H	£3.21	2	£6.1	75%	80%	£1.1	£1.2	£0.0	£1.8	£4.8	5
I	£0.64	2	£6.8	90%	90%	£4.1	£4.5	£0.0	£2.0	£5.0	3

ECV = (I x SI x Cp-OC) x Tp −C

I = Present value of income stream

Cp = Likelihood of commercial success

Tp = Likelihood of technical success

ECV = Expected commercial value

SI = Strategic importance score

OC = Present value of on-going costs

C = Present value of project costs.

Table 15.2 'More bangs for the bucks' selection

Project name	*ECV (m)*	*Project cost PV (m)*	*ECV/Project cost PV Analyses*	*Rank*
Project A	£9.2	£2.7	£3.37	3
Project B	£0.5	£2.7	£0.20	8
Project C	£9.9	£2.6	£3.88	2
Project D	£5.0	£6.4	£0.78	5
Project E	£2.2	£7.3	£0.30	7
Project F	£0.6	£6.6	£0.09	9
Project G	£1.0	£1.7	£0.57	6
Project H	£4.8	£1.1	£4.41	1
Project I	£5.0	£4.1	£1.23	4

Divide the Expected commercial value (ECV) by the limiting resource, in this case Project cost, to determine which projects make best use of that resource. Then select those which make greatest use until the constraint is met. This results in the selection of six projects: H, C, A, I, D and G, slightly more than the pure 'Economic value' method in Figure 15.1 and using £18.7m of the £20m budget.

This approach favours projects with certain characteristics: those that:

- are closer to launch;
- have relatively little left to be spent on them;
- have a higher likelihood of success;
- use less of the scarce or constraining resource.

It also requires financial or other quantitative data. This can be particularly problematic in the early stages of a project. Probabilities can also be difficult to determine, whilst none of the scoring techniques take account of portfolio balance.

Visualization techniques

Visualization techniques build on scoring methods but present the output in such a way that the decision maker can gain a better understanding of the non-financial factors. This is done by plotting each project on a matrix with axes representing key decision influencing factors. For example, using the factors, benefit versus risk, you would choose the projects which are in the 'less risky, most beneficial' quartile (Figure 15.1). This type of presentation is often called a 'bubble diagram'. The limitations of this method are that that there are only two dimensions, one represented by each axis. A third dimension can be added by using the size of the 'bubble' to indicate a factor such as project size. To use more dimensions, it is necessary to invent creative formulae for weighting a collection of factors into a single one, like the example in Table 15.1. Bubble diagrams are, however, relatively simple to construct and can help decision makers understand a potentially complex set of projects or work. They can also give a concise view of portfolio balance. On the other hand, the output can be misleading or even manipulated and, as a minimum, basic management sense should be used to verify the model. Such presentations also tend to favour supposedly strategic projects over those yielding a real financial return and, unless you are careful in their use, can lead to an unbalanced portfolio.

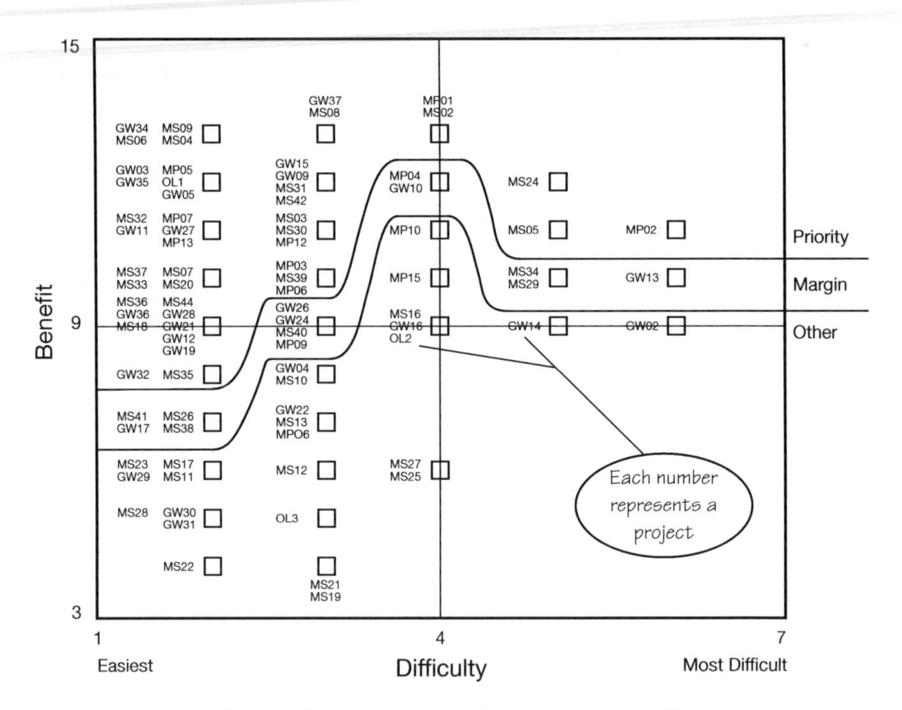

Figure 15.1 Example of using a matrix to aid the selection of projects

Each project is plotted on a matrix with axes representing key decision-influencing factors; in the example shown, this is benefit versus difficulty. Those projects which are in the 'less risky, most benefit' quartile (top left) were chosen for priority review.

Balanced optimization

Some organizations now use portfolio optimization concepts, with computerized models applied if the analysis becomes complex. In these, the business objectives are stated in quantitative terms, usually a mix of financial figures and quality of service indicators. The candidate projects are fed into the model, together with constraints, such as cashflow and resources. The application then derives an 'optimum' mix to meet the prescribed targets. This becomes a scenario, as the objectives, funding or resource amounts can be changed to generate further possible mixes. 'Essential projects' and dependencies can also be incorporated (Figure 15.2).

Such techniques have the added advantage that the timing of the projects can be considered. Hence a project can be chosen to start at different points in time to fit within the constraints, without it actually being rejected outright because it cannot be scheduled in immediately.

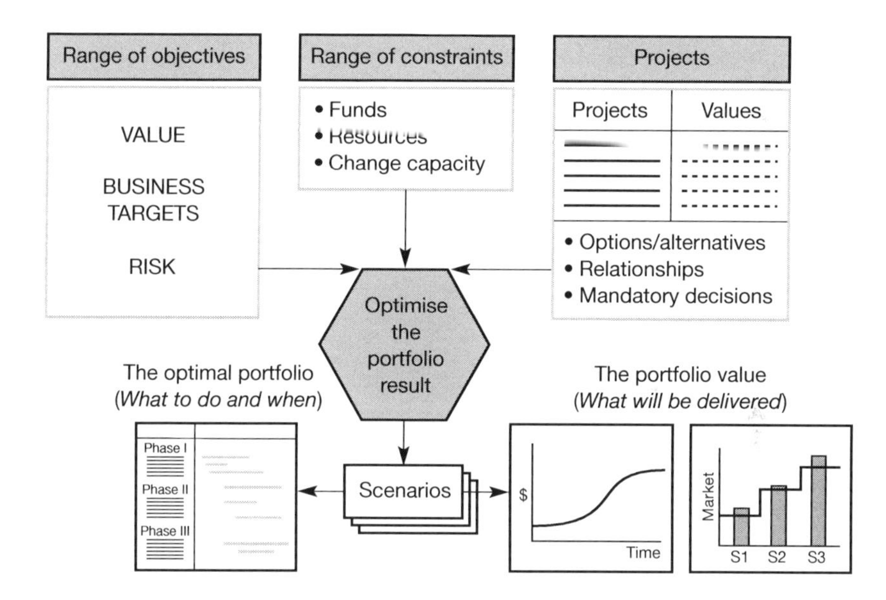

Figure 15.2 Balanced optimization

A range of business objectives, constraints and a set of candidate projects are used as the data to create a number of scenarios. The objective is to use optimization to identify which group of projects and timings takes you closest to your objectives, whilst taking into account other factors, such as risk.

The output from such models can be very enlightening and stimulate some productive discussion, which, on its own, can improve the quality of the decisions made. Of interest, one model I saw allowed any project to be forced into the business portfolio, such as the 'chief executive's pet project'. Alternative scenarios could then be generated (with and without the 'pet project') and a judgment made as to the effect of doing this project on the whole portfolio. Portfolio optimization is more informative than the previous methods discussed in this chapter but does require specialized knowledge to use it effectively. Beware, however, there are some commercial offerings which do not result in the right outputs. Like any modelling technique, senior management need to have faith in data used. Mind you, if they do not trust the basic data, no rational method will satisfy them!

The scorecard prioritization approach outlined earlier in this chapter is often cited as the only credible form of analysis available. Yet, this is not the case. Balanced optimization, using mathematical techniques, can perform the analysis more comprehensively, faster and with a closer representation of the real-world complexities. Experience shows that not only is such analysis possible, but it can also be trusted. It should not replace management judgment but should support it by enabling complex factors such as benefits, risks, relationships, timing and constraints to be analyzed and drawn together, enabling senior executives to apply judgment from a far better starting point than other methods yield. As modelling algorithms improve, the use of these techniques is likely to become more widespread, especially when coupled with simulations which include risk. In many organizations, senior managers still believe the more projects they undertake, the more likely they are to achieve the results they want whilst (in reality) they are simply overloading the people and slowing everything down. If balanced optimization and simulation can help to reduce the incidence of such mis-directed behaviours, the savings and benefits for the organization who use them will be significant.

Keeping the pipeline flowing

An organization found that its pipeline of development projects was blocked. There were too many projects (about 140) being undertaken, and few were being completed. The organization decided they needed to get these projects under control and delivering. First, each project was aligned to a to a life cycle stage (similar to that in Chapter 8) and then ranked on a matrix, based on difficulty versus benefit (such as in Figure 15.1). The objective was to include the least difficult projects which gave the most benefit and were almost complete into the portfolio and terminate the remainder. The exercise was not without difficulties, but it did result in a smaller and more focussed portfolio of about 90 projects. Instead of only one or two projects being completed each month, the delivery rate shot up to three or four a week being completed. The matrix selection method used was known to be imperfect as it favoured short-term revenue-generating projects over longer-term strategic projects. However, it was considered adequate for the task required at that point in time. The senior leadership, however agonized over the type of tool to use when the next batch of projects needed prioritizing. As it turned out, they did not need to prioritize for over six months. The project sponsors, during the initial investigations, had already identified potential blockages and changed the approach and scope of their projects accordingly. The portfolio review group was able to let all new projects continue. Twelve months in and no tool had yet been devised. However, the portfolio was still under control, and projects were being still being completed at the rate of two to three a week.

Is selection worth doing better?

Of course it is! Returning to Figure 1.1, there is no point in becoming really great at the art of project management and then doing the wrong projects. In the earlier sections I have drawn out the pitfalls relating to the different techniques. Do not let that put you off; just use this as knowledge to approach the problem with your eyes 'wide open'. Just because something is difficult, that doesn't mean it isn't worth doing. Even a technically or academically poor selection process is of more value than none, simply because of the debate it will create among the senior team. If they are discussing this topic, you are halfway there. If in doubt, think of the improvements that others have realized:

Even a technically or academically poor selection process is of more value than none

- in one organization the overall return through optimizing a project portfolio was a massive 15% increase in the total estimated return;
- research has shown a potential advantage of 19% in average growth and 67% in profit for those achieving excellence in portfolio management (see Chapter 30 for more on this).

Benefits on this scale can never be attained by a finance-led slash and burn, cost-cutting approach to business planning. It would seem the rewards are there for those organizations which rise to the challenge.

Perhaps what remains is an issue of credibility. How can senior executives become confident that some approaches are practical and can be used to turn what they perceive as 'theoretical benefits' into bottom line results? Some areas of management practice are now evolving which, if combined, can lead to far better results. These include:

- benefits estimation;
- balanced optimization;
- decision support.

Estimating benefits can be made more accurate

It is now common for organizations to require an estimate of benefits to justify any investment. Major economic crisis such as the austerity in 2018, the credit crunch in 2008, and the collapse of the dot-com bubble in 2000, have accelerated this trend. It is no longer acceptable to simply assert that the latest technology or general improvements in service quality as reason enough for investment. The business benefits must now be quantified.

Improved market intelligence, combined with benchmarking and multi-disciplinary team working, can support much better estimates of benefits

Improved market intelligence, combined with benchmarking and multi-disciplinary team working, can support much better estimates of benefits. If the enterprise itself makes the effort to lay out this intelligence, with clear analysis of current performance, the sponsors of projects can prepare better estimates and save time whilst doing so.

Business planning is serious; without it there is very little basis on which to select the projects or other components of your business portfolio. Project selection is the primary influence on the future direction of your business. The projects you select represent the changes in direction, without which tomorrow will merely be a poorer version be of today.

The popular finance-based tools tend to give poorer results on their own than when combined with other tools. The additional tools bring the strategic imperative to the fore to help achieve balance and take into account risk. When embarking on this, the scoring methods are an easy entry point, but in my opinion, balanced optimization is where we should be aiming; it uses the same data as scoring models but gives a far richer and more useful result.

The meetings when project selection decisions are made can be better managed, to take advantage of improved data and analysis. Strategy setting sessions are often carefully orchestrated, with extensive intelligence provided to assess current performance and evolving business trends. Scenario analyses are usually built in. A similar approach can be taken for portfolio decision making.

Portfolio management is moving more to a process, which is repeated at regular intervals, rather than an annual budgeting and lobbying round. To support this, those who facilitate the function can design the sequence in which performance, supply and demand are considered to lead to more rational decisions. Technology can be introduced to enable the evaluation of scenarios and options.

Don't lose touch with reality, even if you have great ideas

Workout 15.1 – How do you select your projects?

This workout goes to the heart of how you drive your business. We have already looked at who makes selection decision in Workout 13.1. This workout looks at how they make those decisions. If your organization is already running to a defined approach then answering this question will be easy; you simply call up the appropriate process. But is that enough? Even if you have a defined approach, ask yourself, are those making the decisions and those impacted by the decisions noting whether the approach is actually working or are some of the symptoms looked at in Chapter 1 still apparent? Be honest as you'll be fooling no one except yourself.

If you have no defined approach, you'll need to ask those who make the decisions how they do it. What do they take into account? Do they use any specific methods or criteria? Does the approach relate to specific types of projects? How are other projects dealt with? Make notes and keep a list of any comments and queries you have.

In both cases make sure that the five factors illustrated in Figure 11.3 are taken into account, namely:

- strategic alignment;
- balance;
- risk;
- aligned capabilities;
- capacity for change.

You should now have a list of approaches and what type of work they apply to. You should also have an understanding of any gaps or concerns from different stakeholders. By collecting these 'facts' and 'opinions' you have a foundation on which to look at how to improve the selection approach. You might also find the decision makers are wrongly assigned and that could take some sorting out, especially if they are working on an old 'departmental' model . . . which brings us to the reason why this book exists to promote an agile and integrated approach to managing an organization.

16

Directing business portfolios

A process-based approach

Business portfolio management processes

The supporting processes

Implications for a business portfolio sponsor or manager

You need to make sure that the interfaces from the process for directing and managing the portfolio's components are clear and unambiguous. You will also need to make any decisions which you have not delegated to others.

"First say to yourself what you would be; and then do what you have to do."

EPICTETUS, 50–135 AD

- **The business portfolio manager sets the way everything else is managed.**
- **Make the interface to organization management clear.**
- **Define the roles and their respective activities and deliverables.**
- **Decide what can be tailored.**

Business portfolio management processes

Chapter 10 looked at a process model for managing a project, which includes a process called 'Manage higher level'. The management of a business portfolio represents the 'Manage higher level' process, except when a project is part of a programme (for this see Chapter 20). Business portfolios, however, can include not only projects but also programmes and other related work. This can become very complicated, especially as 'other related work' can be anything which is not a project, which itself might or might not be part of a programme. For this reason, the process model shown here refers to a 'business portfolio component'. This reflects the terms used in the international standards (see Chapter 29 for more on standards), where a component could be a sub-portfolio, a programme, a project or any other, defined, related work (refer back to Figure 3.3).

The business portfolio management processes are shown in Figure 16.1 and described as following sections.

Initiate a new business portfolio

The purpose of this process is for the management board to provide the instruction and brief for creating a new business portfolio. This could be in response to the organization's changing environment as a way of refocussing the strategic direction. This should include appointing the business portfolio sponsor accountable for setting up the portfolio and for its on-going direction.

Provide direction and review business portfolios

Unless an organisation is very small, it is likely to have more than one business portfolio. The purpose of this process is for the management board to make sure that the business portfolios, as a whole, cover the needs of the organization. From this process, targets and objectives are set and overall performance measured at organizational level. Any issues which cannot be resolved at business portfolio level should be escalated to here and dealt with. Similarly, there might be risks which need to be handled at organization level as they might impact a number of business portfolios.

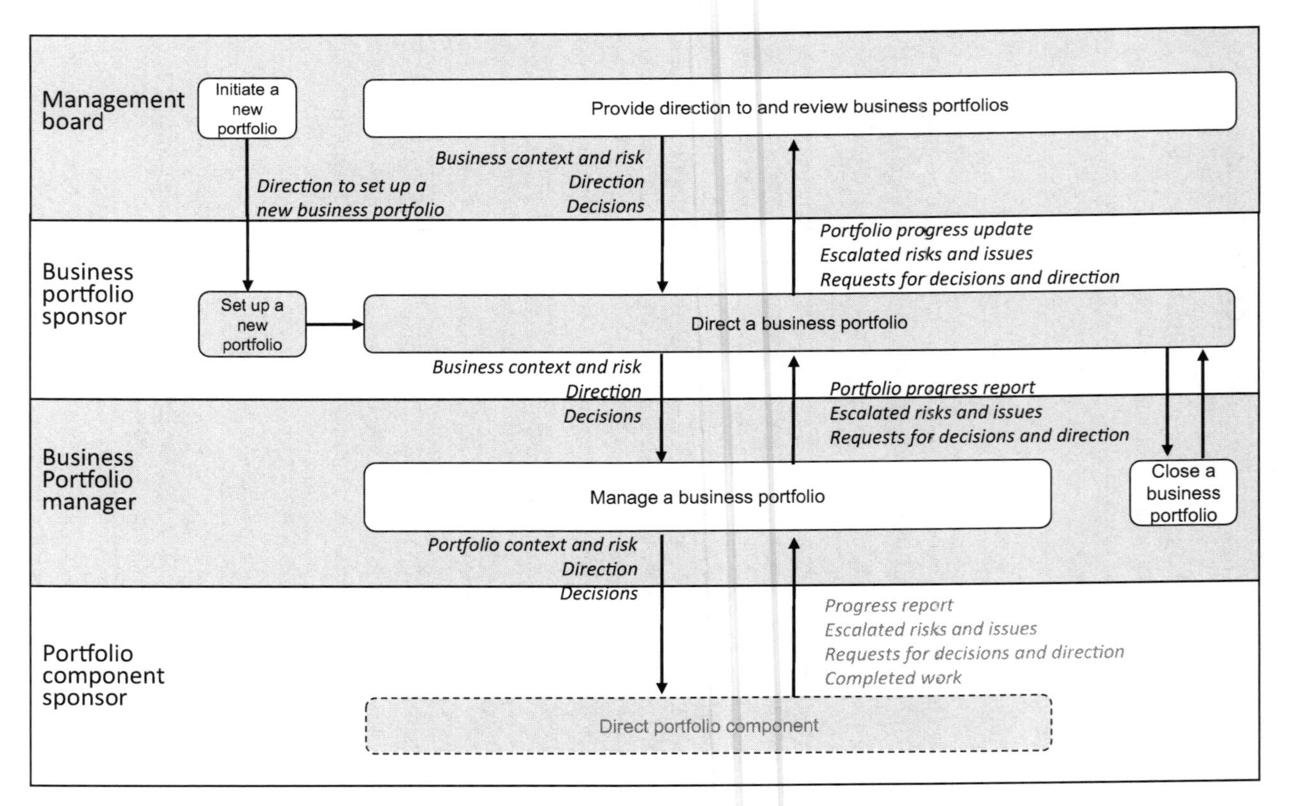

Figure 16.1 Portfolio management processes

The key management activities and their relationships (inputs and outputs) are shown here, with each activity in a swim lane to show which role is accountable. Notice the 'management board' lane; this represents the highest authority in the organization, accountable for all the business portfolios. This is the group (or person) to whom the business portfolio sponsor is accountable.

Set up a new business portfolio

The purpose of setting up a new business portfolio is to ensure that all the necessary roles are filled, initial plans developed and methods and processes (with supporting systems) designed. This should include defining the decision-making authorities and processes for submitting and approving portfolio components. In addition, the different business portfolio components and their management methods should be defined together with criteria for categorizing and selecting these portfolio components. The planning horizon for the portfolio should be defined together with the frequency of updates. Different business portfolios might have different planning horizons and refresh frequencies; it depends on how fast the environment is changing.

Direct a business portfolio

This process is undertaken by the business portfolio sponsor to ensure the business interests of the organization are paramount and reflected in the objectives of the business portfolio. This mainly comprises proactively tuning objectives for the business portfolio in response to the organization's changing environment and circumstances as well as reacting to any escalations. There is more about sponsorship in Chapter 5.

Manage a business portfolio

Define and plan the business portfolio

The business portfolio should be defined and planned to meet the objectives set by the business programme sponsor and agreed with the management board. When planning the business portfolio:

- strategic objectives, context and priorities should be understood, together with the current status of the business portfolio and its components;
- potential new portfolio components should be categorized and evaluated, based on their degree of strategic fit, expected benefits, efficient use of funds and risk. The views of stakeholders should be understood and considered;
- portfolio components should be prioritized and selected, based on the results of the evaluation, taking into account the performance of existing portfolio components;
- each work component should be traceable to and from an aspect of the organization's strategy and objectives;
- the plan should be collated with interdependencies identified between components within and outside the business portfolio;
- once approved, the business portfolio plan should be baselined and any changes approved by the appropriate authority.

A record of the portfolio's components should be kept up to date, including: the component type; responsible persons; status (for example: proposed, in progress, suspended, terminated, completed); the position in the business portfolio hierarchy; significant interdependencies between components under different sponsors.

Figure 16.2 shows the key activities, which are described as follows.

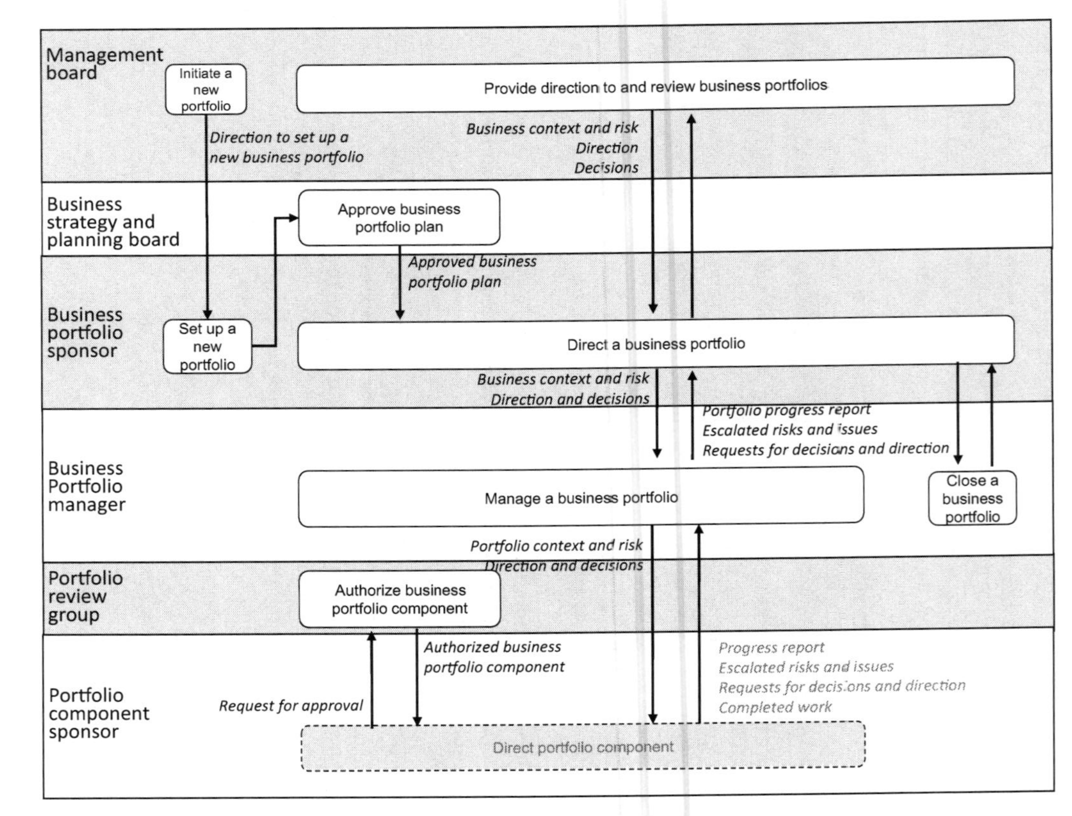

Figure 16.2 Manage a business portfolio – more detail

The 'manage a business portfolio' activity in Figure 16.1t can be broken down into more detail, as shown here. There are numerous ways this can be depicted, but the main features are shown.

Validate the business portfolio's objectives and strategy

The business portfolio's objectives and strategy should be periodically reviewed to ensure:

- they are still current and affordable;
- the right programmes, projects and other work are being undertaken to meet those objectives.

If not validated, corrective action needs to be taken to amend the portfolio's strategy and objectives or adjust the portfolio's components.

Monitor business portfolio delivery

The business portfolio should be monitored and analyzed with respect to:

- outcomes, and benefits realization;
- adherence to cost, schedule or other defined constraints;
- delivery of primary outputs;
- availability of finance;
- current capacity and capability constraints in the organization and supply chain;
- current level of portfolio risk, including those related to interdependencies;
- reaction of impacted parties and other stakeholders.

Stakeholders should be monitored and engaged, with new stakeholders identified and existing stakeholders revaluated.

New risks and issues should be identified and existing ones managed. Action should be taken to keep the portfolio on plan and reflect any constraints. Existing work components might need to be amended, rescheduled or terminating. Corrective and preventative actions might trigger the need for new portfolio components or scope changes in existing components.

Report business portfolio performance

Business portfolio performance should be reported against the agreed plan, including, but not limited to, financials, benefits, important milestones and risk. Additional analysis and commentary might be needed to explain variances. Reporting should reflect both achievement to date and a forecast for future performance.

Authorize the start of a portfolio component

New portfolio components should be identified, defined and authorized to start when indicated in the plan or as required by organizational priorities. Before being initiated, the business portfolio manager should confirm the strategic alignment, financial, resources and technical capability are available and that the component does not conflict with or duplicate other work.

When approving the start of a portfolio component, the problem or opportunity needs to be understood, even though the solution and implementation approach might not yet be known.

Direct business portfolio component

This process is not part of the business portfolio management but represents the interface to the business portfolio's components, with each respective component sponsor acting as the accountable person. For project components see Chapter 10 and for a programme component see Chapter 20.

The supporting processes

Figure 10.2 showed the most commonly used supporting processes for project management and the relationships between them. These are also applicable to business portfolio management. Most of the topics essential to business portfolio management are described in Part V of this book but you might wish to add others, to reflect the needs of your organization.

Implications for a business portfolio sponsor or manager

Think 'top-down'

Check that the business environment hasn't changed so much over time as to make the portfolio's components either irrelevant or sub-optimal.

The business portfolio sponsor or manager represents the 'higher authority' for any constituent programmes, projects or other portfolio components. and therefore, deciding what work needs to be started (and when) is part of this role. Make sure that the interfaces from the process for directing and managing the portfolio's components are clear and unambiguous. The business portfolio sponsor/manager also needs to make any decisions which have not been delegated to others and, in some cases, might also take on a formal programme or project sponsor role. Check that the business environment hasn't changed so much over time as to make the portfolio's components either irrelevant or sub-optimal. Finally, ensure each component achieves whatever it was intended to achieve, bearing in mind risk. This doesn't mean that every part of the portfolio has to be successful; that is very unlikely. It does, however, mean that the business portfolio is moving in the right direction.

Roles

The process model in Figure 16.1 includes the primary roles. The business portfolio and planning board and the portfolio review group from Chapter 11 have not been explicitly shown. The permutations of individual responsibilities and those of numerous boards are limitless and often changing. In some cases, boards or groups are subservient to an individual and sometimes it is the other way around. There is no single right way of defining this, except that such relationships are fundamental to good governance and need to be defined and understood by those involved. Such boards are often used to ensure cross-functional cohesion and avoid the trap many organizations fall in to where a single function works in its own interests rather than those of the whole organization. For example, if, by default you want portfolio components to be approved by a portfolio review group, which acts across a number of business portfolios, then this could be added as an explicit lane (see Figure 16.3). Likewise, if the plans for each portfolio have to be approved by a particular planning and strategy board, which is distinct from the management, this could also be added.

Processes

Figures 16.1 and 16.2 show just two possible architectures for directing and managing a business portfolio. It is possible to assemble the activities in a number of ways to emphasize different approaches or to reflect an organization's culture. It is better to keep a consistent approach from top to bottom in how different aspects of the process are described. Do not change terminology without a good reason; the more intuitive the processes, the more likely they are to be used. Remember, you rely on each component of the business portfolio being managed effectively so take an interest in the processes for those; do not abdicate that responsibility. Make sure the processes are defined in sufficient detail to be useful and do not include spurious detail. Ironically, the less experienced teams are, the more process they seem to need! That is why process alone is not enough; you need to make sure people are competent to undertake their assigned roles; the more senior the role, the more important it is. Just because a person has a senior rank in the organization, it doesn't mean they are, miraculously, an expert at doing everything.

Just because a person has a senior rank in the organization, it doesn't mean they are, miraculously, an expert at doing everything.

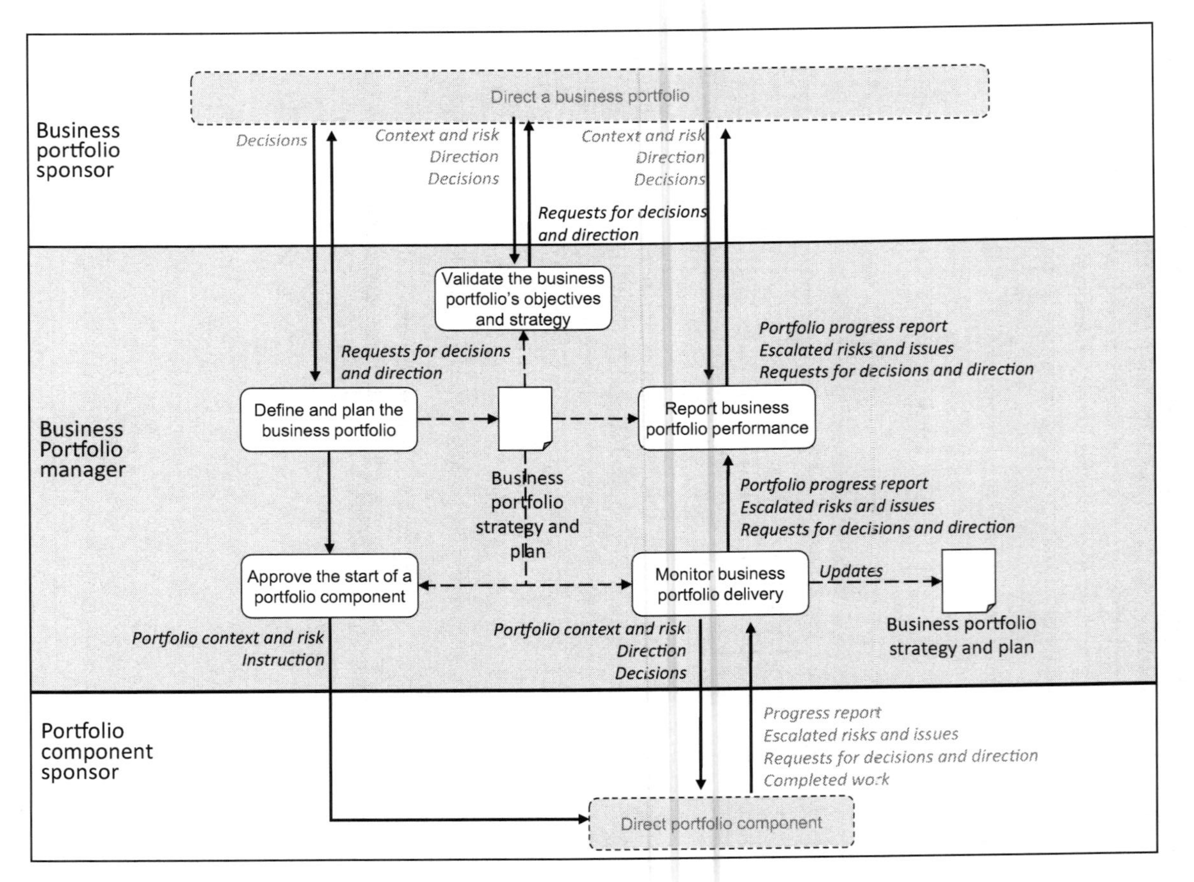

Figure 16.3 Portfolio management processes – an alternative

This model builds on Figure 16.1 by showing the business strategy and planning board and the portfolio review group as explicit lanes rather having them 'hidden' in the next level of detail. How you depict your processes should reflect the way you want governance to work in your organization.

Tailoring

Not every programme, project or other portfolio component will need to use all the available processes. Further, the extent to which each process is used can vary, such as from programme to programme or even within a programme or project. In addition, commercial obligations in contracts associated with the work should not conflict with the defined processes. Allowing tailoring is, therefore, essential; this gives the manager of any portfolio component the freedom to define the detail and rigour for the application of each process. If working within an enterprise-defined method, tailoring should only be done when it adds value, not as a matter of personal preference. Tailoring should be undertaken on a cascade basis, as shown in Figure 16.4. The higher level sets the degrees of freedom within which all lower levels operate. Those working at the lower levels have to tailor and choose their working methods within those constraints. One of the decisions a business portfolio manager needs to make is to decide the degrees of freedom they will allow for those managing the business portfolio's components.

Tailoring should be undertaken on a cascade basis

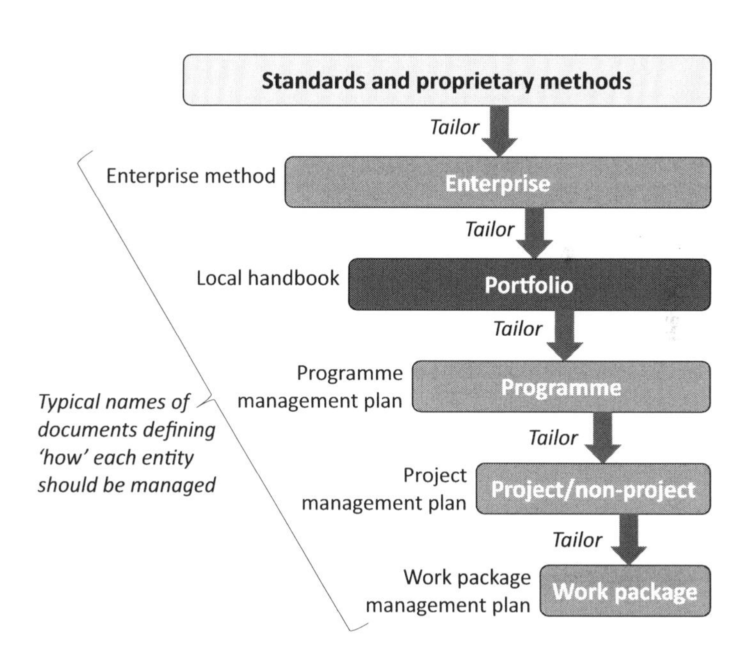

Figure 16.4 Tailoring – a cascade

The higher levels set degrees of freedom within which all lower levels operate. Those working at the lower levels can tailor and choose their working methods within those constraints. The business portfolio manager should decide what degrees of freedom they will allow for those managing their components.

Workout 16.1 – Building your own business portfolio management processes

Use the figures in this chapter as a guide to start building your own business portfolio management process. Make sure you include all the important roles, deliverables and activities.

Define what boards or groups are need in addition to the roles in Figure 16.1. These might be added as a separate swim lane or as a lane at the next level of detail. How you design and present this depends on what messages you want to send.

Pay attention to the interface to the business portfolio components (such as programmes and projects). This needs to be tightly defined so that people know the boundaries of their authority, who they are accountable to and the default line of reporting and escalation.

Once you have your own version of Figure 16.1 you can start defining the next level of activities, such as in Figure 16.2. Draw on publicly available content such as this book, AXELOS' *Management of Portfolios* and the British and international standards for the detail (see Chapter 29).

PART IV
PROGRAMME MANAGEMENT

"Organizing is what you do before you do something, so that when you do it, it is not all mixed up."

A. A. MILNE, 1882–1956

In this part of the book, I look at programmes, how programme management is distinct from project management and portfolio management and how you should organize your work to reflect those distinctions.

- **Programmes are governed through a business case.**
- **Focus on the outcomes needed to achieve your benefits.**
- **Keep a list of all the projects and other work you are undertaking and the interdependencies between them.**
- **Know where the risks are, both within and between the components of the programme.**
- **Make sure the components of your programme are being directed and managed effectively and you have the resources to sustain momentum**

How to use Part IV

Before using Part IV of this book, you will need to be familiar with Parts I, II and III. The boundaries between project management, programme management and portfolio management are not necessarily distinct. When working through this part of the book, consider whether the chunks of work you have called 'programmes', fit this model or whether the work might be better managed using a different approach. I can't give you the answers, you'll need to work that out for yourself. The workouts in Part IV are designed to help managers challenge their thinking. As programmes share many of the characteristics of projects and portfolios, you might also find adapting workouts for Parts II and III useful.

17

Programme management

What is different about programme management?

What does a typical programme look like?

Programme life cycles?

Simplify, simplify, simplify

Prerequisites for effective programme management

Don't think in terms of whether the work is a project or a programme but rather whether it is better to ***manage*** *the work as a project or a programme.*

"The wise man doesn't give the right answers, he poses the right questions."

CLAUDE LEVI-STRAUSS, 1908–2009

- **Programmes share many of the characteristics of portfolio s and projects; make use of those similarities.**
- **Understand why you have chosen to manage your work as a programme.**
- **Keep track of what work your programme comprises.**
- **Choose the scope of each component of your programme carefully; minimize dependencies.**
- **Simplify your plan; it should tell a coherent story.**

What is different about programme management?

This is not an easy question to answer, not least because there are so many different views on what a programme is (or is not). The team creating the international standards on portfolio, programme and project management started by defining a standard for project management (ISO 21500:2012) and then worked on the standard for portfolio management (ISO 21504:2015). The standard for programme management followed a few years later (ISO21503:2017). The programme management standard was the last to be created because it took so long to reach a consensus on what a programme is. Everyone acknowledged that a programme is something between a project and a portfolio, but a precise definition was difficult to agree.

Project or programme?

At one time, a project was distinguished from a programme by saying projects created outputs, but programmes create outcomes. This approach was dispelled in Chapter 3 as it totally negates the concept of business led project management. The outputs-based method is still used but, thankfully, is gradually disappearing. Another approach is to regard programmes as bigger than projects, taking longer, being more complex and exhibiting a greater degree of uncertainty and complexity. This might be true for many programmes but it is not necessarily true for all programmes. Projects can also be very complex, uncertain and large. For this reason, trying to distinguish a programme from a project by using such characteristics alone, can be misleading.

Projects and programmes have several similarities as both are:

- time-bound, having a beginning and an end;
- governed through a business case and need to be justified on a case by case basis;
- have a defined objective;
- require a team to undertake them, outside normal line management authority;
- use common supporting practices, such as risk management (see Part V).

Whilst a programme can be undertaken in phases, such phases are not the equivalent of a project's stages,

To repeat Chapter 3, don't think in terms of whether the work is a project or a programme but rather whether it is better to *manage* the work as a project or a programme. A project, as defined in Part II, comprises a life cycle, where each stage of the life cycle has a number of work packages within which the 'real work' takes place. Generally, the project manager manages the project as a whole and oversees each stage of the project. If a project does not have life cycle stages, it can be managed as a work package. Whilst a programme can be undertaken in phases, such phases are not the equivalent of a project's stages, as is explained later in this chapter.

Programme management is needed when the extent and type of work makes it untenable to manage all the work as a series of project stages within a single project. The work is too extensive for a single individual to manage in detail and might require the delivery of a number of outputs and outcomes over a period of time. In such circumstances, the 'power-distance' of the programme manager from the people doing the 'real' work is greater, than for a project manager.

- A project manager generally manages the people (team managers) who are leading the teams producing the specialist deliverables.
- A programme manager manages the project managers (and managers of any other work components) and is therefore at least one step further removed from the 'real work'. Programme managers manage managers.

Programme or portfolio?

In many ways a portfolio and a programme can be seen as so similar, the distinction is not always clear. Both:

- are more extensive than a single individual can deal with;
- have a degree of uncertainty and complexity;
- comprise programmes, projects and other work;
- deliver several outputs and outcomes over a period of time;
- should realize benefits, in line with defined objectives.

The distinguishing factors are:

- programmes are governed through a business case, whilst business portfolios are governed through a business plan (usually approved annually);
- programmes should be of a finite (even if uncertain) duration, whilst business portfolios might have no perceivable end point.

Business portfolio management is more concerned with managing an organization as a whole, with each chunk of change (such as a programme or a project) needing to be justified in a business case and achieved within the constraints of the business plan.

A business portfolio manager is at least one step further removed from the real work than a programme manager. This increasing power-distance between 'the top' and the 'real work' can result in sluggish decision making if delegation of authority isn't appropriately defined.

Business case or business plan?

A reminder.

A **business case** is used to authorize the commitment of resources and spend for a specific purpose over a specified period. It is updated only when its constraints have been breached.

A **business plan** covers a fixed period (usually based on financial years). It is a statement of intention and the available funds and resources. It results in budgets being set, with managers having to comply with rules for spending the funds. A business plan does not provide any authorization or commitment of resources, although it does create an expectation that they will be authorized.

Harness the similarities

The higher you are in the work breakdown structure, the more holistic your thinking needs to be.

The fact that a programme shares some of the characteristics of a project and some of the characteristics of a portfolio means that many of the management techniques discussed in this book and in *The Project Workout* can be applied to both. The obvious shared techniques, called 'supporting activities or processes', are dealt with in Part V of this book. What changes is the perspective of the user of those processes. The higher you are in the work breakdown structure, the more holistic your thinking needs to be. For example, a manager of a work package would be solely concerned with managing individual risks and escalating those they could not deal with to the project manager. A programme manager, on the other hand, needs to look at the whole landscape of risks to identify patterns and common causes that potentially impact their programme. They should be concerned with managing the totality of risk and making sure this is addressed and there is contingency in the right places.

At the margins, a choice can be made as to whether a particular piece of work is to be managed as a project, programme or business portfolio (Figure 17.1). For example, Chapter 15 explains some techniques to select the projects and other work to put in the business portfolio; the same techniques can be used to select which projects should be included in a programme and when.

Figure 17.1 Choosing the appropriate management approach

In some cases, you can make a choice as to whether a particular piece of work can be managed as a project, programme or business portfolio.

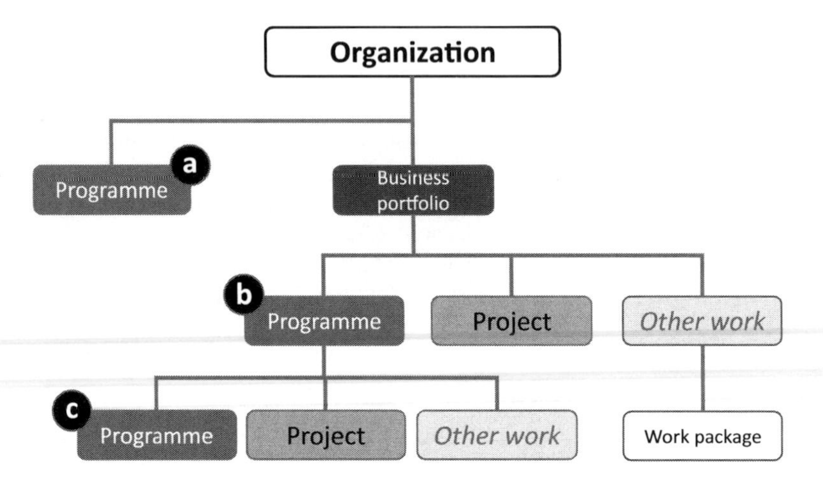

Figure 17.2 Programmes in the context of organizations and portfolios

A programme could be standalone within an organization (a) or it might be a component part of a portfolio (b). In addition, a programme can also be part of a higher-level programme (c).

Programmes in the context of an organization or portfolio

A programme could be standalone within an organization or a component part of a business portfolio (Figure 17.2). In addition, a programme can also be part of a higher level programme (in other words, a sub-programme or tranche). The context will not necessarily affect the processes used when managing a programme, but it will put different constraints on:

- the programme sponsor and their freedom to direct the programme;
- the programme manager in terms of their freedom to manage the programme.

Similarly, a programme manager constrains the freedom of the project managers of the projects within their programme. The context affects governance because the work breakdown structure forms a fundamental line of accountability (who is accountable to whom and for what; see Chapter 4).

The context affects governance because the work breakdown structure forms a fundamental line of accountability

What does a typical programme look like?

A programme comprises components, such as projects and 'other work' and however it is depicted, each component should be obvious. Four different approaches are commonly used to depict a programme, all of which are different viewpoints on a programme's plan:

- network;
- schedule;
- outcomes and benefits;
- list.

Do not fall into the trap of defining a programme based on the pre-determined organization structure. An organization structure should be designed to support the programme's work content. All too often, people start with an organization structure and then wonder why programmes become complicated as they struggle to manage the interdependencies.

The network

If you can't draw the network, you can't manage the programme. The network shows the interdependencies between the component parts of the programme with each box representing a project or other work component. It should be derived from the benefits map (see Chapter 21). The network diagram shows the order in which the work components need to be done, driven by logic, rather than resource or funding constraints. The precise nature of each dependency needs to be understood and defined. Dependencies should represent a deliverable, output or an outcome from one work component, which is required by another work component. A work component that only delivers an output is often called an 'enabler' or 'enabling project'.

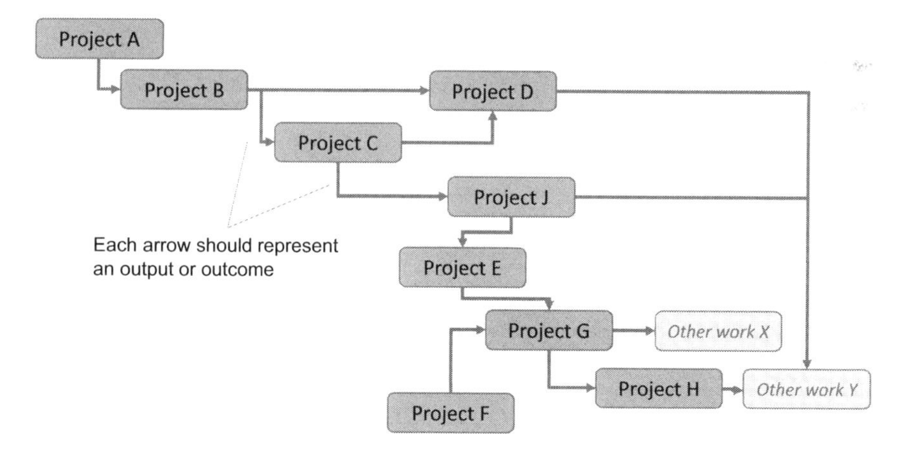

Figure 17.3 A network diagram for a programme

The lines in a network shows the interdependencies between the component parts of the programme. Each line should represent a deliverable, an output or an outcome.

Do not be tempted to think of dependencies in terms of, "It depends on the weather," "It depends if the resources are available" or "It depends if we have the money." These are valid issues but are dealt with in other ways. The first (weather) is a risk; the other two are constraints that need to be checked before a decision to start work is made.

The schedule

The schedule shows when each component of the programme starts and ends. It can also show key milestones within each component, such as project gates or other decision points, outputs, outcomes and points when benefits streams are triggered. The logic in the network is used to build an initial version of the schedule by placing them in the order the dependencies determine; for this reason, the names and number of components should match those on the network diagram. The network and schedule diagrams are simply different ways of viewing the same information. The manager of each component should have an achievable plan, taking into account funding, costs and resource constraints. They should also have a view on risks. When it comes to creating the programme's schedule, the components need to be placed such that overall time, resource, cost and funding constraints are respected and overall risk is acceptable whilst, at the same time, achieving the stated objectives. This often means placing buffers on the interdependencies so slippage in one component does wreck the entire schedule by knocking into and delaying the following components. An example of buffering is shown in Figure 17.4. Many

This often means placing buffers on the interdependencies so slippage in one component does wreck the entire schedule

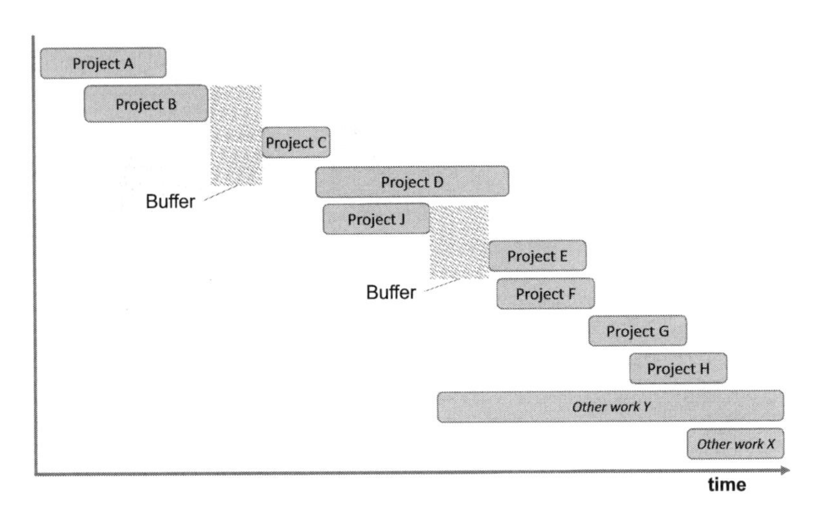

Figure 17.4 A schedule for a programme, showing the buffers

The example from Figure 17.3 is now shown as a schedule. Notice the buffers that protect Project C from slippage in Projects A and B and the buffer which protects Project E. Buffers are a pragmatic way of planning contingency against overall schedule slippage.

business managers dislike the idea of adding buffers into the schedule and see this as needlessly delaying the programme. Likewise, finance managers often view buffers as a waste of money and neglect the 'risk' element. This is where the skill and experience of a programme manager counts: every buffer in the schedule needs to be justified and the consequences of removing them understood. The difficulty is that very few components are likely to be on time, and so the whole schedule is in a constant state of flux. The key is to focus on the milestones that really matter and manage the size and placing of the buffers to protect those 'key milestones'. For many programmes, slippage of some components can be inconsequential and an over emphasis of bringing everything in on time can actually have the opposite effect. This approach is an extension of the concepts developed by Eli Goldratt in his critical chain techniques for project planning.

Upgrade of Reading station

Reading station serves four routes:

1. the main line operating from west of Paddington station in London, with services to Wales and Cornwall;
2. connections to Guildford and Gatwick airport and the North Downs;
3. an electric suburban line linking Reading to London Waterloo Station;
4. north-south routes to Birmingham, Northern England, Scotland, Winchester, Southampton and Bournemouth.

The £850m programme lasted from 2011 to 2015, and the component parts included:

1. a new Thames Valley signalling centre;
2. four new platforms on the north side of the station;
3. a new south side platform and platform extensions for Waterloo line services;
4. grade separation of the track on the east side of the station;
5. a new train maintenance facility to the west of the station replacing the existing facility;
6. a new transfer deck and escalators to platforms;
7. grade separation by provision of elevated mainline to the west of the station facilitating improvements to Cow Lane Bridge;
8. grade separation of the western chord from Oxford Road Junction to Westbury Line junction;
9. extensive track layout reconfiguration;
10. provision for Crossrail services and introduction of AirTrack services to London's Heathrow Airport.

The scheduling challenges are that the railway needs to keep operating, often limiting working time to a few hours in the night or bank holiday closures, when major works, such as rolling a 1000 tonne bridge in to position, happen. Miss one of these deadlines and there could be a year's delay.

Outcomes and benefits

Programmes are set up to realize outcomes and benefits. For this reason, a time-based (schedule) view on when outcomes will be delivered and benefits realized is needed. The trigger points should be identified by milestones in the schedule. Benefits should be looked at as money oriented but can be difficult to track, predict and measure. For this reason, outcomes can be used as a leading indicator and are more practical to implement. Figure 17.5 builds on Figure 17.4 to show this.

Let's look at an example. The Reading station upgrade case study created five additional platforms (outputs) which enabled the following outcomes:

- a minimum of four additional train paths per hour in each direction;
- 125%improvement on through line platform capacity;
- 38%improvement in service performance.

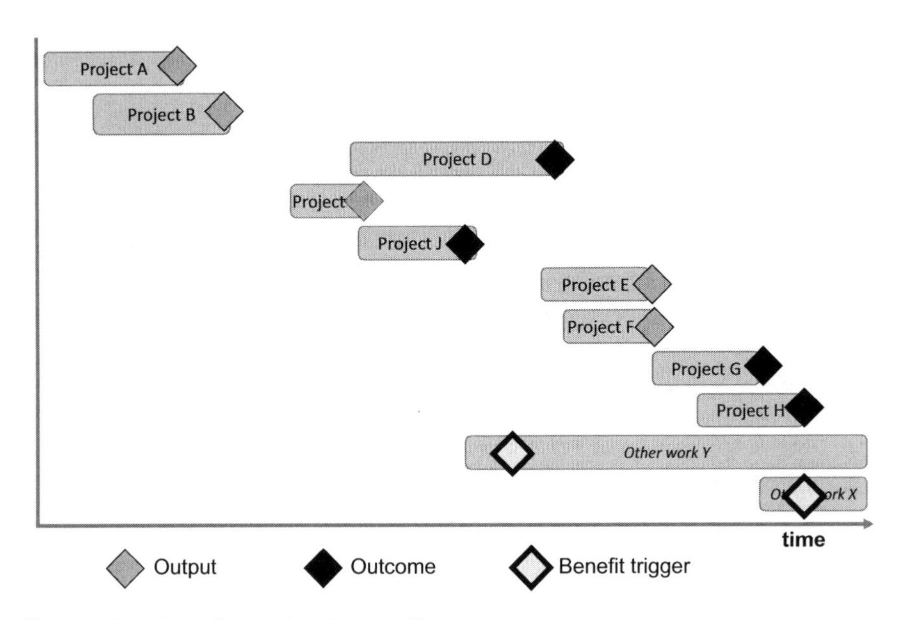

Figure 17.5 Benefits and outcomes from a programme

The example from Figure 17.4 now has the outputs, outcomes and benefits triggers shown. These are what the sponsor is really looking for.

These outcomes can be measured, whereas the economic and social benefits in terms of increase in GDP and growth of local economies on the lines which pass through Reading are difficult to assess. Further, the analysis required could also mean that the results of any measurement could lag by up to a year.

When looking at a programme from a benefits or outcome perspective, the trigger and measurement points for the outcomes and benefits need to be linked to the schedule. Look at:

Outcomes and benefits need to be linked to the schedule

- the benefits mapping technique described in Chapter 21 which describes the essential linkage from outputs to outcomes to benefits;
- Figure 11.1 in Chapter 11 on business portfolio management, which shows that rewards are reaped from existing operations, whilst creating new opportunities through undertaking projects. This also applies to programmes.

The list

Lists can be powerful and for a programme sponsor or manager, having a list of the component parts of the programme is a simple yet effective way of keeping control. Like the network, schedule and outcomes and benefits, the list is simply another way of viewing the same information. As a minimum the 'list' should include the:

- name of the component; always use the same name;
- type of component; is it a 'sub-programme', 'project' or other defined work component;
- sponsor's name, the business leader;
- manager's name, the person managing the component (e.g., project manager).

People's names are important as you'll need to know who to talk to; on a large programme, people can churn through roles continuously, and memory is not always reliable.

Look at Chapter 28, which describes the systems and applications needed to support programme management and what a typical list looks like. The list can be expanded to form a status report, highlighting key milestones, outcome achievement, benefit triggers, financial figures and risks. Notice that these are the same systems needed for business portfolio management, it is just that you are focussing in on a particular part of the work breakdown structure.

Programme life cycles?

Beware the simplistic life cycle

The use of the term 'life cycle' can be problematic, even when dealing with projects, the main criticism being that it isn't a 'cycle'. As demonstrated in Chapter 8, however, the project life cycle is a powerful way of managing risk on projects, which is a tool every programme manager needs! When it comes to programmes, the life cycle can be confusing as there are so many different views. The commonest approach is to design a programme's life cycle as an extension of a project life cycle, comprising several phases, such as shown in Figure 17.6.

Such an approach looks logical and seems to deal with every aspect of a programme. Is it, however, useful to a programme manager? The purpose of chunking up work into components such as work packages, stages, phases is to make the programme easier to direct and manage. As Figure 17.6 (a) shows, the simple life cycle described earlier might make sense for some straight-forward programmes, although it does raise questions:

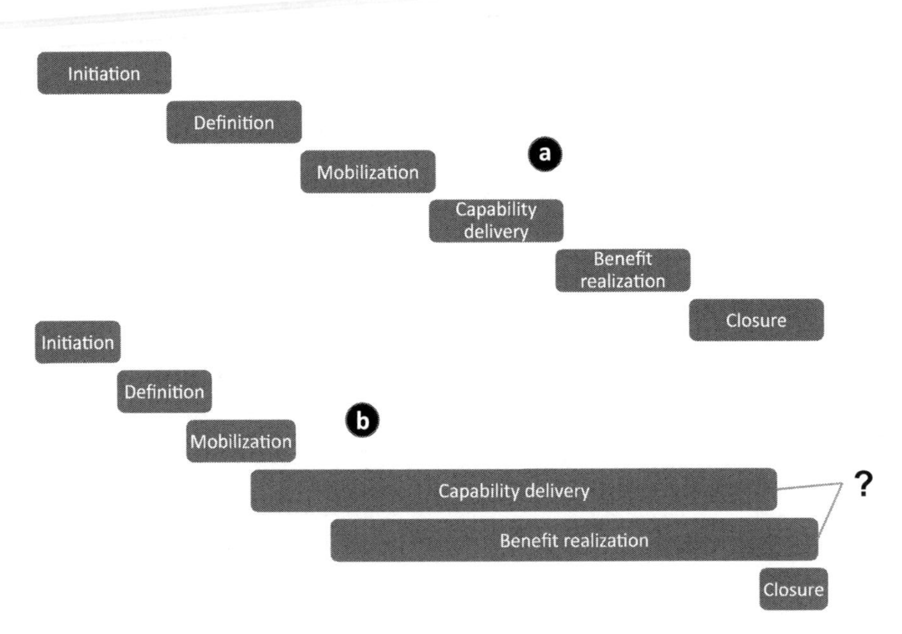

Figure 17.6 The limitations of a simplistic life cycle for a programme

(a) shows a simplistic life cycle for a programme. Each block represents a programme phase. In practice benefits realization would start as soon as the first project delivered an outcome and so the sequential nature of 'capability delivery' to 'benefits realization' is unlikely to be as shown. (b) shows how it is more likely to appear, with significant overlap between 'capability delivery' and 'benefits realization'.

- Why not manage this as a project?
- Where is the decision to actually put a capability into service?
- What is the decision point which starts 'benefits realization?'

If, however, the programme has a large number of projects, each of which triggers a new benefits stream, a simple life cycle would lead to a significant overlap between 'capability delivery' and 'benefits realization' (as shown in (b)): this split is of little use to management.

More terminology to confuse people

In this chapter I refer to 'phases', using the term in its standard dictionary meaning: "a distinct period in a series of events or a process of change or development." In programme management literature, standards and methods alternative words are used. The most common are 'tranche' and 'wave'. By using such distinctive words, authors can add additional features as distinctions. For example, 'tranche' is used in *Managing Successful Programmes®* to (rightly) make a programme *phase* distinct from a project *stage*. Wave is often used in the context of major change, where each wave adds a distinctly new set of outcomes.

Building a programme life cycle which works for you

Unless you are undertaking work similar to that which you have done before, you cannot start with a model programme life cycle. The life cycle should be built to suit the work needed. The key considerations are:

- placement of key decisions;
- the logic flow over time;
- the timing of outcomes.

Decisions are key

How a programme is divided into life cycle phases or any other component parts should be driven by the decisions needed

Decisions are key in life cycle design; senior managers make decisions and so every work component should be preceded by a decision. In other words, how a programme is divided into life cycle phases or any other component parts should be driven by the decisions needed and not just the type of work undertaken.

Chapter 8 introduced the term 'gate' in respect of decision points prior to the start of a project stage. Do programmes have 'gates?' The obvious answer is 'yes' as they are simply decision points. Following this logic, a phase of a programme should also be preceded by a decision to start that phase. But what about the decision to start the first project or work component in that phase; does that require a decision, and, if so, who should make that decision? Chapter 8 describes how a decision at the 'initial investigation gate' is required to start a project. It seems, therefore, that we would need to have a decision both at programme level and at project level. This could be wasteful of senior management time as, if the first project is not ready to be started, the phase is not ready either. The two decisions are tightly linked. The decision to start the phase and start the project are the same decision. This simple example shows that from a programme sponsor or manager's viewpoint, closely related decisions can be stacked vertically into a single decision and the choice of decision maker is paramount. The decision maker in the previous example, ought to be the programme sponsor (or higher) as the starting of the first project represents a major commitment to the entire phase. If you really want to separate the decisions, the criteria for starting the first project must include a check that the phase has already been approved to start.

Another decision which could be elevated from project level to programme level is when an output is released for use. The decision to put a capability into service or launch a product is fundamental and, in many cases, the reputation of the sponsoring organization is at stake. It is a matter of the level of risk which is acceptable. Figure 17.7 illustrates this, showing the examples of decisions which could (or should!) be elevated to programme level. Stacking or separating decisions is a matter of choice. By stacking them, the senior leadership is drawn into the programme at depth, at key points, keeping them visibly in touch with the realities as seen from the lower-level management perspectives. It also makes senior management acutely aware of the immediate impact of their decisions and the concerns of their lower-level managers.

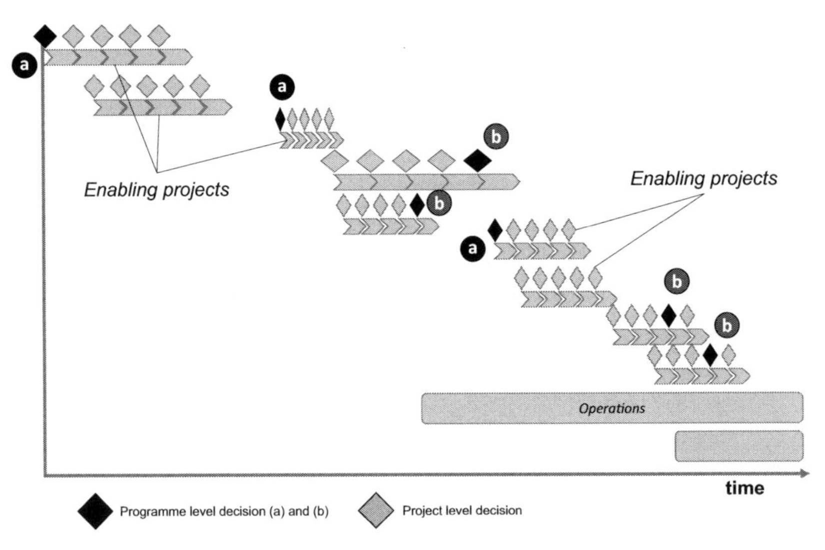

Figure 17.7 Positioning key decisions at the right level

Programme level decisions need to be made when starting a new phase (a). This is usually a significant strategic decision. Decisions are also neede when releasing a capability for use (b) for example, at a project's release gate shown in Figures 8.4 and 8.5. Other decisions could be made at the project level, depending on perceived risk and value.

Logic flow over time

The network and schedule introduced earlier, together with an understanding of the timing of outcomes and benefits triggers is the primary clue to structuring the programme. Unless you understand this, any plans you make will be rootless. It is true that this could change as the programme progresses, but that is just a fact of programme life; the external context changes as does the knowledge gained inside the programme.

Often the logic flow is determined by the type of programme undertaken. Whilst there might not be a generic programme life cycle, there can be models for different types of programmes.

A practical approach

A programme has a beginning, middle and end, and these distinctions should be respected by the life cycle.

The 'beginning' focusses on looking for solutions to problems and building as complete as possible view of what the end-state looks like. This might be an aircraft, a new high-speed rail link or a radically changed business. Whatever the vision prompting the programme, it has to be made more concrete in terms of the outcomes needed. At the beginning, you might not even know whether you want to manage the work as a programme or as a project. The beginning is concerned with initiating and defining the programme.

The 'middle' should be focussed on creating whatever is needed and ensuring the prerequisite changes happen. This is the meat of the programme, and it is likely to dwarf the 'beginning' in scale and complexity. It can take so long, that to many people working within it, the beginning is forgotten (or was never known about); the middle can feel like 'business as usual'. Whatever is developed or created could be released as a single entity, in a series of waves or it might roll out incrementally, with hundreds of small changes gradually building up to the end state. The middle is concerned with mobilization, capability delivery, business change and benefits realization.

The 'end' should be focussed on closing the programme down. In reality, this is about dismantling the programme's governance framework and ensuring any ongoing aspects are taken on within the organization's governance framework. Hopefully this would be a gradual handover as each capability comes into service or each new change is embedded. The end is concerned with demobilization, disposal and redeployment.

From this simple model, the programme can be grown to fit the need. Figures 17.8 to 17.11 are some examples.

In Figure 17.8, the programme is depicted as a simple three phase programme. Incremental benefits realization and outcomes are shown, together with a hand over to business as usual at the end of the programme.

Figure 17.9 shows an extension to Figure 17.8 as the 'middle' is now undertaken in three phases (you could call them tranches or waves). Each phase can be managed

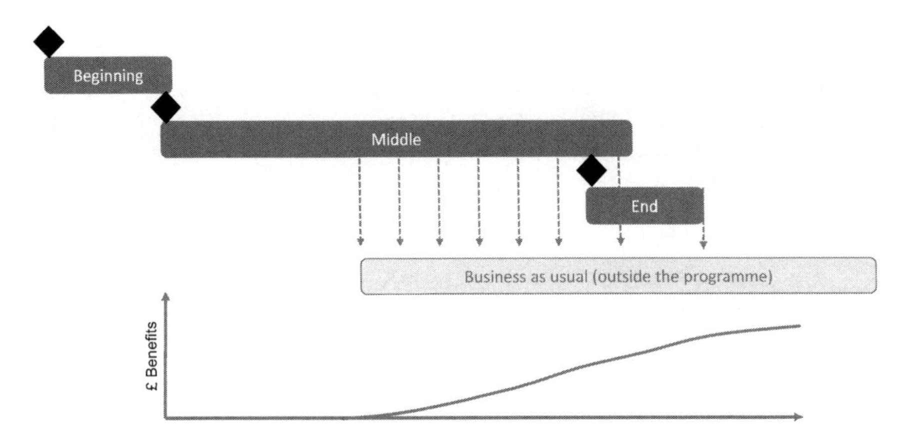

Figure 17.8 A simple, three phase programme with beginning middle and end

Incremental outcomes and associated benefits realization are shown, together with a final hand over to business as usual at the end.

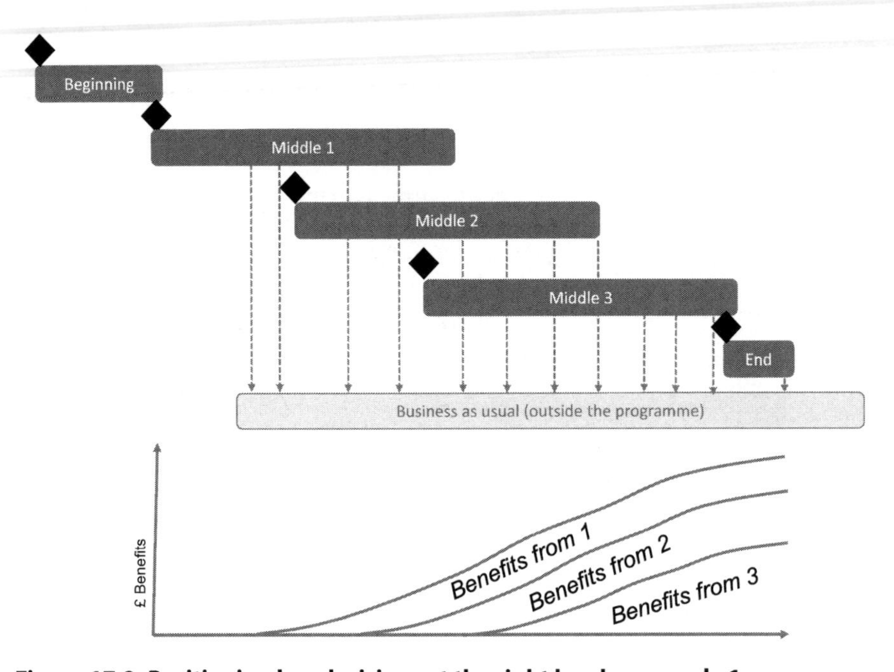

Figure 17.9 Positioning key decisions at the right level – example 1

The programme is shown as being undertaken in three phases (you could call them tranches or waves). Each phase can be managed as a sub-programme' with its own mobilization period. In this, the programme is delivering into an on-going 'business as usual', with each phase managing the operations within the scope of the programme until it is sufficiently embedded to hand over to routine business governance outside the programme.

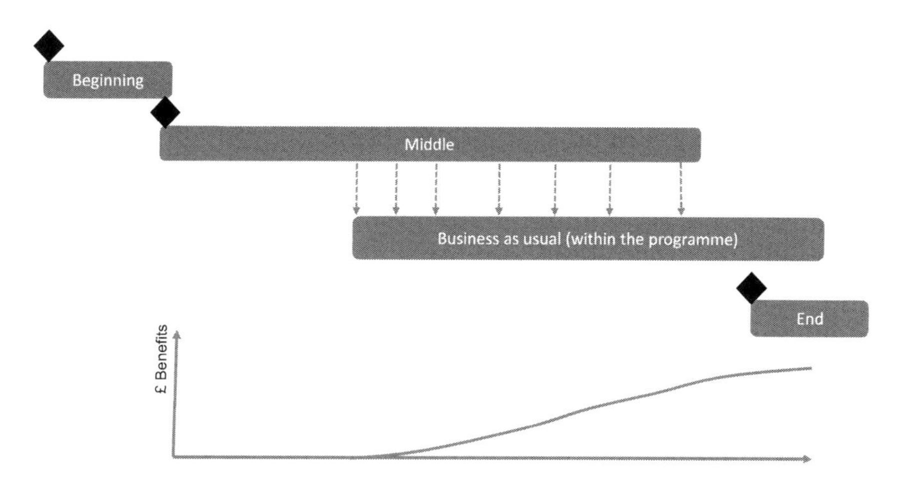

Figure 17.10 Positioning key decisions at the right level – example 2

Unlike Figure 17.8, this programme is self-contained and includes the entirety of operations within the programme. At the end, operations might cease altogether or there could be a handover to another supplier. This model is typically used for outsourced service provision.

as a sub-programme with its own mobilization period, which could be managed as a project. In this example, the programme is delivering into an on-going 'business as usual' environment, with each phase managing the operations within the scope of the programme until it is sufficiently embedded to hand over to routine business management outside the programme.

Figure 17.10 is similar to Figure 17.8 but the programme is more self-contained. For example, this is how an outsource or oil field exploitation could be managed, with the entirety of operations within the programme. At the end, operations might cease altogether (such as when an oil reserve or mine is depleted), or there could be a handover to another supplier (in an IT outsource situation).

Figure 17.11 builds on Figure 17.10 but has three distinct focusses, each is a sub-programme which can itself have all the combinations of 17.8 to 17.10 within it. The permutations are limitless and there is often no obvious 'right' design. For example, the configuration in Figure 17.11 could be managed as a business portfolio with four programmes within it as shown in Figure 17.12.

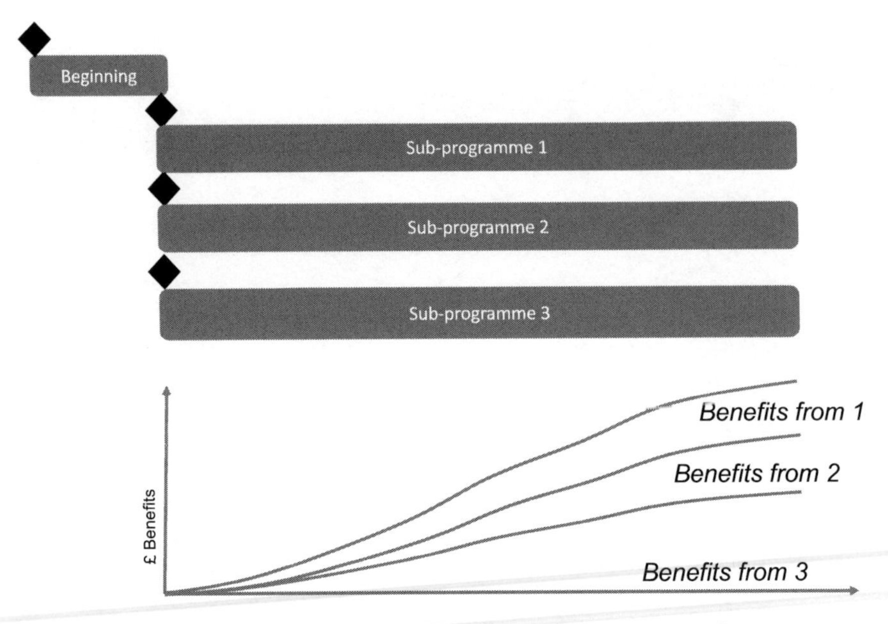

Figure 17.11 Positioning key decisions at the right level – example 3

Each 'middle' part has its own distinct focus and is managed as a sub-programme which can itself have all the combinations of 17.8 to 17.10 within it.

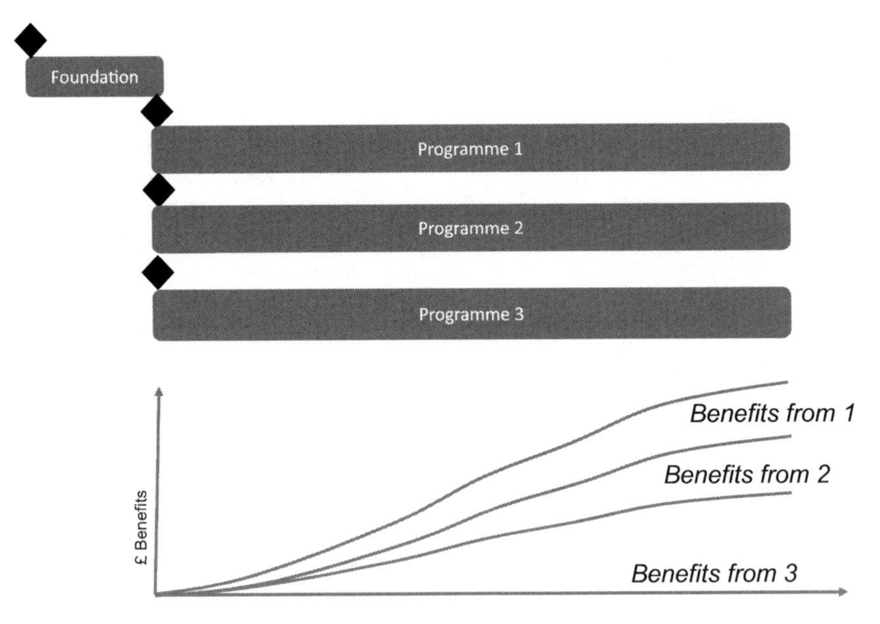

Figure 17.12 Positioning key decisions at the right level – example 4

The configuration in Figure 17.11 could be managed as a business portfolio with four portfolio components, including three programmes.

Simplify, simplify, simplify

Programmes can be very complicated and the simpler the structure, the more likely they are to stay in control. If, through the logic flow and schedule, people can understand the 'grand scheme', the likelihood of gaps or overlaps in scope will diminish. Local decisions will not negate other decisions, teams will not be placed in contentious conflict (say, arguing about priorities or resources). Simplification should be sought in:

- the logic flow and deciding the component parts of the programme;
- decision making;
- keeping spans of control manageable.

The examples used in the figures in this chapter are themselves simple, with only 11 components: nine projects and two 'other work'. Many programmes have hundreds of components, but the same principles apply. Analyzing the programme and designing its structure can be difficult. If it was easy, there would be no need for programme managers; after all, a programme manager's job is concerned with designing the programme with an effective governance and management framework to deal with complication and complexity. Part of this is the organization design, which is covered in Chapter 18.

Reducing interfaces

I worked on the planning for a business transformation programme in a large manufacturing company. This involved consolidating operations onto one site whilst redefining the product portfolio to remove underperforming products. In addition, the management structure was to be redesigned taking into account that only one site needed managing, rather than five. The programme comprised seven projects with about 200 interdependencies. By careful re-scoping of the programme's components, I was able to reduce the interdependencies to only seven. Fewer interdependencies meant each project sponsor could make local decisions, knowing they would not affect anyone else and the programme manager could concentrate on delivering the programme as a whole rather than acting as an arbitrator on a myriad of dependencies.

Prerequisites for effective programme management

Programme management is not a capability an organization can just pick up informally and run alongside their usual operations. Introduce anything new and it will most likely come into conflict with the status quo. The key is not to be taken by surprise. As described later, in Chapter 30, implementing programme management often needs to be programme managed. It also needs close attention to people, both within and beyond the programme team. Running just one programme in an organization can also have repercussions if careful consideration is not given to how it fits into the rest of the organization.

Workout 17.1 – Programme management in an immature organization

When initiating a programme in an immature organization, consider the following.

1. The impact on governance within the organization; who has authority over whom? Who deals with any disputes?
2. How to ensure the programme is really aligned with the organization's strategic and operational objectives?
3. How will the programme and organization's structures co-exist?
4. How to enable people to work across and within organizational boundaries?
5. How to assign your people and make decisions regarding using their knowledge, skills and abilities?
6. How will conflicting priorities between organizational and operational functions be handled?

Unless you can answer these questions:

- as a CEO (or related business leader), you are threatening the very success of the programme, before it has even started. In other words, top-down failure is likely;
- as a programme sponsor or manager, you are embarking on a turbulent path and might have to fight to achieve any progress. Your programme will take longer and cost more as every interface problem will have to be solved as it occurs.

Listen to your what your team is trying to tell you

18

Who does what in a programme

Roles

A programme manager cannot be a master of all that is required and so a team needs to be developed which has the necessary breadth of skills and experience.

"No one can whistle a symphony. It takes a whole orchestra to play it."

H E LUCCOCK, 1885–1960

- **Ensure single point accountability from top to bottom.**
- **Design boards to suit the need and the organizational context.**
- **Decide which central functions are needed.**
- **Make sure the roles reflect all the work needed.**
- **Do not confuse roles with the job titles.**
- **Separate assurance from support.**

Programme accountabilities

Single point accountability for all roles

The primary roles the of programme sponsor and programme manager were introduced in Chapter 4 as an essential aspect of governance. Figure 18.1 builds on this to show an example of a programme organization structure. The permutations are limitless, but this example does show the features you are likely to need. In this organization structure I have assumed:

- single point accountability is maintained, where an individual holds the authority, rather than a body (such as a board) for every component of the programme as defined in its work breakdown structure. This would normally include projects and 'other work' such as 'business as usual' operations.
- a range of 'central functions', which provide direction and support that affect all or many of the work components. These are a particular form of 'other work' but are not directly in the delivery line.

The roles in Figure 18.1 are supported by detailed descriptions. Again, these are examples as the detail would need to reflect the circumstances.

Boards and the senior roles

Two boards are shown in Figure 18.1:

- an executive programme board, chaired by the programme sponsor;
- a programme control board, chaired by the programme manager.

These are included as it is unlikely on any significant programme that the individuals undertaking the programme sponsor and manager roles would act alone. Some organizations might even mandate that such boards should be formed for

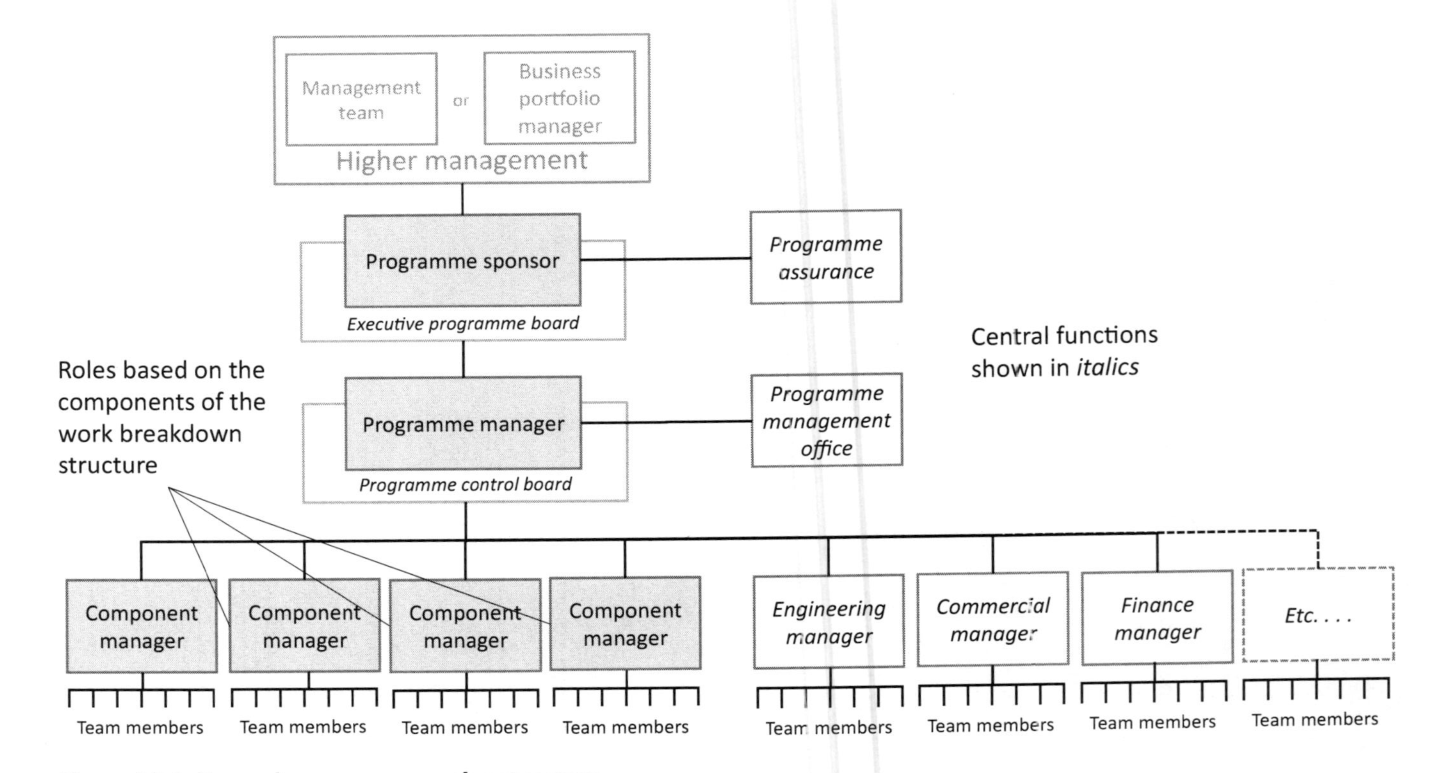

Figure 18.1 Example programme roles structure

The organization structure comprises the roles supporting the work breakdown structure (for components such as projects) and the central functions. The central functions provide consistent direction and support for activities that affect all or many of the components.

programmes greater than a defined size to prevent too much power being vested in a single individual.

The sponsor would normally want a group of people to verify the direction set and the decisions made. There might also be a corporate board, for example, with specific responsibilities, such as assurance and risk. Members might be non-executive to avoid the problems of 'group think', where the board members are so focussed on success that they miss obvious problems. In this approach, the programme sponsor is like the chairman of a corporate board.

Similarly, the programme manager is likely to need advice from senior members of the programme's leadership team, each providing specialist advice and able to contribute to decisions. In this respect, the programme manager role is like the chief executive of a company. This approach is likely for very large programmes.

Alternatively, the programme sponsor can be equated with the chief executive officer role, and the programme manager with a chief operating officer role. This is neither a wrong nor a right comparison; it is simply a way of describing to people who are not familiar with the extent of the programme sponsor and programme manager roles, the importance of, and relationship between, the roles.

An alternative programme organization structure is shown in Figure 18.2, where the programme manager is one step further removed from the 'real work' by having one or more delivery managers accountable for the delivery components of the programme.

Do not worry about the names of the boards supporting the programme sponsor and manager; make them appropriate to your circumstances and context. For example, in some organizations the term 'board' is reserved for the highest-level body only, so the programme control board might be called the senior programme management team. Similarly, do not worry about the use of the term 'manager' and 'director', for example 'delivery manager' versus 'delivery director'. What the roles do is more important than the job title people are given to support their actual or self-perceived status.

Just part of the problem

A brief scan of the accountabilities emphasizes the wide range of skills needed to direct and manage a programme and that many of them need to be filled by specialists. A programme manager cannot be a master of all that is required, and a team needs to be developed with the necessary breadth of skills and experience. This is often easier said than done.

Whilst the structures in Figures 18.1 and 18.2 show the roles and the relationship between them, this is only part of the problem. For large programmes the teams often need to be organized into departments, which has implications for the management of the programme overall; this is dealt with in Chapter 19.

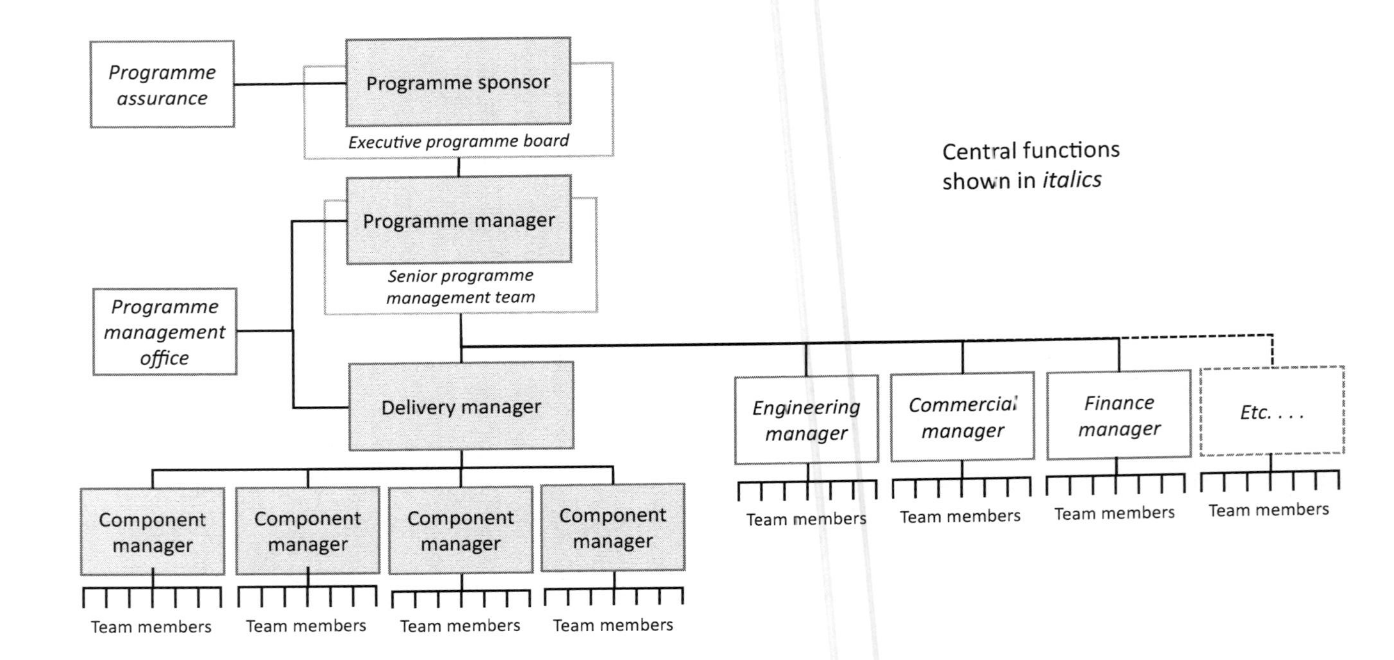

Figure 18.2 An alternative programme organization structure

The programme manager is one step further removed from the 'real work' by having one or more delivery managers accountable for the delivery components of the programme.

Make sure everyone understands their roles and how they fit together

Programme sponsor

The programme sponsor is accountable to the business portfolio sponsor for ensuring a programme meets its objectives, delivers the required outcomes and realizes the required benefits. The programme sponsor owns the business case, is accountable for all aspects of programme governance and may appoint an executive programme board. The programme sponsor's accountabilities include:

- owning the vision for the programme, providing clear leadership and direction;
- providing policy and direction on all aspects of the programme and ensuring that higher level policy is adhered to;
- providing overall direction and leadership for the work in the programme, with personal accountability for the outcomes and business benefits for the organization;
- developing, maintaining and agreeing (with higher level management) the programme business case and plan;
- achieving all assigned and agreed business objectives, such as those for sales, revenue, strategic outcomes, profit, cash flow and schedule to ensure the business plan is realised;
- setting targets for programme team members;
- securing the investment and resources required to set up and run all aspects of the programme;
- being accountable for approving the governance arrangements within the programme by ensuring investments in any sub-programmes, projects and services are established and managed in line with the organization's policy and requirements;
- chairing and attending such strategic level governance bodies as defined and agreed with the customer (where appropriate) and higher management;
- undertaking or assigning sponsorship for any sub-programmes, projects and services within the programme;
- managing the interface with key senior stakeholders including the customer and higher management; ensuring all communications are effective and progress is accurately and timely reported;

- owning and managing the strategic risks and opportunities facing the programme, including holding, delegating and allocating contingency funds;
- maintaining the alignment of the programme's objectives to the organization's wider strategic objectives, addressing issues and providing advice and direction as needed;
- undertaking programme assurance on an on-going basis supported by specialist advisors, where appropriate;
- commissioning reviews and audits of work within the programme to ensure continued alignment with strategy, confirming on-going capability to deliver and measuring on-going achievement of benefits to the organization.

If the programme is being undertaken for a client or customer, the programme sponsor is accountable for the relationship with the client and the formal contractual agreement (see Chapter 26).

Executive programme board

The executive programme board, usually chaired by the programme sponsor, is accountable for supporting the programme sponsor in undertaking his/her role:

- ensuring the business objectives remain valid and appropriate, and approving any changes to them;
- advising on the governance arrangements for the programme;
- reviewing overall progress and setting direction;
- analyzing the gaps between expectations and reality;
- managing escalations and making decisions if the organization's business objectives are at risk;
- controlling the effective undertaking of the contract.

Programme manager

The programme manager is accountable to the programme sponsor for establishing the governance framework and for the day-to-day management of a programme, to deliver the desired outcomes and realize the required benefits.

The role requires the effective co-ordination of the constituent projects and other components, together with their interdependencies and any risks and other issues that may arise. The programme manager is also accountable for the effective and efficient undertaking of the programme and use of the organization's and customer resources (if any). The programme manager's accountabilities include:

- ensuring the integrity of the programme. Focussing inwardly on the internal consistency of the programme; and outwardly on its coherence with infrastructure

planning, interfaces with other programmes and enterprise technical, shared service and specialist standards;
- planning and managing the overall programme including pro-actively monitoring the programme, making all assigned decisions, resolving issues and initiating corrective action as appropriate. Escalating issues to the programme sponsor, where the resolution falls outside delegated authorities or competence;
- operating the programme's governance within the organization's overall governance arrangements;
- ensuring that the outcomes (business changes) from the programme are achieved on time, within the allocated programme budget and that such changes are bedded in and unlikely to revert;
- ensuring that the outputs from the programme are to the required quality, to schedule and within the allocated programme budget, in accordance with the approved programme plan and governance arrangements;
- formally initiating projects and other work components, as defined in the programme plan, including allocating budgets and targets;
- securing the resources needed for the assigned work, including senior delivery staff appointments, materials, facilities, partners and third-party suppliers;
- managing communications and reporting to operational level and (where relevant) external stakeholders;
- ensuring compliance with the programme's procedural documentation and approving (through delegation) such documentation and subsequent changes;
- initiating management level reviews of the programme to ensure continued alignment with strategy and confirming on-going capability to deliver.

Programme control board

The programme control board, usually chaired by the programme manager, is accountable for supporting the programme sponsor by:

- agreeing direction, reviewing progress, managing key issues and risks (as escalated) and agreeing actions to keep the programme on track to meeting its objectives;
- ensuring consistent communications to the business and, if appropriate to eternal stakeholders, customers and suppliers;
- advising the programme manager on the response to any risks or issues which have been escalated;
- reviewing changes to the programme scope, plans and approach.

Other leadership roles

Whilst much of the work on a programme is likely to be undertaken in project or operational work packages, the managers of those programme components are unlikely to have total freedom to manage their assigned work as they see fit; this can be not only inefficient but also undesirable. They are likely to have to share consistent approaches in terms of management practices and standards relating to the outputs they are producing. For this reason, a programme is likely to have a number of central functions which can promote consistency and provide specialist services for the programme as a whole. The most common are described in the following.

Programme management office

A programme management office should provide expertise, specialist advice and guidance on programme management and, as such, support the programme manager to establish the most appropriate governance arrangements and implement planning and control mechanisms, methods, processes and tools. This can include all the topics in Parts V and VI of this book, including the routine administrative functions.

See Chapter 27 for more detail on support roles and how to decide what is appropriate in your case.

Engineering

Many programmes, such as those for infrastructure or information systems, need all elements of the solution to be built to the same standards to ensure compatibility. For example, a turbine must fit into the building which houses it; applications need to share data; a train needs to fit on the tracks and between platforms. For this reason, there is often a role, supported by a team, accountable for the integrity and utility of the overall solution and for setting standards. The name of the role varies depending on context and custom. Two common ones are 'Chief Engineer' and 'Solutions Architect', but there are many more.

Commercial

If a programme has a lot of suppliers, or is being undertaken for a client or customer, it is common for there to be a specialist commercial role on the programme to manage procurement and to advise managers on contractual matters. For large programmes, this can be a self-contained department within the programme with its own supporting information systems. In other cases, the roles might be provided on a part-time basis from a corporate commercial department or a third party.

See Chapter 26 for more detail on commercial management.

Finance

It is common for there to be a specialist financial role on a programme, to manage the finances and ensure financial regularity. For large programmes, this can be a self-contained department within the programme, sometimes with its own financial systems. In other cases, the role might be provided on a part or full-time basis from a corporate financial department using the corporate financial system.

Human resources

Programmes often require a lot of people to be recruited, either by promotion from within the programme, secondment from the sponsoring organization or through direct recruitment. In addition, because of the length of time programmes can last, the full range of human resource management services are often needed, including performance management, training and development, industrial relations, payment and reward and leaving employment. For large programmes, this can be a self-contained department within the programme with its own human resource systems. In other cases, the roles might be provided on a part or full-time basis from a corporate human resource department.

Change and benefits management

Change management roles can be the most contentious to organize. In the example organization structure, I have shown the role as reporting to the programme manager. Some approaches have this role by-passing the programme manager to report directly to the programme sponsor. The argument from advocates of this approach is:

1. the programme sponsor is accountable for the benefits;
2. the business change manager's aims are to see change happens and benefits are realized; therefore,
3. the business change manager should report to the sponsor.

If, however, the business change manager reports to the programme sponsor directly, the programme manager can no longer be accountable for an essential part of the programme: the business changes. This can lead to the programme equivalent of 'an IT project' and a 'business project' and becomes a recipe for confusion and power struggles. This approach probably stems from people's experience (or perception) of programme managers being 'technical' and not having change management skills. In my view, a programme manager should manage the entire programme, otherwise they cannot be called a 'programme manager'. The composition of the team needs to cover all the specialist roles needed (including change and benefits management) and no single person has all the skills. Weaknesses should be treated as a risk and a focus for assurance. Chapter 25 explains the breadth of research and techniques available for managing change and Chapter 21 deals with benefits management.

Business change manager

The business change manager should focus on outcomes and benefits realization and is accountable to the programme manager for identifying, defining and tracking benefits. The business change manager requires detailed knowledge of the business environment in which the benefits are to be realised. In particular, they need to have good relationships with the key influencers in the business and an understanding of the management structures, politics and culture.

Ideally, the business change manager should have on-going operational responsibilities within the business area and their participation in the programme can be considered part of their normal responsibilities to ensure the change resulting from the programme is accepted into the business. In the context of customer programmes, the business change manager is likely to have a close and enduring relationship with the client.

The business change manager's accountabilities include:

- liaising with the programme manager to ensure that the work of the programme, including the scoping of each project and work component, covers all necessary aspects required to deliver the products or services that enable business change (outcomes) and hence to the expected business benefits which support strategic objectives;
- preparing people for change and leading transition from the 'as-is' to the 'to-be' state to ensure 'business as usual' activities are maintained whilst the change is integrated into the business. Working with the programme manager to schedule deployment of outputs to minimize adverse impacts on the business and maximize benefits;
- establishing mechanisms to realize and measure benefits;
- managing the realization of benefits and ensuring that continued accrual of benefits can be achieved and measured after the programme has been completed;
- managing the network of change agents, if any.

Benefit owner

This role is sometimes called the outcome owner or business owner. The benefit owner is accountable to the business change manager for owning the realization of one or more benefits and embedding capability in their area of the business.

The benefit owner is the person best placed in the business to ensure the assigned outcome and related benefit is realized. This will often be an operational manager/ business department head, with responsibility for the area realizing the benefit. As such, they should be involved in selecting and setting up appropriate measures for that outcome. The benefit owner's accountabilities include:

- gaining approval of the forecast/target values for that outcome (from the sponsor);
- achieving the forecast/target values for all measures selected for the outcome/ benefit they own;
- agreeing joint contributions/targets, where measures selected have also been targeted by other programmes.

Change agent

The change agent (also known as the change champion) is primarily focussed on embedding change and realizing benefits in their area of the business. Change agents are often accountable to a business change manager.

The change agent's accountabilities include:

- embedding and championing the change in their area of the business;
- reporting progress and highlighting risks to benefits realization.

Programme assurance

Assurance covers all interests of sponsorship, including business, user and supplier needs. It should be independent of the programme manager and programme support. Tasks can include:

- recommending to the programme sponsor that programme or project reviews should be held and (when directed) undertaking those reviews;
- carrying out any both informal and formal reviews as required.

Specific responsibilities include assuring:

- fit with the overall business strategy;
- focus on the business need is maintained;
- the programme remains viable;
- business requirements, user needs and expectations are being met and managed;
- risks are being controlled and contained;
- an acceptable solution is being developed;
- the right people are being involved;
- applicable standards are being met;
- the scope of the programme is not 'creeping upwards' unnoticed;
- internal and external communications are working;
- legislative, regulatory or contractual constraints are being observed;
- the needs of specialist interest stakeholders (for example, sustainability, safety, security) are being observed.

See Chapter 4 for more on assurance.

Programme support

Programme support provides expertise, support services, specialist advice and guidance on aspects of programme and project management, primarily for the governance of programmes and projects. They are often called a programme management office.

Working with the programme manager, programme support helps establish the most appropriate governance framework and implements the necessary planning and control mechanisms, methods, processes and tools. Programme support can act as the focal point for lessons learned and as a central source of expertise and advice using any methods and specialist support tools.

See Chapter 27 for more on programme support offices.

Workout 18.1 – Defining the programme's organization

If you have no defined organization chart, it is unlikely that those involved will understand what they are meant to do. Even members of self-defining teams need to define how their team works!

Take any of your programmes and using the roles and example charts in Figures 18.1 and 18.2 draw up a chart for the programme.

1. Ensure you understand what each line between the roles means. Remember in matrices an individual can be accountable to two or more people for different activities or deliverables.
2. For each role on the chart, summarize, or if already defined, write up what each role is accountable for and who they are accountable to.
3. Look for where I have described a role, but you don't have an equivalent. Bear in mind you might use different role names to me.
4. Look out for areas where roles could come into conflict. For example, in relation to management versus engineering, or in relation to change management, where it is important that each knows their limits of authority. These are common areas where there are problems.
5. Don't confuse job title with roles. They might look the same but can be different. A single jobholder might undertake a number of roles.
6. Adjust the organization chart and the role definitions as appropriate.

19

Organizing your programme

Two fundamental choices

Shared resources

Dedicated resources

A hybrid model

The systems needed to support this

What is a workstream?

Some example programme organizations

Programme structures are very varied and need to be designed to suit the programme being undertaken. For large programmes, the structure can be similar in scale to that for a medium sized company. Simpler programmes tend to reflect typical project structures.

"Under a good administration, the Nile gains on the desert. Under a bad one, the desert gains on the Nile."

NAPOLEON BONAPARTE, 1769–1821

- **Consider who can commit resources when designing your organization.**
- **Make the matrix work within the programme.**
- **Use the work breakdown structure for primary accountabilities.**
- **Do not sacrifice effectiveness for efficiency.**
- **Do not use the term 'workstream'.**

Two fundamental choices

Programme structures are varied and need to be designed to suit the programme being undertaken. For large programmes, the structure can be similar in scale to that for a medium sized company. Simpler programmes tend to reflect typical project structures. One reason for this relates to how the programme is resourced. Look back at Lesson 7, in Chapter 2: "Use dedicated resources for each category of development and prioritize within each category." This lesson demonstrated that it is easier to make decisions if you have control of the resources. For a company, it therefore recommended the organization is managed as a set of business portfolios, each with dedicated resources. By doing this, the portfolio manager can make decisions on deploying resources with minimum reference to other senior managers. This makes decision making simpler and hence quicker. We can apply the lesson to a programme, as shown in Table 19.1.

In practice, a hybrid between the two extremes can be used where it is impractical or inefficient for a programme to own all the resources it needs. Some resources can be shared across the wider organization, for example, specialist resources, whilst the bulk of resources could be dedicated to the programme for the time needed. Whichever model is used, and it might change as the programme moves through its life cycle, make sure the matrix (see Chapter 3) is at the heart of it.

Table 19.1 Different sourcing models for a programme

Model	*Advantages*	*Disadvantages*
Share resources with other programmes, projects and work and draw on resources when needed.	Resources are likely to be used more efficiently.	Might require a number of managers to be consulted, who have different (potentially conflicting) priorities.
Dedicate resources to a programme	Minimizes dependencies across programmes Quicker, local decisions	Limits conflicts in priority Potentially inefficient use of resources

Shared resources

If a 'shared resources' model is used, the standard matrix organization applies, as shown in Figure 19.1. This might be within a business portfolio (as shown in the figure) or for the organization as a whole. The programme and its components would have to fit into the same prioritization, selection and authorization processes as the rest of the work the business is undertaking. Whilst the strategic fit for each component of the programme should be tightly linked to that of the programme as a whole, their relative priorities might change. When authorizing a new project (or stage within a project), the business portfolio manager might put a higher priority on a project outside the programme rather than one within the programme, even if the programme as a whole is seen as 'high priority'. One would hope such a decision would be taken transparently and in full knowledge of the implications for legitimate business reasons: for instance, certain specialist staff might be needed to resolve a regulatory issue, which if not dealt with, could force the company into default, incurring fines, damaging reputation and threatening future revenue opportunities.

In practice, a hybrid between the two extremes can be used where it is impractical or inefficient for a programme to own all the resources it needs

In the shared resource model, the programme sponsor is likely to have to refer every decision requiring the commitment of resources, to an external decision-making body (such as the portfolio or investment review groups in Chapter 13). If these

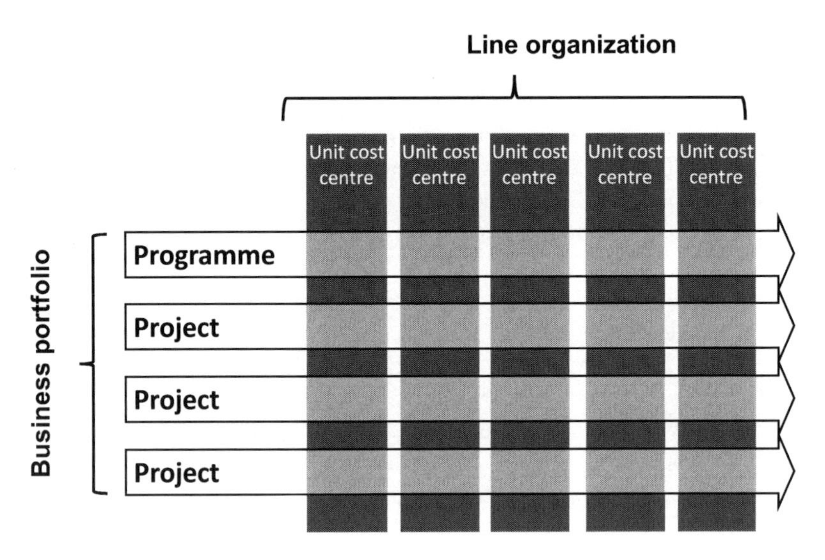

Figure 19.1 Shared resources

This figure shows an organization matrix structure where resources are shared across the organization. People are assigned to projects (or other work) from whichever cost centre they belong to.

decision-making bodies are working efficiently, it should not be a problem, but it does mean there is a risk of the programme sponsor's priorities being overruled by a higher authority. All the factors discussed in this book concerning good matrix management apply, and this is still preferable to the often 'he who shouts loudest' approach of traditional hierarchical organizations.

Managing people is not just a numbers game

** In Rome, chariot race teams (named by colours) attracted fanatical support.*

Dedicated resources

A dedicated resources approach should be used, when the programme is either the whole of, or a very significant part of, the sponsoring organization, or even a separate legal entity. Example programmes lending themselves to this approach relate to:

- infrastructure programmes such as High Speed 2 and Crossrail in the UK;
- outsources, where the supplier not only runs a service but has an obligation to improve current services and develop new services over a number of years. It is not unusual for such arrangements to last five to ten years and cost hundreds of millions of pounds;
- product or service management, where a product or service line (or parts of it) are managed as whole. Existing products or services need to be sold and supported, updated and replaced by new products or services.

The applications of programme management are limitless. It can be used wherever work has to be ordered logically and structured to achieve a defined objective.

Having decided that resources are to be dedicated to the programme, the organization structure needs to be designed. In order to have basic financial and management control over the work, people should be assigned to cost centres with a line manager. Work is then assigned to them from one or more of the component parts of the programme.

If there are a large number of people involved (hundreds or even thousands), it is impractical to hold the resources in a single pool (cost centre) and draw on them as and when needed; a single resource (or line) manager could not cope. The resources would need to be allocated to several units, each with a line or resource manager to ensure their people are assigned the right work at the right time and the basic work-related needs are cared for. This includes training and development and well-being. This means that the programme needs to have its own matrix structure, such as that shown in Figure 19.2. Here, the programme is organized into five cost centres, from which its component projects and other work draw on resources as needed. This model is similar to that needed for a business portfolio, shown in Figure 19.1. Such a programme would therefore need to have the same management functions as a business portfolio, described in Part III, namely:

Such a programme would therefore need to have the same management functions as a business portfolio

- work would need to be approved and initiated at the right time Chapter 13);
- resource availability would need to be checked prior to being committed (Chapter 14);
- work components (such as projects) would need to be selected (Chapter 15).

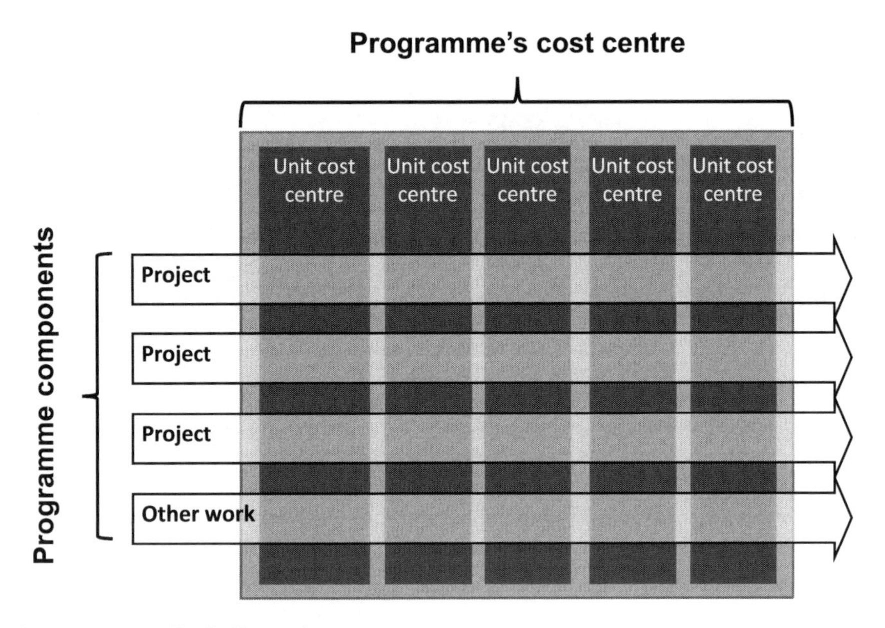

Figure 19.2 Fully dedicated resources

The programme has been shown as being organized into five cost centres, from which its component projects and other work components draw on resources as needed.

The external portfolio or investment review group in the shared model would become internal to the programme. Only very high value decisions would need to be referred to higher management, in accordance with the organization's formal scheme of delegation.

To a project manager on a large programme, decision making might not look much different to that experienced by a stand-alone project manager within a portfolio, but at least the decision makers would all be reporting to the same programme sponsor and aligned to the same objectives.

A hybrid model

The downside of a fully dedicated resource model is use of resources can become inefficient. Whilst inefficiency, on its own, it not necessarily bad, as we saw in Part II, effective organizations tend to do better than merely efficient ones. The only time efficiency really counts is if operational efficiency strategy is selected. It might be that the organization has some very specialist teams it can deploy across the organization but does not want to or cannot dedicate them to a particular programme or project. This might be because those people's skills are rare and cannot be easily developed or bought in. In these circumstances, the programme needs to have a structure which supports dedicated resource management but also enables people to be assigned from outside the programme when needed. This is shown in Figure 19.3. In this model, the programme manager mostly draws on resources from his own cost centres (a) but can (if needed) draw on resources from other cost centres (b). Projects outside the programme should not usually draw on the programme's dedicated resources in its cost centres (X). When resource commitment decisions are needed, they can be made by the programme's management team if resources come from the programme's own cost centres. Where resources come from outside the programme, the decision would have to be elevated to business portfolio level. It can be looked at as a matrix within a matrix.

The downside of a fully dedicated resource model is use of resources can become inefficient.

Isn't this just secondment?

Surely, I don't need to bother with a hybrid structure, I can just second people into the programme; can't I? Yes, you can, but secondment usually involves a person changing cost centres on a temporary basis. By seconding a person, you are actually dedicating the resource to the programme, albeit on a temporary basis. What if the programme needed this person or team every Monday, and they were required on other work on the other days? You are unlikely to keep 'moving the person' around. With a properly functioning matrix structure, you don't need to.

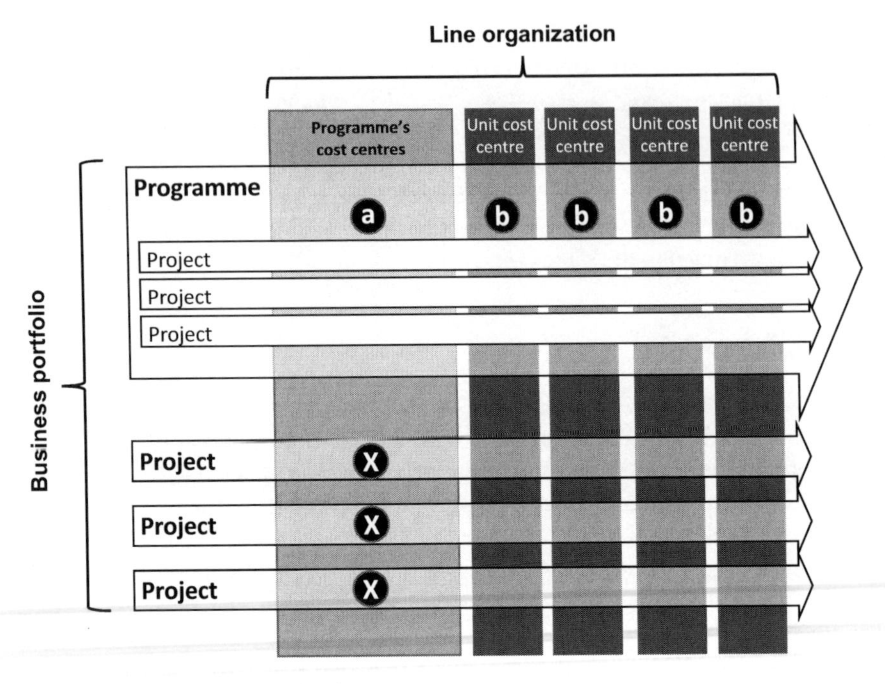

Figure 19.3 Hybrid organization

In this model, the programme manager mostly draws on resources from his own cost centres (a) but can (if needed) draw on resources from other cost centres (b). Projects, outside the programme, should not usually draw on the Programme's dedicated resources in its cost centres (X).

The systems needed to support this

On the face of it, the hybrid structure might look complicated, but it is no more complicated than the basic matrix structure and can be supported by the same systems and processes. All that differs is deciding who should be made accountable for which decisions, and this has to be done anyway, even without a formal matrix structure. In fact, the matrix used in this way, simplifies accountabilities and also makes it clear when decisions need to be elevated. Once this is working, pragmatic short cuts can be made. For example, not needing to wait until the next portfolio level review board meeting if only a few people were needed, and their line managers are happy to assign them. The assignment could be made and then reported at the next meeting. See Chapter 28 for more on systems and tools.

What is a 'workstream'?

How many times have you seen the term 'workstream' used in relation to programmes? It seems to be widely used but without any consensus on what it is. After some research, I found that this word does not exist as a management entity in the formal project management related methodologies, bodies of knowledge or in the international standards. *Managing Successful Programmes* does, however, define it as: "The logical grouping of projects and activities that together enable effective management. Workstreams may delineate projects against a variety of criteria". It goes on to say that the aim is to enhance management control by grouping certain types of work and concentrating dependencies as much as possible within the workstreams. This advice appears only in a 'tip' and not as part of the mainstream text. The boundaries of a workstream could be by any criteria, the commonest being:

- by discipline, such as all the work done by the training specialists;
- by location, such as the 'Africa' workstream, meaning all the work done in Africa;
- by output, such as software, meaning all the work related to software development.

In other words, it is related to how the work breakdown structure is designed. An entity such as a 'workstream' is not needed to manage a programme. In fact, in the wrong hands this could be dangerous as its use could result is the old-fashioned and discredited hierarchical organization. Say, a programme's outputs require specialist teams in system architecture, IT infrastructure, data migration, software development, testing, training and business change. If the programme is structured into discipline related

An entity such as a 'workstream' is not needed to manage a programme.

Figure 19.4 Workstream organization: Do not use this approach!

If you structure the programme into discipline related workstreams, you simply end up with a traditional silo organization with no cross-functional elements nor any focus on outcomes and business objectives.

workstreams, this could result in an organization such as that shown in Figure 19.4. Then, each head of workstream is asked to plan their people's work (i.e., create a workstream plan) and required to liaise with their counterparts across workstream boundaries to join it all up. In other words, you have created a traditional hierarchy with no cross-functional elements or focus on outcomes and business objectives; every lesson in Chapter 2 of this book would have been ignored.

Delineating the departments in a programme by discipline, however, is often a good approach but only by putting in place the cross-functional elements (such as projects) can the work be truly programme managed (such as in figures 19.1 to 19.3).

My advice – don't use it!

I am sure people will still use the term, perhaps because it can be an excellent fudge or perhaps it just sounds like you know what you are talking about; consultants use it a lot. My advice is to avoid using the word as there are well defined, plain English, alternatives.

This book does not use the term 'workstream' in its recommended approaches for all the reasons given earlier. The term is, however, in common use, and as we are not living in George Orwell's *1984*, you can use the term 'workstream' if you really want to. If, however, you do choose to use it, consider exactly what you want it to mean and what management procedure would be used to manage it; if you cannot determine that, do not expect anyone else in your team to understand you.

One reason for the prevalence of the use of the term might relate to the lack of programme management maturity in organizations. Consultants contracted to help an organization which has little concept of programme and matrix management tend to replicate the single dimension hierarchies those organization's leaders are familiar with and then give them a memorable (though meaningless) name.

Reasons not to use the term 'workstream'

1. It is jargon.
2. There is no consensus on what it is and therefore a huge scope for misunderstanding.
3. It does not appear in a reputable dictionary; not even Microsoft's spell checker recognizes it!
4. It cannot be translated.
5. It is not needed; other defined words do a better job.

Some example programme organizations

As the range of programme organizations is theoretically infinite, I cannot give you a structure that will work in all circumstances. I can, however, give you three examples, derived and simplified from real life. By studying these and undertaking Workout 19.1 you should be able to start reviewing or designing your own programme organization.

Share resource programme example

The first example is based on a shared model. It is derived from a multi-million pound business operating across the world providing outsourced, bespoke information technology services. The model is based on a government or multi-national company contracting the services to the provider. On winning the business, the provider would mobilize their teams. Once the team is in place, the services would be transitioned from an existing provider and formally taken over by the new provider in an 'as is' state. The new provider then operates the services and starts to transform them, adding new services, making existing ones better, stripping out costs and taking advantage of new technologies. Transformation might be on-going after an initial wave and could continue until the contract is up for renewal. If the contract is won, service continues; if lost, service is transitioned to a new supplier. In such companies, there could be over 50 of these types of contracts underway at any one time, all drawing on the same pool of resources.

Each contract is run as a programme

Each contract is run as a programme with a number of component parts, dealing with mobilization, transitioning services, transforming services and running the services. Mobilization, transition and transformation are shown as separate phases, which might, depending on the scale of the work, simply have one project within each or, for more extensive work, several projects. For example, a number of services might need to be transitioned and transformed at different times and in different locations.

Each project would be run using the same project management method but with different project life cycles:

- mobilization project: three life cycle stages;
- transition project: three life cycles stages;
- transformation project: five life cycle stages.

The structure is shown in Figure 19.5. The only predictable dependencies are that the definition of the first transition project cannot start until the programme has been mobilized, and in many cases, mobilization is not trivial. The first transformation project could start at any time after this, depending on whether it relies on an existing service or results in a brand new service. The programme can become complicated very quickly, and unless the component parts and interdependencies have been defined, the programme manager can easily lose control.

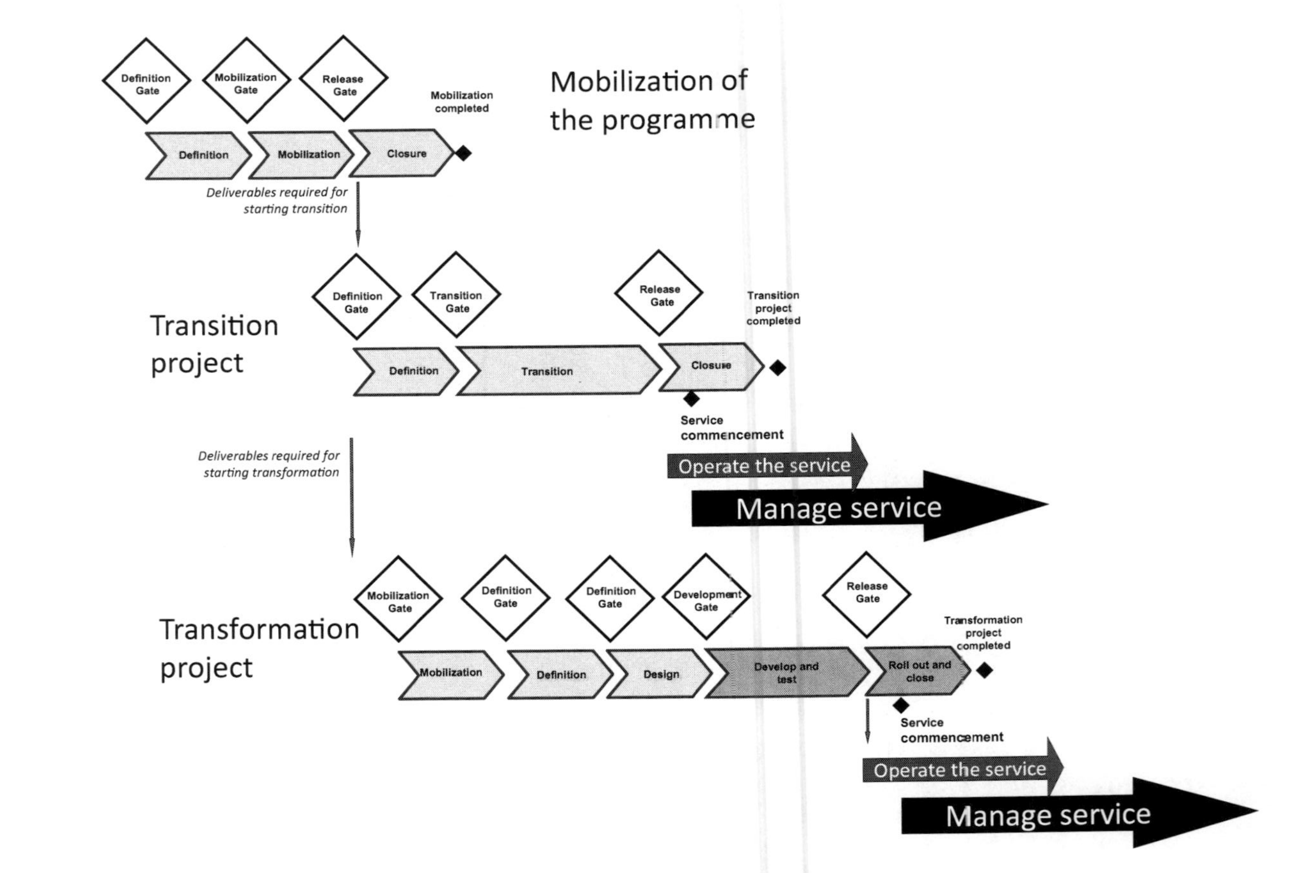

Figure 19.5 The building blocks for this programme are the individual project life cycles

The four building blocks for the programme, mobilization, transition, transformation and service management. In addition to these, there might also be some central services.

Dedicated resource programme example

The second example is of a major 'software as a service' provider. The core applications are built to a common architecture but targeted at different sectors (A, B and C). About 40 applications are to be developed and deployed at several hundred locations. Deployment of the software at each location requires the installation of specialist hardware, data cleansing and migration, staff training and disposal of old kit. Naturally, everything must be tested in terms of performance, security and function at each location and a local administration and operations team set up. The programme was set up with its own matrix.

The programme was set up with its own matrix.

The programme's vertical structure was divided into four main functions, covering:

- development of the services, run by a development director;
- deployment of the services, run by a deployment director;
- running the live services;
- central programme management services (such as finance, HR, PMO, etc.).

Each was then subdivided into its specialisms and staffed to undertake all the work required of it. See Figure 19.6.

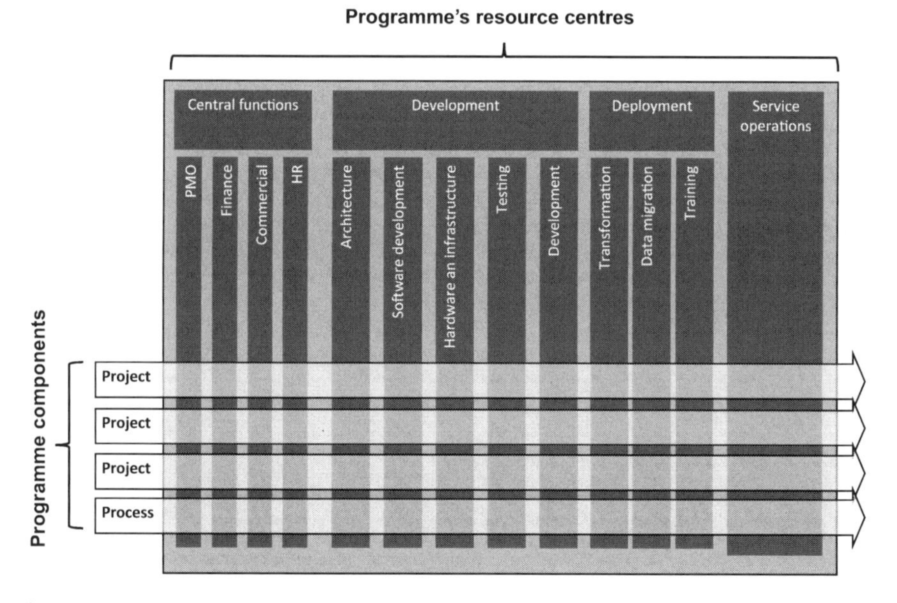

Figure 19.6 The programme's matrix structure

The programme's vertical structure was the cost centre hierarchy was divided into four main functions covering development of the services, deployment of the services, running the live services and central programme management services (such as finance, HR, PMO, etc.). Each was then subdivided into its specialisms and was staffed to undertake all the work required of it.

The programme's horizontal structure comprised the programme components covering the planning, management, development, deployment, operation and retirement of the services. Development, deployment and retirement were run as projects. The on-going operation of the platform and services were managed as business processes. These included the maintenance of the platform and service architectures as well as the local configuration at each location. See Figure 19.7.

Service development

All the services were built to similar standards which were set and governed by a chief engineer. Each of the three sectors had a platform on which their services could be built. The platform enabled interoperability across the services in a sector and common standards enabled interoperability across all three sectors.

The platform and service developments were each run as a five-stage project, with points of interdependencies identified.

Service deployment

Each deployment of the service at a location was run as a four-stage project.

As each new service was developed, deployment tools and training had to be prepared as soon as the application was stable. Then, training versions of the applications could be set up with training data. Data cleansing could start as soon as data specifications had been defined but data migration could not begin until the core application was stable and data cleansed. These critical points of dependency were defined and closely monitored.

The first deployment of the application was therefore heavily dependent on the application moving through its development path successfully. Any delays would reverberate throughout the programme and need protecting with a 'buffer'. An added complication was that training often required temporary training facilities, which had a lead time for set up; on top of that, staff required at least six weeks' notice for the training.

Once the first of type deployments had been completed, the risks associated with each subsequent deployment moved from being primarily dependent on the development of the service, to simply those risks associated with the respective deployment location. As lessons could be learned from deployment to deployment, overall risks decreased as the number of completed deployments rose.

Figure 19.8 shows the project life cycle for the development and deployment projects and the dependencies between them.

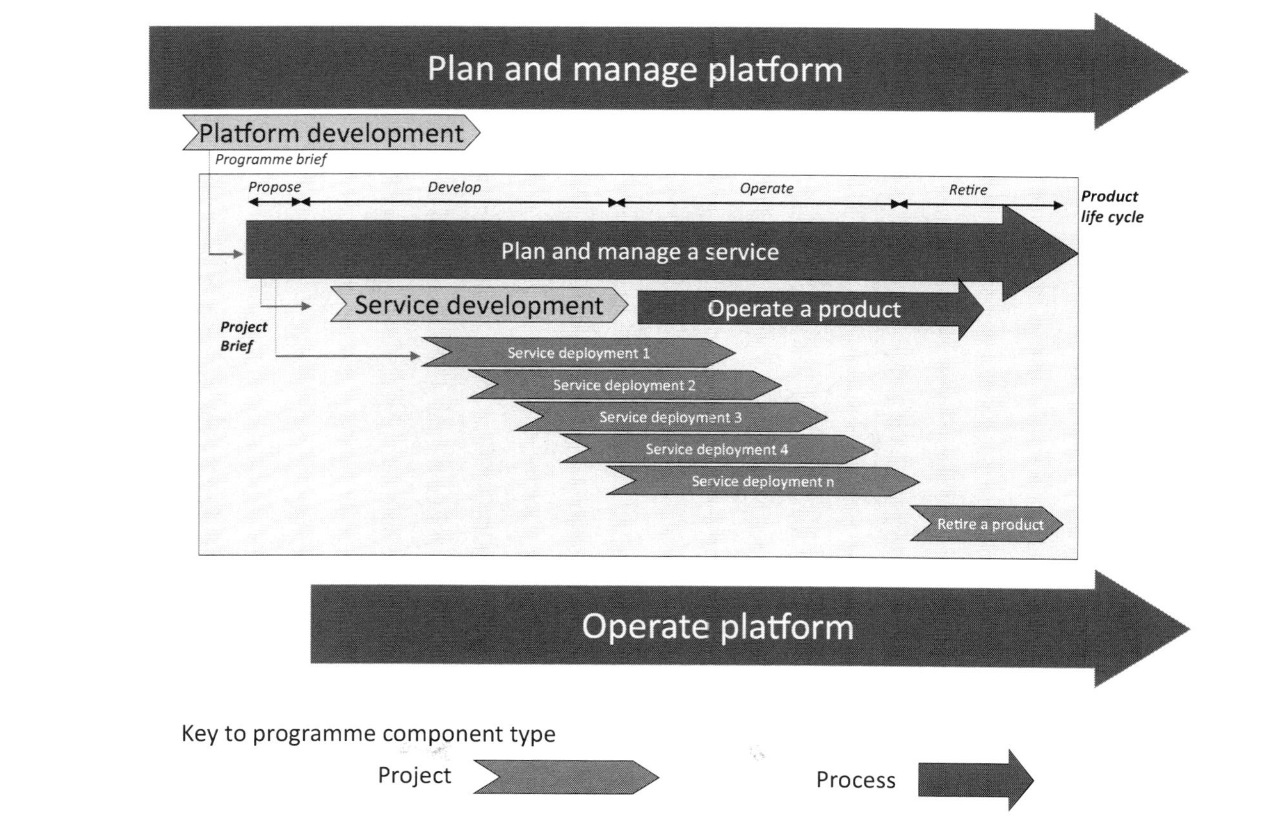

Figure 19.7 Platform development, service development and deployment

A high-level view of the programme's horizontal components: platform development and operation, service development and operation and deployment at multiple locations.

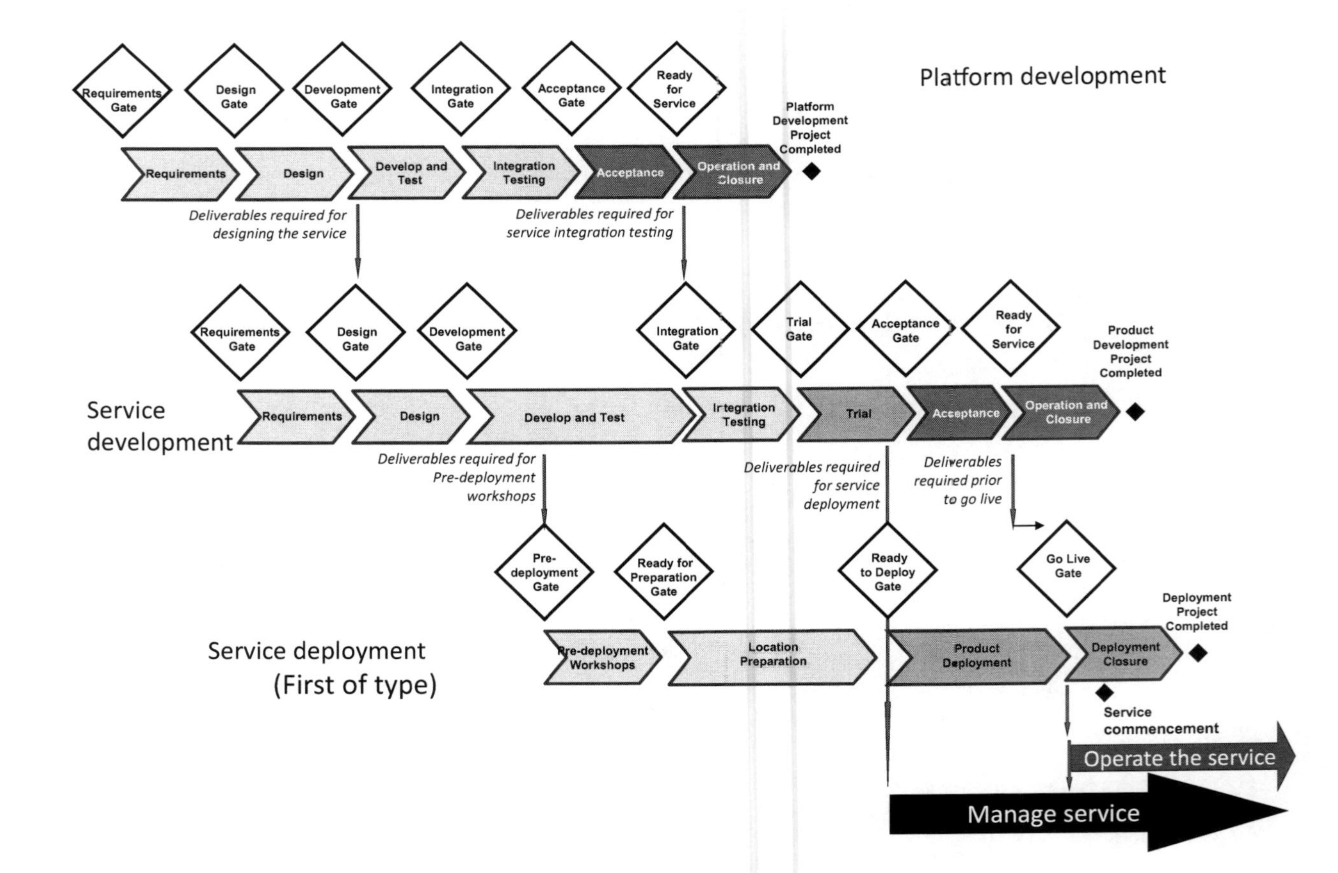

Figure 19.8 Project life cycles and dependencies

The programme comprises three primary project life cycles. At the top, the development of the platform. In the middle, the development of a service, using the platform's capabilities. At the bottom, the deployment of the first instance of the service to its user location. The choice of project life cycle can significantly influence a programme manager's control.

High Speed Two (HS2) phase 1

The last example illustrates a large infrastructure programme. The UK government is planning a new high-speed rail network, from London to Birmingham and to Manchester and Leeds, known as HS2. It is intended to improve the transport network and boost the economy. The initial plan is for a new railway line between London and the West Midlands running at speeds of up to 250mph – faster than any current operating speed in Europe – and would run as often as 14 times per hour in each direction. This would be followed by a second phase, running services from Birmingham to Manchester and Leeds.

Phase 1 is far more complicated than a design, build and operate project, despite having a single 'go live' date. An undertaking of this scale cannot be managed as a single project along the lines described in Chapter 8. It requires many projects, integrating civil structures in multiple locations (track, tunnels and viaducts), new buildings, power supplies, high-tech signalling and state of the art rolling stock. If the sequencing of any one part of the work is wrong and the risks underestimated, delays are inevitable. Figure 19.9 is an indicative schedule and illustrates the range of work required. Notice a large number of components run in parallel for up to eight years; this is significant and each of these is probably a programme in its own right. This is a classic case of programmes containing programmes looked at in Chapter 3. The power-distance from the overall programme manager to works managers on the ground is very large, which means that information flows can be distorted as reports feed up the line of accountability. A slight bias at one level can become grossly misleading at another level.

If the sequencing is wrong and the risks underestimated, delays are inevitable.

A diagram as shown in Figure 19.9 is a good start at understanding the make-up of the programme but is not sufficient to really grasp the risks. Additional information is required, namely:

- the dependencies between the components;
- the dates of indisputable deliveries which are indicative of progress;
- the risk of each component;
- the buffers in place to manage the risks.

These only deal with schedule. The landscape becomes more complicated when also considering costs and cash flow. This is a good reason for using the same work break down structure for the programme's costs as for the schedule. The management of a programme requires the manager to define and track a myriad of moving parts (programme components), which means that unless those parts are themselves built on good practice, the management of the whole programme is at risk.

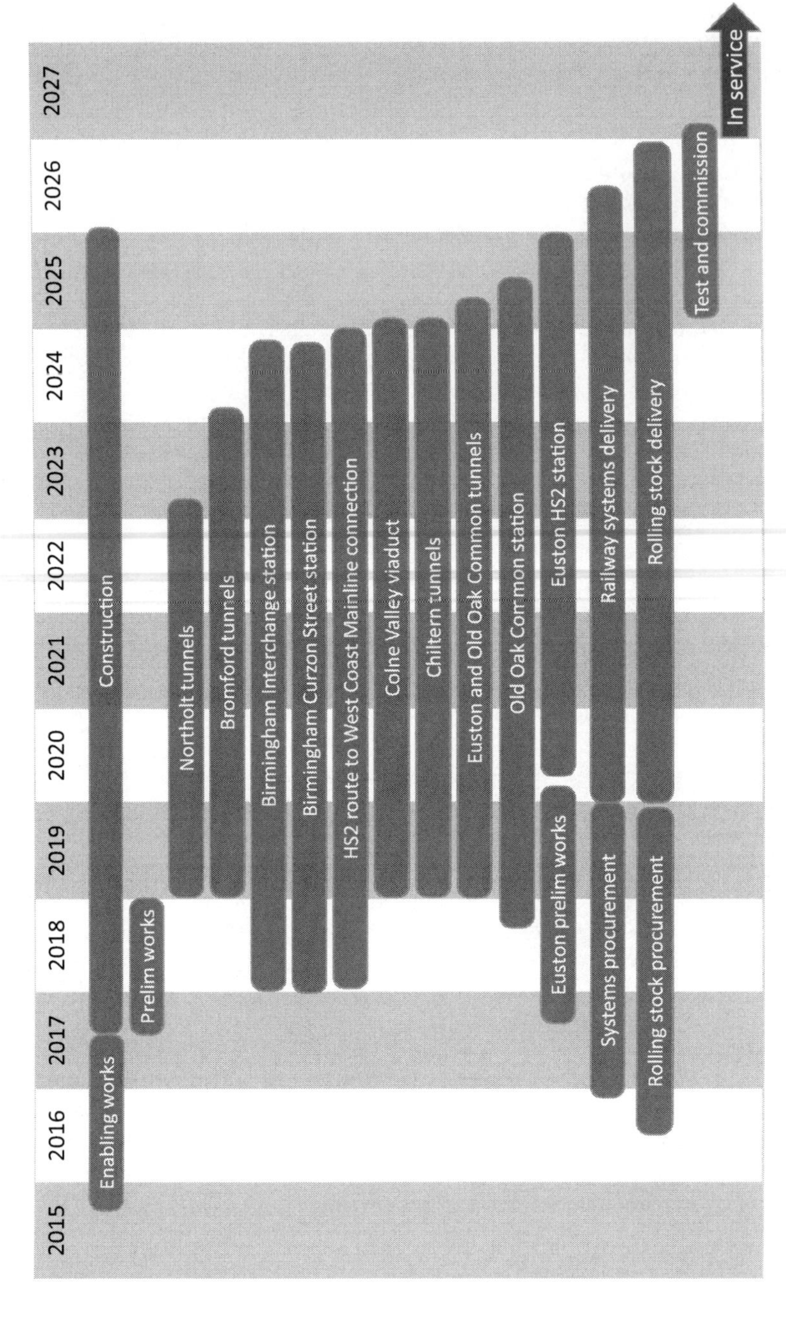

Figure 19.9 Indicative HS2 schedule and packages

This is an indicative schedule, and this illustrates the range of work required. A large number of components run in parallel for up to eight years, and each of these is probably a programme in its own right.

Workout 19.1 – Your overall programme organization

In Workout 18.1 we built an organization chart for a programme. In this workout, we'll look at 'organization' in a more holistic way, and this might require you to amend your organization chart as the organization chart and roles should reflect how everything else is put together. Like many aspects of management, getting to an approach that works is often iterative as you work on different aspects, each of which can affect the others. Think back to Figure 2.2 which shows even culture and behaviours can have a significant impact. There is no 'single right way' to organize a programme. Good results can be achieved from any number of organization designs. Every successful programme organization, however, should have certain characteristics. Whether reviewing an existing programme or defining a new one, check the points listed as follows. Use tables or diagrams to illustrate how the programme fulfils these needs, using the figures in this book to prompt the most appropriate representation. One diagram will not be able to demonstrate everything. Remember, if you cannot explain why your programme is organized in a particular way, your managers definitely won't understand it!

Significant milestones

The points in time should be defined when:

1. benefits are triggered;
2. outcomes can be indisputably recognized;
3. significant outputs can be indisputably verified as having been completed;
4. finance becomes available;
5. regulatory matters have been concluded.

Programme components

6. The components of the programme are defined such that they lead to one of the significant milestones.
7. Each different type of component is defined: for example, a definitive project life cycle for project components.
8. Components are as self-contained as they can be: minimum dependencies on other components.
9. The deliverables, outputs or outcomes comprising the interdependencies are defined.
10. The sequencing of components reflects the risks; higher risk work is given more time (buffers) to protect the end dates.
11. The risks of each component are understood and built into the plan (schedule and cost).
12. The levels of 'safety' managed at each level in the work break down structure are defined and reflect the risks at that level. No 'sandbagging'!
13. The constraints on the management of each component are known and taken into account in the plan: for example, two components being undertaken at the same location.

Financing and procurement

14 It is known how funds to pay for the programme are to be raised.
15 The procurement packages follow the component definitions.
16 The contracts take into account the knock-on effect resulting from delays.
17 The plan takes account of risks 'transferred' to contractors, but which, in truth, belong to the promotor. Liquidated damages might be irrelevant!

Resourcing

18 The organization and/or the supply chain can provide sufficient, skilled resources to undertake the work economically.
19 The resource model (shared, dedicated or hybrid) has been designed and managers on both dimensions of the matrix understand their authority and that of their colleagues.

20

Directing and managing a programme

A process-based approach

Programme management processes

The supporting activities

Implications for a business portfolio or programme manager

The most important aspect of programme management is being able to break up the work into manageable chunks to ensure the flow of work, and dependencies are obvious and such that each component is as self-contained as possible.

"A bad beginning makes a bad ending."

EURIPEDES, c500–406 BC

- **Make programme governance seamless across management boundaries.**
- **Organize your programme to harness the matrix.**
- **Allow tailoring, without losing control.**

Programme management processes

The programme management processes are summarized in Figure 20.1, with the arrows depicting information flows.

Programme components

As a reminder, a programme can comprise two types of work components:

- project-related work, as described in Part II of this book;
- other work (work not managed as a project).

Project work

'Project-related work' was described in Part II and involves the building, development or creation of outputs for new capabilities or services, or the withdrawal of existing capabilities or services. A project can, however, also include the work involved in transforming an organization to ensure outcomes are achieved (change management, described in Chapter 25). Change management ensures that the outputs are actually used, and the organization is transformed so that the benefits are more likely to be achieved. It is an approach advocated in Isochron's D4 method, using 'Recognition events™' and 'Value flashpoints™' (Fowler and Lock, 2006). Chapter 10 of this book includes a process model for project management.

As a programme is likely to comprise more than one project, it is necessary to have a process for managing them, with a gating process to ensure that each stage of a project is approved to start when it is meant to (if the risks are acceptable).

Other 'non-project' work

'Other work' relates to work which is not run as a staged and gated project but is essential as part of the programme. A common example relates to operating the capabilities and services developed in the programme, including the measurement of performance and benefits. 'Other work' also applies to the management-the programme, for example, running the programme management office, the other specialist functions, such as for engineering, commercial and finance, as described in Chapter 18. Just as the process and rules around running a project have been defined in Part II, it

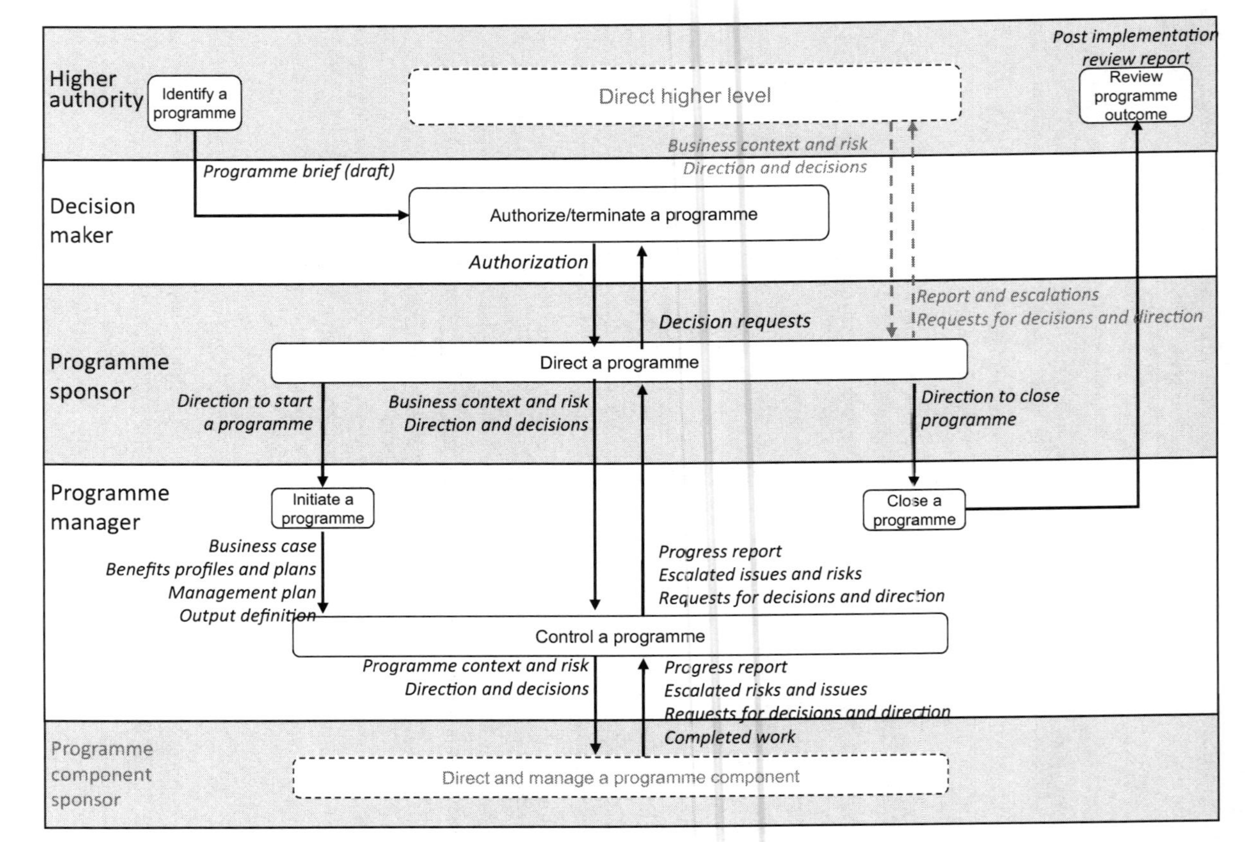

Figure 20.1 Programme management processes

The key programme management processes and their relationships (inputs and outputs) are shown here, with each activity in a swim lane to show which role is accountable. Notice the 'higher authority' lane. Who undertakes this depends on the context; this could be a higher-level programme manager, business portfolio manager or another corporate role. This is the person to whom the programme sponsor is accountable.

is also necessary to define the process and rules relating to the management of 'other work'. As other work can be almost anything you choose to make it, I cannot provide a model for you. The characteristics for such a process should, however, include:

- a role for who is directing the work (equivalent to a project sponsor);
- a role for the day-to-day management of the work (equivalent to a project manager);
- rules for how to initiate work: who makes the decision, what deliverables are required;
- rules for how the work is to be managed and progress reported;
- rules for closing the work.

Notice that 'other work' can harness the same supporting processes (described in Part V of this book) as used for portfolios, programmes and projects.

Direct higher level

For a programme, the higher level could be a business portfolio or a bigger programme. Another term used to represent the higher level is 'sponsoring organization'. Its purpose is to ensure a programme continues to be valid; that is to say, aligned to the higher-level organizational objectives and is justifiable. This is where any of the programme sponsor's queries are answered, escalations dealt with and decisions and direction made. If the higher level is a business portfolio, the business portfolio management processes are used (see Chapter 16).

Identify a programme

Identifying a programme is the first step in launching a programme. If the programme is internal to an organization it should be identified within a business portfolio as a need or opportunity, derived from the business strategy and plan. The people within the business area who require the programme to be undertaken (for the benefits it will realize) are the 'higher authority' or 'sponsoring group'. In a contracting context, if the programme is related to a bid for a customer, the identification happens as part of putting the bid response together.

The primary output from this activity is a programme brief, summarizing why an organization's senior management wants to undertake the programme and outlining their expectations. Note that the programme is not started through the immediate creation of a programme management plan and full programme plan. In programmes, the complexity and amount of work need to develop these can be so great that they can themselves be an expensive and extensive undertaking. For this reason, a shorter programme brief is created, to ensure strategic alignment and explain why the programme needs to be created. This is then used as the basis for selecting the appropriate programme sponsor, manager and team.

How do I know it is a programme?

At the very start, you might not know if the works needs to be managed as a programme or as a project. You might have to do a lot of work to determine this. For this reason, the programme brief and project brief need to have very similar content or even be the same document. Following on from that, the activities in initiating a project and initiating a programme would be so similar that it wouldn't matter if what you first thought was a project turned out to be better managed as a programme (or vice versa).

Authorize/terminate a programme

The purpose of this process is to ensure a programme is started in the knowledge that it is still required, has a viable plan and the risks are acceptable. In addition, the process is used to suspend (place on hold) a programme if there are doubts over its viability and, if necessary, terminate it. It is also the process in which programme-wide change requests are approved.

As in the equivalent process for project management (Chapter 10), I have not presumed who the ultimate decision maker should be. In some cases, the programme sponsor can be the decision maker, in others, the 'higher level authority' or a corporate board could be the decision maker. In practice, an organization's 'scheme of delegation' determines who has the delegated authority to make a particular decision. This is organizational and context specific.

Direct a programme

This process is undertaken by the programme sponsor who should ensure the programme is always viable in business terms. If the programme becomes unviable, it must either be changed (see Chapter 23) or terminated. Activities include ensuring the programme manager and team are aware of the changing business context and risks, requesting and receiving direction from the sponsoring group, dealing with requests and direction from the programme manager and reporting on the programme status to the sponsoring group and key stakeholders. The programme sponsor is also accountable for engaging senior stakeholders. The scope, complexity and size of a programme can be such that the programme sponsor might delegate certain aspects of the role to others (which would be defined in the programme management plan). Such delegation does not, however, absolve the programme sponsor from overall accountability for the success of the programme.

Initiate a programme

As soon as the programme brief is approved the 'initiate a programme' activity is triggered. This means setting up the programme correctly from the start. Note however, this does NOT mean defining the solution and fixing the plan; for large or complex programmes, the overall solution and plan is likely to evolve as a number of investigative projects come to fruition.

The programme brief (from identifying a programme) forms the basis for initiating a programme and the programme manager is accountable for ensuring that it happens. The programme's internal processes are defined within this process. The key tasks include mobilizing the cross-functional team, reviewing lessons from previous programmes, identifying and engaging stakeholders, determining how quality will be managed and outline planning of the programme. Large programmes often need the establishment of several capabilities to ensure effective management and probably include a programme management office and programme infrastructure, covering:

- procedures;
- house style;
- intranet;
- document and information management facilities;
- specialist tools such as for planning, risk and issue management, change control, configuration management, requirements management, testing and so on.

The programme's governance arrangements should be defined, taking into account the needs of the key stakeholders and (if relevant) the customer. Each governing body should have clearly defined terms of reference and responsibilities. All this is documented in the programme management plan. If your organization has an enterprise programme management approach, each programme team need only cross-refer or define any tailoring, dramatically simplifying and reducing the extent of the programme's documentation.

Work also needs to be undertaken to develop:

- a future state to be created by the programme (AXELOS's Managing Successful Programmes calls this a 'blueprint');
- develop an initial, outline programme plan for achieving this and;
- justification through a business case.

Often, programme delivery is phased (undertaken in 'tranches'). Phases are convenient ways of segmenting a large or complex programme to gain early benefits, facilitate understanding and simplify the planning aspects. They can be regarded as 'sub-programmes'. Those phases which are well into the future need not be planned in detail until necessary. For many programmes, even if the business need remains stable, plans for achieving the desired outcomes are likely to alter during the course of the programme. Programme management is ideally suited to this ambiguous form of business activity. The 'initiate a programme' activity includes work that will itself be undertaken as a project or simply as a 'work package'.

Control a programme

The programme manager is accountable for controlling the programme on a day-to-day basis to ensure delivery of the outcomes and benefits realization remains on track. Throughout the programme the programme manager should receive reports and confirmation of completed deliverables, outputs, outcomes and benefits from the project and other component managers. Progress should be reported to the programme sponsor and key stakeholders. In many programmes, suppliers are engaged to create the outputs or operate services. It is the programme manager's accountability, through the programme team, to ensure that these are run effectively, supported by specialist supplier managers where appropriate (see Chapter 26).

A key activity is the issue of an instruction, by the programme manager, to start work on a project or other type of work.

Close a programme

Programme closure can happen in three circumstances:

- the programme is completed;
- the programme is terminated because the risks have become unacceptable or a problem has arisen which cannot be resolved;
- the context has changed (for example a business takeover, reorganization or competitor activity), which means the programme is no longer needed.

The decision to close a programme is usually made by the programme sponsor, often in consultation with, or with the agreement of, the sponsoring organization.

The programme manager should decommission the programme and prepare a programme closure report to confirm the state of the programme at the point of time when it is closed. This should include a summary of the lessons learned. The report forms the basis for formal approval of programme closure by the programme sponsor and, if needed, higher authority. On receipt of formal approval, the programme manager should manage the final closure actions:

- delivery of outputs and achievement of outcomes to date should be confirmed;
- responsibilities for on-going risks, issues, actions and benefit tracking should be handed over to, and accepted by, the appropriate business authorities;
- documentation and information should be securely archived;
- the team and any temporary facilities should be demobilized
- stakeholders should be informed, facilities decommissioned and the programme team members reassigned.

Review programme outcome

A review of the programme's outcomes should be undertaken to determine the degree of success. The higher authority should ensure a review is undertaken to assess of the extent to which benefits realization and operational performance have met, and are likely to continue to meet, the objectives and expectations stated in the business case. Lessons should be captured and communicated.

If the programme has a significant amount of operational work within its scope, this review can happen towards the end the programme (rather than after closure) as the outcomes and benefits can be assessed from real-life operational experience. In other words, combine it with the closure review. Don't have multiple reviews for sake of it.

The supporting activities

The management processes described earlier outline 'integrating activities' that the programme sponsor, programme manager and core programme team need to undertake. They do not necessarily describe how some of those activities are undertaken. The detail for many of these, such as managing risks and issues, controlling change (as in baselined plans), managing information and so on, should be defined in a set of supporting processes (which might not be unique to programme management). Documenting the supporting processes separately ensures:

- the management procedures are as concise as possible;
- common supporting procedures can be used across all programmes and projects;
- variants of the procedures can be slotted into place for use on specific types of programme or project;
- a common tools strategy can be deployed.

The support processes are described in Part V of this book. To make these processes mutually consistent, they need to be designed as part of the overall architecture, showing how each part relates to the other parts. Figure 20.1 shows an example of how you could organize the supporting activities.

Implications for a business portfolio or programme manager

Make governance seamless

Chapter 3 discussed the ambiguities that often arise in relation to programmes. Whilst it is usually obvious where a portfolio sits in a corporate structure and what a project exists to achieve, the same cannot be said for programmes. A programme sits between these extremes and of the three management entities, the programme is usually the most diverse and hardest to define. If a programme also comprises other programmes, life can become very complicated and, as a result, management focus lost. For this reason, it is imperative to define the position of a programme with respect to the higher authority or entity it belongs to. It should also be designed to respect the management of its component parts. Governance must flow seamlessly across the management boundaries and senior management on both sides of a boundary need to understand each other's roles and viewpoints.

Organize to harness the matrix

The most important aspect of programme management is being able to break up the work into manageable chunks to make the flow of work and dependencies obvious and such that each component is as self-contained as possible. A diagram of a well structure programme should need little explanation; its structure should tell the story. The easier it is for each component manager to understand their place in the wider programme and the needs of their colleagues managing the other components, the

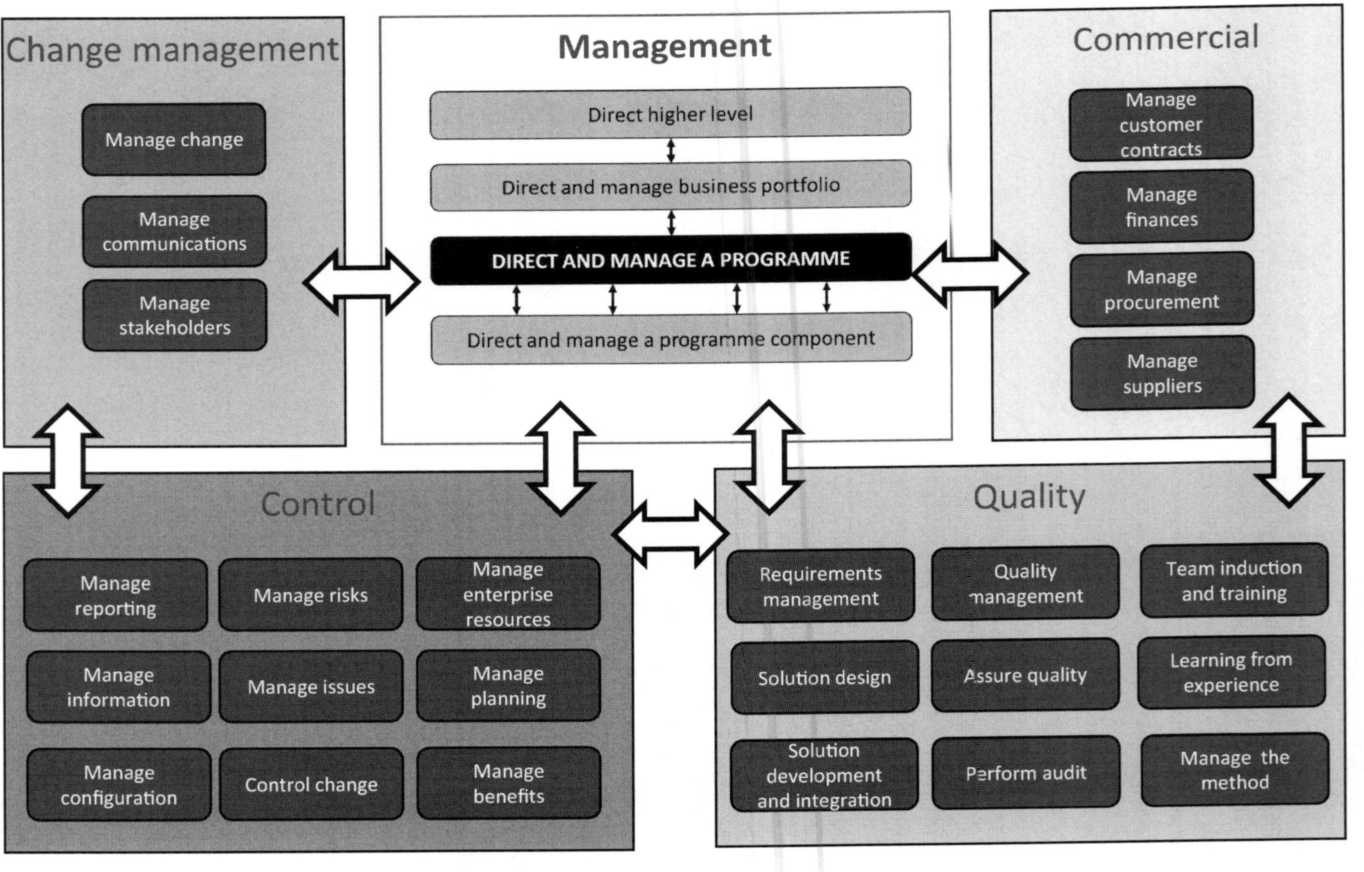

Figure 20.2 Supporting processes

Some of the most commonly used supporting processes are shown here, grouped in the same way as in Part V. Unless you define an overall architecture showing how these relate to each other, you will find the interfaces between processes become muddled, which in turn leads to muddled accountabilities and gaps where processes interface.

better the programme will run. In this respect, programme management is mainly concerned with organizing an often large, changeable, seemingly ambiguous workload. Traditional department management will not work; a programme which mirrors an organization's traditional functions is likely to fail for the same reason a siloed corporate organization can fail. Good programme managers really know how to make the matrix work and can build the management systems to make them work.

Tailor without losing control

Tailoring is the act of adapting a standard process or procedure to make it more applicable to a specific project or programme. It is concerned with ensuring the management effort is appropriate and proportionate to the work being undertaken to achieve the desired result. Tailoring, however, must be constrained as it is necessary to ensure governance is seamless across all the entities being managed. Each lower level entity should be directed and managed in accordance with the 'rules' set at the next higher level but with certain freedoms allowed to make sure they are applied appropriately. This is shown in Figure 20.3. Notice, it mirrors Figure 16.4 and follows the work breakdown structure, emphasizing the best practices described in Chapter 4 on governance.

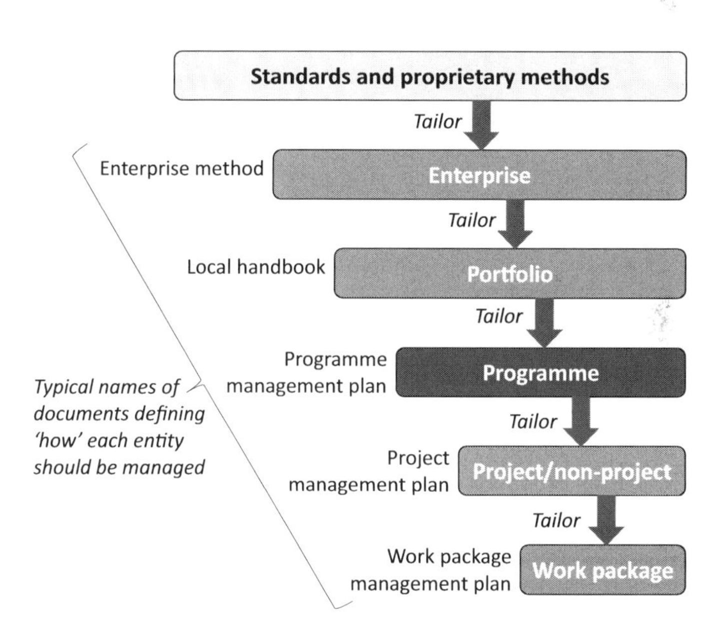

Figure 20.3 Cascade for tailoring

The management framework for a programme should be tailored from the enterprise and portfolio levels. The management of the programme's projects and other work should be tailored from the programme's management framework.

PART V

THE SUPPORTING ACTIVITIES

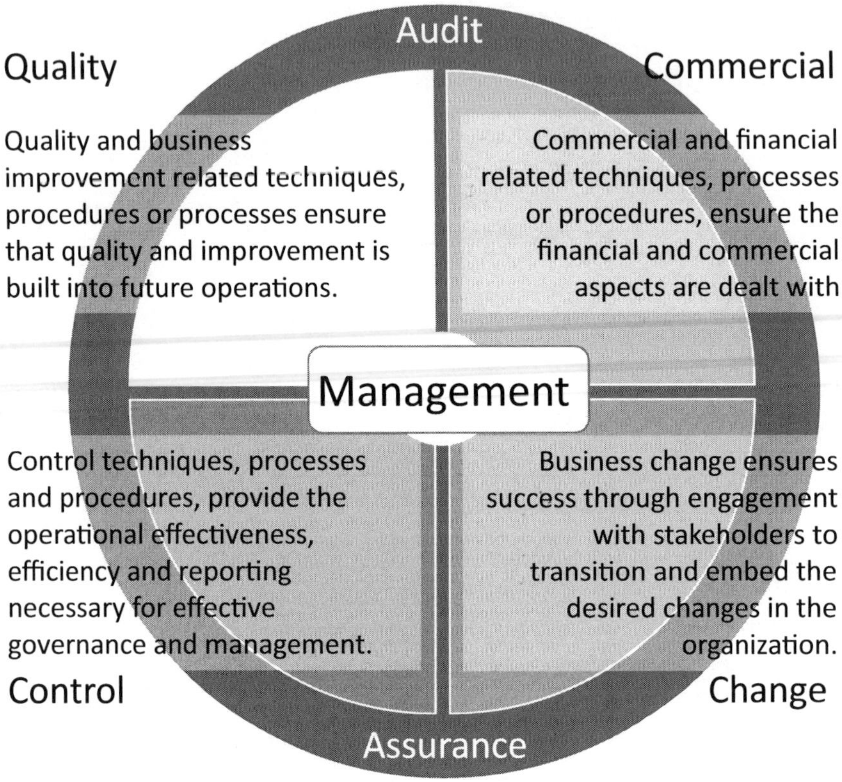

Figure 21.1 The supporting activities

Throughout the life cycle of a business portfolio or programme you need to be assured you are in control, confident your solution is the right one, your commercial imperatives are being dealt with and the business changes you need are actually happening.

"Probabilities guide the decisions of the wise."

MARCUS TULLIUS CICERO, 106–43 BC

This part of the book deals with the techniques that are needed, whether you are managing a business portfolio, programme, project or any other type of work.

- **Be in control – understand your constraints and risks.**
- **Continuously validate your solution is the right one.**
- **Make sure the changes you need are actually happening.**
- **Be aware of your commercial imperatives and constraints.**
- **Make sure your assurance regime is working.**

How to use Part V

Benefits are what you hope to get out of all the money and effort spent in your programmes and portfolios; Chapter 21 looks at some approaches you can take. Chapters 22 and 23 summarize the essential supporting activities that are covered in detail in *The Project Workout*, putting them in a programme and portfolio managed context. These are what every sponsor and manager should know about. Chapter 24 looks at what is needed to create the right solution to your business challenges, as there is no point in having brilliant methods for managing the work if the outputs from the work don't meet the need. Helping people to change the way they behave or work is a vital prerequisite to realizing the benefits, so change, whether transformational or incremental, is something you need to understand (Chapter 25). All of this often has to be undertaken within a web of commercial arrangements; you have to be able to state clearly what you want your suppliers to do and also understand what your obligations are (Chapter 26). As a business portfolio or programme manager you are unlikely to be an expert at all of this, but you need to know enough to ask challenging questions; after all, you are still accountable!

21

Why we do it

Benefits

Benefits driven change

Legitimate benefits

Benefits and planning

Value drivers and the business plan

The business case

A seemingly great business case might not be so good when the risks are taken into account.

"Forethought we may have . . . but not foresight."

NAPOLEON BONAPARTE, 1769–1821

- **Be clear what drives your organization's value.**
- **Make sure you know the impact in money terms.**
- **Understand the outcomes you need to generate the benefits.**
- **Always consider the risks.**
- **Aim for robust business cases which can be compared.**

Benefits driven change

Throughout this book and its companion, *The Project Workout*, I have emphasized that projects and programmes should exist to benefit the organization which is sponsoring them. If there is no benefit, there should be no project or programme. In Chapter 6, I explained the differences between 'business driven' as opposed to 'enabling' projects and that the delivery of an output, on its own, is not enough to realize the benefits needed. It is also necessary to change the way people work or behave or, in the case of social projects, live. Those changes in themselves can affect the choice of solution (or output). Too often, people focus on a solution in terms of what they will create and having decided that, determine the changes which are needed to embed that solution in the work and lives of the people who are affected; in other words, change is treated as an 'add-on'. By taking a 'whole system' approach to deciding the solution, as described in Chapter 24, every part of the solution matters and 'change' is treated as an integral part of the solution. In other words, when defining a solution, the change aspects need to be considered at the same time as the technical aspects and determined for each option. Planning for change starts in the very first phase of a project or programme. Further, the outputs and outcomes should demonstrably support the benefits you aspire to achieve. This linkage is shown in Figure 21.2. In this diagram:

- outputs represent the main parts of the solution;
- outcomes represent the changes needed if the benefits are to be realized;
- benefits are what is gained (such as revenue, cost saving, increase in gross domestic product.)

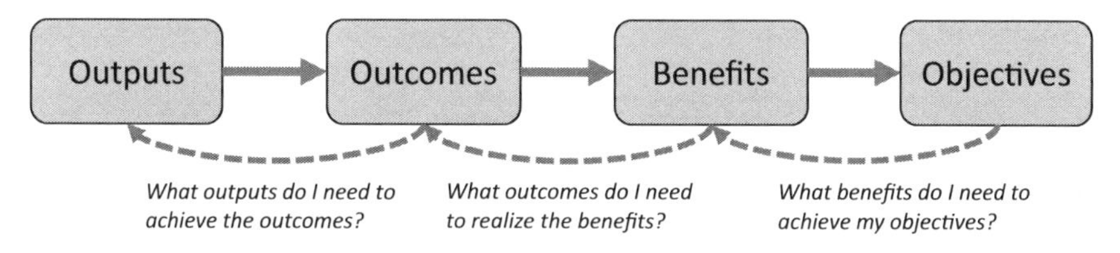

Figure 21.2 Benefits mapping

In benefits mapping, outputs represent the main parts of the solution, outcomes represent the changes needed if the benefits are to be realized and benefits are what you will get out of it in whatever terms you measure benefits (such as revenue, cost saving, increase in Gross Domestic Product). There should be two-way traceability from outputs to benefits.

Figure 21.2 is called a **benefits map**, and they can come in many different forms, but all aim to ensure that a solution is complete and sufficiently defined to ensure the benefits can be realized. They are used to validate two-way traceability from output to benefit and vice-versa. When everyone is focussed on delivery, the needs which initiated a project can become divorced from the outputs a project produces; benefits maps make sure the linkage is maintained. When push comes to shove and a project needs to be trimmed back due to overspends, slippage or budget cuts, having a benefits map will ensure the right work is addressed with no unforeseen side effects. Note the similarity with traceability in Chapter 24, where every aspect of a solution is traced back to a specific requirement.

When everyone is focussed on delivery, the needs which initiated a project can become divorced from the outputs

Traceability

Two-way traceability is a very powerful way to make sure your project, programme and business portfolios make sense. Everything is linked to something, whether it be an objective to an output, a requirement to an element of a solution, or a package of work to a contractor. Two-way traceability ensures that you have everything covered and, when changes are needed, you can determine the impact. This can be a nightmare of record keeping; however, with good discipline and the right configuration management tool to support you, it is easier now than it has ever been, but you do have to plan for it.

Achieving the benefits by accident

The managers of a large, multi-national company frequently found the benefits from their projects were realized but not in the way they expected. Some benefits listed in the business cases did not materialize, whilst others (not in any business case) appeared unexpectedly and often compensated for, or exceeded, the benefits they lost. A colleague with considerable experience in this field made the harsh (but probably true) comment that the senior managers in that organization were clearly not aware of the linkages in the benefits map, nor did they understand how the business worked in terms of value drivers. He then added, however, that the consistency with which this happened probably meant that the management of the company had a sound intuitive grasp of how the business worked, even though they could not yet formally translate that into reliable predictions of performance. In other words, people who really know the business came up with a good solution most of the time, despite their analysis being somewhat flawed. Imagine what they could have achieved if their analysis was right and their projects tuned to maximize the benefits?

Legitimate benefits

Realizing benefits is the sole reason for a company's existence. If there are no benefits, there should be no company and hence no business portfolios, programmes, projects or operations.

To be 'legitimate', work within a company must satisfy at least one of the following conditions:

- condition 1 – maintain or increase profitable revenue to the business, now or in the future;
- condition 2 – maintain or reduce the operating costs of the business, now or in the future;
- condition 3 – maintain or reduce the amount of money tied up within the business, now or in the future;
- condition 4 – support or provide a solution to a necessary or externally imposed constraint (e.g., a legal or regulatory requirement).

In short, benefits are about making more money, using existing resources and assets more efficiently and staying in business. Words such as 'growth', 'efficiency', 'protection' and 'demand' are frequently used, reflecting an organization's focus at any point in time. The value of a company is determined by its ability to maximize its risk-adjusted cash flow generation consistently. It follows, then, that companies should focus on those factors that help them generate more cash for longer periods of time and with the least risk possible. These are called value drivers.

For public sector organizations, the story is similar but focusses more on delivering a government's or council's policies whilst ensuring value for money. Thus, the conditions could be:

- condition 1 – maintain or increase income (mainly from taxation) to the organization, now or in the future;
- condition 2 – maintain or reduce the operating costs of the organization, now or in the future;
- condition 3 – maintain or reduce the amount of money tied up within the organization, now or in the future;
- condition 4 – support or provide a solution to a necessary or externally imposed constraint (e.g., an international treaty obligation).

Benefits and planning

Effective identification, analysis, planning and tracking of benefits should ensure benefits are realized in practice. This implies having an agreed upon, definitive set of benefits to start with. Stakeholders have different expectations regarding the benefits to be realized, framed by how they view the programme or project. This is why the choice of programme or project sponsor (see Chapter 5) is so important. If a business

It is better to have what appears to be a sub-optimal output that can be implemented than a theoretically perfect output which cannot be implemented

portfolio or programme manager selects a project sponsor with a completely different viewpoint, the entire portfolio could be disrupted as strategic alignment will be broken. It is, however, important to understand the different perspectives of stakeholders and take them into account when developing the outputs and implementing the associated changes. It is better to have what appears to be a sub-optimal output that can be implemented than a theoretically perfect output which cannot be implemented; the former will provide some benefit, the latter, none.

Benefits should be assessed for a number of output/outcome options before a solution is chosen and included in a business case; potentially conflicting pressures, such as performance, scope, time, cost and benefits need to be balanced with risk. Remember to focus on net benefits by including 'dis-benefits'. When asked what benefits result from a particular course of action, often people only state the positive benefits leaving the negative aspects out. Make sure both are covered.

Whilst the programme or project sponsor is accountable for overall benefits, as they own the business case, they will often need to assign a benefits owner to forecast and monitor each benefit. This might be for a particular benefits measure over all or for the same measure within a defined area. For example, if the benefit measure was revenue from a particular new product, this might have a single owner, the product manager, or it might be devolved to an owner in each geographic area the product is sold in.

New benefits might emerge as the work progresses whilst stakeholder expectations might change, making it essential to reassess benefits throughout the duration of the work. This is why, for projects, the business case is assessed prior to the start of each new stage in the project life cycle. For programmes, the programme business case would need to be assessed every time a new tranche or programme phase begins and when significant project stages or other work are started.

Plans should include milestones which relate to benefits

Plans should include milestones which relate to benefits as the realization of benefits is what you really want. People are used to including milestones for when outputs are delivered but milestones relating to benefits are not so commonly seen. The problem is that benefits are seldom realized in one lump. Benefits are usually realized over a longer period and so discrete milestones are not very helpful. The answer is to include milestones which represent the outcomes which, when achieved, enable the benefits to be realized. For example, if your project benefits show a considerable saving in costs by closing one office and consolidating your operations into a single site, the milestones to track could be:

- office vacated;
- confirmation of final rent payment.

The first means it is no longer necessary to pay for running the building on a day-to-day basis, whilst the second means rent is not payable. These outcomes lead to directly tangible, financial benefits and are good milestones to keep an eye on. If they slip, the benefits will slip. In fact, from a sponsor's perspective, milestones signifying outcomes are far more useful than those representing outputs as they show real progress in business terms. Such milestone should relate to the **conditions of satisfaction**, the circumstances under which the project or programme can be declared a success. A useful, alternative name for the milestones which represent observable changes is **recognition event**®. This term was coined as part of the Dimension Four method. Other milestones which can be tracked are called **value flashpoints**®, which mark the start in an observable change in cash flow. In terms of benefits mapping, recognition events® represent the outcomes and value flashpoints® the benefits. Together they provide an easily understood way for senior management to track progress towards their strategic objectives, without getting bogged down in the minutiae of measurement and analysis.

Workout 21.1 – Outputs – Outcomes – Benefits

Consider your project, programme or business portfolio:

1. What are the overriding business objectives for the organization?
2. What benefits do you need in order to meet these objectives?
3. What are the business changes (outcomes) needed to generate the benefits?
4. What enablers or deliverables (outputs), do you need to enable the outcomes?
5. Which components (projects or other work) of your portfolio are these outputs and outcomes delivered?

Draw a map, like the one here, showing the linkage for your project, programme or business portfolio.

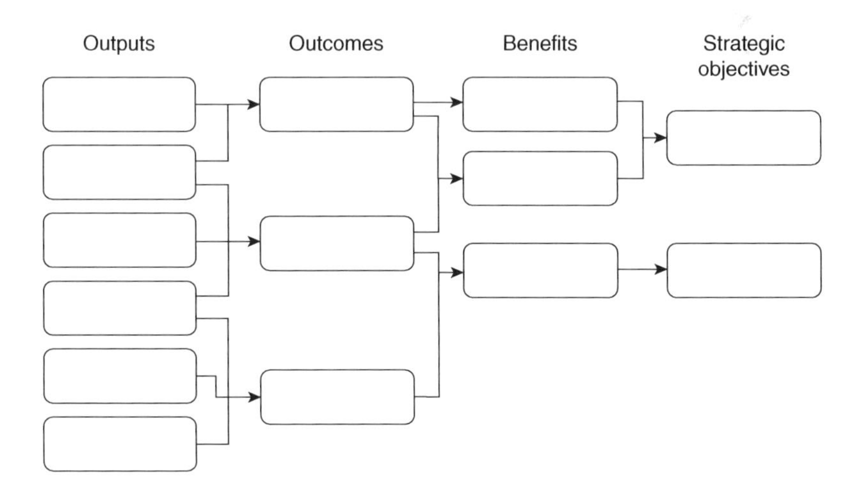

Look for (real) opportunities to bring benefits forward

* M IV now called the M4 motorway from England to Wales.

Value drivers and the business plan

If you have worked in mergers and acquisitions, you might be familiar with how due diligence is carried out to assess the value and the liabilities of the target company. Managers in acquiring companies look at the variables of the target company which drive its costs, revenues and asset value. This approach is also useful when aiming for greater efficiency and effectiveness in your own organization. The objective is to identify the set of value drivers specific to the organization which can be checked off against the organization's chart of accounts. Examples of value drivers for a commercial company are as follows, but you may have more or different ones in your organization:

1. REDUCED PERSONNEL COSTS
   - Driven by reduced head count
   - Driven by reduced/avoided recruitment
   - Driven by reduced employment overheads
2. REDUCED COST OF OWNERSHIP OF ASSETS
   - Driven by reduced maintenance costs
   - Driven by reduced security costs (including losses)
3. REDUCED COST OF RECTIFICATION
   - Driven by reduced effort per error on investigation and recovery
   - Driven by reduced volume of re-supply per error
4. PROFITABLE ACQUISITION
   - Driven by profitable acquisition of valuable estate
   - Driven by profitable acquisition of valuable IT systems
   - Driven by profitable acquisition of valuable production assets/plant
5. IMPROVED PROFITABLE SALES INFRASTRUCTURE
   - Driven by enhancement of profitable new sales personnel skills and relationships

- Driven by acquisition of profitable improvements to sales processes
- Driven by acquisition of new company data and knowledge that are put to profitable use in sales

If you know what drives your organization's costs down and its revenues and asset values up, you can compare these against the business changes your programme or project will enable and see how this drives benefits realization. This technique enables a sponsor to identify the benefits, which usually go far beyond those envisaged when working within imposed, budget-cutting targets.

One of the useful spin-offs of value drivers is how the analysis can increase a team's understanding of where an organization's money comes from. It can also turn up unexpected drivers, which may enhance or devalue the benefits.

Understanding the value drivers is essential from a business portfolio perspective. If you understand the drivers, you can be more specific on the programmes, projects and other work you need to initiate. In fact, the business plan should be based on a thorough understanding of the value drivers.

Workout 21.2 – What drives your organization's value?

This is probably the toughest workout in the book and goes to the heart of how you derive your benefits. The business leaders usually have the best idea of what the drivers are.

1. Build on Workout 21.1, by identifying the recognition events® (outcomes) and value flashpoints® (benefits) necessary to achieve your objectives.
2. Using the list of drivers in this chapter as a prompt, note what you believe are your organization's value drivers. The number can be limitless, but for most organizations, there are five to ten value drivers which are material.
3. Test this assumption by taking the value flash points in step 1 and matching them to one (or more) of your assumed value drivers.

The business case

Initial and full business cases – a progressive approach

A business case is a document which sets out to justify taking a particular course of action.

Benefits for programmes and projects are usually documented at a high level in a business case. A business case is a document which sets out to justify taking a particular course of action. The aim is to convince senior stakeholders and decision makers that the project or programme is a good use of resources. For all but the simplest projects, business cases are usually developed progressively over a number of life cycle stages. The early versions are usually differentiated from the complete version by calling them 'outline', 'initial' or similar, with the completed business case often being referred to as a 'full' business case. You should be able to match the type of business case against the project life cycle as done in Figures 8.4 and 8.5. Avoid the use of the term 'final' business case, as this implies this is the last version of the business and that it will never change. In practice, a 'full' business case is likely to require updating to reflect the changing context of the project or programme and the progress being made. The only final business case is the one which stands at the end of the project or programme.

The initial business case

Using the two-step approach in Chapter 8, the initial business case for a project should include the business rationale for the programme or project, outlining (not detailing!) WHY you need it, WHAT options you intend to work on, HOW you will do it and WHO is needed to make it happen. It is also used to authorize the funding for at least the next stage of the project. The initial business case does not comprise a full analysis but only sufficient detail to enable you to decide if it is worth continuing. The initial business case includes:

- a preliminary assessment of the financial aspects of the proposed development;
- a definition of the work which would be required to meet these, including an outline of the requirement in terms of customer/user 'feel', technology, commercial, market needs and desired outcomes. There may be a number of options at this point in time;
- a description of how the work will be organized in terms of roles and governance.

The initial business also enables the evaluation of the work against the existing strategies and goals of the company to confirm its strategic fit and determine if it is likely to be viable in business, technical, operational and customer terms.

The full business case

The full business case provides the definitive appraisal for the programme or project. It is derived from the initial business case and feasibility report, together with the outputs from other investigative work. It is the document on which the decision is made to authorize funding for the remainder of the work and the building in of costs and benefits to the business portfolio's business plan. The document is 'live' and under strict version control for the remainder of the programme or project.

The first business case?

In the typical project life cycle in Chapters 8, the very first gate is governed by a 'Proposal' rather than a business case. The reason for this is because there are so many interpretations and versions of what a business case is, that if people have in mind a 'full business case' when asked to justify the project being started, they could mistakenly believe all the investigative work has to be undertaken before the programme or project is even started, which would completely nullify the advantages of a staged approach. Add to this that many people still take a contractor viewpoint and do not believe a programme or project has started until actual development or building work begins, so you can see there is scope for confusion. It is not wrong to call a 'proposal' a business case, but do beware of the dangers if your people are not fully aligned in the way these words are used and how they link to the project life cycle.

A programme's business case

The trigger for re-assessing a programme's business case is when individual projects or major pieces of other work are initiated

A programme's business cases should follow the same principles as a project's business case as it serves the same purpose, namely to justify the work being undertaken. The only difference is that it has been decided that the work should be managed as a programme rather than as a project. The problem is that programmes, unlike projects, do not have stages and so the checkpoints for assessing the business case cannot be tied to a life cycle. The business case needs to be treated as a continuum, starting as an outline (or initial) case and gradually becoming more detailed and (hopefully) less volatile as the programme proceeds. The trigger for re-assessing a programme's business case is when individual projects or major pieces of other work are initiated. In some circumstances the constituent projects could have their own business cases, whilst in other circumstances, a project might not need a business case at all, having been justified at programme level.

Analysis approach

As a business case is used to justify whether particular work should proceed, it necessarily includes, or relies on, a great deal of analysis. The approaches used are numerous, and most organizations tend to develop their own methods and codify them. For example, the UK government has its *Green Book*, which together with its supplementary guidance runs into hundreds of pages. By having a common approach to analysis, the benefits of different solutions or projects can be compared. For private sector organizations, discounted cash flow and internal rate of return are the most popular approaches, as they take account of the cost of borrowing. The analysis is financially based and includes taxation, borrowing and other financial aspects. In the public sector, the approach is based on how the work will benefit the economy as a whole, and not just the sponsoring organization. For both however, the analysis of cash flow, the setting of a discount rate and an understanding of where the funds are to be obtained are paramount. A good project is not good if there is no money to pay for it!

It is therefore best to think in terms of ranges rather than absolute values

Remember, however, that everything in the business case is a forecast and therefore uncertain, both in terms of timing and values. It is therefore best to think in terms of ranges rather than absolute values and to look at the sensitivity of different assumptions for a number of scenarios. In other words, look at and analyze the risks. A seemingly great business case might not be so good when the risks are considered.

Deliberately misleading the decision makers

Business cases are very important documents, as they are the basis for major decisions. They are not, however, without their faults, especially in highly charged political situations. A programme or a project's business case does not stand or fall on its own merits. There is always strong competition for investment within any organization, and any individual business case needs to pass the test of comparison or competition with others. From the viewpoint of those developing a business case, there can be no guarantee of creating a winner, even if, on its own, it makes sense. For this reason, it might be tempting to 'overegg' the benefits in a business case. This does, however, add a greater risk of failure and may also serve to de-motivate the team when they realize the targets they have to achieve are impossible; it can result in the rejection of the project by key stakeholders who may challenge or reject any exaggerated benefits claims.

Strategic misrepresentation is the planned, systematic distortion or misstatement of fact (some call it 'lying') to further an agenda or strategy in response to incentives in the budget process. Jones and Euske applied it to public sector budgeting in a paper they wrote in 1991. They argued that strategic misrepresentation is a predictable response to a system of rewards in a highly competitive 'game' where resource constraints are present. They found it is used both by budget advocates and controllers and, at times, by both sides of the left–right political spectrum. The study concluded that no amount of moral handwringing over the evils of strategic misrepresentation is likely to lessen the practice. Rather, the system of incentives that triggers strategic misrepresentation requires reform if the behaviour is to be discouraged. In 2013, The UK's National Audit Office published a report, *Over-Optimism in Government Projects*, which describes how 'optimism bias' and other dysfunctions can distort key investment decisions; it investigated the causes of 'strategic misrepresentation' and provided case studies to illustrate the effect. Like Jones and Euske 22 years earlier, the report found the incentives in many organizations "to be over-optimistic are very strong, and disincentives relatively weak." The report also points out that "decision-makers seek short-term recognition and rewards, and are often not in the same role when the project is under way and issues emerge." Although written from the perspective of government projects, these findings are also relevant in the private sector, for which a number of studies have also been done. As I have a said a few times in this book, organizational success requires far more than having good processes and trained people. Having the right environment and behaviours is vital; we touched on this point in the chapter on governance (see Chapter 4).

No amount of moral handwringing over the evils of strategic misrepresentation is likely to lessen the practice.

Workout 21.3 – Five questions to challenge your business case

This workout can be done at any point in the project, but the earlier the better. These are good questions for auditors and project assurance as well for the project team to 'test' themselves.

1. Does the programme or project fit your organization's business strategy?
2. Have alternative options for realizing the benefits been investigated. Why were they rejected?
3. Is the work affordable? Will the organization have the funds available when needed? If it generates some or all of its own funds, what are the risks associated with this?
4. Does the solution represent value for money, whether produced internally or by suppliers?
5. Is the programme or project achievable? Do you have (or can you acquire) the capability and capacity?

22

Planning and controls

What are my control levers?

Planning: working out how to get there

Monitoring and reporting: so you don't get lost

Whilst these topics apply from business portfolio to work package in concept, the way you undertake them differs. The higher up the breakdown structure you are working, the more holistic your perspective needs to be.

"Life can only be understood backwards, but it must be lived forwards."

SOREN KIERKEGAARD, 1813–1855

- **Focus on outcomes and benefits.**
- **Make sure your plan is viable and robust.**
- **Ensure progress is verifiable: check what you've been told.**
- **Don't micromanage the levels below you.**

What are my control levers?

Regardless of whether you are directing a business portfolio, sponsoring a programme or project, or managing a work package, you will need to:

- develop a viable plan;
- monitor progress against that plan;
- identify what is likely to go wrong and what has gone wrong and sort them out;
- make sure everyone is working with the right information.

The first two points are covered in this chapter and the second two in Chapter 23. Whilst these four activities are often treated as separate topics in methods, standards or textbooks, in practice there is a continuous flow between them. When asked to advise on course content for entry level and intermediate project managers, I found the topics to be covered were the same, but how they should be dealt with was not. The difference was that the intermediate level not only included more techniques, but more importantly, the topics were taught in an integrated way. In real life, information does not arrive in neat packages, clearly labelled, "I am a risk, save me for when you next look at risks." In practice, you might not even know if the information is even factual and people do not always use the 'right words' when they communicate. A risk might be described as an issue or as a 'bit of a problem'; they might simply make statements with no indication as to what it is. It is up to the manager who receives the information to make judgements concerning what the information represents, if it is true or significant and if any preventative or corrective action is needed. If action is needed, it is possible to move from identifying an issue, to requesting a change and replanning the work, thus passing through a number of the topics. This could happen very rapidly, say within an hour in a meeting, or it could take days or weeks.

The relationships between the control topics in are shown in Figure 22.1. Without a diagram such as this, the interfaces between the topics can become unclear, which, in turn, can lead to confused accountabilities. Whilst these topics apply from business portfolio to work package in concept, the way they are undertaken differs. The higher up the breakdown structure, the more holistic your perspective needs to be. Remember,

The higher up the breakdown structure, the more holistic your perspective needs to be.

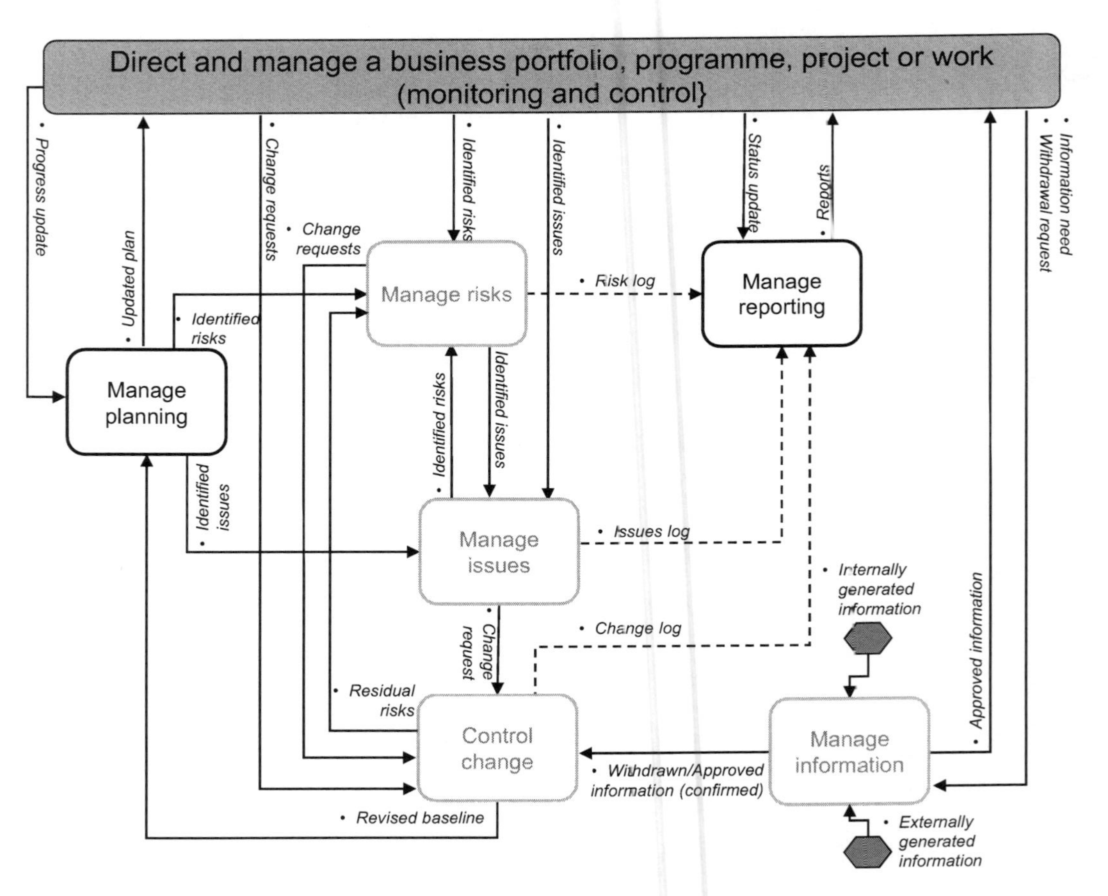

Figure 22.1 The relationship between control activities

The key control activities and their relationships (inputs and outputs) are shown here. Unless you define an overall architecture such as this, you will find the interfaces between processes become muddled, which, in turn, leads to muddled accountabilities. These apply from business portfolio to work package.

Chapter 4 on governance showed that the breakdown structure is fundamental to assigning tiered accountabilities and each level owns any gaps or overlaps which might appear in the levels below. Accountability includes being accountable for all the topics covered in this chapter.

Planning: working out how to get there

What is a plan made up of?

Planning ensures your objectives are likely to be delivered within the defined constraints. Constraints include not only schedule, resources, costs and scope but also risk and benefits. A plan has to be viable and breaching any one of these constraints could mean needing to rethink what you are doing. In business portfolio management terms, that could lead to revaluating the whole of your business.

Plan at an appropriate level of detail

A plan should be based on a hierarchy showing each work component's place, with single point accountability assigned for every component and activity, reflecting the structure in Figure 3.3, Chapter 3. When planning a business portfolio, you would need to be able to identify every programme, project and work item within the portfolio.

Plans need to include the level of detail appropriate to the planning level and the needs of those viewing or using the plan. For example, a manager of a work package would need a different level of detail to a programme manager. The work package manager would need to know, by name, who is working on each deliverable, the activities needed to create the deliverable and order they need to be done, when a deliverable is due to be completed and when different resources need to be mobilized. A programme manager might simply be interested in when the work package is likely to be completed, how much it is likely to cost and when the outcomes are planned to happen.

Plans need to include the level of detail appropriate to the planning level and the needs of those viewing or using the plan.

Depending on the level (portfolio, programme, project or work package), a plan might include forecasts of benefits, milestones, activities, schedule, cost and resources, with associated assumptions, constraints, critical paths(s) and risk.

Know your interdependencies

Dependencies between programmes and projects and other work need to be identified. Just as a project manager needs to know which activities have to be completed before another can be started, so a programme or portfolio manager needs to understand the order each component of the portfolio or programme should be undertaken. This is not as a simple as knowing start and end dates, as dependencies usually occur at milestones part-way through the work and not at completion.

Plans can wobble

The danger is that too much attention could be paid to meeting interim dates rather than meeting the dates which really matter.

Dates in portfolios and programmes are rarely fixed or predictable. Some work will take longer than expected, other tasks completed more quickly. The whole system is always in a state of flux. The danger is that too much attention could be paid to meeting interim dates rather than meeting the dates which really matter. For a project, a date which matters is the ready for service gate (see Chapter 8), which is the decision point prior to benefits starting to be realized. As outcomes and benefits are the only reason a programme or portfolio exists, outcomes and benefits should always be the primary focus of a portfolio or programme plan; this is what the whole organization is driving towards. You should therefore ensure that you have, within your programme or portfolio plan, milestones which represent the outcomes (recognition events®) and benefits (value flashpoints®). These were discussed in Chapter 21. Without understanding how each stream of benefits connects with the work on the ground, the benefits plan can end up being little more than a pipe dream. How many organizations have finance plans which demand a stated revenue stream together with a stretch target on cost reduction, but no foundation in reality? A chief finance officer saying, "Reduce costs by 15%" doesn't make it happen in practice. The higher the stretch target, the greater the risk is of it not being met. Every plan includes a level of risk, which should never be ignored. I can promise you £21m for an investment of £1, if you are willing to accept the probability of me delivering is only 1 in 14,000,000 (these are the odds of winning the jackpot in The National Lottery®).

Assurance and decision making take time

Remember, a plan should include and allow for assurance and decision making. As we saw in Chapter 4 on governance, business leaders' ability to make decisions often constrains the speed with which a plan can be undertaken. This applies, not only to decision making within your organization but also within the other organizations you are depending on. A classic example is obtaining planning permission; the time this can take is notoriously unpredictable, and even then, obtaining it is not certain. If the business portfolio plan includes the need for a new building or facility, you are blocked until the requisite permissions are granted. Other examples include obtaining wayleaves, regulatory approvals and, for those involved in national infrastructure programmes, might include the passing of an Act of Parliament.

Know your baseline

Once approved, plans should be baselined and progress regularly monitored and analyzed. Many argue that it is impossible to 'baseline' a portfolio plan as it is a continuous churn of work being added and completed. That, however, is taking a very narrow, project-based, view of baselining. No matter what level you are working at in the hierarchy, only baseline the parts that matter at that level. For a work package, you might baseline the start and end of each activity, whilst for a programme or portfolio you might only need a list of all the components with the associated decision points and the milestones representing the prime interdependencies, outcomes and when benefits start being realized. Each lower level manager can then be allowed the freedom to develop their plans within those constraints. For a portfolio, the working portfolio plan is the baseline. Every time a project is added, the mere fact of approval means it has been incorporated into the portfolio's baseline; no separate 'approvals' are needed. The only aspects of a portfolio plan which would require separate approval are the 'top-down' targets, set as part of business planning. The degree of freedom a higher-level manager gives a lower-level manager is often called **tolerance** and can apply to any constraint, not just scope, costs and schedule.

Each lower level manager can then be allowed the freedom to develop their plans within those constraints.

How will you know when you've got there?

Benefits driven planning

Planning for things you know nothing about

The fundamental starting point of planning is knowing where you want to end up. What is your vision? How will you know when you have arrived? Without a destination, you are simply a traveller consuming vast amounts of money and energy on the way. In Chapter 9, we looked at Obeng's project types which dealt with varying degrees of knowledge concerning the end point of a project. This model can also be used in the management of business portfolios and programmes. As a reminder, the project types are repeated in Table 22.1.

Logically, if a project can be any one of the four types, the portfolio or programme a project is a part of can take on the characteristics of that project. If a business portfolio has a 'lost in a fog' project within it, the plan for the portfolio as whole has to take that into account. It doesn't necessarily mean the entire portfolio is lost in a fog, as the 'foggy' part might simply be a small element of the scope and the risks associated with it might be insignificant. On the other hand, one 'lost' project could mean the

Table 22.1 Obeng's project types can be applied to programmes and portfolios

Project type	*Type of change it helps create*	*Application*
Painting by numbers	Evolutionary	Improving your continuing business operations
Going on a quest	Revolutionary	Proactively exploring outside current operations and ways of working
Making a movie	Evolutionary	Leveraging existing capabilities
Lost in a fog	Revolutionary	Solving a problem or exploring areas outside your current operations and ways of working

Adapted from Eddie Obeng *Putting Strategy to Work* (London: Pitman Publishing, 1996)

entire portfolio or programme is at risk, if everything which follows relies on it. What would be the point of a beautifully designed Mars lander if the launch vehicle was incapable of getting the payload safely into orbit?

Planning for programmes and portfolios needs to take into account the 'unknown'. Chapter 11, on business portfolios, discusses how a portfolio comprises current business operations and 'new stuff', such as projects. We also saw there needs to be 'white space' representing future work that cannot be detailed yet. Without such white space, an organization would be paralyzed and unable to respond to new threats and opportunities. A business portfolio always requires future 'white space' within it, and so it always has an element which is either a 'quest' or 'lost in a fog'. The plan for the business portfolio needs to roll in a way such that the white space is always pushed out into the future, as it is replaced by more solid work and the fogs and quests become 'painting by numbers' activities. The task of the portfolio or programme manager is to balance the mix of work to ensure benefits can be reliably and consistently realized in line with the portfolio's business plan.

Planning should be iterative and progressive

Planning should be iterative and progressive, with more detail for the immediate future than the more distant work. The scope of the work should be refined and clarified as it progresses, always recognizing the overall risk and the acceptable level of risk for each component at each level of the hierarchy. For business portfolios and programmes, it is useful to recognize the current level of certainty by, for example, using ranges or confidence indicators when stating benefits, costs and timescales. All too often a 'single figure', such as the capital cost of a rail or road programme can become fixed in people's minds, who soon forget the number came from an early feasibility study. Using this initial figure as a baseline means you will always have a poor view of project performance. The staged, project life cycle described in Chapter 8 of this book, is a good basis to manage this. Estimates at the start of the project are less reliable than those towards the end, otherwise there is no point in having any investigative stages. Table 22.2 shows a hypothetical project's expected cost of overtime and the story looks like one of relentless escalation of costs, finishing with an apparent 96% overspend. On the other hand, Table 22.3 uses ranges and shows how, as the project

Table 22.2 Absolute cost overruns

Stage	*Initial investigation gate*	*Detailed investigation gate*	*Development gate*	*Trial gate*	*Release gate*	*Project completion*
Estimated cost at completion	£120m	£130m	£140m	£155m	£170m	£176m (actual)

progresses, the envelope becomes narrower and the outcome cost is within the range of the original estimate – a very different story. Figure 22.2 shows the same information as a graph. The range of the final cost is shown by the upper and lower lines and shows, as work progresses, the spread decreases. The middle line shows an 'absolute figure'. Whist this always sits within the range, it appears to show relentless escalation. By using ranges, you are can indicate the level of uncertainty at each point through the life cycle. This also illustrates the importance of using quoted figures. Every figure has a level of uncertainty associated with it; if you deliberately use a low figure you might be misrepresenting the actual situation (see the section on strategic misrepresentation in Chapter 21).

By using ranges, you are can indicate the level of uncertainty at each point through the life cycle.

Planning techniques to reflect instability

For all but the simplest business portfolio and programme plans, planning techniques reflecting the inherent instability caused by so many moving parts are needed. It is delusional to pretend everything will come in on time and to budget and that consequently the required level of benefits you need will be realized. No matter how detailed the planning, it will never reflect what will actually happen. That is not to say that producing a plan is pointless; in fact, it is the producing of the plan which really matters. By developing a plan, which takes into account the risks and dependencies, the team will develop a greater understanding of the dynamics of the plan and be able to choose a strategy which is more likely to meet their needs at an acceptable level of risk. For this reason, planning should be a collaborative activity, involving team members advising on different aspects of the work. Estimates should be justifiable through evidence or experience such as by using reference class forecasting, consensus or learnings from previous work. Standard project planning techniques described in *The Project Workout* are useful but need to be adapted to make them appropriate for business portfolio and programme planning. This includes using:

- benefits mapping;
- sensitivity analysis;
- scenario analysis;
- simulation and probabilistic modelling.

Table 22.3 Cost overruns as ranges

Stage	*Initial investigation gate*	*Detailed investigation gate*	*Development gate*	*Trial gate*	*Release gate*	*Project completion*
Estimated cost at completion	£90m to £220m	£100m to £200m	£110m – £180m	£140m-£175m	£170m-£180m	£176m (actual)

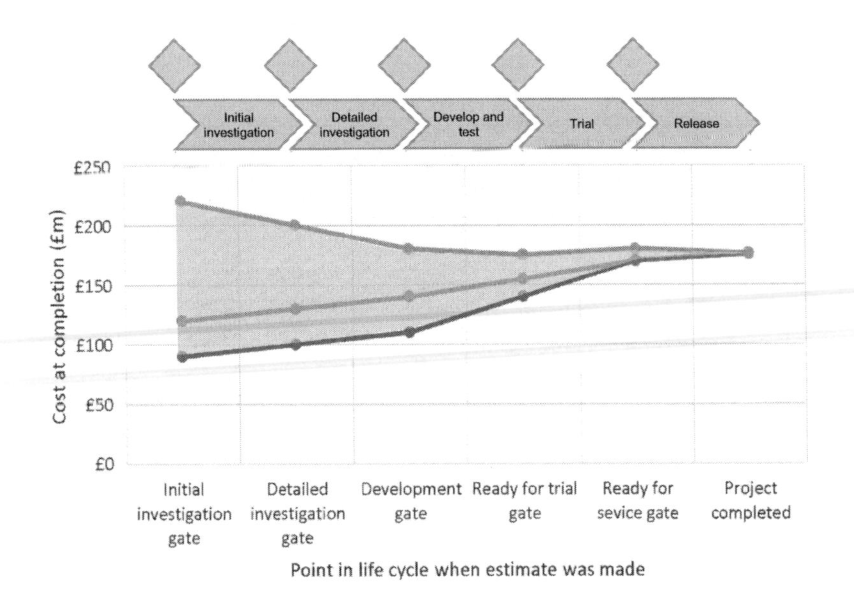

Figure 22.2 Working in ranges

This graph shows the advantage of thinking in ranges rather than absolute figures. It uses the same figures as in Tables 22.2 and 22.3. The range of the final cost is shown by the upper and lower lines and shows, as work progresses, the spread decreases. The middle line shows an 'absolute figure'. Whist this always sits within the range, it appears to show relentless escalation. By using ranges, you can indicate the level of uncertainty at each point through the life cycle.

Benefits mapping back from the future to the present

Benefits mapping was covered in Chapter 21. It is, in concept, a very simple technique for making sure that the deliverables you produce result in some benefit. It ensures traceability from work on the ground to the achievement of business objectives. An effective way of using the mapping technique is to imagine a point in the future when your current aims have been fulfilled and then work backwards, progressively asking, what needed to happen to get to here? In this way, you can move from the future to the present, adding the required outcomes and outputs along the way, identifying only those which are needed. This technique is called **back-casting**: using the desired result (outcome) of a project or programme as the basis and starting point for planning. This means planning is initially conducted working backwards from completion. There are a number of variants of this technique, but all show:

- which benefits contribute to specific business objectives;
- the outcomes needed to realize those benefits;
- the outputs needed to enable the outcomes (business changes).

When used in a portfolio or programme management context, such maps can help decide on how the work should be divided into its component parts. The idea is to ensure:

- only what is necessary to achieve the objectives is included;
- minimize the dependencies.

A simple example is shown in Figure 22.3, where four projects (P1 to P4) are used with two other work components (W1 and W2) to effect the changes needed to achieve the stated objective.

By making the streams in the benefits map as independent as possible, the number of stakeholders is reduced and decision making localized. This enhances the likelihood of achieving successful results. The technique can be used at project level, with an extension on the left to include the deliverables which make up each output (this is described in *The Project Workout*).

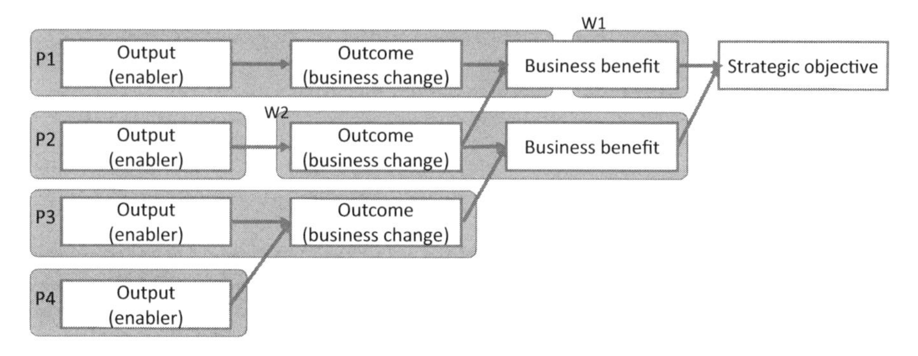

Figure 22.3 Benefits mapping with multiple streams

A benefits map explains how the outputs will lead to outcomes (business changes), which in turn lead to specific business benefits that support strategic objectives. In this representation I have over laid four projects (P1 to P4) with two other work components (W1 and W2) to show how the scope of each builds up to effect the changes needed to achieve the stated objective.

Reducing interdependencies in a programme

I was given the task of looking at a plan for a complex change programme for a manufacturing organization. There were six projects and about 400 activities. The complexity was due to over 50 interdependencies between the projects. I printed out a network chart of the programme and laid it out on the factory floor like a carpet. A half-day of study and marking up resulted in a much simpler schedule. There were still six projects but now only five interdependencies. The original project scope had been defined largely on departmental lines but by focussing on outcomes, I was able to create relatively independent projects, giving each project sponsor greater degrees of freedom to direct their projects without the need to involve the others.

Sensitivity analysis

Risk is not always binary. In practice, there can be a range of effects, with impacts ranging from the disastrously negative to the unbelievably positive. Such items are easily identified and relate to assumptions such as market rates, customer usage, plant efficiency, inflation, customer demand, cost forecasts and timing. Uncertainty usually has a greater impact on benefits than cost and schedule. Sensitivity analysis is used to review the impact on viability of a possible range of values for each assumption made. In this way, you can decide which assumptions are substantive to the business case or plan and need to be addressed further. For example, in Table 22.4, we see viability is more sensitive to percentage moves in tariffs than in costs.

Risk is not always binary.

Table 22.4 Example sensitivity analysis

Assumption		*– 20%*	*– 10%*	*+10%*	*+20%*
Change in cost	**NPV ($)**	215k	416k	764k	987k
	IRR	14%	32%	52%	67%
Change in tariff	**NPV ($)**	10k	234k	865k	1234k
	IRR	9%	17%	16%	102%

Scenario analysis

Scenario analysis takes sensitivity analysis a step further by looking at alternative futures. A scenario comprises a set of compatible assumptions, chosen from the risk and sensitivity analysis, which describes the future. This often requires a model to be built so the different assumptions can be used consistently. e.g., fewer customers can lead not only to less revenue but also to less cost of sales, whilst fixed costs remain the same. Scenarios are great way to investigate the pros and cons of different strategies (hence plans) to achieving your objectives. Within this, each primary scenario can be further investigated in terms of how well it might perform, looking at forecasts which are:

- optimistic;
- most likely;
- pessimistic.

Thus, for a pessimistic scenario, you might assume a late project completion date with a cost overrun, slower customer take-up and usage and more severe downward price pressures than anticipated. This can be tabulated, as in Table 22.5. As for sensitivity analysis, the aim is to provide decision makers with an objective view of the consequences of their decisions, enabling them to balance the possible opportunities (upside) with the associated threats (downside).

Table 22.5 Example scenario analysis

Parameter	*Pessimistic*	*Most likely*	*Optimistic*
Timing of RFS	2 months late	On time	2 weeks early
IT cost	$450k	$340k	$320k
Customer take-up	+5%	+12%	+15%
Usage	35 minutes/day	50 minutes/day	65 minutes/day
Tariff erosion	−15% annual	−5% annual	−5% annual
IRR %	−6%	40%	87%
NPV ($k)	−1767	2990	3875
Payback	No payback	3 years	2 years

Simulation and probabilistic modelling

Simulation can be used to support sensitivity and scenario analyses and help analyze a portfolio, programme or project and investigate the possible results from different courses of action. Simulation is a relatively new but little used technique but, with the growth of artificial intelligence and more widely available tools, it is likely to become more widespread. As always, different industries are likely to pick up on different aspects of simulation, related to their own needs. There is no standard or categorization for business simulation, but simulators tend to have two different purposes in the context of portfolio and programme management:

- numeric: enabling you to provide different values for the parameters required in the business model;
- scenario based: a way of seeing the impact of following different strategies.

In the fields of project management, the numeric based approach has been used for longest. It relies on the application of a range of durations, costs and benefits associated with the key activities for a programme or project. This is input as:

- the lowest likely value;
- the most likely value;
- the highest probable value.

The simulation software analyses the network of activities, using assigned probability distribution curves to calculate a range of likely benefits, costs and durations with a set of overall probabilities. Figure 22.4 shows the results of a simulation in terms of cost and schedule. It is a powerful way of investigating how the work might end up and can help in isolating particularly problematic aspects of the work. It also drives home the message that, in reality, there is not one 'critical path' but a whole range of near-critical paths which require attention. It is also sobering to see how many simulation runs result in the same end date but with radically different intermediate milestones. This highlights that at the programme and portfolio level you need to track only the milestones which matter.

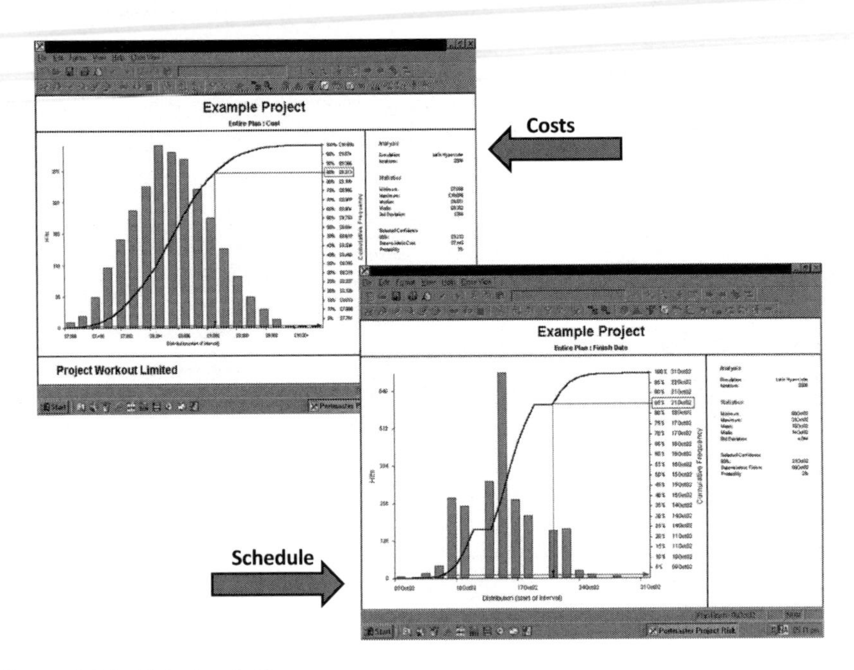

Figure 22.4 Risk simulation

The figure (created using Oracle Risk Manager®) shows typical outputs you can expect from a Monte Carlo analysis. At the top is a histogram for costs, so you can place a percentage confidence measure on completing the project within a stated cost. The bottom screen is the same project but shows the variation in schedule for a range of confidence percentages. In this example, we can be 85%confident the project will be completed by 21 October and for less than £9,200k.

Scenario based simulations take an entire business or a significant part (business portfolio!) and model the possible outcomes under different sets of decisions and assumptions. These are most commonly used in universities and business schools as training aids but, with care, can be used on real businesses. The balanced optimization approach to selecting projects looked at in Chapter 15 is an example of a simulation application which can be used to decide the content and timing of each component of a business portfolio. They are still in their infancy, but even simple models can promote good results simply by being the focus of discussions when planning a programme or business portfolio. The problem is such tools can be seductive because they:

- can induce unrealistic expectations; the computer does it all at the press of a button;
- are ONLY a simulation and have limitations designed into it. You need to know the limits for a model's use;
- can promote sub-optimization, which, like detailed planning, is spurious in the wrong context.

That said, the right simulation used for the right task will lead to better thought through strategies.

But I thought this was about planning, not risk?

Yes, the techniques described earlier are more about risk than planning. Risk, however, is an inherent feature of any plan, and the two cannot be divorced. Any plan has risk associated with it. The task it to create a plan which is viable and can be delivered at an acceptable level of risk. Every control mentioned in this chapter is intrinsically linked to the others and have to be treated as a whole.

Don't forget your resource, capacity and capability constraints

No matter how well thought through the schedule, without the resources, nothing will happen.

Resource, capacity and capability management balances the supply and demand for resources (such as people, equipment, material and facilities) to be deployed when needed. This is an inherent part of planning. No matter how well thought through the schedule, without the resources, nothing will happen. Resources can come from within your organization, by recruiting, or from your supply chain. The balance depends on your business or operating model. Even if you use suppliers for almost all that needs to be done, you will still need a core team, as an 'intelligent client' to oversee it . . . and will have to be confident the supply chain can actually deliver.

You will need to have a comprehensive view of future resource needs and identify possible shortfalls and how to deal with them. If insufficient resources are available, you will have to revaluate the components of your programme or portfolio and choose an alternative approach which is not constrained. See Chapter 14 for more about resources.

Workout 22.1 – Planning from the future

This workout can be done at any level in the work breakdown structure and can cover any defined scope of work, such as an entire programme or a work package within a project. You'll need a large wall, flipchart markers and a good supply of Post-It Notes®. Try to have as wider team as possible do this workout together as a 'team'.

1 Write each of your objectives down on a Post-It Note®. Place these on the far right of your wall.
2 Write down the outcomes (business changes) that need to be in place if your objectives are to be achieved. Write each outcome on a separate Post-It Note. Place these to the left of your objectives. Draw a line from each outcome to one or more objectives which it enables. Try to position the Post-It Notes® so you don't have too many lines crossing. The objectives and outcomes represent your 'future'.
3 Write down the outputs (one per Post-It Note®) that enable each of the outcomes. Place these to the left of the outcomes. Draw lines from each output to the outcomes it enables. Try to minimize the number of lines which cross.
4 You now have a benefits map which can be converted into the basis of a plan. For each output, decide what deliverables are necessary to create each output. Place these to the left of the outputs. Draw lines from each deliverable to the outputs it enables. Try to minimize the number of lines which cross.
5 Keep adding deliverables to the left until you reach 'today'.
6 Having created a chain of deliverables, go through the flow again but add in the activities that would be needed to produce each deliverable. Try to minimize cross-overs but do include dependencies. You might not be able to define some parts as you don't know enough about that area of the plan. In these cases, put in a dummy activity and add some investigative work. You might notice that the plan has some distinct clusters of activities; these might be a clue to your work breakdown structure.
7 Make a guess at how long each activity might take. Think in terms of ranges rather than absolute figures, as this will help you consider risk. The network of activities and the durations should enable you to create a draft bar chart. Is the overall duration likely to be acceptable? If not, consider alternative approaches.
8 Once a high-level plan has formed, different members of the team can work on more detail within their own part of the plan. This will enable then to check, by looking at the detail, if anything is missing from the overall plan.

The exercise will give you and the tram undertaking it, a good idea of the work needed and the relationship between different teams. You'll have looked at different options and discussed their merits enough to make some risk-based decisions on the overall strategy. The benefits for those doing this are that they gain a common understanding of their own areas of interest and those of the other people they are relying on.

Monitoring and reporting: so you don't get lost

The way the plan is constructed determines how you monitor it. If you have built your plan correctly, it should include all the aspects you need to keep an eye on. Monitoring is not just about looking at what has been achieved but is also concerned with what the future is likely to hold. Forecasts need to take into account progress to date, prevailing assumptions and risks and then, based on estimates of future performance, predict what the situation will be in future periods. Unlike projects, portfolios have no 'completion date', making 'estimates at completion' irrelevant. You need to look at estimates in given time periods (such as annual, quarterly, monthly), which should be synchronous with the organization's financial year but go beyond the end of the last planned piece of work. This could be many years into the future. Very long-lasting programmes should have 'estimates at completion' but can be so long that the estimates, say each quarter, are more useful for on-going control.

The control cycle

The control cycle, shown in Figure 22.5, is at the heart of monitoring and reporting and is used to make sure you are on track to deliver the outcomes needed.

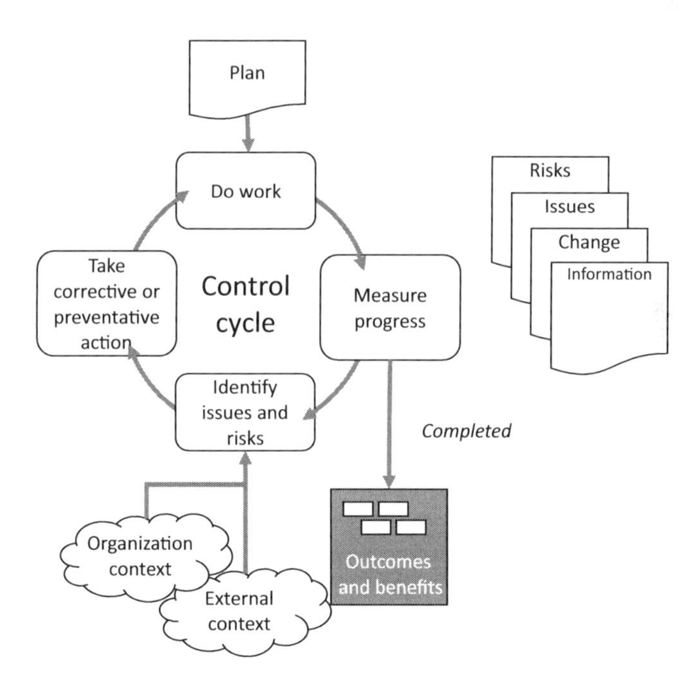

Figure 22.5 The control cycle

The control cycle is at the heart of monitoring, controlling and reporting and is used to make sure you are on track to deliver the outcomes needed.

This model has been in use for a long time in a number of different forms and is applicable to monitoring the classic project dimensions such as, risks and issues, progress of any change requests, timescale, costs and resources needed. From a portfolio or programme perspective, add:

- interdependencies;
- progress towards realizing the benefits;
- robustness of the outcomes;
- quality of the outputs;
- outside influences.

Do not ignore this last point because context is always changing, and unless the sponsors of the work being undertaken within the portfolio or programme are kept informed, and update their respective managers, they might make the wrong decisions. Many programmes and projects fail 'top-down' and as a portfolio or programme manager, it is your job to avoid this. The more the leaders within the programme or portfolio understand about the business context of their work, the better they can undertake their role.

The frequency you go around the control cycle depends on the level in a portfolio and different types of work required and should match the regular reporting calendars set organizationally. For regular reporting, the frequency can range from daily, which is used in agile techniques and also the roll-out or provisioning of some services, to quarterly, for some high-level boards. Reporting might be 'ad-hoc', such as reporting high-priority issues. It also ensures that the management team(s) and interested parties are aware of the current status and outlook, particularly with respect to the likelihood of achieving the objectives. The frequency of reporting is usually driven by:

- the stakeholders' actual or perceived needs for information;
- managers' perceived needs to stay informed and their assessment of risk;
- organizational practice set, say, by a programme management office or other overseeing body.

Synchronous reporting?

Do not make the mistake of trying to synchronize the reporting across all levels in a portfolio or programme.

Do not make the mistake of trying to synchronize reporting across all levels in a portfolio or programme. It might sound logical for everyone to report on the same cut-off date and time, but bear in mind each report is simply a guess at a point in time, and a few days or even weeks difference in reporting dates is not going to bring an organization to its knees. What matters is how much you can rely on the reports; do they contain sufficient information to base your decisions on? In fact, the 'monthly report' syndrome can work against good governance. If everyone is required to report, say, on the last Friday of the month:

- focus will be on reporting for the few days leading up to it;
- work schedules (and personal schedules) will be disrupted to ensure the report authors are available (no leave; no customer meetings!);

- some managers will ask for reports from sub-ordinates a week earlier for checking (so much for synchronicity);
- applications for reporting will be overloaded for just a few days a month and under used the rest of the time;
- a mentality of getting the report submitted on time takes over from producing a useful report (quality suffers).

Finally, the recipients of the reports will be deluged in information in the space of a few hours, thereby reducing the likelihood of them paying the right level of attention to the content (or even reading any of it). Reporting in such circumstances can degrade into non-value-added 'lip-service' activity.

An alternative approach is to let each team agree reporting frequencies with the report recipients in terms of the allowable time lapse between reports and timing. This enables reports to be produced and submitted at any convenient time but ensures the currency of the information. But surely, for monthly reports, it could be up to 30 days out of date? Yes, but not every report will be out of date by that much, as they will be spread throughout the month, whereas with a single reporting date, everything will be out of date by up to 30 days! The actual frequency of the control cycle can change and need not be consistent across a portfolio, programme or project. For instance, daily or weekly reporting on one project might be necessary, whilst bi-weekly on others could be adequate (see Figure 22.6).

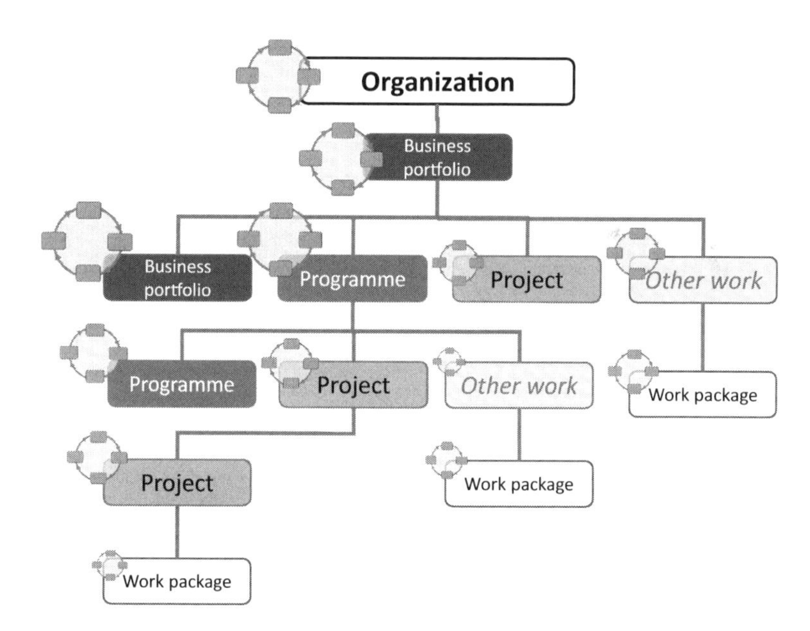

Figure 22.6 Different reporting frequencies for different needs

The actual frequency of the control cycle can change and need not be consistent across a portfolio, programme or project. For instance, daily or weekly reporting on one project might be necessary, whilst bi-weekly on others could be adequate.

Eventually, if the supporting systems and applications are right, you should be able to draw off reports on any population at any time and have a view on the reliability of the report's information. This is discussed further in Chapter 27, which looks at support tools.

An accurate watch?

Remember the old story about a stopped watch being more accurate than one which runs slow because it is 'on time' twice a day, whilst a slow watch never tells the right time? Is your reporting any different? Isn't approximately right usually good enough, when the costs of 'dead right' are so high and of spurious benefit?

What should a report include?

Reporting should be designed to meet the needs of the identified report recipients, both in terms of content and timeliness. The range of possible reports is vast, and I never cease to be amazed at some of the 'slide-ware' works of art some consultants produce. With this in mind, reports need to be easy to create; the more information that can be gathered automatically and the easier they can be assembled, the better. A report for a component of a business portfolio, like a programme or a project, should highlight progress towards the achievement of outcomes, whether the current work scope is likely to be completed to plan, the prevailing risks and issues and any decisions or direction required. Appropriate milestones (such as project gates) and performance indicators should be included in the report. Performance indicators should reflect the delivery method used (e.g., backlog for agile delivery). For work components which are not project based, reports should comprise the key performance indicators for whatever the core work comprises.

Every report should state the period or date the report relates to and the date on which the report was published, or if live, created. The form of a report should be appropriate and proportionate to the work being reported on. Figure 22.7 is an example of a report showing the financial figures for a project and each of its stages. The layout includes details for the current month, current financial year and for the life of the project. This same format could be used for a programme or a business portfolio, where each line in the report would represent a programme or business portfolio component. By using the same layout for the reports, you make them easier for people to read and understand. Familiarity with the layout and what each data point represents means the reports are less likely to be misinterpreted, and any rogue figures are spotted quickly. *The Project Workout* includes a wide selection, including Gantt, slippage, burn-down and burn-up, milestone, resource usage, financial project life and year reporting.

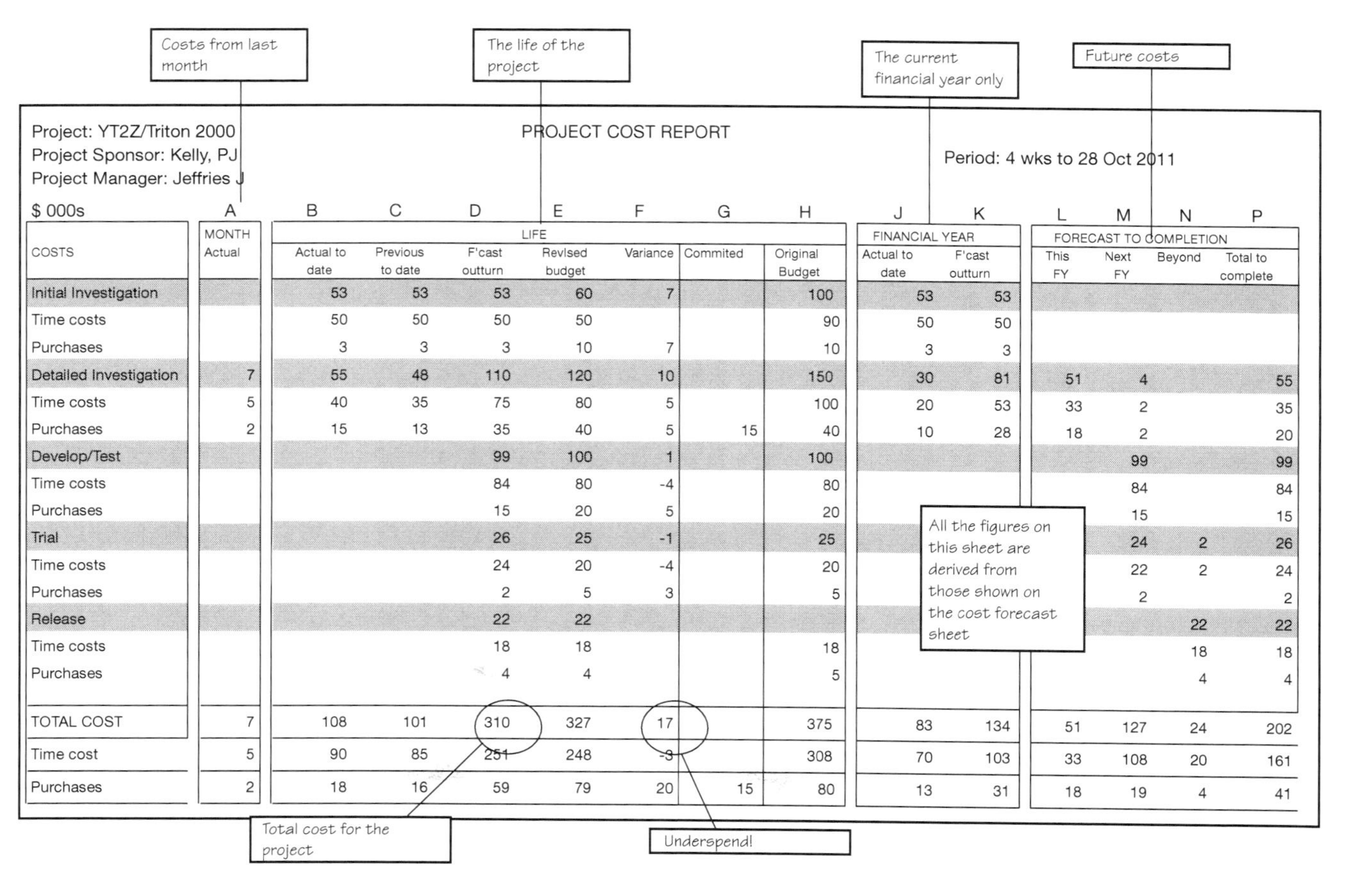

Project: YT2Z/Triton 2000
Project Sponsor: Kelly, PJ
Project Manager: Jeffries J

PROJECT COST REPORT

Period: 4 wks to 28 Oct 2011

$ 000s	A	B	C	D	E	F	G	H	J	K	L	M	N	P
	MONTH	LIFE							FINANCIAL YEAR		FORECAST TO COMPLETION			
COSTS	Actual	Actual to date	Previous to date	F'cast outturn	Revised budget	Variance	Commited	Original Budget	Actual to date	F'cast outturn	This FY	Next FY	Beyond	Total to complete
Initial Investigation		53	53	53	60	7		100	53	53				
Time costs		50	50	50	50			90	50	50				
Purchases		3	3	3	10	7		10	3	3				
Detailed Investigation	7	55	48	110	120	10		150	30	81	51	4		55
Time costs	5	40	35	75	80	5		100	20	53	33	2		35
Purchases	2	15	13	35	40	5	15	40	10	28	18	2		20
Develop/Test				99	100	1		100				99		99
Time costs				84	80	-4		80				84		84
Purchases				15	20	5		20				15		15
Trial				26	25	-1		25				24	2	26
Time costs				24	20	-4		20				22	2	24
Purchases				2	5	3		5				2		2
Release				22	22								22	22
Time costs				18	18			18					18	18
Purchases				4	4			5					4	4
TOTAL COST	7	108	101	310	327	17		375	83	134	51	127	24	202
Time cost	5	90	85	251	248	-3		308	70	103	33	108	20	161
Purchases	2	18	16	59	79	20	15	80	13	31	18	19	4	41

Figure 22.7 Example financial report

A report such as this gives you, on a stage-by-stage basis, all the key financial information you should require: actual costs, forecast costs, commitments for the project as a whole and by financial year; it is derived directly from the data in Figure 14.2.

What skills does a report author need?

Some people are great at writing reports; others are not. Unfortunately, the skill of a person in writing a report might not match their skill in their specialist discipline; great technicians can be poor report writers! The best way to improve the quality of reports is to coach the authors towards writing succinct and value-added reports. If you do not provide feedback, do not expect reporting to improve. If you are the author, ask a peer to look at your report and coach you if necessary. This might sound like a lot of time to invest but good information is at the heart of good management and trustworthy reporting will save far more time than it costs. Do not be tempted to rewrite reports for people; they will become demoralized and just leave it to you.

Workout 22.2 – Setting up your reporting regime

Use the following prompts to help you define or review your reporting regime:

9 Reporting should reflect the information and timeliness needs of the stakeholders, especially those with responsibilities for some aspect of governance. For each report:
   a the report should be focussed on the future and likely outcome for the work covered;
   b the content of the report should be relevant for the readers of the report;
   c it should be clear why the report recipients would want to read what has been written and what, if any, action is expected as a result of the report;
   d the report should indicate the level of confidence of the manager in any forecasts;
   e risks and issues should be worded clearly and unambiguously;
   f data on the report are consistent with those on any subsidiary reports or data.

10 There is evidence that reports are being read and, where necessary, being acted on.

11 The weight of the reporting regime should be appropriate to the work being undertaken, required accuracy of the report and the competence of the people undertaking it.

12 The reporting regime should protect your commercial position and collateral, with respect to customers, partners and suppliers.

13 The basic planning elements should be in place to collect the level and detail of reporting required (for example, if project costs are to be tracked, the cost codes need to be created to capture this).

14 A repository should be set up where reports are available for recipients and archived.

15 A permissions structure should be defined for the reporting repository, enabling those who need to publish and see reports to do so.

23

Risks, issues, change control and information

Your job as a director or manager is to filter the incoming information and make judgements concerning what the information represents, if it is true or significant and if any preventative or corrective action is needed.

> *"No-one is so brave that he is not disturbed by something unexpected."*
>
> JULIUS CAESAR 100 BC – 44 BC

- **Do not micromanage the levels below you.**
- **Continually look for the invisible hand which will thwart you.**
- **Ensure that information can be relied on for making decisions.**

What are my control levers?

Chapter 22, covered planning, monitoring and control. This chapter looks at risks, issues, change control and information management. Remember these topics, whilst presented separately, are intimately linked and flow from one to other and back very quickly. The relationships between the control topics are shown in Figure 23.1.

Risks, issues and change control

Risk and issue management ensures objectives are more likely to be achieved, bearing in mind uncertainty, unexpected events and threats or opportunities which originate from:

- undertaking the work;
- using the solution;
- the external environment.

A **risk** is an uncertainty of outcome. A positive risk is called 'opportunity'; a negative risk is a 'threat'.

An **issue** is a relevant event that has happened, was not planned and requires management action. It could be a problem, benefit, query, concern, change request or a risk that has occurred.

Change control is the formal process through which changes to a plan are introduced and approved. Changes are recorded on a change log. Change control ensures only beneficial or necessary changes to the baseline are implemented after the impact of the change has been assessed.

Figure 23.2 shows how risk, issues and changes relate to each other; a risk will become an issue if the event occurs or assumption proved false. Issues can be resolved either within the scope of the work as currently defined or via a change request. Most processes show these are managed one at time, with each being taken through a process until resolved. In a portfolio or programme context however, it is the holistic management of them that matters. Any process has to allow for:

- escalation to a higher level in (or even outside) the breakdown structure;
- the bundling of items to be resolved as a group.

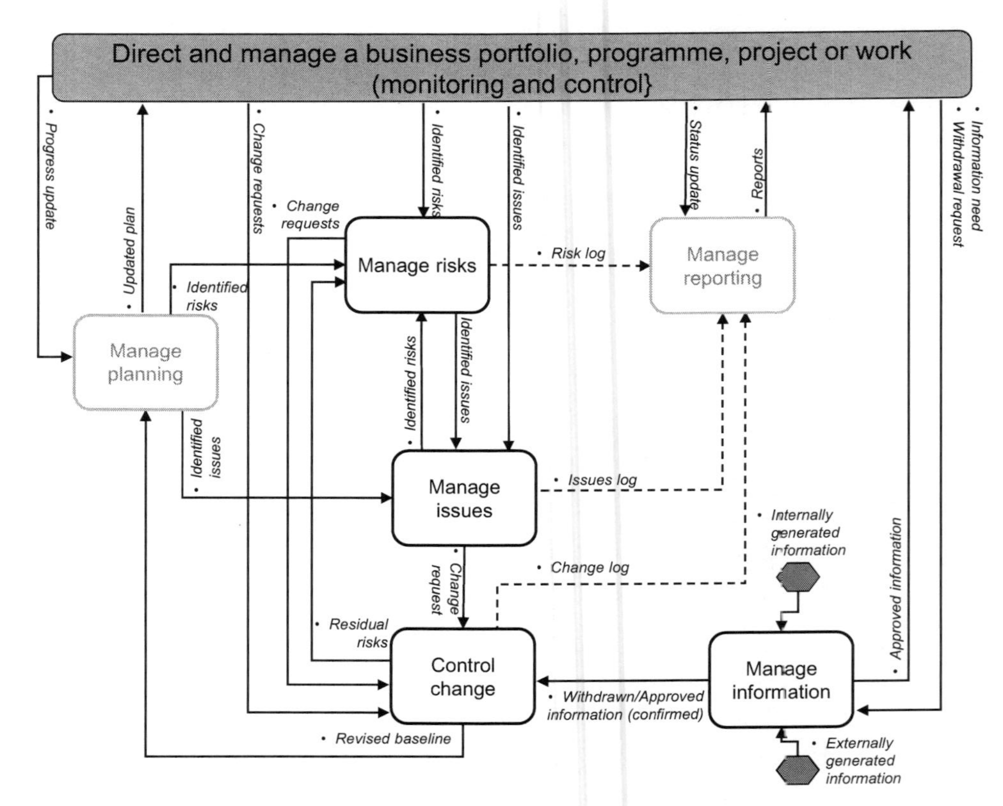

Figure 23.1 The relationship between control activities

The key control activities and their relationships (inputs and outputs) are shown here. Unless you define an overall architecture such as this, you will find the interfaces between processes become muddled, which, in turn, leads to muddled accountabilities. These apply from business portfolio to work package.

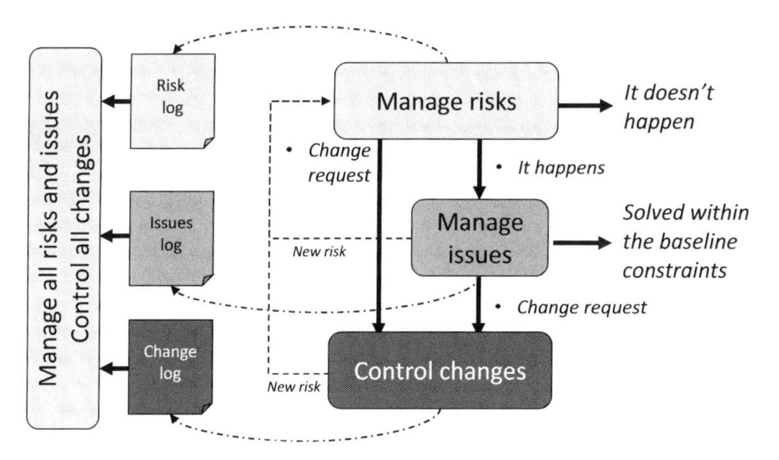

Figure 23.2 Risks, issues and change control

A risk will become an issue if the event or occurrence occurs. Issues can be resolved either within the scope, as currently defined or via a change. Risk, issues and change requests can be managed 'one at a time' and as a group.

Often individual risks or issues cannot be resolved as they are symptoms of an underlying problem which until identified, cannot be resolved. Similarly, change requests might simply be proposed solutions to the same issue, seen from different perspectives. Solving the same issue in multiple ways will not solve anything. The phrasing of a risk, issue or change request is fundamental to finding a solution.

Risks: what might happen

How much can you take?

Overall risk should be managed within the organization's risk appetite and tolerance.

- **Risk appetite** is the amount and type of risk that an organization is prepared to seek, accept or tolerate. Risk appetite is the general level of acceptable risk.
- **Risk tolerance** is an organization's readiness to bear the risk after risk treatments have been applied. Risk tolerance can be limited by legal or regulatory requirements. It is more specific than risk appetite and applies to individual risks.

The business portfolio or programme sponsor or manager needs to determine (and keep reconfirming) the risk appetite. It could depend on factors such as an organization's culture, industry sector, competitor behaviour or the strength of the organization's capabilities and assets (a cash rich organization is more likely to have a greater risk appetite than a poor one).

If risks become unbearable, in other words exceed the risk appetite, action needs to be taken. If it relates to a programme or project that might mean terminating it, which is usually easier said than done.

The management of risks and issues on small projects or work scopes is relatively straight forward. A simple risk and issues log is usually adequate for keeping track of what needs attention. Unfortunately, even at this basic level of management, such logs can be neglected and seen as white elephants. Either a risk is identified but no management action is taken, or risks and issues do not even appear on the logs. A simple test is to conversationally ask people what their greatest fears or concerns are at that moment and you will soon be able to cross check any formal logs to see if they are recorded. You should also ask how the plan takes into account specific risks; all too often plans simply do not reflect the risks!

Is it likely? And, so what?

Risk has two dimensions, often depicted in a risk matrix:

- probability – how likely it is to happen (usually as a % probability);
- impact – so what if it does happen? Impact should relate to the stated objectives, which could be influences by any of the constraints, such as benefits, timescale, cost, quality, etc.

A high risk is one which is likely to happen AND which will severely damage the chances of achieving the stated objectives. If a risk has no impact, it is not a risk at all. Figure 23.3 is a simple risk matrix illustrating this.

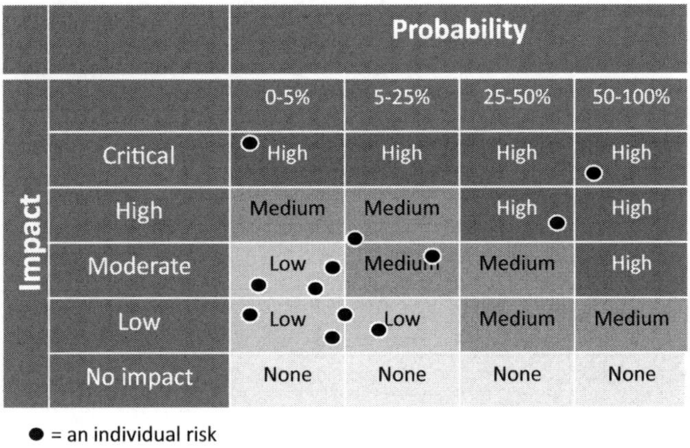

		Probability			
		0-5%	5-25%	25-50%	50-100%
Impact	Critical	High	High	High	High
	High	Medium	Medium	High	High
	Moderate	Low	Medium	Medium	High
	Low	Low	Low	Medium	Medium
	No impact	None	None	None	None

● = an individual risk

Figure 23.3 A simple risk matrix

A risk matrix can be used to categorize risks based on the probability of occurrence and their impact, should they materialize. They can also be used to look at clusters of risks to help gauge the overall risk faced by a programme or a business portfolio.

A risk matrix can be used to determine the risk category (high, medium, low). The key is to ensure the probability and impact parameters are defined in a way which suits your circumstances. Risk can be very difficult to define. For example, if I was to say that an aeroplane has a low risk of crashing, you might fly on it. Whereas, in the example matrix, 'low' can mean up to 15% or a one in seven chance of crashing, you might think again. You also need to look at the perspective of different people. It might be that your organization can lose £1m without any real harm. It is low impact. For an individual project within your organization, that loss might be more than the entire spend. The project would need to be terminated: the impact is critical. In order to reconcile these differences of viewpoint, risk matrices can be constructed with different probability/impact criteria and applied depending on the perspective of the user.

Don't ignore risks; do something!

Risks are managed with two types of measures.

- A **risk action** (or treatment) is a task that changes how a risk is managed. Normally an action will add or improve a risk control. Actions do not affect the net risk exposure.
- A **risk control** is a measure already in place to help manage a risk, either by making the risk less likely or by reducing the impact if it occurs. Controls have an influence on the net risk exposure – the risk faced today.

Many possible options exist for 'risk actions', including:

- **prevention** – countermeasures are put in place either to stop the threat or problem occurring or prevent it having any impact (avoidance);
- **reduction** – the actions either reduce the likelihood of the risk occurring or limit the impact on the project to acceptable levels;
- **transference** – the impact of the risk is transferred to a third party, such as a contractor or insurance company organization. This approach is beneficial as it should lead to a reduction in the total amount of funds held in contingency;
- **contingency** – actions are planned (contingency plan) which will come into effect in sufficient time to manage the risk;
- acceptance – the company organization decides to go ahead and accept the possibility that the risk might occur and is willing to accept the consequences;
- **exploitation** – in relation to opportunities, mine it for all its worth!

Different publications use various terms for the categories associated with risk actions but generally have the same effect; it is a matter of choosing what makes sense in your organization. Choosing category headings is not a 'make or break' decision, as what is important is taking appropriate action; categories are simply useful prompts as to what that action might be.

The main difference between controls and actions is that controls are already in place, whilst actions are tasks that are planned to be done. For example, an installed fire extinguisher is a risk control, whilst the related action would be to procure and install the fire extinguishers. Actions have completion dates which should be tracked. Controls have no completion dates, as there is no progress to track; instead their effectiveness needs to be monitored. This means that controls reduce the net (current) risk exposure but actions do not. By looking at all the controls together, the net risk exposure can be calculated. Target risk exposure can be worked out by considering all the controls and actions together. Project managers are generally used to managing risks on projects in terms of risk actions; however, the control aspect of risk management tends to be forgotten, as it is related more to business-as-usual and operations, in other words, 'other work'. Risk controls therefore take on greater importance in business portfolio and programme management.

Risk controls therefore take on greater importance in business portfolio and programme management.

A simple example of risks actions and controls

There is a risk of fire breaking out in a building. The risk actions could be to use flame retardant materials and install fire doors, fire exits, emergency exit signs, an alarm system, sprinklers and fire extinguishers. These then become 'risk controls'. Having taken an action to put these controls in place, you need to make sure they are still effective. Are the exits blocked? Does the sprinkler work? Are the fire extinguishers in place and within their 'use by' date? Many health and safety aspects have to be covered by risk controls.

Planning for the unthinkable

An area where risk controls are crucial for an organization is for business continuity.

Business continuity concerns planning and preparation to ensure that an organization:

- can continue to operate during and after a serious incident or disaster;
- is able to recover to a normal operational state within a reasonably short period.

Typical incidents that business continuity can account for include flooding, cyber-attack, supply chain failure or losing a key employee. To ensure business continuity three elements need to be considered:

- **resilience:** critical business functions and the supporting infrastructure are designed in such a way to be materially unaffected by relevant disruptions, for example through the use of redundancy and spare capacity;

- **recovery:** arrangements are in place to recover or restore critical and near-critical business functions that fail for some reason;
- **contingency:** the organization has the capability and readiness to cope adequately with whatever incidents occur, including those that were not, and or could not have been, foreseen. Notice this is another example of 'white space' (see Chapter 14).

In terms of business continuity, contingency preparations constitute a last-resort response if resilience and recovery arrangements prove to be inadequate.

Expect some roadblocks on the way

Keeping something back, just in case

The money held in reserve just in case it is needed to treat a risk is called a **contingency fund**. Because such funds are not actually being used, there is often pressure from finance managers to keep them to a minimum; however, choosing what that minimum is can be problematic. If every project and operations manager was to hold contingency funds for everything that might go wrong with what they are accountable for, it could bankrupt the organization; working capital would be left unused. Some risks might be worth taking from an organizational perspective but not from a project or operational perspective. In such cases, these 'unaffordable project risks' can be accepted by higher level business portfolio or programme managers in the organization who hold the necessary funds. They expect something will go wrong, but do not know where or when, so rather than distribute the contingency funds, they retain a proportion centrally. Something will go wrong, but it is hardly likely everything will go wrong at the same time, and so the fund held can be smaller than the total needed if the funds were distributed. The organization is, in effect, acting as its own insurer or might even be using an external insurer for some risks. The business portfolio hierarchy in Chapter 3 should be used as the basis

Something will go wrong, but it is hardly likely everything will go wrong at the same time

for the escalation, acceptance and holding of contingency funds; contingency should be retained at an appropriate level in the work hierarchy and authorized, if needed. The holding of contingency funds can be tiered with the next higher level, taking accountability for all its lower levels. In this way, a programme manager can be allocated a certain level of funds to cover specific risks and other risks will be covered by the business portfolio manager. The programme manager, in turn, can allocate contingency funds to a project manager, if appropriate.

Just as it is necessary to have contingency funds, it is also essential to have 'contingency time' to deal with work coming in late. As we learned earlier, plans wobble and can have a detrimental impact on the dates required for interdependencies, delivery of outcomes and start of benefits realization. A business portfolio or programme manager needs to understand the risks associated with any delays of interdependencies and, where necessary, put a buffer in to ensure the downstream work is not too damaged by upstream delays. Initially, this might appear to make the work take longer, but often, accurately predicting when a new capability goes live is more important than it happening earlier. In many cases the cost of delays, say with suppliers, can outweigh any benefits of early completion. It is a balancing act.

Holistic view of risk management

Risk management is far more than identifying and tracking risks in a log. Good risk management is a perspective that needs to be taken on all aspects of a business portfolio or programme and built into the way they are managed and into the design and operation of the solutions. As an example, in Chapter 8 the staged project life cycle is itself a fundamental to the effective control of project risk and covers commercial, solution and operational dimensions.

Black swans

Nassim Nicholas Taleb first discussed 'black swan' events in his 2001 book *Fooled By Randomness*, which concerned financial events; in his 2007 book *The Black Swan*, he extended his thinking to cover events outside of financial markets. Until the Dutch discovered black swans in Australia in the late seventeenth century, the term 'black swan' was a metaphor for 'impossible', rather like 'flying pigs'. In Taleb's work, a black swan is an event outside the realm of regular expectations, carries an extreme impact and, despite its outlier status, human nature rationalizes it in retrospect to claim it could have (should have!) been predicted. By definition, a black swan event is not predictable based on previous experience and so trying to predict it is pointless. The aim is to make society robust enough to survive the event and exploit its opportunities.

Bengt Flyvberg applied the same thinking into the realm of major project failure, particularly IT projects. He talks about 'avoiding black swans' and suggests a stress test to determine if an organization should undertake a particular project. His tests were that the organization should be able to survive an individual project which goes over budget by 400% with only

25% to 50% of predicted benefits being realized plus 15% of the project portfolio exceeding its budget by 200%. He goes on to recommend work is organized into smaller chunks to limit risk and that reference class forecasting should be used when planning. The survival of an organization in the event of the failure of a major project cannot be managed by the project sponsor or manager; the survival of the organization depends on effective business portfolio management.

Workout 23.1 – Risks

Consider the following with respect to your business portfolio or programme:

1 Look at the programmes or project in your business portfolio. What would be the effect on your organization of a black swan event such as a major overspend and a crash in expected benefits?
2 Look at your portfolio and determine how much of it could go wrong before it destroyed your organization. Is the limit acceptable?
3 Are you holding contingency at the right level in the organization? Have any of your projects been assigned large contingency funds for highly unlikely events?
4 When using simulation techniques, what distribution curve do you use for probabilities? Is it normal or skewed? Does it represent the world as you know it?

How you react to the findings from the earlier questions very much depends on your risk tolerance . . . or more accurately the tolerance of the person taking the risk. If an individual might suffer very little in the event of organizational collapse, they might be the wrong person to be making the decisions. On the other hand, they might simply be realistic. For example, putting a project in its own legal entity can be a good way of protecting the mother organization in the event of failure . . . and might be a worthwhile gamble if the regards are rich enough. It can also be a matter of ethics.

Issues: what has happened

Issues management is about recording, handling and resolving any event or problem which either threatens the success or represents an opportunity to be exploited. Examples of problem issues are:

- the late delivery of a critical deliverable;
- a reported lack of confidence by users;
- a lack of resources to carry out the work;
- the late approval of a critical document or deliverable;
- a reported deviation of a deliverable from its specification;
- a request for additional functionality;
- a recognized omission from the project scope.

Examples of opportunity issues are:

- a contract negotiation is concluded early;
- a breakthrough on a new technology cuts months off the development time;
- a new, cheaper source of raw materials is located;
- the enrolment of key stakeholders happens sooner than planned;
- a contract tender comes in significantly less than the pre-tender estimate.

Issues can be seen as an extension of risks, except that probability is always certain (or so close as to make no difference). By taking this approach, the same impact criteria and management approaches can be applied.

Expect a large number of issues to be raised at the start of any new venture or at the start of a new phase in the venture. These will mainly be from people seeking confirmation that aspects they are involved with have been covered. This is a rich source of feedback on stakeholder concerns as well as a check on completeness of the scope and plan.

Make sure you record issues, even if you have no time to address them or cannot yet find a person to manage the resolution. Just making issues visible can sometimes be enough to start resolving them.

Just making issues visible can sometimes be enough to start resolving them.

Workout 23.2 – Resolving issues – from breakdown to breakthrough

The following steps, if used in full, are an effective and powerful way of resolving issues. Followed rigorously, they will enable you to 'breakthrough' an issue which is blocking progress. The toughest part is to declare that you have a problem. but doing so puts you in a position of responsibility and enables you to proceed. Be careful, however; the natural tendency is to dwell on what is wrong: what is wrong with you, or with the project, or with 'them'. Steps 3 to 8 should be done in a facilitated workshop, with those who have a stake in the issue, recording the input from the group on flip charts. Follow all the steps and do them in the right order. Do not jump ahead.

1. **Declare that you have an issue!**
   Tell everyone who could possibly have an impact on resolving the issue, even those you do not want to know about it. Do not hide the issue. Merely putting it in your issues log is not enough. Actively tell people!
2. **Stop the action.**
   Call everything around the issue to a halt. Do not react. Do not try to fix it. Relax.
3. **What, precisely is the issue?**
   Exactly what did or didn't happen? When? Distinguish between fact, gossip and rumour. Then, describe the issue in one sentence. This is the sentence you should write in the issues log.

4 **What commitments are being thwarted?**
Which of your commitments is being thwarted, stopped or hindered by the issue? Remind yourself of the reasons for the project in the first place and the drivers for action.

5 **What would a breakthrough make possible?**
What would the resolution of the issue, under these circumstances, look like? What would it make possible? Are you really committed to resolving this and furthering these possibilities? If so, continue. If solving the issue will achieve nothing, then stop now.

6 **What is missing? What is present and in the way?**
Take stock of the entire project. What is the situation now (stick to facts!)? What is missing that, if present, would allow the action to move forward quickly and effectively? What is present and standing in the way of progress?

7 **What possible actions could you take to further your commitments?**
Leave the facts of the current situation and what is missing in the background. Stand in the future, with a breakthrough having been accomplished and create an array of possible actions that brought you to this point. Look outside your paradigm. Think from the future, back to the present.

8 **What actions will you take?**
Next, narrow down the possibilities to those with the greatest opportunity and leverage, not necessarily the safest and most predictable! Then, choose a direction and get back into action. Make requests of people and agree the actions needed. Hold them to account on those actions.

(Adapted, with kind permission of the London Peret Roche Group, from their 'Breakdown to Breakthrough' technology. Copyright © 1992, N J.)

Change control: to stop you falling into chaos

Every change should be justified

Change control should ensure only beneficial or necessary changes to the baseline are implemented. Figure 23.4 illustrates how a standalone project or programme should be viable at all times. If one of the constraints is breached, say it is forecast to cost too much, action has to be taken to make it viable. If that is not possible, then termination might be the best action. For example, I might have a programme in which one of the projects is taking too long and costing too much. It has ceased to be viable. If I was to terminate it, however, there could be follow-on projects which could no longer be undertaken as they depend on deliverables from the first project. Further, despite the delays and cost overruns on the problem project, the programme, as a whole, might still viable. The choice to terminate or not depends on the context of the problem and your level of confidence in any future work.

The choice to terminate or not depends on the context of the problem and your level of confidence in any future work.

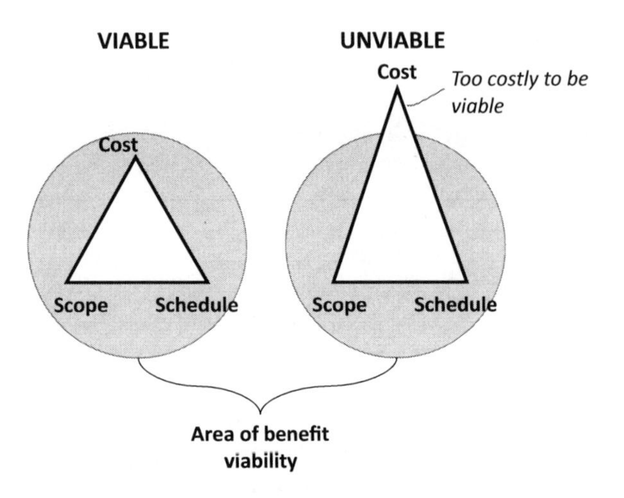

Figure 23.4 Change control and viability

The left-hand project is viable as the benefits can be achieved within the scope, time and cost constraints. However, in the project on the right, the costs have escalated to the extent that the project is no longer viable.

What changes need controlling?

Changes can originate from any stakeholder, including executive management, customers, end users, suppliers or team members. Alternatively, a change might result from a risk or issue which cannot be resolved. The key questions here are:

- what should be change controlled?
- who should have the authority to authorize changes?

There are two sets of information that usually need controlling:

- management information, which includes business cases, plans (schedule, costs, etc.), contracts;
- information relating to the solution, which includes requirements, designs, test plans and specifications and as-built records.

At any point in time, the version of the solution or management information which is currently called the **baseline**. A baseline serves as a point to measure from which is used as a basis for comparison. A plan can only indicate if you are late if you are able to compare the actual time you completed something against the time you planned to have completed it, as defined in the baselined plan.

For a solution, use the baselined specification to check that you have built the right output. Baselines for solutions are generally managed using configuration management, which is covered later in this chapter. Solution baselines often reflect a particular point in the development of the solution, such as a requirements baseline, design baseline, ready for test baseline or as-built baseline.

Who can authorize a change?

Choosing who can authorize a change can be problematic. Many organizations use simple 'cost' based criteria, where the greater the cost, the higher the level of manager required to authorize it. That might work in a simple functional bureaucracy but is totally inadequate in the world of business-driven, cross functional portfolio and programme management. What matters is the degree to which the impact of a change is contained and the level of 'tolerance' a manager has been granted in managing their plan. For example:

- if a change to a project can be managed within the baselined plan plus tolerance and affects nothing outside the project, the project manager should be able to authorize the change;
- if the change takes the plan outside its tolerance, thereby impacting the business case, the project sponsor should be the decision maker;
- if the change delays a deliverable another project manager depends on, causing a ripple through a programme's plan, the programme manager should be the decision maker.

The hierarchy in Figure 3.3 in Chapter 3 is fundamental to allocating decision rights as this same structure is used to build plans, define tiered accountabilities and assign contingency funds. Contracts with suppliers or customers should have specific rules on how changes should be managed and this needs to be reflected in the overall change control process and authorities defined in your own organization, often extending the time from creating a change request to approving the request longer than it would be within a single organization. Table 23.5 is an example.

Table 23.1 Change control decision levels

	Impact of change	*Authorization required by*
A	Change affecting schedule or costs which can be accommodated within assigned tolerance without affecting other work packages.	Team manager
B	Change affecting schedule or costs which can be accommodated within assigned tolerance without affecting other projects.	Project manager
C	Allocation of project contingency within assigned business case tolerance without affecting other projects.	Project sponsor
D	Change that affects other work within the programme and/or has material impact on the project's business and is within the assigned tolerance or is a material change to a listed suppliers' contracts.	Programme Manager
E	Change that affects only work contained within the programme and/or has a material impact on the programme's business.	Programme sponsor

Change can result from a number of sources, such as:

- changes in the business environment (e.g., economics, social factors, competitor action);
- changes in business needs/requirements driven by the sponsor or other stakeholders;
- problems or opportunities which occur during the course of the work;
- modifications or enhancements identified by the team (beware of these!);
- faults detected by the team or users.

Changes have the potential to reduce programmes and projects to chaos,

Changes have the potential to reduce programmes and projects to chaos, making it essential to adopt a formal approach to assessing and authorizing change right from the start.

Here is a summary of a suitable process.

Identify the proposed change and record it in a change log.

Assess the impact of implementing the proposed change on your business case, objectives, benefits, scope, resources, time, cost, quality and risk. Check if at affects any interdependent work. There might be a number of options to consider, including doing nothing:

- If within the respective manager's authority, reject or accept the change proposal.
- If it is outside the manager's authority, refer the decision, with a recommendation, to a higher authority.

Make decision. The change proposal may be:

- accepted for immediate implementation;
- accepted, subject to certain conditions being met;
- accepted but implementation is deferred to a later date;
- rejected (with/without recommendation to include in a later work).

Implement. If the change was accepted:

- update the documentation (like the plan) and information sources;
- inform all interested parties about the change and change of baseline;
- implement the change.

Close the change, when it has been implemented and inform stakeholders.

Now it starts to get complicated!

Changes to your outputs, such as solutions, systems or groups of interrelated deliverables (products) should be controlled through configuration management.

Configuration management is used to describe the tracking and relationship of a group of deliverables through their life cycle. The set of deliverables which are the subject of configuration management are called **configuration items**. Configuration items are treated as a self-contained unit for the purposes of identification and change control. They can be management deliverables or components of a solution, service or system, whether produced internally or by a supplier. This ensures each configuration item is identified in terms of status and version, and the composition of higher-level groupings of those deliverables are compatible and known at all times. Configuration management includes:

- planning the scope of and managing configuration, including choice of configuration items and configuration baseline control;
- configuration status accounting and reporting to ensure those requiring this information are informed; a status report could include:
  - a list of the configuration items that comprise a baseline;
  - the date when each version of each configuration item was baselined;
  - a list of the specifications that describe each configuration item;
  - the history of baseline changes including rationales for change;
  - a list of open change requests by configuration item;
  - defects identified by configuration audits;
  - the status of work with approved change requests by item.
- verifying the accuracy of the configuration records (configuration audit).

Configuration management tends to be associated with engineering or IT related work, but the concept is as applicable to any type of solution. Configuration management usually involves the use of specialist tools. Different industries use different terms and apply it in different ways: for example, parts management in the automotive industry is a form of configuration management. In some cases, configuration management can simply come down to making sure the right version of a user manual is packed with the right version of the product.

Configuration management is key to ensuring traceability and integrity, which is covered in Chapter 24 on quality.

Configuration management is key to ensuring traceability and integrity

Workout 23.3 – Change control

For your existing documentation for your business portfolio or programme:

1. Review how changes are justified
   - a Is it rigorous enough or too rigorous?
   - b Is the associated process working in a timely manner?
2. List the types of output which should be subject to change control
   - a Is this list complete? Look at the examples in this chapter and add anything which is missing.
   - b What grouping are configuration managed? Is this adequate for control purposes?

3 Construct Table 23.5 to show who has accountability for which decisions:
  a Does the level of decision maker reflect the risks involved?
  b Is there a clear path of traceability and escalation?

Is there any formal or anecdotal evidence that change control might not be working effectively?

Information: without it you are ignorant

It's just the CIO's problem . . . isn't it?

Understanding the classification, recording, distribution, storage and destruction of information can be daunting and 'information management' is now a focus for study encompassing behavioural sciences, IT and business modelling. It has a host of associated 'management systems', including enterprise content management (ECM), electronic records management (ERM), business process management (BPM), taxonomy and metadata, knowledge management (KM), web content management (WCM), document management (DM) and social media governance technology solutions and best practices. Notice the two and three letter acronyms appearing; perhaps this is the time to say, "Let the IT and information management professionals sort it out; over to you, Chief Information Officer!" This would be a wrong move, as information is what makes organizations work; the management of information is every manager's responsibility in relation to the domains they are managing. Information is the lifeblood of decision making. The business portfolio manager is therefore responsible for ensuring the people working within the portfolio have the necessary information (physical or electronic) available to them and that it is reliable for undertaking their work and making decisions. The same follows throughout the business portfolio hierarchy, to programmes, projects, other work and work packages.

Information is the lifeblood of decision making.

Know what information you need, including the relationships

Fortunately, you do not need to be concerned with every aspect of information management in all circumstances; focus on what matters in the framework of what you are directing and managing. In the context of this book, we need to concern ourselves with information, which is explicitly mentioned or strongly implied, including information relating to accountabilities, the solution and its development, plans, progress assessments, reviews and audits, contracts, reports and communications. Anything with the word 'baseline' attached is also vital. Some of this information matters more than others and it must be a priority to decide which information, unquestionably, has to be managed. For example, it is obvious that the contracts with your customers and suppliers need to be managed, otherwise you will not know when to pay them, get paid or what to do if things go wrong. You will not even know what is meant to be delivered under the contract. The business plan and business case are also obvious; without them you will not know what has been approved or authorized to be done and why. Other essential aspects are not so obvious, like the work break down structure. Time and again, I have referred a topic in a chapter to the breakdown in Figure 3.3 because this structure is the spine which holds together the many parts of a business portfolio, and is the key to the relationship between many seemingly separate sets of data and information. It is not the only breakdown structure needed, however, and there is another in the Chapter 24 which shows the hierarchical association between different elements of a solution. Again, this breakdown structure helps you to understand relationships. Without knowing the relationship between the different groups of information, a single information set, no matter how good it looks, will be unreliable. You need to be able to 'trace' the path within and across all the different sets of data.

Deal with the documents first

Despite the explosion in the different ways of recording, transmitting, receiving and storing information, much of the work associated with the management of portfolios, programmes and projects is dealt with in conventional documents. Most finance departments want a 'business case document' to approve; contracts and their schedules are prepared as documents. This is document management (just one aspect of information management) and is covered in detail in *The Project Workout*, from where I have taken Figure 23.5 to show what activities need to be covered.

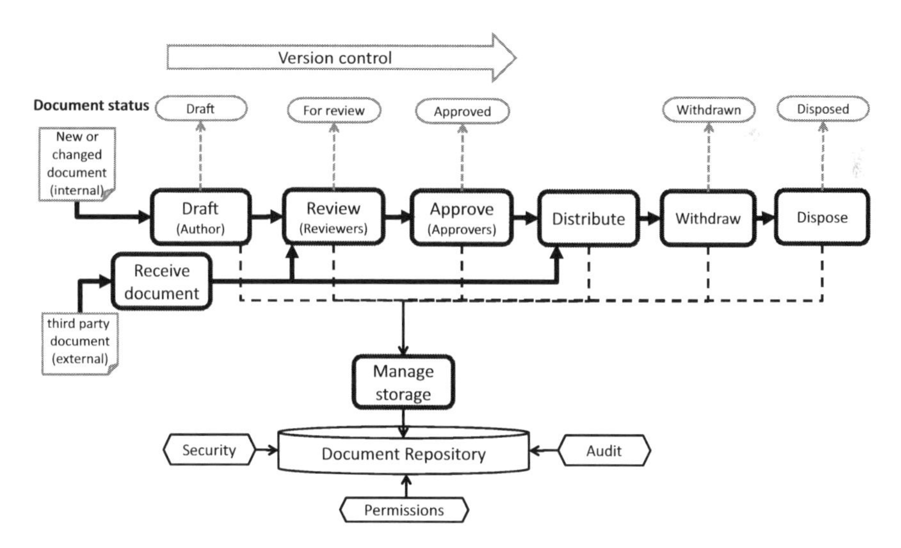

Figure 23.5 A typical document management process

An outline for a complete document management process, which you can either use or adapt to suit your needs.

Documents derive from inside and outside the organization:

- documents from the outside should be recorded on receipt, validated as correct, securely stored, distributed and retrievable by those who need it;
- documents, created within the organization, should be reviewed, approved, version controlled and, when no longer required, withdrawn and archived. The status, security classification and provenance of each should be clear.

In the days when most correspondence was by post or telex, this was easy. Every organization had a post room and a network of filing rooms, with internal couriers delivering letters, telexes, memos and documents to wherever they were needed. Files were filed in rows of cabinets by filing clerks and 'signed out' when a person took them away to consult. Every now and then boxes of files were taken away to archives and some, when deemed no longer needed, were destroyed. These systems did not come about by accident but were designed and evolved to enable documents to be located when needed. Many live and archive, paper-based files still exist as the legacy content is still referred to and of value. Nowadays, rather than just one point of entry into an organization (the post room), information can be received by each individual and in many formats, but the need to manage it has not gone away. In fact, with the increased danger of an unknown number of multiple copies of a document in circulation at any one time, the need for control is even greater if there is to be one reliable source of 'the truth'.

Document management solutions

Document management solutions or systems are, in effect, electronic filing cabinets with the advantage that those with access rights can get what they need from their desk, or remotely, rather than go to a physical location. Commonly used examples are the OpenText™ Content Suite (formerly called Livelink) and Microsoft's shared folders and SharePoint®. Most of the enterprise 'PPM solution' providers include document management as part of their solutions. Given the huge and growing volumes of data within organizations, ensuring consistency of approach and access becomes virtually impossible without an electronic system. For standalone programmes and projects, this becomes more critical as the size of the programme or project increases. Key features of an electronic system to look for are listed as follows:

- The capability to store and retrieve documents effectively; each document must be adequately described to support appropriate retrieval, retention period and security level, status and classification according to your needs and taxonomy.
- Unique referencing; a document and version of a document should have a unique identifier which does not change, even if the document is reclassified or moved. It is likely many documents will need to be referenced from web pages, and having a stable hyperlink, which won't break, is essential.
- Permissions management, to ensure only those who need to can edit documents. It also defines who is able to view documents. Do not tie down 'read only' access

too tightly; this is probably what your security advisors would want on the basis that the only 'safe' document is one that no one can see! The benefit of having document management systems is to enable collaboration and ease of visibility in teams formed of people from any department in the organization. If access is restricted unnecessarily, these benefits will be negated, leading to a large management overhead maintaining access controls. Do make sure you comply with the security rating; for example, there may be no problem letting everyone in the organization have access to your project management templates, but access to commercial information would need to be limited, both for commercial and legal reasons.

- Check in/check out, document locking or document sharing to ensure only one person can edit a document (or part of a document) at any one time. Multiple users should not be able to inadvertently overwrite each other's contributions 'live'.
- Version control, so the latest version is always the most visible, but previous versions are still available, if needed.
- Roll back to correct errors.
- Audit trail to see previous versions of documents and who loaded them and when; some systems also show who has read a document, which is useful to gauge how successful a document is or if the right people are using it.
- An automated back-up and disaster recovery capability, which is used for business continuity in the event of a serious incident.

The document repository need not only be used for the 'key documents' but can also be used for working documents, including risk logs, issues logs and change requests logs, making these vital control tools are accessible and the latest version available to everyone who needs them.

Beyond documents

Much of what used to be held in documents is now held in applications as data assembled to provide the information needed. For example, most 'Enterprise PPM applications' deal with risk logs in this way; spreadsheets are no longer required (thank goodness). Each of the tools has an in-built definition of what its terms mean and the relationship between them; some are customizable, and often you can add your own data fields to sort and select the data to provide reports containing the information necessary for a particular purpose. This is looked at in more detail in Chapter 27. Another example relates to information which defines a solution: Building Information Management (BIM). For now, it is enough to recognize that these are data repositories and information sources. If they are to help, rather than just add confusion, you need to understand the relationships between all these data sources and be able to reference them to the breakdown structures which are

If they are to help, rather than just add confusion, you need to understand the relationships between all these data sources

the spine of your governance framework and the hierarchy of your solution (see ahead to Figure 24.5). Configuration management is a good way to ensure the integrity of groups of related information.

A final legal point

Information, as we know it today, includes both electronic and physical information. People need to be capable of managing this information from creation to disposal, regardless of source or format (data, paper documents, electronic documents, audio, video, etc.) for delivery through multiple channels that includes mobile phones and web interfaces. In many countries this is not a 'nice to have'; it is often mandated in law, such as in the General Data Protection Regulations, which became law throughout Europe in 2018. Any information retained should meet statutory and contractual requirements in the operating environment.

Workout 23.4 – Information management

From your current management documentation, is it clear what information needs to be managed and how?

1 Does the information cover both management and solution specific needs?
2 How does this information relate to the items which require to be change or configuration controlled? There should be a close relationship.
3 Are contractual documents and information explicitly controlled?
4 Do you know how many documents (or information sets) are currently 'live'?
5 Are documents or information sets being withdrawn when no longer needed?
6 Take a sample of 20 pieces of information: for each, is its ownership, version, status and security level clear?
7 Ask a new recruit to the work to describe how information should be managed (be kind! It might not be their fault if they don't know!)

Good document and information management is more a matter of knowing what counts than blindly following processes. That said, the processes, if followed, should help people comply as part of doing their normal work and shouldn't be an obstructive 'add-on'. They are there to protect the business and so knowing what really counts and then tailoring processes accordingly is important. Deal with any issues arising from the questions earlier by emphasizing the risks they pose and how best to contain those risks rather than from the viewpoint of simply 'following the process'. A process has to make sense and help if its managers are to command any respect and if it is too serve a beneficial purpose.

24

Developing a quality solution

You can hardly say you have a 'quality solution' if it is the wrong solution, no matter how perfectly crafted.

"Quality is not an act, it is a habit."

ARISTOTLE, 384–322 B.C.

- **You cannot check everything, so use robust methods and processes.**
- **Understand the whole solution in its context.**
- **Ensure everything is traceable to everything else.**
- **Build quality into how you work, on a day-to-day basis.**

The right solution, built, deployed and used in the right way

What is quality?

Ask any of your colleagues, "What is quality?" and you will receive a range of different answers, taken from whatever course or book they have been reading or from their own experience. Here are a few formal definitions.

- The degree to which a set of inherent characteristics fulfils requirements (CMMI; APM Bok v6, ANSI).
- The ability of a product, service or process to provide the intended value. For example, a hardware component can be considered to be of high quality if it performs as expected and delivers the required reliability. Process quality also requires an ability to monitor effectiveness and efficiency and to improve them if necessary (AXELOS, ITIL®).
- The degree to which the features and inherent or assigned characteristics of a product, person, process, service and/or system bear on its ability to show that it meets expectations or stated needs, requirements or specification (AXELOS, MSP®).

The international standards on portfolio, programme and project management (ISO 21500, 21503, 21504 and 21505) and on system engineering (ISO 15288) do not include a definition of 'quality' as ISO has a policy not to define words where a 'plain English' dictionary definition exists and serves the need. What many of these publications do, however, is provide definitions for the word 'quality' in association with another term, such as in 'quality planning', 'quality assurance', 'quality control' and 'quality improvement'.

Quality management

Quality management ensures outputs are fit for purpose to achieve the objectives; this usually requires four related activities:

- **quality planning** to ensure quality is addressed in the management of a business portfolio or programme;

- **quality assurance** to provide confidence that outputs will match their defined quality criteria;
- **quality control** to monitor specific results to determine compliance with the specified designs;
- **quality improvement** to identify ways to eliminate causes of unsatisfactory performance.

Quality planning and assurance

Quality planning and assurance are concerned with the way work is managed and carried out, aiming to ensure there are no defects (or minimum acceptable defects) in the first place; fixing defects can be expensive. It is estimated that the later an error is detected, the more costly it is to rectify with some researchers claiming that rectifying a software error during live running is 100 times more costly than the same error if detected during design. As a business portfolio or programme sponsor or manager, you cannot personally supervise everything and need to define a management framework to build in quality with the necessary checks and balances to assure your objectives are achieved. This should include the methods, processes, tools and resources to be used and the type of quality controls needed.

Quality control

Quality control can be looked on as a back stop to detect errors. A term associated with quality control is 'verification'. **Verification** checks the correctness of a solution (or part of a solution) to confirm that it matches the specified design. It should be aimed at detecting faults or failures. The four commonest approaches are:

- **inspection:** non-destructive examination of a product or system using one or more of the five senses;
- **demonstration:** manipulation of the product or system as it is intended to be used to verify the results are as planned or expected;
- **test:** ensuring the system produces a predefined output when using a predefined series of inputs, data or stimuli;
- **analysis:** using models, calculations to study different results.

Different deliverables lend themselves to different methods of verification

Different deliverables lend themselves to different methods of verification and, in some cases, the methods can be combined. For example, a dock-side container crane might undergo commissioning trials (demonstration) in which it must lift a given weight over a minimum distance and height, plus show that the safety measures cut in if that weight or lift reach is exceeded. In addition, calculations would be made to show the crane is safe to operate in different wind conditions (analysis), as you can hardly wait for the next hurricane to see if it is blown over. In a single programme, it is likely all four methods will be used, due to the wide range of deliverables.

Verification can be applied to interim or final deliverables, to the whole solution or just part of it, at any time in the life cycle of a business portfolio or programme. For example, a component supplier in the car industry would have to make sure the parts supplied meet the specification; the assembled car would undergo a different set of checks to make sure it is fit to be handed over to a customer.

Quality improvement – learning from experience

Having decided how you will develop a particular deliverable, it is still possible that defects will emerge or that the deliverable itself does not quite meet the need. Assuming the development approach is not totally inappropriate, quality improvement approaches can be used to improve the quality or efficiency of how the work is undertaken. Learning from experience avoids repeating the same mistakes and helps spread improved practices to benefit current and future work. At the start of any new activity, those involved, together with key stakeholders and subject matter experts, should identify lessons from their previous experience and apply them when developing their plans and working methods. Once work is under way, lessons should be continually captured, evaluated and action taken to mitigate delivery risk and facilitate continual improvement of the final outputs and services. From an organizational perspective, however, it is wasteful if just one team learns and applies these lessons and their experience goes no further. If an organization, whether portfolio or programme, is to improve overall, the owners of standards, processes, methods, guidance, tools and training, should update their knowledge sources and communicate learning as appropriate to ensure everyone in the organization benefits. That, of course, assumes you have such roles and people know who they are. Once a programme and project management method has been established, most of the lessons are concerned with the costs of not applying the guidance at the right time to result in better costing and training rather than changes to the method. The greatest number of lessons tend to come from undertaking the specialist work itself, where often the methods are not defined and owners not assigned, making it difficult to capture and harness the experience to benefit others. Figure 24.1 shows the symptoms of a bad and indicators of a good learning cycle.

The greatest number of lessons tend to come from undertaking the specialist work itself

Making sure you do not build the wrong thing brilliantly

Building something exactly as designed does not, necessarily, mean it is what is needed or meets the underlying requirements. Whilst verification is about 'building it right', validation is concerned with 'building the right thing'. **Validation** ensures the right problem is being addressed and the solution is likely to meet the requirements when operating in its intended environment. This requires you to make sure this is built into your whole approach to quality. You can hardly say you have a 'quality solution' if it is the wrong solution, no matter how perfectly crafted. Validation needs, therefore, to be part of quality planning, assurance control.

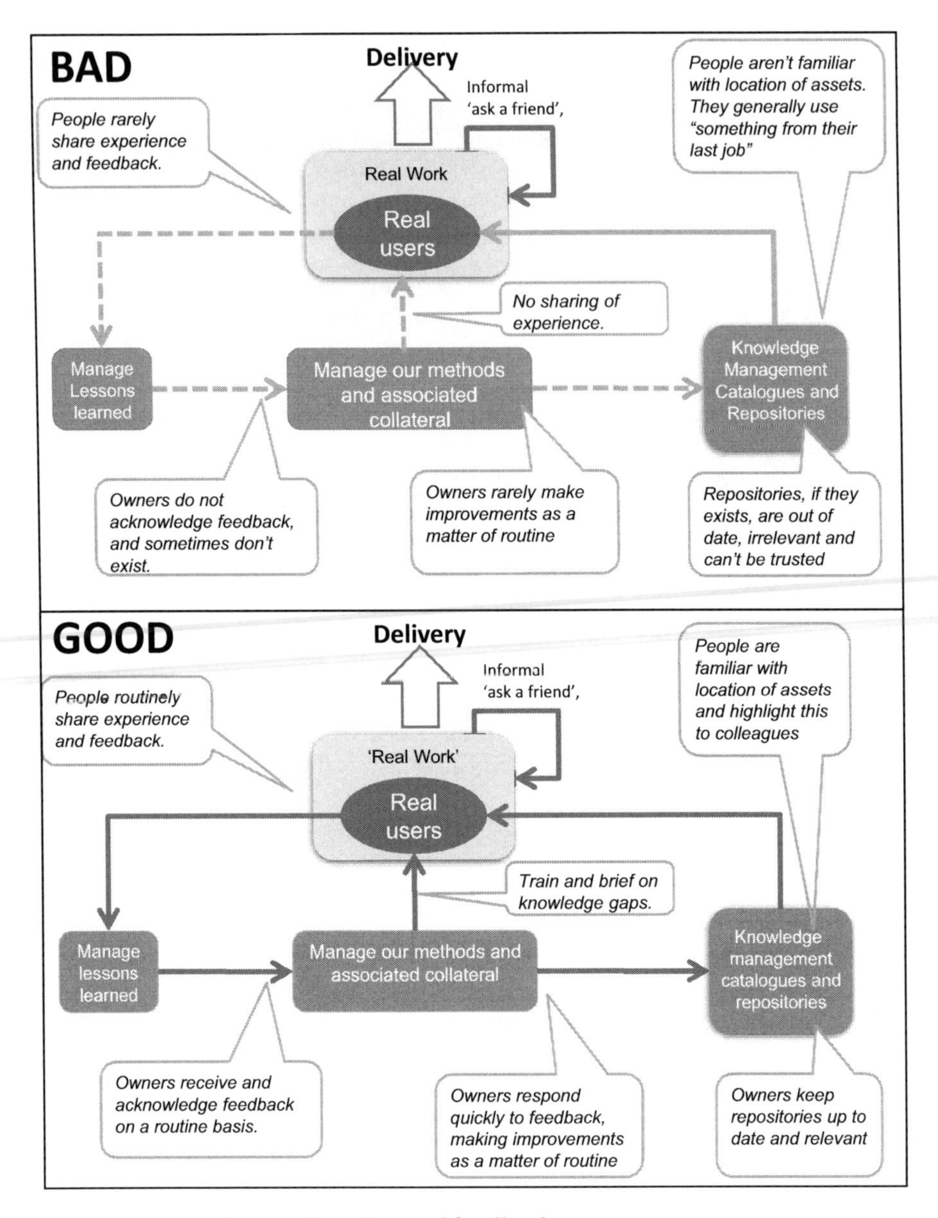

Figure 24.1 Continuous learning and feedback

The symptoms of a bad and indicators of a good learning and improvement cycle.

It is essential to plan the way you undertake work to validate that you are dealing with the right problem and that your proposed solution will meet the need. Such checks should not just look at the design but look at performance directly against

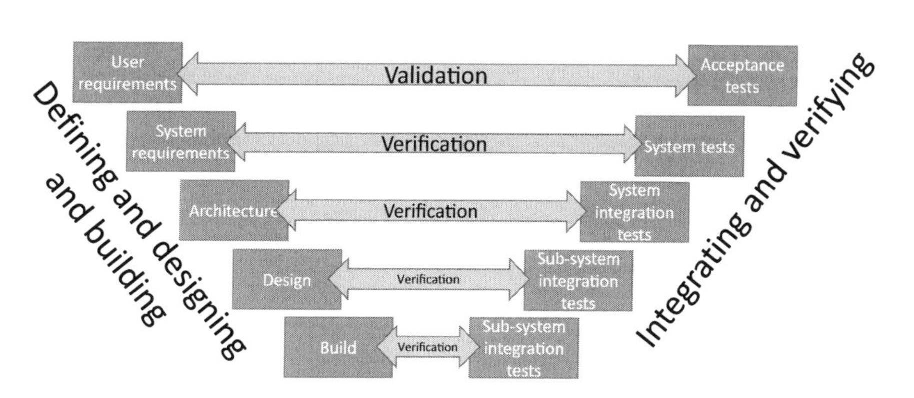

Figure 24.2 The classic V model

The classic V model shows how the different aspects of design relate to each other and to the level of verification. It is most suited to more complicated solutions in order to decide on your verification and validation strategy. In practice they can be multiple layers of systems within systems within systems.

validated requirements. The classic engineering 'V' model shown in Figure 24.2 shows this relationship.

Validation should be applied, throughout the life cycle, to the solution or a significant part of it and be aimed at demonstrating stakeholder satisfaction. Like verification, validation may be iterative in nature with solution, design and requirements evolving as work progresses, such as in many agile delivery methods.

Systems thinking improves the quality of solutions

Systems thinking

Project managers tend to think about quality as ensuring a particular deliverable is accepted by the customer, usually involving some form of 'quality check' (verification). In business-led portfolio, programme and project management, however, you need to think much wider than that. To achieve your business objectives, you need to make sure that you introduce a solution which meets the needs of various people involved in its creation and use and that its use can be, and is, embedded into your organization, or wider society; hence the importance of validation. Stakeholders can include the end customer of the solution, the people who develop the solution and those who manufacture or build it, maintain it and demobilize or dispose of it. It might be necessary to consider those who have no direct involvement but are in some way affected or perceive themselves to be affected. For example, people living near a major road or railway could be affected by the noise; this could lead to a design which limits noise to acceptable levels. In other words, you need to think holistically about what you intend to do, after all, if anything goes wrong with any part of it, it will be your responsibility. If you think this sounds like stakeholder management, you are right; I told you many aspects of this book are interrelated. Taking a holistic approach is often referred to as

systems thinking. **Systems thinking** is an approach to integration that is based on the belief that the component parts of a system will act differently when isolated from the system's environment or other parts of the system. Systems thinking sets out to view systems in a holistic manner and concerns an understanding of a system by examining the linkages and interactions between the elements that comprise the whole of the system. In this context the word 'system' is used in its wider meaning, not as an alternative for computer or IT system. Systems thinking is essential to quality; if you do not know how all the various parts of a solution work together, or even what they are, you cannot be confident it will lead to achieving your objectives. Taking this viewpoint, it is little wonder that the colleagues you asked what 'quality' is, might give such a range of answers. Each would be looking at quality from their own perspective. Can a person use the product? Is the service being delivered reliably? Will it work at 40,000 feet? Can 150,000 people access it at the same time? Is it secure? Will it survive falling off a cliff? Can I upgrade it whilst it is still running? Can I demolish it safely? What affect will it have on 'xyz'? Can I really get two million people to use this service? Some will be thinking about developing the solution, others about keeping it working and how it might affect other things which are going on, and some will be concerned about what happens when it is no longer needed. In other words, different people will have different interests during the phases of the system's life cycle, and all of these views are valid.

Systems thinking is essential to quality

Systems thinking is NOT about technology

Much of the language in this chapter is engineering based, but do not be put off if you are operating in a non-technical sector. The idea that a solution needs to be thought of in a holistic way and ought to meet the needs is fundamental to any sector.

What is a 'system'?

A **system** is a collection of different components or elements that work together to produce results which exceed that contributed, independently, by the components parts. The value of the system as a whole is created by the relationships, interconnections and interactions between the components of the system. The components can include people, hardware, software, facilities, policies, processes, facilities and information. The results include system level qualities, properties, characteristics, functions, behaviours and performance. The focus is to create an effective solution to a defined need, problem or opportunity. This requires a multi-disciplinary approach to handling both the management and specialist activities to transform a set of needs into a supportable solution within defined constraints. In other words, the management of a business portfolio or a programme cannot be separated from the development of the solution.

As a system is made up of many parts, there are various ways of depicting them, none of which can show the features in a way that is understood by, or is of value to, all stakeholders. For this reason, different representations are used to show different aspects. These are limitless but can include:

- the system hierarchy, showing how each component of the system is progressively broken down into lesser components;
- layout model which shows the relative positions of system components, such stores and docks in warehouses or general arrangements for road and rail infrastructure;
- logical modelling deals with gathering business requirements and converting those requirements into a model;
- physical modelling involves the actual design of a database according to the requirements established during logical modelling;
- functional model, which is a structured representation of the activities, actions, processes, operations within the modelled system or subject area;
- the behaviour of the system;
- the structure, for example data architecture;
- temporal model showing the state of a system at a particular point in time.

Hierarchy and ownership

The system hierarchy is used to break a system into its component parts, so that you know what each part of the solution comprises. It can also be used as the basis for assigning accountability for the different aspects of the solution. Just as in a work breakdown structure, the higher-level manager is accountable for all associated lower level work (including gaps and overlaps); by using a system hierarchy, responsibility can be assigned for the integrity of the system (or part of the system) and its sub-systems and components as shown in Figure 24.3. The more

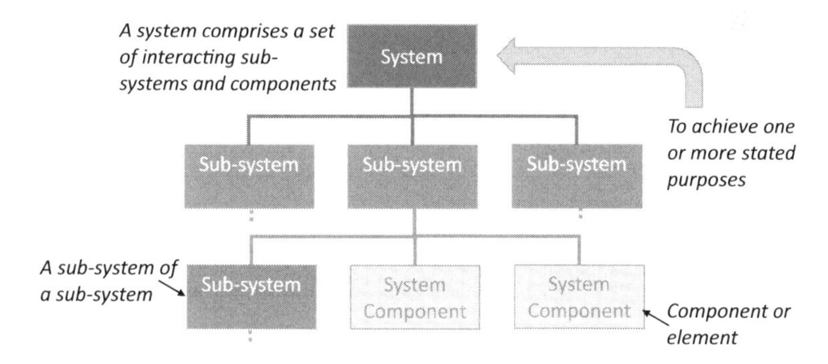

Figure 24.3 System hierarchy

The system hierarchy is used to break a system into its component parts, so that you know what each part of the solution comprises. It can also be used as the basis for assigning accountability for the different aspects of the solution.

interconnected an organization and its services are, the more effort is needed to manage the solutions. For convenience, let us call the person accountable for a solution the 'architect'. If the business portfolio requires a common approach to its solutions, an enterprise architect would be needed to define and manage these. Each programme and project would also need a programme or project architect, accountable for the solution (or part of solution) being delivered. In other words, the ownership follows the system hierarchy and, where suppliers are involved, can jump organizational boundaries.

COTS products can be seductive as they are apparently ready-made, but they also have their problems

In many cases a 'sub-system' or component might be provided by a third party, possibly by what is termed a 'COTS' (commercial off-the-shelf) product. The job of the person accountable for the whole system is to make sure all these parts work together. COTS products can be seductive as they are apparently ready-made, but they also have their problems:

- suppliers might exaggerate their capabilities and a paper-based assessment is not always enough to identify the this;
- some requirements might only be partially met, and missing functions always seem to be promised in the next release or version;
- future compatibility and support can be uncertain;
- the product might contain unwanted features with unknown side-effects;
- manufacturers can have a 'take it or leave it' attitude;
- interfaces can be problematic.

Some organizations develop their own 'home-made' COTS products for reuse and have a system of internal certification to ensure they are used in the right situations.

PRINCE2® product-based planning

The system hierarchy is the equivalent of what is referred to as a product breakdown structure in PRINCE2®. Like all methods and standards, PRINCE2® has its own terminology, using 'product' where other approaches might use terms such as 'deliverable', 'component', 'element' or 'artefact'.

Systems of systems

In many cases, a solution cannot be designed as an independent system as it relies on other, independently managed systems to meet the requirements. In these cases, a system of systems has to be used. A system of systems brings together a set of systems for a task that none of the systems can accomplish individually. A **system of systems** is a collection of components, which:

- can operate independently, fulfilling a purpose on their own;
- are independently acquired and managed;
- can maintain a continuing operational existence independent of the system-of-systems.

Logically, if a solution is to work within a given environment, that environment becomes part of the 'system'. If you are using systems thinking, always investigate the boundaries between sub-systems and systems which make up the solution to identify which interfaces represent a risk. It can become very complicated, and it is easy to lose track of which system is being talked about, especially as one person's system can be perceived as another person's sub-system or even component! For this reason, the term **system of interest** is used to focus on a particular system based on a specific purpose (or purposes). Figure 24.4 shows an example of a system of systems with a system of interest highlighted. An example of a system of systems is an aircraft, the air traffic control system, the passenger management system, the baggage handling system, the runway and taxiways and the terminal building. Each can me managed and operated independently, but if a traveller is to arrive at their destination, all these need to work together.

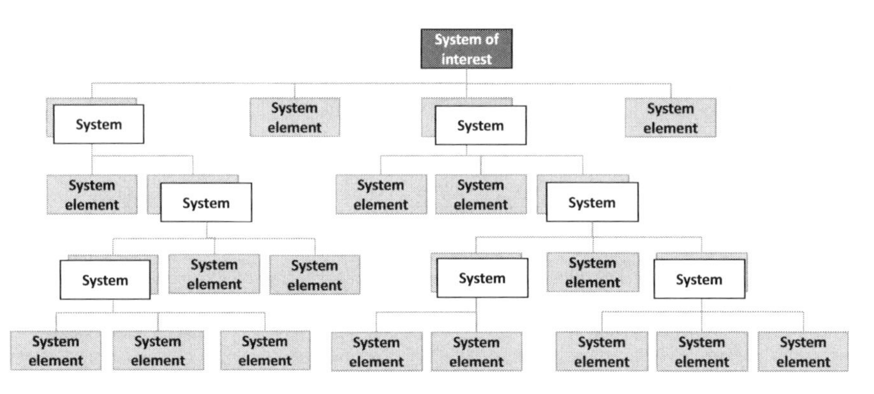

Figure 24.4 System of systems and system of interest

The 'system of interest' is the one you are focussing on. Whilst the diagram implies a hierarchical relationship, in reality there are an increasing number of systems that, from one or more aspects are not hierarchical, such as networks and other distributed systems.

Black-box and white-box models

A common technique is to model the system as a black-box, which only exposes the features of the system that are visible to an external observer and hides the internal details of the design. This includes externally visible behaviour and other physical characteristics, such as the system's mass or weight. A white-box model of a system, on the other hand, shows the internal structure and displays the behaviour of the system.

Black-box and white-box modelling can be applied to the next level of design, decomposition, to create a black-box and white-box model of each system component.

Some definitions of 'system'

Sometimes definitions of 'system' can be confusing in themselves, yet all are converging on similar characteristics but emphasize different aspects.

BS ISO/IEC/IEEE 15288

Combination of interacting elements organized to achieve one or more stated purposes Note 1: A system is sometimes considered as a product or as the services it provides.

Note 2: In practice, the interpretation of its meaning is frequently clarified by the use of an associative noun, e.g., aircraft system. Alternatively, the word 'system' is substituted simply by a context-dependent synonym, e.g., aircraft, though this potentially obscures a system principles perspective.

Systems Engineering Handbook, **INCOSE**

An integrated set of elements, sub-systems or assemblies that accomplish a defined objective. These elements include products (hardware, software, firmware), processes, people, information, techniques, facilities, services and other support elements.

System Engineering Body of Knowledge

A system is "a collection of elements and a collection of inter-relationships amongst the elements such that they can be viewed as a bounded whole relative to the elements around them."

System Engineering, coping with complexity **Stevens, Brooks, Jackson, Arnold**

The definition of a system depends on one's view of the world. . . . Often synonymous with product, in this sense, it is an artefact that draws on integrated, constituent parts, each of which does not individually possess the required overall characteristics.

The system life cycle

The word 'system' is often used synonymously with 'product' or 'solution', and the life cycle takes a system through time from 'concept' to 'retirement'. The form of the life cycle depends on the context. For example, if the product is manufactured, one of the phases would relate to the period of time when the product is being manufactured. If the solution is a 'one-off' creation, manufacturing is irrelevant. The name of the final stage might reflect the nature of how the system is 'ended'. For example, the term 'decommission' would be more appropriate to a nuclear power station, than 'disposal', whilst 'deactivation' might lead one to believe it is simply turned off and left there for eternity. Table 24.1 gives two examples of formal system life cycles, one from the UK's Ministry of Defence and the other from an international standard, ISO 15288:2015.

Notice the differences. The MoD has:

- a phase purely for demonstration so that a particular weapons system, for example, is validated prior to full scale production;
- an 'in service' phase which covers ISO 15288's two phases: 'utilization' and 'support' (ISO shows these diagrammatically as happening simultaneously).

In other words, system life cycles can and should be designed to emphasize what is important with respect to the type of system being delivered.

System life cycles can and should be designed to emphasize what is important with respect to the type of system being delivered

The system life cycle is important in terms of business or organizational sustainability. If your solution is to be sustainable in both business and environmental terms, you need to build into the solution design how and where it will be used, manufactured, supported and, eventually, disposed of. A cheap solution to build might be expensive to run or decommission. A system life cycle is, therefore, a useful tool for breaking down the phases of a solution's life and helping you focus on what is needed in each phase. It is also valuable as a means of ensuring you know the current status of a solution and its constituent parts.

Table 24.1 Example system life cycles

UK Ministry of Defence, CADMID	*ISO 15288:2015*
Concept	Concept
Assessment	Development
Demonstration	
Manufacture	Production
In service	Utilization
	Support
Disposal	Retirement

The other point to note is that different systems or variants are often developed for specific environments and uses during the system's life cycle. The version of an aircraft used for flight trials is different from a production model, as it might carry simulated passenger loads and measurement equipment to record the aircraft's behaviour during the trials. If you are developing a computer system you might need, in addition to the operational environment, environments for software development, integration, prototyping, testing, data migration, installation staging, pilots and training. All these uses and environments have to be taken into account.

A major omission

A complex suite of clinic software was being developed; environments were planned for development, testing and data migration. To save money, environments were stripped and repurposed as and when needed. Unfortunately delays in testing meant that no environments were available for continuing development. In addition, the 'go live' sequence required an additional environment for staging the software prior to implementation. In all, a number of new environments were needed to maintain momentum, each of which needed to mirror the live environment; at £7m each, this was not a trivial change.

Don't confuse your life cycles!

Programme and project life cycles

Chapter 8 of this book introduced the project life cycle. A project life cycle is only part of the overall system life cycle. Projects are often used at the start of a system life cycle to develop a solution and put it into operation. A project might also be used to upgrade the solution during its system life cycle and decommission a solution at the end of the life cycle. In other words, the project life cycle relates to only part of the system life cycle, and a system life cycle may comprise any number of project life cycles. For this reason, system life cycles can take on the same characteristics as a programme life cycle, with the system life cycle phases being represented by programme life cycle phases. In fact, the role of a product manager and a true programme manager (as opposed to a manager of multiple projects) are closely related.

System Development Life Cycle (SDLC)

Another term people are often confused about is 'system development life cycle'; they often think that this is synonymous with a system life cycle. These terms are not the same and the clue is in the use of the word 'development'. A systems *development* life cycle is a way of *developing* of an application. It would be clearer to describe this as a method or process and leaving the term 'life cycle' to relate to the project within which the application is being developed. Consider life cycles as governed by time and, as you cannot go back in time to correct any errors, you have to correct them at whatever stage or phase it is discovered. On the other hand, development methods and processes can be iterative and can happen in any project stage or even during the in-service period.

Simple, complicated and complex systems

So far, we have talked about a system in terms of the solution or solutions needed to be implemented to achieve the business objectives. If the solution is simple, understanding it and its interactions with the environment it works within, is not normally be a problem. In such situations, the full power of business portfolio and programme management is hardly likely to be needed. It starts to become more of an issue when considering:

- a business portfolio for a major company, with numerous products and services, many of which are built on common platforms, operating across the world;
- a programme for the development of a new aircraft, high speed railway, frigate, social benefits policy.

In other words, it starts to get 'tricky', 'complicated' or even 'complex'. Whilst the words 'complex' and 'complicated' are often used synonymously, it is useful to consider them as distinct.

- A **complicated system** is one which involves the management of a large number of requirements and parts comprising a solution and the level of coordination and specialist expertise needed to manage them. On the whole, the outcomes from a complicated system are reproducible and predictable. For example, an aircraft should be designed to take off and land safely, every time.
- A **complex system** is one where the relationships between the parts of the system are not always reproducible or predictable. Here the elements have a degree of self-organization and can evolve, having emergent behaviour. For example, whilst an aircraft can be designed to take-off and land safely, the pilot could behave in a way as to make this unsafe and the system has to be designed to take this into account. In this respect, pilot selection and training needs to be considered as an essential part of the system.

Complex systems cannot be 'solved' but need to be managed

A system can be very complicated but not complex at all. Likewise, a system can be simple but very complicated. Why does this matter? Complicated systems can be solved by using the right amount of logic and computing power, whereas complex systems cannot be 'solved' but need to be managed; this difference needs to be reflected in the management approach taken. To manage a complicated system, it is necessary to understand and coordinate a vast number of elements comprising the solution (configuration management). To manage a complex solution, it is essential to navigate an emerging landscape, observe, interpret, learn and act. The classic example of a complex system is one where people are an essential element and their behaviour, either as individuals or groups, determines the outcome. This is where 'management of change' is needed, which is covered in Chapter 25. That does not mean complexity cannot result from solutions where the 'people' aspect is less apparent. As the world moves towards being more interconnected, what used to be a standalone system can now be made up of a federation of independently managed systems, each with their own increasingly complicated operating rules (a system of systems). In such circumstances, can we really be sure that a change in one might not have unpredictable consequences in other connected systems, even if certain protocols are followed? If the development of a solution depends on a raft of suppliers, each looking after their own business interests, how can we be sure that the decisions they make will be aligned to the interests of the organization requiring the solution as a whole? Quality depends on being able to deal with complicated aspects of a solution but also with identifying and managing sources of the complexity. In this respect, verification is best for dealing with 'complicated' and validation with the 'complex'.

Verification is best for dealing with 'complicated' and validation with the 'complex'

Traceability

Changes to the solution and plan are inevitable (see Chapter 23). Without knowing how everything is connected, it is impossible to assess the impact on any risks, issues or changes. Requirements should always be traceable to elements of the solution. Elements of the solution should always be traceable to the plan. If work is being done by contractors, each contract should be traceable to an element (work package) of the plan. Knowing the connection between contracts, requirements, solution, plan and all their sub-parts is known as **traceability**.

This is illustrated in Figure 24.5, which shows traceability between the plan, contracts and solution. Traceability can highlight gaps; for example, Figure 24.5 highlights two gaps:

- work package (a) is reflected in the programme scope but is not reflected in any contract; the implication being that this work is being done in-house;
- solution element (b) is not reflected in the work scope for the programme; it therefore won't be built.

Traceability is easier to do in theory than in practice as it requires a well-structured plan, set of requirements, solution and contract strategy, together with an effective configuration management system to draw it together (see Chapter 23). This could be a lot of data.

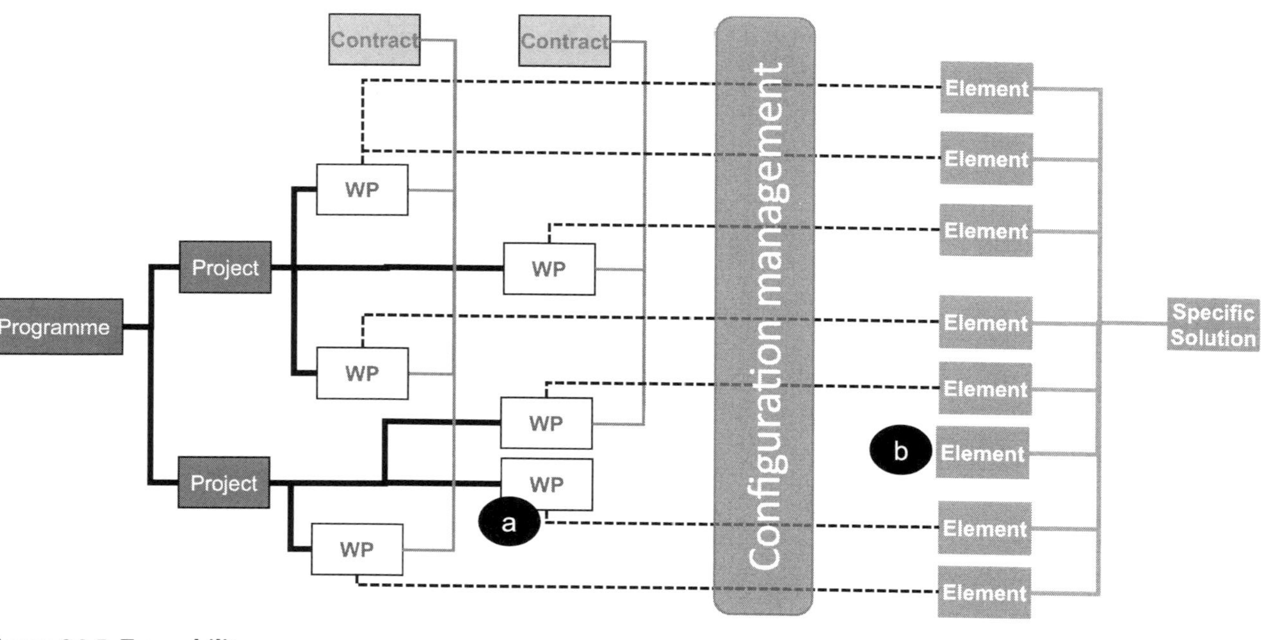

Figure 24.5 Traceability

Requirements should always be traceable to elements of the solution. Elements of the solution should always be traceable to the plan. If work is being done by contractors, each contract should be traceable to an element (work package) of the plan. Work package (a) is reflected in the programme scope but is not reflected in any contract. Solution element (b) is not reflected in the work scope for the programme.

Workout 24.1 – Testing the completeness of your solution and plan

Changes to the solution and plan are inevitable. Without knowing how everything is connected, it is impossible to assess the impact on any risks, issues or changes. You need to be able to answer (and prove!) 'yes' to the following questions.

1. Is every element of your solution reflected in a work package?
2. Is every work package traceable back to the element(s) it is creating?
3. Do your contracts reflect all the work packages done 'by others'?
4. Is every work package reflected in the programme/project plan?

This is not an easy exercise and might require you to work on it at multiple levels in the plan and system hierarchies, using separate diagrams or matrices to illustrate different aspects.

Building quality into how you work

The way you approach the specialist work is critical to quality and achieving the results you want. The methods used for undertaking the work should be defined and include appropriate approaches for both verification and validation. Different development approaches are appropriate in different circumstances; for example, an iterative, agile delivery approach would be suitable for developing a digital service but not necessarily for the power bogey on a railway engine. Not only should the working approaches be defined, but the people using them should have the appropriate level of training and experience to undertake their assigned role.

Whilst it is not possible to have a generic process to 'develop anything', it is possible to say what needs to be described in a process or method and to put them in the context of the system life cycle. In brief, you need to:

- understand what the requirements really are;
- design the right solution;
- build the right solution;
- deal with any defects.

Remember, even though the sequence of these could infer a life cycle, as processes they can happen at any time during the life cycle. Figure 24.6 shows an example process. Whilst it appears sequential, like a waterfall development approach, the 'rework' loops show that it is neither a life cycle nor waterfall. The boxes simply show activities which need to be done and the flow between them, including any rework. All of these could be undertaken in a single project stage, such as in agile approaches. Further, the figure shows the points at which configuration management attention is required and how defects are dealt with. Notice the configuration management points are where activity moves from one process to another, making sure that those working on them know what version of the requirements, or design, say, they are working under.

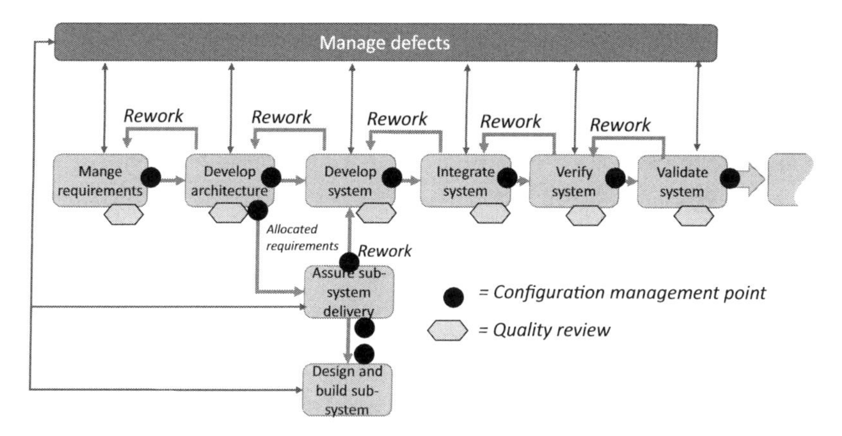

Figure 24.6 An example solution development process

Figure 24.6 shows an example process. Whilst it appears sequential, like a waterfall development approach, the 'rework' loops show that it is neither a life cycle nor waterfall.

Understanding the needs

Unless the real requirements are understood, it is impossible to provide the right solution.

Unless the real requirements are understood, it is impossible to provide the right solution. **User requirements** are statements that translate or express a stakeholder's needs and associated constraints and conditions. The user requirements are the starting point of any programme or project and should be addressed in the initial phases and are likely to be refined and elaborated and evolve with the design, often for a number of alternative options, until a solution is defined and a viable solution is agreed. Even then, requirements can continue to change right through development and into operation.

System requirements represents a user requirement which has been interpreted into a technical form to enable the design of a component of the solution. Multiple iterations might be needed to fully understand the requirements, which might take place over several project stages. The requirements should cover all phases of the solution's life cycle (including development, in-life and disposal). Requirements are not just concerned with the end users of a solution, but all users such as the public, end users, operational and maintenance staff, developers, constructors and manufacturers. A mechanic who maintains a train is just as much a 'user' as the driver, passengers, steward or guard. Requirements also go beyond the 'functions' to be undertaken and can include aspects such as accessibility, availability, resilience, performance, scalability and security. These are often the most difficult to design for, and it is not simply a matter of applying them to each component separately. For example, it is often the interfaces between components and behaviour of the whole system that determines security or performance; for this reason, it is essential to know at which level in the system hierarchy requirements (and hence validation) are applied. Requirements should also include any relevant statutory and regulatory constraints.

As a system comprises a hierarchy of components, it is normal for some requirements to be assigned to lower-level components. Such assignments as called **allocated requirements**. They can be:

- direct requirements, where a requirement is passed, complete to a sub-system or component;
- indirect requirements, where a mathematical or modelled analysis is used to distribute the requirement across several components;
- derived requirements, which is a result of higher-level design choices and not necessarily related directly to a user requirement.

Requirements should be uniquely identifiable, current, mutually consistent, understandable, unambiguous, prioritized and validated.

Requirements should be uniquely identifiable, current, mutually consistent, understandable, unambiguous, prioritized and validated. Requirements should be confirmed in a baseline and any changes controlled (see Chapter 23). Use Workout 24.2 to check the requirements in your portfolio or programmes.

When working to a deadline, don't forget quality

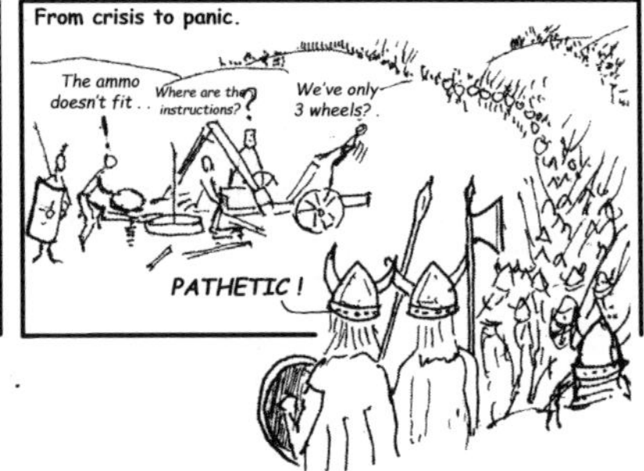

Workout 24.2 – Requirements

The following is a checklist to challenge whether requirements are being adequately managed.

For all requirements:

Method driven	The management of requirements is based on a defined methodology.
Completeness	The requirements cover both external (e.g., customer) and internal needs and also business, product (functional, non-functional and constraint) and process needs.
Integrated	The decomposition of requirements to enable more detailed understanding is formally managed.
Measurable	Performance measures are used to provide managers with information on how well requirements management is being undertaken. These should be defined in the methodology being used and may include: **Requirements** Number of requirements verified against plan. Number of requirements in plan/ Total number of requirements **Requirements stability** Number of obsolete requirements Number of new requirements Number of requirements to be determined Number of modified requirements Number of unchanged requirements

For each requirement:

Uniquely identifiable	The requirement addresses one and only one thing. Get rid of any ambiguities, spot duplicate requirements, and improve how requirements can be traced. Each requirement must have an agreed upon interpretation.
Current	The requirement has not been made obsolete by the passage of time.
Consistent	The requirement does not contradict any other requirement and is fully consistent with all authoritative external documentation.
Understandable and unambiguous	The requirement is concisely stated without recourse to technical jargon, acronyms (unless defined elsewhere in the Requirements document) or other esoteric verbiage. It expresses objective facts, not subjective opinions. It is subject to one and only one interpretation. Vague subjects, adjectives, prepositions, verbs and subjective phrases are avoided. Negative statements and compound statements are prohibited.

Verifiable	The implementation of the requirement can be determined through one of four possible methods: inspection, demonstration, test or analysis.
Traceable	The requirement meets all or part of a business need as stated by stakeholders and authoritatively documented. Make sure that you can trace the requirements from the original need, via the plan, through to what is finally delivered.
Prioritized	You need to classify each requirement according to an agreed set of importance criteria.

Designing the right solution

A solution should be designed to ensure the requirements can be met and will lead to the desired outcomes and benefits. A range of solutions (design approaches, design concepts or preliminary designs) that potentially satisfy the requirements should be considered and a solution recommended which best meets the need and recognizes the organization's appetite for risk. The design might evolve as requirements are elaborated and design progresses and should include all the outputs needed for the solution to achieve the desired outcomes.

For complicated and complex solutions, the entire solution should be considered with progressive decomposition into its constituent components, including those undertaken and implemented by suppliers. Interactions between elements and the operating environment should be known, taken into account and tracked, using configuration management.

The way that something is built can often dictate significant aspects of its design and so 'buildability' needs to be designed into the solution. This makes it necessary to develop a strategy defining the approach, as part of the design, to be taken for sequencing, delivery and integration of the components of the solution, including any special environments or facilities required. A tangible example of this is the construction of a block of flats using pre-formed components for both the structural and finished elements (like bathroom or kitchen pods).

Building the right solution

Solution development and integration ensures the solution is built in a defined way, such that all its components work together within the required operating environment. This applies to physical as well a digital component. Generally, each component is likely to be built and verified 'standalone' prior to integration into a sub-system or the overall system. Verification can be at various levels of detail as the component is created. Final verification can be in a test harness which simulates the component in its operating environment, prior to actual integration. Activities should be included to validate that the component is going to meet the stakeholders' needs.

Dealing with defects

No matter how good your processes or skilful your people, mistakes will happen, and you need to have a robust way of dealing with them. Those working in software development should be familiar with 'defect management' in the context of fixing programming errors as a result of failures in testing. A **defect** is an identified error within an approved deliverable and can be applied to any deliverable, whether interim or final. For example, a requirement, a test specification or integration strategy. Earlier we discussed how a system can be divided into a life cycle and that the later a defect is discovered, the greater the cost of fixing it. The cost of fixing defects (and hence the cost of (poor) quality) can be determined by using a specific cost code (see Chapter 28) for recording this work. You can also track how good you are at spotting defects. If the processes and method are working well, a defect should be spotted within the life cycle stage it was introduced. Comparing when a defect was identified in relation to when it was introduced gives a measure of quality for your development approach and quality control processes. A defect which is not spotted in the stage it was introduced, is known as an **out of stage defect**. For example, a design error should be identified during the detailed investigation stage of a project, when the design was approved. If discovered later, say in develop and test stage, it is an out of stage defect.

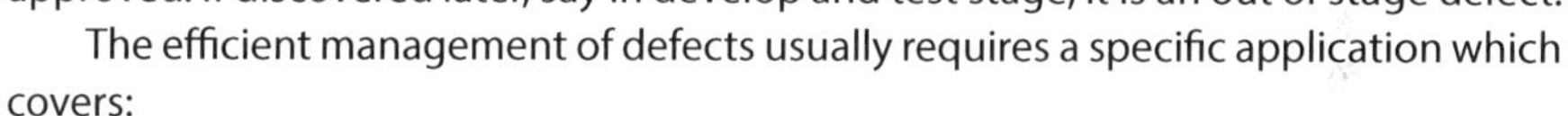

The efficient management of defects usually requires a specific application which covers:

- raising the new defect, by describing it in as much operational and environmental detail and the impact the defect will have on the programme/project objectives if not resolved within a given timeframe;
- triaging the defects, deciding priority and responsibility for resolution;
- planning for and resolving the defect;
- reporting on defects.

The identification of a defect might trigger the raising of an issue and the resolution might need a formal change (see Chapter 23). In some cases, the apparent defect is found not be a defect at all as it complies with the specification, in which case, it might be the specification that is defective, or even the requirements the specification was derived from. You can now see why traceability is so important.

25

Coping with all that change

Management of change – it's all about people!

Stakeholders – people you should not ignore

Change saturation

A brief history of change

There is no silver bullet change method

Getting people fit for work – induction and training

The management of change focusses on people, often called stakeholders; stakeholders are those who are impacted by, or perceive themselves to be impacted by, a change.

"When you are finished changing, you're finished."

BENJAMIN FRANKLIN, 1706–1790

- **Change should always be driven by vision and benefits.**
- **How much change management is needed depends on the likely impact on people.**
- **Project management and change management are complimentary.**
- **Change management can be a subset of project management and vice versa.**
- **Be very specific in how you tailor your approach on a case-by-case basis.**

Management of change – it's all about people!

The vison as a starting point

All leaders should have a vision of the future they want to create. They must also be able to communicate that vision to others; a vision which isn't shared and understood is just empty words. Except when dealing with relatively simple change or an obvious crisis, simply instructing or asserting that 'something should happen' is seldom enough. The vision:

- sets the direction;
- dictates the benefits and outcomes needed;
- should energize and motivate people to align around an objective and 'make it happen'.

Programme and project management is simply a way of structuring and managing the vast array of different activities and dependences needed. The key person is the sponsor (see Chapter 5).

Change is vital to progress

Change is all about delivering the desired outcomes.

The purpose of managing change is to prepare, equip and support organizations and people to change their approach and, where appropriate, behaviours, to enable an organization's leaders to realize the benefits needed to achieve the vision. In other words, change is all about delivering the desired outcomes. For example, if a new IT system (output) is not used, it serves no purpose as only by using it can the business change (outcome) and reap the rewards (benefit). This linkage, from outputs to benefits is often called 'benefits mapping' and was looked at in Chapter 21. Figure 25.1 builds on this, showing outcomes as the vital link between the outputs that are delivered and the benefits to be realized. Notice it should be possible to explain the mapping from left to right and right to left. This is another example of the two-way traceability and an essential feature of many of the concepts discussed in this book.

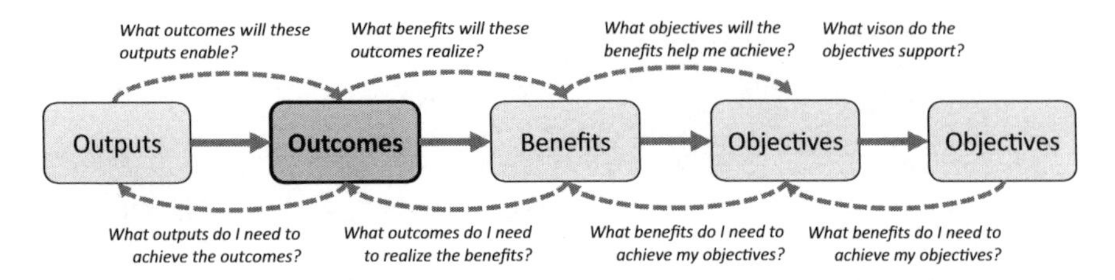

Figure 25.1 Outcomes within benefits mapping

In benefits mapping, outputs represent the main parts of the solution, outcomes represent the business or societal changes needed if the benefits are to be realized and benefits are what you will get out of it in whatever terms you measure benefits (such as revenue, cost saving, increase in Gross Domestic Product). There should be two-way traceability from outputs to outcomes to benefits to objectives.

Stakeholders – people you should not ignore

Engaging stakeholders

Delivering outcomes usually means someone, somewhere must do something differently, something new or stop doing what has been done for years. For major initiatives, this could mean tens of thousands of people have to change the way they work or behave. For a government, this could mean millions of people are affected. The management of change, therefore, focusses on people. These are often called stakeholders; **stakeholders** are any individual, group or organization that can affect, be affected by, or perceive itself to be affected by an initiative (programme, project or activity). Notice the word 'perceive'; with the rise of social media and pressure groups, there now seems to be an endless procession of people who are offended on behalf of someone they do not know or who promote a cause that does not directly affect them. They can often prove more difficult to deal with than the people who are actually affected . . . and do not assume they are always wrong!

Stakeholder or interested party?

ISO 9001:2015 (Quality management systems) started using the term 'interested parties' in place of 'stakeholders'. The authors were following the lead from ISO 14001:2015 (Environmental management) substituting the term 'stakeholders' with 'interested parties' on the basis thapeople with 'an interest' could affect quality and so need to be recognized. The definition for 'interested parties' is identical to that used in other publications for 'stakeholder'. My preference is to use the term 'stakeholder' in relation to portfolio, programme and project management as it is more inclusive and implies even disinterested people might be (or even should be) treated as stakeholders.

The 'poll tax' and 'yellow vests'

In extreme cases, stakeholder power can lead to an initiative being abandoned. The introduction of the 'Community Charge' in the UK in 1989 was a dramatic example. The change proposed by the government was to move from local tax being raised on 'property value' to a flat rate tax being levied on individuals within a household instead. One of the desired outcomes was to promote more interest in how the local authorities spent their taxes and hence restrain escalating council budgets. Opponents of the Community Charge were soon joined by opponents of the government generally; the Community Charge was soon dubbed a 'poll tax' in the media, an historically emotive term in the UK. Riots ensued in many cities and towns, and the Community Charge was repealed. Indirectly, it also led to the removal of the prime minister a year later. The French government faced an even greater reaction to its programme in 2018, in the, already established, 'yellow vest protest movement', where months of riots, sparked off by fuel tax rises, grew to encompass broader anger over the president's economic policies.

The needs and concerns of stakeholders (whether real or perceived) need to be addressed sufficiently to enable the business portfolio, programme or project's objectives to be met. Stakeholders are a source of risk and therefore, on occasions, adjustments to the objectives or solution are necessary to accommodate them. The weight of stakeholder opinion might also force you to face reality and abandon your approach entirely or look for a different way to achieve your objectives (see the case study).

Stakeholders should be identified and their interests and expectations understood. This is often not a trivial task. Depending on the nature of the change aimed for, stakeholders could be outside your organization. Think about:

- your customers and suppliers and your suppliers' suppliers;
- pressure groups;
- how the media might react to what you are doing;
- the institutions, especially if your work relates to government, security, armed forces or regulators.

Having identified the stakeholders (either as individuals or as groups) and understood their motivations, fears and drivers, next, decide how to engage each in a coordinated and appropriate way. Depending on the stakeholder, engagement might be done in a number of ways, including face-to-face contact, meetings or through collaborative working approaches, such as many 'agile' approaches. Mass media communications might be needed to reach wider stakeholder groups, in which case social media, adverts, TV bulletins, press releases and websites containing what you need or want people to know might be required. For small changes, stakeholder engagement could be undertaken relatively informally but for large scale changes which require to be programme managed, a more formal engagement plan would need to be drawn up, implemented, monitored and updated to reflect newly emerging stakeholders and existing stakeholders' attitudes. Stakeholders' attitudes will and should change throughout the work. After all, one of the purposes of stakeholder engagement is to change attitudes, and your work should be the trigger for many changes. On the other hand, people are likely to be influenced by opinion formers outside the programme as well; this might be positive or negative as far as you are concerned. For this reason, stakeholder attitudes need to be reassessed, updated and validated throughout the work.

> *"Four hostile newspapers are more to be feared than a thousand bayonets."*
>
> *NAPOLEON BONAPARTE, 1769–1821*

Communications

Communications management is closely allied to stakeholder engagement. There is little point of identifying and analyzing stakeholders' needs, only to ignore them. Communication is therefore an essential aspect of change management, vital for ensuring stakeholders contribute to the successful delivery of the work or, at least, do not stand in the way.

Communications need to be designed and coordinated to ensure the right messages are addressed to the right audience, at the right time and in a way which is acceptable to the recipients. All communications should be planned to match the stakeholders' needs, fears and hopes. It is also necessary to understand if communications have been effective and feedback mechanisms and effectiveness measures should be designed. Depending on the stakeholders, communications might be through press releases/news channels, adverts, posters, social media, websites and leaflets. This requires specialist managers, meticulous planning and attention to detail. It is essential communications build trust as any mistakes, perceived spin or errors can be extremely damaging, to government or a private organization alike. Good communications need to be authentic and seen to be authentic. Again, the boundaries between telling the truth, part of the truth or selective truths is a fine one and the ethics of the organization and the individuals involved are paramount.

Practical detail and methods on stakeholder engagement and communications can be found in *The Project Workout*. You can also find advice in the UK government's functional standard: GovS011, Communications.

Workout 25.1 – Reviewing communications

You are likely to have to approve communications. A poorly drafted communication can cause untold damage. Use the following to review an individual communication:

1. Is the intention of the communication clear? Is it obvious what should be the result of a person receiving this? Why are you using this communication?
2. Is it clear who the communication is addressed to? Is it designed from their viewpoint?
3. Is the chosen media appropriate to both the subject and the target people? Think about accessibility, age preferences and style.
4. Is the message clear and unambiguous? Is it factually correct? Are there any gross omissions? Could it be wilfully misinterpreted?
5. Has the communication been trialled on a representative sample of target recipients?
6. Is the timing right? Why send it now?
7. What are the risks of sending this communication? Have they been addressed and are they acceptable?
8. Is the cost proportionate to the benefits expected from the communication?
9. How will you know if the communication is successful?

Change saturation

The amount of change an organization can handle is not fixed nor arbitrary. **Change saturation** is when an organization and its people cannot absorb any more change. Organizations can reach change saturation because no one has a high-level view of the entire portfolio of change nor of the collective impact of those changes, on the people who are affected. In other words, the organization's leaders keep piling more and more change on their own people (and possibly their customers and suppliers), as each new 'good idea' comes along. Change can be internally generated, such as a reorganization, or externally generated, say through a takeover. Governments (especially when there is a change in the ruling party) are notorious for forcing change through, regardless of the risks and weariness of those impacted.

In many organizations, it is common practice to just manage a portfolio of projects, leaving the 'business as usual' to others to sort out. This practice, however, does not provide a view of how the changes triggered in each programme are going to impact the people, nor what the total effect is likely to be on 'business as usual'. When the cumulative and collective impact of change is not monitored and managed, problems can arise, which could prevent each project's objectives being fully achieved. In fact, it can be worse than that: the whole organization could grind to a halt, rather like a computer's CPU if it spends more time managing itself than the user applications. The consequences can be seen at the individual, project and organizational levels:

- individuals can become disengaged, frustrated, fatigued, resistant, confused and more cynical and sceptical of the current changes underway and future changes being introduced because they are already dealing with so much change;

- projects do not realize their expected benefits, as there is a lack of resources to devote to each project, changes are not sustained, and projects fail to gain momentum because priorities are ignored and resources are scarce;
- organizations (such as a business portfolio or programme) operating at or past the point of change saturation, can experience higher staff turnover, declining productivity, increased absenteeism and loss of focus on simply running the business.

Remember, it is not just your own organization you need to worry about. You might be able to cope with launching a raft of new products or services, but can your supply chain cope? Can your customers cope? I am sure if Microsoft® launched a new operating system every three months, wanting its customers to update their laptops every time, their customers might become a little jaded and look for an alternative provider.

You might be able to cope with launching a raft of new products or services, but can your supply chain cope?

Doing too much might mean achieving nothing at all

An organization had about 140 new product development projects under way. It was only delivering one or two new products a month, mostly broken. Hardly anything was being achieved of any business value, despite everyone working at capacity and vast amounts of money being spent. The number of projects was reduced by a third to about 90. Within months, four to five projects were being completed every week, mostly working. The organization had totally transformed its delivery record by:

- reducing people's workload,
- cutting the spend;
- the weight of change their people had to shoulder.

Does this sound familiar?

I hope, as you are reading this chapter, you can hear echoes from previous chapters in this book. Think of the purpose of 'business portfolios' where the projects and other work, including business as usual, are managed together. Remind yourself of the cause and effect diagram in Figure 1.1 and the four bases in Figure 2.1. Everything is connected. This why silo management does not work. No single part of this book can be used in isolation, each part has to work with and build on every other part. My single biggest challenge in writing the book was determining the order of the chapters, as understanding it is not a sequential exercise!

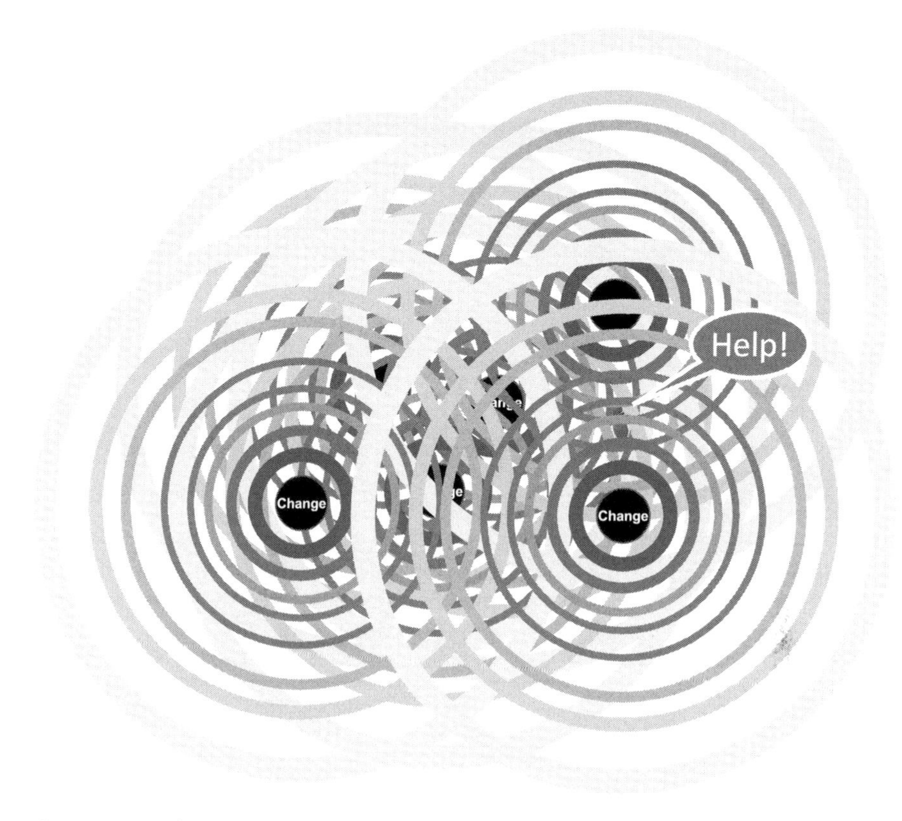

Figure 25.2 Change on change can look like chaos

Imagine a pebble is tossed into a still pond, where the pebble represents a change and the pond your organization or environment. The ripples will be predictable and understandable. As each new pebble is dropped into a different part of the pond, the water becomes turbulent. If you are a pond-skater, life could become very stressful and look like chaos. Perhaps it is time to find a different pond.

Finally, think about the individual's perspective. A person might be able to cope with one, two or three changes at once, but as more are added, it is easy to lose sight of what is triggering what and it might start to feel like chaos. Imagine a pebble is tossed into a still pond, where the pebble represents a change and the pond is your organization and its wider environment. The ripples from a single pebble are predictable and understandable. As each new pebble is dropped into a different part of the pond, the water becomes more turbulent (Figure 25.2). Life in that pond could become very chaotic and stressful. Perhaps it is time to find a different pond, or stop throwing stones!

People are at the heart of change (and resistance)

McKinsey and Company and several other researchers say about 70% of all change initiatives fail. This figure is hotly disputed by many commentators, but even if exaggerated, a real figure would probably still be far in excess of what is acceptable and represents a significant amount of waste in corporations and governments. There could be many reasons for failure on this scale, and a number of them are covered in Part I of this book, which demonstrates organizations with unclear strategies (or even no strategy) and have no rational way of managing their portfolios, making the failure of programmes and projects almost inevitable. This book is concerned with putting in place an environment to address that shortfall. People are, however, at the heart of change, and their actions are not always rational nor predictable. People always add to complexity, and if people are part of the solution, you need to address this complexity and not just concentrate of the 'complicated' yet more predictable technical aspects of the solution. The project life cycle is a key tool in dealing with this and trial stages (as described in Chapters 8 and 9) help to tackle such unpredictability, but actually observing behaviours is also essential. The following might be common signs of resistance but, at the same time, could be genuine concerns:

- postponing meetings on a regular basis *or they might really be busy*;
- attacking the detail to find one flaw and use it to discredit the whole concept *or they really could be experts in the area concerned*;
- promising everything but doing nothing *or they might simply lack the resources*;
- referring to the 'real world' to infer the proposal is an academic pipe dream *or they might have spotted real flaws*;
- asking for more detail and no matter how much you give, it is never enough *or they really do have a genuine concern*;
- flooding you with detail to 'prove' you do not understand what you are doing, *or they are passionate about helping you see another point of view*;
- silence – you want people to act, never assume silence as meaning consent *or they might be busy on other things*;
- attacking your methodology asking so many questions about the method, there is no opportunity to discuss the real issues raised by the change, *or they might have experience which they wish to share.*

Do not limit your degrees of freedom

Change can be planned to happen in any of the component parts of a business portfolio or programme. Do not assume projects create outputs and programmes create change. Whilst some methods and writers might take this approach, I would advise not limiting degrees of freedom. Some changes can be introduced in a project, whilst others might be best implemented as 'other work'. It depends on the context.

A brief history of change

Psychological and engineered

The management of change was originally seen as the domain of psychologists or academics and often referred to (in a derogatory way) as 'the pink and fluffy stuff' simply because it had no engineering foundation.

Change management methods started to be developed alongside a number of academic 'change models'. The psychological approaches emphasize how humans react, whilst the engineering approaches focus on the measurable elements of the business. The application of different models has implications for the way organizations and their leaders regard change, the way change is managed and even the effectiveness of any change initiatives.

Project managers versus change managers – who is the boss?

Sometimes there is tension between 'project managers' and 'change managers'. Project management is sometimes criticized for not dealing well with the 'people' side. But if people have traditionally scoped projects based on outputs and appointed project managers based on their technical expertise, this is hardly surprising. Just think how many times you have heard people say that implementing new working approaches, based on new technology, requires:

- an 'IT project' led by IT specialist;
- a 'business project' led by businesspeople.

In crude terms, the IT people are saying the job of ensuring people use the system is not IT's problem; if the 'business' cannot specify what is wanted and get people to use it, then IT cannot be blamed. The problem is no one actually says who, precisely, the 'business' is. I have shown this approach in Figure 25.3. An alternative approach is shown in Figure 25.4, which treats the change initiative as a single project with a single sponsor. In this approach there is no one outside the team to blame if things are missed, do not join up or simply go wrong. The expertise of all the team is focussed on the desired outcomes with the realization that technical changes can be used to solve people issues and vice versa.

Whilst project management was born in the engineering disciplines, it was soon realised that it was effective for managing any type of initiative. The first edition of *The Project Workout* took this approach in 1997, as did the first edition of *PRINCE2®*. Nevertheless, many people still insist that project managers are incapable of managing change, probably because their only experience of project managers is of those with a narrow technical background. The term programme manager was used by some to cover the business change aspects as

Whilst project management was born in the engineering disciplines, it was soon realised that it was effective for managing any type of initiative.

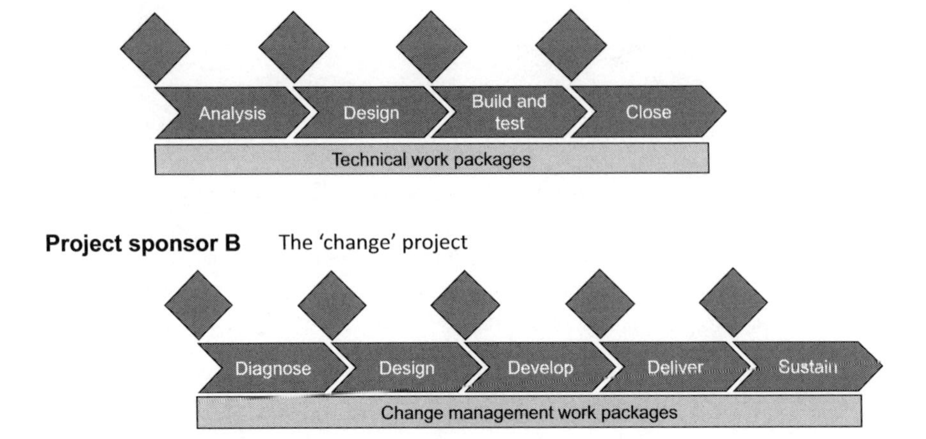

Figure 25.3 Treat change as a separate 'business' project

An approach, often seen in immature organizations, where the business change and technical aspects are treated as separate projects, under different sponsors and often in different portfolios.

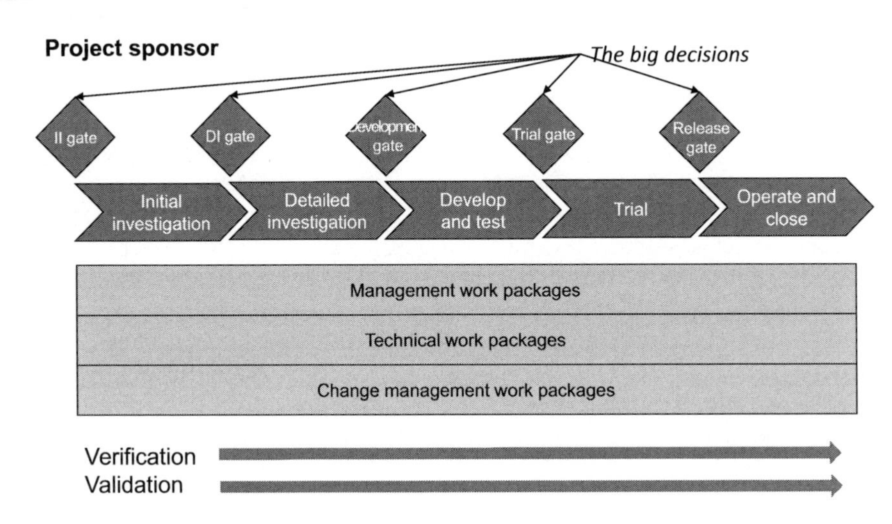

Figure 25.4 Treating change as part of a single, overall project

An alternative approach to Figure 25.3, which treats the change initiative as a single project with a single sponsor. In this approach there is no one outside the team to blame if things are missed, don't join up or simply go wrong.

the idea that a project manager could actually be a business and people focussed individual was beyond their paradigm. As a result, it is still frequently believed that projects create outputs and programmes deliver change and benefit, which is a misconception dispelled in Part I of this book. Nevertheless, a new profession is being born, with institutes and associations growing up to fill what they see as a knowledge gap. Two of these are the:

- Change Management Institute (CMI), founded in 2004, which is competency based;
- Association for Change Management Professionals (ACMP) founded in 2009, which is subject (knowledge area) based.

A comparison of the respective scope and their stated relationship to project management are shown in Table 25.1. The CMI, sees project management and change management as working closely together whereas the APCM sees the disciplines as distinct. I have highlighted (in bold text) those topics which have chapters in this book, just to emphasize the cross-over.

Sometimes there are arguments over whether the change manager is at a higher level of accountability to a programme manager or project manager or vice versa. A practical approach to this often emotive difference of opinion is to keep it simple. The manager of a programme is the programme manager and the manager of a

Table 25.1 Two different views on change management

	Change Management Institute	*Association for Change Management Professionals*
Perspective on project management	Project and programme management professionals' fast-developing profession provides powerful tools to define, plan and control change initiatives in organizations. They offer structures and processes that reassure organizations that change could be managed.	Project management and change management are complementary yet distinct disciplines that may overlap during change delivery and are often interdependent when delivering value to the organization.
Topics covered	Defining change Change impact Change readiness Sustaining systems **Stakeholder strategy** **Communications and engagement** **Education and learning support** **Managing benefits** Facilitation **Personal and professional management** Organizational considerations **Project management**	Change initiative scope **Leadership/sponsorship engagement** Sustainability **Stakeholder management and engagement** **Communications** **Learning and development** **Measurement and benefits realization** **Resource management** **Risk management**

*Note: topics in **bold** are covered in other chapters in this book to illustrate the cross-over between disciplines.*

project is a project manager. The fact that the programme or project is a change initiative is irrelevant. What is pertinent is that the management team has the right skills and experience to manage the work. It might be that the project manager is a highly skilled change manager and can undertake this aspect themselves, or it might be that a specialist change manager is required as part of the team, just like there should be specialists in other disciplines.

The legion battles through the change curve

There is no silver bullet change method

The idea that there is a single change management method which can be used in all circumstances is as ludicrous as thinking that any one method is right for every software development challenge. Change management is simply another categorization of a type of work that needs to be undertaken as part of a business portfolio's scope. How change is approached depends on the nature of the change needed and the context. Once this is understood, choose an approach to suit the need, drawing on the many models and methods published (a few of which are highlighted later in this chapter). Whilst considering this, think about change happening in three distinct steps:

- make the change wanted;
- make the change happen;
- make the change stick.

Making the change wanted

Making the change wanted is the fundamental step when the needs of the business are analyzed to determine the nature of the change (outcome) needed. No matter how compelling the need, if people do not want the change, it is unlikely to happen. This is when the idea has to be sold:

- first that change is necessary;
- second that the particular change proposed is the right course of action.

The leaders should create a compelling storyline to inform stakeholders why it is not in their best interest for the organization to remain in its current state and then go on to work out what changes are needed.

The burning platform

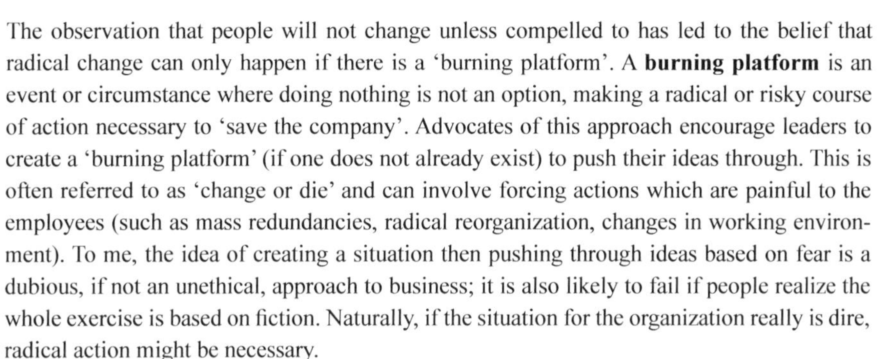

The observation that people will not change unless compelled to has led to the belief that radical change can only happen if there is a 'burning platform'. A **burning platform** is an event or circumstance where doing nothing is not an option, making a radical or risky course of action necessary to 'save the company'. Advocates of this approach encourage leaders to create a 'burning platform' (if one does not already exist) to push their ideas through. This is often referred to as 'change or die' and can involve forcing actions which are painful to the employees (such as mass redundancies, radical reorganization, changes in working environment). To me, the idea of creating a situation then pushing through ideas based on fear is a dubious, if not an unethical, approach to business; it is also likely to fail if people realize the whole exercise is based on fiction. Naturally, if the situation for the organization really is dire, radical action might be necessary.

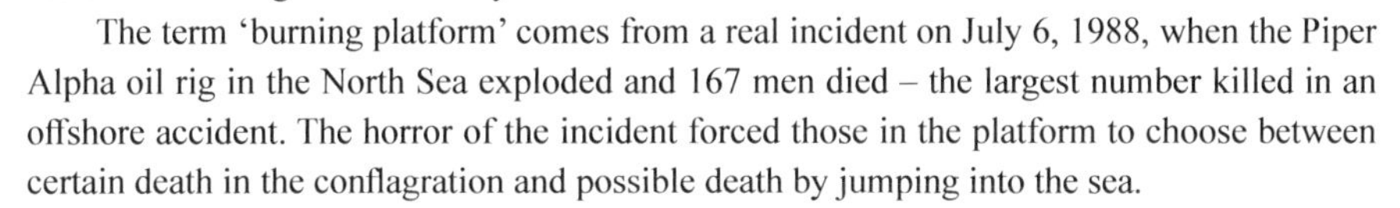

The term 'burning platform' comes from a real incident on July 6, 1988, when the Piper Alpha oil rig in the North Sea exploded and 167 men died – the largest number killed in an offshore accident. The horror of the incident forced those in the platform to choose between certain death in the conflagration and possible death by jumping into the sea.

Making the change happen

Making the change happen is when much of cost arises and important work undertaken, such as re-structuring the organization to achieve the benefits. For many IT-intensive organizations, IT delivery takes most of management's attention and the change management aspects are often neglected, resulting in difficulties later in converting the IT outputs into valued outcomes. One could (and should) ask, however, "How can you design an IT system without understanding the users' needs and how it will be implemented?"The answer is by taking an outcome focussed approach to programme and project planning, the right weight will be applied to the many different activities needed and at the same time the solution can be continuously validated to confirm it is correct and will be used in the organization. By giving the change agenda pre-eminence during this step, you reverse the common approach of defining the project from an analysis of outputs and deliverables and, instead, look first at what outcomes (i.e., business changes) are needed in order to determine the scope of work.

Making the change stick

Making the change stick means that people do not regress to their previous working and behavioural patterns.

Notice that the project life cycle in Chapter 8 is designed to include the earlier steps, although always remember that project management is just one management approach, and others might be more appropriate in different contexts.

Change management models and methods – some examples

Although the number of change management methods and models available might be overwhelming at first, it is important to understand them sufficiently enough to:

- either choose what you need to deploy your changes;
- or for you to act as an 'intelligent client' when dealing with specialists on the subject.

An **intelligent client** is one who is capable of specifying the requirements to external participants and managing the delivery of outcomes. As a programme or business portfolio manager, you do not need to be the expert on everything, but you have to know enough to ask the right questions, challenge advice given and make the decisions which are rightfully yours.

The following is a short commentary on a number of change models. I have given enough information for you to follow up and research each further, should you need to.

Lewin's change model (1947)

This model, generally attributed to Kurt Lewin, is still one of the most popular, probably because it has just three steps, namely:

- Unfreezing involves overcoming inertia and dismantling the existing 'mind-set'. It must be part of surviving. Defence mechanisms have to be bypassed.
- Make changes, typically during a period of confusion and transition. There is an awareness that the old ways are being challenged, but there is not yet a clear picture as to what will replace them.
- Freezing, especially when the new mind-set is being established and comfort levels are returning to previous levels.

This model is good if your business requires in-depth analysis and improvements.

Beer's six step model (1990)

Michael Beer (1990) and his colleagues suggested most change initiatives have been guided by a theory of change that is fundamentally flawed as it is assumed that changes in attitudes lead to changes in behaviour. Beer advocates the exact opposite and prescribes solving specific business problems by concentrating on reorganizing employees' roles, responsibilities and relationships in small units where goals and tasks can be clearly defined. The aim is to build a self-reinforcing cycle of commitment, coordination and competence. Beer's six step model comprises:

- mobilize commitment;
- develop shared vision;
- foster consensus, competence and commitment'
- spread the word about the change;
- institutionalize the change through formal policies;
- monitor and adjust as needed.

One advantage of this model is that it forces a focus on the task and putting in place long-term processes, procedures and policies, rather than creating them in an ad-hoc, temporary manner. Also, being at team and task level, it enables much of the detail of the changes to be determined from the middle of the organization, with the direction set from the top.

Bridges's transition model (1991)

Bridges's transition model comprises:

- ending, losing and letting go;
- the neutral zone;
- the new beginning.

As the name suggests, Bridges' transition model is focussed on guiding people through a period of change (transition) and is more of a mood predictor. It forces you to look through the eyes of those being changed. It does not, however, deal with deciding, designing and implementing the actual changes themselves. As such, it is a good addition to other methods.

Kotter's eight step model (1996)

This is probably one of the more famous methods and comprises eight steps:

- step 1: Establishing a Sense of Urgency;
- step 2: Creating the Guiding Coalition;
- step 3: Developing a Change Vision;
- step 4: Communicating the Vision for Buy-in;
- step 5: Empowering Broad-based Action;
- step 6: Generating Short-term Wins;
- step 7: Never Letting Up;
- step 8: Incorporating Changes into the Culture.

Kotter's model is great as a checklist but lacks a step-by-step process (despite it naming each element as a 'step') and should be complemented with other approaches to make up for its shortcomings.

Linda Ackerman-Anderson and Dean Anderson (2001)

This method comprises nine steps:

- preparing;
- creating organizational vision;
- assessing design requirements;
- designing the desired state;
- analyzing the impact;
- planning and organizing for implementation;
- implementing the new state;
- celebrating/integrating the new state;
- course correcting as the new state takes hold in the organization.

Nudge: Thaler and Sustein (2008)

This is one of the more 'people-focussed' approaches and often used in the UK government. It comprises seven steps:

- define your changes clearly;
- consider changes from your employees' point of view;
- use evidence to show the best option;
- present the change as a choice;
- listen to feedback;
- limit obstacles;
- keep momentum up with short-term wins.

Nudge theory is great for engaging the people the changes most depend on (usually, but not always, your employees) and often turning them into your most active champions. However, nudge, if used on a large scale, requires a lot of resources. Further, it is not a complete change method and it is best to combine it with another model.

ADKAR by Proscii

This is a proprietary method. It comprises five steps, which form a mnemonic to help people remember them:

- Awareness (of the need to change);
- Desire (to participate and support the change);
- Knowledge (on how to change);
- Ability (to implement required skills and behaviours);
- Reinforcement (to sustain the change).

If (and it is a big 'if'), you already know what you want to change and why it is important, ADKAR can be used with confidence in making the changes happen and keeping trust with those who are the subjects of the changes.

The Satir change management model

The Satir change model takes individuals through a journey, in five steps, from the 'old world' to the 'new world'.

- late status quo;
- resistance;
- chaos;
- integration;
- new status quo.

This model is good for measuring people's reactions to a change and reassuring them along the way. Like Bridges's model, it is a good tool but needs to be used with other approaches. It has parallels to Kübler-Ross's change curve which focusses on a person's emotional response to change (denial, anger, bargaining, depression, acceptance).

Other models

Other models and approaches include:

- 'being' versus 'doing' which focusses on planned one-on--one conversations (How High Impact leaders communicate; Phil Harkins;1999);
- skills based, which advocates that the most important elements a leader can bring are passion, conviction and confidence in others; leading others to follow their dream, stretching their horizons and encouraging others to do the same (The enduring skills of change leaders; Rosabeth Moss Kanter: 1999);
- storytelling, which primarily uses the power of stories to convey intent and meaning to persuade, motivate and inspire in ways that cold facts, bullet points and directives cannot (Story Factor; Annette Simmons: 2006).

Getting people fit for work – induction and training

Earlier, I drew out stakeholder engagement and communications as special aspects for the management of change as they are needed on every business portfolio, programme and project. Similarly, in organizations, training is a vital aspect of change because it enables people to undertake their current roles and prepare for new roles. This should not, however, happen solely in the context of change management. Every business portfolio and programme should be built on a defined management approach and those involved need to understand the part they play in it. Very few publicly available methods and models include this facet of management (an exception is CMMI), but it makes sense that people ought to be skilled and competent to undertake their roles. I would always prefer to work

I would always prefer to work with skilled and competent people and mediocre processes than mediocre people and brilliant processes.

with skilled and competent people and mediocre processes than mediocre people and brilliant processes. The processes used for inducting people into your programme can be based on the same principles as inducting people into a new role as part of a change programme. It is just the context and content that changes. The same goes for training. Business portfolios and programmes can be very long. Ten years is not unusual. Many people are likely to spend a substantial and informative part of their working lives on such programmes and need to be able to develop and grow into new roles. Just using whatever the 'enterprise approach' from their corporate HR is often not enough. Programmes can become distant from their sponsoring organization and often need their own corporate infrastructure and can be large enough to sustain such an overhead; a big programme can dwarf most small and medium-sized companies.

Induction of people who are new to their role

Induction is concerned with making sure those new to a role understand what is expected of them and how to work with colleagues. As a minimum, this should include:

- introductions to colleagues;
- making sure the necessary facilities are made available;
- a briefing on the work, both the overall context and their specific role;
- the processes to be followed and methods to be used;
- training required for their role;
- providing appropriate security access (buildings, computer networks, facilities).

Do not expect someone to join the team and find their own way. In the early days they are more likely to worry about getting lost in the building and where and when to get coffee and lunch than the intricate details of their job, so don't neglect basic human needs. If a person is to be an asset to the team, they need to feel welcome and be able to locate a familiar, friendly face to help them in the first few weeks.

Training and development

Training and development should be designed to build people's skills in the types of work they are required to do. This has to be undertaken on two dimensions, against:

- the topics each person needs to know;
- an individual's expected and actual level of expertise in each topic.

Not everyone needs to be an expert at everything, but the team, as a whole, has to be competent to undertake the work. Different people have different strengths and weaknesses and personal preferences, but unfortunately many human resource departments do not recognize this when recruiting. 'People specifications' for the ideal candidate are designed and used to mark each applicant on a score card. As a result, a team of managers constructed with this approach can be deficient as a team, as a vital skill or attribute might be missing from all the applicants.

Having determined what people need to be capable of, the big question is to decide how best to provide such training or development. Training can be face to face in seminar format, or it could be by working through computer-based routines. The greater the need for people interaction, the more beneficial a face-to-face approach is. For management topics, the discussion between delegates can be as instructive as formal lectures and case work. Basic 'for information' training can be done in isolation using computer-based training; topics such as corporate ethics, data protection and basic security lend themselves to this. No doubt, with the rapid development of artificial intelligence, immersive computer training in a virtual reality environment will become possible. Much of the technology already exists in the gaming sector but, at present, the cost of development does not warrant the market size.

Each training or development intervention should be defined and designed, with trials as an essential part of the development approach. The training suppliers (whether in-house or external) need to be selected and be credible for the subjects they cover. Once launched, the relevance and effectiveness of the course needs to be monitored and the course updated when necessary.

Workout 25.2 – Training

You probably will not have all the information necessary and will need to work with your management team on this workout. Keep to the critical roles to start with or this could become a daunting task.

1. List the key roles in your business portfolio programme (or project)
2. List the topics and skills you require each role to have and the extent of expertise required. Note different roles might require different levels of expertise. Use the topics in this book or a published competency framework, such as from the International Project Management Association, Association for Project Management or the UK government's Project Delivery Capability Framework.
3. Determine to what extent the individuals undertaking each role meet the required level of competence.
4. Note the gaps: use these as the basis for designing training and development interventions.
5. Note those with higher level skills in some topics than their role requires. These are worth keeping a note of as they can be used to fill shortfalls elsewhere, even if you do not change their role formally.

26

Sorting out all those contracts

The importance of contracts

What constitutes a 'contract'?

Forms of contract

The contract life cycle

Procurement

Supplier management

Strategic supplier management

It is almost inconceivable to direct or manage a business portfolio or a programme without having to deal with contracts.

"Disagreement may be the shortest cut between two minds."

KAHLIL GIBRAN, 1883–1931

- **Make sure the contract covers all needs and eventualities.**
- **Choose the form of contract to suit the need.**
- **Take care when apportioning risk.**
- **Understand the market power you and your potential suppliers have.**
- **Contract signature is just the start; making it work is what matters.**
- **Focus more effort on the most important suppliers.**

The importance of contracts

It is almost inconceivable to direct or manage a business portfolio or a programme without having to deal with contracts. For some organizations, the bulk of their work is undertaken by third parties, whether for building infrastructure or for outsourcing. Chapter 3 describes how, for some organizations, such as a contractor, large parts of their business are driven by contracts. Contracts can therefore exist for any part of any business portfolio or programme.

A contract might be between the organization and its customer (a customer contract) or between the organization and its suppliers (supplier contract). As discussed in Chapter 3, suppliers might also have their own suppliers, often called sub-contractors (see Figure 26.1). There is no difference, in law, between a customer

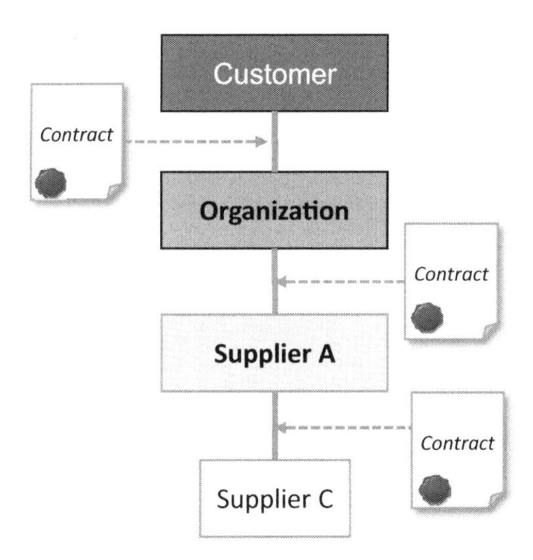

Figure 26.1 Different contexts for contracts

A contract might be between the organization and its customer or between the organization and its suppliers. As we also saw in Chapter 3, suppliers might also have their own suppliers.

contract or a supplier contract. This is simply a convenient way of describing the context for the contract, relative to your own organization. A customer and a supplier are parties to the contract. **Parties** are those with a legal, contractual relationship. A party can be any legal entity such as a person, or in the context of this book, most likely a formally constituted company, partnership or public sector or charitable body.

This book does not go into the technicalities of contract law but simply describes some of the basics to highlight what to look out for, when to call on specialist help and what questions to ask. I have based this chapter on English law, and there will be differences in other jurisdictions; nevertheless, the topics covered are ones of general interest and, if working outside English law, you will need to know the implications on your business portfolio or programme.

English contract law evolves continuously as it builds on case law, resulting from judgements made over 150 years of disputes. The fact that contract law is based on case law has practical implications; in the case of a dispute, there is no easy way for the layman to find out what their legal position is. Further, if your problem has not arisen before, there is no precedent to follow; judges will decide on the merits of the individual case. Contract law in the UK is based on some, occasionally conflicting, expectations. These are:

- an organization's people know the law and in areas where the law is developing fast (such as environmental, health and safety and data protection), the organization needs to take steps to ensure they are kept up to date;
- it is assumed all commercial organizations have the competency to negotiate contracts and therefore have to live with the terms of any contract they sign. Further, that they know how to draft and interpret contracts correctly. This is a big assumption;
- an organization is technically or professionally skilled to carry out the work it has contracted to do;
- the parties comply with the rules set out in the contract; providing the parties comply, the law does not require people to be 'fair' in the way they comply.

The contract period for a relationship is often so long that all circumstances cannot be foreseen

Contracts can either involve a transaction, being the purchase or sale of a product, or a relationship carried out over a period of time, often many months or years. Whilst it might be possible for a contract for a transaction to include all the rules governing the parties, this is not usually the case for a contract involving a relationship. The contract period for a relationship is often so long that all circumstances cannot be foreseen. For this reason, such contracts need to include rules on how to develop and change the contract itself over time. The relationship between the parties and their behaviours is of paramount importance and a mutual appreciation of what is 'fair' is essential. Contract law is primarily based on transactions and does not deal with relationships very well, as there have been relatively few disputes reaching the courts. As such, this aspect of contract law is undeveloped and not easy to predict. In fact, the number of disputes has generally decreased over the years with the introduction of mediation, adjudication, arbitration and conciliation, together with the use of new forms of contract which promote cooperation between the parties.

What constitutes a 'contract'?

A **contract** is a legally binding promise (written or verbal) by one party to fulfil an obligation to another party in return for consideration. For a contract to be legal it has to comprise four key elements:

1 **offer**: one of the parties has to offer the terms of the contract. An offer has to be 'complete', including the full terms of the intended contract. A conditional offer is not valid until the conditions have been met. A rejection, instantly terminates the offer, as does a counter-offer;

2 **acceptance**: the other party accepts, in full, the terms within the validity period of the offer. Often a contract specifically excludes any communications leading up to the final offer, the assumption being that anything required for the contract should be written in the contract;

3 **consideration:** payment, exchange of goods, services or similar, which must be of some value but can be nominal;
4 **intent to create legal relations**: the parties to a commercial agreement are presumed to have the intention of it being legally binding unless it clearly states otherwise in the agreement.

Whilst this might look simple, in the context of programmes and projects, the route to achieving agreement for a significant work scope can be lengthy, often involving many steps along the way. This might involve a sequence of negotiations between the parties, starting with an invitation or enquiry and followed by a series of offers, which are negotiated until the full terms are agreed. In effect, the original offer is superseded by an offer and acceptance, resulting in the outcome of the negotiations. In such circumstances, it is easy to lose sight of who is making an offer to whom and on what. With the number of people involved, it is also easy to lose sight of who has authority to do what. It is therefore essential to avoid any implied (or actual) agreement until you are satisfied that the terms are acceptable.

it is easy to lose sight of who has authority to do what.

The people representing the parties need to have the legal capacity to agree the contract. When the party to a contract is an organization, the contract must relate to activities within its memorandum of association (or equivalent for other types of organization) and the persons involved (including agents) should have the necessary authority to act on behalf of that organization. It is therefore advisable, when negotiating a contract, or any subsequent variations, to understand your own authority limits and those of the people representing the other party.

An offer can be revoked (unless under deed or seal) at any time before it is accepted. This relies on there being clear and unambiguous communications between the prospective parties. Under English law, there are rules concerning this. Every person is responsible for their own communications and it is the sender's responsibility to:

- check the recipient's understanding;
- make sure the addressee and address are right;
- accept the risks that the communications might be lost or corrupted between being sent and received.

Remember, in the context of contracts which concern relationships, the previous applies whenever a variation needs to be agreed as, in effect, the contract is being rewritten. This is why formal change control processes are so essential (see Chapter 23).

Communication rules

1. A letter accepting an offer takes effect from the moment it is properly posted.
2. A telegram accepting an offer takes effect the moment it is sent.
3. The revoking of an offer takes place from the moment it is delivered.
4. All other letters take effect the moment they are received.
5. All electronic communications (such as fax, email, telex or message) are effective when received.
6. Spoken communications are effective when heard and as heard.

Forms of contract

What is in a contract?

A contract sets out the relationship between the parties and so needs to include everything necessary for that purpose. Usually, a contract includes:

- a statement of scope; what is within the remit of the contract;
- a means to measure the performance of the contract. This might be in the form of required delivery dates, quality criteria or service level agreements;
- general and specific contract terms and conditions; these can be in the form of specifications and drawings as well as text;
- payment mechanisms;
- how to deal with breaches of the contract.

The order these are presented in the written contract and the headings used will differ from contract to contract, depending on previous, similar contracts or any standard form used.

Standard forms of contract

Due to the complexity of contracts involving relationships it is preferable, where they exist, to use standard forms of contract rather than invent every contract anew. Different industries publish forms of contract recommended for use in particular circumstances; some forms of contracts comprise whole suites of options which can be adopted. Standard forms of contracts have a number of advantages over bespoke contracts:

- they are built on the knowledge and experience of a large number of contributors and take into account preceding case law;
- they are developed by independent cross-industry experts and so tend to be impartial;
- parties become familiar with them, therefore:
    - tendering is easier as the risks to each party are better understood;
    - interpretation, in use, becomes standard;
    - they are often already tried and tested in the courts and so, in the event of disputes, the 'right' interpretation becomes more predictable.

The wording of a contract

Contracts comprise two sets of terms:

- **express terms**, which are the words, as written in the contract;
- **implied terms**, which are not written in the contract.

Express terms can take a number of forms and serve several purposes. For example, a dimension on a drawing is a term of the contract, as is the specification for materials. Other terms can include access rights, payment process, clauses to report potential delays or cost increases, what to do if work is actually delayed, how long documents should take to review and how to agree changes to the contract. Good contract terms protect the parties to a contract by covering all foreseeable eventualities, thereby helping to avoid disputes and potentially costly litigation.

Express term can be split into three further categories which determine what remedy or action is allowable if the term is not met. These are:

- **warranty** terms, treated by the parties as not important and, if breached, will not substantially impact the contract. The principle remedy is damages;
- **condition** terms, treated by the parties as significant and can lead to either damages or termination of the contract. Conditions should relate to the primary objectives of the contract, namely:

    - the timescale for delivery;
    - the requirements;
    - statutory obligations (implied terms);
    - any terms which are specifically described as conditions or state that triggering of termination might result of a breach;
- **intermediate** terms, are everything else. The remedy is usually damages but in serious circumstances can lead to termination of the contract.

An implied term can come about from one of three sources:

- first, they are terms which are required in order to comply with the statutes;
- second, they can come about as a matter of 'custom and practice' within a particular industry, type of business or activity;
- finally, they can be the result of judgements in law, either on the particular contract or when a court has decided a term should be included in contracts as a matter of public policy.

Check what is really in your contract

Penalties and damages

You will often hear people talk about 'penalty clauses' in contracts. There is no such thing, at least in English law. A contract is a voluntary commercial undertaking and not criminal. Penalties, i.e., punishment, only apply in criminal law. When people refer to 'penalty clauses' they are usually referring to liquidated damages.

Damages are set by a court after a breach of contract. Damages can be avoided through agreement by the parties in the form of a commercial settlement, avoiding the need for further action.

Liquidated damages are pre-determined and written into the contract. They usually relate to late completion of work, either in total or for an intermediate milestone (sometimes called a 'key milestone'). As they usually relate to delays in the schedule, they are sometimes called 'delay damages'. Liquidated damages have to be based on genuine estimates of losses a party might incur in the event of say, a contractor being late in achieving a particular milestone. They should not be set so high as to be punitive nor to frighten the other party. Nor should they be a blanket provision, covering a range of different breaches which, in reality, would have different financial implications on the other party. The inclusion of pre-determined liquidated damages in a contract helps the tendering party assess their risk in financial terms, as they know exactly what their liability would be in the event of a breach of contract. Liquidated damages clauses can therefore lead to a lower tender price, as the contractor is not taking a risk on what a court might decide if there is a dispute later. Liquidated damages are usually deducted from the interim payments to a contractor by the named contract manager or administrator and are calculated using the formula in the contract; they do not need to reflect actual losses. Liquidated damages are often capped at a maximum level to stop them running out of control; again, this can lead to lower tenders as overall liability for the related events is limited. The use of liquidated damages is classed as a breach of warranty and not a breach of condition, so the contract cannot be terminated as a result; the payments are made, and the contract continues.

To balance the risk between the parties, a contract should also include provisions to safeguard the contractor over delays they are not responsible for. There should, therefore, be conditions set for extending the completion dates to reflect this. This is why your change control process and delegated authorities need to reflect the contracts you have signed.

Your change control process and delegated authorities need to reflect the contracts you have signed

Understanding particular words in a contract

Different forms of contract often use different words to describe the same issue – for example, 'liquidated damages' and 'delay damages'. Seemingly innocent words can often take on very significant meanings, such as the word 'key'. Many contracts include 'key milestones' which, if missed, can incur liquidated damages. For this reason, you really do need to know what words mean in the context of the contract. Most contracts include a list of definitions and this should be your starting point. If using a standard form of contract, there might be a body of case law to define specific terms used in the contract.

The contract life cycle

The contract life cycle encompasses activities, starting with the identification of the need for a contract, through contract award, to the contract ending. Whilst there are many ways to describe a contract life cycle, it can be looked at as having two main phases, as shown in Figure 26.2.

The first phase, procurement, deals with verifying the need for a contract, deciding the appropriate contract strategy, selecting the supplier and agreeing to the

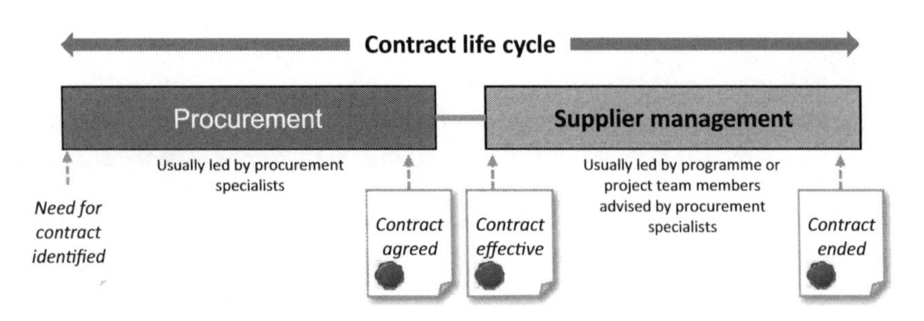

Figure 26.2 Typical contract life cycle

The contract life cycle comprises two parts. The first deals with verifying the need for a contract, deciding the contract strategy, selecting the supplier and agreeing to the contract. The second part deals with managing the contract itself.

contract. This is usually led by procurement or commercial specialists, with the business needs provided by other programme or project team members.

The second phase, supplier management, deals with managing the contract itself in terms of oversight, to ensure obligations are met. This second phase is normally led by the programme or project team members most associated with the work being carried out, supported by commercial advisors. The shift of accountability is important, as it is within the second phase that:

- shortfalls, errors and omissions in the contract are identified;
- poor commercial practices can lead to disputes, cost overruns or delays.

In both phases, overall responsibility rests with the most senior person with management accountability. For example, in the case of a contract for a programme, the programme sponsor would need to have ultimate decision-making authority within their own delegated authorities. Bear in mind that a supplier might have numerous contracts with your organization, and so it can get complicated; this is looked at later in the chapter.

Whilst the commercial team might be celebrating the signing of a contract, in business terms no value or benefit has been gained at that point in time (just costs and obligations!); benefits and value will only become apparent as the contract proceeds. The commercial team might be somewhat premature in their celebrations. On the other hand, a good contract, poorly administered by the programme or project team, can be wrecked through poor practice and inappropriate behaviours. For this reason, all managers associated with the administration of a contract should have a good understanding of the contract and a working knowledge of day-to-day commercial practice . . . and know when to ask for help.

For a transaction-based contract, the second phase can be very short, simply comprising confirmation that the goods have been received intact. For a relationship-based contract, however, this phase can cover a number of years.

Different words

In this book, I have used the term 'procurement' to cover the activities leading up to the contract being signed and 'supplier management' to cover the activities relating to carrying out the contract after it comes into effect. There are no commonly agreed upon definitions, and others include:

1 procurement, covering the period leading up to signature and then on to the end of the contract;
2 sourcing, instead of procurement;
3 contract management instead of supplier management.

I am sure there are other terms people use. Make sure, however, you understand the terms used in your organization or there could be misunderstanding over who is accountable for what, as the case study shows.

It's not my responsibility!

A large organization was unifying and rationalizing its processes and methods across all their divisions. One of the processes was for procurement. In that organization, the word 'procurement' covered the entire contract life cycle and the process users included procurement specialists as well as the line and project managers and their teams. During the reorganization, the newly recruited head of procurement refused to cover the supplier management processes on the basis of it being something 'his team' of procurement specialists was not accountable for. As most of the contracts were long term and based on relationships, this left a large gap in the organization's operating processes. It also meant that the people who were accountable for supplier monitoring and performance (who were not commercial specialists) had no written processes or guidance to help them; they had to create their own. This was a clear case of 'silo thinking' working against the best interests of the organization.

Procurement

It can be very complicated

When done well, procurement ensures products or services bought as part of resourcing the work or developing the outputs are of the appropriate quality, represent value for money and can be delivered within an acceptable level of risk. The path leading from the identification of a need for a contract to awarding the contract can be long and complicated. There is no single 'right route'; as you should have realized from reading this book, context matters. The following questions need to be answered.

- Should we do it ourselves, rather than ask a supplier?
- Which suppliers should be considered?
- Is a multi-step approach best, with pre-qualification of potential suppliers and subsequent filtering to produce a short-list?
- Should it be an open tender or other form of selection?
- What pricing model would be best? Fixed price, time and materials?
- How should payments to the supplier be made and on what basis?
- What form of contract should we use?
- Where are the risks?

On top of this, there are often statutory or regulatory restrictions which can limit an organization's choices. In many cases, funding agencies, such as development banks, impose conditions relating to the means of choosing a supplier and the form of contract to be used. Consequently, this work is usually undertaken by commercial specialists.

OJEU

OJEU stands for the Official Journal of the European Union and is the publication in which all tenders from the public sector, valued above a certain financial threshold according to EU legislation, must be published. The thresholds are set every two years and the legislation covers organizations that receive public money. Prior to Brexit, organizations in the UK such as local authorities, NHS Trusts, MOD, central government departments and educational establishments were all covered by this legislation. Around 2500 new notices are advertised every week; these include invitations to tender, prior information notices, qualification systems and contract award notices. In January 2018, the thresholds in the UK were:

- £118,133 for Central Government;
- £363,424 for Defence and Security;
- £181,302 for other contracting authorities;
- £65,630 for small Lots.

Understanding the business need and risk

For a contract that is part of a programme, the programme's context is the context for the contract. If a programme or part of a programme, such as a project, has been properly initiated, the business need should be clear in the brief. The 'why' should be a given, but the 'what' needs to be understood. Understanding what is needed comes about through the activities discussed in Chapter 24, which describes how to come up with a solution, bearing in mind any relevant constraints. As such, the feasibility and design activities need to take into account the commercial realities if a workable solution is to be achieved. This emphasizes the cross-functional nature of good programme and project management and the need for mixed teams. Once you have decided the organization cannot create the goods or provide the required service itself, sourcing the solution becomes the only option. For this reason, it is often necessary to look at a range of options and solutions before reaching a conclusion. You also need to check that what you want can, in reality, be provided by the market. Generally, markets fall into one of four categories:

Design activities need to take into account the commercial realities

- perfect competition: many buyers and sellers, none being able to influence prices;
- oligopoly: several large sellers who have some control over the prices;
- monopoly: single seller with considerable control over supply and prices;
- monopsony: a single buyer with considerable control over demand and prices.

Factors to consider are included in Workout 26.1, which shows the commercial specialist should, in this sense, be part of the design team. Having developed a good understanding of the market and any limitations, consider how risk should be apportioned between the parties. If you are asking a supplier to work for you, it is either because you do not have the in-house capacity or capability. In the former case, you are likely to have the expertise to understand the nature of the work. With the latter, however, you might be somewhat uninformed and need to employ consultants to fill that knowledge gap (another contract!). Many organizations try to put as much risk as possible on their suppliers, but often this proves futile and usually resulting in a higher price. If things go wrong, it is not necessarily just the suppler who will suffer. If a supplier fails, usually the other party fails too and that failure can, in terms of reputation, be more severe. Workout 4.3 uses one method for considering the relative strengths of parties in a contract.

A supplier failure of Olympic scale

G4S won a trophy contract worth £248m to provide 10,400 security guards for the London 2012 Olympic Games. Two weeks before the start of the games, however, G4S admitted not being able to meet its contractual commitments. The UK government had to step in, using the armed forces. Eventually, G4S took an £88m loss after paying a settlement for breach of contract. The Group Chief Executive, surprisingly, retained his role, but two high profile directors lost their jobs. If the government had been unable to fill the gap created by the failure of G4S to meet its obligations, the games might have had to be cancelled, with a severe damage to the reputation of the UK and its businesses. Some risks cannot truly be transferred, even if you have a contract!

Workout 26.1 – Reviewing the market

Take a situation where you need a supplier to provide a component of your solution, whether it is an asset or a service. Before starting to select suppliers consider the following.

1. How is the market structured? Consider the number and relative strength of buyers and sellers and degree of collusion among them, level and forms of competition, extent of product differentiation and ease of entry into and exit from the market
2. Are there organizations in the market capable of delivering what you need?
3. Bearing in mind market demand for similar services, has the market the capacity to deliver what is required for you and their other customers?
4. Is the market mature and hence prices and range of solutions relatively stable?
5. How competitive is the market? Are you likely to achieve value for money?
6. How secure is the market? Is delivery likely to be disrupted by external national or global issues? Are the suppliers themselves stable and likely to remain in business?

Deciding you sourcing strategy

Having understood the business needs and the wider market context, engage the market to verify your research and gain the views of potential suppliers. The advantage of such early engagement is that suppliers have an opportunity to understand your needs and can often influence the solution for the better. Be careful, however, to ensure that individual suppliers do not skew the contract requirements in their favour prior to any tendering, such as by suggesting specifications, which can only be fulfilled by their proprietary product. For effective procurement, prior to any tendering or selection the following need to be covered.

- Translate the business needs into contractual requirements. The rules for writing good requirements for a contract are the same as for doing the task in-house, except that any shortcomings are likely to be more obvious in the form of claims. See Chapter 24 for more on requirements.
- Decide what route to market you will use. For example, will it be open competitive tender, single supplier negotiation, design competition? Different industries have different customs and practices, but you need not always follow such customs. A lot can be learned by harnessing experience across a number of sectors.
- Decide the pricing model, including how risk is allocated. Risks are best allocated to those who can best manage them.
- Choose the form of contract you will use (see earlier).
- Set the criteria for evaluating suppliers. Many organizations are required to ensure that procurement is open and not subject to bias. For this reason, be very clear on the factors to be considered when coming to a decision.
- Set out the timescale for delivery of the contract obligations.

Workout 26.2 – Evaluating your suppliers' circumstances

Take any one of your suppliers, or prospective suppliers, and consider whether any of the following factors influence their ability to deliver their obligations under the proposed contract:

1. financial standing, stability, especially in terms of cash flow to sustain the business or any outstanding provisions for on-going debts or possible events;
2. prior delivery experience, in terms of time, cost and quality and performance record;
3. involvement in recent or on-going lawsuits, which might indicate their propensity for litigation;
4. ethical stance and whether it is supportive or contradictory to your own organization;
5. security in terms of maintaining commercial, data, physical and personal security, where relevant.

Do your selection criteria cover the items listed?

If you have doubts with one of your prospective or actual suppliers on any of the listed items, consider not inviting them to make an offer or, if they are already appointed, treat this as a risk and manage it accordingly (Chapter 23).

Making the contract

As discussed earlier, each contract should be designed to reflect the type and method of delivery and reliability of the supply chain. Its scope should include all necessary documentation and tools required for the operation of the service or product. If your strategy is right, this should follow when choosing the form of contract and actually drafting the detailed terms. Risks applicable to a contract should be identified and apportioned within the contract to the parties best placed to manage the risk and each party's liabilities and obligations should be clear. The contract should define how the supplier should be paid for delivering the requirement and take account of the:

Risks applicable to a contract should be identified and apportioned within the contract to the parties best placed to manage the risk

- risk appetite of both contracting parties and the risk allocation approach;
- level of scope definition and consider the extent to which the scope is expected to change;
- cost of potential future options.

You should be confident that those invited to participate can do what you need and you would be happy to work with any of them; this is why many procurements have a 'request for information' and/or 'pre-qualification' phases. You should also be very clear on how you will select a supplier before you ask for offers so that all the information you need is provided. Selection is usually made against a set of criteria comprising those which have to be complied with and those which enable differentiation between suppliers.

Having received offers from the prospective suppliers, it is now necessary to select which supplier you want to undertake the work. Evaluation criteria should be defined to enable you to differentiate between suppliers' offers and should consider both priced and unpriced factors. The objective is not usually to select the cheapest offer but to identify the most advantageous offer, including but not limited to:

- quality;
- deliverability;
- price;
- relevant capability, knowledge and skills;
- whole life costs;
- security;
- risk;
- ethics.

For extensive, long lasting contracts, evaluating the offers can require significant analysis to determine what the impact is on overall cost for different scenarios. In such cases, you will probably need to use the more advanced risk analysis methods discussed in Chapter 23, such as simulation, cost modelling, sensitivity analysis and scenario analysis. For example, one of your suppliers might be sourcing their materials from overseas and hence, depending on the payment model, changes in trade tariffs and exchange rates might be relevant, as could actual security of delivery. In other examples, the actual volume of a service might not be predictable, and some suppliers might be more expensive for lower volumes than others or charge a premium for higher volumes, even if it costs them far less. Remember, 'fair' is whatever you agree to!

Supplier management

Mobilizing the contract

Build relationships – we are all people

The contract has been awarded and now the real work with your supplier begins. The procurement specialists have had their celebration, nursed their hangovers, stepped back and are working on the next procurement. Unfortunately, that is what often happens, leaving the incumbent manager, who might not have even been involved in the procurement, to do the best they can. Contract award is often the trigger for the management of the contract to pass from a commercial specialist to a team manager, project manager or programme manager within whose scope the contract is a part. In some cases, a contract can be very extensive, and a number of people might manage a part of it, for example, on a geographic basis and the handover could be to a number of people. As with any handover, the risks can be high, and relationships need to be built between those who have to put the contract into effect.

The opening weeks or months of a new contract are vital to how the contract will run in practice. Get this right from the start and the contract will progress far more smoothly than if it is hurried or ignored. Like all human activity, the critical element is building the relationships between those who will be working together, often over a long period of time. There needs to be an atmosphere of mutual trust and shared objectives. That is not to say people should always agree, but that they respect the views of the other party as being authentic. Underlying this, there should be a common understanding of each party's contract obligations.

Down to earth with a thump

A multi-billion-dollar supplier of leading-edge capabilities in 'software as a service', 'platform as a service', 'infrastructure as a service' and 'data as a service' was in negotiation with a major communications company with whom they already had a relationship and which they wanted to extend. The fact finding and requirements meetings were held over a number of weeks at the supplier's offices, with experts from both companies going through the business needs, leading to a genuine, common understanding. The meeting rooms were comfortable and those involved supplied with coffee, tea, soft drinks and an extensive buffet lunch every day. The week after the contract was signed, the communications company team arrived to find a different group of people to work with and were told there was no budget for refreshments, and they should bring their own. The change from pre-award to post-award was very marked and the team had to effectively start again in building an understanding of the business needs and in developing the working relationships. They wondered what they had signed up for.

Decide how you will work together in practice

Because of the number of people who might be involved after contract award, it is unreasonable to assume everyone has read the contract and understands its implications. Even 'plain English' contracts can include obscure but vital obligations which could be missed or misunderstood. For this reason, on many large contracts a set of roles,

Processes should be put in place to present the commonly used parts of the contract

responsibilities and processes should be put in place to present the commonly used parts of the contract in a practical form for day-to-day use. This is often called a **contract management plan** and should include:

- a listing of the contract management team, including their roles and responsibilities;
- contract risk management approach;
- how contract contingency should be held and when it may be approved for use;
- the processes and tools required to support contract administration, monitor delivery and manage performance.

As with all documentation, the contract management plan can be a physical document, a set of documents, a set of linked web pages or a mixture of all three.

It is important to recognize which elements of the contract management plan are limited by the contract and which relate to the internal business of the contracted party. For example, approval of contract contingency is likely to be solely the business of the contracted party and does not concern the other party. How a person runs their business is their concern. Other such activities might be how to:

- drive continuous improvement;
- validate invoices;
- track costs;
- measure benefits realization.

On the other hand, many processes can arise as a result of the contract itself and would impact both parties. In effect, key elements of the contract can be translated into processes which, if people follow them, ensure compliance with certain contract provisions, without the need for them to read and interpret the contract for themselves. Such activities could include:

- the conduct of meetings between the parties (purpose of meetings, who attends, how frequent, quorum, authority of attendees, approval and status of minutes);
- tracking delivery against contractual obligations;
- providing instructions to the supplier;
- issuing formal notices (such for possible delays or change notes);
- managing contract disputes;
- monitoring operational performance, assuring quality;
- controlling contract changes.

In these cases, it is essential to agree the processes and interfaces with the other party. Often a contract uses the phrase, 'in agreement with', and it is often these clauses that need to be represented in a process. The contract says 'what' must be done, but an agreed upon process should define 'how' to do it in practice. This implies the parties need to start working together to agree to such

The parties need to start working together to agree to such practicalities.

practicalities. This helps build a common understanding of the contract and shapes the relationship before anything contentious arises.

Notice that some of the 'internal' business processes can impact the contract driven processes. For example, issuing a change note to a supplier might require prior approval to use contract contingency. For this reason, the processes need to be designed as a complete system rather than set up on an ad-hoc basis. Processes developed in an ad-hoc way tend to have loose ends which can prove expensive to sort out or even lead to an inadvertent breach of contract.

Formal contract roles

You need to be familiar with the roles and terms in any contracts you are working on. They are usually capitalized in the contract to denote their importance. I have given some examples from different forms of contract to show the variety of terms used.

The customer is referred to by different names in different contracts, for example:

- Client – NEC4;
- Employer – FIDIC.

The contract administrator role title differs between forms of contract. The details of the role also differ, as they need to reflect the particular form. Usually they are part of the customer's organization, but in some cases, they are independent (such as architects or consulting engineers) and subject to a separate contract. Contract administrators are always required to act impartially, regardless of their relationship to the parties to the contract they are administering.

- Contract administrator: JCT;
- Project Manager: NEC4;
- The 'Engineer' (or Engineer's Representative): FIDIC.

Mobilization can take a long time

Translating the contract into practical activities is only a small part of mobilization for a contract. Many contracts are managed as programmes or projects and so everything that applies to initiating a programme or project also applies to a contract. The contract only exists because you cannot do the work yourself. Context, scale and complexity are everything. Mobilizing a single consultant can be done in days, but mobilizing a major infrastructure project can take many months. In some instances, the mobilization activities are significant enough to be run as a project within a programme. The obvious examples are:

- mobilizing for construction, where the site has to be taken over and prepared, site offices built, plant procured and wayleaves and planning permissions for temporary works applied for;
- mobilizing for an outsource, where not only the facilities and people need to be found but also a plan for taking on services from an incumbent suppler might be needed.

Unfortunately, there is often too much pressure from the customer's senior management to see visible progress on the 'real work'

Unfortunately, there is often too much pressure from the customer's senior management to see visible progress on the 'real work' and, as a result, mobilization planning can be skimped and time scales compressed. This often leads to the contract going into a schedule breach almost from the start. Time lost here is seldom caught up unless you have specifically added float into your schedule to cover the risk. That, however, costs the supplier money, puts the offer price up and, as a result, the supplier might lose the contract to a competitor who is less principled. Again, it comes down to relationships and mutual trust.

Don't lose the procurement team's experience

So where are the commercial specialists? Hopefully they would not have stepped back fully. As they were involved in the intricacies of procurement, they are a vital source of information and can help smooth mobilization to ensure the contract management plan faithfully reflects the contract. In addition, they can act as relationship brokers, making introductions and providing a stakeholder analysis to help the incoming team find their way through the people maze (see Chapter 25).

Why are you already three months late?

It was three months into the contract and the customer's and supplier's representatives were ready for their newly instituted weekly site meeting. The site was in an isolated location 6,000 miles from the supplier's base and 3500 from the customer representative's base.

Customer's representative: "Would you mind explaining why you are already three months late?"

Supplier's representative: "Ah. We have been hardly working."

The customer's representative passed the dictionary across the table, open at 'hardly'.

Supplier's representative: *Laughing*. "I have inadvertently been truthful! I meant we have been working hard . . . but not on site."

Customer's representative: *Also laughing*. "Could you explain that please?"

Supplier's representative: "Mobilizing to this location is risky and therefore we are doing most of the equipment checks as some pre-assembly prior to leaving our home port, rather than here. Our ships leave in about one month and within two months we should be on, or slightly ahead of schedule. The risk of equipment failure or missing materials is also minimized."

The supplier had thought through the risks very carefully, bearing in mind the isolated location and the time it took to deal with any missing equipment or materials. This was exemplary. What they had failed to do was tell the customer representative that they had decided to move the checks from site to their own base, over 6,000 miles away. As a result, the customer's team had been mobilized to the wrong location. In this case, this was easily remedied, as there was time to relocate the quality team.

Putting the contract into effect

Having mobilized the contract and agreed to the practicalities of how the parties will work together, it is time for the supplier to actually start delivering. This is when the contract management plan (or whatever you choose to call it) is put into effect. In practice, the activities fall into two types, those related to:

- supplier performance and delivery;
- contract administration.

Supplier performance and delivery

The work associated with managing suppliers' performance is similar to managing your own performance, except that you have to do it within the constraints of a contract. Delivery of goods and services need to be managed and performance and quality monitored to ensure you get what you expect from the contract. Where performance is unlikely to or does not meet the requirements of the contract, preventative and/or corrective action should be taken to remedy the situation, such as through formal notices or by invoking a performance improvement plan. Remember, such actions have to be carried out within the constraints of the contract, or in agreement with the supplier. Sometimes a customer has little leverage on a supplier, apart from terminating the contract as they have no powers to investigate, intervene or even help. Termination is always damaging to both parties. Some contracts include clauses to enable a customer to audit or review the supplier's work, allowing extensive powers of disclosure. This ensures the customer is well informed and can also form a basis for helping a failing supplier. Unfortunately, reviews and audits can be perceived as something to be avoided or scraped through (like an academic exam) rather than an opportunity for improvement. Again, it is all about attitude, trust and relationships.

If a customer behaves in a heavy-handed way when exercising their powers of disclosure, they are unlikely to find a supplier cooperative. On the other hand, if the review or audit is focussed on real issues with a view to helping the supplier resolve them, the supplier is likely to be more supportive.

Any contract lasting for an extensive period needs to be reviewed periodically to make sure it still reflects the parties' relationship, current risks, market conditions and the organization's business needs. The global, political, economic context is always shifting, and sometimes a contract is no longer fit for purpose, or it might be delivering something that is no longer needed. These risks should have been highlighted during the procurement phase and contract clauses inserted to deal with such eventualities. Unfortunately, 20–20 foresight is not always possible, nor do identified risks play out within the expected boundaries. It can be tough, but that is why we need effective business leaders for our portfolios and programmes. At some point, risks cannot be contained within a single project or even programme. Risk has to be elevated to portfolio or organizational level. As shown in Part III on business portfolio management, an organization can afford some failures but not for everything to fail.

A clear case for contract termination?

The software supplier's product had failed performance testing . . . dramatically. It simply wasn't scalable. The supplier was a small, specialist company and had previously introduced the software as a stand-alone application in individual organizations. The software, under the new contract, was, however, required to operate over many hundreds of locations from a central server. Despite this, the functionality was exemplary, and no other product came near to it in capability. Under the terms of the contract, the failure of performance testing was a material breach of contract, which could lead to termination and, in turn, bankruptcy for this supplier. Termination would, however, have left the customer with a problem: no supplier at all and being in breach of their own contract with their customer. Rather than terminate the contract, the customer provided its own expertise to redesign the supplier's product such that it could work at scale. The contract was revised to reflect the new approach and the software was launched with only a short delay. The result was a classic win-win that management theory says we should always look for in commercial relationships.

Contract administration

Many people shy away from anything with the term 'administration' in it; just look at Chapter 23 on information management for an example; information management includes information relating to contracts. Contract administration is necessary to ensure the terms of the contract are upheld by all parties, obligations are fulfilled, payments made, contract changes formalized, disputes managed to a conclusion and records kept. Without effective contract administration, you are leaving yourself open to significant claims and, if you end up in court, the loss of any case taken against you. Remember, as a commercial organization you are presumed to be competent at contract management in fact, not just image. You have to 'be' good, not just 'look' good.

If contract administration is treated as a chore to do after hours when the 'real work' is finished, you are on the wrong track. Contract administration should be encompassed in your processes and good practices. In other words, by people doing their jobs properly, they automatically deal with the 'administrative' aspect of a contract. This is why translating contract clauses into processes as part of mobilization is so important. Finally, ensure the activities and milestones required as part of a contract are added into the detailed programme, project or work package plans as part of progressive planning; it is almost impossible to add them all from the start. In this way (always assuming you actually manage your plan), they will not be forgotten and the linkage between the work activities is not lost. From the plan, you should be able to see every contractual delivery, milestone and payment point. If you are using good planning software, you should also be able to filter the plan to show just the contract related accountabilities, activities and milestones and assess the contractual implications of any slippage or other variances.

It sounds like a lot to do, and often it is. Remember, no one is forcing you to have a contract with anyone; it is simply a means for you to achieve your aims, and neglecting it is actually neglecting your own business interests. If, however, you have to prioritize your time, make sure you concentrate on two aspects:

- paying the supplier what they are due;
- keeping track of changes.

An unpaid supplier is an unhappy supplier

An unpaid supplier is an unhappy supplier, and unhappy suppliers can become difficult to work with. Keep tight control over contract related expenditures and make sure your supplier is paid in a timely manner, in accordance with the contract. You might not agree with the detail of every invoice, but most good contracts for long-term relationships have interim payment mechanisms, where the supplier can be paid in such circumstances (interim payment) but the actual amount is not finalized until the work (or section of the work) is completed. This keeps things moving and stops minor disputes from escalating into major stand-offs.

Contract changes can run out of control, leading to cost overruns and delays. For that reason, you need to ensure that:

- each change is necessary, or beneficial;
- the process used reflects the contract;
- there is an audit trail of contractual changes for audit and continuity/handover purposes;
- the relevant people approve the changes prior to implementation; and
- evidence is retained in case of a later dispute,

Contract transition

When the contract involves taking on a service from an incumbent supplier, mobilization needs to be planned to take into account the outgoing supplier's transition plan.

Contract transition ensures, in cases where a service is passed from one supplier to another, that a complete and smooth handover is conducted, with no unplanned interruption to service.

Transition goals and responsibilities need to be defined, agreed and activities allocated to the responsible parties, including, but not limited to:

- data handover;
- supplier staff transition;
- contingency plans.

These need to be included in the respective contracts. The transition from one supplier to another is not always easy to manage because the outgoing supplier has little to lose, as they have already lost the next contact. Incentives and/or liquidated damages might need to be included to make sure they fulfil their part of the work. The incoming supplier will not usually be willing to take the blame for any failings in the handover and is likely to claim compensation from the customer.

Contract exit

Contact exit happens either when the contract scope is completed or when the contract is terminated early. Early termination of a contract should be a last resort only enacted after other provisions for the delivery of the contract, including contractual remedies for improving performance, have been exhausted. When early termination provisions are enacted, all measures to minimize the cost and impact of the termination should be considered. On contract exit, all information systems should be updated, staff and facilities (if any) reassigned and the contract documentation archived in accordance with the organization's information retention policy and procedures.

Contract exit is very similar to closing a project, and many of the activities described there are relevant. However, for contract exit, the contract needs to be followed scrupulously, ensuring formal notices are delivered, final certification is carried out (if any) and final payments are made. This often involves settling outstanding claims and balancing them against liquidated damages. In some cases, this can still be happening many months after practical closure.

Strategic supplier management

So far, everything in this chapter has looked at individual contracts. In practice, few business portfolios or major programmes have a single contract associated with them; they are likely to have many tens or (for portfolios) even hundreds of contracts. If this is your situation, you have an opportunity to make the management of your contracts more effective and efficient by:

- sharing management approaches across the contracts;
- leveraging your buying power where similar products and services are required across the business portfolios or programmes;
- building special relationships with suppliers who you value.

This requires you to segment your contractual spend along a number of different dimensions, known as categories, the most common being the:

- type of product or service being provided;
- value of the contract to the organization;
- risk associated with the contract.

Categories can include any characteristic which helps analysis and decision making with respect to how your contracts are managed.

Type of product

Segmentation by type of product or service enables you to determine if it is worth creating in-house expertise on using specific forms of contract and model contract management plans. By doing this centrally, you can save each contract team having to decide this for themselves each time. Naturally, this calls for a 'central team' or individual who is accountable for that work (often called a category manager) and the benefits to the organization as a whole have to be significant enough to warrant such an overhead. Example types are office supplies, technology, professional services, facilities and utilities. The specific types which are procured frequently are the candidates for category management if the total cost is significant.

Value

By looking at value, you are focussing on what the contract is worth to you. Value does not necessarily relate to the contract price and is probably the most difficult to pin down. Some organizations never do and use the contract price as a surrogate measure for value.

Risk

Risk is associated with value. The key question is, "What will happen to my business if this goes wrong?" By looking at value and risk, you can make sure that the effort you put into procurement and supplier management is appropriate and proportionate, whether by category or on individual contracts. Intuitively, it makes sense to spend more time and expertise on the high value, riskier contracts but actually deciding which ones these are requires some analysis. In other words, ensuring the form of contract and contract management plan not only reflects the category of contract but is also tailored to reflect the value and risk of each contract. Always remember that whilst you can theoretically transfer risk to a supplier, if things do go wrong, your reputation might suffer, no matter what the contract says.

Like any management activity, you need to be clear on what you want to get out of category management, as that determines the work necessary and the relationships you will need to build. The commonest is to make savings on contractual spend, but benefits can go far beyond this. This is normally documented in a category strategy (see Workout 26.3), supported by a plan.

Category management

Category management is a strategic approach which focuses resources on specific areas of spend, enabling you to fully leverage procurement decisions on behalf of the whole organization. The results can be significantly greater than traditional transactional-based purchasing methods. Best-in-class procurement organizations are increasingly turning to category management as an effective way to drive greater value and growth for the business. A structured category management approach not only helps generate higher savings but also improves supplier performance, mitigates supply risks and drives innovation and continuous improvement.

Workout 26.3 – Category strategy

Analyze your overall contract spend and identify possible categories. For each category:

- determine your historic category spend;
- estimate possible future demand. You might need a few scenarios if your future is unclear;
- determine the opportunities which could be realized as part of a category plan;
- identify who you need to talk to and gain agreement from (stakeholders). How will you go about this? See Chapter 25 for more on stakeholder management;
- determine, based on this rough analysis, whether the management of particular categories will be worthwhile, taking into account the effort needed. If so, undertake a fuller analysis, taking specialist advice.

Segmenting your suppliers

Having looked at categories of spend, determine which suppliers you work with most and the total amount of money you spend with them.

Organizations can segment their suppliers in different ways, depending on what they want to achieve. One useful approach is to use the following:

- basic suppliers, where there are many alternatives and risk to you of an order not being met are low;
- approved suppliers, where alternatives exist and the risk to you of an order not being met can be contained;
- key suppliers, where some alternatives exist but changing supplier might expose you to higher risk in the event of an order not being met;
- strategic suppliers are critical to you staying in business or, if you are in the public or voluntary sectors, maintain your service.

Notice how a supplier is categorized is dependent on the impact on your organization in the event of a delivery failure. Contract price might be irrelevant. This way of categorizing contracts enables you to decide how much commercial management effort you need to apply. This in turn can help you decide which processes to use and what experience the person managing the supplier needs to have. Clearly, strategic suppliers should have more attention than basic suppliers.

Relationships between customers and strategic suppliers need to be collaborative and of mutual benefit, aimed at:

- reducing risk to both parties;
- securing supply, so you can rely on it;
- improving operational efficiency for both parties;
- improving value for money for you and for your supplier's suppliers;
- further improving the relationship.

For example, some customers pay slightly higher prices for some goods and services so that they can stabilize the supply chain and rely on it. What use is a cheaper product if it isn't available when you need it? Getting the mix right is not always easy.

Managing contracts collectively on a supplier by supplier basis requires a certain amount of organization. Figure 26.3 shows an example where Supplier A has multiple contracts within Programmes 1 and 2 and for Department 3. Each contract would need a contract manager, and each programme and department has a lead to ensure a consistent approach within their areas of accountability. At portfolio (or organization level), there is a strategic relationship management owner accountable for the overall relationship and harnessing of any synergies or buying power. This overall owner is the primary contact between the portfolio and the supplier and, as such, deals with any escalated issues in the interests of the wider organization and maintaining a beneficial relationship. Naturally, the contract managers and strategic relationship management leads would deal with all day-to-day activities with their remits.

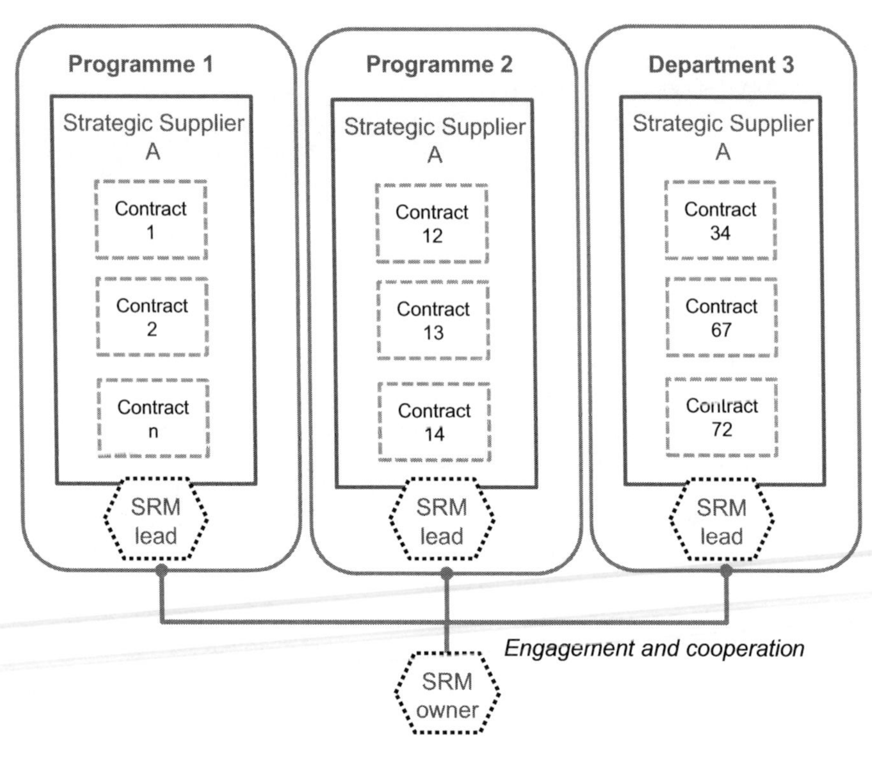

Figure 26.3 Example of strategic supplier management

Supplier A has multiple contracts for Programmes 1 and 2 and for Department 3, each of these has a lead to ensure a consistent approach within their areas of accountability. At portfolio (or organization level), there is an owner who is accountable for the overall relationship with the supplier and for harnessing any synergies and buying power.

Avoid confusing your categories!

When identifying your categories and suppliers, use different approaches so it is clear whether you are talking about a category or a suppler.

Use plain English and self-evident names rather than numbers or letters, as people can forget which way round numbers go: for example, is a tier 1 supplier more important than a tier 4 supplier? It depends on your definitions, and different organizations take a different view. Similarly, it might be clear to you that a 'gold supplier' is more important than a bronze supplier, but what does that mean? I would argue people would intuitively understand what a 'key supplier' is, as opposed to a 'silver supplier', even if they have the same definition.

Workout 26.4 – What sort of supplier?

Look at each of the suppliers you use most and ask yourself:

- what is their level of involvement in your business?
- what product or service are they providing and to what degree?
- what is their impact do they have on your core business?
- is this relationship mutually beneficial?
- if they ceased trading tomorrow, what would happen to your business?

If they seem critical to your business, ask yourself:

- what steps you taking to expand the relationship?
- what steps they are taking to expand the relationship?
- is there potential for a more formal partnership of some sort?

Notice these last questions all infer the need for a relationship between you and the supplier and the more critical the supplier, the deeper that relationship needs to be.

Also, look through your supplier's eyes:

- how critical is your business to them?
- what damage would be done to their business if you terminated the contract or you ceased trading tomorrow?

Some customer supplier relationships can be very unbalanced, and that can influence how you want to build the partnership, or even if you want to.

PART VI

IMPLEMENTING THE FRAMEWORK

Whoever wishes to foresee the future must consult the past.

NICCOLO MACHIAVELLI, 1469–1527

In Part VI, I will look at what you need to consider to start using the concepts outlined in this book and its companion, *The Project Workout*.

- **Harness the power of matrix management.**
- **Decide what specialist and administrative support is needed.**
- **Integrate finance tools with your other management tools.**
- **Define what publicly available standards and methods you will base your approach on.**
- **Build up your capability in steps, based on good practice; consolidate before moving on.**

How to use Part VI

Part VI takes you through a series of topics which are essential to implementing a portfolio, programme and project approach in your organization. The workouts in Part VI are designed to help you understand and consider what your options are if you want to put this book into practice. They include ideas from a range of industries and organizations, demonstrating the 'art of the possible'. I can't prescribe what is right for you. As we learned in Part I, everything needs to suit its context, and each set of circumstances is different. If yours is a large organization, you'll probably find little is consistent among the various departments, adding to your change challenge. Remember to use the rest of this book, especially Chapter 25, on change management, to keep you on the right track.

27

Supporting the management of portfolios, programmes and projects

Some organizations are well on their way to managing themselves 'out of their functional boxes'. Most are not.

"Great things are not done by impulse, but by a series of small things brought together."

GEORGE ELIOT, 1819–1880

- **Decide what roles are needed to run your business.**
- **Determine what support the senior role holders need.**
- **Design your support office to serve the needs of senior management.**
- **Make the names of your offices self-evident.**

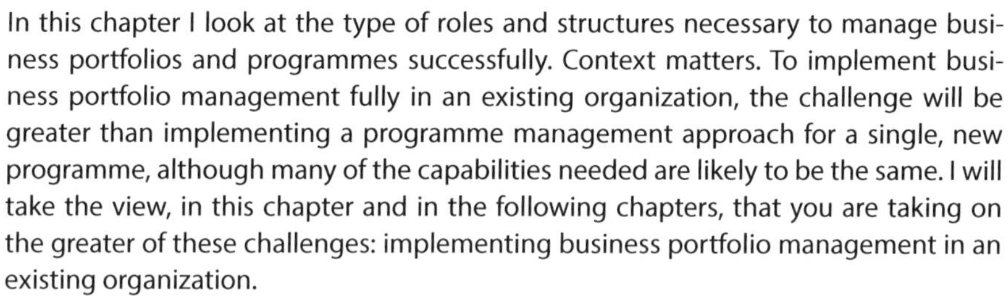

In this chapter I look at the type of roles and structures necessary to manage business portfolios and programmes successfully. Context matters. To implement business portfolio management fully in an existing organization, the challenge will be greater than implementing a programme management approach for a single, new programme, although many of the capabilities needed are likely to be the same. I will take the view, in this chapter and in the following chapters, that you are taking on the greater of these challenges: implementing business portfolio management in an existing organization.

As we saw in Chapter 2, putting this book into practice means you will need to consider the:

- processes and methods required to ensure work is undertaken consistently;
- structures and accountabilities so everyone knows what they are accountable for and who they are accountable to;
- systems, applications and tools required to undertake the work effectively and efficiently;
- culture and behaviours which will either 'make it or break it'.

These should not be treated in isolation, as each will affect the others, as shown previously in Figure 2,2.

Flipping from vertical to horizontal

The aim is to be able deploy people anywhere in the organization where they can, due to their mix of skills and competences, add the greatest value. Functional and departmental barriers will need to be broken down to the extent that the word 'cross-functional' becomes unnecessary. In effect, the purely cost-centre based, functional structure, which was so important in the 'old days', becomes secondary to the value driven business processes and change projects which work across it. In such an environment, reorganization, as a means of responding to problems, becomes less necessary (now what are the new executives going to do to prove they have arrived?).

The power base of the leaders of vertical functions was that they controlled the people, the budgets and decisions within their respective domains. Often the decisions were ones which, ideally, should have been taken on an organization-wide basis, but often were not. As discussed in Chapter 3, if the organization has programmes or projects crossing the functions, the power of the programme or project managers was often weaker than the functional directors.

The power bases of value-driven agile organizations are associated more with the roles of people and groups than their job titles or position in a departmental hierarchy. Consequently, the important structures will be those associated with sponsorship and decision making; these are the activities which will determine the future shape of the organization. They will be more associated with directing and coaching than managing.

The power bases of value-driven agile organizations are associated more with the roles of people and groups than their job titles

'Direction' should be horizontal, across whole organizations and not just vertical parts of it. Of course, every function needs a 'person at the top' to ensure work undertaken is of the right standard, that people are happy, and the 'architectures' are robust. However, because someone is an exceptional people manager or gifted technical expert does not automatically bring the breadth of knowledge, skills or competence to direct a corporation, or even the ambition to be a director! The corporate world is full of people promoted beyond their levels of competence through no fault of their own.

Some organizations are well on their way to managing themselves 'out of their functional boxes'. Most are not. The decrease in importance of functional hierarchy is not going to happen by decree. It has its place and its uses. Much of the day-to-day work in many organizations is ideally suited to a departmental approach provided the hand-offs and process flows are efficient and uninterrupted. Problems and limitations become most apparent when it comes to change. Before you loosen the reins of traditional cost centre management, you need to build alternative management frameworks and systems. Do not 'fly blind'. Once in place, they will be so useful that the old hierarchies will become less relevant.

Seamless reorganization

An organization ran itself on a full matrix. It knew all its costs both by cost centre and project and activity. The structure was stable for many years, but the emergence of new services and a more unified approach to the market required a reorganization of its departments. This took about three months to put in place. However, financial reporting and work continued as usual as nearly everyone was working to a set of roles relating to prescribed accountabilities. Although there were no departments for a time, it made little difference in day-to-day work or reporting. They were already used to working across boundaries.

You need a matrix

A delegate at a conference said they had found moving to a business portfolio management approach very difficult and that it just created havoc. I asked her to describe what happened. It seems they reorganized the entire company on a cross-functional basis and dismantled the former departmental structure. No wonder it failed. They hadn't instituted matrix management but simply created a different silo structure, so had none of the mechanisms for building in the flexibility a properly constructed matrix provides.

Workout 27.1 – Can you reorganize and maintain visibility, accountability and control?

If you dismantle the functional structure of your organization for, say, four months, in whole or in part, would you be able to maintain operational management visibility, control and reporting during the change period?

If not, what are the blockages? These blockage are clues to where your matrix is lacking.

Leadership – from the top and the side

If you are serious about business portfolio management, you need to realize that it does not run itself. It needs leadership to establish its profile and enforce the accountabilities. The opportunity might have been recognized by a few middle-management enthusiasts in various parts of the business and they might even get as far as agreeing some common methods and practices for running projects. However, that is not enough to reap the full rewards. The senior management team has to want to do this; after all they are accountable for running the business.

The senior management team has to want to do this; after all they are accountable for running the business.

Cost centres will still be needed after the new approach has been implemented, so it is not necessary to demolish any part of your organization. Keep it running as it is and then layer the horizontal structures over the top. There is probably a weak matrix at the moment, so you will not make matters worse. Once the horizontal structures and tools are in place, run them in parallel to ensure the horizontal management reports give the information required and do not conflict with your vertical reports.

If this is to work, there must be a common set of processes for the horizontal structures, and people need to be in place to design and manage these. This means having roles for the following:

- top level accountability for the adoption and direction of the full environment across the whole organization, preferably reporting directly to the CEO, deputy CEO or COO. I call this a **business portfolio management director** and provide a typical set of accountabilities in the following section;
- specific accountability for the operational architecture (accountabilities, process, systems and culture). I often refer to this person as **business portfolio design authority** and provide a typical set of accountabilities in the following section.

The former should be an established leader in the organization and could undertake the role together with other accountabilities. The latter is likely to be a specialist and full-time role, supported by a team to cover the range of activities needed.

Always check your stakeholders continue to support you

Business portfolio management director

The business portfolio management director is accountable to the chief executive officer (or equivalent) for ensuring business change is planned, directed and managed in an effective and efficient way using appropriate portfolio, programme and project management techniques. This includes:

- championing good value business and benefits-driven culture;
- introducing, maintaining and improving common management frameworks, processes and methods, including for business planning, project selection and project authorization;

- creating an environment in which programme and project sponsors, managers and teams are developed and recognized for their skills;
- recommending changes to senior management to improve the effectiveness and efficiency for delivering business change;
- providing independent reviews of projects.

Once the new way of working is established, this role should be subsumed into the chief operating officer's accountabilities as, after all, the chief operating officer is responsible for how the organization operates.

Business portfolio design authority

The business portfolio design authority is accountable to the business portfolio management director for acting as guardian for the organization's 'best practice' methods, processes, tools, systems and templates for authorizing and undertaking portfolios, programmes and projects. In particular:

- developing the processes, methods and tools required for portfolio, programme and project management;
- updating, supporting and obtaining user feedback (including lessons learned) on the project environment and future developments;
- developing and communicating changes to the environment;
- ensuring that the management frameworks and associated controls are in place and used throughout the organization;
- preparing and leading briefings on the management frameworks and their use;
- ensuring the availability of a consistent and complete range of training and development;
- ensuring recruitment and selection tools and processes are available for portfolio, programme and project management related appointments;
- ensuring that the processes interface at a high level with other core processes within the organization;
- providing consulting, coaching and facilitation.

Roles should not be designed in isolation

When designing roles and accountabilities, check that they are mutually compatible. Accountability cannot be designed in isolation but should be defined in relation to the other accountabilities with which it interfaces. Never design an accountability which undermines another. For example, notice the business portfolio management director is not accountable for benefit realization as that sits with the respective business portfolio sponsors (see Chapters 4 and 5). In the accountability descriptions given in this book I have taken the view that accountability for delivery and benefit realization pass through the business portfolio-programme-project chain, but that the methods are owned, for the total organization, by the business portfolio management director.

PMOs or support offices – who supports whom on what?

An organization needs to support its people in undertaking their roles, especially senior roles, where they need to be focussed on their job rather than the administration which sustains it. In addition, they cannot be expected to be experts at everything they are accountable for and need to have trusted and reliable people to advise them. This brings us to the subject of 'PMOs'.

What is a PMO?

What exactly is a 'PMO' and what should it do in relation to business portfolio management? PMO is a three-letter acronym which people often use so loosely that, on its own, it can be meaningless. Here are a few variations of 'PMO' that I have come across:

PMO is a three-letter acronym which people often use so loosely that, on its own, it can be meaningless.

- project management office;
- programme (program) management office;
- portfolio management office;
- enterprise project management office;
- strategic project management office.

There are many more variations and a number of these include the word 'support', such as 'project support office' and 'project support'.

PMOs have evolved from dealing with administrative aspects to taking on an increasingly important role in ensuring the consistency of governance (especially decision making processes), promoting best practice, managing risk and finances. The people who design and run such offices are specialists in their own right and can have an extraordinary impact on an organization's business performance. For this reason, some now see the term 'support' as demeaning or trivializing the role, even though, in plain English, it simply means 'giving assistance to'.

Whilst many proprietary methods define a 'PMO' role, they often have different purposes, and hence activities associated with them also differ. As with many project management related topics, there is no single, commonly agreed definition or approach; create your own, drawing on whatever experience is available (including this book!).

There is no single, commonly agreed definition or approach;

I find the easiest way to approach this is to:

- assume such an office has no accountabilities of its own;
- decide which roles the office supports;

- look at which aspects of the supported roles a support office can facilitate or add value to.

Then look at the discrete accountabilities associated with each supported role and decide which will benefit from a support service. This will give a list of what the support office needs to do. Workout 27.2 provides a step by step approach. You might find the list is very short and focussed. It might, however, be very wide ranging; if so, consider if a single office is the best way to provide the service. It might be better to design a network of support offices, each supporting different roles, but which in total provides the services you require.

How the offices undertake the support services very much depends on:

- whether the aspects of the roles supported are optional or mandatory;
- the overall culture of the organization.

If the activities are optional, the support office will need to rely on 'pull' influencing styles in order to move forward. If the aspect being supported is mandated by policy, then assertion can be used: see Chapter 5 on leadership and influencing styles. If the organization culture is loose, allowing senior managers a high degree of freedom in how they carry out their accountabilities, the support office is unlikely to be accepted if it takes a very prescriptive approach – in which case, you could use your finance department as the tough guys.

Finally, you need to determine the required competencies and volume of work (throughput) the offices need to cope with so that you can decide on staffing levels. For instance, will a central office supply all services to everyone? Will it expect some services to be provided by 'local' offices or expect some accountabilities to 'serve themselves' whilst using tools and methods which are centrally owned?

The key roles to be supported

In Chapter 4, I proposed a set of accountabilities for business portfolio management. which can be used to draw up an accountability model for the entire organization (Figure 27.1). Notice, I have added the accountability for a business portfolio management director, which I introduced at the start of this chapter. Against each of these accountabilities you can list the services you feel need to be provided in your organization and the extent to which that service is supplied. By doing this, it soon becomes evident that the needs of the accountabilities are very distinct, and hence the roles of the support offices are different. For example, supporting a project manager in planning and risk management is totally different from supporting a business portfolio manager on business strategy and planning.

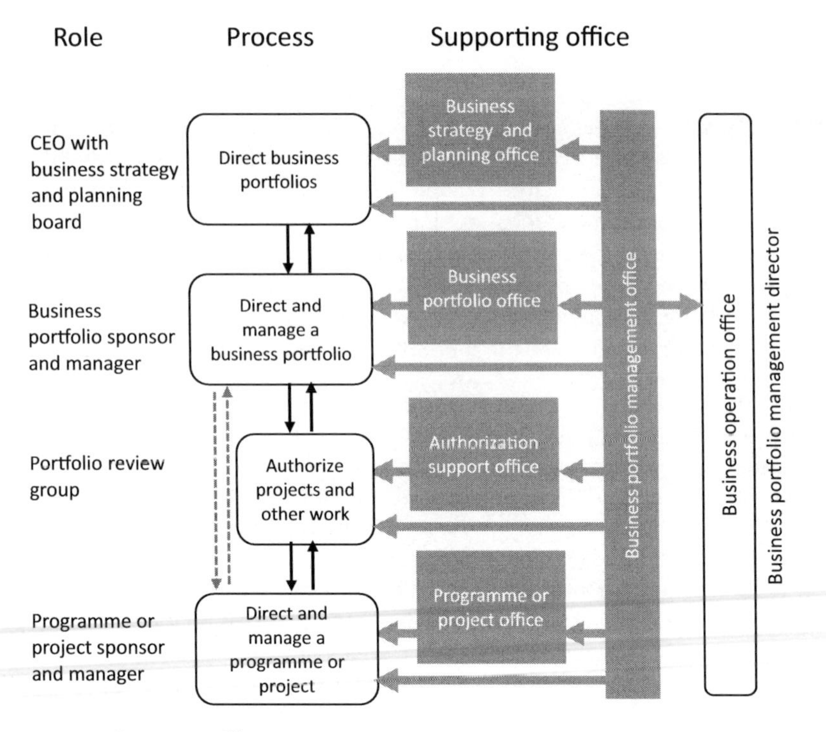

Figure 27.1 Support offices

When deciding which support offices, you need, think first of the roles which need supporting. Then decide what aspects of the roles would benefit from a support service and the extent to which that service needs to be supplied. Then consider location; does the support need to be local to those being supported? Look to combine office where it makes sense.

What should I call the offices?

There is no set standard for naming support offices. What the United States calls a 'Project Office', the UK calls 'Project Support'. One person's PMO is another person's enterprise programme office. You will find every conceivable combination of the words 'programme', 'project', 'support', 'management', office' and 'organization'. Where possible, name the offices after the entity, role, or group it supports. Hence, a 'project support office' supports a 'project', a 'programme support office' supports a programme and 'business portfolio office' supports a business portfolio. If an office supports a particular programme or project, name the office after that programme or project, e.g., 'Titan Project Support Office'. You will not believe how many phone calls I used to receive from '*the* project office' with little clue as to which of about 40 were calling! You will, of course, have to fight your way

Where possible, name the offices after the entity, role, or group it supports.

through the 'project' versus 'programme' debate when choosing names (see later). Next, ensure each office has a role description comprising a few lines of summary and the individual activities bulleted. The summary can then be used liberally in communications, so there is little doubt as to who the office supports. If you have an aversion to the word 'support', use management or, even, nothing at all, such as:

- business portfolio management office; business portfolio office;
- programme management office; programme office;
- Titan project management office; Titan project office.

Support (or management) offices – some examples

The permutations for designing an office infrastructure are limitless and can be daunting. Project Workout 27.2 provides a process to follow in defining your own, but to bring this to life, the following illustrates a snapshot of a typical support office set-up, which can be used as a basis for developing your own ideas. Do note, however, that the service level provided by the offices very much relates to the maturity of the organization in respect to portfolio, programme and project management. As the organization matures, the range of services the office provides will increase and its focus is likely to shift. In the early days much time will be spent on basic administration, project control, understanding the staged framework and helping people understand and use them. Once this is established, such support will be available either from local offices or colleagues on a less formal basis. The offices will have moved on to implementing or improving other aspects of capability. Support office staff should be proactive in continuously pushing corporate capability forward.

The business operations office

The business operations office, enterprise programme office or as it is sometimes presumptuously called, the 'centre of excellence', is the focal point for expertise related to business portfolio, programme and project management. It supports the business portfolio management director, ensuring the organization has an environment commensurate with its level of maturity. It sets the 'way we work' for the organization in relation to all portfolios, programmes and projects by providing methods and systems; a key role in this respect is the portfolio management design authority. If suitably supported by the right financial information, the office can also provide aggregated performance reports to senior management for each business portfolio, with a specific focus on benefits realization.

Other services offered by the office can include the following:

- undertaking independent reviews of projects;
- developing, procuring and selecting project management support tools and systems;
- monitoring resource usage across the organization;

- providing consulting and coaching and advising project sponsors and managers in carrying out their roles. This can range from simple 'response to phone calls' to providing a full facilitation, coaching and consulting service on specialist topics such as project set up, risk management, benefits management, business change, planning and project closure;
- maintaining standards for recruitment and development of project management staff (often working with the human resources department);
- providing support office services (see later);
- providing trained project management staff for assignment to projects.

This office could be combined with that of the business strategy and planning office and the authorization support office (see later) to create an extremely powerful grouping which not only provides methods but also helps those accountable drive strategy through delivery to benefits realization.

Business strategy and planning office

The business strategy and planning office supports the CEO and business strategy and planning board in the development, update and monitoring of the business plan. The focus here is strategic, and most large organizations have a group who do this. The change here, is to start them thinking in terms of a portfolio approach and considering any interfaces between the business portfolios. There is usually only one such office for an organization, unless it comprises semi-autonomous divisions, which are run almost independently.

Business portfolio office

Each business portfolio office should support the respective business portfolio sponsor and manager and be at the heart of driving the business portfolio's strategy and plan. Key to this is developing the blueprint (description of target operating model) and plan and then implementing them through initiating and running programmes, projects and other work components, together with managing benefits realization.

Services offered by such offices can include the following:

- checking documents prior to submission through the authorization process;
- managing the flow of documents for authorization, whether locally authorized or by higher authority;
- providing a secretariat service for the business portfolio sponsor and manager and communicating the outcomes and decisions;
- undertaking independent reviews and audits of work within the portfolio;
- providing consolidated reporting within the business portfolio;
- assisting in identifying and engaging stakeholders;
- monitoring resource usage within the business portfolio;

- consulting, coaching and advising programme and project sponsors and managers in carrying out their roles;
- providing support office services (see later);
- providing trained project management staff for assignment to projects.

If the business portfolio includes external projects (those for clients/ customers), it could also include a sales and bid management capability.

The authorization support office

The authorization support office supports the portfolio review group (see Chapter 13), verifying who the decision makers should be, ensuring flow of information to the decision makers (authorization process) and providing a secretariat for running decision-making meetings, communicating the results, updating systems (e.g., releasing cost codes) and archiving the relevant documents securely. In addition, this office could provide a quality advisory and review service for the documentation, which is submitted for authorization, to ensure the decision makers have the right information. The office could also provide a commentary or brief suggesting aspects the decision makers should focus on or challenge.

Programme or project office

The programme or project office(s) supports programme or project sponsors and, in particular, project managers in their accountabilities. This can range from ad hoc advice and guidance to providing a fully resourced service for tasks such as project planning, procurement or contract management, if not already provided by specialist central functions. These offices also tend to provide administrative services. A number of models are used and the extent to which a service is provided can vary significantly, including:

- a single office providing services to a number of key projects;
- a single office providing a service to all projects, regardless of size;
- a number of offices each providing services to a number of key projects;
- a number of offices each providing a service to all project within a business portfolio;
- each programme or major project having its own office, staffed from centrally owned resources;
- each project organizing its own arrangements for support.

Typical activities undertaken by the programme or project offices include:

- secretariat for programme or project board meetings;
- maintaining and operating the communications and stakeholder plans;
- administering change control, risk logs, issues logs and action lists;
- setting up and maintaining information management (paper based and electronic);
- establishing and operating information management procedures;

- maintaining plans (data collection and tools update for cost, schedule, scope and interdependencies);
- administering the quality review process and standards;
- reviewing key documents (e.g., business cases);
- administering document control and configuration management;
- assisting with the drafting of reports;
- administering contracted-in resources and facilities;
- ensuring compliance and best use of corporate methods;
- providing specialist knowledge, tools and techniques;
- assurance reviews.

Workout 27.2 – Fighting your way through the office fog

This workout should be undertaken with the design authority and other key advocates of project and program management. It should be carried out after you have established the key roles and accountabilities for your program management framework. If these are not yet completed, use the roles and accountabilities provided in this book, but do remember to check back later to see if they are still valid for your organization. If some support offices already exist, include the managers of them in your workout and determine where they sit with respect to the new roles and accountabilities. You should allow up to a day for this, not including the write-up and agreement after the workshop is completed.

1. Using a paper-covered wall, construct a table which includes the roles and accountabilities in your framework. (There is a model to get you started on the CD-ROM.)
2. Put a tick against each accountability/activity for which you believe support would be beneficial.
3. Against each accountability requiring support, decide what the support may comprise. Use three levels of support (high, medium and low), describe on a Post-It Note what that means in practical terms. Place the notes on the wall chart. Select which level of support you feel should be provided by marking the relevant Post-It note with a different coloured note (you may change your mind later). In writing these, consider the style and mandate you want the offices to have. Use active verbs to describe the service, being as specific as possible, e.g., assist; advise; guide; review; recommend; provide; own; enforce; decide; instruct. Be specific about who owns, develops or uses a process/method.
4. Name any existing support offices in the right-hand columns. For each existing support office, write on a Post-It Note what service it provides against the relevant accountabilities. If it provides a service for an unlisted accountability, add it to the bottom of the chart.
5. Based on the support requirements and the existing provision (if any), decide on an initial guess for different support offices. Name these in the right-hand columns.
6. Transfer the 'desired support service' Post-It from step 3 to the column for the support office which you think is best placed to provide the service.

7 Take a break! Clear your head.
8 As a group, run through the accountabilities of each office. Look for opportunities to consolidate services into fewer support offices.
9 For each office, decide its primary location, being the best location from which to provide the service. Some offices may be 'virtual', with staff residing in different locations.
10 Briefly outline the type of infrastructure the offices will need to operate. For example, shared intranets, document management systems and project support tools are usually essential for modern program management.
11 For each office, define the type of people required to staff it. Purely administrative activities need lower-qualified staff than activities requiring specialist knowledge and skills.
12 Based on your knowledge of the volume of projects and work involved, take a view on the numbers of people required. Decide if they all need to be full-time staff or if some roles (e.g., coaching) can be supplied by practicing managers on a peer-to-peer basis.

You now have a detailed set of accountabilities for your offices, together with an outline of staffing, location and infrastructure needs. This is sufficient to include in a project plan for implementing your office structures.

28

Tools and systems

Ensure users with differing requirements can view the data and information they need, in a format convenient for them.

"I've got a little list. I've got a little list."

W. S. GILBERT, 1836–1911

- **Design your tools to support each role.**
- **Think 'integrated' even if you don't integrate your tools in practice.**
- **Ensure your finance systems help to manage the business not just costs.**
- **Use tools to help drive change.**
- **Understand your tools landscape and identify significant gaps.**

The tools to help it work

You need a list!

"The most useful thing I have is a list of what I'm meant to be working on," said a senior manager of an application development function. The people in his function worked on applications for numerous projects, dealing with marketing information, finance, billing and customer services. He had learned that it was impossible for his function on its own to prioritize this workload, decide what needed to be done, when and what could safely be postponed. The outputs his function produced were valueless unless combined with the outputs from other functions. By having an agreed 'list' of projects, he is now clear which projects the organization wants done and that no others should be worked on. In addition, the staged framework (see Chapter 8) ensures that any particular part of the project does not proceed ahead of the others, and full checks on resource availability have been carried out. This 'list' is a key control to help manage a portfolio of projects and ensures that work around the organization is aligned. For a business portfolio, the list of projects needs to be extended to become a list of business portfolio components, i.e., programmes, projects and other work.

What does the business portfolio 'list' look like?

As soon as lists are mentioned, the words 'databases', 'spreadsheets' and 'management information systems' spring to mind. These are the 'tools' to make managing the 'list' easier. All too often, however, these systems are too complicated with a tendency to be taken over by the technical people who create them. Keep in perspective that they are only there to help the organization achieve its objectives and should be suited to the processes, systems and culture they serve. A key purpose of any set of tools is reporting. It does not matter how good the data input is; if you do not get useful information out, tools prove to be empty shells at best and totally misleading at worst. You will find that if people cannot get the information they need out of a tool, they will not bother to put anything in, no matter how much you plague them or how important it is to you!

If you do not get useful information out, tools prove to be empty shells

Tools as reinforcers for cultural shift

Good tools can help support the drive to move culture in a particular direction. If, for example, you want a projects environment where personal accountability is key, then having people's names visible and attached to accountabilities can be powerful. This is especially so if the management information system holding that data is easily accessible to those named people and those dependent on them.

Making accountabilities visible

An investment approval process in a major organization required that all the departmental managers impacted by the project had to sign the front sheet in ink. The logic was that each department paid for its part of the investment from its annual budget (whether capital or operational). The result was a sheet with anything up to 25 signatures on it. Somewhere in that forest of names was the real decision maker . . . or was there? A new process was instituted to make it clear who was actually making the decision. The process still requires the impacted functions to review and commit to the project; however, no signatures are required. The only signatures are those of the decision makers:

Somewhere in that forest of names was the real decision maker

- the project sponsor;
- the director of the department with overall project management accountability;
- the director with the budget which will fund the project (i.e., the business portfolio manager).

It is clear who is accountable for the decision – the person:

- who wants it;
- who does it;
- who pays for it.

"No snowflake in an avalanche ever feels responsible."

STANISLAV LEE

Management information needs

Your 'list' needs to be designed to ensure users with differing requirements can view the data and information they need, in a format convenient for them. They need to be able to:

- select the data they want to view;
- sort the data in an order to suit them;
- report in a format which serves their needs.

Information systems for keeping track of a business portfolio generally centre around three sets of data:

- resources;
- non-financial data;
- financial data.

Chapter 14 dealt with resources. The other two sets are covered in the following sections. Finance functions tend to have specialist accounting systems dealing with the 'money matters'. These systems are not primarily designed for holding the non-financial data needed, but many systems are now capable of being configured to deal with the wide range of ways people want to manage their businesses and manipulate their data.

Don't think a technical solution is always the best solution

Lists: keeping tabs on your projects and other work

To keep track of your projects and other work within a business portfolio, you will need a definitive list of the requests for new proposals and the work currently in progress. The following gives the basic requirements.

Capturing the new proposals

A proposal needs to be logged with a unique reference number from the moment a sponsor wishes to declare its existence. This MUST be prior to the initial investigation gate. It can be entered as early as when a portfolio strategy or plan is created and flags up the need for a potential project and hence the earmarking of funds. A proposal document need not be created before a request is logged, although sufficient information must be available to describe, in outline, the business objectives, desired outcomes and required benefits of the potential project.

A proposal is converted via the initial investigation gate to a project as an initial investigation and on into the staged framework, as described in Chapter 13.

It should be possible to track back from any project in progress to find where the original request/proposal came from. In addition, if a request/proposal is converted to a project, it should be possible to see whether the project was in fact completed or terminated early. 'Key word searches' are useful to analyze the population of activities based on any of the header or other data for each proposal (e.g., rejected, terminated, etc.).

The 'list'

There is a need for a central database which holds the data on each business portfolio, individual projects and items of other work. If implementing full business portfolio management, this system(s) should contain all work being undertaken in the organization. If business portfolio management is being partially implemented, the system needs to contain only what you have decided is in scope. As a reminder of the options, look at Chapter 12 again. The system should provide information in support of decision makers, resource managers, business planners and programme and project sponsors. Also, remember the needs of people managing programmes, projects, other work and work packages. You will be relying on these people to supply much of the data, and there needs to be something in it for them to warrant the effort.

Defining the relationships between components of the portfolio

Each component needs to be categorized; for example, 'project' or 'programme', and there should also be categories for different types of 'other work'. The relationship between each component must be defined to show which projects are stand-alone, part of a specific programme and what other work is in a programme. This is shown, by example, in Figure 28.1 which is built up from the principles in Figure 3.3. This example shows which work components are part of the TSR2 programme. The structure is essential to good governance, and a practical way to apply the tiers of accountability looked at in Chapter 4. Whilst there should only be one definitive structure for running the organization at any one time, good information systems allow the establishment of a number of different structures. This can be useful if reorganizing the business portfolios to reflect the future direction of the organization. The new structure can be constructed and monitored 'in shadow' until the time it is cut over to become the new, defined structure. For example, SAP® has a simple user interface for building such structures, where each component can be 'dragged and dropped' into position and

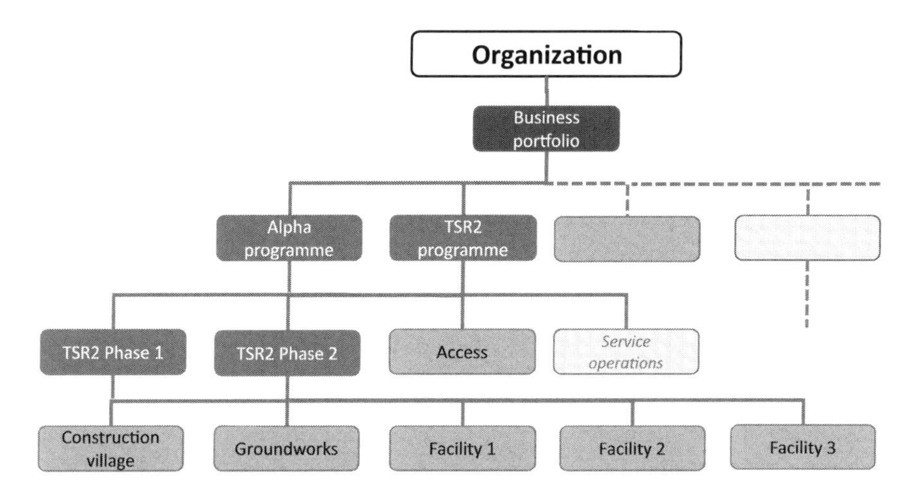

Figure 28.1 Relationships between components of the portfolio are vital

In this example, built on the same principles as Figure 3.3, we can see what makes up the TSR2 programme. The programme comprises two phases (each managed as a programme), with phase two having five projects for the village, groundworks and facilities. There is also an access project and 'other work' representing service operations.

any number of separate structures held at any one time. When a component is moved, it takes all its history and forecasts with it, so nothing is lost on the way.

As a minimum, for each component of the business portfolio, you will need:

- header data (name, accountabilities, etc.);
- interdependencies with other work;
- milestone data;
- cost data;
- progress information;
- useful and targeted reporting.

Project header data

The following data should be held for each project:

- project number, project name, business objectives, project framework stage, project sponsor, project manager;
- which business portfolio the project belongs to;
- which programme the project is part of (if any);
- status (proposed, in progress, on hold, terminated or completed)
- the people, platforms, systems, processes and products impacted by the project;
- specific header data which are relevant to specific categories or types of projects.

Header data for other work

The header data for other work very much depends on your business model, its associated value chain and the business processes required. There should be specific header data for each category of 'other work'. For example, if 'other work' relates to business-as-usual activities, each category of 'other work' could relate to a cross-organization business process within a value chain, such as 'serve customer'. The header, in this case might be:

- business process reference number, name, business objectives, sponsor, manager;
- which business portfolio the business process belongs to;
- which value chain the business process is part of;
- status (proposed, in progress, on hold, terminated or completed)
- the people, platforms, systems, processes and products impacted by the project;
- specific header data which are relevant to that particular type of work.

Interdependencies

The project definition of each project should include its interdependencies. A dependency is a deliverable produced by one project, which is needed by another project in order to achieve its targeted benefits. There can also be dependencies between other categories of work. It is essential that interdependencies are visible, defined and maintained. It must be possible to enquire:

A dependency is a deliverable produced by one project, which is needed by another project

- which project(s) or work depend on this project/work;
- which project(s) or work this project/work depends on.

A simple list of projects and work and those which it depends on might be sufficient but if the data is to be used as a decision support tool to enable business portfolios and the business impacts seen, more detail is necessary. This could comprise the planned and forecast dates for the transfer of each key dependent deliverable.

Milestone data

The information system should hold milestone schedule data as original baseline (with date set), current baseline (with date set), achieved dates (if completed) and forecast dates (for uncompleted milestones) for the following:

- for projects: the gates in the staged framework (detailed investigation gate, development gate, trial gate, release gate, release, project completed);
- for other work: any important dates it is necessary to track, usually relating to significant decisions;
- additional manager-defined milestones in addition to those already stated.

Cost data

If costs are held in a separate financial system, it is useful to extract summary level information into the management information system to enable reporting on mixes of financial and non-financial information. The information system should hold:

- for projects:
  - actual costs to date for the project by project stage;
  - forecast costs to completion by project stage.
- for other work:
  - actual costs to date;
  - forecast costs to completion.
- costs in two categories:
  - manpower (time costs);
  - external purchases.

See Figure 28.2 for an example.

Benefits forecasting data

The information system should hold the 'benefits' forecast, both in 'plan' form (i.e., as per the authorized business case) and as a forecast (i.e., the estimated outcome at the current point in time). This could also be in the form of 'conditions of satisfaction'.

Progress information

The system should be able to be used as a corporate reporting repository, capable of producing a standard report for each project or work category. For example, for projects this would include:

- key header data;
- business objectives;
- progress summary and outlook;
- financial summary;
- milestones;
- issues and risks;
- changes (via formal change management).

Reporting generally

The requirement is to provide a range of user roles with targeted, selected and sorted reports to meet their needs. Users will require either:

- detailed reports on individual projects or other work categories; or
- a summary reports for portfolios of projects or other work categories as selected, sorted using any of the other data field criteria.

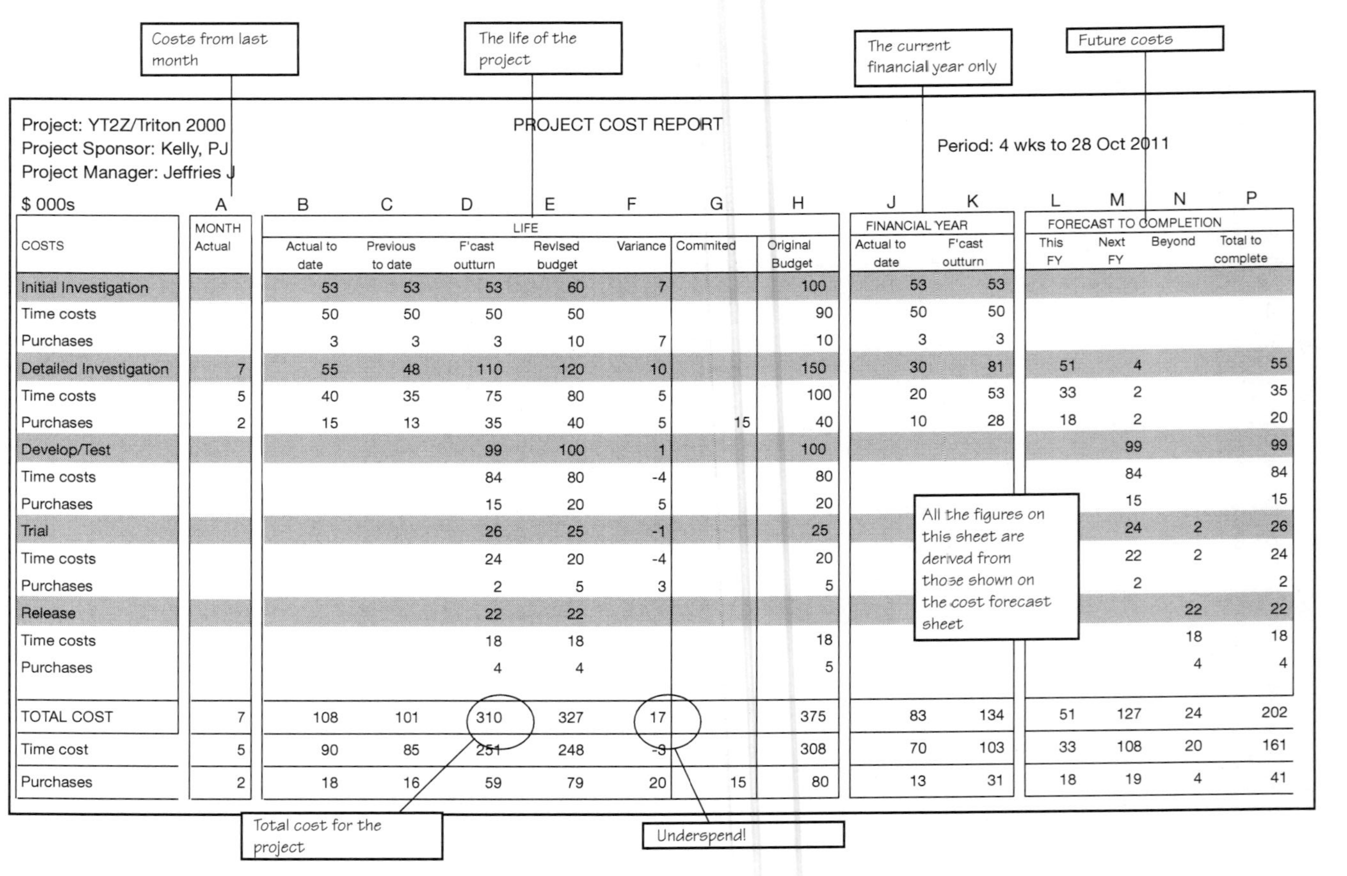

Project: YT2Z/Triton 2000
Project Sponsor: Kelly, PJ
Project Manager: Jeffries J

PROJECT COST REPORT

Period: 4 wks to 28 Oct 2011

$ 000s

	A	B	C	D	E	F	G	H	J	K	L	M	N	P
	MONTH	LIFE							FINANCIAL YEAR		FORECAST TO COMPLETION			
COSTS	Actual	Actual to date	Previous to date	F'cast outturn	Revised budget	Variance	Commited	Original Budget	Actual to date	F'cast outturn	This FY	Next FY	Beyond	Total to complete
Initial Investigation		53	53	53	60	7		100	53	53				
Time costs		50	50	50	50			90	50	50				
Purchases		3	3	3	10	7		10	3	3				
Detailed Investigation	7	55	48	110	120	10		150	30	81	51	4		55
Time costs	5	40	35	75	80	5		100	20	53	33	2		35
Purchases	2	15	13	35	40	5	15	40	10	28	18	2		20
Develop/Test				99	100	1		100				99		99
Time costs				84	80	-4		80				84		84
Purchases				15	20	5		20				15		15
Trial				26	25	-1		25				24	2	26
Time costs				24	20	-4		20				22	2	24
Purchases				2	5	3		5				2		2
Release				22	22								22	22
Time costs				18	18			18					18	18
Purchases				4	4			5					4	4
TOTAL COST	7	108	101	310	327	17		375	83	134	51	127	24	202
Time cost	5	90	85	251	248	-3		308	70	103	33	108	20	161
Purchases	2	18	16	59	79	20	15	80	13	31	18	19	4	41

Figure 28.2 Keeping track of your accountabilities!

A report, such as this, gives you, on a stage by stage basis, the key financial information you should require: actual costs, forecast costs and commitments for the project as a whole and by financial period.

So users:

- select which projects or work they are interested in (based on the data stored in the information system;
- sort the data in the order they need (at least three levels of sort criteria);
- choose a report from a set of prescribed templates at a full, summary and/or analysis level. This can be either printed or exported to external applications.

The standard reports should be either:

- qualitative (i.e., non-numerical);
- or quantitative (cost-based, benefit based, timescale), with subtotals and totals.

Examples:

1. A project sponsor may select report showing all the projects and other work he/she is sponsoring.
2. A director may select a report of all the projects being sponsored by her and anyone else in her function.
3. Or she may select a report of all the projects which will benefit her function.
4. A line manager may select report of all the projects which are being managed by his staff.

Active and passive reporting

Always distinguish between active and passive reporting. If you want stakeholders to know something, tell them. Do not expect them to consult a database to find out if anything in it is critical for them to know. Databases and information systems are passive and do not assume that anyone will look at them. Even if 'push' notifications are sent, unless designed well, the volume of notifications can be so large and of indiscriminate priority no one pays them any attention; so make sure you maintain regular contact with your key stakeholders.

Simple reporting in action

A multi-national company was implementing an SAP® finance and procurement system across its worldwide operations. It also built a 'list' of all projects in its business portfolios, using OpenText™'s Livelink system, which mined financial data directly from SAP® and was capable of real-time 'select, sort, choose your report' reporting as described earlier in this chapter. During the pre-cutover checks for the implementation of SAP® in the USA, the finance manager visiting from the UK found that the USA's project portfolio had about $35m committed funds on

24 projects. On looking at the reporting from LiveLink, it was noted to be about $70m on 31 projects. Seven projects seemed to be missing from the SAP report. The finance team spent a morning trying to trace the reason for the discrepancy. A different finance manager (USA based) ran the report again in SAP® and found his results matched those when using Livelink. The difference between to two apparently similar SAP® queries was found to be due to the finance managers having been given access to different data sets. The first manager (from the UK) hadn't been given access to the full set and so SAP® automatically limited its search to what that person was entitled to see according to the credentials against that person's SAP profile. The Livelink utility on the other hand did not filter any data based on user profile and so always returned a full set.

Many of the finance managers found the reporting interface in SAP® complicated and prone to such 'user errors' and as a result, preferred to use the simplified reporting via Livelink, which was originally designed for the business portfolio and project managers. In fact, the Livelink based reporting covered about 90% of the finance team's day-to-day needs, with the more powerful native SAP® reporting needed only for the more specialist queries.

Harnessing digital technology

One of the biggest advances in project management over recent years is the provision of digital environments for displaying business information. Everything we have talked about in the preceding sections has very much been for the benefit of those directing and managing business portfolios. Whilst essential for corporate management, to the teams who actually enter data into databases (rather than use aggregated reports from the databases), it can be seen as 'non-value-added bureaucracy'. In many cases, such tools duplicate the project manager's own records and systems.

It is an obvious step to 'web enable' the project list. This has two advantages:

- roll out of the tools is simplified as the key interface is through a web browser (such as Edge, Chrome or Safari);
- the information can be made available to anyone who needs it. The more people who use it, the more likely those supplying the data are to keep it current.

The next step, however, is to turn the digital environment into tools the project manager and team can use on a day-to-day basis. For this to happen, a number of additional features are needed, such as document libraries, control logs, action lists and social media. In this way, the basic data collection for central reporting and tracking is drawn from the actual data the project managers use and most of the drudge associated with central reporting systems is eliminated; it becomes a secondary effect of 'doing the project properly'.

A number of criteria need to be considered if such digitally-enabled environments are to be effective.

- Someone must be accountable for the system and its features. These tools always attract a wonderful array of ideas for possible enhancements. Unless someone has a very good handle on the architecture and how it fits the portfolio, programme and project management methods in the organization, destructive complexity and inconsistencies will be introduced;
- Someone has to be accountable for the data quality. Every project manager or work component owner should be accountable for his or her own data but above that level, someone needs to check at business portfolio level, the overall integrity. The introduction of a 'quality score' is a good method for assessing this. The score should be designed to tell users of the data the extent to which they can 'trust' the portfolio reports which are generated;
- Anyone who needs access should be given access. If half the team are 'locked out' behind a firewall, any information they need will have to be duplicated elsewhere. It truly needs to be an enterprise-wide system and might even need to include suppliers and contractors;
- Manually duplicating data which is held in other systems should be avoided. If it can be drawn on directly, then do so. Systems based on open architectures are particularly good for this;
- User response time has to be acceptable. If adding data or drawing off reports takes too long, people will not use it.

What would such a system look like?

There are an increasing number of digital portfolio, programme, project and knowledge management environments on the market. They enable you to direct, manage and coordinate teams and information, regardless of where they are based or which organizations people belong to.

Features, complexity and reporting

When deciding the features for your management environment, you will find that the options are endless. The more features you have, the more complicated the system will become and the more errors will be introduced, leading to a drop off in trust for users of the system. Look for systems built on a core of base features, each of which enables a high degree of user configuration at both corporate, business portfolio, programme and project levels and with an obvious use in real life. There might be some features you do not need yet (or at all); see if you can 'disable' these so they do not clog your screens with 'useless' clutter. Again, this should be at all levels. Many software suppliers make their profit from customizing their offerings. On the face of it, this can look very customer-focussed but can also be a very expensive and not necessarily fruitful pathway if you are not really clear on what you want or need. The design of all systems is based on an assumed business model. If your customization conflicts with the system's assumed business model (for example, a totally different view on how to allocate access permissions), the impacts can be very unpredictable.

Designing new reports and creating better ways to present information is non-intrusive to the system architecture but adds value for the user.

However, one area that I feel customization should be given free rein in is reporting. Systems are useless if they do not convert data into meaningful information through screen based, printed and exported reports. Designing new reports and creating better ways to present information is non-intrusive to the system architecture but adds value for the user.

Apart from the usual project management features, the following capabilities can be useful.

- Organization: the ability to assign roles and put people in teams (such as user groups, decision-making bodies).
- News: on-line newspaper to keep your team and wider stakeholder community up to date without boring them with the standard progress report!
- Communications: integrated e-mail, storing the e-mails with the project rather than on a corporate e-mail server 'somewhere' no one can get at.
- Meetings: agenda, minutes linked to actions.
- Notifications: the system tells you when something you want to keep an eye on changes.
- Social (business!) media: on-line discussions – great for capturing lessons learned and quality reviews.
- Timesheets: if you need to track time and there is no corporate system.

Some test questions, when you are looking for a tool

There are so many tools currently on the market choosing one for illustrative purposes would not be fair on other providers and might lead you to choose a tool, simply because I have used it in this book. In addition, new technologies and innovative approaches are appearing all the time and what is available as this book is written will be different from what is available when you read it. I have therefore provided a basic set of 'can I' or 'how does it' questions to ask any supplier to get a feel for a particular tool and how it works. Make sure they actually show you how it works rather than just explain it or show you a set of slides.

Make sure they actually show you how it works

What methodologies does this support?

Any tool should be able to support the best practices and principles found in this book but adaptable to fit virtually any method or standard. Ask to be shown examples, say for PRINCE2®.

Does it give me what I need in my role?

The system should recognize who you are through your 'login' details. From here, you should be taken to a 'My home portal' (or similar) which should summarize what you are accountable for in each of your roles, with links to all elements of the system relating to you (including existing projects, outstanding issues, actions, etc.). You should be able to see any work packages, actions, risks, issues or changes allocated to you and the project or work component they relate to.

How can move around the system?

By using the menu options, you should be able move to different areas of the system;

Can I look at project life cycle-based information?

You should be able to identify every project and its project life cycle stages. You should then be able to drill down in each stage to individual work packages, with schedule, costs and other associated data. You should also be able to see how many and the cost of projects in each life cycle stage.

How do I see the details on a project or work component?

Selecting any project or work component should enable you to see that project's detail in a structured way. You should be able to read a high-level description of the project, together with a summary of the key data and then access all the detailed information about the project. This approach should enable the project sponsor, project manager and team to keep track of risks, issues, milestones and many other aspects of the project.

Management accounting systems

The missing dimension

"What we do is more important than where we sit in the organization." This might be what we feel but it is not what many of our management accounting systems measure or report. Currently many organizations count money in only two dimensions:

- a cost centre code (against whose budget money is spent);
- an analysis code (what it is spent on).

In other words, they are still rooted in traditional vertical control structures. They do not say how the money is applied, i.e., what is actually done with it along the horizontal value-based dimension of the matrix. Sometimes this is attempted by using a cost centre code or an analysis code to capture the essence of where money is applied. For example, a cost centre is opened to capture costs for a particular project. Whilst this might be pragmatic, it does not serve the full management accounting needs of the organization of the future.

A third dimension of accounting is needed to cover the use to which funds are put, regardless of what they are spent on and which cost centres resource them. This is an 'application code' and in essence, a 'source and application of internal funds', which is useful at a grass roots management level as well as at the senior management level.

So, the three dimensions are:

- cost centre code – **which** department is sending the money;
- analysis code – **what** it is spent on;
- application code – **why** it is being spent.

The sum of each should always equal the same number as they are just different ways of looking at the money used in the organization. It is essential this balance is made or 'leakage' of funds or 'cheating' will be possible.

The application code

Cost centre codes and analysis codes are familiar concepts, but what does an 'application code' look like? There should be three mutually exclusive application code types:

- **P type**: creates change; taking us from what we do now to what we do tomorrow, i.e., projects.
- **A type**: 'business as usual' processes. In the steady state, e.g., retaining and acquiring customers, doing management tasks (business processes).
- **X type**: down time such as sickness, leave, training.

Typically, X type is about 15 to 20%of total 'people' expenditure. Who really knows, however, how much is spent on running the existing business (A type) as opposed to changing it (P type)?

A 'PAX' type of management accounting system gives the knowledge to sharpen our focus and ensure that only those things which are important to meeting our strategic objectives are done, rather than merely keeping track of who spends the money. Consider the picture of the business when using the traditional cost centre code approach shown in Table 28.1.

The costs in each cost centre are known (the shaded part) (cost centre 1 = 20, cost centre 2 = 30, etc.), but we have no idea *how* the money and people are applied. This

Table 28.1 Cost centre based

	Total spend
Cost centre 1	20
Cost centre 2	30
Cost centre 3	40
Cost centre 4	10
Total organization	**100**

Table 28.2 Three cost dimensions

	Down time	Process activities			Projects		Total
	X	A1	A2	A3	P1	P2	
Cost centre 1	4	10	4	–	2	–	20
Cost centre 2	7	5	10	–	3	5	30
Cost centre 3	10	10	–	–	20	–	40
Cost centre 4	2	–	–	8	–	–	10
Total organization	**23**	**25**	**14**	**8**	**25**	**5**	**100**

is revealed when a third dimension is added, giving us a richer picture of our business, shown in Table 28.2.

For the first time, organizations can be run based on 'what counts', i.e., why we spend money matters more than who spends it

Why we spend money matters more than who spends

In this environment, cost centres become 'homes' where 'pay and rations' are sourced and experience and expertise fostered. Many cost centres will be focussed on particular activities, but that is not a prerequisite. The application code tells why they are doing something:

- away on paid leave?
- being trained?
- performing as part of the 'business as usual' task?
- contributing to a project?

By introducing the third dimension on all our costs (people included), we will know what we are applying ourselves to. The advantage is that the balance of power moves away from cost centre managers as the 'fund-holding barons' of the old hierarchical organization towards the flat structured 'what we do is important' new corporation AND . . . the key management tool (the management accounting system) will support this.

Management by accountability will thrive, as accountabilities are tied to application codes which operate across the whole organization, regardless of the cost centre to which the person holding the accountability belongs. In this way, any person can sponsor or work on any project or activity anywhere in the organization without you losing control of the finances or the head count. For example, Figure 28.3 (later in this chapter) shows a typical financial report for a project sponsor. It shows the person is sponsoring five projects, one of which is terminated, one on hold and three in progress. This person is accountable for over $1m spent across the organization.

As the three dimensions must balance, there is little scope or benefit for 'cheating'. If a project is running over budget, there is no point in hiding its cost within another project or activity even if the owner would accept it! It would merely 'rob Peter to pay Paul' and different performance indicators would move in opposite directions accordingly.

It would stop the racket of 'head count' restrictions or targets because it would no longer matter how many people are in a cost centre, as you would be concentrating more on what they did. There would be no need to push people out of the 'home' cost centre to do a 'project' only to fill their position with another person (net effect equals one more head).

This might sound a radical approach, but it is within the capability of many organizations. It would require 'time sheeting for all' but it is done already (e.g., everyone fills in sickness notes, paid leave forms, etc.). In addition, as the bulk of employees only do one 'A type' application and some 'X types', time sheets could be generated by default with only the exceptions requiring input. This would give organizations' managers the freedom to deploy anyone anywhere, not 'lose them', and know what they are doing. Thus, 'doing projects' or 'special activities' stops being dangerous; no longer will they be the fast track to redundancy!

Further, as we are in a rapidly moving world, by adopting the management approach given here, reorganizations will become less necessary and can be done at any time in the financial year. P, A and X will be the way businesses are run.

The requirements for such a system, incorporating project costing, would be that each application code should have:

- a unique reference number;
- costs captured against a work breakdown structure, representing, for project, at
    - least the stages of the project life cycle;
- forecasts set;
- viewing capability with or without absorbed overheads;
- the staged authorization of funds;
- three status for transaction postings:
    - open for forecast only;
    - open for cost and forecast;
    - closed.

Reporting should be flexible to reflect the life of a project, the current financial year and the future, enabling interest groups (such as project sponsors) to see their own projects as a portfolio.

Figure 28.2 is an example, which shows the costs associated with Phillipa Brixham's sponsorship portfolio. If your management accounting system is linked to your project database, these data could also appear. Similar reports could be produced, selecting and sorting from any of the data which are held in the accounting system, with the ability to summarize any level of the business portfolio's work breakdown structure.

Bookkeeping!

Always distinguish between the management of costs from a management accounting perspective and a financial perspective. The latter relates to 'bookkeeping' and where the transactions appear in the formal chart of accounts. In the management of projects, this is of little or no use. Managing the actual spend and cash flow provides far greater control.

This report is for a particular sponsor

PROJECT SPONSOR PORTFOLIO REPORT

Project Sponsor: Brixham, Phillipa

Period: 4 wks to 28 Sept 2011

$ 000s

No	PROJECTS	A	B	C	D	E	F	G	H	J	K	L	M	N	P
		MONTH	LIFE							FINANCIAL YEAR		FORECAST TO COMPLETION			
		Actual	Actual to Date	Previous to Date	F'cast Outturn	Revised Budget	Variance	Commited	Original Budget	Actual to Date	F'cast Outturn	This FY	Next FY	Beyond	Total to Complete
In progress															
755	Inventory free warehouse Phase 1	12	56	44	214	220	6	43	200	56	182	126	32		158
828	International acquisition B	14	72	58	167	150	-17	12	150	60	120	60	30	5	95
627	Logistics Management System IV	23	567	544	590	600	10	34	600	234	257	23			23
On hold															
832	Automated HR Appraisals		124	124	156	160	4		150	32	64	32			32
Terminated															
721	Improve Customer Support		12	12	24	24			110	12	24	12			12
TOTAL PORTFOLIO		49	831	782	1151	1154	3	89	1210	394	647	253	62	5	320

The total line shows the sum of the projects that the person is sponsoring

Figure 28.3 Typical financial summary for a sponsor

This report shows the financial summary of Phillipa Brixham's sponsorship portfolio. This report shows that she is accountable for $1.15m authorized spend on five projects, one of which has been terminated and another put on hold. Only one of her projects, 828, is forecasted to overspend.

Putting your systems together

Previous sections covered the three primary information needs (resources, non-financial and financial) and how they could be handled in information systems. We have also seen how resource management relates to cost forecasting and how this in turn builds into the business plan. Each system is targeted at a particular need; however, they are all related. Figure 28.4 shows the relationship in diagrammatic form. Actual expenditure on your projects is captured by the accounting system (the shaded boxes). These costs can be handled on both a project-focussed basis and on a more traditional, cost centre basis. Forecast of manpower (person hours) is costed and then combined with the forecast of purchases to produce an overall cost forecast for the projects.

At the point marked 'A', the manpower forecasts are taken off and collated to give an early view of resource needs for line managers and the organization as a whole. Once the actual costs and forecast costs are collected, they can be combined to produce the project financial accounts and summary reports. They can also be fed into the project database and combined with other, non-financial data, to produce an overall reporting capability. Where you keep your data and how the reports are produced, will depend very much on the systems you have in your organization, but regardless of this, the overall logic and flow should be similar to that examined here. It will not be easy to put in place, but if you have a vision of the future of your enterprise system's strategy, you will gradually be able to build the full set. Simple, separate systems may be the most pragmatic way to start, even if it means some temporary duplication of data and the risks that entails. It is better than not having a view of your business portfolios.

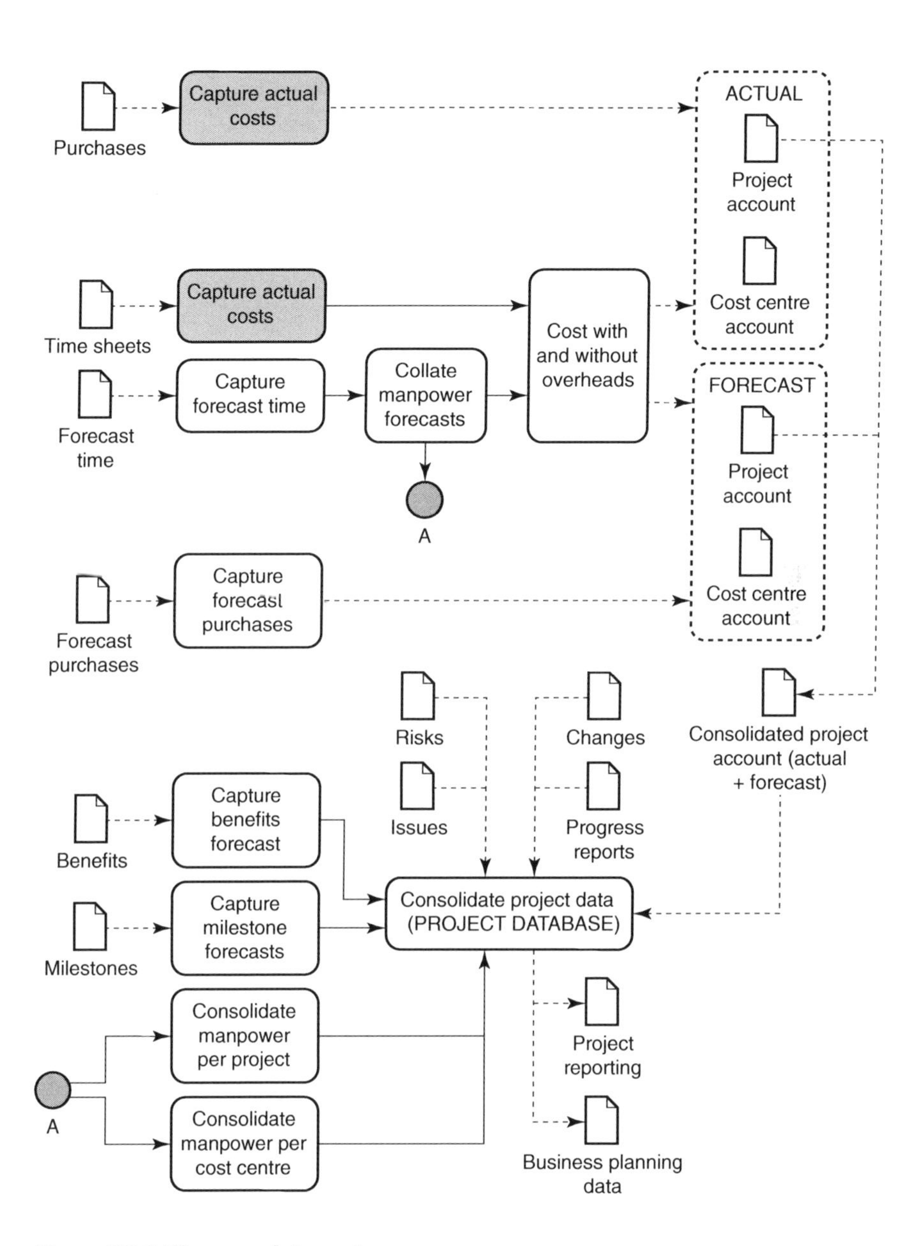

Figure 28.4 The complete system

This diagram shows the links between resources, costs, benefits within the management systems. The outputs include both reporting and the necessary inputs required for business planning.

Workout 28.1 – Your tools landscape

1 Look at the table of contents for this book and decide which aspects of programme and portfolio management would benefit from having supporting information systems.
2 Draw up a grid on a flip chart or large whiteboard, like the one in the diagram. Include any additional aspects you have chosen.
3 Enter what tools you currently use, if any, to support each requirement, in the appropriate box.
4 Consider each box in the grid and discuss how discrete or integrated each tool is and how this might affect the effectiveness of your organization. Discuss those boxes with no tools associated with them. Add any particular problems to an issues log.

The BusinessOptix application discussed in the Introduction has a feature to do this type of analysis.

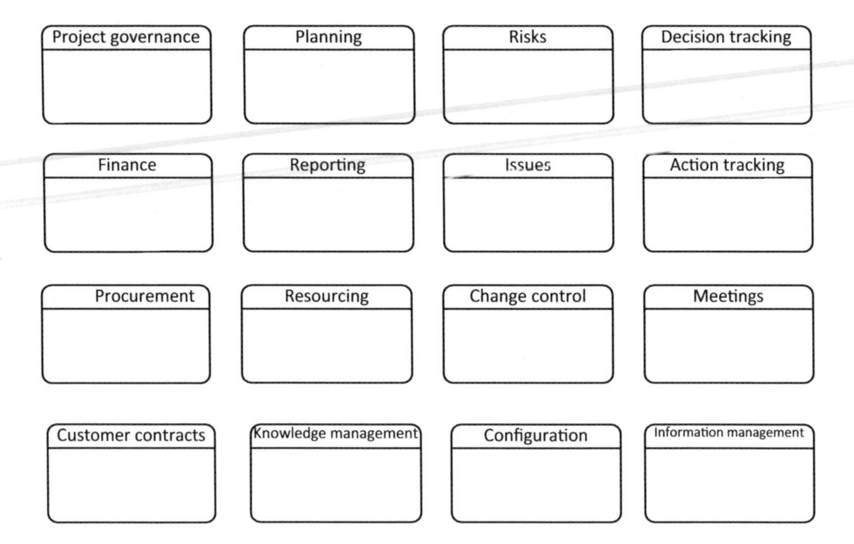

Workout 28.2 – Your own tools, joining up with finance

1 Make an enlarged copy of Figure 28.4. Mark it up with highlighter pens, indicating the elements you currently have in place (shade in yellow) and those parts which you already plan to put in place (shade in another colour).
2 Are the elements you have shaded designed to be compatible with each other?
3 On a flip chart:
   a list elements which are missing;
   b list the data which would be contained within these elements;
   c list the information you are lacking as a result.
4 Consider, based on what you have in place, what actions you could take to fill any gaps you have identified in the systems environment supporting your business portfolios.

29

Standards and methods

Do they matter?

What is the difference between a standard and a method?

Standards

Key methods

Other sources of best practice

Comparing the methods and standards

A word of warning

There is an ever-growing range of 'methods', 'standards' and 'guides' dealing with portfolio, programme and project management. It can all get a bit daunting.

"A man who makes no mistakes does not usually make anything."

BISHOP WILLIAM CONNOR MAGEE, 1821–1891

- **A standard can be used to help assess the completeness of any method.**
- **A method is intended for practical use.**
- **Take what you need from the published sources to build your capability.**

What is the difference between a standard and a method?

In the context of business portfolio management:

- a standard, such as ISO21504:2015, defines *what* needs to be done and *why* but not *how* activities are done;
- a method, such as MoP® (Management of Portfolios), provides not only a set of activities to be done, together with roles, but also techniques for undertaking those activities.

As such:

- a standard can be used to help assess the completeness of any method;
- a method is intended for practical use.

Organizational approaches to business portfolio management normally fit within the definition of a 'method', as they are designed for practical use within a specific organization. They might be derived directly from a method like PRINCE2® or based on particular standards. By including techniques and templates, a method is far more prescriptive (and helpful!) about the way a particular activity should be undertaken; for that reason, methods are longer and more detailed than standards. For example, *ISO 21504:2015, Guidance on Portfolio Management*, has 25 pages, whilst AXELOS's method, *Management of Portfolios*, has 154 pages.

Many organizations use these terms in different ways. 'Standard', 'method' or 'process' might not be always applied in the way as I have used them in this book, nor in the way you use them in your workplace. Some people use 'methodology' rather than 'method' and arguments over which is right can get heated! Some publications seem to cross over the previous definitions, being a hybrid of a 'standard' and a 'method'. Do not worry; what is important is that what you produce is of use in your organization and the terminology fits the way words are used within the organization. Whatever words you choose to call the parts of your approach, use them consistently.

This chapter is where the most acronyms and jargon are found as authors seem to love them! Further, different publications are not easily comparable as different concepts, structures and terminology are used. Do not be daunted by this. You will only need to refer to the standards and methods if your role requires it – for example if you are the owner of an enterprise wide portfolio, programme and project management method.

Publicly available standards, methods and other sources of best practice are a consensus among the authors of what they agree is important. As such, they do not usually break new ground in terms of thought leadership and tend to lag behind good practice. It can take a long time for the experts involved to reach a consensus! Nevertheless, they are usually reliable and form a good basis on which to build your own organization's methods

It can take a long time for the experts involved to reach a consensus

What is *The Programme and Portfolio Workout*?

The Programme and Portfolio Workout is neither a method nor a standard. It is a textbook. It can, however, be used as a core source to create a practical method and so become your 'training manual'. As *The Programme and Portfolio Workout* also supports the concepts in many standards and proprietary methods, it can also be used in conjunction with them. As 'tailoring' is now a feature of all standards, this book gives a view of what really counts when directing and managing a business portfolio or programme to help you understand how these different approaches can be used together.

Standards

What is a standard?

A standard is an agreed way of doing something, or an agreed set of quality criteria for a product or service. Standards were first promoted as a way of encouraging trade for buyers to trust that the products on offer are fit for purpose. Standards cover a wide range of activities and products and can be:

- **normative standards**: prescriptive and set requirements which must be met, as in a specification. The word 'shall' is used in these, for example, "The outer dimensions shall be less than 3mm";
- **informative standards**: for guidance, such as a code of practice. The word 'should' is used in these. Project management related standards tend to fit into this category. For example, "The project manager should tailor the management processes."

The language used in standards is carefully chosen; each standards body has its own rules, usually described in a standard! The British Standard Institute has *BS 0, A standard for standards – Principles of standardization*, with an accompanying rule book. Table 29.1 includes some of the key uses of English, designed to avoid ambiguity. For example, in common speech, 'may' could mean you might do something or that you have permission to do something; 'will' could be a prediction of the future or it could be an instruction, "You *will* come to my office at 9:00am, sharp!" When writing your own methods and processes, pay attention to the syntax to avoid ambiguity.

Table 29.1 Use of English in standards

Word	*Implications*	*Alternative phrases*	*Notes*
shall	**Requirements** – content from which no deviation is permitted if compliance with the document is to be claimed.	*is required to* *it is required that* *has to* *only . . . is permitted* *it is necessary* *needs to*	Do not use 'must' as an alternative for 'shall'. Do not use 'may not' instead of 'shall not' to express a prohibition.
should	**Recommendations** – content denoting a suggested possible choice or course of action deemed to be particularly suitable without necessarily mentioning or excluding others.	*it is recommended that* *ought to*	
may	**Permission** – expression demoting approval, consent or opportunity to do something.	*is permitted* *is allowed* *is permissible*	Do not use 'possible' or 'impossible' in this context.
might	**Possibility** – expression denoting expected or conceivable outcome.		Use in informative text only
can	**Possibility and capability** – expression conveying expected or conceivable outcome and the ability to do or achieve a specified something.	*be able to* *there is a possibility of* *it is possible to*	Use in informative text only
will	Ambiguous term, do not use		Implies the ability to predict of the future
must	Ambiguous term, do not use		Reserved for legal compliance.
Is/are	A description		

In the context of this book, standards improve the effectiveness of portfolio, programme and project management by drawing attention to the key principles and activities required. The standard becomes a 'checklist' against which an organization's method can be checked. Standards also seek to define the use of words in a particular context.

Once established, standards can promote continuous improvement. They should be being periodically reviewed and updated to ensure the latest consensus on best practice is included and any omissions or clarifications are dealt with. In this way, all users of standards benefit from the collective experience and feedback of other users. Standards authorities, like the International Standards Organization, require a standard is formally reviewed at least every five years to check it is still current and relevant.

National and international standards

Official standards, with international and national recognition, tend to come from three different sources. The numbering convention usually makes it clear:

- National standards, such as BS (British), DIN (German), NF (standard), ANSI (USA), SS (Swedish), JIS (Japan);

- European standards, denoted 'EN', are used throughout Europe; these are automatically adopted by EU member states;
- International standards, denoted 'ISO', may be used throughout the world.

Adoption by individual countries is optional. For example, in the UK, an adopted international standard is denoted as 'BS ISO'.

Standards on portfolio, programme and project management

The international standards most pertinent to this book are:

- ISO 21500: (currently being drafted) *Project, Programme and Portfolio Management – Context and Concepts*;
- ISO 21502: (currently being drafted) *Project, programme and portfolio management – Guidance on project management* (replaces 21500:2012);
- ISO 21503:2017 *Project, programme and portfolio management – Guidance on programme management*;
- ISO 21504:2015 *Project, programme and portfolio management – Guidance on portfolio*
- management;
- ISO 21505:2017 *Project, programme and portfolio management – Guidance on governance.*

This book covers the scope of all these. *The Project Workout* covers ISO21502 and part of ISO 21505.

Other useful standards in the context of business portfolio and programme management include:

- ISO 9000 family on quality management;
- ISO 31000:2009 *Risk management*;
- ISO/IEC/IEEE 15288:2015 *Systems and software engineering – System life cycle processes.*

The ISO 9000 family on quality management

The ISO 9000 family addresses various aspects of quality management and contains some of the best-known ISO standards. These standards provide guidance and tools for companies and organizations to ensure their products and services consistently meet customer requirements. If your organization seeks to be or is required by regulation to be 'ISO 9001 certified', your portfolio, programme and project management processes and method will need to comply. The quality family includes:

- ISO 9001:2015: *Quality management systems – Requirements (the certifiable standard)*;
- ISO 9000:2015: *Quality management systems – Fundamentals and vocabulary (definitions)*;
- ISO 9004:2009: *Quality management systems – Managing for the sustained success of an organization (continuous improvement)*;

- ISO 19011:2011: *Guidelines for auditing management systems.*

Obtaining certification to ISO 9001 should be considered to be a first step, the base level of a quality system and not a complete guarantee of quality. For this reason, some organizations are perceived as only going through the motions, badge collecting, to achieve their certification rather being serious about using the approaches in the standards to improve business performance.

ISO 31000:2009 *Risk management*

ISO 31000:2009, *Risk management* – can be used by any organization, regardless of size, activity or sector. Using ISO 31000 can help increase the likelihood of achieving objectives, improve the identification of opportunities or threats and effectively allocate and use resources for risk treatment. ISO 31000 cannot be used for certification purposes but does provide guidance for auditors. It enables organizations to compare their risk management practices with an internationally recognized benchmark, providing a sound basis for effective management and corporate governance.

ISO/IEC/IEEE 15288:2015 *Systems and software*

ISO/IEC/IEEE 15288:2015 *Systems and software engineering – System life cycle processes* is targeted at those in systems engineering but covers much of the same ground as the project management standards, albeit in a different way. It concerns those systems that are man-made and are configured with one or more of the following system elements: hardware, software, data, humans, processes (e.g., processes for providing service to users), procedures (e.g., operator instructions), facilities, materials and naturally occurring entities, which just about covers everything from a railway network to missiles. I take the view that you can learn from anyone and what works in one industry or situation can be transportable and bring a competitive advantage in another context. ISO/IEC/IEEE 15288:2015 defines a set of processes and associated terminology which can be applied at any level in the hierarchy of a system's structure. Selected sets of these processes can be applied for managing and performing the stages of a system's life cycle. It provides processes to support the definition, control and improvement of the system life cycle processes used within an organization, portfolio, programme or a project. I have used this standard as the basis for much of the content of Chapter 24 on quality, but reinterpreted for a broad application, not just for what is generally thought of as 'systems'.

Obtaining national and international standards

Standards tend to be expensive, but many organizations pay a subscription to download copies under a licence agreement. Many university libraries also have a subscription and so lecturers and students can obtain copies 'free' for academic purposes.

UK government functional standards

The UK Government has its own set of Government Functional Standards, designed to be used by government departments and their agencies. The aim is to bring a mutually understood 'government way' for conducting business to work across organizational barriers and enable 'joined up government'. A range of business functions are included, including project delivery, digital services, finance, commercial, property, security and HR. The project delivery standard, *GovS002: Project delivery*, covers portfolio, programme and project management and is the only standard published to date which integrates all three topics in a single document. It has 40 pages, and its scope is represented in Figure 29.1.

Obtaining UK government functional standards

The UK government's transparency and open licence policy means any of their standards can be downloaded free from the 'gov.uk' website.

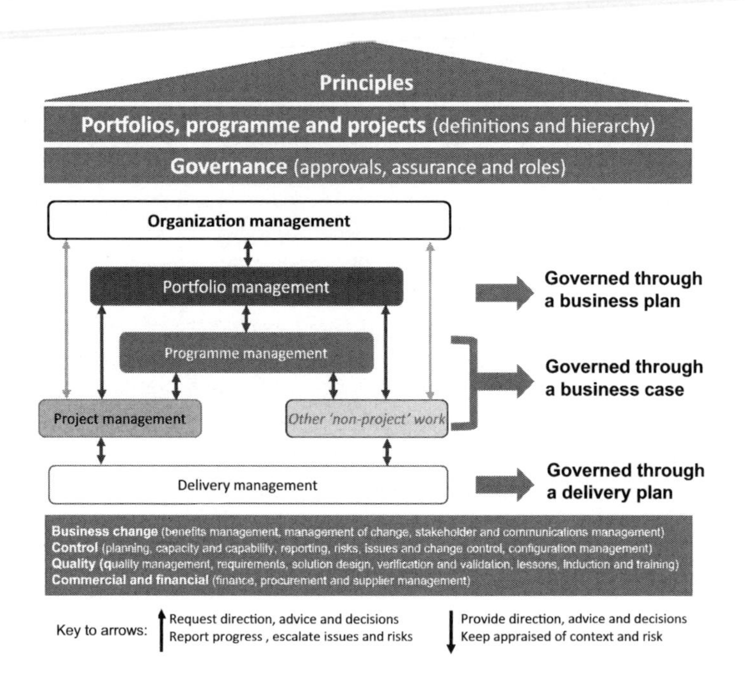

Figure 29.1 Structure and scope of the UK government's project delivery standard

The project delivery standard covers portfolio, programme and project management as an integrated set of practices.

Key methods

A method is a collection of practices, rules, tools and instructions used by teams or individuals to achieve a specific result. It defines how to do something and generally includes documentation and tools, but users are responsible for the identification and planning of the relevant component for their specific tasks. As such, a method provides flexibility but requires each user to tailor it to suit the work needed to be done. The mostly widely used, publicly available methods are:

- *Management of Portfolios* (MoP®);
- *Managing Successful Programmes* (MSP®);
- *PRINCE2®* for project management.

These were originally developed by the UK government's Cabinet Office (Office of Government Commerce) and are now owned by AXELOS, with the government holding a 49% share. These three methods are mostly built on the same principles but as they were developed at different times by various authoring teams, the terminology and processes are not always seamless. The interfaces are obvious, and these slight niggles can be avoided by suitable tailoring. This suite of methods is supported by training and examinations with associated accreditations.

Management of Portfolios (MoP®)

The MoP® (*Management of Portfolios*) guidance provides senior executives and practitioners responsible for planning and implementing change, with a set of principles, techniques and practices to introduce or re-energize portfolio management. MoP® helps organizations answer the fundamental question: "Are we sure this investment is right for us and how will it contribute to our strategic objectives?" Investment is the key word because portfolio management is about investing in the right change initiatives and implementing them correctly.

Management of Portfolios comprises 12 portfolio management practices, grouped within two cycles.

- The definition cycle contains a series of broadly sequential practices (i.e., 'understand' generally comes before 'categorize', which usually comes before 'prioritize', etc.), although, in practice, there are often overlaps;
- The delivery cycle is different in that the practices here are undertaken broadly simultaneously. The cycle analogy is still applicable as the individual initiatives go through the programme or project life cycle and, as portfolio delivery is linked to the strategic planning, financial and risk management cycles.

There is common ground between this book and ISO 21504, except that *Management of Portfolios* defines a 'portfolio' as "the totality of an organization's investment (or segment thereof) in the changes required to achieve its strategic objectives." It is therefore more constrained in scope than this book or ISO 21504, which both allow anything you need to be defined within a portfolio and, at its limit, means the portfolio can cover the whole of the organization. Hence, I use the term 'business portfolio' in this book as a reminder of this.

Managing Successful Programmes (MSP®)

Managing Successful Programmes (MSP®) provides a framework whereby large, complex change can be broken down into manageable, inter-related projects. The method comprises a set of principles and processes for managing a programme, which are founded on best practice. It is designed to be adapted to meet different needs and circumstances and has been adopted by both public and private sector organizations. This method has certainly had a big impact on how programmes are regarded and was at the forefront of advocating that business change being an essential part of a programme's scope. It defines a programme as:

> *A temporary flexible organization structure created to coordinate, direct and oversee the implementation of a set of related projects and activities in order to deliver outcomes and benefits related to an organization's strategic objectives. A programme is likely to have a life that spans several years.*

The important phrase to note is 'a set of related projects and activities'. It recognizes that a successful programme needs more than projects. The detail of the method, however, limits such activities to those involved with business change. Two of its process are:

- delivering the capability: it assumes this is done through projects;
- realizing the benefits: it is assuming this is done through business change activities.

Earlier editions of *Managing Successful Programmes* were not as prescriptive allowing you to choose whatever management approach suited the circumstances. There is no reason why business change should be managed as a project and why the delivery of some capabilities cannot be managed in a 'non-project' way. The other quirk is that whilst the MSP programme manager is responsible to the senior responsible owner (i.e., programme sponsor) for leading and managing the programme as a whole, the business change manager role is responsible to the senior responsible owner for the business change and benefits realization. In other words, it appears that the programme manager can be circumvented by the business change manager for much of the programme's scope. The manual does not make clear how this should work in practice and, for programmes, the range of different circumstances is so vast that perhaps trying to pin this down is not possible. Notwithstanding, these issues, the method is respected and can be tailored to be more flexible. For example, BT adopted it in a tailored form, which allows the flexibility and single point accountability advocated in this book.

One of *Managing Successful Programmes'* strengths is the inclusion of benefit mapping, which emphasises the link for outputs to capability to outcomes to benefits. If more business leaders had this mind-set, then fewer projects would fail.

PRINCE2®

PRINCE2® was first published in 1996, and is used not just in the UK, but in more than 150 countries worldwide. Expectations for its use have been set by successive UK governments, with the aim of improving project performance in both the public and private sectors to benefit the country as a whole. Consequently, many other countries follow this lead, partly because as there is very little alternative 'open copyright' material available for organizations to draw on. *PRINCE2®*'s scope covers all the roles and processes needed to direct, manage and undertake a project.

The scope of *PRINCE2®* is similar to that covered by BS6079, but being a 'method', it includes far more detail and defines specific techniques, the main ones being:

- business case; looked at in detail in *PRINCE2®*, but the use of the document and its development through the project life cycle are identical to that defined in BS6079;
- exception management, as a technique, this is not prescribed in the British Standard;
- product-based planning; the British Standard is non-prescriptive, but both documents end up with the same planning components, covering benefits, cost, resources, schedule and scope;
- health checks.

The recent update of *PRINCE®* in 2017, emphasized the need for tailoring the method and also started to open up the idea that its 'products' could be outcomes, as well as outputs.

There is also a version of *PRINCE2®*, which specifically shows how it can be used in the context of agile delivery methods. If you are interested in agile delivery in the context of project management, look at the *DSDM Agile Project Framework*, from the Dynamic Systems Development Consortium. This uses the classic life cycle (staged) approach to project management and demonstrates how it is used to encompass the iterative approaches to development which are core to agile delivery.

Other sources of best practice

Standards and methods are not the only publications available; there are others from a range of international and national organizations that come in many forms, such as knowledge bases, maturity models and competency frameworks. Some are described here, though this is by no means a comprehensive list:

- Professional bodies, such as the:
  - UK's Association for Project Management;
  - USA's Project Management Institute;
- International Project Management Association;
- Capability Maturity Model Integrated (CMMI®), from the Software Engineering Institute;
- GAPPS, Global Alliance for Project Performance Standards.

Professional bodies

In the UK, the primary professional body is the Association for Project Management, which received its Royal Charter in 2017. In the UK, chartered status means an organization is recognized as meeting rigorous criteria enabling it to be a self-governing profession. Many other countries have similar professional bodies. In the USA, the Project Management Institute takes on this role, styling itself as "the leading not-for-profit professional membership association for the project management profession," and its resources and research "deliver value for more than 2.9 million professionals working in nearly every country in the world."

National professional bodies are a good source of information, often producing white papers on new approaches long before they are officially adopted within the formal standards, guides or bodies of knowledge. Such articles tend be more practical than many of the academic papers produced by universities.

The Association for Project Management

The Association for Project Management's Body of Knowledge provides a foundation for portfolio, programme and project management, across all sectors and industries. It sets out the areas of knowledge a manager should have to be successful. It covers context, people aspects, delivery and interfaces.

- **Context** includes governance, sponsorship, life cycle, success factors and maturity, as well as the project in relation to operation management and strategy.
- **People** aspects cover interpersonal skills, including communication, conflict management, delegation, influencing, leadership, teamwork and negotiation, as well as professionalism ethics.
- **Delivery** covers the classic project management techniques, providing guidance on integrative management, planning (scope, schedule, resource), risk management and quality.
- **Interfaces** includes topics such as accounting, health and safety, law, sustainability and security.

Whist it has its own glossary of terms and seeks to be internally consistent, the authors recognize different terminology is be used and gives some frequently used alternatives. Each section in the document has references for further reading in terms of relevant standards, books and papers.

The APM's Body of Knowledge, unlike many other publications mentioned in this chapter, is not process based, thereby recognizing there can be 'many right ways' to undertake the activities associated with portfolio, programme and project management.

The Project Management Institute

The Project Management Institute has a range of publications, the core of which it terms its 'foundational standards'. These provide a base for project management knowledge and represent the four areas of the profession: project, programme, portfolio and the organizational approach to project management. They are the foundation on which particular practice standards and industry-specific extensions are built. These publications have been adopted (in whole or part) by the American National Standards Institute (ANSI) as the USA's national standard. They are listed here, with their respective ANSI numbers:

- *A Guide to the Project Management Body of Knowledge* (PMBOK® Guide), Part 2 of which contains ANSI/PMI 99–001–2017, The Standard for Project Management;
- *The Standard for Program Management – Fourth edition* (ANSI/PMI 08–002–2017);
- *The Standard for Portfolio Management – Fourth edition* (ANSI/PMI 08–003–2017);
- *The Organizational Project Management Maturity Model* (OPM3®) – Third Edition (ANSI/PMI 08–004–2013);
- *The Standard for Business Analysis* (ANSI/PMI 17–005–2017).

In addition, the PMI has practice standards and frameworks which describe particular tools, techniques or processes identified in its foundational standards. The ANSI and PMOBoK are due to be updated in 2020.

The International Project Management Association (IPMA),

The IPMA is an umbrella organization for about 70 national bodies, including the UK's APM, and provides a global network giving its member bodies a large degree of autonomy. IPMA promotes professional growth through its conferences and relationships with corporations, government agencies, universities and colleges, as well as training organizations and consulting companies. Three of the IPMA's flagship publications are:

- Individual Competence Baseline (IPMA ICB4®) outlines the competences by describing 29 competence elements, organized into three competence areas ('Eye of Competence'): Perspective, People and Practice. All competence elements are detailed with the required knowledge and skills. Key Competence Indicators (KCIs) provide the definitive indicators for successful project, programme and portfolio management.
- Project Excellence Baseline (IPMA PEB®) outlines the concept of excellence in managing projects and programmes. It serves as a guide to organizations and practitioners in assessing the ability of their project and programme teams to achieve project excellence.
- Organisational Competence Baseline (IPMA OCB®) outlines 18 competences to deliver an organization's vision, mission and strategic objectives in a sustainable manner. It describes how the governance and management of projects, programmes and portfolios should be analyzed, assessed and improved.

Capability Maturity Model Integrated for Development (CMMI-DEV)

CMMI looks at maturity. Whilst skills and competencies are a feature of an individual's capability, maturing refers to the capability of an entire organization. To achieve maturity, the model states an organization has to consistently and repeatedly be able to undertake a number of specified 'practices', depending on the maturity level claimed. The term 'practice' is used as CMMI assessors are concerned with what people actually do in their day-to-day jobs, rather than what their processes say they should do. A single CMMI practice may correspond to one or more 'processes' or procedures. CMMI can therefore be used to check a project management approach, whether on a single project (CMMI maturity level 2) or on all an organization's projects (CMMI maturity level 3 and above). CMMI-DEV covers general practices, project management, process management, support and engineering practices.

The general practices cover how to manage a process or method. For example, General Practice 2.3 is to "Provide resources: Provide adequate resources for performing the process, developing the work products and providing the services of the process." In other words, make sure you have the people and other resources needed to do the work you want to do. General Practice, 2.4 is "Assign Responsibility: Assign responsibility and authority for performing the process, developing the work products, and providing the services of the process." In other words, ensure someone is accountable, as in Chapter 15.

CMMI does not specifically differentiate between portfolio, programmes or projects but leaves the user the freedom to interpret the scope as they see fit. CMMI's project management practices are defined under their process groups.

- Integrated Project Management is about managing a project, involving the stakeholders.
- Project Monitoring and Control is concerned with providing an understanding of the project's progress so appropriate corrective actions can be taken.
- Project Planning is concerned with establish and maintain plans defining project activities. Notice, like Project Workout, BS6079 Part I and PRINCE2, it treats planning in a holistic way.
- Quantitative Project Management is a step up from monitoring and control and takes a metrics-based view on this.
- Risk Management is aimed at identifying potential problems so risk handling activities can be planned and called on if needed.
- Supplier Agreement Management is about buying products and service from suppliers (procurement).

CMMI does not contain information on how to undertake the practices leaving that to the manager to decide. By including the engineering activities within its scope, however, it shows how these and project management rely on each other. If you are working in a system engineering-based organization, such as aerospace, automotive and construction, then this is a useful perspective. Other CMMI models include CMMI for services and CMMI for acquisition, which deal with how to be a good supplier and a good client. The three CMMI models can be used together and share many practice areas.

I have more on this model in Chapter 30, looking at corporate maturity.

GAPPS, Global Alliance for Project Performance Standards

The Global Alliance for Project Performance Standards (GAPPS) was formed to provide a neutral platform for all parties interested in the leadership and management of projects, including professional associations, public and private sector organizations and academic institutions. The primary aim is to promote mutual recognition and transferability of project management standards and qualifications by providing a reliable source of comparative information. Everything the GAPPS produces is made available, free of charge, on its website.

The GAPPS has developed an approach to categorizing projects based on management complexity. The framework uses tools to differentiate roles based on the complexity of the programmes or projects managed. For example, for project management, the tool identifies seven factors affecting the management complexity of a project. Each factor is rated from 1 to 4, using a qualitative point scale, and the factors are totalled to produce a management complexity rating for the project. This was used as the basis for development of two levels of Project Manager Standards: G1 is for a moderately complex project and G2 for a very complex project. A score below a G1 is considered to be a simple project. The comparisons of different standards and methods are made against the GAPPS set of project management competencies, from which an overall percentage coverage for each standard is derived. For example, the extract that follows shows that the IPMA's competency standard (ICB3) and *PRINCE2®* have the greatest coverage. A detailed look at the results on the website shows where the differences lie.

Table 29.2 Comparison of different project management publications' coverage

	AIPM 2008 **(Australia)**	*ANCSPM 2011* **(Australia)**	*ICB3 (IPMA)*	*ISO 21500*	*P2M* **(Japan)**	*PMBoK 2008* **(PMI)**	*PRINCE2 2009* **(AXELOS)**
Very complex project % coverage	65	70	98	54	73	70	92
Moderately complex % coverage	69	74	99	58	81	79	93

Source: GAPPS, Comparison of project management standards, 27 Feb 2014

Comparing the methods and standards

Comparing methods, standards, bodies of knowledge and the like is fraught with difficulty as they serve different purposes and have different structures. They also cover the topics in various ways, particularly regarding how some topics are grouped. For example, all cover the topic of 'risk', but the methods go into it in more detail. In addition, new versions are being launched on a continual basis. The most relevant and complete standard for covering project management only is BS 6079:2019, *Project management – Principles and guidelines for the management of projects*. The scope of ISO 21500:2012 is more limited and wholly encompassed in BS6079, although work is under way to widen the scope when next issued as ISO 21502.

Portfolio management is covered by Management of Portfolios and ISO 21504. MoP has a slightly wider range of topics and has more depth. The same applies to programme management with Managing Successful Programmes and ISO 21503. The UK Government's GovS002 covers everything within the other documents except institutionalizing the approaches in an organization. GovS002 is, however, written at a higher level than the other documents and so does not include so much detail. Figure 29.2 is an indicative comparison of the relative scope of the documents and serves

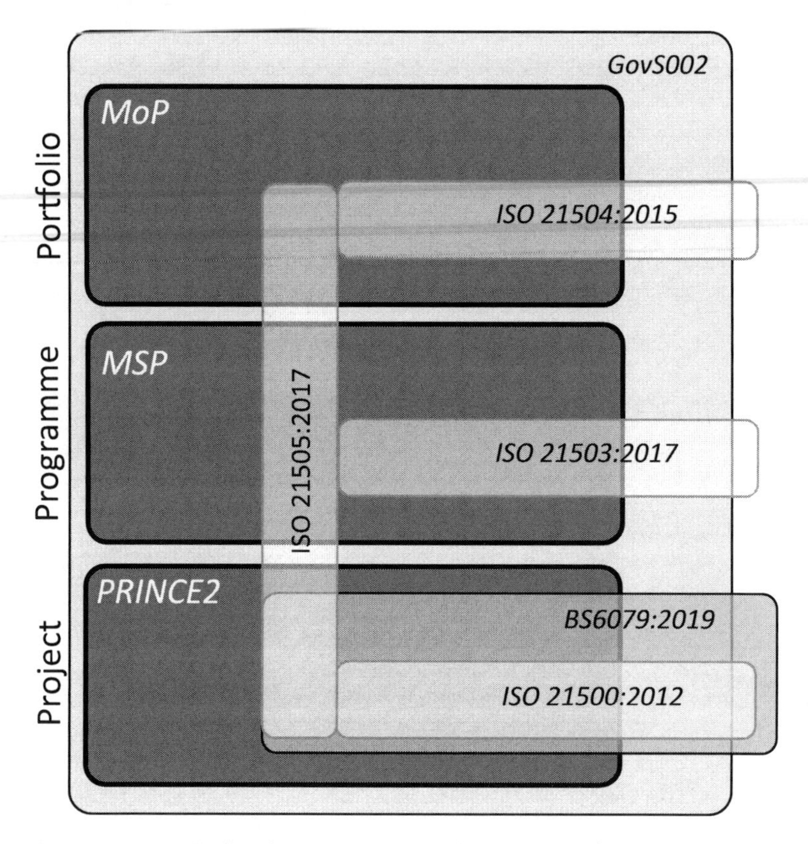

Figure 29.2 An indicative comparison of the scope of various documents

Comparing the scope of documents is fraught with difficulty as they follow different principles, go to varying degrees of depth and use different language. In addition, new versions are always being launched. This figure illustrates that none of the documents covers everything, so, if you are designing a PPM method, you need to be familiar with them all and apply what you need.

to illustrate that if you are implementing a portfolio, programme and project management approach in your organization, you need to be familiar with them all and select what you need in your business context. You can create your own comparisons using Workout 29.1.

A word of warning

There is an ever-growing range of 'methods', 'standards' and 'guides' dealing with portfolio, programme and project management. It can all get a bit daunting. On top of that, all these standards and methods are updated on a rolling basis, so be sure to check the editions you are working from are current. Remember, each is simply a consensus of the respective authors' opinions and will not necessarily contain everything you need or reflect your own views. You will need to tailor and adapt them to suit your organization. If you have a corporate method, most people will not need to read any of these, as they should be using your published method; it is the creators of the method who will need an in-depth knowledge of what the rest of the world is currently saying.

Where a standard or published method can be useful

A large company based in the USA required its suppliers to manage their project in accordance with PMI's PMBoK. The UK based supplier did not actually use the PMBoK as the basis for its method or its training. It was however able to demonstrate to that potential client that its corporate method covered every aspect of the PMBoK, and more besides. This was presented in a slim document explaining, section by section, how this was achieved. The potential client was satisfied with this and subsequently a contract was signed. That same supplier also had explanations of how their method complied with PRINCE2® and the BSI and ISO standards, as other potential customers required alignment with those.

There's no point in speeding if you are on the wrong road

Workout 29.1 – Checking your method against a standard or proprietary approach

If you need to (or want to) check your method against a published standard, such as BS6079 or PRINCE2®, you will need to list the clauses in the standard and then show where those are reflected in your method. The table that follows shows how you could organize a spreadsheet to do this.

Clause no.	*Clause title*	*Covered Y/P/N*	*Where covered in method*	*Comment*
<name of source standard or method>				
		Y = it is covered P = it is partially covered N = It is not covered	List thc specific references in your method where the clause is covered. There might be a number of these.	Add any comments explaining how a clause is reflected in your method

Your method might be structured in a different way to the source standard you are checking against. There is nothing wrong with that. The structure of a standard and the structure of a method can be different. Where they are different, however, you might need to do some deeper analysis, as the context of a clause or part of a method can have a significant impact on how it is used or interpreted.

30

Putting it into practice

The implementation task is very large, but not so large that you should give up now! Implementing business portfolio management is not a single project.

> *"If there are obstacles, the shortest line between two points may be a crooked one."*
>
> BERTOLT BRECHT, 1898–1956

- **Recognize that different organizations are at different levels of maturity.**
- **Be 'light' and 'tight' in the right places.**
- **Ensure your approach can be tailored, when tailoring adds value.**
- **Use consultants, your own staff and other organization's experience.**
- **Do try to build everything at once; take a phased and considered approach.**
- **Grasp opportunities for embedding new capabilities as they arise.**
- **Be patient, but consistent and persistent.**

Advice from other organizations

You have read and understood the book, bought into the principles and now you want to apply them to your organization. There are some projects going on, but you are not quite sure how many. You do not know what stage in the project framework they are. You might not know who wants the benefits or even who is managing them. You now want to do something about it – but what?

I asked a number of organizations what their advice would be to anyone introducing business portfolio management to an organization as a whole, or one particular cross-functional activity such as product development. All the advice given matched that found in any good book on the management of change (see Chapter 25). However, despite this consensus of common sense, much of this advice is ignored by many companies, to their cost!

> *"It is the true nature of mankind to learn from mistakes, not from example."*
>
> FRED HAYLE

Without good, timely decisions, the business, as a whole, will suffer

'Top management' support was always stated as essential, particularly if it goes to the heart of, "How we want to manage our business." This is one of the few business processes where top management is required to 'live' the process rather than leave it to others. This is where top management not only trigger new ventures but also act as a key link in the chain, steering the business to meet new challenges and grasp emerging opportunities and making decisions. Without good, timely decisions, the business, as a whole, will suffer. One chief executive of a major engineering group, rightly, held back his implementation for six months until convinced that every member of his senior team was really committed. This was in an organization where cross-functional working and project management concepts were already well established.

Other valuable advice included:

- do not underestimate the training and coaching effort needed;
- do not underestimate the resources needed to support implementation;
- do not underestimate people's ingenuity in resisting the changes;
- use champions embedded in the business to promote the new approach;
- roll it out in parts – you can't do all of it at once.

Finally, keep any supporting documentation simple. One organization had all their basic process summarized on ten A4 sheets of paper! This was supported by a number of more detailed guides to aid the users with particular aspects.

Of course, you have to direct and manage your business regardless of whether you have a business portfolio approach to aid you or not. Many organizations have operated as functional hierarchies for years and not even heard of words such as 'matrix', 'cross-functional' or 'project'. By the same token, there are organizations today where the use of the word 'cross-functional' is no longer needed. They always work in teams, drawing on the most appropriate people from across the organization to work together in pursuit of objectives. They cannot conceive of any other way to work effectively. I know which sort of organization I would rather work in!

A business portfolio approach will give you the capability to know:

- what you are doing to change your business in pursuit of your strategy;
- the interdependencies between the different components of your portfolio;
- the benefits and risks you are signed up to.

It does this by making the work you are doing, especially projects, and hence the implementation of strategy, very visible. It does not reduce or affect your discretion to direct and manage your business as you see fit. In fact, it gives you the knowledge to enable you to make better informed decisions and delegate more than ever before. Programmes or projects can be assigned to your colleagues and subordinates but, because they are visible and defined, you do not lose sight of them.

Implementing business portfolio management entails introducing complex changes encompassing processes, systems, accountabilities and culture. This book gives an insight into the processes, systems, accountabilities and cultures that have been shown to work best but it is impossible to be prescriptive about how it should be implemented in your organization. The easier parts to start work on are the processes and systems because they are tangible and can be written down and created. Structure and culture, however, are another matter. As soon as you start changing the structures, say, for decision making, the defence mechanisms of those who feel threatened will rise. Similarly, just because you have a process, it does not mean that some will do nothing but pay lip service to it. They might even ignore it if they can. You need to grow a culture which wants to play the game and engages all your people, from top to bottom. Earlier in this book I talked about the organization which always looked to 'people problems' when a process broke down. They had learned that this was usually the root cause of breakdowns, rather than the process itself. I also described how business portfolio management is one of the few business processes which senior management take a part in rather than watch from afar. It is, therefore, vital that your implementation includes full account of the roles that those key people are to take. Remember, this is not just about processes and project managers but running a business in totality.

Remember, this is not just about processes and project managers but running a business in totality.

Corporate maturity

One of the greatest obstacles to the effective implementation of business portfolio management is the corporate culture, with respect to cross-functional accountabilities from top to bottom. There are a number of maturity models published to help organizations plan their way through the 'improvement maze'.

Capability Maturity Model® Integration *(CMMI®)*

CMMI®, from the Software Engineering Institute, is an established set of maturity models. Each maturity model defines four 'maturity levels', with distinct criteria and associated best practices. CMMI®, according to its official website, is described as follows:

> *CMMI® is a process improvement approach that provides organizations with the essential elements of effective processes. It can be used to guide process improvement across a project, a division, or an entire organization. CMMI® helps integrate traditionally separate organizational functions, set process improvement goals and priorities, provide guidance for quality processes, and provide a point of reference for appraising current processes."*

In other words, CMMI®'s models seek to be a set of best practices, which, if followed, will lead to business advantage. It has four levels of 'maturity'. The levels for the development model (CMMI® Development), which is the one most closely associated with programme and project management are:

- Level one, is where most people are: ad hoc project management. In fact, by definition everyone not at level 2 or above is at level 1!
- Level two, means you can do one project at a time, but maybe all your projects are done differently.
- Level three means there is a common way of undertaking all your projects. This is the minimum level I advocate, as evidenced by this book.
- Level four means you are truly metrics driven and an organization optimizing its performance.

If you target a particular maturity stage, then level 3 is where you need to aim. Each level defines a set of process areas and criteria to meet. Failure in just one small part of one process area means you fail to achieve that level. Alternatively, you can use their 'continuous representation', where you choose what process areas to concentrate on based on your own priorities rather than those of the people who wrote the model. Instead of achieving a 'maturity level', you will achieve a 'capability level' on the chosen process area

The CMMI® handbook is not a gripping read. It is the only book I've read which I needed to go on a course to know what it really means to say! That said, once you get through the style and the jargon, there is a lot of sense in it. Used properly and supported by the right consultants, CMMI® can make a difference to organizations in the engineering sectors. Some major corporations and government departments (especially in the USA) require it as a pre-requisite to bidding. That can be its success and its downfall as many organizations may take CMMI® on in order to 'get the badge' rather than really make a difference to their business operations.

I have used CMMI® and can reconcile it with my own ideas in this book and in *The Project Workout*. It does, however, show its IT industry roots in the writing style and perhaps that is why it can be difficult to understand. One unique feature is that the maturity model covers not only portfolio, programme and project management but also the management of specialist work, which it calls 'engineering'. It argues that no matter how good you are at 'management', if you cannot do the fundamental work required to realize your solution, you are hardly likely to succeed.

PRTM

Another maturity model I have used to great effect was developed in the 1980s by PRTM (a management consultancy specializing in high technology businesses, later taken over by PwC). Unlike CMMI®, it has a five-level model, starting at not being capable of undertaking projects at all, to being able to undertake whole herds of projects: portfolio management. I like this model as it acknowledges the 'ignorant' who have no realization of the benefits business-led project management can provide and also recognizes, in its highest maturity level, the importance of organizations working together (partnering), which is increasingly common today. It is the only model I have come across which explicitly places partnering at the top level. The logic is, if you are unable to work effectively within your own organization, how do you expect to work with another one? Research related to the CMMI model bears this out, where they found that if two organizations are to work effectively together, they need to be at a comparably high level of maturity.

If you are unable to work effectively within your own organization, how do you expect to work with another one

Both the PRTM and CMMI® models have the characteristic that movement through the stages of the maturity model are progressive; you must have attained and continue to maintain maturity at all lower levels of maturity. In other words, you cannot skip a level. This makes sense. To have a reliable view over your portfolio, you need to be assured that each component in the portfolio is being managed in a

Table 30.1 PRTM's maturity model explained [in one piece, not split over a page]

PRTM maturity model			*Comment*
Level 0	Informal	Informal practices based on individual experience.	**The Ignorant** – These organizations do not realize the importance and the power a staged project framework gives them. They spend little time on the early investigative stages and waste much effort in the later development stages. Their 'project' success rate is low. These organizations are inefficient and ineffective at implementing business projects.
Level 1	Functional	Excellence within functions, but not across functions.	
Level 2	Project excellence	Functions aligned for effective execution from concept to market.	**The Enlightened** – These organizations realize that a project framework is powerful. They spend a significant amount of time on the investigative stages and become excellent at terminating unwanted projects and doing thorough groundwork for those they wish to continue. Their project success rate is high. However, these organizations are operating below 'optimum' efficiency but are far more effective at implementing business projects than Stage 0/1 organizations.
Level 3	Portfolio excellence (Business Programs)	Processes in place to achieve aligned product and corporate strategy, platform and technology leverage, portfolio balance and excellence in project selection and execution.	**The Leaders** – These organizations can run not only individual projects but also portfolios of projects. They have a firm grasp on their strategy and what implementation looks like. Consequently, the proportion of time spent on investigative stages as a whole decreases as they are able to screen their proposals more effectively. (Note: the proportion of time spent on investigative stages on individual projects is still high.) They are able to select projects for their portfolio, taking into account constraints such as resources, funding and risk. Their project success rate is high. These organizations are both efficient and effective at implementing business projects.
Level 4	Co-development excellence (Partnering)	Core processes linked across to internal and external business partners for maximum leverage.	**The Leaders PLUS** – These organizations can run not only their own projects, but are also effective at working with other organizations, which is key in partnering.

reliable way. For example, a business portfolio is hardly likely to be run well if none of the projects is under control.

PRTM's research showed it is not effective to move up a stage without sufficient mastery of the preceding stages. It also shows how productivity can increase by up to 50% for those on Stage 4, as opposed to Stage 1, with commensurate improvements in growth, profit and time to delivery. Stages 0 to 2 can, to a greater or lesser extent, be driven by forward-thinking middle managers, whereas Stages 3 and 4 are impossible to attain unless senior management want it. Excellence at this level really does come down to a question of: "How do we want to direct our organization?" If you are a business leader, that is the choice.

P3M3

If you are aligning your working methods with the AXELOS PRINCE2®, MSP® and MoP® approaches (see Chapter 29), you are likely to come across the P3M3 maturity model. Whilst part of the AXELOS suite, it can be used for assessing an organization, regardless of the portfolio, programme and project management methods used. Its five maturity levels are roughly equivalent to the five used by the CMMI® model and are characterized in Table 30.2.

Again, like the CMMI® model, the P3M3 model focusses on a number of practice areas or perspectives. The perspectives group together one or more processes and are as follows:

- organizational governance;
- management control;
- benefits management;
- risk management;
- stakeholder management;
- finance management;
- resource management.

A feature of P3M3 is that it allows you to review just one (or several) of the perspectives in one or more models. This can be useful to gain a better understanding of an organization's overall effectiveness in, for example, risk management or resource management. This is similar to the CMMI® continuous capability approach.

Workout 30.1 – Where does your gut tell you that you are?

Think about your organization in light of the descriptions in Table 30.1 and 30.2:

1. Which level of maturity do you honestly believe you are at now?
2. Which level are you aiming for in your implementation and what timescale?
3. Are you clear on the business reason for wanting to improve?

Table 30.2 High-level descriptors of P3M3 maturity levels [do not split over a page break]

Maturity	*Portfolio*	*Programme*	*Project*
Level 1: Awareness of process	Does the organization's board recognize programmes and projects and run an informal list of its investments in programmes and projects? (There may be no formal tracking and documenting process.)	Does the organization recognize programmes and run them differently from projects? (Programmes may be run informally with no standard process or tracking system.)	Does the organization recognize projects and run them differently from its on-going business? (Projects may be run informally with no standard process or tracking system.)
Level 2: Repeatable process	Does the organization ensure that each programme and/or project in its various portfolios is run with its own processes and procedures to a minimum specified standard? (There may be limited consistency or coordination between portfolios.)	Does the organization ensure that each programme is run with its own processes and procedures to a minimum specified standard? (There may be limited consistency or coordination between programmes.)	Does the organization ensure that each project is run with its own processes and procedures to a minimum specified standard? (There may be limited consistency or coordination between projects.)
Level 3: Defined process	Does the organization have its own centrally controlled portfolio processes and can individual initiatives flex within these?	Does the organization have its own centrally controlled programme processes and can individual programmes flex within these processes to suit the particular programme?	Does the organization have its own centrally controlled project processes and can individual projects flex within these processes to suit the particular project?
Level 4: Managed process	Does the organization obtain and retain specific management metrics on its whole portfolio of programmes and projects as a means of predicting future performance? Does the organization assess its capacity to manage programmes and projects and prioritize them accordingly?	Does the organization obtain and retain specific measurements on its programme management performance and run a quality management organization to better predict future programme outcomes?	Does the organization obtain and retain specific measurements on its project management performance and run a quality management organization to better predict future performance?
Level 5: Optimized process	Does the organization run continual process improvement with proactive problem and technology management for the portfolio in order to improve its ability to predict performance over time and optimize processes?	Does the organization run continual process improvement with proactive problem and technology management for programmes in order to improve its ability to predict performance over time and optimize processes?	Does the organization run continual process improvement with proactive problem and technology management for projects in order to improve its ability to predict performance over time and optimize processes?

Source: © Copyright © AXELOS Limited 2016

Formal, informal, light or tight?

Processes define the activities to be undertaken, who is involved, and usually include templates for important and frequently used documents (such as the business case and programme management plan) and hyperlinks to relevant web pages and work-flow tools. They can also include product descriptions with quality criteria, guidance in the form of booklets (online and/or physical) and videos, which act as educational vehicles for the team.

The degree of formality is a matter of context, culture and choice. It ranges from being very prescriptive (process-driven) to being much looser, giving the manager a large degree of freedom on the detail (this is often called method-driven). Some organizations are clear on the difference between 'process' and 'method' and find the distinction useful whilst, for others, it is irrelevant. It is very much a matter of how the words are perceived and used in your organization.

Recent focus has been on improving programme and project management success rates by using reliable, repeatable processes. CMMI®, discussed earlier in this chapter, is based on the assumption that the quality of the output is highly influenced by the quality of the process used. Many (but not all) organizations have gained significant improvements as a result but not all. Consequently, there is growing concern that an overemphasis on 'process' or being 'process obsessed' might have the opposite effect to that intended. There is little point of having process for process sake; as we saw in Chapter 2, there should only be a process if it adds value. For this reason, 'methods' are gaining more attention.

A method defines the broad approach, leaving much of the detail for the user to define. Methods are less prescriptive than processes, which can be seen as a straitjacket. For this reason, many believe that 'management', being more of an art, is better defined in terms of method rather than process. Again, the context and words used in your organization might paint another picture; the terms 'process', 'activity' and 'practice' are used differently and often interchangeably in different organizations, published methods and standards. Do not, however, confuse the freedom 'methods' give over a pure process approach with how 'tight or light' your management is.

Both business portfolio and programme management need to be tight in terms of ensuring that everyone is aligned on:

- strategy;
- business objectives;
- interdependencies;
- overall risk.

Business portfolios and programmes, by their nature, are usually too large to be predictable enough to let an unmanaged and unaligned plan drive them.

With both a 'method' or 'process' approach, the management practices and activities can be looked at as falling into three main groups:

- **Management processes or methods,** which ensure the portfolio or programme as a whole, including its component parts, is adequately governed, integrated,

under enough control and likely to meet the defined objectives. This is the core of the process set. See Chapters 10, 16 and 20.
- **Supporting processes or methods**, which determine how a particular facet of management is undertaken (for example risk management). Such processes include the detail and may be used within the components of a portfolio or programme or even outside. Typically, they comprise processes for the control, quality and commercial work, such as described in Part V of this book.
- **Specialist processes or methods**, which are dependent on the type of outputs to be developed and outcomes expected (for example a software development process or method). These are outside the scope of this book but as they form part of the context, can have a significant effect on success. For this reason, in the process set recommended in this book, I have included processes, under the 'quality' heading in Chapter 24, which can be used to ensure:
  - requirements are collected;
  - the solution, as a whole, is designed;
  - the solution is built, verified and validated.

Justifiably different – tailoring

You might be wondering, as you read this book, whether the implied 'one size fits all' approach is practical. Can you really direct and manage a small internal project using the same processes as for a major multi-million-dollar programme? Common sense says this cannot be right . . . and usually common sense is right! All organizations are different, and all have an emphasis on different types of project. The principles and building blocks in this book are applicable to all of them but the detail might need to differ. Chapter 9 looked at how to adapt a standard project framework to suit different circumstances by 'tailoring' the approach for specific needs and documenting this in the business case. Similarly, any aspect of any topic in the book can be tailored. For example, you should decide, based on your circumstances, what project life cycle to use, how the risk log should look and how the business case should be constructed. Having defined these, you need to ask:

- what differences will I permit?
- what parts are mandatory?

These are your **tailoring limits**. They enable the users of your processes and methods to alter some aspects of the standard approach to meet their needs. Programmes and projects are self-defining, in that the business case and its management approaches define not only *why* you are undertaking a project but also *how* to undertake it. In other words, it will state what tailoring you have applied. Approval of the such documentation should imply approval of any tailoring. 'Difference' is a fact of life and tailoring should be used to enable people to take an appropriate but proportionate different approach to managing and undertaking their work but stopping it becoming a 'free-for-all'.

Finding help in implementing a project management approach

Finding help in putting the principles and practice outlined in this book into effect can be daunting. The options include:

- asking a consultant;
- asking your in-house experts;
- finding out how others solve this problem (benchmarking).

Consultants

Employing an outside consultant is an obvious and frequently used choice but their solutions might be resisted from within the organization. 'We're different', 'That's too theoretical and 'You don't understand how complicated our business is' are commonly heard objections. Unfortunately, much good experience, advice and money are wasted if an organization lacks trust and belief in what its consultants are saying. However, before you ignore the complaints of your people, consider whether the consultants chosen (or proposed to be used) really do know their subject and understand your particular business sector. Check a number of consultancies and ask their former clients for references. If possible, make some site visits and find out what the people on the ground think. Making a wrong move at the start could be catastrophic. Having made the selection, the benefits the consultant will bring include expertise and broad experience. In addition, they are able to challenge and coach your senior team to an extent internal staff are often reticent to do.

Internal experts

Many organizations use their own people. They are cheaper than consultants and might even have been recruited from top consulting firms in the first place. However, if regarded as a 'prophet in their own country who is not believed', they may have less credibility than an external consultant. When considering using your own people, check them out as thoroughly as you would an external consultant. Look for evidence that they really know what they are talking about and their ability to deliver the goods.

Benchmarking

Nowadays, the use of 'benchmarking' is becoming commonplace. It is invaluable in both the commercial and the non-commercial sectors for improving performance and finding better ways of structuring and running organizations. Looking at other organizations enables you to see beyond your own immediate problems at how others really operate. Often benchmarking merely confirms that the approach you are proposing or taking is correct but can have the additional benefit of suggesting alternative and illuminating approaches experienced by others. If benchmarking is to work, you must, however, be receptive to new ideas or even old ones you have previously discarded.

If benchmarking is to work, you must, however, be receptive to new ideas

Use all three sources of help

if trust in the proposed solutions is to be generated, I have found that using a combination of consultants, internal staff and benchmarking is the most productive route through the implementation maze because:

- consultants can give a dispassionate view based on their own specialist knowledge and bring considerable experience in a particular field;
- in-house experts will know their own organization, its culture and style and will also have to live with any solutions adopted;
- benchmarking gives a wider perspective ("Other organizations really do it that way!").

A strategy for implementation

Boil the ocean and eat an elephant

The implementation task is very large but not so large that you should give up now! Implementing a business portfolio approach is not a single project and cannot be done in one hit, as the scale of the changes needed are too extensive. It is necessary to split the task into smaller parts, each of which should satisfy a particular need and give a definite benefit. Each of these parts should be run as a project, using all the discipline that a projects approach entails. Then ease your way forward, a step at a time, to reap the rewards early. As a start you could use the tools, techniques, lessons and principles in this book and *The Project Workout*. What better test is there for a project framework than to use it in its own creation!

One word of warning: be very firm on maintaining the principles that business portfolio management relies on. As the framework starts to bed in, it will throw other processes and procedures within your organization into sharp relief. Sometimes it will show them up to be inadequate. This is not necessarily the fault of the new approach; the other procedures might always have been inadequate but were hidden under a pile of inefficiency and confusion. Alternatively, it might be that the side effects of the new approach had been missed during trials. The temptation is always to stop and fix every 'new problem'. Resist this. Keep on implementing the parts you decided to implement. If the 'new' problems have been lying unnoticed for a number of years, a few more months should do no great harm. If you stop to fix every glitch you find, you will end up being diverted to do more and more until you will indeed be trying to eat the elephant whole or boil the entire ocean.

Get real!

A board of senior managers was listening to a presentation on the findings of a benchmarking study (Part I of this book!). A few of them were shaking their heads, commenting, "The approaches being presented are not used in the 'real world.'' The chief executive stopped the presentation stating, "You might think these approaches don't work but the organizations we talked to are highly respected and successful and they do use them. This is the real world: forget about what you think we could or could not do in this organization and listen."

How do we make decisions?

The design of the basic staged, project life cycle was completed. It was agreed. It was ready to be introduced when one small question was raised:

Executive:	"The gates require us to make decisions – how do we do that? Could you design a decision-making process for us first? We need that before we go any further. We need to know how to prioritize."
Project champion:	"Why do you need that now? All I've done is design a management life cycle for projects. I haven't touched decision making yet. You make decisions on these things now, so continue as you are until we work out a better way and get the information infrastructure in place."

What had happened, in fact, was that by rationalizing one part, decision making was shown to be lacking. You cannot 'process' decision making; only process the points when they need to be made. It is possible, however, to provide the information required to enable informed decisions to be made; but that relies on having a basic framework within which to manage in the first place. Delaying the implementation of the project life cycle until decision making is in place would not necessarily solve the problem and would probably lead to implementation being delayed until all process components (resources, business planning, fund management, etc.) were defined and approved. In practice, this could mean that nothing is ever implemented.

Watch out for gaps in your scope

Building your implementation strategy

When undertaking complex change or business process re-engineering, often the advice is that it should be done in tranches, moving from one 'temporary mode of operation' or 'island of certainty' to another. Put some change in place, let it settle, put some more in place. This assumes a linear and sequential transition from one state to another. It also assumes that the overall implementation order and configurations at for each tranche can be planned in advance (see (a) in Figure 30.1).

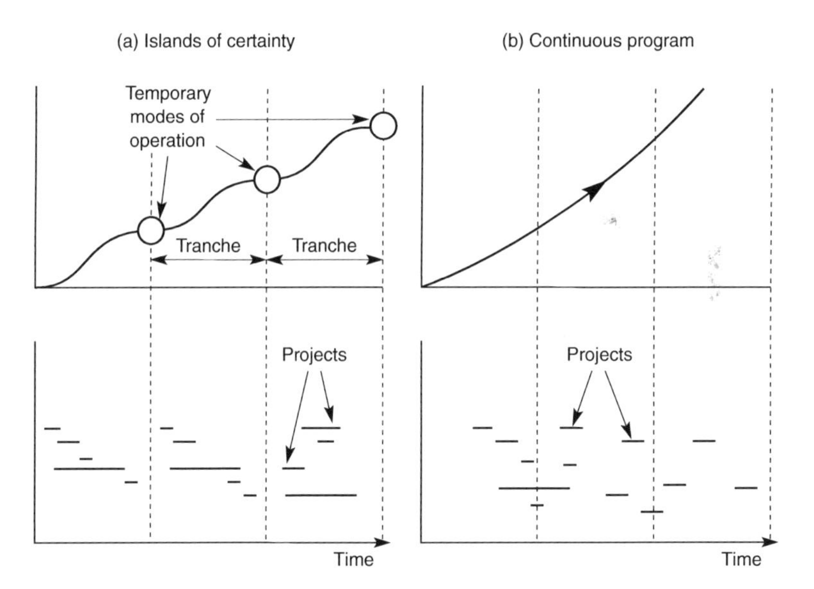

Figure 30.1 Islands of certainty and progressive change

Often the advice on implementing complex change is undertake a first tranche of changes, pause to allow the new changes to bed in (island of certainty or temporary mode of operation) and then move on with the next set of changes. In contrast using a strategy of continuous change, moving from configuration to configuration, will give you the freedom to choose whether to carry on without limiting yourself to what may be arbitrary islands.

The advice to split the implementation up into projects and hence manage them as a programme is sound. The concept of progressing from one planned state to another, however, is not always realistic. The implementation will not be a 'paint by numbers' programme. Overall, it will start off as a fog and you will need to feel your way forward. A detailed road map showing the islands of certainty might impose constraints on your freedom to capitalize on implementation opportunities as they arise. After all, the power of programme management is to be flexible and proactive rather than being restricted to a plan which seemed a great idea last year. Using a strategy of continuous change, moving from configuration to configuration, will give you the freedom to choose whether to push forward or pause every time a new capability is delivered (see (b) in Figure 30.1). Such decisions must be taken in the knowledge of the prevailing workload in the organization and level of acceptance achieved so far.

Assume that you have decided to split implementation up into projects as follows:

- high-level design of the final state;
- staged project life cycle and project management;
- decision making;
- strategic alignment;
- fund management;
- release management;
- resource management;
- business planning and forecasting.

Depending on where your organization is now, you will have a certain amount of confidence in your current operational capabilities for each area of implementation covered by these projects. For you, some of the projects listed here will be paint by numbers, some will be quests and others might even be fogs (for a reminder of these, see Chapter 9).

Starting with the paint by numbers projects will give you more confidence in delivery and hence in securing some benefits. As for the others, you will not know how long they will take, nor the order in which they can be completed. Neither will you be sure on the timing, as much of the change relies on the development of culture. So you cannot predict any further islands of certainty – you are in uncharted territory. The starting point has affected the implementation strategy from the very first day. Do not despair; concentrate on the changes you want to happen. Define these in terms of outcomes with 'conditions of satisfaction' and then work out, through backcast planning, how they were achieved.

A possible implementation strategy is:

Project set 1. Build a high-level picture of what you ultimately want to achieve and define a programme of possible projects – classify them as paint by numbers, fog or quest. This picture is often called a 'blueprint' and should never be confused with a programme definition.

Project set 2. Implement the staged framework and project management method. Experience from both CMMI® and PRTM has demonstrated that unless you can do at least one project at a time (level 2), you cannot progress to the required higher levels of maturity.

Project set 3. Implement any other paint by numbers projects you have identified. You must look for early benefits if the programme is to be seen as credible.

Project set 4. Work on the remaining quests and fog projects when you have resource available, implementing them as soon as they become clear and the conditions in the organization are right.

The overall design (Project set 1) is critical to sound implementation. This book is a reference to help identify and design the elements of the management framework for your organization. You will also need to know how you are currently dealing with all the activities which will still need to be undertaken in your future project state (i.e., know your present mode of operation, its strengths and weaknesses). Do not spend too long on this; you need only know enough to make sure that your new management framework fits into the organization with no gaps. Designing the new framework can be dealt with on an iterative basis. You will not design it correctly the first time and are bound to make a few mistakes. Accept this and plan for it. A very effective way of designing and validating the framework is to take a part of it and trial it on a number of projects. Use the learning from this to refine the approach before moving into wider implementation.

After completing the overall design, implement the staged framework itself (Project set 2). The benefit of putting this in place first is that it provides the hooks that all the associated processes need to lock onto. The teams undertaking the other projects will have a known reference point to join onto. They cannot help but align to each other as they are all referenced to the same anchor (represented by the gates in the project life cycle). The work scope for this set should include basic guides outlining the framework, together with foundation training for programme and project sponsors, programme and project managers, line managers and team managers. You should also have project coaches available to guide newcomers; training, on its own, is seldom sufficient.

The choice of the next implementation projects is critical (Project set 3). They must be those you know how to do and which will remain stable once in place. They should be ones which, when coupled with those that follow, will ensure sustainable progress. In this way, a launch pad is built quickly to progress the remainder of the implementation. Decision making and establishing a project list should be a high priority in this set

You are then ready to undertake your remaining projects (Project set 4) in any order, at any time, creating continual change towards your objective rather than moving from island to island in any predesigned order. This does not mean that there will be no critical dependencies between projects nor any overall programme plan.

On the contrary, in order to have this flexibility you must be sure of your high-level design and of the possible configurations you might pass through on the way. It also might be that the particular systems or related processes in your organization will require some elements to be completed before others. Consider this in the investigative stages of each project and design your operational configurations accordingly. To do this, it might be necessary to implement temporary systems, structures and processes. For example, to maintain control, you will need to have a list of the projects and other work in your business portfolio. That does not mean you need the finished database. A simple spreadsheet can be enough to start off which can act as a prototype to help decide the requirements for a final system.

You should also try to ensure that one of the early projects provides useful management information and reporting for the decision makers and others involved in the process. Reporting makes the process visible and serves as a driver of behaviour. Again, this helps set the scene for a cultural shift. Provided the newfound knowledge is used responsibly, the shift will be in the right direction. If the new information is used to expose and punish 'wrong doers', do not be surprised if people become less enthusiastic about the change and work to undermine it.

When undertaking any of the projects, do not assume you need do them throughout the whole organization at the same time. It is usually better to implement the new way of working on a particular sub-portfolio of cross-functional projects, for example, product development. Use this as the vehicle to refine and bed in the new processes, systems and structures and to start growing the new culture. Remember, business projects are usually, by nature, cross-functional; therefore, you will not be able to implement this function by function. Do consider, however, that if you implement in a phased way, there will be some boundary issues where people will insist that certain projects are 'outside the new process'. Expect and accept this. Many people will insist that they can move their projects forward quicker outside the project framework and a few of them might be right, in the short term at least. As the disciplines become better established, the advantages of working within a known framework will become obvious; projects will meet their objectives. I recall one project manager who spent more time avoiding using a new approach than would have been involved in getting on and using it.

As some of your process infrastructure may be broken before you even start, the order the remaining projects are introduced does not matter. Choose the order which suits your own circumstances and the timing of when the quest and fog projects come to fruition (Figure 30.2). At the start, you will notice inefficiencies, but these will reduce as more of the 'final configuration' comes into being. People might even start to solve some problem areas outside the formal programme. As they will be aligned to the core principles and project life cycle, there will be little danger of conflict. In this way, certain parts of the organization can adopt certain elements before others if it suits their needs at that point in time. The fact that people do this is evidence of the approach gaining acceptance naturally, and part of the cultural shift is happening.

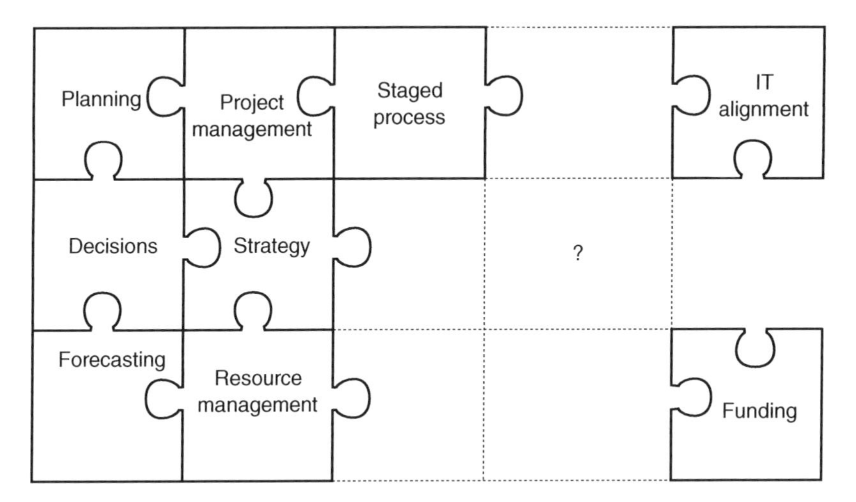

Figure 30.2 Implementation of a portfolio, programme and project management approach

Think of implementation as if it was a complicated jigsaw. The work from Project set 1 will give you a view of the final picture, although some parts may be fuzzy. Fill in the new pieces as projects are completed. The picture will become clearer as more of the pieces are in place. Do not think of it as building a wall. In a wall it is not possible to put the coping stone on until the bricks below are in place. With a jigsaw, you can put any pieces in place as, and when, you see fit.

What do I do with the existing processes?

There will most probably be some parts of your organization already using a projects approach. They might also be backed up by excellent good practice tools and guides. Should you ask them to throw these away in favour of an, as-yet unproven, organization-wide approach? If you try, you will meet resistance. Your aim is to ensure that change in your business is managed well and properly directed, not to force people into a straitjacket. Make sure you involve the key players who are champions of their local project processes. Have them design the detail of the new process, adding whatever they can from their own toolkits. Do not insist they follow the new process from day one. Start off by saying it is for those people in the organization who have nothing and for the senior managers who will act as project sponsors or project board members. Then ask them to show how their local processes align to the new one. Where possible, ask them to adopt any new terminology (especially stages, gates and key roles) and templates. Over time, the local processes will converge on a single 'best way'.

How long will this take?

The time taken to establish viable business portfolio management depends very much on your starting point. In an organization used to cross-functional working, which puts more emphasis on role than formal job description, much of the culture will already be established. If, however, your organization is a very functional-led hierarchy where rank is highly prized, the change will be a shock. If you have stable and active leadership, the speed with which you can move forward will be faster than if your leadership suffers frequent change. In fact, if your organization is one where change is relentless, implement in bite-sized chunks so that at least part of the jigsaw is established prior to a change at the top. Many implementations have failed, as they never quite got there before the old top team went. Nevertheless, a period of two to five years for fully establishing a completely integrated business portfolio approach is common.

A project life cycle, together with its associated project management documentation and training, can be launched within six months of a decision to move forward. After that, aim to have another major piece of the jigsaw in place every three to six months. Remember, one factor influencing rate of change is the state of the business processes and culture in aspects which influence projects. The better they are, the quicker you can move forward.

A project life cycle, together with its associated project management documentation and training, can be launched within six months of a decision to move forward.

Being held accountable

If you are an invisible project sponsor or manager on an invisible project which few people know exists, let alone what it is for, you might take your accountabilities less seriously than if your name is published to the organization in a list against the project with key milestones appended. In the former case, failure can be hidden and objectives can be recast to suit performance. However, in the latter you are being asked to deliver on a 'promise' and can be held accountable. This may sound hard, but remember, the project has been approved in full knowledge of the risks and stopping the project, if circumstances dictate it, is a success; you are not expected to be Superman or Wonder Woman.

Appendix A: Glossary

This appendix provides the definitions for the terms used in *The Programme and Portfolio Workout*. It also includes some commonly used alternatives so you can understand the book in the context of your current programme and portfolio management knowledge and so that you can tailor the concepts and terms used in the book to suit your situation.

Key cross references are shown in *italics*.

Accountability What you can count on a person doing. That person and only that person can be called to account if a task they have accountability for is not done or is not done adequately. Note that this book and *The Project Workout* distinguish between 'accountability' and *responsibility*.

Activity Individual components of work that must be undertaken to complete the *stages* of a project. Each activity should be defined in terms of its start and end dates and the name of the person accountable for its completion. Common alternative: task.

Approval The term used when an individual accepts a deliverable as fit for purpose such that the project can continue. Note that this book and *The Project Workout* distinguish between 'approval' and '*authorization*'.

Assumption An assumption is made when an unknown is taken to be a fact. Assumptions can be tested using sensitivity analysis and often pose a *risk* to a project. An assumption is used so that work can continue without the full facts being available.

Assurance Assurance is the systematic set of actions necessary to provide confidence that work remains aligned to strategy and viable in terms of costs and benefits (business assurance), checking that the users' *requirements* are being met (user assurance) and that a suitable solution and outcomes are being delivered (specialist or technical assurance).

Authorization The decision which triggers the allocation of the resources and funding. Authorization is needed to carry on a project and to provide the project sponsor and project manager with the authority to undertake the project or the part of the project which has been authorized.

Backcasting Using the desired end result (*outcome*) of a project or programme as the basis and starting point for planning. This means planning is initially conducted working backwards from completion.

Bar chart A visual representation of a schedule, showing the start and finish dates of the activities a project and its stages, work packages and activities. Each *activity's* duration is shown as a horizontal bar, the ends of which correspond to its start and end dates. *Baseline*, actual and forecast dates can be shown on the same chart. A bar chart is also known as a *Gantt chart*.

Baseline A baseline serves as a point to measure from, which is used as a basis for comparison. In a *portfolio*, *programme* and *project* context baselines typically apply to *plans* and to sets of data relating to the solution (such as requirements baseline, design baseline).

Benefits The quantifiable and measurable improvement resulting from an outcome which is perceived as positive by a stakeholder and which makes the investment worthwhile. Benefits are normally expressed in monetary or resource terms. Benefits are expected when a change is conceived. Benefits are realized as a result of activities undertaken to effect the change. Examples include, quantified increases in revenue, decreases in costs, reductions in working capital and/or increase in performance.

Benefits map A diagram linking *outputs* to *outcomes* to *benefits* to objectives.

Blueprint A description of the 'future business or organization', its working practices and processes, the information required and the technology needed. It is the fundamental sourcebook describing a programme or project's *outcome* and *output* in terms of 'feel', 'technology' and commercial and customer/user needs. It is the document which integrates all the individual systems, processes and platform requirements and specifies how they should work together. This is also called a target operating model.

Board (programme or project) Body established to monitor a programme or project and assist the sponsor in delivering the *outcomes* and realizing the *benefits*. Sometimes called a steering group or steering board.

Brainstorming A technique for generating ideas in a group.

Budget Planned, approved cost for the project. See, also, *baseline*.

Buffer A term used in *critical chain* for the centralized management of schedule. There are two types of buffer:

- feeder buffer: protects the start of a critical chain activity from a delay of an upstream dependent non-critical chain activity. A project can have many feeder buffers.
- project buffer: protects the project end date from variability in the duration of the tasks in the *critical chain*. For a single project, the size of the buffer depends on the number and duration of the critical chain activities and the degree of risk associated with each.

Burning platform A burning platform is an event or circumstance where doing nothing is not an option.

Business case A document (or set of information) providing the justification for undertaking (or for continuing) a programme or project, defining the financial and other benefits the project is expected to realize, together with the schedule and other constraints within which the project is to operate. This is can be prepared in stages.

Business continuity Business continuity concerns planning and preparation to ensure that an organization:

- can continue to operate during and after a serious incident or disaster;
- is able to recover to a normal operational state within a reasonably short period.
- Three elements should be considered:
- resilience: critical business functions and the supporting infrastructure are designed in such a way to be materially unaffected by relevant disruptions, for example through the use of redundancy and spare capacity;
- recovery: arrangements are in place to recover or restore critical and near-critical business functions that fail for some reason;
- contingency: the organization has the capability and readiness to cope adequately with whatever incidents occur, including those that were not, and or could not have been, foreseen. Notice this is another example of *white space*.

Business portfolio A business portfolio comprises current benefit generating business activities, together with a loosely coupled but tightly aligned *portfolio* of programmes, projects and other work, aimed at realizing the benefits of part of a business plan or strategy.

Business portfolio, programme and project management is an integrated way of meeting an organization's ambitions, driving better decisions and increasing the likelihood of successful *outcomes*.

Business portfolio office A *support office*, which supports the roles of the business portfolio sponsor and manager. Alternatives include enterprise programme office, portfolio management office.

Business portfolio plan A part of the organization's business plan which focusses on the targets (benefits) and resources of a particular *business portfolio.*

Capabilities Building blocks of systems, processes and competence which are combined with other capabilities to provide an organization with operational potential.

Capacity buffer A *Critical Chain* term. Protective time placed between projects within the drum resource.

Change control The formal process through which changes to a *plan* are introduced and approved. Changes are recorded on a change log. (Not to be confused with the *management of change.*) Change control ensures only beneficial or necessary changes to the *baseline* are implemented after the impact of the change has been assessed.

Change log A list, maintained as part of change control, of all proposed and actual changes. Also called change register.

Change saturation Change saturation is when an organization and its people cannot absorb or cope with any more change.

Closure Formal 'end point' of a project, either because it is complete or has been *terminated* early. Closure is formally documented in a closure report.

Commitments Orders placed and hence the money, although not yet spent, committed as part of an agreed contract.

Complexity In the context of this book is an indicator of how difficult it is to undertake a programme or project:

- absolute complexity relates to how inherently difficult the work is to undertake, regardless of the organization undertaking it;
- relative complexity deals with how difficult an individual organization would find undertaking the work.

Conditions of satisfaction Conditions, which if met, enable the project to objectively be termed a success. These should be indicative of *benefits* realization. *Recognition Events*™ and *Value Flashpoints*™ are special types of condition, used in the Isochron methodology.

Configuration management A discipline, normally supported by software tools, which gives management precise control over the *deliverables* of a project (or components of a solution or an operational environment) and ensures the correct version of each part of a system is known and documented.

Configuration item The set of *deliverables* which are the subject of configuration management.

Consideration Payment, exchange of goods, services or similar, which must be of some value but can be nominal.

Constraint Defined restriction or limitation imposed on a project or operational work. A constraint limits a manager's freedom of action.

Contingency fund The money held in reserve just in case it is needed to treat a risk.

Contingency plan An alternative plan of action to be followed in the event of a *risk* occurring.

Contract A legally binding promise (written or verbal) by one party to fulfil an obligation to another party in return for consideration.

Contract terms Contracts comprise two sets of terms:

- express terms, which are the words, as written in the contract;
- implied terms, which are not written in the contract.

Contracting organization A contracting organization identifies an opportunity through market analysis, or an invitation to tender, prepares a response and then, if successful, undertakes the work as a programme or project.

Cost plan Document detailing items of cost associated with a project, in categories (*work packages*) relating to the schedule plan. See, also, *budget* and *baseline*.

Critical chain The critical chain of a single project is the sequence of dependent activities that would prevent the project from being completed in a shorter interval, given finite resources.

Critical path The path through a *network* of activities, taking into account dependencies, in which late completion of activities will have an impact on the project end date or delay a key *milestone*.

Critical success factors Factors to ensure the achievement of *success criteria*.

Culture Culture comprises two elements:

1. The norms and behaviours of a group (the way things are done here!)
2. Unconscious programming of the mind, leading to a set of similar collective habits, behaviours and mind-sets.

Customer programme or project A programme or project undertaken for a customer or client with the primary benefit gained being the revenue as payment for the services provided. See, also, *internal programme or project*.

Damages Damages are a sum of money awarded in compensation for loss or injury. Damages are set by a court after a breach of contract. Liquidated damages are predetermined and written into the contract.

Defect A defect is an identified error within an approved *deliverable* and can be applied to any deliverable, whether interim or final. See, also, *out of stage defect*.

Deliverable Output produced by the project, e.g., a report, system or product. Deliverables may be:

- Intermediate or temporary, used only during the undertaking of a project;
- Final, comprising part of the outputs from the project.

Each key deliverable should be defined in the *project definition* section of the *business case* document and represented by a *milestone* on the project plan. Alternatives: product, work product, asset.

Dependency A constraint on the sequence and timing of activities in a project. Activities may be dependent on other activities within the same project (internal dependency) or on activities/deliverables from other projects (*interdependency*).

Detailed investigation stage The second stage within the project framework, when a feasibility study is undertaken to choose the best solution from a range of options and when the chosen solution is defined in sufficient detail for delivery to start.

Detailed plan Developed throughout the project, from the *summary plan*, breaking down the forthcoming stage into manageable work packages and activities.

Duration The amount of time required to complete an *activity*. It is calculated as the finish date – the start date.

Earned value (1) A management technique which analyses and determines project progress by comparing the amount of work planned with what was actually earned and what was actually spent. Earned value is usually measured in currency units but effort or notional points may also be used; the key is that the actual measure and the plan need to be the same units.

Earned value (2) A method for integrating scope, schedule and resources and for measuring project performance. It compares the amount of work which was planned with what was actually earned with what was actually spent to determine if cost and schedule performance are as planned.

Effective Successful at realizing an objective.

Efficient Providing progress or performance with minimal waste of resources.

Emergency project A project required as a result of a business issue which will severely damage the organization if not addressed without delay. These projects may cause previously committed projects to be allocated a lower priority or to be *terminated* to release resources.

Enabling project A project which has no direct benefit for the sponsoring organization and so is not viable on its own merit. Such projects should be part of a programme and enable something else to happen, which would lead to *outcomes* and *benefits* being realized.

Escalation To increase the awareness and ownership of a problem or *issue* to a level in the organization where the required resources, expertise and/or authority can be applied to resolve that *issue*.

Estimate An approximate calculation or judgement of the value, number, quantity or extent of an element of a *plan*. In project management, an estimate may be considered 'soft' or 'hard':

- a soft estimate is one in which only a low level of confidence can be placed.
- a hard estimate is one in which you have high confidence.

Feeder buffer See *buffer*.

Float The amount of time an activity may be delayed without delaying subsequent activities. Float (also called slack) is a mathematical calculation and can alter as the work progresses and changes made to the plan. Float is measured in units of time, so an activity on the critical path has zero float. If an activity has some float, however, it can be done later.

- free float measures the time that an activity can be delayed without affecting any succeeding activity;
- total float measures the amount of time an activity can be delayed without affecting the end of a project.

Fog Project (walking in a fog) Formally known as an open project, this type of project occurs when you are unsure of both what is to be done and how.

Gantt Chart See *bar chart*. Henry Laurence Gantt, an American mechanical engineer, is recognized for developing the Gantt chart.

Gate The point, preceding each stage, at which all new information converges and which serves for:

- quality control checks
- prioritization
- a point from which to plan forward
- a go/no go decision point.

Governance Governance defines relationships and the distribution of rights and responsibilities among those who work with and in the organisation. It determines the rules and procedures through which the organization's objectives are set and provides the means of attaining those objectives and monitoring performance. Importantly, it defines where accountability lies throughout the organization.

Idea A possibility for a new or enhanced capability, system, service or product. This is written up as a *proposal*.

Impact The marked effect or influence of one action on another.

Impact assessment A study undertaken to determine the effect of an *issue* or *risk* on the project. An impact assessment is required as part of *change control* and as part assessing the advantages of taking one course of action over another (options).

Intelligent client An intelligent client one capable of specifying the requirements to external participants and managing the delivery of outcomes.

Interdependence If Project B requires a *deliverable* from Project A, in order to achieve its objective, project B is dependent on project A. Dependency is when a deliverable is passed from one project to another.

Internal programme or project A programme or project which an organization is undertaking directly for its own benefit. For example, an internal project may be the development and roll out of a new billing system. See, also, *project* and *customer project*.

Internal Rate of Return (IRR) A method used to determine the value of a project. The discount rate at which the value of the opportunity will be zero. In principle, the higher the IRR, the 'better' the opportunity, but this guideline should be used with caution as other factors, such as cash flow and risk, may be more important.

Issue An issue is a relevant event that has happened, was not planned and requires management action. It could be a problem, benefit, query, concern, change request or a *risk* that has occurred.

Issues log A list, maintained as part of issue management, of all issues and their status. Alternative: issues register.

Late activity An *activity* which is forecast to end later than the *baseline* plan finish date. This is reported on a late activities report.

Life cycle The life cycle provides a phased structure for governing the work and underpinning the delivery plan, from start to finish. Life cycles can be applied to a portfolio, service, product, system, programme or project.

Link A relationship between *dependent* activities.

Liquidated damages See *damages*.

Management of change A term often used to describe the action of transforming an organization from one state to another. Alternative phrases are management of business transformation and change management. Not to be confused with *change control*, which is a technique used on projects to ensure that alterations to the project schedule, scope, *benefits* and cost are introduced in a regularized way.

Management plan A documented description of how something is to be managed, in terms of the approach, methods and processes required to be used. For example, project management plan, contract management plan, risk management plan.

Method A collection of practices, rules, tools and instructions used by teams or individuals to achieve a specific result. A method defines principles and provides documentation and tools. It is the responsibility of users to identify and plan the relevant component to carry out their specific tasks. As such, a method provides flexibility but requires each user to choose and organize the set of activities relevant for the programme or project. A method may comprise one or more procedures, supported by guides and templates. Alternative: methodology, although some people define a method as distinct from a methodology.

Milestone A major event (often representing the start of a *stage*) used to monitor progress at a summary level. Milestones are activities of zero duration.

Mission A mission states the purpose of the organization, why it exists, what it does and who for.

Movie project (making a movie) Formally, a semi-open project, where the means are known but not the *output*.

Net Present Value (NPV) The value calculated by projecting the future cash flow and discounting the value of future years' cash at the discount rate to give its notional value today.

Network chart or diagram A diagram which shows dependencies between project *activities*. Activities are represented as boxes or nodes and the activity relationship is shown by arrows connecting the nodes. Often called a PERT chart.

Offer In a contractual context, one of the parties to a *contract* has to offer the terms of the contract. An offer has to be 'complete', including the full terms of the intended contract.

Opportunity An uncertainty that could have a positive impact on objectives or benefits. See, also, *risk*.

Originator The person who conceives an *idea* or need for a new development or enhancement and publishes it in the form of a *proposal*. This person can come from any function or level in the organization.

Other work Other work is work within a business portfolio or programme, which is not managed as a project. Sometimes called 'other related work' or 'non-project work'.

Out of stage defect A *defect* which is not spotted in the stage it was introduced.

Outcome The result of change, normally affecting real-world behaviour or circumstances. Outcomes are desired when a change is conceived. Outcomes are achieved as a result of the activities undertaken to effect the change; they are the manifestation of part or all of the new state conceived in the *blueprint*. In a portfolio, programme and project management context, this means the result of change, affecting real-world behaviour or circumstances through a programme, project or business operation. Outcomes are desired when a change is conceived and are achieved as a result of the activities undertaken and *outputs* produced to effect the change. Desired outcomes, if achieved, usually produce a *benefit* for the organization.

Output A specialist product (the tangible or intangible *deliverable* or set of deliverables) is produced, constructed or created as a result of a planned activity. Outputs, if used, will result in an *outcome* or business change.

Parties In a contractual context, parties are those with a legal, contractual relationship.

Phase See *stage* and *tranche*.

Pilot A pilot is the ultimate form of validating a new development and its implementation plan prior to committing to the full-scale release. It is undertaken using a sample of potential customers and users. This would normally take place in the *trial stage* although may, in some cases, a pilot can be treated as a limited release.

Plan The information detailing the *benefits*, *schedule*, *resource*, costs and *risks* for a defined piece of work, such as a programme, project or work package.

Portfolio A generic term for a grouping or bundle of programmes, projects and other work collected together for management or reporting convenience: e.g., the collection of projects sponsored by an individual is his or her sponsorship portfolio; those projects managed by a person is a management portfolio; the set of projects within region is the regional portfolio. See, also, *business portfolio*, which represent a specific type of portfolio required for effective governance.

Portfolio review group The term used in this book for the body accountable for the authorizing work within an organization, business portfolio or programme. There is no industry standard for this.

Post implementation review (PIR) A review, three to six months after the end of the project, to establish whether:

- the predicted benefits were delivered;
- the most effective operational processes were designed;
- the solution really met the business needs, both for users and customers;
- the changes have been sustained and are likely to remain so; sometimes referred to as being 'sticky'.

The post implementation review checks the *effectiveness* of a project as opposed its *efficiency* which is reviewed as part of project *closure*. Alternative: Post-project review, Post investment review.

Post investment review (PIR) A review, three to six months after the end of the project, to assess whether the expected *financial benefits* are being achieved. This checks the financial effectiveness of a project. A post investment review is included in a *post implementation review*, but often finance departments insist on the financial aspects being covered in a separate document to the operational aspects.

Process A series of actions or steps taken to achieve a particular end, with defined inputs, outputs, resource needs and constraints.

Programme A programme is a tightly coupled and tightly aligned grouping of projects and other work managed as a temporary, flexible organization created to coordinate, direct, oversee and deliver outputs, outcomes and benefits related to a set of strategic objectives.

Progamme management office (PMO) A *support office*, which supports the roles of the programme sponsor and manager. Alternatives include programme support office, programme office.

Progress bar chart A bar chart which shows the actual and forecast dates for each *activity* compared with the *baseline* plan dates.

Progress report Regular report from a manager to the next higher manager and other stakeholders summarizing the progress of a programme, project or work package, including key events, benefits realized milestones not achieved and issues and outlook for the future.

Product A term used in some project *methods* in place of *deliverable*. Hence the terms 'product breakdown structure', which identifies, in a hierarchical way, the deliverable/products required, and 'product flow diagram', which identifies each deliverable's derivation and the dependencies between them.

Project A project, in a business environment, is a piece of work with a beginning and end, undertaken in *stages*, within defined cost and time constraints, directed at achieving stated business *outcomes* and *benefits*. A project can be standalone within a *business portfolio* or part of a *programme*. See, also, *internal project* and *customer project*.

Project buffer See *buffer*.

Project definition A section within the initial and full *business case* which summarizes a project in terms of the benefits, expected outcome, what will be done, how it will be delivered and what business need the project supports.

Project support office (PSO) A group set up to provide certain administrative and other services to the project sponsor, manager and team. A project support office can provide services to several projects in parallel. See, also, *support office*.

Promoting organization Identifies a business, strategic or political need, translates this into a set of objectives and, using a programme or project as the vehicle of change creates the outputs and business changes needed to ensure those objectives are met.

Proposal A short document prepared by the *originator* for the initial investigation gate review which outlines the proposed project, its fit with current strategy and, if known, the impact on the organization, broad estimates of benefits, cost and expected time to completion.

Quality The totality of features and characteristics of a *deliverable* that bear on its ability to satisfy stated and implied needs. Also defined as 'fitness for purpose' or 'conforms to requirements'. Hence, 'quality criteria' are the conditions a deliverable must meet to be accepted as fit for purpose.

Quality assurance Providing confidence that outputs will match their defined quality criteria;

Quality control Monitoring specific results to determine compliance with the specified designs.

Quality improvement Identifying ways to eliminate causes of unsatisfactory performance.

Quality management Ensuring outputs are fit for purpose to achieve the objectives.

Quality planning Determine how to ensure quality is addressed in the management of a business portfolio or programme.

Quality review A review of a *deliverable* against an established set of quality criteria.

Quest project (going on a quest) Quest projects are formally known as semi-closed projects. You are clear what is to be done but have no idea about how to do it.

RAG (red – amber – green) A simple status reporting method, enabling the reader of a report to grasp very quickly, whether a project is likely to achieve its objectives or not. RAG stands for Red – Amber – Green:

- red means there are significant issues with the project that the project team and project sponsor are unable to address;
- amber means there are problems with the project but the team has them under control;
- green means that the project is going well with no significant issues, although it may be late or forecast to overspend.

The RAG status is usually based on a manager's own assessment of the situation and is useful for highlighting those projects or work which have difficulties. Some organizations set the RAG status automatically by systems, e.g., when a project is forecast to overspend. Some organizations use 'BRAG', where the 'B' is blue and denotes completed.

Ready for service (RFS) The *milestone* prior to the *release stage*, by when prerequisite project work, testing and trials have been completed and full operational support is in place. This is either prior to, or coincident with, the *release gate*.

Recognition event™ A real life happening that when it occurs, tells a sponsor and other stakeholders that one particular expectation of the project plan has been met. This is a term used in the Isochron method. See, also, *Conditions of satisfaction*.

Release gate The point prior to the release stage, when the decision is made to put the capability, product or service into operation.

Release Generic term used to denote when an output from a project is put into service, e.g., a product is launched into the market, an information or management system goes live, a new process is made operational. It should not be confused with *ready for service*, which is the point when all capabilities are ready to use but have not yet been put to use.

Release stage The final stage in the staged project framework during which the final output is launched and put into service.

Requirements Requirements are statements that translates or expresses a need and its associated constraints and conditions.

- Allocated requirements are those requirements provided from a higher-level system element to a lower level element.
- System requirements System requirements represents a user requirement which has been interpreted into a technical form to enable the design of a component of the solution.
- User requirements User requirements are statements that translates or expresses a stakeholder's need and its associated constraints and conditions.

Resource buffer A resource buffer is used in critical chain schedule management to provide early warning, from one *critical chain* activity to another critical chain activity, for an activity to start.

Resource levelling is when the planned assignment of resources is changed to ensure no over or under commitment of the resources. The aim is to be as evenly spread as possible.

Resource loading is when resources are assigned to activities in a plan so that their over- and under-allocation can be determined.

Resource manager A person in each unit and function accountable for knowing the future assignment of resources to processes and projects.

Responsibility What a person is or feels, responsible for. It assumes they have a commitment, beyond their own *accountabilities*, to act responsibly to ensure the project objectives are met.

Review A formal assessment of something with the intention of recommending changes if necessary. For a project as whole, a review is to ensure the business objectives will be achieved (project *assurance*); for deliverables, a review ensures the deliverable is fit for purpose. Reviewers are contributors to a decision but do not actually make the decisions (see *approval*).

Risk A risk is an uncertainty of outcome. A positive risk is called 'opportunity'; a negative risk is a 'threat'.

Risk action A risk action is a task that changes how a risk is managed. Normally an action will add or improve a control. Actions do not affect the net risk exposure. Possible actions are:

- prevention – countermeasures are put in place either to stop the threat or problem occurring or prevent it having any impact (avoidance);
- reduction – the actions either reduce the likelihood of the risk occurring or limit the impact on the project to acceptable levels;
- transference the impact of the risk is transferred to a third party, such as a contractor or insurance company organization. This approach is beneficial as it should lead to a reduction in the total amount of funds held in contingency;
- contingency – actions are planned (contingency plan) which will come into effect in sufficient time to manage the risk;
- acceptance – the company organization decides to go ahead and accept the possibility that the risk might occur and is willing to accept the consequences;
- exploitation in relation to opportunities, mine it for all its worth!

Alternative: risk treatment.

Risk appetite The amount of risk the organization, or subset of it, is willing to accept.

Risk log A list, maintained as part of risk management, to track all risks and their status. Alternative: risk register.

Risk control A risk control is a measure already in place to help manage a risk, either by making the risk less likely or by reducing the impact if it occurs. Controls have an influence on the net risk exposure – the risk faced today.

Risk tolerance Risk tolerance is an organization's readiness to bear the risk after risk treatments to achieve its objectives. Risk tolerance can be limited by legal or regulatory requirements. It is more specific and applies to individual risks.

Single point accountability The concept that any *activity*, or *work package*, at any level in the *work breakdown structure*, has only one named person accountable for it.

Slippage See *Late activities.*

Sponsor The person who sees a commercial possibility in an idea and agrees to take ownership of the proposal. Once a programme or project is approved, the sponsor is accountable for realizing the benefits to the business. Typically, he/she will:

- chair the programme or project board;
- appoint the programme or project manager;
- ensure that the delivered solution matches the business needs;
- represent the business and users in key decisions;
- approve key deliverables;

- resolve issues which are outside the programme or project manager's control;
- be the primary risk taker.

Sponsoring group The driving force behind a programme or project, which provides the investment decision and top-level endorsement for the rationale and objectives of the work.

Stage The natural high-level breakpoints in the project *life cycle* (e.g., initial investigation, detailed investigation, develop and test, trial and release). A stage represents the *phase* of a project. Note some standards and methods use the word 'phase' in place of 'stage' as used in this book.

Stakeholder Any individual, group or organization that can affect, be affected by, or perceive itself to be affected by an initiative (programme, project or activity)

Stakeholder influence map A diagram used to depict the influence individual stakeholders have on others. The objective is to identify the routes by which key influencers and decision makers can be enrolled in the project's objectives.

Standard A required or agreed level of quality or attainment.

Strategic misrepresentation The planned, systematic distortion or misstatement of fact to further an agenda or strategy.

Subproject A tightly aligned and tightly coupled part of a project. Subprojects are usually run to their own staged *life cycle*.

Success A successful portfolio, programme or project achieves its business objectives and outcomes and realizes the expected benefits. Success is formally measured against the *conditions of satisfaction* and *benefits* stated in a business portfolio plan or in a programme or project *business case*. Different *stakeholders* have their own views on whether a project is successful, regardless of what the business case may say.

Success criteria Criteria used for judging if the programme or project is successful (see *conditions of satisfaction*).

Summary plan Initial part of the evolution of the schedule, resource and cost plan, developed at the start of the work, defining the overall targets and key dates.

Support office A group of people providing administrative and/or specialist services to defined roles in the project management environment. Hence, *project support office*, *programme support office* and *business portfolio office*.

System A system is a collection of different components or elements that work together to produce results which exceed that contributed, independently by the components parts.

- A complicated system is one which involves the management of a large number of requirements and parts comprising a solution and the level of co-ordination and specialist expertise needed to manage them.
- A complex system is one where the relationships between the parts of the system are not always reproducible or predictable.

System of interest System of interest is used to focus on a particular system based on a specific purpose (or purposes), usually to highlight one of the systems among many in a system of systems.

System of systems A system of systems is a collection of components, each of which can be regarded as system, and which:

- can operate independently, fulfilling a purpose on their own;
- are independently acquired and managed and can maintain a continuing operational existence independent of the system-of-systems.

Systems thinking Systems thinking is an approach to integration that is based on the belief that the component parts of a system will act differently when isolated from the system's environment or other parts of the system. Systems thinking sets out to view systems in a holistic manner and concerns an understanding of a system by examining the linkages and interactions between the elements that comprise the whole of the system.

Tailoring Tailoring is the act of adapting a standard process or procedure to make it more applicable to a specific project or programme. It is concerned with ensuring the management effort is appropriate and proportionate to the work being undertaken to achieve the desired result.

Tailoring guidelines describe what can and cannot be modified in a process or method; they may also provide examples of tailoring.

Target operating model See *blueprint*.

Termination The premature *closure* of a project due to an issue which cannot be addressed or because the risks have become too high.

Theory of constraints The theory expounded by Eli Goldratt which led to the development of *critical chain* schedule management.

Threat An uncertainty that could have a negative impact on objectives or benefits. See, also, *risk*.

Tolerance The degree of freedom a higher level manager gives a lower level manager.

Traceability The ability to trace both forward and backward. (for example, from requirement to an element(s) of the solution and from the solution element back to requirement(s)) It can also be applied in other areas, such as to output-outcome-benefits mapping and solution-plan mapping.

Tranche the term used in *Managing Successful Programmes* for a group of projects or other work components in a programme, structured around a distinct step change in capability and benefits realization. A tranche is a phase of a programme.

Trial stage A trial of a capability in same environment as the customer or user will use it. Often denoted as a beta trial under special trial agreements.

Validation Validation ensures the right problem is being addressed and the solution is likely to meet the requirements when operating in its intended environment

Value driver The things which increase revenue or decrease cost or increase asset value in the organization.

Value flashpoint™ A *milestone* at which a particular cash *benefit* starts to be realized. In the Isochron method, value flashpoints are used to map financial implications of the project to the organization's accounts and ties all project activity and investment to the points where benefits start. See, also, *Conditions of Satisfaction*.

Value management A technique used in the investigative stages of a project to ensure deliverables are clearly defined and matched to business needs and solutions represent value for money whilst remaining fit for their intended purpose. Do not confuse this with *earned value*.

Values Values influence behaviours and the way an organization achieves the *outcome* defined in its *vision*.

Verification Verification checks the correctness of a solution (or part of a solution) to confirm that it matches the specified design. It should be aimed at detecting faults or failures.

Vision A vision sets out the organization's aspirations for the future. See also *mission*.

White space Unassigned resources which are available to work on future projects. White space is required at short notice for initial investigations and at medium notice to resource future projects after the detailed investigation gate. Without white space, organizations are unable to change themselves without taking resource from previously authorized and committed work.

Work breakdown structure (WBS) A structured hierarchy of *work packages*.

Work component A defined and managed part of a portfolio or programme, such as a lower level portfolio, programme, project, other related work or work package. Hence, portfolio component and programme component.

Work package A work package is a set of information relevant to the creation of one or more deliverables or outputs. It comprises a description of the outputs required and details of any constraints; it is managed through its work plan.

Index

Note: page numbers in *italic* indicate a figure on the corresponding page. Page numbers in **bold** indicate a table on the corresponding page. Page numbers with a 'n' plus a number indicate a note on the corresponding page.